Human Resources Management in Canada

Canadian

Twelfth

Edition

Gary Dessler
Florida International University

Nita Chhinzer
University of Guelph

Nina D. Cole
Ryerson University

PEARSON

Toronto

Vice-President, Editorial Director: Gary Bennett
Editor-in-Chief: Nicole Lukach
Acquisitions Editor: Nick Durie
Marketing Manager: Leigh-Anne Graham
Developmental Editor: Paul Donnelly
Project Manager: Jessica Hellen
Manufacturing Specialist: Jane Schell
Production Editor: GEX Publishing Services
Copy Editor: Leanne Rancourt
Proofreader: Lila Campbell
Compositor: GEX Publishing Services
Photo and Permissions Researcher: Strand Acquisitions Inc.
Art Director: Julia Hall
Cover and Interior Designer: Miriam Blier
Cover Image: Henrik Sorensen / Getty Images

Credits and acknowledgments of material borrowed from other sources and reproduced, with permission, in this textbook appear on the appropriate page within the text and on p. 541.

10 9 8 7 6 5 4 3 2 1 [WC]

Library and Archives Canada Cataloguing in Publication

Dessler, Gary, 1942–
    Human resources management in Canada / Gary Dessler, Nita Chhinzer, Nina
D. Cole. -- Canadian 12th ed.

Includes bibliographical references and indexes.
ISBN 978-0-13-260486-4

    1. Personnel management -- Textbooks. 2. Personnel management—
Canada -- Textbooks. I. Chhinzer, Nita II. Cole, Nina D. (Nina Dawn) III. Title.

HF5549.D49 2013   658.3   C2012-904916-6

ISBN 978-0-13-260486-4

Human Resources Management in Canada

Canadian

Twelfth

Edition

Dedication

To my mother
—G.D.

I would like to dedicate this book to those students who consistently demonstrate the ability to integrate, analyse and transfer knowledge, both within the classroom and outside of it. Your excellence keeps me inspired.

—N.N.C.

To Peggy Martin
—N.D.C.

Brief Contents

Preface xvii

Part 1 Human Resources Management in Perspective 1

Chapter 1 The Strategic Role of Human Resources Management 1

Chapter 2 The Changing Legal Emphasis: Compliance and Impact on Canadian Workplaces 25

Chapter 3 Human Resources Management and Technology 56

Part 2 Meeting Human Resources Requirements 87

Chapter 4 Designing and Analyzing Jobs 87

Chapter 5 Human Resources Planning 119

Chapter 6 Recruitment 143

Chapter 7 Selection 173

Part 3 Developing Effective Human Resources 208

Chapter 8 Orientation and Training 208

Chapter 9 Career Development 238

Chapter 10 Performance Management 261

Part 4 Total Rewards 293

Chapter 11 Strategic Pay Plans 293

Chapter 12 Pay-for-Performance and Financial Incentives 322

Chapter 13 Employee Benefits and Services 351

Part 5 Building Effective Employee–Employer Relationships 381

Chapter 14 Occupational Health and Safety 381

Chapter 15 Managing Employee Separations: Foundations of Employee Engagement, Communication, and Turnover Management 415

Chapter 16 Labour Relations 439

Part 6 Global Issues in Human Resources Management 466

Chapter 17 Managing Human Resources in a Global Business 466

Notes 492

Glossary 516

Name and Organization Index 526

Subject Index 529

Photo Credits 541

Table of Contents

Preface xvii

| PART ONE | Human Resources Management in Perspective 1 |

Chapter 1 The Strategic Role of Human Resources Management 1

The Strategic Role of Human Resources Management 2

A Brief History of HRM 3

Strategic HR The HR Role Continues to Evolve 9

Environmental Influences on HRM 11

Global HRM Lin Congyin Prizes His Staff 15

Growing Professionalism in HRM 18

Chapter Summary 20
Key Terms 21
Review and Discussion Questions 21
Critical Thinking Questions 22
Experiential Exercises 22
Running Case 23
Case Incident 24

Chapter 2 The Changing Legal Emphasis: Compliance and Impact on Canadian Workplaces 25

The Legal Framework for Employment Law in Canada 26

Legislation Protecting the General Population 29

Workforce Diversity The Evolution of Thought on Sexual Harassment in Canada 37

Global HRM UK Court Awards $1.7 Million to Bullied Employee 39

Employment Equity Legislation 44

Employment/Labour Standards Legislation 47

Respecting Employee Privacy 48

Chapter Summary 51
Key Terms 52
Review and Discussion Questions 52
Critical Thinking Questions 53
Experiential Exercises 53
Running Case 54
Case Incident 55

Chapter 3 Human Resources Management and Technology 56

Human Resources Management and Technology 57

The Strategic Importance of Technology in HRM 57

Strategic HR Google Tackles Retention Issues with "Predictive Attrition" 58

The Impact of Technology on the Role of HR 58

Human Resources Information Systems (HRIS) 61

Selecting and Implementing an HRIS 69

Electronic HR 73

Entrepreneurs and HR Cronus Technologies 77

A Brief History of the Evolution of HR Technology 78

Trends in HR and Technology 79

Global HRM Outsourcing HR Functions 81

Chapter Summary 81
Key Terms 82
Review and Discussion Questions 83
Critical Thinking Questions 83
Experiential Exercises 83
Running Case 84
Case Incident 84

PART TWO   Meeting Human Resources Requirements 87

Chapter 4   Designing and Analyzing Jobs 87

Fundamentals of Job Analysis 88

Step 1: Review Relevant Background Information 90

Strategic HR 90

Step 2: Select Jobs to be Analyzed 93

Step 3: Collecting Job Analysis Information 98

Step 4: Verifying Information 105

Step 5: Writing Job Descriptions and Job Specifications 106

Entrepreneurs and HR A Practical Approach to Job Analysis and Job Descriptions 110

Step 6: Communication and Preparations for Revisions 114

Chapter Summary 114
Key Terms 115
Review and Discussion Questions 115
Critical Thinking Questions 115
Experiential Exercises 116
Running Case 117
Case Incident 118

Chapter 5   Human Resources Planning 119

The Strategic Importance of Human Resources Planning 120

Forecasting the Availability of Candidates (Supply) 123

Entrepreneurs and HR Succession Planning and Family Businesses 127

Strategic HR Pumping Up People Supply 129

Forecasting Future Human Resources Needs (Demand) 130

Planning and Implementing HR Programs to Balance Supply and Demand 134

Chapter Summary 139
Key Terms 139

Review and Discussion Questions 140
Critical Thinking Questions 140
Experiential Exercises 140
Running Case 141
Case Incident 142

IIIIIIIIIIIIIIIIIIIIIIIIIIIIIIIIIIIIIIIIIIII   **Chapter 6   Recruitment 143**

The Strategic Importance of Recruitment 144

The Recruitment Process 146

   Global HRM Recruiting European Candidates 147

Developing and Using Application Forms 147

Recruiting from within the Organization 151

Recruiting from Outside the Organization 154

Recruiting a More Diverse Workforce 165

   Strategic HR Attracting the Younger Generation 166

   Workforce Diversity The Disconnect in Recruiting People with
                Disabilities 168

Chapter Summary 168
Key Terms 169
Review and Discussion Questions 169
Critical Thinking Questions 170
Experiential Exercises 170
Running Case 171
Case Incident 172

IIIIIIIIIIIIIIIIIIIIIIIIIIIIIIIIIIIIIIIIIIII   **Chapter 7   Selection 173**

The Strategic Importance of Employee Selection 174

   Entrepreneurs and HR Employment Testing and Interviewing 176

Step 1: Preliminary Applicant Screening 180

   Workforce Diversity Principles for Assessment
                Accommodations 181

Step 2: Selection Testing 181

Step 3: The Selection Interview 190

Step 4: Background Investigation/Reference Checking 197

Step 5: Supervisory Interview and Realistic Job Preview 199

Step 6: Hiring Decision and Candidate Notification 199

Chapter Summary 200
Key Terms 201
Review and Discussion Questions 201
Critical Thinking Questions 202
Experiential Exercises 202
Running Case 203
Case Incident 204

Appendix 7.1 A Guide to Screening and Selection in Employment 205

PART THREE   Developing Effective Human Resources 208

||||||||||||||||||||||||||||||||||||||||||||||| **Chapter 8   Orientation and Training 208**

Orienting Employees 209

Strategic HR Onboarding: The First Step in Motivation and Retention 210

The Training Process 214

Strategic HR The Role of Training and Orientation in a Tough Economy 215

Step 1: Training Needs Analysis 218

Step 2: Instructional Design 222

Steps 3 and 4: Validation and Implementation 227

Step 5: Evaluation of Training 227

Training for Special Purposes 230

Chapter Summary 233
Key Terms 233
Review and Discussion Questions 234
Critical Thinking Questions 234
Experiential Exercises 234
Running Case 235
Case Incident 236

||||||||||||||||||||||||||||||||||||||||||||||| **Chapter 9   Career Development 238**

Career Planning and Development 239

Workforce Diversity Career Development for Older Workers 240

The Evolution of Career Development 240

Managing Transfers and Promotions 245

Management Development 246

Global HRM Leadership Development in the Asia-Pacific Region 247

Strategic HR Brewing Up Management Trainee Programs 250

Leadership Development 254

Chapter Summary 256
Key Terms 257
Review and Discussion Questions 257
Critical Thinking Questions 257
Experiential Exercises 258
Running Case 258
Case Incident 259

||||||||||||||||||||||||||||||||||||||||||||||| **Chapter 10 Performance Management 261**

The Strategic Importance of Performance Management 262

The Performance Management Process 262

Step 1: Defining Performance Expectations 262

Global HRM Performance Appraisal Criteria in China 264

Step 2: Providing Ongoing Coaching and Feedback 264

Step 3: Performance Appraisal and Evaluation Discussion 266

Workforce Diversity Watch for Cultural Biases in Assessing Employees 276

Strategic HR Jaguar Land Rover Formal Appraisal Discussion Training 284

Step 4: Determine Performance Rewards/Consequences 286

Step 5: Career Development Discussion 286

Legal and Ethical Issues in Performance Management 286

The Future of Performance Management 288

Chapter Summary 288
Key Terms 289
Review and Discussion Questions 290
Critical Thinking Questions 290
Experiential Exercises 291
Running Case 291
Case Incident 292

PART FOUR   Total Rewards 293

Chapter 11 Strategic Pay Plans 293

The Strategic Importance of Total Employment Rewards 294

Strategic HR Rewards Program Effectiveness at the World's Most Admired Companies 296

Basic Considerations in Determining Pay Rates 297

Establishing Pay Rates 299

Pay for Knowledge 310

Pay for Executive, Managerial, and Professional Jobs 311

Pay Equity 313

Workforce Diversity Women Work for Free as of September 17 314

Chapter Summary 316
Key Terms 316
Review and Discussion Questions 317
Critical Thinking Questions 317
Experiential Exercises 318
Running Case 319
Case Incident 320

Chapter 12 Pay-for-Performance and Financial Incentives 322

Money and Motivation 323

Incentives for Operations Employees 324

Workforce Diversity Targeting Incentives for Life Stage 325

Incentives for Senior Managers and Executives 328

Strategic HR Bank CEOs Take a Pay Cut 334

Incentives for Salespeople 334

Incentives for other Managers and Professionals 337

Organization-Wide Incentive Plans 338

Developing Effective Incentive Plans 340

Employee Recognition Programs 342

Entrepreneurs and HR Recognition and Incentives for Entrepreneurs 343

Chapter Summary 345
Key Terms 346
Review and Discussion Questions 346
Critical Thinking Questions 346
Experiential Exercises 347
Running Case 348
Case Incident 349

||||||||||||||||||||||||||||||||||||||| **Chapter 13 Employee Benefits and Services 351**

The Strategic Role of Employee Benefits 352

Strategic HR AltaGas Benefits Drive Successful Competition for Talent 352

Government-Mandated Benefits 353

Voluntary Employer-Sponsored Benefits 359

Workforce Diversity Gen Y's Benefits that Work 362

Global HRM Defined Benefit Pension Problems and Solutions Around the World 367

Employee Services 369

Flexible Benefits Programs 373

Benefits Administration 375

Chapter Summary 376
Key Terms 377
Review and Discussion Questions 377
Critical Thinking Questions 378
Experiential Exercises 378
Running Case 379
Case Incident 380

PART FIVE   Building Effective Employee–Employer Relationships 381

||||||||||||||||||||||||||||||||||||||| **Chapter 14 Occupational Health and Safety 381**

Strategic Importance of Occupational Health and Safety 382

Basic Facts about Occupational Health and Safety Legislation 383

What Causes Accidents? 389

Workforce Diversity Guiding Young Workers in Health and Safety 393

How To Prevent Accidents 394

Strategic HR Top Management Commitment to Safety at Steelcase Canada Pays Off 396

Entrepreneurs and HR Small Business Safety Calculator 397

Occupational Health and Safety Challenges in Canada 398

Employee Wellness Programs 409

Chapter Summary 410
Key Terms 411
Review and Discussion Questions 411
Critical Thinking Questions 412

Experiential Exercises 412
Running Case 413
Case Incident 414

||||||||||||||||||||||||||||||||||||||||||||| Chapter 15 Managing Employee Separations: Foundations of Employee Engagement, Communication, and Turnover Management 415

The Importance of Managing Employee Separations 416

Managing Turnover 416

Fairness in Employee Separations 426

Effective Employee Communication 432

Strategic HR Forensic Technology: Improved Engagement Fuels Company Turnaround 434

Chapter Summary 435
Key Terms 435
Review and Discussion Questions 436
Critical Thinking Questions 436
Experiential Exercises 436
Running Case 437
Case Incident 438

||||||||||||||||||||||||||||||||||||||||||||| Chapter 16 Labour Relations 439

Introduction to Labour Relations 440

Workforce Diversity Collective Agreement Puts Aboriginals First 442

Strategic HR UFCW Forms a "Super Local" 443

The Labour Relations Process 445

The Impact of Unionization on HRM 460

Chapter Summary 461
Key Terms 462
Review and Discussion Questions 462
Critical Thinking Questions 462
Experiential Exercises 463
Running Case 464
Case Incident 464

PART SIX   Global Issues in Human Resources Management 466

||||||||||||||||||||||||||||||||||||||||||||| Chapter 17 Managing Human Resources in a Global Business 466

The Globalization of Business and Strategic HR 467

How Intercountry Differences affect HRM 467

Workforce Diversity Mummy Crew in Monster Trucks 468

Global Relocation 470

Strategic HR Employee Engagement Program Drives Business Results at DHL 472

Considerations in Global HRM 474

Repatriation 481

Managing Global Workers within Canada 482

Global HRM Successful Integration of Immigrants in Canada 485

Chapter Summary 487
Key Terms 488
Review and Discussion Questions 488
Critical Thinking Questions 488
Experiential Exercises 489
Running Case 489
Case Incident 490

Notes 492

Glossary 516

Name and Organization Index 526

Subject Index 529

Photo Credits 541

The twelfth edition of *Human Resources Management in Canada* shows students how human resources are the most important assets in organizations today. Human resources continue to provide a source of competitive advantage for organizations in a hyper-competitive, global environment. The strategic importance of human resources management (HRM) activities is emphasized throughout the book, using recent examples from the Canadian employment landscape. Knowledge of HRM is important for supervisors and managers in every field and for employees at every level—not just those working in HR departments or aspiring to do so in the future. This book is designed to provide a complete, comprehensive review of HRM concepts and techniques in a highly readable and understandable form for a wide audience: students specializing in HRM and those in business programs, supervisory/managerial staff, and small-business owners.

As in previous editions, the Canadian twelfth edition provides extensive coverage of all HRM topics, such as job analysis, HR planning, recruitment, selection, orientation and training, career development, compensation and benefits, performance appraisal, health and safety, and labour relations. Practical applications are highlighted with *Tips for the Front Line* and *Hints to Ensure Legal Compliance* icons in the margins. *Research Insights* are also highlighted, and *Ethical Dilemmas* are presented for discussion.

NEW TO THE CANADIAN TWELFTH EDITION

Revised Introductory Chapter. The first chapter has been revised to provide a comprehensive overview of the strategic importance of HR, highlighting the evolution of HR over the years, the advances in measuring HRM's contribution to the bottom line, and HRM's critical role in strategy implementation.

Reformatted and Updated Legal Emphasis. Chapter 2 was refocused from diversity management and now develops a clearer understanding of the comprehensive and often overlapping areas of legislation that affect the employment relationship. This includes a discussion of key legal cases, potential outcomes and remedies to violations, as well as a discussion about employer rights related to employment.

Significant Discussion of Managing Decline. Chapter 15 was rewritten to focus on the impact and management of turnover (quits, layoffs, termination, etc.). This includes a focus on legal, psychological and communication issues.

More Coverage on the Impact of Globalization on HR. Further discussion on the impact of globalization on HR was added throughout with a focus on both Canadian organizations interactions on a global scale, as well as the impact of immigrants on the Canadian labour force. Specific sections, such as performance management (in addition to performance appraisal), the impact of immigration on the labour force, and employability skills, are introduced.

Integrated Chapters. Rather than approaching topics as isolated silos, the book highlights areas of overlap in order to present HRM as an integrated set of topics.

Boxed Features. The four boxed features—*Workforce Diversity, Strategic HR, Entrepreneurs and HR*, and *Global HRM*—have been updated and revised in all chapters.

Required Professional Capabilities (RPCs). Each chapter indicates where the specific required professional capabilities are discussed. These RPCs are set out by the Canadian Council of Human Resources Associations for students preparing to write the National Knowledge Exam.

KEY FEATURES OF THE CANADIAN TWELFTH EDITION

Highlighted Themes

WORKFORCE DIVERSITY

The Disconnect in Recruiting People with Disabilities

The good news is that employers want to hire people with disabilities, and qualified candidates are available. But putting employers and job seekers together needs improved coordination to create more success stories. Employers have bottom-line reasons for building workforce diversity. Inclusiveness is a competitive advantage that lets an organization better connect with a diverse community and customer base. Inclusiveness provides access to a larger pool of strong job candidates in a time of skills shortages and enhances an organization's reputation as an employer of choice.

So why aren't more employers tapping into the wealth of human potential in people with disabilities? After all, as a group they make up roughly 13 percent of the working-age population. That is precisely what the Canadian Abilities Foundation set out to determine in its recently completed Neglected or Hidden study, the findings of which may surprise employers.

Likely the most revealing finding that illustrates the need for a new employment strategy for people with disabilities is the disconnect that exists among employers, people with disabilities, and the service providers who help these individuals enter the workforce.

With few exceptions, these stakeholders just don't seem to know how to communicate with one another,

if they are fortunate enough to find one another in the first place. The commitment and passion of workers with disabilities and those assisting them is sound. Meanwhile, hundreds of disability-related organizations across Canada provide some level of employment support to their clients. The Neglected or Hidden study suggests that the number of Canadian employers willing to hire people with disabilities should be more than adequate to meet the availability of disabled job seekers.

The good news is that a small number of disability organizations have made significant inroads in their regions by using employer partnerships. One example is the Dartmouth Work Activity Society in Nova Scotia, which started its new approach with just a single employer "partner" who was highly satisfied with the services provided. EmployAbilities, a full-time service agency serving Edmonton and northern Alberta for more than 35 years, has also launched a partnership-building strategy. A unique feature of the agency's approach is its partnership with the local chamber of commerce through which it offers advice on disability issues to employers.

Source: Adapted from A. Prost, "Successful Recruiting from an Untapped Source," *Canadian HR Reporter* (January 16, 2006), pp. 11–12.

- **Workforce Diversity.** The *Workforce Diversity* boxes describe some of the issues and challenges involved in managing the diverse workforce found in Canadian organizations. The broad range of types of diversity addressed include generational/age, ethnic, gender, racial, and religious.

STRATEGIC HR

IKEA Canada doesn't just want to fill jobs; it wants to partner with people. It recruits unique individuals who share the corporate values of togetherness, cost consciousness, respect, and simplicity. IKEA listens and supports each employee to identify his or her needs, ambitions, and capabilities. Employees are expected not to ask others what they should be doing but to ask themselves and then get on with it. It is important for IKEA employees to have a strong desire to learn and the motivation to continually do things better, because the IKEA way of working is less structured than that of many other organizations.

IKEA Canada employee Ingeborg, a sales co-worker who is 71 years young, says, "Everyone asks me why I am still working. I tell them I love my job. There is always a great atmosphere in the store; I really enjoy the company of my managers and co-workers. We work together very well."

Source: Adapted from IKEA Canada, www.ikea.com/ms/en_CA/jobs/simply_ikea/index.html and www.ikea.com/ms/en_JP/jobs/true_stories/ingeborg/index.html. (Accessed April 6, 2009). Used with permission from IKEA Canada.

- **Strategic HR.** These boxes provide examples that illustrate the ways in which organizations are using effective HRM policies and practices to achieve their strategic goals.

ENTREPRENEURS and HR

A Practical Approach to Job Analysis and Job Descriptions

Without their own job analysts or even their own HR managers, many small-business owners need a more streamlined approach to job analysis. A resource that includes all of the possible positions that they might encounter, with a detailed listing of the duties normally assigned to these positions, exists in the National Occupational Classification (NOC) mentioned earlier. The practical approach to job analysis for small-business owners presented next is built around this invaluable reference tool.

Step 1: Develop an Organization Chart
Drawing up the organization chart of the present structure comes first. Then, depending on how far in advance planning is being done, a chart can be produced that shows how the organization should look in the immediate future (say, in two months), as well as two or three other charts showing how the organization is likely to evolve over the next two or three years.

Step 2: Use a Job Analysis Questionnaire
Next, a job analysis questionnaire can be used to determine what each job entails. A shorter version of one of the more comprehensive job analysis questionnaires, such as that in Figure 4.5, may be useful for collecting job analysis data. An example of a job summary for a customer service clerk follows:

Answers inquiries and gives directions to customers, authorizes cashing of customers' cheques, records and

returns lost credit cards, sorts and reviews new credit applications, and works at the customer service desk.

Step 3: Obtain a Copy of the National Occupational Classification (NOC) and Related Publications for Reference
Next, standardized examples of the job descriptions needed should be obtained from the NOC website at www.hrsdc.gc.ca/eng/workplaceskills/noc/index.shtml. A related publication entitled *Job Descriptions: An Employers' Handbook* is also available for download ing from the NOC website at www.hrsdc.gc.ca/eng/workplaceskills/noc/employers/emplr_handbooks.shtml.

Step 4: Choose Appropriate Job Titles and Job Descriptions and Copy Them for Reference
For each department, the NOC job titles and job descriptions that are believed to be appropriate should be chosen. The NOC definition will provide a firm foundation for the job description being created. It will provide a standardized list and constant reminder of the specific duties that should be included.

Step 5: Complete the Job Description
An appropriate job description for the job under consideration can then be written. The job analysis information, together with the information from the NOC, can be used to create a complete listing of the tasks and duties of each of the jobs. The working conditions section can be completed once all of the tasks and duties have been specified.

- **Entrepreneurs and HR.** Suggestions, examples, and practical hints are provided to assist those in smaller businesses who have limited time and resources to implement effective HRM policies and procedures.

• **Global HRM.** In recognition of the increasing impact of globalization, topics highlighted in the *Global HRM* boxes include cultural issues in retirement plans, employment contracts in Europe, and the importance of personal relationships for business success in China.

Additional Features

Learning Outcomes. Specific learning goals are defined on each chapter-opening page.

Key Terms. Key terms appear in boldface within the text, are defined in the margins, and are listed at the end of each chapter.

Current Examples. Numerous real-world examples of HRM policies, procedures, and practices at a wide variety of organizations, ranging from small service providers to huge global corporations, can be found throughout the text.

Full-Colour Figures, Tables, and Photographs. Throughout each chapter, key concepts and applications are illustrated with strong, full-colour visual materials.

Web Links. Helpful Internet sites are provided throughout the text and are featured in the margins.

End-of-Chapter Summaries. At the end of each chapter, the summary reviews key points related to each of the learning outcomes.

End-of-Chapter Review and Discussion Questions. Each chapter contains a set of review and discussion questions.

Critical Thinking Questions. Each chapter contains end-of-chapter questions designed to provoke critical thinking and stimulate discussion.

Experiential Exercises. Each chapter includes a number of individual and group-based experiential exercises that provide learners with the opportunity to apply the text material and develop some hands-on skills.

Running Case. The running case at the end of each chapter illustrates the types of HRM challenges confronted by small-business owners and front-line supervisors. It is accompanied by critical thinking questions, which provide an opportunity to discuss and apply the text material.

Case Incidents. Case incidents can be found at the end of each chapter. These cases present current HRM issues in a real-life setting and are followed by questions designed to encourage discussion and promote the use of problem-solving skills.

Supplements

Human Resources Management in Canada, Twelfth Edition, is accompanied by a complete supplements package.

MyManagementLab

www.mymanagementlab.com

The Moment You Know

Educators know it. Students know it. It's that inspired moment when something that was difficult to understand suddenly makes perfect sense. Our MyLab products have been designed and refined with a single purpose in mind—to help educators create that moment of understanding with their students.

MyManagementLab delivers proven results in helping individual students succeed. It provides engaging experiences that personalize, stimulate, and measure learning for each student. Students and instructors can make use of the following online resources:

- **Study Plan:** MyManagementLab offers chapter pre-tests that generate personalized Study Plans that show students exactly the topics that require additional practice. The Study Plan links to multiple learning aids, such as student PowerPoint slides, the eText, and glossary flashcards. After students work through the learning aids, they can take a post-test to measure their improvement and demonstrate their mastery of the topics.

- **Audio Glossary Flashcards:** This study tool provides a targeted review of the Key Terms in each chapter. The Audio Glossary Flashcards allow learners to select and listen to the specific terms and chapters that they would like to study. The cards can also be sorted by Key Term or by definition to give students greater flexibility when studying.

- **Pearson eText:** MyManagementLab also includes an eText version of *Human Resources Management in Canada* including a complete Glossary and Index. This dynamic, online version of the text is integrated throughout MyManagementLab to create an enriched, interactive learning experience for students. Users can create notes, highlight text in different colours, create bookmarks, zoom, and click hyperlinked words and phrases to view definitions and go directly to weblinks. The Pearson eText allows for quick navigation to key parts of the eText using a table of contents and provides full-text search.

Instructors and students can also access Chapter Quizzes, Case Assessments, Annotated Text Figures, and many additional study tools designed to engage learners and improve student understanding.

Instructor Supplements

- **Instructor's Manual with CBC Video Guide.** This comprehensive guide contains a detailed lecture outline of each chapter, descriptions of the discussion boxes, answers to review and critical thinking questions, answers to the case questions, hints regarding the experiential exercises, and helpful video case notes.

- **Test Item File.** This comprehensive test bank contains more than 1500 multiple-choice, true/false, and short essay questions.

- **PowerPoint® Lecture Slides.** This practical set of PowerPoint lecture slides outlines key concepts discussed in the text, and includes selected tables and figures from the text.
- **Clicker PowerPoint® Slides.** This set of Clicker-ready slides is suitable for use with any Personal Response System.

Most of these instructor supplements are also available for download from a password-protected section of Pearson Canada's online catalogue (vig.pearsoned.ca). Navigate to your book's catalogue page to view a list of the supplements that are available. See your local sales representative for details and access.

- **Pearson Canada/CBC Video Library.** Pearson Canada and the CBC have worked together to provide six video segments from the CBC series *The National*. Designed specifically to complement the text, this case collection is an excellent tool for bringing students in contact with the world outside the classroom. These programs have extremely high production quality and have been chosen to relate directly to chapter content.
- **MyTest.** MyTest from Pearson Canada is a powerful assessment generation program that helps instructors easily create and print quizzes, tests, and exams, as well as homework or practice handouts. Questions and tests can all be authored online, allowing instructors ultimate flexibility and the ability to efficiently manage assessments at any time, from anywhere. MyTest for *Human Resources Management in Canada*, Twelfth Edition, includes more than 1500 multiple-choice, true/false, and short essay questions.
- **CourseSmart.** CourseSmart goes beyond traditional expectations—providing instant, online access to the textbooks and course materials you need at a lower cost for students. And even as students save money, you can save time and hassle with a digital eTextbook that allows you to search for the most relevant content at the very moment you need it. Whether it's evaluating textbooks or creating lecture notes to help students with difficult concepts, CourseSmart can make life a little easier. See how when you visit www.coursesmart.com/instructors.
- **Technology Specialists.** Pearson's technology specialists work with faculty and campus course designers to ensure that Pearson technology products, assessment tools, and online course materials are tailored to meet your specific needs. This highly qualified team is dedicated to helping schools take full advantage of a wide range of educational resources by assisting in the integration of a variety of instructional materials and media formats. Your local Pearson Canada sales representative can provide you with more details on this service program.

CourseSmart for Students

CourseSmart. CourseSmart goes beyond traditional expectations—providing instant, online access to the textbooks and course materials you need at an average savings of 60%. With instant access from any computer and the ability to search your text, you'll find the content you need quickly, no matter where you are. And with online tools like highlighting and note-taking, you can save time and study efficiently. See all the benefits at www.coursesmart.com/students.

Other Resources

- **HR Management Simulation.** A great online simulation is available for students. Access code cards can be packaged with the text for an additional charge. Please see http://www.interpretive.com/rd6/index.php?pg=hrm&sid=1 and contact your Pearson representative for more details.

- **Pearson Custom Publishing (http://www.pearsonlearningsolutions.com/higher-education/).** Pearson Custom Publishing can provide you and your students with texts, cases, and articles to enhance your course. Choose material from Darden, Ivey, Harvard Business School Publishing, NACRA, and Thunderbird to create your own custom casebook. Contact your Pearson sales representative for more details.

- **Your Pearson Sales Representative.** Your Pearson rep is always available to ensure you have everything you need to teach a winning course. Armed with experience, training, and product knowledge, your Pearson rep will support your assessment and adoption of any of the products, services, and technologies outlined here to ensure our offerings are tailored to suit your individual needs and the needs of your students. Whether it's getting instructions for MyTest software or specific content files for your new online course, your Pearson sales representative is here to help.

ACKNOWLEDGMENTS

The manuscript was reviewed at various stages of its development by a number of peers across Canada, and we want to thank those who shared their insights and constructive criticism.

Stan Arnold, Humber College

David Berrington, Sauder School of Business, UBC

Anna Bortolon, Conestoga College

Elizabeth Clipsham, Capilano University

Katrina Di Gravio, University of Waterloo

Thomas Foard, University of Guelph-Humber

Sarah Holding, Vancouver Island University

Helen MacDonald, Nova Scotia Community College

Cheryl Meheden, University of Lethbridge

James O'Brien, University of Western Ontario

Melanie Peacock, Mount Royal University

Chet Robie, Wilfrid Laurier University

Aaron Schat, McMaster University

Andrew Templer, University of Windsor

Bryan Webber, Vancouver Island University

At Pearson Canada, we are very grateful to Nick Durie, Acquisitions Editor; Leigh-Anne Graham, Marketing Manager; Paul Donnelly, Developmental Editor; Jessica Hellen, Project Manager; and all the other people behind the scenes who have helped make this edition possible.

A special note of thanks is extended to research assistant My-Binh Trung.

Gary Dessler
Florida International University

Nita N. Chhinzer
University of Guelph

Nina D. Cole
Ryerson University

About the Canadian Authors

Dr. Nita N. Chhinzer

Dr. Nita N. Chhinzer is an Assistant Professor of Human Resources at the Department of Business, University of Guelph. Her research is concentrated on Strategic Human Resources Management, with a strong focus on downsizing practices, procedures, and ethics. Her program of research includes securing a stronger understanding of downsizing activity in the Canadian context, with an aim to affect public policy and legislation regarding layoffs. She has gained international recognition with conference participation including Athens, Greece; Paris, France; Dubai, UAE; and many North American speaking engagements. From May 2012–2017, Dr. Chhinzer is the recipient of the prestigious Fellowship in Leadership, HRM and Work.

Dr. Nina D. Cole

Dr. Nina Cole has over 30 years of experience in human resources management as a practitioner, consultant, researcher, and professor. She worked in business for 12 years as an HR management consultant and an HR manager with federal industries. Since 1990, she has worked as an academic, teaching and conducting research in human resources management and organizational behaviour. Dr. Cole is currently an Associate Professor at the Ted Rogers School of Management at Ryerson University in Toronto. She has been an active member of the Administrative Sciences Association of Canada, the Human Resources Professionals Association, and numerous other academic, industry, and community groups for many years.

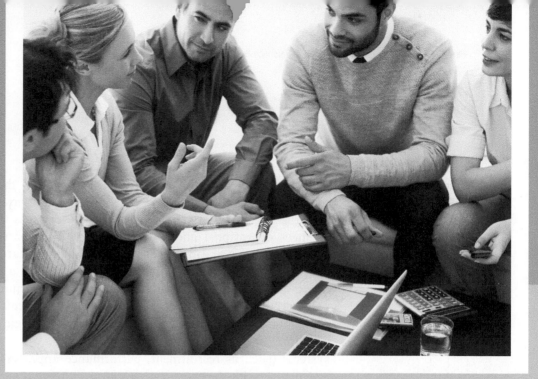

CHAPTER 1

The Strategic Role of Human Resources Management

LEARNING OUTCOMES

AFTER STUDYING THIS CHAPTER, YOU SHOULD BE ABLE TO

DEFINE human resources management and **ANALYZE** the strategic significance of human resources management.

DESCRIBE the two categories of activities required of HR managers and **DISCUSS** examples of each.

DISCUSS the internal and external environmental factors affecting human resources management policies and practices and **EXPLAIN** their impact.

DESCRIBE the three stages in the evolution of HRM.

EXPLAIN how HRM has changed over recent years to include a higher-level advisory role.

REQUIRED PROFESSIONAL CAPABILITIES (RPC)

- Advises on the status of dependent and independent contractors and determinants of employee status

- Contributes to improvements in the organization's structures and work processes

- Gathers, analyzes, and reports relevant business and industry information (including global trends) to influence the development of strategic business HR plans

- Develops business cases for HR activity

- Stays current with professional knowledge

- Fosters and promotes the advancement of the profession

- Keeps current with emerging HR trends

- Guides and facilitates change in organizational culture or values consistent with business strategy

- Provides support and expertise to managers and supervisors with respect to managing people

- Monitors expenditures and timelines

THE STRATEGIC ROLE OF HUMAN RESOURCES MANAGEMENT

human resources management (HRM) The management of people in organizations to drive successful organizational performance and achievement of the organization's strategic goals.

Human resources management (HRM) refers to the management of people in organizations. Human resources professionals are responsible for ensuring that the organization attracts, retains, and engages the diverse talent required to meet operational and performance commitments made to customers and shareholders. Their job is to ensure that the organization finds and hires the best individuals available, develops their talent, creates a productive work environment, and continually builds and monitors these human assets. They have the primary responsibility for managing the workforce that drives organizational performance and achieves the organization's strategic goals.[1]

More specifically, HRM involves formulating and implementing HRM systems (such as recruitment, performance appraisal, and compensation) that are aligned with the organization's strategy to ensure that the workforce has the competencies and behaviours required to achieve the organization's strategic objectives. It is crucial that the HR strategy be aligned with the company's strategic plan (see **Figure 1.1**).

Just as important as the financial capital that is required for an organization to operate, the knowledge, education, training, skills, and expertise of a firm's workers represent its increasingly valuable **human capital**. More and more organizations are awakening to the importance of human capital as the next competitive advantage.[2]

human capital The knowledge, education, training, skills, and expertise of an organization's workforce.

Research studies over the past two decades have confirmed that effective HR practices are related to better organizational performance.[3] Organizational benefits range from employee empowerment to extensive training that affects the productivity of employees.[4] The resource-based view of the firm suggests that human resource practices contribute to the development of embedded knowledge of a firm's culture, history, processes, and context, which are non-imitable.[5]

RPC

Develops business cases for HR activity.

FIGURE **1.1**   Linking Company-wide and HR Strategies

Source: © Gary Dessler, Ph.D., 2007.

More specifically, three HR practices (profit sharing, results-oriented performance appraisal, and employment security) have strong relationships with important accounting measures of performance (return on assets and return on equity).[6] High-performance HR practices (comprehensive employee recruitment and selection procedures, incentive compensation and performance management systems, and extensive employee involvement and training) have a positive relationship with turnover, productivity, and corporate financial performance (gross rate of return on capital).[7]

A BRIEF HISTORY OF HRM

HRM has changed dramatically over time and has assumed an increasingly strategic role. The demands on HR staff and expectations regarding their role have evolved as HRM has changed. HR practices have been shaped by society's prevailing beliefs and attitudes about workers and their rights, which have evolved in three stages.

Scientific Management: Concern for Production

scientific management The process of "scientifically" analyzing manufacturing processes, reducing production costs, and compensating employees based on their performance levels.

Frederick Taylor was the driving force behind **scientific management**, the process of "scientifically" analyzing manufacturing processes, reducing production costs, and compensating employees based on their performance.[8] As a result, management practices in the late 1800s and early 1900s emphasized task simplification and performance-based pay. Such incentives were expected to lead to higher wages for workers, increased profits for the organization, and workplace harmony. Taylor's views were not accepted by all management theorists. For example, Mary Parker Follett, a writer ahead of her time, advocated the use of self-management, cross-functional cooperation, empowerment, and managers as leaders, not dictators.[9]

The Human Resources Movement: Concern for People and Productivity

human resources movement A management philosophy focusing on concern for people and productivity.

HRM is currently based on the theoretical assumptions of the **human resources movement**. Arriving at this joint focus on people and productivity involved four evolutionary phases.[10]

Phase 1

In the early 1900s, HRM—or personnel administration, as it was then called—played a very minor or non-existent role. During this era, personnel administrators assumed responsibility for hiring and firing (a duty formerly looked after by first-line supervisors), ran the payroll department, and administered benefits. Their job consisted largely of ensuring that procedures were followed.

Phase 2

As the *scientific management movement* gained momentum, operational efficiency increased but wage increases did not keep up, causing workers to distrust management. The resulting increase in unionization led to personnel departments serving as the primary contact for union representatives. Following the depression of the 1930s, various pieces of legislation were enacted, including a minimum wage act, an unemployment insurance program, and protection of workers' right to belong to unions. Legal compliance was subsequently added to the responsibilities of personnel managers. During the 1940s and 1950s, personnel managers were also involved in dealing with the impact of the *human relations movement*. Orientation, performance appraisal, and employee relations responsibilities were added to their job.

Phase 3

The third major phase in personnel management was a direct result of government legislation passed during the 1960s, 1970s, and 1980s that affected employees' human rights, wages and benefits, working conditions, health and safety, and established penalties for failure to meet them. The role of personnel departments expanded dramatically. They continued to provide expertise in such areas as compensation, recruitment, and training but in an expanded capacity.

outsourcing The practice of contracting with outside vendors to handle specified business functions on a permanent basis.

Technological advances resulted in outsourcing much of the operational HR activities. **Outsourcing** involves contracting with outside vendors to handle specified business functions on a permanent basis. Although using outside experts to provide employee counselling and payroll services has been common for many years, the outsourcing of other specific HR functions, including pension and benefits administration, recruitment, management development, and training, has become increasingly common.[11]

For example, Air Canada, CIBC, BMO Financial Group, Hewlett-Packard Canada, IBM Canada, Calgary Health, and TELUS have all outsourced part or all of their administrative HR functions. During the latter part of this era, the term "human resources management" emerged. This change represented a shift in emphasis—from maintenance and administration to corporate contribution, proactive management, and initiation of change.[12]

Phase 4

The fourth phase of HRM is the current phase, where the role of HR departments has evolved to that of helping their organization achieve its strategic objectives.[13] HR activities have become ubiquitous, where not only the HR department but also every line manager has responsibilities related to employees as they move through the stages of the human-capital life cycle: selection and assimilation into the organization, development of capabilities while working in the organization, and transition out of the organization. **Figure 1.2** highlights core job requirements that are found in non-HR roles that were traditionally limited to the HR department, thus providing further evidence for the permeation of HR skills throughout the organization. Thus, all potential managers must be aware of the basics of HR to succeed in their respective roles. HR professionals often serve as subject matter experts or in-house consultants to line managers, offering advice on HR-related matters, formulating HR policies and procedures, and providing a wide range of HR services.

A 2011 national survey of HR professionals identified five critical pieces of knowledge required by HR professionals today. Presented in priority order, they are business acumen, an understanding of employment law and

FIGURE **1.2** Traditional HR Responsibilities in Non-HR Roles

Senior Managers

- Senior managers may specialize in areas such as finance, marketing, or human resources or in the sale of a particular product or provision of a particular service
- Establish objectives for the company and formulate or approve policies and programs (Strategy: Chapter 1)
- Authorize and organize the establishment of major departments and associated senior staff positions (Designing and Analyzing Jobs: Chapter 4)
- Allocate material, human, and financial resources to implement organizational policies and programs; establish financial and administrative controls; formulate and approve promotional campaigns; and approve overall personnel planning (HR Planning: Chapter 5)
- Select middle managers, directors, or other executive staff (Selection: Chapter 7)
- Coordinate the work of regions, divisions, or departments (Designing and Analyzing Jobs: Chapter 4)

Financial Auditors and Accountants

- May supervise and train articling students, other accountants, or administrative technicians (Orientation and Training: Chapter 8)

Supervisors, General Office and Administrative Support Workers

- Coordinate, assign, and review the work of clerks engaged in word processing, record keeping and filing, operating telephones and switchboards, data entry, desktop publishing, and other activities involving general office and administrative skills (Performance Management: Chapter 10)
- Establish work schedules and procedures and coordinate activities with other work units or departments (Career Development: Chapter 9)
- Resolve work-related problems and prepare and submit progress and other reports (Legal: Chapter 2)
- Train workers in job duties, safety procedures, and company policies (Occupational Health and Safety: Chapter 14)
- Ensure smooth operation of office equipment and machinery, and arrange for maintenance and repair work (Occupational Health and Safety: Chapter 14)

Industrial and Manufacturing Engineers

- Plan and design plant layouts and facilities
- Study new machinery and facilities and recommend or select efficient combinations (Performance Management: Chapter 10)
- Develop flexible or integrated manufacturing systems and technological procedures (Technology: Chapter 3)
- Conduct studies and implement programs to determine optimum inventory levels for production and to allow optimum use of machinery, materials, and resources (HR Planning: Chapter 5)
- Analyze costs of production (Strategic Pay Plans: Chapter 11)
- Design, develop, and conduct time studies and work simplification programs (Employee Benefits and Services: Chapter 13)
- Determine human resource and skill requirements and develop training programs (Orientation and Training: Chapter 8)
- Develop performance standards, evaluation systems, and wage and incentive programs (Financial Incentives: Chapter 12)
- Establish programs and conduct studies to enhance industrial health and safety or to identify and correct fire and other hazards (Occupational Health and Safety: Chapter 14)
- Supervise technicians, technologists, analysts, administrative staff, and other engineers (Performance Management: Chapter 10)

Nursing Coordinators and Supervisors

- Supervise registered nurses, licensed practical nurses, and other nursing personnel (Performance Management: Chapter 10)
- Evaluate patients' needs and ensure that required nursing care is delivered (Strategy: Chapter 1)
- Assist in the establishment of unit policies and procedures (HR Planning: Chapter 5)
- Assist in the selection, evaluation, and professional development of nursing personnel (Selection: Chapter 7, Orientation and Training: Chapter 8, Career Development: Chapter 9)

continued

University Professors and Lecturers

- Teach one or more university subjects to undergraduate and graduate students (Strategy: Chapter 1)
- Prepare, administer, and grade examinations, laboratory assignments, and reports (Performance Management: Chapter 10)
- Direct research programs of graduate students and advise on research matters (Designing and Analyzing Jobs: Chapter 4)
- Conduct research in field of specialization and publish findings in scholarly journals or books (Career Development: Chapter 9)
- May serve on faculty committees dealing with such matters as curriculum planning and degree requirements and perform a variety of administrative duties (Designing and Analyzing Jobs: Chapter 4)
- May represent their universities as speakers and guest lecturers (Employee Benefits and Services: Chapter 13)
- May provide professional consultative services to government, industry, and private individuals (Legal: Chapter 2)

Source: O*NET OnLine, www.onetonline.org, (accessed October 3, 2011).

legislation, talent management, broad HR knowledge, and employee–labour relations knowledge.[14] The results align with an overall trend of increased expectations of HR professionals, suggesting that there are core competencies that those responsible for HR activities (within the HRM department and outside of it) must secure to help deliver value to the organization (see **Figure 1.3**).

Credible Activist A core HR competency is that of being both credible (respected, listened to, trusted) and active (takes a position, challenges assumptions). Both of these qualities are required to help an organization optimize the value added from its human resources.

The activist role is shared with non-HR positions as well. For example, a recent study conducted by Monster.com found that 73 percent of CEOs spend more than 25 percent of their time on talent-related activities, with three in every five identifying employee satisfaction/engagement as a key goal for their job, and three of every four identifying retention of high-performing employees as one of their goals.[15]

Culture and Change Steward The ability to appreciate, help shape, and articulate an organization's corporate culture includes understanding, guiding, and reacting to both internal and external stakeholder expectations. HR staff has a responsibility to shape and support a culture of change as well as develop programs, strategies, or projects to embed desired change throughout the organization.

Intense global competition and the need for more responsiveness to environmental changes put a premium on **employee engagement**, the emotional and intellectual involvement of employees in their work, such as intensity, focus, and involvement in his or her job and organization. Engaged employees drive desired organizational outcomes—they go beyond what is required; understand and share the values and goals of the organization; perceive that there are opportunities for growth, development, and advancement; enjoy collegial relationships with managers and co-workers; trust their leaders; and regard the success of the organization as their success.[16] According to an analysis of a Hewitt Associates database (over 4 million employees from

RPC

Guides and facilitates change in organizational culture or values consistent with business strategy

employee engagement The emotional and intellectual involvement of employees in their work, such as intensity, focus, and involvement in his or her job and organization.

FIGURE **1.3**   HR Competency Model

almost 1500 companies), there is a strong positive relationship between engagement and organizational performance (sales growth and total shareholder return).[17]

Talent Manager and Organizational Designer As traditional linear career paths change, the importance of an HR professional's ability to effectively manage human resources has become more critical as employees enter, exit, or move up, down, or across the organization. In this vein, HR specialists must embed theory, research, and practice into the processes, policies, and structures of an organization.

HR professionals and line managers play a pivotal role in *lowering labour costs*, the single largest operating expense in many organizations, particularly in the service sector. Doing so might involve introducing strategies to reduce turnover, absenteeism, and the rate of incidence of occupational illnesses and injuries. It could also mean adopting more effective recruitment, selection, and training programs. At one international tire manufacturing firm, adopting a behaviour-based interview strategy as the basis for selection of entry-level engineers resulted in savings of $500 000 in three years. These savings were due to lower turnover, lower training costs, and improved capabilities of the engineering staff because of a better fit.[18]

Strategy Architect HR professionals significantly contribute to strategy by integrating internal stakeholder and external stakeholder expectations. Through identifying, forecasting, and facilitating organizational responses to an ever-changing internal workforce and often volatile external pressures, HR plays an active role in the establishment and execution of overall strategy.

RPC

Monitors expenditures and timelines

strategy The company's plan for how it will balance its internal strengths and weaknesses with external opportunities and threats to maintain a competitive advantage.

Traditionally, **strategy**—the company's plan for how it will balance its internal strengths and weaknesses with external opportunities and threats to maintain a competitive advantage—was formulated without HR input. But today HR professionals are increasingly involved in both formulating and implementing organizational strategy. A survey of over 1100 corporate managers in Canada found that three-quarters of them strongly believe that the HR function contributes significantly to the overall success of their company and view having an HR professional on staff as a strategic advantage.[19]

Operational Executor Leading HR researcher Brian Becker says, "It isn't the content of the strategy that differentiates the winners and losers, it is the ability to execute."[20] HR specialists are expected to be **change agents** who lead the organization and its employees through organizational change. Making the enterprise more responsive to product or service innovations and technological change is the objective of many management strategies. Flattening the pyramid, empowering employees, and organizing around teams are ways in which HRM can help an organization respond quickly to its customers' needs and competitors' challenges.

change agents Specialists who lead the organization and its employees through organizational change.

Policy drafting, adaption, and implementation, as well as employees' administrative needs, were traditional roles that HR fulfilled. In recent years the efficiency in dealing with operational issues has significantly improved through the use of technology, shared services, or outsourcing. However, much of the expertise in operational aspects of employee-related policies remains largely within the HR professional's realm of responsibility.

environmental scanning Identifying and analyzing external opportunities and threats that may be crucial to the organization's success.

Resources Consulting
www.cfthr.com/en/index.php

HR Dept
www.hrdept.co.uk

Business Ally Organizational goal setting and development of business objectives is highly dependent on external opportunities or threats. HR professionals, together with other organizational managers, play a role in what strategic planners call **environmental scanning**, which involves identifying and analyzing *external* opportunities and threats that may be crucial to the organization's success. These managers can also supply competitive intelligence that may be useful as the company formulates its strategic plans. Details regarding a successful incentive plan being used by a competitor, impending labour shortages, and information about pending legislative changes are examples.

HR professionals can also add value to the strategy formulation process by supplying information regarding the company's *internal* strengths and weaknesses, particularly as they relate to the organization's workforce. HR professionals not only understand the value and social context of the business, but they are also increasingly relied on to determine how an organization should be structured and how work can be integrated to ensure financial success.

RPC

Provides support and expertise to managers and supervisors with respect to managing people

As highlighted in the Strategic HR box, the evolution of HR is far from done. HR's transformation has been underway for several years, but progress has been somewhat inconsistent because of lack of senior management support and the fact that many non-HR managers still view HR as a cost centre. Many HR professionals need to acquire more broad-based business knowledge and skill sets to be considered and respected as equal business partners by other executives in the company.[21] In a few organizations HR remains locked in an operational mode, processing forms and requests, administering compensation and benefits, managing policies and programs, and overseeing hiring and training.[22]

Table 1.1 illustrates the different focus of operational versus strategic HR activities.

STRATEGIC HR

The HR Role Continues to Evolve

The current shift in human resources management as a department and as a profession will continue to undergo evolution well into the 2020s. There are five major forces driving this change:

1. **Changing Technology.** Technology has helped automate basic HR functions, including managing day-to-day transactions and employee self-service systems. Rather than maintain HR technology experts in-house, nearly half of companies outsource operational functions of HR (payroll, benefits administration, employee education, recruitment processes, and workforce analytics). And rather than commoditizing or marginalizing HR functions, the shift has actually freed up HR professionals from these repetitive tasks to concentrate on more critical functions, such as decreasing turnover, focusing on the quality of talent secured, and developing leaders within the organization.

2. **New Rules.** Corporate accounting scandals that plagued the early 2000s resulted in a more focused alignment of organizational activities with new laws and compliance expectations. The financial crisis that started in 2008 included a series of additional regulations and expectations of organizational accountability. In this highly volatile environment with high accountability expectations, HR's role is increasingly strategic, including helping the organization recover from changes and comply with new regulations.

3. **Succession Planning.** Fifty percent of companies do not have a succession plan in place for their CEO. Tales of disruptive, hastily planned, and overall unsuccessful succession plans highlight the importance of identifying, grooming, and supporting potential successors within an organization. HR's role extends significantly beyond operational tasks to think critically about the complexities, time, and contingencies that must be considered in succession planning. Thus, HR executives are critical to organizational success through development and management of a comprehensive succession planning process.

4. **Identifying Top Talent.** While some companies argue that all employees must be motivated, educated, rewarded, and evaluated, others argue that a better return on investment can be secured by focusing on a smaller portion of workers (for example, the top 3 percent of all employees). HR is continually asked to establish a commitment to talent development that is fair, realistic, aware of limitations, and sustainable. A thoughtful set of criteria for assessing and managing talent goes well beyond administrative activities to include an integrative and strategic approach to HR.

5. **A New Breed of HR Leaders.** The rise of the CHRO (chief HR officer) or CTO (chief talent officer) confirms the seriousness and intent of many boards of directors in elevating and recognizing the role and capabilities of HR in an organization's leadership. Including HR in the C-suite highlights the importance of talent management and HR's perspective on organizational issues. HR's participation at the highest level of organizational decision making marks the transformation of the role of HR from operational expert to strategic expert in a concrete way.

Measuring the Value of HR: Metrics

Today's HR professionals need to be able to measure the value and impact of their organization's human capital and HRM practices. The use of various **metrics**, or statistics to measure the activities and results of HR, is now quite common. Traditional operational measures focused on the amount of activity and the costs of the HR function (such as number of job candidates interviewed per month, cost per hire, and so on), but today's measures need to reflect the quality of people and the effectiveness of HRM initiatives that build workforce capability. These new measures provide critical information that

metrics Statistics used to measure activities and results.

TABLE 1.1 Operational versus Strategic HR	
Operational	**Strategic**
Skills	Concepts
Administrative tasks	Planning
Reactive	Proactive
Collecting metrics/measurements	Analyzing metrics/measurements
Working to achieve goals and objectives	Setting the goals and objectives
Following the laws, policies, and procedures	Interpreting, establishing, and revising the laws, policies, and procedures
Employee focus	Organizational focus
Explaining benefits to employees	Designing benefit plans that help the organization achieve its mission and goals
Setting up training sessions for employees	Assessing training needs for the entire organization
Recruiting and selecting employees	Workforce planning and building relationships with external resources
Administering the salary/wage plan	Creating a pay plan that maximizes employees' productivity, morale, and retention
Always doing things the same way	Recognizing that there may be better ways of doing things; recognizing how changes affect the entire organization—not just HR
Works within the organizational culture	Attempts to improve the organizational culture

Source: D.M. Cox and C.H. Cox, "At the Table: Transitioning to Strategic Business Partner," *Workspan* (November 2003), p. 22.

can be linked to organizational outcomes like productivity, product or service quality, sales, market share, and profits. For example, the percentage of first-choice job candidates accepting an offer to hire indicates the strength of the organization's employment brand in the marketplace and directly affects the quality of the workforce.[23]

balanced scorecard A measurement system that translates an organization's strategy into a comprehensive set of performance measures.

Many organizations are using the **balanced scorecard** system that includes measures of the impact of HRM on organizational outcomes. The balanced scorecard approach translates an organization's strategy into a comprehensive set of performance measures. It includes financial measures that tell the results of actions already taken. It complements the financial measures with operational measures of organizational, business unit, or department success that will drive future performance. It balances long-term and short-term actions and measures of success relating to financial results, customers, internal business processes, and human capital management.[24] For example, one measure relating to HRM is the percentage of senior management positions with fully job-ready successors ready to move up.

ENVIRONMENTAL INFLUENCES ON HRM

There are numerous external and internal environmental influences that drive the strategic focus of HRM. To be effective, all managers, including those with responsibility for HR, must monitor the environment on an ongoing basis, assess the impact of any changes, and be proactive in responding to such challenges.

External Environmental Influences

Six major external environmental influences on HRM will be discussed: economic conditions, labour market issues, technology, government, globalization, and environmental concerns.

Economic Conditions

Economic conditions affect supply and demand for products and services, which, in turn, have a dramatic impact on the number and types of employees required as well as on an employer's ability to pay wages and provide benefits. When the economy is healthy, companies often hire more workers as demand for products and services increases. Consequently, unemployment rates fall, there is more competition for qualified employees, and training and retention strategies increase in importance. Conversely, during an economic downturn, some firms reduce pay and benefits to maintain workers' jobs. Other employers are forced to downsize by offering attractive early retirement and early leave programs or by laying off or terminating employees. Unemployment rates rise and employers are often overwhelmed with applicants when vacancies are advertised.

productivity The ratio of an organization's outputs (goods and services) to its inputs (people, capital, energy, and materials).

Productivity refers to the ratio of an organization's outputs (goods and services) to its inputs (people, capital, energy, and materials). Canada's relatively low productivity growth rate is of concern because of increasing global competition. To improve productivity, managers must find ways to produce more outputs with current input levels or use fewer resources to maintain current output levels. In most organizations today, productivity improvement is essential for long-term success.

primary sector Jobs in agriculture, fishing and trapping, forestry, and mining.

secondary sector Jobs in manufacturing and construction.

tertiary or service sector Jobs in public administration, personal and business services, finance, trade, public utilities, and transportation/communications.

Employment trends in Canada have been experiencing dramatic change. The **primary sector**, which includes agriculture, fishing and trapping, forestry, and mining, now represents only 4 percent of jobs. Employment in the **secondary sector** (manufacturing and construction) has decreased to 19 percent of jobs. The sector that has grown to represent 77 percent of jobs, dominating the Canadian economy, is the **tertiary or service sector**, which includes public administration, personal and business services, finance, trade, public utilities, and transportation/communications.

Since all jobs in the service sector involve the provision of services by employees to individual customers, effectively managing and motivating human resources is critical. Although there are some lesser-skilled jobs (in housekeeping and food services, for example), many service-sector jobs demand highly knowledgeable employees.

Labour Market Issues

Increasing Workforce Diversity Canada's workforce is among the most diverse in the world. Diversity refers to the attributes that humans are likely to use to tell themselves "that person is different from me." These attributes include demographic factors (such as race, gender, and age) as well as values and cultural norms.[25]

The proportion of visible and ethnic minorities entering the Canadian labour market is expected to continue growing at a faster pace than the rest of the population. Today, Canada admits more immigrants per capita than any other country. About two-thirds of visible minorities are immigrants, and approximately 20 percent of the Canadian population could be visible minorities by 2017. Ethnic diversity is also increasing. Currently, more than 200 different ethnic groups are represented among Canadian residents.[26]

As the employment rate for women has continued to converge toward that for men, organizations are accommodating working women and shared parenting responsibilities by offering onsite daycare, emergency childcare support, and flexible work arrangements. Women are now the primary breadwinners for 29 percent of dual-earner couples in Canada.[27]

The Aboriginal population is young and growing at a rate almost twice that of the rest of the Canadian population.[28] Young Aboriginal people represent an untapped source of employees who are still facing considerable difficulty in obtaining jobs and advancing in the workplace.

Canadians with disabilities continue to confront physical barriers to equality every day. Inaccessibility is still the rule, not the exception. Even though studies show that there are no performance differences in terms of productivity, attendance, and average tenure between employees who classify themselves as having a disability and those who do not, persons with disabilities continue, on average, to experience an unemployment rate that is 50 percent higher than that for the able-bodied population and an average income that is 17 percent lower.[29]

Another aspect of diversity is generational differences. There are four generations in the workplace, and nearly half of all Canadians say they have experienced a clash with workers older or younger than themselves. On the other hand, about one-quarter of workers say they don't notice age differences and another one-quarter think this situation provides an excellent learning opportunity.

Traditionalists Individuals born before 1946.

The senior group are the **Traditionalists** (also known as the Silent Generation), born before 1946. They grew up in era of hardship, including a world war and the Great Depression, and they tend to be quiet, loyal, and self-sacrificing. Although many have retired, many remain in the workforce.[30] For example, Walmart employs many seniors, even into their 90s, as greeters in their stores.[31]

Baby Boomers Individuals born between 1946 and 1964.

The **Baby Boomers**, born between 1946 and 1964, are the largest group in the workforce. They grew up in a time of major optimism and change amidst the moon landing and the women's movement. They tend to be career-focused workaholics who experienced a lot of competition in the workplace and are driven to succeed. Boomers are just beginning to retire and as a result the ratio of people not in the labour force (children under the age of 16 and seniors) per hundred people in the working population is expected to increase rapidly, from 44 per hundred in 2005 to 61 per hundred in 2031.[32] There are significantly fewer workers in later generations. This will create a labour shortage because a large, experienced group will be leaving the labour force and there will not be enough workers behind them to take over their jobs.

Generation X Individuals born between 1965 and 1980.

Generation X (individuals born between 1965 and 1980) is a much smaller group than the Boomers and were originally called the Baby Busters. This group grew up as divorce rates skyrocketed, and they were the first technology-literate generation. They tend to be independent and believe that security comes from transferability of skills rather than corporate loyalty. They can provide "out-of-the-box" thinking that can help companies deal with uncertainty. Flexible work–life arrangements and continuous skill development are valued by this generation.[33]

Generation Y Individuals born since 1980.

Generation Y (also known as Millennials and the Net Generation), born since 1980, are the children of the Baby Boomers, who have a reputation for being over-involved parents.[34] Members of this sizable group are beginning to enter the workforce. Although they are techno-savvy, comfortable with diversity, and eager to make a contribution, they tend also to be impatient and action oriented. They expect to change jobs frequently. New approaches to work and career management will be required to keep this group challenged.[35] For example, almost 90 percent of recent graduates in one survey said that they would deliberately seek out an employer with corporate social responsibility behaviour that reflects their own values. Unfortunately, businesses have been slow to catch on.[36] A summary of the attitudes/values/expectations and key characteristics of each generation is shown in **Table 1.2**.

Half of Canada's population has some postsecondary education (trades, college, or university).[37] Given the higher expectations of the better-educated labour force, managers are expected to ensure that the talents and capabilities of employees are fully utilized and that opportunities are provided for career growth.

RPC

Keeps current with emerging HR trends

TABLE 1.2 The Four Generations

	Traditionalists 1922–1945	Baby Boomers 1946–1964	Gen Xers 1965–1980	Gen Ys 1981–2000
Attitudes, Values, and Expectations	• Loyalty • Respect for authority • Dedication • Sacrifice • Conformity • Honour • Privacy • Stability • Economic conservatism	• Optimism • Involvement • Team oriented • Personal growth and gratification • Youthfulness • Equality • Career focused	• Independence • Self-reliance • Pragmatism • Skepticism • Informality • Balance	• Confidence • Diversity • Civic duty • Optimism • Immediate access to information and services
Key Characteristics	• Compliant • Stable • Detail oriented • Hard-working • Dedicated • Fiscally frugal • Trustworthy • Risk averse • Long-term focused	• Driven to succeed • Team player • Relationship focused • Eager to add value • Politically savvy in the workplace • Competitive	• Techno-literate • Flexible and adaptable • Creative • Entrepreneurial • Multitasker • Results driven • Individualistic	• Techno-savvy • Collective action • Expressive and tolerant of differences • Eager to accept challenges • Innovative and creative

Source: Adwoa K. Buahene and Giselle Kovary. Reprinted with permission from *HR Professional* (October/November 2007).

An Ethical : Dilemma

The maintenance department supervisor has just come to you, the HR manager, voicing concern about the safety of two of her reporting employees whom she recently discovered are functionally illiterate. What are your responsibilities to these employees, if any?

contingent/non-standard workers
Workers who do not have regular full-time employment status.

RPC

Advises on the status of dependent and independent contractors and determinants of employee status

RPC

Contributes to improvements in the organization's structures and work processes

On the other hand, a startlingly high proportion (26 percent) have only marginal literacy skills, meaning their ability to understand and use printed and written documents in daily activities to achieve goals and to develop knowledge and potential is limited. A frightening reality is that inadequate reading and writing skills have replaced lack of experience as the major reason for rejecting entry-level candidates.[38] About 15 percent of working-age Canadians are *functionally illiterate*—unable to read, write, calculate, or solve problems at a level required for independent functioning or the performance of routine technical tasks.[39] Functional illiteracy is exacting a toll not only on individual social and economic opportunities, but also on organizations' accident rates and productivity levels.

Non-Standard or Contingent Workers For the last 30 years or more, the labour market has undergone major structural changes with the growth of **contingent (or "non-standard") workers**, meaning workers that do not fit the traditional definition of permanent, full-time employment with the same employer on an indeterminate basis. The forms of employment involving part-time, fixed-term, temporary, home, and standby workers, those who have more than one job, and the self-employed have become so significant numerically that they now affect about one-third of the workforce. More women fall into this category than men.[40] Non-standard work is often poorly paid, offers little or no job security, and is generally not covered by employment legislation. Some are calling for these laws to be updated so that contingent workers are provided the same legal protection as other workers.[41]

Technology

From Twitter to Facebook to videoconferencing setups that make it seem like everyone is in the same room, there is a wide range of technology available to organizations today. All of this technology can make working in and managing a dispersed workforce easier and can enable people to work anywhere and everywhere. The workplace of today includes "hotels, cafes and conference venues, as well as public areas of lounges and airports."[42] However, it has also brought new concerns as the line between work and family time has become blurred.[43]

Questions concerning data control, accuracy, the right to privacy, and ethics are at the core of a growing controversy brought about by the new information technologies. Sophisticated computerized control systems are used to monitor employee speed, accuracy, and efficiency in some firms. More firms are also monitoring employee email, voice mail, telephone conversations, and computer usage, and some now monitor employee behaviour using video surveillance.[44]

Government

Various laws enacted by governments have had and will continue to have a dramatic impact on the employer–employee relationship in Canada. One of the factors that makes employment law in Canada so challenging is that there are 14 different jurisdictions involved. Each of the ten provinces and three territories has its own human rights, employment standards, labour relations, health and safety, and workers' compensation legislation. In addition, about 10 percent of the workforce (including employees of the federal government and Crown corporations, chartered banks, airlines, national railways, and the Canadian Armed Forces) is covered by federal employment legislation.

Although there is some commonality across jurisdictions, there is also considerable variation. Minimum wage, overtime pay requirements, vacation entitlement, and grounds protected under human rights legislation, for example, vary from one province/territory to another. Furthermore, some jurisdictions have pay equity and employment equity legislation while others do not. This means that companies with employees in more than one jurisdiction have different rules applying to different employees. There are, however, certain laws that apply to all employers and employees across Canada, such as employment insurance and the Canada/Quebec Pension Plan.

Globalization

globalization The emergence of a single global market for most products and services.

The term **globalization** refers to the emergence of a single global market for most products and services. This growing integration of the world economy into a single, huge marketplace is increasing the intensity of competition and leading most organizations to expand their operations around the world.[45] Firms in other parts of the world are also seeing human resources as a source of competitive advantage, as discussed in the Global HRM box.

GLOBAL HRM

Lin Congyin Prizes His Staff

Lin Congyin is the founder and chairperson of Jiumuwang Western-Style Fashional Clothes Co. Ltd. in Quanzhou, the third-largest city in Fujian province in China. His company makes men's trousers and has led the segment's market share for seven consecutive years, beating out more than 110 000 garment enterprises in China. For Lin, the most valuable assets of his undertaking are not capital, products, or brand: "Staff is paramount," he says. In the clothing industry, which has a high employee turnover rate, Jiumuwang's rate always stands at no higher than 1.5 percent, the lowest among his competitors. "Without my staff, we wouldn't have such a renowned brand with a reputation of high quality."

No matter how busy he is, Lin always makes time to sign birthday cards for all his 8000 staff, almost every day. And he has incorporated a monthly birthday party into his routine. "Just imagine a big party for at least 500 people every month," he says with excitement.

Lin has insisted on providing free annual physical examinations for every staff member for the past 10 years.

Moreover, he arranges the same package vacation for all of his staff, including cleaners, every year. "It's my responsibility to take care of all the staff."

"It's quite simple to explain: as a boss, staff is earning your money or helping you to make money," he says. "If being concerned with staff helps you make fortune, then they should be respected," he says. "When I started Jiumuwang, I realized this principle."

Jiumuwang creates a career path tailored to every new staff member when they join the company. "We provide training to help promote staff's abilities. As a result we gain a talent pool," he says. Earlier this year, the All-China Federation of Industry and Commerce and Federation of Trade Unions awarded Lin the National Outstanding Entrepreneur award for staff caring. "If we respect staff and offer them training, their value will be priceless," says Lin.

Source: Adapted from Li Fangfang, "Lin Means Business," *China Business Week* (March 31–April 6, 2008), p. 12.

There are increasing numbers of multinational corporations—firms that conduct a large part of their business outside the country in which they are headquartered and that locate a significant percentage of their physical facilities and human resources in other countries. For example, Toyota has a large market share in the United States, Europe, and Africa, and is the market leader in Australia. Toyota has factories all over the world, manufacturing or assembling vehicles like the Corolla for local markets. Notably, Toyota has manufacturing or assembly plants in the United States, Japan, Australia, Canada, Indonesia, Poland, South Africa, Turkey, the United Kingdom, France, and Brazil, and has recently added plants in Pakistan, India, Argentina, the Czech Republic, Mexico, Malaysia, Thailand, China, and Venezuela.[46]

Globalization means that HR professionals need to become familiar with employment legislation in other countries and need to manage ethical dilemmas when labour standards are substantially lower than those in Canada. Companies doing business in sub-Saharan Africa, for example, have to deal with a high death rate among employees with AIDS. Some are paying for antiretroviral drugs to keep their employees alive.[47]

Environmental Concerns

Environmental concerns have suddenly (some might say finally) emerged as an issue for people, particularly the younger generations.[48] Sustainability, climate change, global warming, pollution, carbon footprints, extinction of wildlife species, ecosystem fragility, and other related issues are increasingly important to people around the world. There is increasing evidence that interest in environmental issues is motivating the behaviour of employees, and that they are concerned about whether they work for environmentally responsible companies. Companies like Fairmont Hotels have made environmental stewardship a priority for almost 20 years. They have found that developing a reputation as an environmental leader and demonstrating corporate social responsibility have not only helped them to gain market share, but have also been a strong employee retention tool.[49]

Employees are increasingly concerned with social responsibility, including environmental responsibility, on the part of their employer.

Internal Environmental Influences

How a firm deals with the three internal environmental influences of organizational culture, organizational climate, and management practices has a major impact on its ability to meet its objectives.

Organizational Culture

organizational culture The core values, beliefs, and assumptions that are widely shared by members of an organization.

Organizational culture consists of the core values, beliefs, and assumptions that are widely shared by members of an organization. Culture is often conveyed through an organization's mission statement, as well as through stories, myths, symbols, and ceremonies. It serves a variety of purposes:

- communicating what the organization "believes in" and "stands for"
- providing employees with a sense of direction and expected behaviour (norms)
- shaping employees' attitudes about themselves, the organization, and their roles
- creating a sense of identity, orderliness, and consistency
- fostering employee loyalty and commitment

All managers with HR responsibilities play an important role in creating and maintaining the type of organizational culture desired. For example, they may organize recognition ceremonies for high-performing employees and be involved in decisions regarding symbols, such as a logo or the design of new company premises. Having a positive culture has a positive impact on employer branding, recruitment, retention, and productivity.

Organizational Climate

organizational climate The prevailing atmosphere that exists in an organization and its impact on employees.

Organizational climate refers to the prevailing atmosphere, or "internal weather," that exists in an organization and its impact on employees.[50] It can be friendly or unfriendly, open or secretive, rigid or flexible, innovative or stagnant. The major factors influencing the climate are management's leadership style, HR policies and practices, and the amount and style of organizational communication. The type of climate that exists is generally reflected in the level of employee motivation, job satisfaction, performance, and productivity. HR professionals play a key role in helping managers throughout the firm establish and maintain a positive organizational climate.

Employees in fast-food establishments are taught how to provide courteous, efficient customer service.

Management Practices

Management practices have changed considerably over the past decade, with many HRM implications. For example, the traditional bureaucratic structure with many levels of management is being replaced by

empowerment Providing workers with the skills and authority to make decisions that would traditionally be made by managers.

flatter organizational forms using cross-functional teams and improved communication. Since managers have more people reporting to them in flat structures, they cannot supervise their employees as closely and employee **empowerment** has greatly increased.

GROWING PROFESSIONALISM IN HRM

RPC

Stays current with professional knowledge

Fosters and promotes advancement of the profession

Today, HR practitioners must be professionals in terms of both performance and qualifications.[51] Every profession has several characteristics: (1) a common body of knowledge; (2) benchmarked performance standards; (3) a representative professional association; (4) an external perception as a profession; (5) a code of ethics; (6) required training credentials for entry and career mobility; (7) an ongoing need for skill development; and (8) a need to ensure professional competence is maintained and put to socially responsible uses. Every province has an association of HR practitioners (Prince Edward Island is included in Nova Scotia's) that currently assumes dual roles: first, as a professional association serving the interests of its members, and second, as a regulatory body serving the public. These two roles sometimes conflict, such as when the disciplinary role of a regulator conflicts with the professional interests of a member.[52]

Canadian Council of Human Resources Associations
www.cchra.ca/en/

World Federation of People Management Associations
www.wfpma.com

The Canadian Council of Human Resources Associations (CCHRA) is the 40 000-member national body through which all provincial HR associations are affiliated. The CCHRA is in turn a member of the World Federation of People Management Associations (WFPMA). The International Personnel Management Association (IPMA)–Canada is the national association for public-sector and quasi-public-sector HR professionals.

Other important associations for HR specialists include the Canadian Industrial Relations Association; WorldatWork for compensation and rewards issues; health and safety associations, such as the Industrial Accident Prevention Association, the Construction Safety Association, and Safe Communities Canada; and the Canadian Society for Training and Development.

certification Recognition for having met certain professional standards.

The Certified Human Resources Professional (CHRP) designation is a nationally recognized **certification** for Canadian HR professionals (there are approximately 21 000 of them at present).[53] Managed by the CCHRA and administered through provincial HR associations, the CHRP is similar to other professional designations, such as Chartered Accountant (CA) and Professional Engineer (P.Eng.); it recognizes members' qualifications and experience based on established levels of 187 required professional capabilities in seven functional dimensions: (1) professional practice; (2) organizational effectiveness; (3) staffing; (4) employee and labour relations; (5) total compensation; (6) organizational learning, training, and development; and (7) occupational health, safety, and wellness. The national certification requirements are shown in **Figure 1.4**. A recently launched SHRP designation (Senior Human Resources Professional) is aimed at professionals who possess other internationally recognized designations (for example, the US Society for Human Resource Management), or a work history demonstrating leadership, advisory capabilities, strategic orientation, a breadth of general business knowledge (not just limited to HR), and significant impact of their organization and profession.

In addition to the international- and national-level broad HR designations, a series of more specialized or specific professional designations in Canada allows those who may be interested in specialized areas to gain recognition for a deeper level of subject matter expertise. **Table 1.3** highlights a series of additional HR designations.[54]

FIGURE 1.4   National CHRP Certification Requirements

Please note that throughout the certification and recertification process, provincial variations may apply. Always contact the provincial HR association of which you are a member to ensure you have the most updated information that applies to you (www.hranb.org/cchra-member-association.php).

A. Initial Certification

To fulfill the academic requirements for the CHRP designation, a candidate must:

1. Become a member of a provincial human resources professionals association; and

2. Pass

(1) The National Knowledge Exam® (assesses knowledge of major human resources functions), and

(2) National Professional Practice Assessment® (measures human resources "experience"); must be written within 5 years of passing the National Knowledge Exam®. (Please note that the NPPA is not mandatory in Quebec and Ontario.)

As of January 1, 2011, CHRP Candidates—those who have passed the National Knowledge Exam® (NKE) – will require a minimum of a bachelor's degree from an accredited college or university in order to register for the National Professional Practice Assessment® and qualify for the CHRP designation. In some provinces, the degree requirement varies, or additional requirements may be applicable. Please contact your provincial HR association for more details.

B. Sign the National Code of Ethics (or your provincial association's equivalent)

C. Recertification

Every three years, all CHRPs will be required to recertify based on a set of professional development criteria, including seminars, conferences, volunteer work, or continuing education. Provincial variations may apply.

Source: Adapted from Canadian Council of Human Resources Associations, *What Is the CHRP Designation?* www.cchra.ca (July 29, 2009). Reproduced with permission of the Canadian Council of Human Resources Associations.

TABLE 1.3   Professional HR Designations in Canada (as of 2006)

Designation	Designation Holders in Canada
Certified Human Resources Professional (CHRP)	18 000
Group Benefits Associate (GBA)	1430
Registered Professional Recruiter (RPR)	1200
Canadian Payroll Manager (CPM)	1200
Certified Employee Benefits Specialist (CEBS)	896
Payroll Compliance Practitioner (PCP)	850
Certified Compensation Professional (CCP)	734
Retirement Plans Associate (RPA)	652
Canadian Management Professional (CMP)	550
International Personnel Management Association (IPMA) – Certified Practitioner	266
Registered Assessment Specialist (RAS)	250
Certified Training and Development Professional (CTDP)	250
Registered Professional Trainer (RPT)	200
Compensation Management Specialist (CMS)	174
Global Remuneration Professional (GPR)	37
Senior Professional in HR (SPHR)	37

Source: Adapted from S. Klie, "Senior HR Designations Unveiled," *Canadian HR Reporter*, July 7, 2009. Reprinted by permission of Canadian HR Reporter. © Copyright Thomson Reuters Canada Ltd., (2012) Toronto, Ontario, 1-800-387-5164. Web: www.hrreporter.com

Chapter SUMMARY

1. Human resources management (HRM) refers to the management of people in organizations. Strategic HRM involves linking HRM with strategic goals and objectives to improve business performance. In more and more firms, HR professionals are becoming strategic partners in strategy formulation and execution.

2. The two major stages in the evolution of management thinking about workers were (1) scientific management, which focused on production, and (2) the human resources movement, in which it was recognized that organizational success is linked to operational and strategic management of labour.

3. Core roles HR professionals must fulfill today include the roles of talent manager, culture/change steward, strategic architect, operational executor, business ally, and credible activist. These roles are shared with managers and executives in the organization, with HR professionals often assuming roles of advisers or subject matter experts.

4. Activities of employee management, empowerment, training, and guidance are often shared between managers in the organization (executive and line managers) and HR professionals. Therefore, managers, executives,

and HR personnel are all influential in effective human resources management.

5. Human resources activities are now being seen as falling into two categories. The first is the traditional operational (administrative) category, where HR hires and maintains employees and then manages employee separations. The second is the more recent strategic category, where HR is focused on ensuring that the organization is staffed with the most effective human capital to achieve its strategic goals.

6. A number of external factors have an impact on HRM, including economic factors, labour market issues, technology, government, globalization, and environmental concerns.

7. There are numerous professional designations that will boost a career trajectory in human resources. The most basic of these is the Canadian Human Resources Professional (CHRP). However, additional designations exist that are important and may be influential in building expertise and careers in management or human resources management.

MyManagementLab

Visit MyManagementLab to access a personalized Study Plan and additional study tools for this chapter.

Key TERMS

Baby Boomers *(p. 12)*
balanced scorecard *(p. 10)*
certification *(p. 18)*
change agents   *(p. 8)*
contingent/non-standard workers *(p. 14)*
employee engagement *(p. 6)*
empowerment *(p. 17)*
environmental scanning *(p. 8)*
Generation X *(p. 13)*
Generation Y *(p. 13)*
globalization *(p. 15)*
human capital *(p. 2)*
human resources management (HRM) *(p. 2)*

human resources movement *(p. 3)*
metrics *(p. 9)*
organizational climate *(p. 17)*
organizational culture *(p. 17)*
outsourcing *(p. 4)*
primary sector *(p. 11)*
productivity *(p. 11)*
scientific management *(p. 3)*
secondary sector *(p. 11)*
strategy *(p. 8)*
tertiary or service sector *(p. 11)*
Traditionalists *(p. 12)*

Review and Discussion QUESTIONS

1. Describe the transformation that HR underwent over the years. Discuss how changes in internal and external factors contributed to the evolution in HR.

2. Describe the role of HR in strategy formulation and strategy implementation.

3. Describe how the external environment influences HR.

4. Differentiate between organizational culture and organizational climate.

5. Describe the multiple jurisdictions related to employment legislation affecting HRM in Canada.

6. Discuss the six core competencies required of HR professionals. Identify how these competencies are also embedded in the roles of line managers, senior managers, and C-level executives in an organization.

7. Explain how HR has become professionalized and describe the value of this professionalization.

Critical Thinking QUESTIONS

1. Explain how demographics and workforce diversity have had an impact on the organization in which you are working or one in which you have worked. What policies or practices did managers or HR in the organization have in place to help assist with the management of a diverse internal labour force?

2. Explain how changing economic and competitive pressures have had an impact on the organization in which you are working or one in which you have worked. How has your business responded to these pressures?

3. A firm has requested your assistance in ensuring that its multigenerational workforce functions effectively as a team. What strategies or programs would you recommend? Why?

4. Choose a non-HR role you have had in your previous jobs. Identify how you used the core competencies of HR professionals in that role and how it affected your job performance.

Experiential EXERCISES

1. Working alone or with a small group of classmates, interview an HR manager and prepare a short essay regarding his or her role in strategy formulation and implementation.

2. Review job ads for five senior HR roles on job posting websites or corporate websites. Identify common competencies required for those roles as per the ads. Contrast these required competencies (both implied and explicit) with the core HR professional competencies highlighted in this chapter. Discuss the most consistently required competency and the impact of that competency on organizational success.

3. Review job ads for five executive roles (such as CEO, vice-president, or president) on job posting websites or corporate websites. Identify common competencies required for those roles as per the ads. Contrast these required competencies (both implied and explicit) with the core HR professional competencies highlighted in this chapter. Discuss the most consistently required competency and how it is important in non-HR roles.

4. According to a 2011 study of the world's most attractive firms (released by Universum), the top 10 employers for career seekers with a business background were (in priority order): Google, KPMG, PricewaterhouseCoopers, Ernst & Young, Deloitte, Microsoft, Procter & Gamble, J.P. Morgan, Apple, and Goldman Sachs. In groups, review the company websites of these organizations to determine the corporate strategy, objectives, and markets that these organizations target. As a team, discuss the similarities and differences among the strategies, objectives, and markets of these 10 employers. Explain how these factors might affect Generation Y perceiving these companies as desirable employers.

5. Using the sample balanced scorecard template provided by your professor, in pairs develop a balanced scorecard measure for a hypothetical company in the retail urban clothing sector. This company has many stores in large and small cities in Ontario and Quebec. Be sure to take into consideration current economic conditions as you develop your measures.

   Exchange your completed set of measures with another pair. Compare and contrast your measures. Is one set "better" than the other? Why or why not? Debrief as instructed.

Running CASE

Introduction

The main theme of this book is that HRM—activities like recruiting, selecting, training, and rewarding employees—is not just the job of a central HR group, but rather one in which every manager must engage. Perhaps nowhere is this more apparent than in the typical small service business, where the owner–manager usually has no HR staff to rely on. However, the success of such an enterprise often depends largely on the effectiveness with which workers are recruited, hired, trained, evaluated, and rewarded. To help illustrate and emphasize the front-line manager's HR role, throughout this book we will use a continuing ("running") case based on an actual small business in Ottawa's high-tech region. Each segment will illustrate how the case's main players—owner–managers Jennifer Lau and Pierre LeBlanc—confront and solve HRM problems each day by applying the concepts and techniques presented in that particular chapter. Here is some background information you'll need to answer questions that arise in subsequent chapters.

LearnInMotion.com: A Profile

Jennifer and Pierre graduated from university as business majors in June 2008 and got the idea for LearnInMotion.com as a result of a project they worked on together their last semester in their entrepreneurship class. The professor had divided the students into two- or three-person teams and asked them to "create a business plan for a high-tech company." The idea the two came up with was LearnInMotion.com. The basic idea of the website was to list a vast array of web-based, CD-ROM–based, or textbook-based continuing education-type business courses for working people who wanted to take a course from the comfort of their own homes. Users could come to the website to find and then take a course in one of several ways. Some courses could be completed interactively on the web via the site; others were in a form that was downloadable directly to the user's computer; others (which were either textbook or CD-ROM–based) could be ordered and delivered (in several major metropolitan areas) by independent contractor delivery people. Their business mission was "to provide work-related learning when, where, and how you need it."

Based on their research, they knew the market for work-related learning was booming. At the same time, professional development activities like these were increasingly Internet-based. Tens of thousands of on- and offline training firms, universities, associations, and other content providers were trying to reach their target customers via the Internet. Jennifer and Pierre understandably thought they were in the right place at the right time.

Jennifer's father had some unused loft space in Kanata, Ontario, so with about $45 000 of accumulated savings, Jennifer and Pierre incorporated and were in business. They retained the services of an independent programmer and hired two people— a web designer to create the graphics for the site (which would then be programmed by the programmer) and a content manager whose job was to enter information onto the site as it came in from content providers. By the end of 2008, they also completed upgrading their business plan into a form they could show to prospective venture capitalists. They sent the first version to three Canadian venture capitalists. Then they waited.

And then they waited some more. They never heard back from the first three venture capitalists, so they sent their plan to five more. They still got no response. But Pierre and Jennifer pressed on. By day they called customers to get people to place ads on their site, to get content providers to list their available courses, and to get someone—anyone—to deliver textbook- and CD-ROM–based courses, as needed, across Canada. By May 2009 they had about 30 content providers offering courses and content through LearnInMotion.com. In the summer, they got their first serious nibble from a venture capital firm. They negotiated with this company through much of the summer, came to terms in the early fall, and closed the deal—getting just over $1 million in venture funding—in November 2009.

After a stunning total of $75 000 in legal fees (they had to pay both their firm's and the venture capital firm's lawyers to navigate the voluminous disclosure documents and agreements), they had just over $900 000 to spend. The funding, according to the business plan, was to go toward accomplishing five main goals: redesigning and expanding the website; hiring about seven more employees; moving to a larger office; designing and implementing a personal information manager (PIM)/calendar (users and content providers could use the calendar to interactively keep track of their personal and business schedules); and last but not least, driving up sales. LearnInMotion was off and running.

QUESTIONS

1   What is human resources management and does it have a role to play in this organization? If so, in what ways specifically?

2   What environmental influences will affect the role that human resources management could play within this organization?

Case INCIDENT

Jack Nelson's Problem

As a new member of the board of directors for a local bank, Jack Nelson was being introduced to all the employees in the home office. When he was introduced to Ruth Johnson he was curious about her work and asked her what the machine she was using did. Johnson replied that she really did not know what the machine was called or what it did. She explained that she had only been working there for two months. She did, however, know precisely how to operate the machine. According to her supervisor, she was an excellent employee.

At one of the branch offices, the supervisor in charge spoke to Nelson confidentially, telling him that "something was wrong," but she didn't know what. For one thing, she explained, employee turnover was too high, and no sooner had one employee been put on the job than another one resigned. With customers to see and loans to be made, she continued, she had little time to work with the new employees as they came and went.

All branch supervisors hired their own employees without communication with the home office or other branches. When an opening developed, the supervisor tried to find a suitable employee to replace the worker who had quit.

After touring the 22 branches and finding similar problems in many of them, Nelson wondered what the home office should do or what action he should take. The banking firm was generally regarded as a well-run institution that had grown from 27 to 191 employees in the past eight years. The more he thought about the matter, the more puzzled Nelson became. He couldn't quite put his finger on the problem, and he didn't know whether to report his findings to the president.

QUESTIONS

1   What do you think is causing some of the problems in the bank's branches?

2   Do you think setting up an HR unit in the main office would help?

3   What specific functions should an HR unit carry out? What HR functions would then be carried out by supervisors and other line managers? What role should the Internet play in the new HR organization?

Source: Claude S. George, *Supervision in Action: Art Managing Others,* 4th Ed., ©1985. Reprinted and Electronically reproduced by permission of Pearson Education, Inc., Upper Saddle River, New Jersey.

MyManagementLab

Visit MyManagementLab to access a personalized Study Plan and additional study tools for this chapter.

CBC To view the CBC videos, read a summary, and answer discussion questions, go to MyManagementLab

2

The Changing Legal Emphasis
Compliance and Impact on Canadian Workplaces

LEARNING OUTCOMES

AFTER STUDYING THIS CHAPTER, YOU SHOULD BE ABLE TO

EXPLAIN how employment-related issues are governed in Canada.

DISCUSS at least five prohibited grounds for discrimination under human rights legislation, and DESCRIBE the requirements for reasonable accommodation.

DESCRIBE behaviour that could constitute harassment.

EXPLAIN the employers' responsibilities regarding harassment.

DESCRIBE the role of minimums established in employment standards legislation and the enforcement process.

DISCUSS HR's role in ensuring compliance with employment legislation in Canada.

REQUIRED PROFESSIONAL CAPABILITIES (RPC)

- Identifies and masters legislation and jurisprudence relevant to HR functions

- Ensures that the organization's HR policies and practices align with human rights legislation

- Promotes a productive culture in the organization that values diversity, trust, and respect for individuals and their contributions

- Assesses requests for HR information in light of corporate policy, freedom of information legislation, evidentiary privileges, and contractual or other releases

- Contributes to the development of information security measures issues

THE LEGAL FRAMEWORK FOR EMPLOYMENT LAW IN CANADA

A 2011 survey conducted by Queen's University in partnership with the Human Resources Institute of Alberta (HRIA) and the International Personnel Management Association (IPMA) asked 451 HR professionals to identify the top five critical pieces of knowledge required in their roles. While business acumen was identified as the most critical piece of knowledge, employment law/legislative awareness and talent management were tied for second position.[1] While HR professionals are expected to provide guidance, training, programs, and policy developments that are legally defensible, the actions of supervisors and managers as agents of the organization must also abide by legislated rules and regulations. The risk of expensive lawsuits and their impact on employer branding or reputation requires an awareness of employment law within the organization that extends well beyond just the HR professionals.

There are a number of distinct sets of responsibilities that exist between the employee and employer, including formal and informal expectations. There is a mutual expectation of each party to maintain the employment relationship by fulfilling their own responsibilities within the relationship. For example, there may be an implied, informal expectation from an employee's point of view that as long as they attend work for the scheduled number of hours, they can expect job security and continued employment from the employer. Such informal and personalized expectations are difficult to manage and correct if one party feels that the other has violated the expectations within the mutual relationship. As a result, the influence and impact of formal expectations (largely established through legislation and the interpretation of it) plays a significant role in the Canadian workplace.

The primary objective of most employment legislation in Canada is to prevent employers from exploiting paid workers, assuming that an implicit power imbalance exists in the employment relationship (in favour of the employer).[2] While employers have a right to modify employee work terms and arrangements according to legitimate business needs, employees have a right to be protected from harmful business practices. In this regard, the government's role is to balance employee and employer needs through the development and maintenance of employment legislation. The judicial system provides a forum for interpreting legislation according to the precedents past judicial rulings have established.

Canadian employment legislation is largely modelled on the US National Labor Relations Act with three significant differences. First, the Canadian population is more inclined to accept and expect government-mandated regulations about organizational activities, since Canadians are generally more receptive to governmental regulatory intervention than the US public.[3]

Second, in the United States the historical notion of "employment at will" allowed either the employee or employer to break the relationship (with no liability) provided that no autonomous employment contract exists and employees are not represented by a collective bargaining unit. In Canada, employers are permitted to terminate employment without a reason provided they ensure reasonable notice is given to workers. In return, the employee is permitted to quit, strike, or otherwise cease employment without penalty, provided that they align with the legislation pertaining to such events.

Finally, the US employment legislation model is largely centralized. In contrast, the primary responsibility for employment-related laws resides with the provinces and territories in Canada. Today, provincial/territorial employment laws govern approximately 90 percent of Canadian workers. The remaining 10 percent of the workforce are employed in the federal civil service, Crown corporations and agencies, or businesses engaged in transportation, banking, and communications, which are all governed by federal employment legislation. Thus there are 14 jurisdictions—10 provinces, 3 territories, and Canada as a whole—for employment law.

As highlighted in **Figure 2.1**, at the broadest level all persons residing in Canada are guaranteed protection under constitutional law, particularly the Charter of Rights and Freedoms. The regulations set forth in the Charter are not employment specific, but all employers must abide by them because they are fundamental, guaranteed rights to all persons residing in Canada. There are also provincial human rights codes that ensure the rights of every Canadian are protected and that all persons are treated with equality and respect. Discrimination based on protected grounds highlighted in the legislation is prohibited not only in the employment relationship but also in the delivery of goods and services. Therefore, while the Charter of Rights and Freedom and human rights codes extend beyond just the employment relationship, they both have a significant impact on workplace practices.

FIGURE 2.1   Multiple Layers of Canadian Legislation Affecting Workplace Practices

Affects general population

↑
Canadian Charter of Rights and Freedom—Basic rights guaranteed to all persons residing in Canada

Human Rights Legislation—Protection from discrimination in employment relationships and the delivery of goods and services

Employment Standards Legislation—Establishes minimum terms and conditions of the employment relationship within each jurisdiction (e.g., minimum wages, hours of work, maternity leave)

Ordinary Laws—Protection under context- or content-specific laws affecting workplaces (like Occupational Health and Safety)

Collective Bargaining Agreement—A legally binding agreement establishing minimum terms and conditions of employment affecting unionized positions

Employment Contract—A contract between an individual employee and their employer regarding specified employment conditions in specified roles
↓

Affects specific employees and conditions

Source: Chhinzer, 2011

RPC

Identifies and masters legislation and jurisprudence relevant to HR functions

Government of Canada
http://canada.gc.ca

regulations Legally binding rules established by special regulatory bodies created to enforce compliance with the law and aid in its interpretation.

Hints TO ENSURE LEGAL COMPLIANCE

There is also a series of employment-specific legislation in Canada that employers must abide by, such as the Employment Standards Act, which vary slightly by jurisdiction. There is a great deal of commonality to the legislation, but there are also some differences. For example, vacations, statutory holidays, and minimum wage standards are provided by all jurisdictions, but specific entitlements may vary from one jurisdiction to the next. Therefore, a company with employees in different provinces/territories must monitor the legislation in each of those jurisdictions and remain current as legislation changes. Ensuring legality across multiple jurisdictions can be complex, since it is possible for a policy, practice, or procedure to be legal in one jurisdiction yet illegal in others.

There are laws that specifically regulate some areas of HRM—occupational health and safety (occupational health and safety acts are reviewed in Chapter 14), union relations (labour relations acts are reviewed in Chapter 16), and pensions and compensation (pay equity acts, the Income Tax Act, and others are discussed briefly in Chapter 13).

Yet even more specific is the issue of contract law, which governs collective agreements and individual employment contracts. Such laws impose specific requirements and constraints on management and employee policies, procedures, and practices. For example, a collective bargaining agreement is a contract regarding the terms and conditions of employment that both employees and employers must abide by legally. In non-unionized roles, individual employment contracts are often signed prior to the commencement of the employment relationship and create an individualized legal contract that employees and employers must abide by.

In addition to the legislation above, Canada has also inherited the English system of tort law. Tort law is primarily judge-based law, where the precedent and jurisprudences set by one judge through his or her assessment of a case establishes how similar cases will be interpreted. Tort laws are often separated into two categories: intentional torts (for example, assault, battery, trespass, intentional affliction of mental distress) and unintentional torts (for example, negligence based on events where harm is caused by carelessness).

To avoid flooding the courts with complaints and the prosecutions of relatively minor infractions, the government in each jurisdiction creates special regulatory bodies to enforce compliance with the law and aid in its interpretation. Such bodies, which include human rights commissions and ministries of labour, develop legally binding rules called **regulations** and evaluate complaints.

Within these various levels of legislation there is a sense of hierarchy. The more general the impact of the legislation, the more it supersedes lower levels of legislation. For example, a collective bargaining agreement cannot agree to wages less than the minimum wage established in the provincial Employment Standards Act. Likewise, the Employment Standards Act cannot violate the minimums set forth in the Charter of Rights and Freedom.

There are two opposing interpretations of Canadian legislation. Employees often choose to view the regulations as a statutory floor and expect to receive higher than the minimum requirements (more than the minimum wage, minimum entitlement for vacation days, minimum entitlement for severance pay, and so on). In contrast, employers often prefer to view legislated guidelines as a contractual ceiling and align maximum commitment levels to the minimums established in the guidelines. HR professionals play a critical role in balancing these divergent sets of expectations, with obligations toward both the employees and employers.

LEGISLATION PROTECTING THE GENERAL POPULATION

Human rights legislation makes it illegal to discriminate, even unintentionally, against various groups. Reactive (complaint driven) in nature, the focus of such legislation is on the types of acts in which employers should *not* engage. Included in this category are

1. *the Charter of Rights and Freedoms*, federal legislation that is the cornerstone of human rights in Canada, and
2. *human rights legislation*, which is present in every jurisdiction.

The Charter of Rights and Freedoms

Charter of Rights and Freedoms
Federal law enacted in 1982 that guarantees fundamental freedoms to all Canadians.

The cornerstone of Canada's legislation pertaining to issues of human rights is the Constitution Act, which contains the **Charter of Rights and Freedoms**. The Charter applies to the actions of all levels of government (federal, provincial/territorial, and municipal) and agencies under their jurisdiction as they go about their work of creating laws. The Charter takes precedence over all other laws, which means that all legislation must meet Charter standards; thus, it is quite far-reaching in scope.

There are two notable exceptions to this generalization. The Charter allows laws to infringe on Charter rights if they can be demonstrably justified as reasonable limits in a "free and democratic society." Since "demonstrably justified" and "reasonable" are open to interpretation, many issues challenged under the Charter eventually end up before the Supreme Court of Canada, its ultimate interpreter. The second exception occurs when a legislative body invokes the "notwithstanding" provision, which allows the legislation to be exempted from challenge under the Charter.

Supreme Court of Canada
www.scc-csc.gc.ca

The Charter provides the following fundamental rights and freedoms to every Canadian, including but not limited to:

1. freedom of conscience and religion
2. freedom of thought, belief, opinion, and expression, including freedom of the press and other media of communication
3. freedom of peaceful assembly
4. freedom of association

In addition, the Charter provides Canadian multicultural heritage rights, First Nations' rights, minority language education rights, equality rights, the right to live and work anywhere in Canada, the right to due process in criminal proceedings, and the right to democracy.[4]

equality rights Section 15 of the Charter of Rights and Freedoms, which guarantees the right to equal protection and benefit of the law without discrimination.

Section 15—**equality rights**—provides the basis for human rights legislation, as it guarantees the right to equal protection and benefit of the law without discrimination, in particular without discrimination based on race, national or ethnic origin, colour, religion, sex, age, or mental or physical disability.[5]

Human Rights Legislation

human rights legislation
Jurisdictions specific legislation that prohibits intentional and unintentional discrimination in employment situations and in the delivery of goods and services.

Every person residing in Canada is protected by **human rights legislation,** which prohibits intentional and unintentional discrimination in employment situations and the delivery of goods and services. Human rights legislation is extremely broad in scope, affecting almost all aspects of HRM when applied to the employment relationship. An important feature of human rights legislation is that it supersedes the terms of any employment contract or collective agreement.[6] For these reasons, supervisors and managers must be thoroughly familiar with the human rights legislation of their jurisdiction and their legal obligations and responsibilities specified therein.

RPC

Ensures the organization's HR policies and practices align with human rights legislation

Government of Canada
http://canada.gc.ca

Canadian Human Rights Tribunal
www.chrt-tcdp.gc.ca

Human rights legislation prohibits discrimination against all Canadians in a number of areas, including employment. To review individual provincial and territorial human rights laws would be confusing because of the many but generally minor differences among them, often only in terminology (for example, some provinces use the term "creed," others "religion"). As indicated in **Figure 2.2,** most provincial/territorial laws are similar to the federal statute in terms of scope, interpretation, and application. All jurisdictions prohibit discrimination on the grounds of race, colour, religion/creed, sex, marital status, age, disability, and sexual orientation. Some, but not all, jurisdictions further prohibit discrimination on the basis of family status, nationality or ethnic origin, and various other grounds.

Discrimination Defined

discrimination As used in the context of human rights in employment, a distinction, exclusion, or preference based on one of the prohibited grounds that has the effect of nullifying or impairing the right of a person to full and equal recognition and exercise of his or her human rights and freedoms.

Central to human rights laws is the concept of **discrimination.** When someone is accused of discrimination, it generally means that he or she is perceived to be acting in an unfair or prejudiced manner within the context of prohibited grounds for discrimination. For example, if an employee was discriminated against based on his or her initials or if they wore a black top to work that day, this would fall outside the scope of human rights legislation. The law prohibits unfair discrimination—making choices on the basis of perceived but inaccurate differences to the detriment of specific individuals or groups. Standards pertaining to unfair discrimination have changed over time. Both intentional and unintentional discrimination is prohibited.

Intentional Discrimination

Except in specific circumstances that will be described later, intentional discrimination is prohibited. An employer cannot discriminate *directly* by deliberately refusing to hire, train, or promote an individual, for example, on any of the prohibited grounds. It is important to realize that deliberate discrimination is not necessarily overt. In fact, overt (blatant) discrimination is relatively rare today. But subtle, indirect discrimination can be difficult to prove. For example, if a 60-year-old applicant is not selected for a job and is told that there was a better-qualified candidate, it is often difficult for the rejected job seeker to determine if someone else truly did more closely match the firm's specifications or if the employer discriminated on the basis of age.

differential or unequal treatment
Treating an individual differently in any aspect of terms and conditions of employment based on any of the prohibited grounds

An employer is also prohibited from intentional discrimination in the form of **differential or unequal treatment.** No individuals or groups may be treated differently in any aspects or terms and conditions of employment based on any

FIGURE 2.2	Prohibited Grounds of Discrimination in Employment by Jurisdiction

Prohibited Grounds of Discrimination	Federal	Alta.	B.C.	Man.	N.B.	N.L.	N.S.	Ont.	P.E.I.	Que.	Sask.	N.W.T.	Y.T.	Nunavut
Race	◆	◆	◆	◆	◆	◆	◆	◆	◆	◆	◆	◆	◆	◆
Colour	◆	◆	◆	◆	◆	◆	◆	◆	◆	◆	◆	◆	◆	◆
Creed or religion	◆	◆	◆	◆	◆	◆	◆	◆	◆	◆	◆	◆	◆	◆
Sex	◆	◆	◆	◆	◆	◆	◆	◆	◆	◆	◆	◆	◆	◆
Marital status	◆	◆	◆	◆	◆	◆	◆	◆	◆	◆	◆	◆	◆	◆
Age	◆	◆ 18+	◆ 19–65	◆	◆	◆ 19–65	◆	◆ 18+	◆	◆	◆ 18–64	◆	◆	◆
Mental & physical disability	◆	◆	◆	◆	◆	◆	◆	◆	◆	◆	◆	◆	◆	◆
Sexual orientation	◆	◆	◆	◆	◆	◆	◆	◆	◆	◆	◆	◆	◆	◆
National or ethnic origin	◆			◆	◆	◆	◆	◆	◆	◆	◆	◆	◆	◆
Family status	◆	◆	◆	◆			◆	◆	◆	◆	◆	◆	◆	◆
Ancestry or place of origin		◆	◆	◆	◆			◆			◆	◆	◆	◆
Political belief			◆	◆	◆	◆	◆		◆	◆			◆	
Association				◆	◆		◆	◆	◆			◆	◆	◆
Source of income		◆		◆			◆		◆	◆	◆			
Social condition or origin					◆	◆				◆			◆	
Language								◆		◆			◆	
Pardoned conviction	◆											◆	◆	◆
Record of criminal conviction										◆			◆	
Assignment, attachment, or seizure of pay						◆								

Source: Prohibited Grounds of Discrimination in Canada. http://www.chrc-ccdp.ca/pdf/prohibit_en.pdf, Canadian Human Rights Commission, 2006. Reproduced with the permission of the Ministry of Public Works and Government Services Canada, 2012.

of the prohibited grounds. For example, it is illegal for an employer to request that only female applicants for a factory job demonstrate their lifting skills or to insist that any candidates with a physical disability undergo a pre-employment medical, unless all applicants are being asked to do so.

It is also illegal for an employer to engage in intentional discrimination *indirectly* through another party. This means that an employer may not ask someone else to discriminate on his or her behalf. For example, an employer cannot request that an employment agency refer only male candidates for consideration as management trainees or instruct supervisors that racial minorities are to be excluded from consideration for promotions.

Discrimination because of association is another possible type of intentional discrimination listed specifically as a prohibited ground in several Canadian

discrimination because of association Denial of rights because of friendship or other relationship with a protected group member jurisdictions. It involves the denial of rights because of friendship or other relationship with a protected group member. An example would be the refusal of a firm to promote a highly qualified male into senior management on the basis of the assumption that his wife, who was recently diagnosed with multiple sclerosis, will require too much of his time and attention and that her needs may restrict his willingness to travel on company business.

**unintentional/constructive/
systemic discrimination**
Discrimination that is embedded in policies and practices that appear neutral on the surface and are implemented impartially, but have an adverse impact on specific groups of people for reasons that are not job related or required for the safe and efficient operation of the business.

Unintentional Discrimination

Unintentional discrimination (also known as **constructive** or **systemic discrimination**) is the most difficult to detect and combat. Typically, it is embedded in policies and practices that appear neutral on the surface and that are implemented impartially, but have an adverse impact on specific groups of people for reasons that are not job related or required for the safe and efficient operation of the business. Examples are shown in **Figure 2.3**.

Permissible Discrimination via Bona Fide Occupational Requirements

**bona fide occupational
requirement (BFOR)** A justifiable reason for discrimination based on business necessity (that is, required for the safe and efficient operation of the organization) or a requirement that can be clearly defended as intrinsically required by the tasks an employee is expected to perform.

Employers are permitted to discriminate if employment preferences are based on a **bona fide occupational requirement** (BFOR), defined as a justifiable reason for discrimination based on business necessity, such as the requirement for the safe and efficient operation of the organization (for example, a person who is blind cannot be employed as a truck driver or bus driver). In some cases, a BFOR exception to human rights protection is fairly obvious. For example, when casting in the theatre, there may be specific roles that justify using age, sex, or national origin as a recruitment and selection criterion.

FIGURE **2.3**   Examples of Systemic Discrimination

- Minimum height and weight requirements, which screen out disproportionate numbers of women and people from Asia, who tend to be shorter in stature.
- Internal hiring policies or word-of-mouth hiring in workplaces that have not embraced diversity.
- Limited accessibility to company premises, which poses a barrier to persons with mobility limitations.
- Culturally biased or non-job-related employment tests, which discriminate against specific groups.
- Job evaluation systems that are not gender-neutral; that is, they undervalue traditional female-dominated jobs.
- Promotions based exclusively on seniority or experience in firms that have a history of being white-male-dominated.
- Lack of a harassment policy or guidelines, or an organizational climate in which certain groups feel unwelcome and uncomfortable.

Source: Based on material provided by the Ontario Women's Directorate and the Canadian Human Rights Commission.

The Meiorin case (Supreme Court of Canada, 1999) established three criteria that are now used to assess if the discrimination qualifies as a bona fide occupational requirement. First, is the question of rationale: Was the policy or procedure that resulted in the discrimination based on a legitimate, work-related purpose? Second, is the question of good faith: Did the decision makers or other agents of the organization honestly believe that the requirement was necessary to fulfill the requirements of the role? Third, (and this one is often the most difficult to prove) is the question of reasonable necessity: Was it impossible to accommodate those who have been discriminated against without imposing undue hardship on the employer?

The issue of BFORs gets more complicated in situations in which the occupational requirement is less obvious; the onus of proof is then placed on the employer. There are a number of instances in which BFORs have been established. For example, adherence to the tenets of the Roman Catholic Church has been deemed a BFOR when selecting faculty to teach in a Roman Catholic school.[7] The Royal Canadian Mounted Police has a requirement that guards be of the same sex as prisoners being guarded, which was also ruled to be a BFOR.[8]

Reasonable Accommodation

An important feature of human rights legislation is the requirement for **reasonable accommodation.** Employers are required to adjust employment policies and practices so that no individual is prevented from doing his or her job on the basis of prohibited grounds for discrimination. Accommodation may involve scheduling adjustments to accommodate religious beliefs or workstation redesign to enable an individual with a physical disability to perform a particular task. Employers are expected to accommodate to the point of **undue hardship**, meaning that the financial cost of the accommodation (even with outside sources of funding) or health and safety risks to the individual concerned or other employees would make accommodation impossible.[9] Failure to make every reasonable effort to accommodate employees is a violation of human rights legislation in all Canadian jurisdictions. The term "reasonable" is relatively vague and open to interpretation, which can be found in the precedent that has been established in the legal system. The Supreme Court of Canada recently clarified the scope of the duty to accommodate by stating that it does not require an employer to completely alter the essence of the employment contract, whereby the employee has a duty to perform work in exchange for remuneration. For example, if the characteristics of an illness are such that the employee remains unable to work for the foreseeable future, even though the employer has tried to accommodate the employee, the employer will have satisfied the test of undue hardship.[10]

Human Rights Case Examples

In claims of discrimination, it does not matter if the protected grounds were the primary or heaviest weighted factor in the decision being challenged or if it was one of many considerations made in the decision. If there were 20 criteria used to make a decision, and even one of those criteria violated protection against discrimination as per the applicable human rights legislation, then the entire decision made by the employer can be deemed illegal. Provincial/Territorial human

---

reasonable accommodation The adjustment of employment policies and practices that an employer may be expected to make so that no individual is denied benefits, disadvantaged in employment, or prevented from carrying out the essential components of a job because of grounds prohibited in human rights legislation.

undue hardship The point to which employers are expected to accommodate employees under human rights legislative requirements.

The Job Accommodation Network
http://askjan.org/

Alberta Human Rights Commission
www.albertahumanrights.ab.ca

British Columbia Human Rights Tribunal
www.bchrt.bc.ca

Manitoba Human Rights Commission
www.gov.mb.ca/hrc

New Brunswick Human Rights
Commission
www.gnb.ca/hrc-cdp/index-e.asp

Newfoundland and Labrador Human
Rights Commission
www.justice.gov.nl.ca/hrc

Northwest Territories Human
Rights Commission
www.nwthumanrights.ca

Nova Scotia Human Rights
Commission
www.gov.ns.ca/humanrights

Nunavut Human Rights Tribunal
www.nhrt.ca

Ontario Human Rights Commission
www.ohrc.on.ca

Prince Edward Island Human Rights
Commission
www.gov.pe.ca/humanrights/

Québec Commission des droits
de la personne et des droits de la
jeunesse
www.cdpdj.qc.ca

Saskatchewan Human Rights
Commission
www.shrc.gov.sk.ca

Yukon Human Rights Commission
www.yhrc.yk.ca

rights commissions most often encounter cases related to disability (roughly 50%), gender (including pregnancy) and harassment (roughly 20% combined), and race or ethnicity (roughly 15%), with the remaining protected clauses accounting for an estimated 10% of discrimination claims.[11] In order to clarify how the human rights legislation is applied and the types of discrimination prohibited, a few examples follow.

Disability

Claims of discrimination based on disability make up almost half of all human rights claims. A disability in human rights legislation includes a wide range of conditions, some which are visible and some which are not. In general, a distinction can be drawn between a physical disability and a mental one. A disability may be present from birth, caused by an accident, or develop over time and may include (depending on the jurisdiction) physical, mental, and learning disabilities; mental disorders; hearing or vision disabilities; epilepsy; drug and alcohol dependencies; environmental sensitivities; as well as other conditions. Temporary illnesses are generally not considered to be disabilities under human rights legislation (unless related to a workplace safety claim), but mental disorders, even temporary ones, are included in the definition of a disability. The intent of providing protection from discrimination based on past, present, or perceived disabilities is largely based on the principle of having an inclusive society with a barrier-free design and equal participation of persons with varying levels of ability.[12] Because employers set standards or requirements, they therefore "owe an obligation to be aware of both the differences between individuals, and differences that characterize groups of individuals. They must build conceptions of equality into workplace [or other] standards."[13]

According to the Supreme Court of Canada, the focus of a disability is not simply the presence of it, but the effect of the disability. In a case heard by the Supreme Court of Canada in 2000 against the City of Boisbriand and Communauté urbaine de Montréal, the city had dismissed an employee, Palmerino Troilo, from his position as a police officer because he suffered from Crohn's disease. Crohn's disease is linked to problems with a person's immune system response and people with it have (ongoing) inflammation of their gastrointestinal tract. There is no known cure for Crohn's at the moment.[14] Medical evidence presented in the case indicated that Troilo could perform normal functions of his job, but the city argued that the illness was permanent and could be interpreted subjectively as an indication of future job-related challenges. The judge found that the illness did not actually result in any functional limitations and held that Troilo had been a victim of discriminatory exclusion. In this case, it was not the presence of a disability that was of concern to employment-related legislation, but the impact of that disability on creating job-related functional limitations.

The Supreme Court of Canada has suggested three broad inquiries to determine if discrimination has taken place:

1. Differential treatment: Was there substantively differential treatment due to a distinction, exclusion, or preference or because of a failure to take into account the complainant's already disadvantaged position within Canadian society?

2. An enumerated ground (a condition or clause that is explicitly protected by legislation): Was the differential treatment based on an enumerated ground?

3. Discrimination in a substantive sense: Does the differential treatment discriminate by imposing a burden upon or withholding a benefit from a person? Does the differential treatment amount to discrimination because it makes distinctions that are offensive to human dignity?

Accommodation Although each situation is unique, there are general principles for accommodating persons with disabilities.

First, the accommodation should be provided in a manner that most respects the dignity of the person, including an awareness of privacy, confidentiality, autonomy, individuality, and self-esteem. For example, the requirement for a person in a wheel chair to enter the workplace through the loading dock or garbage room is undignified. Each person's needs are unique and must be considered independently when an accommodation request is made. Persons with disabilities have the fundamental right to integration and full participation; therefore, barriers should be removed to the point of undue hardship. Workplace programs and policies should be designed by inclusion to combat "social handicapping," in which societal attitudes and actions create non-inclusive thinking against people who have no or few limitations. Providing equal access to employment is largely based on the removal of physical, attitudinal, and systemic barriers. Even when all of these factors are considered, there might still be a need for accommodation.

Second, if discrimination does exist it must be legally defensible, in the sense that the company must demonstrate individualized attempts to accommodate the disability to the point of undue hardship. The Meiorin test discussed earlier is used to establish if the company reached the point of undue hardship. Employers have the legal duty to accommodate persons with disability, and the employees have a responsibility to seek accommodation, cooperate in the process, exchange relevant information, and explore accommodation solutions together.[15] Examples of employer and employee responsibilities associated with the duty to accommodate disabilities are highlighted in **Figure 2.4**. Often, accommodations can be made easily and at minimal cost, such as increased flexibility in work hours or break times; providing reading material in digitized, Braille, or large print formats; installing automatic doors and making washrooms accessible; job restructuring, retraining, or assignment to an alternative position within the company.

Third, the duty to accommodate requires the most appropriate accommodation to be undertaken to the point of undue hardship. The principle underlying this condition is that accommodations are unique, numerous, part of a process, and a matter of degree. Rather than an all-or-nothing approach, there may be many options available to accommodate an employee's disability with varying degrees of complexity, resource demands, and effects on work processes. An accommodation can be considered appropriate if it results in equal opportunity to attain the same level of performance, benefits, and privileges others experience, or if it is adopted for the purpose of achieving equal opportunity and meets the individual's disability-related needs. In cases where alternative options preserve the same level of dignity and respect, employers are entitled to select the less expensive or less disruptive option.

FIGURE 2.4   Duty to Accommodate Disabilities: Shared Responsibilities

As a person with a disability

- Tell your employer or union what your disability-related needs are as they relate to your job duties.
- Provide supporting information about your disability-related needs, including medical or other expert opinions where necessary.
- Participate in exploring possible accommodation solutions.

As an employer or union

- Accept requests for accommodation from employees in good faith.
- Request only information that is required to provide the accommodation. For example, you need to know that an employee's loss of vision prevents them from using printed material, but you do not need to know they have diabetes.
- Take an active role in examining accommodation solutions that meet individual needs.
- Deal with accommodation requests as quickly as possible, even if it means creating a temporary solution while a long-term one is developed.
- Maximize confidentiality for the person seeking accommodation and be respectful of his or her dignity.
- Cover the costs of accommodations, including any necessary medical or other expert opinion or documentation.

Source: Policy and Guidelines on Disability and the Duty to Accommodate, published by the Ontario Human Rights Commission in 2000 and found on the Commission's website at http://www.ohrc.on.ca/en/policy-and-guidelines-disability-and-duty-accommodate. © Queen's Printer for Ontario, 2000. Reproduced with permission.

Accommodation of employees with "invisible" disabilities, such as chronic fatigue syndrome, fibromyalgia, and mental illnesses, is becoming more common. An employee with bipolar disorder was terminated when he began to exhibit pre-manic symptoms after waiting for a response from management regarding his request for accommodation. A human rights tribunal in 2008 found that the company had not investigated the nature of his condition or possible accommodations and awarded the employee over $80 000 in damages.[16]

Harassment

The most historic battle for protection against harassment was initiated in 1982, at a time when it was largely interpreted that sexual harassment was not a form of sex discrimination (therefore, not illegal) and it was perceived that employers were not responsible for the actions of their employees. As indicated in the Workforce Diversity box, perspectives on sexual harassment and employers' responsibilities toward protecting employees from sexual harassment have shifted significantly over the last three decades, largely due to a Supreme Court ruling on a case initiated by two young waitresses.

Some jurisdictions prohibit harassment on all prescribed grounds, while others only expressly ban sexual harassment. **Harassment** includes unwelcome behaviour that demeans, humiliates, or embarrasses a person and that a reasonable person should have known would be unwelcome.[17] Examples of harassment are included in **Figure 2.5**. Minority women often experience harassment based on both sex and race.[18]

One type of intentional harassment that is receiving increasing attention is bullying, which involves repeated and deliberate incidents of negative behaviour

harassment Unwelcome behaviour that demeans, humiliates, or embarrasses a person and that a reasonable person should have known would be unwelcome.

WORKFORCE DIVERSITY

The Evolution of Thought on Sexual Harassment in Canada

In August 1982, two young women named Dianna Janzen and Tracy Govereau secured waitressing jobs at Pharos Restaurant in Winnipeg, Manitoba. While the women hardly knew each other and rarely worked together, they were both soon facing a common problem at work. The cook, Tommy Grammas, started groping the women and making sexual advances during each woman's shift at work. As the women resisted the sexual advances, Tommy told them to "shut up or be fired."

Janzen tried to make it clear to Grammas that his actions were inappropriate, which did not stop the unwanted behaviour. When Janzen approached the owner, Philip Anastasiadis, he commented that she "needed to get laid."

Govereau was soon fired from her job, because of her "attitude." Feeling unsupported and embarrassed, Janzen continued working for two months before eventually quitting the job to remove herself from the continually hostile environment. In hindsight, Janzen says she didn't quit right away "because I was naive, because I was young, because I was stupid, because I was putting up with a lot of stuff, because I didn't know my own rights."

Both women filed complaints under the Manitoba Human Rights Code. They claimed that only females ran the risk of being harassed at Pharos, since none of the male waiters, cashiers, or busboys had ever been harassed; thus, sexual harassment was a form of discrimination based on sex.

The adjudicator, Yude Henteleff, set initial damages as deliberately large (by standards at the time), ordering Pharos to pay Janzen $3980 and Govereau (who was out of work longer) $6000. "I didn't exaggerate the damages but I wanted to make people aware of the psychological damage involved with sexual harassment and that it will cost (employers) lots," Henteleff later stated.

Pharos appealed the ruling and the Manitoba Court of Queen's Bench agreed with Henteleff's ruling, but reduced the award to $1480 for Janzen and $2000 for Govereau.

Pharos appealed again, arguing that an employer should not be legally responsible for the actions of its employees (in this case, Pharos should not be responsible for the actions of Grammas). Janzen and Govereau cross appealed, suggesting that the original damages should be restored.

The judges at the Manitoba high court, Justice Charles Huband and Kerr Twaddle, suggested it was "nonsense to say that harassment is discrimination" and that it was inappropriate to expect an employer to be responsible for the actions of its employees or for sexual harassment to be considered discrimination based on sex.

Outside of Manitoba, two similar top court rulings from other provinces provided a sharp contrast to the rulings within Manitoba, so Janzen and Govereau appealed the case again—this time to the Supreme Court of Canada with the help of the Manitoba Human Rights Commission and the Women's Legal Education and Action Fund.

In mid-1989 the case was reviewed by the Supreme Court of Canada. In this historic case, the Supreme Court agreed that the women were sexually harassed at work, that sexual harassment is a form of sex discrimination (and is therefore illegal), and that employers are responsible for their employees' actions.

Up until the ruling, the terms of sexual harassment were not defined and the application of the law was unclear. The real impact of the precedent that this ruling set was that it gave employers and employees an unrestricted definition of sexual harassment that has since been instrumental in capturing a broader level of unwelcomed behaviours at work.

According to Janzen, "The win was the win and that's all that mattered. The dollars attached to it were irrelevant and in terms of what it represented, it's curious to me that anybody would be successful in trying to put a dollar amount to it. And the other point is that it was an award and it wasn't a reality. I've never seen a penny of that. It was to make a point, it wasn't to be punitive. And I think it did make a point."

Source: Summarized from Stephen Hammond of Harassment Solutions Inc., "The Historic Fight Against Sexual Harassment", *Canadian HR Reporter*, Aug 15, 2011, 24, no 14, pp 33. Used with permission from Stephen Hammond, Harassment Solutions Inc.; Harassment is a Form of Discrimination, http://www.chrc-ccdp.ca/en/timeportals/milestones/125mile.asp, Canadian Human Rights Commission, 1989. Reproduced with the permission of the Minister of Public Works and Government Services Canada, 2012.

FIGURE 2.5   Examples of Harassment

Some examples of harassment include:

- unwelcome remarks, slurs, jokes, taunts, or suggestions about a person's body, clothing, race, national or ethnic origin, colour, religion, age, sex, marital status, family status, physical or mental disability, sexual orientation, pardoned conviction, or other personal characteristics;
- unwelcome sexual remarks, invitations, or requests (including persistent, unwanted contact after the end of a relationship);
- display of sexually explicit, sexist, racist, or other offensive or derogatory material;
- written or verbal abuse or threats;
- practical jokes that embarrass or insult someone;
- leering (suggestive staring) or other offensive gestures;
- unwelcome physical contact, such as patting, touching, pinching, hitting;
- patronizing or condescending behaviour;
- humiliating an employee in front of co-workers;
- abuse of authority that undermines someone's performance or threatens his or her career;
- vandalism of personal property; and
- physical or sexual assault.

Source: Anti-Harassment Policies for the Workforce: An Employer's Guide, www.chrc-ccdp.ca/pdf/
AHPoliciesWorkplace_en.pdf, Canadian Human Rights Commission, 2006. Reproduced by permission of the
Ministry of Public Works and Government Services Canada, 2012.

Psychological harassment is often called bullying.

that cumulatively undermine a person's self-image. This psychological form of harassment is much more prevalent and pervasive in workplaces than physical violence.[19] In 2004, a Quebec law prohibiting workplace psychological harassment came into effect with the intent of ending bullying in the workplace. In the first year more than 2500 complaints were received, surpassing expectations to such a degree that the number of investigators was increased from 10 to 34.[20] Saskatchewan prohibits psychological harassment in its occupational health and safety legislation.[21]

This issue is a concern in other countries as well, as described in the Global HRM box.

Employer Responsibility The Supreme Court has made it clear that protecting employees from harassment is part of an employer's responsibility to provide a safe and healthy working environment. If harassment is occurring and employers are aware or ought to have been aware, they can be charged as well as the alleged harasser.[22] Employer responsibility also includes employee harassment by clients or customers once it has been reported. In a recent Ontario case,

GLOBAL HRM

UK Court Awards $1.7 Million to Bullied Employee

A banking employee in the UK was the victim of bullying from four female co-workers over a period of four years. Some examples of her co-workers' behaviour included

- ignoring her or staring silently at her, often with arms crossed, in a way intended to intimidate and unnerve her;

- greeting others within the department in a very overt manner, highlighting that they were not speaking to her;

- talking over her or pretending they could not hear anything she said;

- bursting out laughing when she walked by;

- making crude and lewd comments that made her feel uncomfortable; and

- removing her name from circulation lists, hiding her mail, and removing papers from her desk.

Another male colleague also bullied her by being vulgar, inappropriate, and hostile, trying to undermine her work and authority in the eyes of others.

As a result, she suffered two major episodes of depressive disorder requiring hospitalization and a suicide watch, followed by a period of four years in which she was not able to return to work and in which her capacity to enjoy life to the fullest had been seriously disrupted. The court concluded that she was subjected to a relentless campaign of mean and spiteful behaviour designed to cause her distress, amounting to a deliberate and concerted campaign of bullying.

The court held the employer vicariously liable for the conduct of the co-workers because the managers collectively closed their eyes to what was going on. They awarded damages of $1.7 million, including $1.3 million for future loss of earnings because she had lost her lifetime career.

Source: Adapted from H. Gray, "British Court Punishes Employer that Let Bullying Go Unchecked," *Canadian HR Reporter* (October 9, 2006). Reprinted by permission of Canadian HR Reporter. © Copyright Thomson Reuters Canada Ltd., (2012) Toronto, Ontario, 1-800-387-5164. Web: www.hrreporter.com

---

Sexual Harassment: Your Rights and Responsibilities
www.ohrc.on.ca/en/sexual-and-gender-based-harassment-know-your-rights

sexual harassment Offensive or humiliating behaviour that is related to a person's sex, as well as behaviour of a sexual nature that creates an intimidating, unwelcome, hostile, or offensive work environment or that could reasonably be thought to put sexual conditions on a person's job or employment opportunities.

sexual coercion Harassment of a sexual nature that results in some direct consequence to the worker's employment status or some gain in or loss of tangible job benefits.

sexual annoyance Sexually related conduct that is hostile, intimidating, or offensive to the employee but has no direct link to tangible job benefits or loss thereof.

Bell Mobility was ordered to pay an employee more than $500 000 after a supervisor assaulted her in the office and she developed post-traumatic stress disorder. The company was found vicariously liable for the supervisor's aggressive behaviours and was found to have breached its duty of care to provide a safe and harassment-free working environment.[23]

Sexual Harassment The type of harassment that has attracted the most attention in the workplace is **sexual harassment**. Sexual harassment is offensive or humiliating behaviour that is related to a person's sex, as well as behaviour of a sexual nature that creates an intimidating, unwelcome, hostile, or offensive work environment or that could reasonably be thought to put sexual conditions on a person's job or employment opportunities.

Sexual harassment can be divided into two categories: sexual coercion and sexual annoyance.[24] **Sexual coercion** involves harassment of a sexual nature that results in some direct consequence to the worker's employment status or some gain in or loss of tangible job benefits. Typically, this involves a supervisor using control over employment, pay, performance appraisal results, or promotion to attempt to coerce an employee to grant sexual favours. If the worker agrees to the request, tangible job benefits follow; if the worker refuses, job benefits are denied or taken away.

Sexual annoyance is sexually related conduct that is hostile, intimidating, or offensive to the employee but has no direct link to tangible job benefits or loss thereof. Rather, a "poisoned work environment" is created for the employee, the tolerance of which effectively becomes a term or condition of employment. An Alberta court upheld the dismissal of a male employee who had used profane language, sexually infused talk and jokes, and displayed pornographic and graphically violent images. The employee claimed that he was a misunderstood jokester who had never worked with a female engineer before and blamed the company for not training him on appropriate conduct. However, the court found that the company had embarked on a campaign to recruit women into trade positions many years earlier and that all employees had been provided with diversity training. In addition, the company had also implemented and widely publicized an anti-harassment policy.[25]

Hints TO ENSURE LEGAL COMPLIANCE

Harassment Policies To reduce liability, employers should establish sound harassment policies, communicate such policies to all employees, enforce the policies in a fair and consistent manner, and take an active role in maintaining a working environment that is free of harassment. Effective harassment policies should include[26]

1. an anti-harassment policy statement, stating the organization's commitment to a safe and respectful work environment and specifying that harassment is against the law;
2. information for victims (for example, identifying and defining harassment);
3. employees' rights and responsibilities (for example, respecting others, speaking up, reporting harassment);
4. employers' and managers' responsibilities (for example, putting a stop to harassment, being aware, listening to employees);
5. anti-harassment policy procedures (what to do if you are being harassed, what to do if you are accused of harassment, what to do if you are a third-party employee, investigation guidelines, remedies for the victim and corrective action for harassers, guidelines for handling unsubstantiated complaints and complaints made in bad faith, confidentiality);
6. penalties for retaliation against a complainant;
7. guidelines for appeals;
8. other options such as union grievance procedures and human rights complaints;
9. how the policy will be monitored and adjusted.

Race and Colour

Urban Alliance on Race Relations
www.tgmag.ca/magic/uarr.html

Racism and Racial Harassment: Your Rights and Responsibilities
www.ohrc.on.ca/en/racial-harassment-know-your-rights

Discrimination on the basis of race and colour is illegal in every Canadian jurisdiction. For example, the British Columbia Human Rights Tribunal found that two construction companies had discriminated against 38 Latin American workers brought in to work on a public transit project; the Latin Americans were treated differently than workers brought in from European countries in that they were paid lower wages and provided with inferior accommodation. As a result, the Tribunal awarded each worker $100 000.[27]

Religion

Discrimination on the basis of religion can take many forms in Canada's multicultural society. For example, it is a violation of human rights laws across

Canada to deny time to pray or to prohibit clothing recognized as religiously required (for example, a hijab for Muslim women or a turban for Sikh men). According to a recent survey in Toronto, discriminatory hiring practices and workplace racism toward Muslim women are quite common. Of the 32 women surveyed, 29 said that their employer had commented on their hijab, and 13 said they were told that they would have to stop wearing their hijab if they wanted the job.[28]

A well-recognized case on religion involved Canadian National Railway (CN). An employee, Mr. Bhinder, worked as a maintenance electrician in the Toronto coach yard. As a practising Sikh, he wore a turban both on and off work premises. Four years after Bhinder first started working for CN, the company introduced a rule requiring all employees working in the coach yard to wear a hard hat, citing safety reasons. Bhinder informed management that he was unable to wear the hard hat since his faith prohibited him from wearing anything other than the turban and there was no way he could wear anything under or over it. He was fired and subsequently launched a discrimination case against CN. In 1981, the Canadian Human Rights Tribunal found that the company did discriminate against Bhinder on religious grounds. The company appealed, and two years later the Federal Court of Appeal overturned the Tribunal's ruling, identifying the hard hat as a BFOR. The case was appealed again, and in 1995 the Supreme Court of Canada did find that the rule discriminated against Bhinder on religious grounds, but that the requirement was bona fide. Therefore, it was not considered to be a discriminatory process and CN did not have a duty to accommodate Bhinder.

This case highlights a significant area of concern in dealing with human rights complaints—the length of time and multiple opportunities for appeal that exist within the legislative systems in Canada. This puts considerable pressure on HR and management to be aware of and proactively manage programs and policies in a legally defensible way to at least try to mitigate the likelihood of lengthy and often expensive court proceedings.

Sexual Orientation

Discrimination on the basis of sexual orientation is prohibited in all jurisdictions in Canada. As a result of lawsuits by same-sex couples, the Supreme Court ruled that all laws must define "common-law partners" to include both same-sex and opposite-sex couples.[29] In a recent federal case, a lesbian employee alleged that she was harassed by a co-worker. She made a complaint to her supervisors but felt the complaint was not investigated properly. She alleged that she was given a poor performance review because of her complaint and that her request for a transfer to another work site was denied. The Canadian Human Rights Commission ordered her employer to provide a letter of apology, financial compensation for pain and suffering, and a transfer to another work site. The Commission also ordered a meeting with the employer's harassment coordinator to talk about the complainant's experiences with the internal complaint process.[30]

An Ethical Dilemma

Your company president tells you not to hire any gay or lesbian employees to work as part of his office staff because it would make him uncomfortable. What would you do?

Sexual Orientation: Your Rights and Responsibilities
www.ohrc.on.ca/en/sexual-orientation-and-human-rights

Age

Many employers believe that it is justifiable to specify minimum or maximum ages for certain jobs. In actual fact, evidence is rarely available to support the position that age is an accurate indicator of a person's ability to perform a particular type of work.[31] For example, because of an economic downturn, an Ontario company was forced to lay off staff. The complainant, a foreman, had worked for the company for more than 32 years and was 57 at the time he was selected for termination along with another foreman who was aged 56. Both were offered a generous retirement package. The two foremen who remained were younger than the two released. The vice-president had prepared a note indicating that the two older workers who were terminated were told of the need to reduce people and that they "hoped to keep people with career potential." The Ontario Human Rights Tribunal found that the company engaged in age discrimination on the basis of the good employment record of the complainant, the ages of those selected for layoff compared with those retained, and the vice-president's statement, which was found to be a "euphemism; its meaning concerns age."[32]

Family Status

The Canadian Council on Rehabilitation and Work
www.workink.com

Decisions regarding the specific meaning of discrimination based on family status (the status of being in a parent–child relationship) are evolving.[33] In a recent BC case, an employee whose shift was changed by the employer requested a return to her previous shift because the new shift time made it difficult for her to find a caregiver that could provide for her son's special needs. The employer refused, and an arbitrator upheld the decision, saying that family status did not encompass the many circumstances that arise in regard to childcare needs. However, a court of appeal overturned the arbitrator's decision and adopted a middle ground between a narrow definition of family status as being a parent and a broad definition encompassing all possible parental obligations.[34]

Enforcement

Enforcement of human rights acts is the responsibility of the human rights commission in each jurisdiction. It should be noted that all costs are borne by the commission, not by the complainant, which makes the process accessible to all employees, regardless of financial means. The commission itself can initiate a complaint if it has reasonable grounds to assume that a party is engaging in a discriminatory practice.

Challenges of human rights legislation are heard by the human rights tribunal. The tribunal's primary role is to provide a speedy and accessible process to help parties affected by discrimination claims resolve the conflict through mediation. Once a claim is filed with the human rights commission or tribunal, the organization is notified and given a relatively short period of time (for example, 30 calendar days) to prepare their case. Regardless of whether a formal complaint or an informal accusation has been filed against a company, the employer has a duty to investigate claims of discrimination. Fulfilling the duty to investigate starts with the selection of an appropriate investigator. A checklist to be reviewed when selecting an investigator is provided in **Figure 2.6.**

FIGURE **2.6** A Checklist for Employers when Selecting a Workplace Investigator

1. Internal or external investigators: Many employers select trained internal HR experts to conduct workplace investigations, while others rely on external investigators. Selection is dependent on the resources (time and money) of the firm, the complexities of the case (potential conflicts of interest), the expertise of the in-house staff, and the severity of the case.

2. One investigator or two: The nature of the case may warrant the need for more than one investigator (e.g., one male and one female in the case of a sexual harassment claim).

3. Respecting the mandate: Investigators should be able to maintain the role within the mandate of the task they have been assigned (e.g., fact finder or adviser) and not stray too far off track. Assigned investigators are perceived as agents of the organization, therefore the organization can be held partially accountable for investigator actions.

4. Impartiality or neutrality: Investigators should have no conflict of interest vested in the conditions, persons, or context of the case they are handling.

5. Reliable, thorough, and professional: Although these qualities should go without saying, an investigator is expected to be a competent, effective, and professional communicator throughout the investigation, and must be capable of making credible assessments.

6. Quality of the written report: The details and word selection in the written report can become evidence in a case. Therefore, a high-quality report details "what happened" and assists counsel in their defence.

7. Respects confidentiality: The investigator should only discuss the investigation when required and respect the confidentiality of all parties affected by the investigation.

Source: Chhinzer, N., summary from Module 4 at the HR Law Certificate Program at Osgoode Hall Law School, 2011.

An employer's obligations include the following:

1. Demonstrating an awareness of the issues of discrimination or harassment, including having an antidiscrimination/antiharassment policy in place, a complaint mechanism, and training available for employees

2. Fulfilling post-complaint actions, including assessing the seriousness of the complaint, launching an investigation promptly, focusing on employee welfare, and taking actions based on the complaint

3. Resolving the complaint by demonstrating reasonable resolution and communication

systemic remedies Forward looking solutions to discrimination that require respondents to take positive steps to ensure compliance with legislation, both in respect to the current complaint and any future practices.

restitutional remedies Monetary compensation for the complainant to put him or her back to the position he or she would be in if the discrimination had not occurred (this includes compensation for injury to dignity and self-respect), and may include an apology letter.

If discrimination is found, two forms of remedies can be imposed. **Systemic remedies** (forward looking) require the respondent to take positive steps to ensure compliance with legislation, both in respect to the current complaint and with respect to any future practices. If a pattern of discrimination is detected, the employer will be ordered to cease such practices and may be required to attend a training session or hold regular human rights workshops. **Restitutional remedies** include monetary compensation for the complainant to put him or her back to the position he or she would be in if the discrimination had not occurred (this includes compensation for injury to dignity and self-respect). A written letter of apology may also be required.

The most common reason for restitutional remedies is compensation for lost wages; others include compensation for general damages, complainant expenses, and pain and humiliation. The violator is generally asked to restore the rights, opportunities, and privileges denied the victim, such as employment or promotion.

FIGURE 2.7 Common Remedies Issued by the Human Rights Tribunals

Systemic Remedies (forward looking)	Restitution Remedies (penalties for past events)
• cease and desist the discriminatory practice • change a program to eliminate discriminatory elements, such as offering same-sex benefits under an employee benefit plan • make physical modifications to work places as mandated • develop non-discriminatory action plans • develop employment equity plans • post notices regarding provisions and protection offered to employees under the human rights code • develop information-sharing practices for future programs to allow monitoring of progress toward antidiscrimination goals	• payment of retroactive benefits • reinstatement of employment • payment for lost wages • compensation for insult to dignity, mental anguish, or infringement of rights under the human rights code • make a public apology

Source: Raj Anand, "Human Rights and the Professional Regulator in the 21st Century," pp. 17–18, November 4, 2011. Used with permission from Raj Anand, Partner, WeirFoulds LLP.

The total compensation received by the complainant is generally between $0 and $20 000, with a general range of $10 000 to $20 000 for cases where evidence confirmed discrimination occurred and a restitution was ordered. **Figure 2.7** highlights examples of common remedies issued by a human rights tribunal.

EMPLOYMENT EQUITY LEGISLATION

The Charter of Rights and Freedoms legalizes employment equity initiatives, which go beyond human rights laws in that they are proactive programs developed by employers to remedy past discrimination or prevent future discrimination. Human rights laws focus on prohibiting various kinds of discrimination; however, over time it became obvious that there were certain groups for whom this complaint-based, reactive approach was insufficient. Investigation revealed that four identifiable groups—women, Aboriginal people, persons with disabilities, and visible minorities—had been subjected to pervasive patterns of differential treatment by employers, as evidenced by lower pay on average, occupational segregation, higher rates of unemployment, underemployment, and concentration in low-status jobs with little potential for career growth. An example of **occupational segregation** is that the majority of women worked in a very small number of jobs, such as nursing, teaching, sales, and secretarial/clerical work. Advancement of women and other designated group members into senior management positions has been hindered by the existence of a **glass ceiling**, an "invisible" barrier caused by attitudinal or organizational bias that limits the advancement opportunities of qualified individuals. As you can see in **Figure 2.8**, a survey from 2008 confirmed that the glass ceiling is still intact.

After realizing that simple prohibition of discrimination would not correct these patterns, a number of jurisdictions passed employment equity legislation aimed at identifying and eliminating systemic barriers to employment opportunities that adversely affect these four groups. Employment equity legislation is focused on bringing the four traditionally disadvantaged groups identified above into the mainstream of Canada's labour force. The use of the term "employment equity" distinguishes Canada's approach from the "affirmative action" approach used in the United States. Affirmative action has come to be associated with quotas, which is a divisive political issue.[35]

occupational segregation The existence of certain occupations that have traditionally been male dominated and others that have been female dominated.

glass ceiling An invisible barrier, caused by attitudinal or organizational bias, that limits the advancement opportunities of qualified designated group members.

FIGURE 2.8   The Catalyst Pyramid—Canadian Women in Business

Sources: *Catalyst,* 2008 Catalyst Census of Women Corporate Officers and Top Earners of the FP500 (2009); Catalyst, 2007 Census of Women Board Directors of the FP500: Voices of the Boardroom (2008); Statistics Canada, Labour Force Survey (2008). Reproduced by permission of Catalyst, www.catalystwomen.org.

Employment equity legislation is intended to remove employment barriers and promote equality for the members of the four designated groups. Employers under federal jurisdiction must prepare an annual plan with specific goals to achieve better representation of the designated group members at all levels of the organization and timetables for goal implementation. Employers must also submit an annual report on the company's progress in meeting its goals, indicating the representation of designated group members by occupational groups and salary ranges and providing information on those hired, promoted, and terminated. In addition, the Federal Contractors Program requires firms bidding on federal contracts of $200 000 or more to implement an employment equity plan.

In contrast, mandatory employment equity programs are virtually non-existent in provincial and territorial jurisdictions. Some provinces have employment equity policies that encourage employment equity plans in provincial departments and ministries. Quebec has a contract compliance program where employers in receipt of more than $100 000 in provincial funding must implement an employment equity plan.[36]

employment equity program
A detailed plan designed to identify and correct existing discrimination, redress past discrimination, and achieve a balanced representation of designated group members in the organization.

An **employment equity program** is designed to achieve a balanced representation of designated group members in the organization. It is a major management exercise because existing employees must become comfortable working with others from diverse backgrounds, cultures, religions, and so on, and this represents a major change in the work environment. A deliberately structured process is involved, which can be tailored to suit the unique needs of the firm. The employment equity process usually takes six months. The first step is the demonstration of senior management commitment and support, which leads to data collection and analysis of the current workforce demographics. Following that, there is an employment systems review, which leads to plan development and eventual plan implementation. The last step is monitoring, evaluating, and revising the plan.

Although embracing employee equity or diversity offers opportunities to enhance organizational effectiveness, transforming an organizational culture presents a set of challenges that must be handled properly. Diversity initiatives should be undertaken slowly, since they involve a complex change process. Resistance to change may have to be overcome, along with stereotyped beliefs or prejudices and employee resentment.

The Plight of the Four Designated Groups

Women

Canadian Association of
Administrators of Labour
Legislation
www.caall-acalo.org

Workplace Standards
**www.workplace.ca/laws/employ_
standard_comp.html**

Women accounted for 47 percent of the employed workforce in 2006. Two-thirds of all employed women were working in teaching, nursing and related health occupations, clerical or other administrative positions, and sales and service occupations. There has been virtually no change in the proportion of women employed in these traditionally female-dominated occupations over the past decade. Women continue to be under-represented in engineering, natural sciences, and mathematics, a trend unlikely to change in the near future since women are still under-represented in university programs in these fields.[37]

Every jurisdiction in Canada has legislation incorporating the principle of *equal pay for equal work*. In most jurisdictions, this entitlement is found in the employment (labour) standards legislation; otherwise, it is in the human rights legislation. **Equal pay for equal work** specifies that an employer cannot pay male

Equal pay for equal work specifies that an employer cannot pay male and female employees differently if they are performing the same or substantially similar work.

and female employees differently if they are performing the same or substantially similar work. Pay differences based on a valid merit or seniority system or employee productivity are permitted; it is only sex-based discrimination that is prohibited. This principle makes it illegal, for example, for the Canadian government to employ nurses (mostly women) as "program administrators" and doctors (mainly men) as "health professionals" to do the same job adjudicating Canada Pension Plan disability claims and pay the men twice as much.[38]

It is illegal in every jurisdiction in Canada to discriminate on the basis of disability.

Aboriginals

Most Aboriginal employees in the workforce are concentrated in low-skill, low-paid jobs such as trades helpers. The unemployment rate for Aboriginal people is significantly higher than the rate among non-Aboriginals, and their income is significantly lower.[39]

People with Disabilities

About 45 percent of people with disabilities are in the labour force, compared with almost 80 percent of the non-disabled population. Although 63 percent of people with a mild disability are in the workforce, only 28 percent of those with a severe to very severe disability are working. The median employment income of workers with disabilities is 83 percent of that of other Canadian workers.[40]

Visible Minorities

According to the federal Employment Equity Act, a visible minority is defined as "persons, other than Aboriginal peoples, who are non-Caucasian in race or non-white in colour." Often the terms "visible minority" and "immigrant" are used interchangeably, but these two terms are actually distinct. An immigrant represents a person who was not born in Canada, but resides in Canada for the purpose of settlement. In the 2006 Canadian census, there were almost 6.2 million immigrants in the Canadian population. There were almost 5.1 million persons who self-identified as visible minorities, with the largest representation among South Asians and Chinese, followed by persons who self-identified as black, Filipino, and Latin American. In 1981, 55.5 percent of new immigrants to Canada were visible minorities, but by 2001 that proportion reached 72.9 percent.[41] This suggests that almost three out of every ten immigrants in the last decade were not visible minorities, while there are millions of people born in Canada who are visible minorities, but not immigrants.

KSAs Knowledge, skills, and abilities.

underemployment Being employed in a job that does not fully utilize one's knowledge, skills, and abilities (KSAs).

Traditionally, visible minorities were typically unable to obtain employment that took full advantage of their knowledge, skills, and abilities (**KSAs**), and thus faced **underemployment.** As a result, visible minorities were included as a designated group. A recent study on diversity in the Greater Toronto Area (GTA) highlighted the continuing disadvantaged status of visible minorities. The study looked at 3257 leaders in the GTA in all sectors and found that just 13 percent were visible minorities (even though visible minorities make up half of the GTA population).[42]

EMPLOYMENT/LABOUR STANDARDS LEGISLATION

employment (labour) standards legislation Laws present in every Canadian jurisdiction that establish minimum employee entitlements and set a limit on the maximum number of hours of work permitted per day or week.

All employers and employees in Canada, including unionized employees, are covered by **employment (labour) standards legislation.** The intent of an employment standards act (ESA) is to establish minimum terms and conditions for workplaces pertaining to such issues as wages; paid holidays and vacations; maternity, parental, or adoption leave (or some mix thereof); bereavement leave; compassionate care leave; termination notice; and overtime pay. They also set the maximum number of hours of work permitted per day or week; overtime pay is required for any work in excess of the maximum.

While employer and employee agreements or practices can exceed minimums established in the ESA, neither party can choose to opt out of or waive their rights as established in the ESA. For example, if the ESA minimum requirement establishes a minimum vacation rate of 4 percent of pay, an employment agreement cannot have a provision for only 3 percent of pay as vacation pay, even if both parties consent.

In contrast, the minimums established in the ESA can be exceeded in employment contracts, through collective bargaining agreements (in unionized positions), or based on common law (precedent established by the judicial system). An employer or employee can agree to 5 percent of pay as vacation pay without violating the ESA, for example.

If there is a conflict between the ESA and another contract, the principle of greater benefit is applied. For example, an employment policy or contract that is communicated to employees stating that in the case of a layoff, employees will be provided with one month notice for every year that they worked if they are laid off. The ESA minimum requires the provision of only one week notice per year that an employee worked, up to an eight-week maximum. In this example, an employee who worked for 10 years would be given the greater benefit (10 months of notice before a layoff), not the minimum under the ESA, to preserve the greater benefit to the employee.

While the ESA provides minimum terms and conditions of employment, it is not totally inclusive. Often, students on work exchange programs, inmates on work projects, police officers, independent officers, and others are explicitly excluded from protection under the ESA. In addition, regulations for specific occupations such as doctors, lawyers, managers, architects, and specific types of salespersons modify the applicability of certain sections of the ESA.

Enforcement of the ESA

Governed by federal, provincial, or territorial employment standards acts (ESAs), enforcement is complaint based, and violators can be fined. This occurs through the filing of a formal written or electronic complaint against the violator to the appropriate authorities (often the provincial or territorial ministry of labour). A person, union, or corporation can file a complaint with the ministry for violations, given that the ESA has an interest in mitigating the employment relationships between employee and employers.

Employees are required to give up their rights to sue an employer in civil court once a claim is filed with the ministry of labour. This protects employers from dual proceedings on the same issue, and protects courts from being overwhelmed with duplicate cases. There are also strict limitation periods, establishing the maximum amount of time that can elapse between the violation and the filing of a complaint, with these limits differing based on the violation (unpaid wages, vacation pay, and so on). There is also a general maximum claim limit (for example, $10 000 under the Ontario ESA) for unpaid wages. Under the ESA, employees have been awarded compensation for actual unpaid wages and direct earnings losses, time required to find a new job and expenses to seek a new job, benefit plan entitlements, severance pay, and loss of "reasonable expectation" of continued employment.

RESPECTING EMPLOYEE PRIVACY

Privacy Commissioner of Canada
www.priv.gc.ca

Information and Privacy
Commissioner of Ontario
www.ipc.on.ca

Today's employers are grappling with the problem of how to balance employee privacy rights with their need to monitor the use of technology-related tools in the workplace. Employers must maintain the ability to effectively manage their employees and prevent liability to the company, which can be held legally liable for the actions of its employees.[43] They want to eliminate time wasted (on web surfing, playing computer games, and so on) and abuse of company resources

Hints TO ENSURE LEGAL COMPLIANCE

(such as use of the Internet and email at work for personal and possibly illegal uses, such as gambling or visiting pornographic sites).[44] For example, one employee used workplace computers to access hundreds of pornographic websites, to surf Internet dating sites for hours at a time, and to maintain personal files with sexually explicit images. The employee was dismissed and an arbitrator upheld the decision, stating that the employee had engaged in serious culpable misconduct.[45] Another concern is employee blogging, as a posting intended to be seen by a few friends that includes confidential company information or comments about management can easily make its way to a national media outlet without the author even knowing it.[46]

Employees are concerned with privacy—their control over information about themselves and their freedom from unjustifiable interference in their personal life. The Personal Information Protection and Electronic Documents Act (PIPEDA) governs the collection, use, and disclosure of personal information across Canada, including employers' collection and dissemination of personal information about employees. Any information beyond name, title, business address, and telephone number is regarded as personal and private, including health-related information provided to insurers. Employers must obtain consent from employees whenever personal information is collected, used, or disclosed.[47]

Some employers have resorted to electronic monitoring, which is becoming easier and less expensive as new software is developed, that can track websites visited by workers and the time spent on each.[48] In general, courts in Canada have permitted electronic surveillance as long as there is proper balancing of opposing interests. Employers are given substantial leeway in monitoring their employees' use of the Internet and email, and they are in an even stronger position if there is a written policy in place. The policy should be updated regularly to reflect changes in technology and should address the use of all company technological equipment away from the employer's premises, including laptops, cellphones, BlackBerrys, and so on.[49] **Figure 2.9** provides a sample company email and Internet usage policy.

Video Surveillance

Some employers install video surveillance equipment to prevent employee theft and vandalism and to monitor productivity. Employees must be made aware

An Ethical Dilemma

Is it ethical to use video surveillance of employees? Do you think employees need to be told of surveillance tools if they are used?

of the surveillance. Unions often file grievances against video surveillance, and arbitrators have been reluctant to support it because of privacy concerns. Courts typically assess whether the surveillance was reasonable and whether there were reasonable alternatives available. Generally, they have decided that video surveillance is not reasonable and that other means could be used.[50] The federal, British Columbia, and Alberta privacy commissioners have jointly issued video surveillance guidelines, which are shown in **Figure 2.10**.

FIGURE 2.9   Sample Company Email and Internet Usage Policy

1. Employees shall not use the Internet or email in any manner that may harm the business interests of the employer, subject the employer to liability, or be offensive to other employees.
2. Employees may use the Internet and email for reasonable limited personal use providing such use does not interfere with job performance or employee productivity.
3. Employee personal email shall include a disclaimer that the views expressed therein are not the views, representations, or position of the company.
4. Employees shall not send, retrieve, or archive any material that may be considered discriminatory, harassment, or creates a hostile work environment.
5. Employees shall post no junk mail or spam.
6. Employees shall not access, attach, or store any information that may compromise the bandwidth of the employer's system.
7. Employees acknowledge the employer has the right to and does monitor both Internet and email use.
8. Employees acknowledge that the employer has the right to keep and store any information resulting from this monitoring.
9. Employees acknowledge the employer has the right to block access and filter any material that the employer determines to be inappropriate, offensive, or a threat to the security of the employer Internet and email system.
10. Employer shall consent to give employees the right to store personal information in "personal" files provided said files do not violate any provisions of this Internet and email policy.
11. Employee agrees that the employer may access any email or computer storage file, including personal files, to protect the interests of the employer.
12. Employer shall disclose to all employees the extent of monitoring, the type of reports, the level of detail, and who will receive these reports.
13. Employer shall disclose to all employees who is responsible for enforcement of email and Internet policy, clarifying interpretation of policy, granting employee use exceptions, and resolving disputes.
14. Employer shall disclose to all employees the penalties for violation of the Internet and email acceptable use policy.
15. Employer and employees shall establish a procedure for both parties' involvement in design and implementation of the company's Internet and email policy, including a system for continual evaluation of that policy and procedures for making changes to it as necessary.

Source: Journal of organizational culture, communication and conflict. Online by Arnesen and Weis. Copyright 2007 by ALLIED ACADEMIES. Reproduced with permission of ALLIED ACADEMIES.

FIGURE 2.10   Video Surveillance Guidelines

1. Determine whether a less privacy-invasive alternative to video surveillance would meet your needs.
2. Establish the business reason for conducting video surveillance and use video surveillance only for that reason.
3. Develop a policy on the use of video surveillance.
4. Limit the use and viewing range of cameras as much as possible.
5. Inform the public that video surveillance is taking place.
6. Store any recorded images in a secure location with limited access, and destroy them when they are no longer required for business purposes.
7. Be ready to answer questions from the public. Individuals have the right to know who is watching them and why, as well as what information is being captured and what is being done with recorded images.
8. Give individuals access to information about themselves. This includes video images.
9. Educate camera operators about the obligation to protect the privacy of individuals.
10. Periodically evaluate the need for video surveillance.

Source: Office of the Privacy Commissioner of Canada, "Ten Things to Do," Guidelines for Overt Video Surveillance in the Private Sector (March 2008). Reprinted with permission. www.priv.gc.ca/information/guide/2008/gl_vs0803063.pdf.

Chapter SUMMARY

1. The legal framework in Canada attempts to balance employee and employer rights using multiple overlapping legislative pieces, including legislation aimed at protecting the general public (the Charter of Rights and Freedoms, human rights legislation) as well as more specific legislation (employment equity legislation, employment standards acts, and privacy legislation).

2. The responsibility for employment-related law resides with the provinces and territories; however, employees of the federal civil service, Crown corporations and agencies, and businesses engaged in transportation, banking, and communications are federally regulated. So there are 14 jurisdictions for employment law in Canada—ten provinces, three territories, and the federal jurisdiction. Ninety percent of Canadians are covered by provincial/territorial employment legislation, and 10 percent are covered by federal employment legislation.

3. Harassment includes a wide range of behaviours that a reasonable person *ought to know* are unwelcome. Employers and managers have a responsibility to provide a safe and healthy working environment. If harassment is occurring and they are aware or ought to have been aware, they can be charged along with the alleged harasser. To reduce liability, employers should establish harassment policies, communicate these to employees, enforce the policies, and play an active role in maintaining a work environment free of harassment.

4. All jurisdictions prohibit discrimination on the grounds of race, colour, sexual orientation, religion/creed, physical and mental disability, sex, age, and marital status. Employers are required to make reasonable accommodation for employees by adjusting employment policies and practices, so that no one is disadvantaged in employment on any of the prohibited grounds, to the point of undue hardship. Employers are allowed to put in conditions related to employment that may discriminate, provided that these conditions are bona fide occupational requirements.

5. Employment standards legislation establishes minimum terms and conditions for workplaces in each jurisdiction, and violations of these terms are identified in a complaint-based process, whereby the ministry of labour will investigate violations once employees file a complaint.

6. Privacy legislation focuses on how to balance employee privacy rights with an employer's need to monitor the use of technology-related tools in the workplace. The Personal Information Protection and Electronic Documents Act (PIPEDA) governs the collection, use, and disclosure of personal information across Canada.

MyManagementLab

Visit MyManagementLab to access a personalized Study Plan and additional study tools for this chapter.

Key TERMS

bona fide occupational requirement
   (BFOR) *(p. 32)*
Charter of Rights and Freedoms *(p. 29)*
differential or unequal treatment *(p.30)*
discrimination *(p. 30)*
discrimination because of association *(p.31)*
employment (labour) standards legislation *(p. 47)*
employment equity program *(p. 45)*
equality rights *(p. 29)*
glass ceiling *(p. 44)*
harassment *(p. 36)*
human rights legislation *(p. 30)*
KSAs *(p. 47)*

occupational segregation *(p. 44)*
reasonable accommodation *(p. 33)*
regulations *(p. 28)*
restitutional remedies *(p.43)*
sexual annoyance *(p. 39)*
sexual coercion *(p. 39)*
sexual harassment *(p. 39)*
systemic remedies *(p.43)*
underemployment *(p. 47)*
undue hardship *(p. 33)*
unintentional/constructive/systemic
   discrimination *(p. 32)*

Review and Discussion QUESTIONS

1. Explain how the legal system in Canada is different than the legal system in the United States.

2. Describe the impact of the Charter of Rights and Freedoms on HRM.

3. Differentiate among the following types of discrimination and provide one example of each: direct, differential treatment, indirect, because of association, and systemic.

4. Provide five examples of prohibited grounds for discrimination in employment in Canadian jurisdictions.

5. Explain the purpose of employment standards legislation, and the concept of "the greater good" when assessing these minimums.

6. Define "sexual harassment" and describe five types of behaviour that could constitute such harassment.

7. Define the concepts of occupational segregation, underemployment, and the glass ceiling.

8. What is the test to define if a bona fide occupational requirement exists? What are the three elements of this test?

9. What is the role of privacy legislation in Canada? Describe the act that protects employees' privacy.

Critical Thinking QUESTIONS

1. Go to your provincial or territorial employment (labour) standards website and determine the following:

   • minimum legal age to work in this jurisdiction
   • minimum hourly wages
   • maximum number of hours that can be worked in a week before overtime must be paid

   How does this information apply to you and your friends and family? Did you notice anything else that caught your interest that you were previously unaware of?

2. Prepare a report outlining legally acceptable questions that may be asked at a selection interview with a young female engineer applying for the job of engineering project manager at an oil field in rural northern Alberta with an otherwise all-male group. (Refer to Appendix 7.1 on page 205 for help.)

3. Working with a small group of classmates, search the web for a company in your community that has an anti-discriminatory employment program. Contact the company's HR manager and request more information on the program. Prepare a brief report summarizing its key features.

4. The organization you are working for is relatively new and growing and has no HR department. They have asked you to prepare a briefing about what can and cannot be asked during an employment interview. Given that it is a small organization, management usually conducts interviews. You notice a number of managers huffing about how the law doesn't apply to them and their actions can't result in a lawsuit. In addition to preparing a briefing about the types of questions that can and cannot be asked in an interview, prepare a response to the perception that the law does not apply to the managers in this situation.

Experiential EXERCISES

1. You are an HR manager at a moving company. The owner of your company has just informed you that there are certain jobs, namely the movers, for which he feels minimum strength requirements are BFORs. How would you handle this situation?

2. An employee who has been off for two months with a stress-related ailment has just contacted you indicating that she would like to return to work next week but won't be able to work full time for another month or so. How would you handle this?

3. A supervisor has just approached you to indicate a concern she has with an employee. The supervisor indicates that the employee is often surfing the Internet while at work and fears that not only is this affecting productivity negatively, but is also a violation of the company's rules for Internet surfing using a company computer. The supervisor would like you to ask the IT team to investigate how many hours a day are logged to non-work-related activities for that employee and also asks for a list of websites that the employee visits. What is the role of privacy legislation from the employer and employee perspectives? What additional information would you need to make a decision about next steps? What recommendations can you make to the supervisor to deal with the situation in the short term?

Running CASE

Legal Issues

One of the problems that Jennifer and Pierre are facing at LearnInMotion.com concerns the inadequacies of the firm's current human resources management practices and procedures. The previous year had been a swirl of activity—creating and testing the business model, launching the site, writing and rewriting the business plan, and finally getting venture funding. And it would be accurate to say that in all that time, they put absolutely no time into employee manuals, HR policies, or other HR-related matters. Even the 25-page business plan has no information in this regard. The plan provided considerable detail regarding budgetary projections, competition, market growth, and business strategy. However, it was silent when it came to HR except for containing short bios of the current employees and projections of the types of positions that would have to be staffed in the first two years.

Almost from the beginning, it was apparent to both Jennifer and Pierre that they were (as Pierre put it) "out of our depth" when it came to the letter and spirit of equal employment opportunity laws. Having both been through business school, they were familiar with the general requirements, such as not asking applicants their age during interviews. However, those general guidelines weren't always easy to translate into practice during the actual applicant interviews. Two incidents particularly concerned them. One of the applicants for a sales position was in his 50s, which made him about twice as old as any other applicant. Although Pierre didn't mean to be discriminatory, he found himself asking this candidate such questions as "Do you think you'll be able to get up to speed selling an Internet product?" and "You know, we'll be working very long hours here; are you up to that?"—questions that he did not ask the other, younger candidates. There was also a problem with a candidate for the content manager position. The candidate was a single mother with two children, and Pierre asked her quite pointed questions, such as

"What are your children's ages and what childcare arrangements do you have?" and "This job involves quite a bit of overtime and weekend work. Are you sure your kids won't get in the way of that?" Jennifer thought questions like these were probably okay, but she wasn't sure.

There was also a disturbing incident in the office. There were already two content management employees, Maya and Dan, whose job it was to actually place the course and other educational content on the website. Dan, along with Alex, the web surfer, occasionally used vulgarity, for instance, when referring to the problems the firm was having getting the computer supplier to come to the office and repair a chronic problem with the firm's server. Pierre's attitude was that "boys will be boys." However, Jennifer and Maya cringed several times when "the boys" were having one of these exchanges and felt strongly that this behaviour had to stop. However, Jennifer was not sure language like this constituted harassment under the law, although she did feel that at a minimum it was uncivil. The two owners decided it was time to institute and implement some HR policies that would ensure their company and its employees adhered to the letter and the spirit of the various employment laws. Now they want you, their management consultant, to help them actually do it.

QUESTIONS

1 Is the Employment Standards Act applicable to this employer, as they are situated in Ontario? As LearnInMotion's management consultant, what areas of the act do you feel Jennifer and Pierre need to be aware of in regards to their current employee relations issues? Specifically, what areas would you recommend they include in their new human resource policy manual?

2 Should Pierre and Jennifer put a "respectful workplace policy" in place? If so, develop a draft of this type of policy using the web resources listed throughout this chapter.

Case INCIDENT

A New HR Professional's First Workplace Dilemma

Laura, a recent graduate from a human resources diploma program from a local community college, has just landed her first role as a human resources coordinator at a small bottling company. Upper management has made it clear that they want Laura to make the updating of the current human resources manual her first priority. During her second week on the job, Laura was strolling down the hallway toward the break room to get herself a cup of coffee when she passed the director of marketing's office. As she passed she noticed an inappropriate picture of a woman visible on his computer. Shocked at what she had just seen, Laura continued down the hall, not sure what to do next. Upon returning to her office, Laura decided the best way to start revising the manual was to introduce a policy on appropriate computer use. She felt this would address the problem as she didn't want to start her new job on a negative note by reporting the director of marketing to the CEO without a clear policy in place.

QUESTIONS

1 Do you agree with how Laura handled this situation? If so, why? If not, what would you have done differently?

2 Is it important for this company to have such a policy in place? If so, how can the employment (labour) standards act in your province/territory help in drafting a policy on appropriate computer use?

MyManagementLab

Visit MyManagementLab to access a personalized Study Plan and additional study tools for this chapter.

CBC ⦿   To view the CBC videos, read a summary, and answer discussion questions, go to MyManagementLab

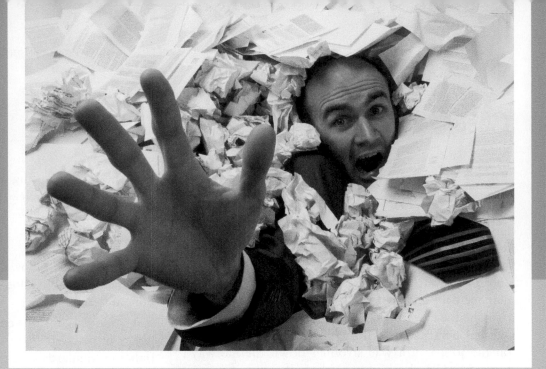

Human Resources Management and Technology

by Julie Bulmash

LEARNING OUTCOMES

AFTER STUDYING THIS CHAPTER, YOU SHOULD BE ABLE TO

EXPLAIN the strategic importance of technology in HRM.

DESCRIBE the impact that HR technology has on the role of the HR professional and the seven core competencies that have emerged.

DEFINE HRIS and describe its main components.

EXPLAIN the key functions of an HRIS and its key stakeholders.

DISCUSS what is meant by e-HR and the benefits of web-enabled service applications.

DESCRIBE the three-step process involved in selecting and implementing an HRIS.

EXPLAIN how HR technology has evolved.

IDENTIFY the key trends in HR technology.

REQUIRED PROFESSIONAL CAPABILITIES (RPC)

- Provides the organization with timely and accurate information
- Ensures compliance with legislated and contractual requirements for information management
- Contributes to the development of specifications for the acquisition and/or development of HR information management systems and for their implementation
- Evaluates alternatives for meeting current and future information management needs
- Contributes to the development of information management systems
- Ensures the availability of information needed to support the management decision-making process
- Ensures HR administrative requirements conform to organizational policies as well as best practices, balancing confidentiality and operational requirements
- Applies principles of project management to HR activities
- Evaluates progress on deliverables
- Assesses requests for HR information in light of corporate policy, freedom of information legislation, evidentiary privileges, and contractual or other releases
- Stays current with professional knowledge

HUMAN RESOURCES MANAGEMENT AND TECHNOLOGY

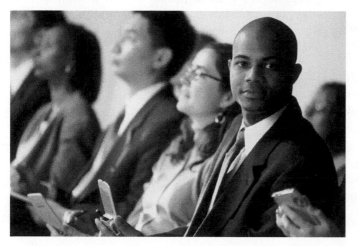

Technology permeates business life today.

When new employees are hired, they are required to provide information such as first and last name, address, emergency contacts, banking information, beneficiary information for pension and benefits, marital status, and social insurance number on a variety of HR and employment-related forms. These are data, and HR has always been the custodian of this data. How the data are used, the type of data collected, how the data are updated, where the data are stored, and the type of system used to collect the data has changed over time, but the need to collect the information relating to hiring, promoting, and terminating employees has not changed. However, the systems that HR uses to capture this data and the importance that HR now places on technology have fundamentally changed. According to a report from Towers Perrin, even in today's uncertain economic times, a third of global organizations are increasing their investments in HR technology while half have maintained their budgets.[1]

This chapter will begin by explaining the strategic importance of technology in HRM. Changes to the role of HR professionals because of their increasing use of technology and the new key competencies that HR professionals must exhibit to deliver superior service to employees will be discussed. Then the role of human resources information systems in managing the human capital of an organization will be reviewed, including web-based electronic HR. Finally, trends in HR and technology will be discussed.

THE STRATEGIC IMPORTANCE OF TECHNOLOGY IN HRM

HR technology Any technology that is used to attract, hire, retain and maintain talent, support workforce administration, and optimize workforce management.

HR technology can be defined as any technology that is used to attract, hire, retain and maintain talent, support workforce administration, and optimize workforce management.[2] This technology can be found in different types of human resource information systems (HRIS), can be used by various stakeholders, such as managers, employees, and HR professionals, and can be accessed in different ways, such as via the company intranet.

There is no doubt that technology has made it easier and faster to gather, collate, and deliver information and to communicate with employees. More importantly, it has the potential to reduce the administrative burden on the HR department members so they are able to focus on more meaningful HR activities, such as providing line managers with the appropriate decision-making tools that will enable managers to make more effective HR-related decisions.[3] Research has indicated that companies who use technology effectively to manage their HR functions will be more effective than those that do not.[4] Perhaps not surprisingly, Google is using technology in an innovative way to help manage employee retention, as discussed in the Strategic HR box.

STRATEGIC HR

Google Tackles Retention Issues with "Predictive Attrition"

Google has worked hard to keep its employees happy. But it is facing some retention challenges as several senior people reportedly have departed in the past year. In response, Google has intensified its efforts in the area of "predictive attrition" to "find situations that may increase the likelihood of some Googlers leaving the company so that managers and HR staff can work on avoiding those very situations," said Wendy Rozeluk of global communications and public affairs at Google Canada in Toronto.

Google is not providing specific details about its analysis, but the algorithm looks at data from employees who have left the company, studying factors such as where people work, team size, and compensation. The tool analyzes less obvious factors that may contribute to the decision to leave the company but identifies groups versus specific people at risk of leaving. For example, are tenured, high-performing engineers in North America more likely to stay or leave than junior ones in Europe?

"As anyone who has observed Google over the years knows, we're serious about keeping our employees happy," said Rozeluk. "What we were looking for was general trends that might indicate an increased likelihood that someone might leave."

Source: Adapted from S. Dobson, "Google Searches for Way to Keep Staff," *Canadian HR Reporter*, July 13, 2009.

Over the next decade, there will be significant pressures on the HR department to manage costs and deliver effective and efficient services. Being responsive and providing service 24/7, 365 days a year across an organization's global networks is the new norm.[5]

A strong strategic relationship between HR and technology will enable HR to achieve three key objectives:

1. *Strategic alignment* with business objectives
2. *Business intelligence*—providing users with relevant data
3. *Effectiveness and efficiency*—changing how HR work is performed by reducing lead times and costs, and increasing service levels.[6]

The expectations are high for HR. Achievement of these objectives will require HR professionals to be very effective at leveraging technology to reduce the time spent on administrative and legal compliance work so that it can focus on delivering strategic services.[7] Demonstrating that HR is adding value to the bottom line continues to be a major challenge for HR. A Mercer survey suggested that over 60 percent of chief financial officers continue to view HR as a cost centre that focuses primarily on executing administrative and compliance functions, and that only 15 percent of them reported that HR was focused on strategic activities.[8]

THE IMPACT OF TECHNOLOGY ON THE ROLE OF HR

The impact of technology has fundamentally changed the HR role. It has enabled HR to decrease its involvement in transactional (administrative) activities and to increase its focus on how to improve its delivery of strategic services. As a result, seven core competencies have emerged that are critical to the development of the HR professional, as shown in **Figure 3.1**. Wayne Brockbank and

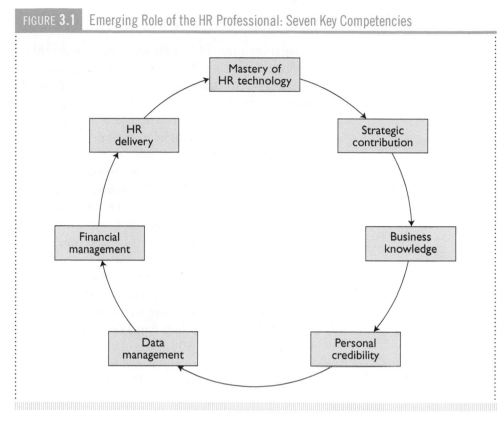

FIGURE **3.1**   Emerging Role of the HR Professional: Seven Key Competencies

Source: Julie Bulmash, 2009.

David Ulrich from the University of Michigan Business School identified five key competencies for HR,[9] and a study by Mercer highlighted two additional competencies.[10] These competencies are mastery of HR technology, strategic contribution, business knowledge, personal credibility, data management, financial management, and HR service delivery.

The traditional HR role has changed in three major ways as a result of the technologically enabled environment: (1) deceased transactional activities, (2) increased client/customer focus, and (3) increased delivery of strategic services.

Decreased Transactional Activities

Technology enables the reduction of the administrative burden, resulting in lowering basic transaction costs. Proactive HR professionals leverage technology to improve the design and delivery of basic HR services. In order to do so, HR professionals develop business knowledge with respect to the key drivers of organizational productivity and become cognizant of costs associated with enhancing efficiencies and effectiveness of the workforce. Reducing administrative and compliance activities through automation is considered necessary if HR is going to liberate itself from these day-to-day activities. Selecting the appropriate technology and ensuring that it is deployed appropriately are very important activities to ensure the organization can meet its goals. A survey published by the Society of Human Resource Management indicated that technical skills such as software and Internet literacy, as well as database skills, are considered most important for the HR specialist to develop[11].

Increased Client/Customer Focus

In organizations, HR deals with many internal customers, including managers, employees, and all the other departments in the organization. These customers expect HR to understand and respond to their requests quickly, reduce bureaucracy, and provide information that is meaningful, useful, and accurate. In today's economic climate, there is a significant need for HR professionals to understand the financial side of organizations, in particular how to help the organization control its people costs.

Managers expect HR to understand their key business issues and to provide relevant and meaningful information to help them make better decisions. For example, managers are responsible for creating and maintaining their staffing budgets. Information about the number of employees who quit or were terminated or the numbers of maternity and other planned leaves is important to help the manager plan more effectively.

Today's employees expect responsiveness, flexibility, and access to information 24/7. To be effective, HR must understand how technology can best meet the needs of their customers. When these stakeholders become more comfortable with the fact that HR is listening and cares about their needs, they will gain respect for HR and trust HR. This trust will lead them to sharing their concerns to a greater degree and trusting HR with their data requirements.

A significant partner of HR is the information technology (IT) department. The next section will focus on how HR can develop a good working relationship with this critical group.

HR and the IT Department: Developing Good Working Relationships

If HR is going to gain credibility with the IT department and work effectively, it must demonstrate its knowledge of and respect for the IT discipline. Specifically, it is important for HR to exhibit knowledge of different types of HR systems, technology delivery methods, best practices of other organizations, and the types of technology enhancements that set these organizations apart. For example, when AT&T long distance services decided to implement an HR/payroll system, HR met with several different vendors to explore the functionalities of the different systems and worked with a team of IT professionals to help them make an informed decision.

In order for HR to build this technological knowledge, they can seek out learning opportunities such as trade shows, meetings with software vendors, formal courses in IT, and reading material about technological trends and issues. Not only will HR practitioners be able to speak the language of IT, but they will also gain a greater understanding of the IT discipline and the challenges facing IT professionals.[12]

Increased Strategic Activities

HR guru Ed Lawler has suggested that HR should consider itself to be a business and that a business must consider the types of products it should offer to ensure sustainability.[13] Those products and services must relate to implementing the organization's strategy, so that HR will be "strategically proactive versus reactive."[14] HR must understand and respond to changing strategic requirements and effectively use technology to reduce the time and effort spent on

---

Gartner Inc.
www.gartner.com

Forrester Research
www.forrester.com

International Data Corporation
www.idc.com

Technology Publications
www.bitpipe.com

Software & Information Industry Association
www.siia.com

International Association for Human Resource Information Management
www.ihrim.org

Society for Human Resource Management
www.shrm.org

RPC

Ensures the availability of information needed to support the management decision-making process maintenance and compliance work so that more effort can be shifted to strategic business needs. Currently, the area of most importance to businesses has been identified as talent management. Managing human capital effectively to positively impact the bottom line is a major focus for executives today.[15]

HUMAN RESOURCES INFORMATION SYSTEMS (HRIS)

There are over 140 human resources information systems being offered by over a hundred vendors in the United States and Canada.[16] The costs of implementing such a system range from $1 000 to $12 million.[17] Licensing fees cost anywhere from three to eight times the cost of the software licence for implementation costs.[18]

Not all companies have the latest and greatest technology, nor do all companies need the most advanced technology. However, all companies do have HR-related information needs. The information needs of a small company with 40 employees may only require the use of a simple Microsoft Word or Microsoft Excel file to keep basic employee data. A company with 3 000 employees manages a greater volume of data, which can be daunting without a more sophisticated tool to store and retrieve data.

human resources information system (HRIS) Integrated systems used to gather, store, and analyze information regarding an organization's human resources.

Also referred to as human resources management systems (HRMS) in the literature,[19] **human resources information systems (HRIS)** can be defined as integrated systems used to gather, store, and analyze information regarding an organization's human resources.[20] These systems consist of software applications that work in conjunction with an electronic database.[21] HRIS enable HR professionals to collaborate with the organization to ensure efficiency and effectiveness of the workforce, become more customer focused, and align their activities to the business plan, thus contributing to the bottom line. Using HRIS technology can help HR automate and simplify tasks, reduce administration and record keeping, and provide management with data and resources.

All these systems have different functionalities (or capabilities) and some are much more complex than others, but they all provide a repository for information/data to be stored and maintained. HRIS possess varying degrees of reporting capability. However, the system must transform basic data into information that is meaningful to managers. This is a challenge facing HR departments today and will ultimately determine whether HR is able to deliver strategic HR services. Much of the data now available to HR comes from a **data warehouse**—a specialized type of database that is optimized for reporting and analysis and is the raw material for managers' decision support.[22]

data warehouse A specialized type of database that is optimized for reporting and analysis and is the raw material for managers' decision support.

The Relationship between HRM and HRIS

HRIS is the composite of databases, computer applications, hardware, and software necessary to collect, record, store, manage, deliver, manipulate, and present data regarding human resources.[23] It is primarily a transaction processor, editor, and record keeper, maintaining employee, organizational, and HR-related data.[24] Its primary function is to provide information to its clients, such as employees, managers, payroll staff, and HR professionals.

It is important to note that the term "systems" refers not just to the technical hardware and software. From an HR perspective, "systems" is about the people, policies, procedures, and data required to manage the HR function. In reality, computer technology is not the key to being successful at managing HR information; what it does do well is provide a very useful tool for "operationalizing" the information, making it easier to obtain and disseminate information and ensuring that the information is specific to the organization's HRpolicies and practices.[25]

An HRIS must allow for the assimilation and integration of HR policies and procedures in addition to operating the computer hardware and software applications.[26] For example, a simple business rule—promotional raises are not to exceed 8 percent of salary—can easily be programmed into the system.

The Major Components of an HRIS

There are several different generic subsystems that comprise an HRIS:[27] administration, recruitment, time and attendance, training and development, pension administration, employment equity, performance evaluation, compensation and benefit administration, organization management, health and safety, labour relations, and payroll, as shown in **Figure 3.2**.

HR Administration

A basic component of an HRIS is its administrative function. The typical information in an HRIS system includes employee name, address, phone number and email address; birth date; hire date; sex; salary; emergency contact information;

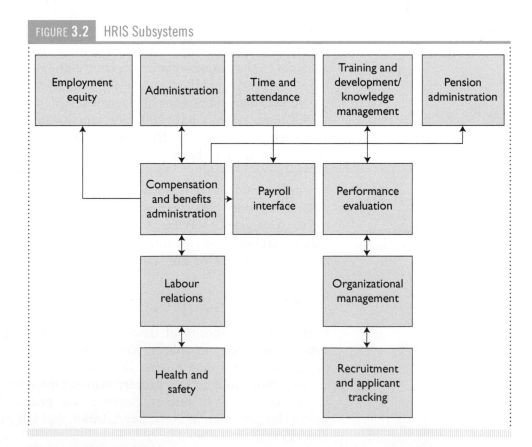

FIGURE **3.2** HRIS Subsystems

Source: Julie Bulmash, 2006.

department code; location; employment status, such as full time, part time, or contract; the start date of each position held; position titles; and benefit information.

Recruitment and Applicant Tracking

One of the first lessons an HR professional learns is not to hire anyone unless the company approves the hiring budget. In organizations that effectively manage their costs, approval for filling a position is a formalized process. This subsystem contains information on the position name and number, the department in which the position resides, whether the position has been approved, and whether the position is going to be a full-time or part-time position. Depending on the sophistication of the HRIS, online forms may be available, and it may be possible to track applicants and scan their résumés for key words identifying skills and experience.

Time and Attendance

Typically, vacation entitlement is based on service. For example, Ontario legislation states that employees are entitled to two weeks of vacation after completing one year of service. However, some organizations may choose to be more generous and may offer three weeks of vacation. To calculate this information the HR specialist would need the hire date, any leaves of absence (paid or unpaid), termination date (if applicable), and any other events that interrupted service. This information can be found in an HRIS. In addition, the company's policy (such as a "use it or lose it" policy) might be programmed into the system. If there are any special rules, this information is also programmed into the system; for example, employees often continue to accumulate vacation on certain types of leaves.

Other data that can be found with respect to time and attendance include information on absenteeism (the number of days an employee was absent), leaves of absence, whether these leaves were sabbatical or personal, parental leaves, and the dates the employee started and ended the leave. Policy details would be programmed; for example, some companies have a policy that states that, if an employee is absent for more than a certain number of days, his or her pay is decreased by a certain amount. **Figure 3.3** shows a related

FIGURE **3.3** PeopleSoft Enterprise Time and Labour Screen

Source: Reproduced with permission of Oracle.

screen from a popular HRIS from PeopleSoft, whose subsystem is called the Enterprise Time and Labour system.

Training and Development/Knowledge Management

This HRIS subsystem includes information about an employee's skills and competencies, training courses and development activities undertaken, and the costs of such activities. It may also contain career planning information in terms of which positions might be most appropriate for particular employees, based on their skills and competencies.

Pension Administration

For organizations that sponsor retirement plans for their employees, information necessary to produce annual pension statements will be recorded. This data includes date of plan entry, normal retirement date, employee elections regarding contributions, and the annual company contribution.

Employment Equity Information

Federally regulated organizations are responsible for annual reporting of their employment equity information to the government. This information, including the types of industry the organization competes in and the geographic region that the organization operates in, can be recorded in the HRIS and easily retrieved to create reports required under the legislation.

Performance Evaluation

New managers need information regarding the performance history of the employees reporting to them and thus must be able to look back at their past ratings. An HRIS can store information regarding ratings, the date these ratings were received, the type of appraisals that were used, and comments about the appraisal, as well as performance objectives and goals that arose out of the performance evaluation process. **Figure 3.4** shows a screen with performance evaluation information from PeopleSoft's Enterprise ePerformance subsystem.

FIGURE **3.4**   PeopleSoft Enterprise ePerformance Screen

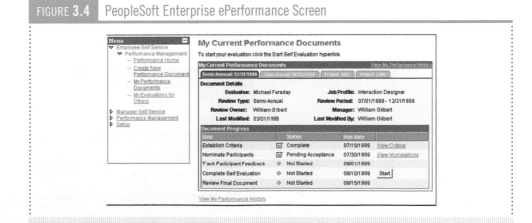

Source: Reproduced with permission of Oracle.

Compensation and Benefits Administration

The HRIS includes information regarding the company's compensation and benefits plans and their policies relating to these plans. For example, information can include the pay increase associated with a promotion, data regarding pay grades and ranges for each position, the bonus structure, and which positions are entitled to a bonus. In addition, information can be entered regarding the type of benefit plans, whether there is a cost-sharing arrangement, and how it would change if an employee took an unpaid leave.

Organization Management

This subsystem identifies the organizational structure and stores job descriptions for each position in the structure. It can also link the positions/jobs to specific workers. It may also have a field to enter the National Occupational Classification (NOC) codes.

Health and Safety

Accidents happen, and organizations are responsible for reporting these accidents to workers' compensation authorities. Information as to the number of accidents, types of accidents, health and safety complaints and resolutions, workers' compensation claims, and workers' compensation forms can also be kept in the system.

Labour Relations

Information such as union membership, seniority lists, grievances, and resolutions can be found in this subsystem.

Payroll Interface

Most HRIS today have a subsystem with information on salary, wages, and benefits to make it easier to interface with the payroll system in accounting. The more sophisticated systems have an ability to interface with external payroll providers such as ADP and Ceridian.

Key Functions of an HRIS

An HRIS is made up of a number of subsystems and data can be stored, maintained, and generated from the system. Through a number of business software applications, these data are then transformed into information. This information is used by different stakeholders, can become essential for business operations, and can aid in decision making.[28] These stakeholders include employees, managers, and HR/payroll professionals.

The key functions of an HRIS are shown in **Figure 3.5**, along with the way in which stakeholders use the information generated.[29] The data in the HRIS can be used to create and maintain employee records, ensure legal compliance, enable managers to forecast and plan their staffing requirements, enable managers and HR to manage knowledge and talent through career and succession planning, ensure the organization is aligned effectively with its strategic plan, and assist managers with decision making by providing the relevant data required to make effective and informed decisions.

FIGURE **3.5** Key Functions of an HRIS

Source: Julie Bulmash, 2006.

RPC

Assesses requests for HR information in light of corporate policy, freedom of information legislation, evidentiary privileges, and contractual or other releases Ensures compliance with legislated and contractual requirements for information management

Create and Maintain Employee Records

A record is established for every employee once they are hired into an organization. This record is maintained throughout his or her period of employment and includes all the details regarding the individual's employment history with the organization, such as personal data (address, telephone number, and so on) and job data (job title[s], salary increases, performance appraisals, and so on). In most organizations, the HRIS administrator is responsible for creating and maintaining these records. Accuracy and timeliness are critical. For example, when an employee is promoted, salary increase information needs to be entered into the system immediately. Over time, managers, the employee, and HR professionals will require access to the employee's record. Typically, employees want to check this data for accuracy, or they may want to use the information to help them advance in the organization, whereas managers and HR use this information to help them make decisions.

Legal Compliance

Information entered into the HRIS ensures that organizations can comply with government regulations by providing data in an accurate and timely manner. Ensuring data integrity and accuracy is very important and a key responsibility of the HR professional. For example, organizations that are subject to employment equity legislation are required to file an annual report. These reports can be generated with ease if this information has been recorded and maintained appropriately. Some HRIS software interfaces directly with the Workplace Equity Information Management System (WEIMS) provided by the government.[30] In this case, the information from the HRIS can be downloaded directly into the required reporting system. Payroll is another example of a function with a multitude of compliance responsibilities, such as the generation of an employee's T4 information.

Forecasting and Planning HR Requirements

Information from the recruitment, training and development, and administrative subsystems, such as number of open positions, types of positions, current employee skills and competencies, job rates (salaries), retirement eligibility, and attrition rates, can be used to help managers develop long-range staffing plans and provide valuable information to human resources professionals.

Talent Management/Knowledge Management

The data that is entered into the system, such as skills, competencies, jobs held, training, and employee development interests, can be used to help managers provide development opportunities for their employees. It will ensure that the appropriate employees are offered positions that will enhance their skills, provide the appropriate training for employees so they can advance in the organization, and highlight an employee's interests and development paths. This information will help HR staff provide more targeted advice and counsel to managers and help HR work more effectively with employees and managers to create a development plan that meets organizational and employee needs.

Strategic Alignment

Information from the system can help organizations align more effectively with their strategic plan. For example, if the organization's plan was to enter into a new market and it required a certain number and type of employees, the data from the system can provide the manager with a barometer as to whether they are moving toward the goal and the manager can leverage the information on the skills employees possess to help the organization effectively obtain the goal.

Enhancing Decision Making: Decision Support Systems

The ability to extract data from the HRIS and use this data not just for information purposes but to improve the quality of decisions made by managers and HR professionals has become important in the effective management of human capital.[31] It is not only a matter of interpreting the data but also using the data within a meaningful context to help managers and HR professionals make effective business decisions.

It is not uncommon for managers to request reports from the HRIS. For example, a manager might be responsible for his or her own salary budget and, when it comes time for annual increases, managers are typically asked to recommend appropriate salary increases for their employees based on their budgets. In order to make a quality decision, the manager might need to confirm each employee's current salary, look at the history of salary increases, review compensation policies, and review the employees' performance history. To make the most informed decision, the manager needs information that is relevant, useful, timely, and accurate.

Human resources might request a report on the number of hires within each department. They may want to look at a particular division to assess how many new hires there were within a given time frame and whether they were full time, contract, or part time. Gathering this information would be an example of using the system to help the HR professional make a decision as to what resources a particular business unit may need in the future.

Some common reports that managers request from the HRIS are basic information reports, including information such as name, address, and phone number; compensation reports such as salary histories; performance evaluations; leaves of absence (length of time, paid or unpaid); number of jobs held and position titles; number of vacation days taken and number outstanding; and types of training taken and skills acquired.

In addition to these reports, managers use the system to perform HR calculations. The Saratoga Institute has identified a list of the most common calculations requested by managers, which include healthcare cost per employee, pay and benefits as a percentage of operating expenses, cost per hire, return on training, voluntary turnover rate, turnover cost, time to fill jobs, return on human capital invested, and human value added.[32]

metrics (workforce analytics)
Statistical measures of the impact of HRM practices on the performance of an organization's human capital.

Metrics, also known as **workforce analytics**, are statistical measures of the impact of HRM practices on the performance of an organization's human capital. An example of a metric is the cost of the HR department per employee, calculated as the total cost of the HR department for a given period of time divided by the total number of employees employed during that time. Metrics can help managers identify opportunities to improve performance and control costs. There are many possible metrics to use, and they are chosen by identifying key HR issues, gathering data from HR and other areas, setting applicable standards for rigour, and ensuring relevance.[33] Leading edge organizations have adopted metrics/workforce analytics and are using sophisticated HRIS capabilities to generate relevant and high-quality data. An example in the area of health and safety is obtaining HRIS data on the number of accidents and injuries and also on the causes of these injuries. Knowing the causes will enable HR to develop the applicable policies and practices to reduce the number of health and safety problems.[34]

Effective HR departments use precision data analysis to aid managers in effective decision making. This ability to contribute to decisions has enabled HR to demonstrate that the effective management of human capital can have a significant and measurable impact on a company's bottom line.[35] **Figure 3.6** summarizes the main user groups for the HRIS and the key information provided to each group.

FIGURE 3.6   HRIS Users

	Employee*	Manager	HR
Record and maintain	✓	✓	✓
Compliance			✓
Forecasting and planning		✓	✓
Talent management/ knowledge management	✓	✓	✓
Strategic		✓	✓
Decision making	✓	✓	✓

*Employee is only able to record and maintain data in the HRIS system if it is web-enabled.
Source: Julie Bulmash, 2009.

SELECTING AND IMPLEMENTING AN HRIS

So far, some generic subsystems of an HRIS, major functions of an HRIS, and the stakeholders who use these systems have been described. Companies vary in terms of their information needs, their existing technology, and their commitment to technology. They are also different in terms of their ability to afford technology, the value they place on HR information, and the people resources they have available to devote to a technology upgrade.[36] A company may only need a very simple system that captures time card and payroll information, or they may need a very sophisticated system that can calculate significant workforce analytics.

Organizations can choose from many different systems in all sorts of sizes and with varying degrees of functionality and sophistication. The choice of technology revolves around two basic questions: (1) What is the desired amount of customization? and (2) What type of system is required/preferred? Organizations can decide whether they want to purchase a standard system and adapt their internal processes to align with the system, or develop a proprietary system, or customize a modular software system to fit the organization's existing processes. Some of the criteria that may affect this decision are the cost of the system, the number of employees, the degree of efficiency, and the company's existing hardware and software. Regardless of the type of system selected, the key reasons for purchase are generally cost savings, faster processing of information, and access to relevant information that will help the organization achieve its goals.[37]

Types of HRIS Systems

An effective HRIS system matches its technical capabilities with the needs of the organization. These needs typically increase with the size of the organization.[38] Smaller firms might use very generic software applications such as Microsoft Excel and Access. These firms might only require payroll and benefits administration, time and attendance reporting, and an employee scheduling function.

Mid-sized firms typically require compliance tracking and reporting, health claims administration, payroll, and compensation and benefits administration. Managers may require information on performance appraisal, time and attendance, succession planning, skills testing, and employee scheduling. Employees may use the system to aid in career development. Mid-sized firms require greater data integration, and the systems will have better backup and recovery capability. They will also allow for many users. In mid-sized systems, all HRIS functions typically flow through one single system so data redundancies can be identified and eliminated. Some popular HRIS vendors for small to mid-sized organizations are Spectrum Human Resource Systems Corporation, Genesys software systems, Best Software Inc., Ultimate Software (UltiPro workforce management), People-Trak, and Organization Plus.[39]

Large organizations typically require greater functionality than mid-sized firms. In addition to those functions mentioned above, these firms will require employee screening, résumé processing and tracking, and additional compliance and reporting requirements like employment equity. They may also require

**enterprise-wide system/
enterprise resource planning
(ERP) system** A system that supports enterprise-wide or cross-functional requirements rather than a single department within the organization.

stand-alone system A self-contained system that does not rely on other systems to operate.

self-service options, which are web-based applications that enable managers and employees to access and manage information directly without having to go through HR or the manager.

The type of HRIS they might require can be part of a larger **enterprise-wide or enterprise resource planning (ERP) system** that supports enterprise-wide or cross-functional requirements rather than a single department within the organization.[40] These systems originated from software that integrated information from the organization's functional areas (finance, marketing, operations, and so on) into one universal database so that financial information could be linked to marketing information and so on. An enterprise-wide system typically includes several HR modules, such as a payroll module and a training and development module. These systems vary with respect to cost, functionality, and robustness, so depending on the organization's requirements, some systems will be more appropriate than others. Some popular ERP systems are SAP, PeopleSoft, and Oracle ERP systems.[41]

The largest ERP systems provider is SAP, a German company that was founded as *Systemanalyse und Programmentwicklung* in 1972 by five former IBM employees in Germany. This acronym was changed to *Systeme, Anwendungen und Produkte in der Datenverarbeitung*, which means "systems, applications and products in data processing," and in 2005 the name was officially changed to SAP AG. SAP products are used by over 12 million people in more than 120 countries, and its market has typically been Fortune 500 companies. Recently SAP has targeted small to medium-sized organizations with some of their new products. SAP is made up of individual, integrated software modules that perform various organizational system tasks such as finance/accounting, controlling, project systems, funds management, materials management, and sales distribution. One of its major modules is the human resource management system (HRMS). These systems are robust, and SAP offers a full range of functionality, HR products, and web-based offerings.[42]

PeopleSoft is a company that provides HRIS, manufacturing, financial, enterprise performance management, student administration, and customer relationship management (CRM) systems to large corporations and governments. It was founded in 1987 by David Duffield and Ken Morris. Its software is well known for its ability to be easily customized so that it can fit the specific business needs of each client. In 2005, PeopleSoft was acquired by Oracle.[43] One company that uses PeopleSoft is the Canadian Imperial Bank of Commerce (CIBC). Their employees are provided with online access to HR services and information. The system enables employees to add dependants to health insurance, change payroll deductions, enroll in benefits programs, calculate pension benefits, and do retirement planning.[44]

HR technology can also be provided by a **stand-alone system**, meaning a self-contained system that does not rely on other systems to operate. These systems are not enterprise-wide, but they do perform specific HR-related functions. Examples include Halogen Software Inc.[45] and Sage HRMS Inc.

Typically, organizations follow a three-step process to choose an HRIS, as shown in **Figure 3.7**. The three steps are (1) adoption phase, (2) implementation phase, and (3) integration (institutionalization) phase.[46]

RPC

Evaluates alternatives for meeting current and future information management needs

FIGURE **3.7**   Three-Step HRIS Implementation Process

Source: Julie Bulmash, 2009.

Phase 1: Adoption—Determining the Need

In this phase, organizations typically engage in a needs analysis to determine what type of system they will purchase. A needs analysis helps the organization decide on what the system should be capable of doing and what the technical specifications will be. It helps the organization develop an information policy about how the information should be managed with respect to storage and access. A needs analysis will also provide the organization with a framework to evaluate vendors of software. There are several main areas to be considered: company background, management considerations, technical considerations, HR considerations, and cost considerations.[47]

Company Background

The industry, the size of the company, and the projected growth are important elements to consider. For example, if the company is very small and has only four people and the HR forecast is to add an additional five people in the next two years, then the type of system that is needed could be something as simple as an Excel spreadsheet. Typically, organizations require HR software after they reach 100 employees.

Management Considerations

Normally, management would have some preconceived views regarding what they want the system to do and the type of software that might be required. They may want a complex system with enterprise-wide capabilities or a stand-alone system.

Technical Considerations

Elements such as hardware, operating systems, networking, databases, and tele-communications all need to be considered. It is important to understand the kind of technology the company currently has, because in some cases integrating new software into existing systems can be costly.

HR Considerations

The HR department must consider its own needs. What type of daily requests and which employee transactions would make the most sense to automate? What types of forms, reports, or listings are maintained? For example, every time management wants to notify the entire organization about some key event, has it been necessary to pull together a list manually? If so, this activity could be automated. The most critical area to be assessed is the decision support activities of HR. As discussed earlier, providing reports to help managers make better decisions is an important activity where HR can add value. The needs assess-ment would identify the types of data required to produce reports, where these data can be found, and how reliable the data are. HR would look at the manual reports currently being maintained and decide how these can be automated.

Cost Considerations

RPC

Applies principles of project management to HR activities

request for proposal (RFP) A document requesting that vendors provide a proposal detailing how the implementation of their particular HRIS will meet the organization's needs.

Organizations may want to have the best possible system, but might not be able to afford all the "bells and whistles." Factored into the price that an organization can afford are considerations such as additional hardware purchases required, the number of additional staff needed during the implementation phase, training costs, and ongoing support costs.

Once the needs analysis is complete, companies send out a **request for proposal (RFP)** to a number of vendors requesting details of how the implemen-tation of their particular HRIS will meet the organization's needs. Then demon-strations of the various systems are scheduled and the system that most closely aligns with the organization's needs is selected.

At this point, the adoption phase is complete, and the organization will move into the implementation phase.

Phase 2: Implementation

In this phase, the company selects a project team that typically includes outside consultants who have knowledge and expertise on the technical side and expertise in change management to help the organization with the implementation. In addition to the outside consultants, there is usually a senior project manager who leads the team, subject matter experts from HR and payroll, and management from the various functional areas across the organization. These managers will be using the system, so it is important for them to ensure that the system is implemented effectively and that their requirements are clearly understood.

RPC

Evaluates progress on deliverables

The activities involved in this phase focus on getting the system "up and running" within a controlled environment so that the system can be tested to ensure that it is functioning in the way the organization requires. The existing data are "converted" into the new system, meaning that the old system data are transformed to be made compatible with the new system. The software is tested and the users are expected to provide feedback before the system goes live.

"Going live" means disengaging any previous HRIS and providing users access to the new system only. In this phase, security profiles are established for the users.

Privacy and Security

There are major privacy concerns when setting up an HRIS because of the sensitive personal nature of much of the data stored there, such as medical claims. Careful decisions must be made regarding who will have access to the computer hardware, software, and databases, and who will be able to modify the databases.[48] Establishing security profiles is a very important activity when implementing an HRIS. The staff members who will be working with the HRIS must be identified and security profiles established. These profiles specify which staff members have access to each screen, which data elements (fields) each staff member can have access to, and which staff members can enter or change data. Security profiles are typically attached to positions in the organization rather than to individuals.

For example, the profile for an HR administrator who enters employee information into the system and who is the point of contact for all changes that employees make to their "tombstone data" would include viewing, entering, and changing data. A line manager's profile typically includes viewing information relating to their employees, but not confidential data that is irrelevant to the work situation, and the profile would not include changing employee records.

A final, critical piece of HRIS security is making sure the system users clearly understand and adhere to the company confidentiality policy and code of ethics. All users need to understand that they must not share passwords, post them in view of others, or compromise them in any way.

Phase 3: Integration

The final step in implementing an HRIS system is to train the users on the system. The organization's goal is for the stakeholders to use the system and reap the benefits identified through the needs analysis. However, many difficulties can arise with the implementation of a new system and, as with any change, people need to become comfortable with it. People often have difficulties transitioning to an HRIS, so the organization can experience inertia.[49]

Employees need to be trained, but even after training they may not feel fully competent and might not use the system. With any new system, stakeholders can underestimate its complexity.

ELECTRONIC HR

electronic HR (e-HR) A form of technology that enables HR professionals to integrate an organization's HR strategies, processes, and human capital to improve overall HR service delivery.

intranet A network that is interconnected within one organization using web technologies for the sharing of information internally.

Electronic HR (e-HR) enables HR professionals to integrate an organization's HR strategies, processes, and human capital to improve overall HR service delivery.[50] By the mid-1990s, organizations were beginning to embrace ways in which to incorporate electronic and computer functions into their HR strategies.[51] Companies continue to look for better ways to manage costs, provide better service, and effectively manage their human capital. e-HR has become integral to helping organizations achieve these goals.

One of the most successful innovations is the migration of HRIS applications onto an intranet.[52] An **intranet** is a network that is interconnected within one organization using web technologies for the sharing of information internally.[53] The Internet has enabled organizations to harness web-based technology and use web-based applications to enhance HR services. A **web-based application** can be accessed from any computer connected to the Internet by using a password-protected login page. More than 90 percent of companies are currently using the web for HR purposes.[54]

web-based application An application that can be accessed from any computer connected to the Internet.

The most significant development in HR technology that enables direct employee access to HR applications is the web-based **HR portal,** which provides users with a single Internet access point for customized and personalized HR services.[55]

HR portal A single Internet access point for customized and personalized HR services.

e-HR and Web-Based Self-Service Trends

The two most popular web-based applications enable HR self-service and therefore save time and reduce paperwork for HR staff.[56] These applications have allowed companies to shift responsibility for viewing and updating records onto employees and managers and have fundamentally changed the manner in which employees acquire information and interact with their HR departments.

Employee Self-Service (ESS)

employee self-service (ESS) Enables employees to access and manage their personal information directly.

Employee self-service (ESS) systems enable employees to access and manage their personal information directly on a 24/7 basis without having to go through their HR departments or their managers. Employees often access ESS systems via the Internet, sometimes using a portal on the company's secure intranet site.

Some common ESS options allow employees to update personal information, such as address, phone number, emergency contact name and number; revise banking information; enroll in benefits programs; research benefit options; view payroll information like salary deductions; record vacation time and sick days; record travel expenses; access HR policies; participate in training delivered via the web; and access company communications and newsletters issued by the HR department. For example, an employee who recently separated from his or her spouse can log on through the company's intranet site, click on the HR portal, and make all the required changes to emergency contact name, beneficiary information, and other benefit details that list the former spouse's name, all from the convenience and privacy of the employee's own home. **Figure 3.8** provides a sample PeopleSoft Enterprise eProfile screen.

ESS systems have fundamentally changed the way employees relate to their HR departments. Employees are able to access information that is relevant only to them, and they no longer need to speak with an HR representative directly for fairly routine data updates. These systems have also helped HR departments manage their operational costs effectively. From the perspective of the HR professional, the responsibility for basic administrative and transactional activities has been shifted onto the employee, which enables HR professionals to have more time to focus on strategic issues.

ESS systems can be very effective. A study by *HR Focus* found that HR generalist workloads were reduced by an average of 15 percent after the introduction of an ESS.[57] Two organizations that have benefited from upgrading their technology and adding ESS are the Toronto Police Services and Time Warner Inc.

For the Toronto Police Services, one of the most time-consuming and onerous activities was the scheduling and payment of both overtime and court time for

FIGURE **3.8**   PeopleSoft Enterprise eProfile Screen

Source: Reproduced with permission of Oracle.

officers. The Toronto Police Services spent over $500 million of their operating budget on salaries, of which $32 million went to paying overtime and court time costs to 7 000 officers. With the implementation of an ESS system, officers were able to revise their schedules online, which in turn reduced administrative costs.[58]

Time Warner's challenge was to find a way to unify its 80 000 employees in geographically diverse regions and give them access to their HR services. They created an employee portal called "Employee Connection." The portal gives employees varying levels of access to benefits enrollment, compensation planning, merit reviews, stock option information, payroll information, administrative HR forms, expense reimbursement forms, and travel planning information.[59]

Management Self-Service (MSS)

management self-service (MSS)
Enables managers to access a range of information about themselves and the employees who report to them and to process HR-related paperwork that pertains to their staff.

Management self-service (MSS) systems allow managers to access a range of information about themselves and the employees who report to them. MSS systems also give managers the opportunity to process HR-related paperwork that pertains to their staff. Managers can view résumés that are on file, view merit reviews, submit position requisitions, view employee salaries, and keep track of employee performance and training histories. Typically, this type of system offers a broader range of services than is available to non-managerial staff. In addition to providing HR-related information, MSS systems often provide managers with additional tools to help them with tasks such as budget reviews, report writing, and authorization of expense reimbursements.

The major benefit of MSS is that it provides managers with ready access to information that is useful both to themselves and to their employees without having to go through a third party. In this way, MSS systems reduce overall company workloads. In fact, research has indicated that when used properly, MSS systems reduce the workload of HR generalists by more than 21 percent because they are not spending that time on planning annual compensation increases, viewing employee histories, initiating requests for positions, or posting jobs.[60]

Managers are receptive to MSS systems because they contribute to data integrity and accuracy. The number of edits to the data decreases, as managers

FIGURE **3.9**   Web-Based Self-Service Applications and Benefits

Source: Julie Bulmash, 2006.

can validate the data right away. In addition, the time needed to process the data improves as the manager can view the information in real time, authorize the activity, and communicate directly with the employee.[61] Imagistics International, formally Pitney Bowes Office Systems, implemented an MSS system. Since the system has been in place, they have reported a significant reduction in administrative costs, process steps, and number of entry errors, and have reported an overall streamlining of their HR reporting process.[62]

MSS can be a very valuable tool, but this technology is currently not as popular as ESS and has been slower to gain acceptance. **Figure 3.9** summarizes web-based self-service applications and their benefits.

e-HR and Talent Management Systems

As mentioned earlier, human capital management has become a key priority in organizations. The importance of acquiring and managing talent has increased and is expected to continue to increase over the next decade. Even in the current uncertain economic times, organizations are dedicating significant resources to this important activity, and the allocation of a sizable portion of HR budget dollars to new talent management technologies is expected.[63]

Talent management systems offer HR an integrated approach to managing its talent. They enable proactive workforce planning, applicant screening, and candidate assessment. They can help HR access employee performance and competency information, run performance management processes, and assign high performers into succession plans. They can also provide increased access to managers so that they can be more effective at compensation planning and budgeting, and offer employees increased access to online career planning tools.

e-HR Vendors

There are numerous vendors in the marketplace offering products to help HR automate its functions. Some are stand-alone applications while others are enterprise-wide solutions. Some software vendors who offer high-quality web-based hiring tools such as applicant tracking and e-recruiting tools are Brass Ring, Deploy, Icarian, Taleo (formally RecruitSoft), and Web Hire.[64] Halogen Software's eAppraisal product is a web-based system for employee performance appraisal. Forms can be created and completed electronically, including 360-degree feedback.[65] ExecuTRACK Software Group has developed software solutions for human capital. Their software can create succession-planning matrices and candidate placement scenarios, as well as many other tasks.[66] OrgPlus software has a sophisticated tool for graphically depicting organizational charts and transforming this information into decision-making tools.[67] The Entrepreneurs and HR box provides an example of a Canadian company that offers innovative HRIS software.

ENTREPRENEURS and HR

Cronus Technologies

Cary and Shaun Schuler were awarded the Young Entrepreneur Award by the Business Development Bank of Canada (BDC). Cary, Shaun, and older brother Rodney founded Cronus Technologies Inc., an IT company located in the heart of Saskatoon's high-tech business area. Cronus specializes in custom software development and project management and has won the prestigious HR Technology Excellence Award for its products. Currently they export to the United States but are developing partnerships in Western Europe.

"The Schulers epitomize a new generation of young Canadian entrepreneurs who, in creating jobs for themselves and members of their communities, are giving a great deal back to the regions that host their businesses," says Michel Vennat, who was BDC president and CEO at the time. "I salute their drive and determination."

Cronus continues to grow as a leading developer of innovative software. It is also a good corporate citizen. The Schulers believe in giving back to the community and have sponsored and made donations to various organizations such as the Arthritis Society, the Hope Cancer Centre, the United Way, and the Dragon Boat Races.

The founders of Cronus Technologies Inc.—Rodney, Cary, and Shaun Schuler.

Source: Business Development Bank of Canada, www.bdc.ca/en/about/mediaroom/news_releases/2003/2003102011.htm?iNoC=1 (accessed June 29, 2006).

However, it is important to note that these systems are enablers only. Understanding how to use the technology effectively to manage talent is critical for HR. Web-based systems have the potential to revolutionize how HR delivers service, but research has indicated that HR is still struggling with how to effectively optimize these new technologies and web-based tools.[68]

Cautions Regarding e-HR

Surveys of ESS and MSS system users indicate that although 80 percent of respondents agreed that web-based self-service systems can lower HR operation costs, only 40 percent believe that their company is actually achieving this result. Two-thirds of those surveyed agree that web-based self-service systems can effectively support the transformation of the HR department into a more strategic partner by redirecting some of their responsibilities onto employees, but only 37 percent actually felt there was a change.[69]

Why does this discrepancy exist? Could it be that employees and managers view this new technology as the "work of HR" and therefore are resistant to using it? Perhaps the technology is not as user-friendly as it should be. The usefulness of this technology will depend on whether the content is considered beneficial and relevant, on how easy the system is to navigate, and on its cultural fit with the organization. Realizing the potential of any new technology means that processes associated with the technology must be changed. People need to use the system in the right way. Only then will they reap the expected benefits.[70]

Another interesting issue to consider is how HR has responded to this new technology. As was mentioned earlier, with these technological developments in place the traditional transactional HR activities are no longer required and, as a result, HR may feel disenfranchised. Implementation of HR technology does not necessarily mean a reduction in the number of HR staff—in fact, the number of staff either increased or remained the same after e-HR was launched.[71] e-HR is about redistributing administrative HR work to provide HR professionals with more time to focus on the strategic activities that add value to the bottom line. The expectations are high for HR in terms of what it is expected to deliver to sustain innovation.[72]

A BRIEF HISTORY OF THE EVOLUTION OF HR TECHNOLOGY

The HR function has evolved significantly in terms of technology. Four main stages of development can be identified: (1) paper-based systems, (2) early personal computer (PC) technology, (3) electronic databases, and (4) web-based technology.[73]

Stage 1: Paper-Based Systems

Initially, HR systems were paper based. These systems operated independently and did not integrate with any other business-related functions. Features were added as needed. Data was typically stored on mainframe computers. The reporting was very rudimentary. HR data was only available to and used by HR staff. It was common for managers during this period to send employees to HR to get all their "personnel" questions answered.

Stage 2: Early Personal Computer (PC) Technology

In the next stage, HR continued to be the only department with access to the data. The fundamental difference was where the data was stored: HR departments began to store data in personal computers (PCs) and on local area network systems. These HR databases were simple, yet able to produce reports that listed basic employee information. Advances in database technology included payroll systems.

Stage 3: Electronic Database Systems

relational database One piece of data is stored in several different data files so that information from the separate files can be linked and used together.

In the next phase, relational database technology emerged. A **relational database** stores one piece of data in several different data files so that the information from the separate files can be linked and used together. This technology provided organizations with the ability to develop more complex reports that integrated several databases.[74] For example, a report could be generated from two different databases—one that included basic information such as name and address, and another containing salary and benefit information—as long as each database included the employee number to link the data.

With the advent of electronic databases, HR systems began to become integrated with other business-related systems, and HR began using information systems to speed up transactional activities. Also at this time the use of the Internet was increasing, and managers began to realize just how powerful a tool it was and the benefits that could be derived from an HR technology perspective.

Leading HR organizations began to purchase ERP systems (including HR modules) that leveraged relational database technology. For example, if a company decided to give all of its employees a salary increase, this information could be recorded on the employee file in the HR system and the financial module could be notified of this increase so that it would automatically debit cash and credit salary expense in the company's general ledger. It was at this point that HR entered fully into the digital world of electronic HR and the term "e-HR" began to appear.

Stage 4: Web-Based Technology

At the present time, most companies use HR technology and the benefits of automation are widely known. The focus has shifted to automating as many transactions as possible to achieve effectiveness and efficiency. Call centres and intranet-based HR systems are becoming widely used by organizations. As was discussed earlier, web-based applications are becoming increasingly popular methods to deliver information. These applications allow users to access the applications from any computer connected to the Internet via a secure, password-protected login page.

An Ethical : Dilemma

A senior manager (a very good friend of your parents) asks if you, the HR administrator, could tell him what his upcoming bonus will be; he has serious financial problems and may have to take out a loan today if his bonus is not high enough. What would you do?

For the most part, HR continues to be the owner of the information; the shift has been in terms of how HR uses the system capabilities. It is minimizing HR time spent on administration by providing tools to managers to take over some of this work. This frees up time for HR staff to focus on making more strategic contributions to organizational effectiveness.

TRENDS IN HR AND TECHNOLOGY

The technology of the future will be about speedy access to accurate real-time information. The ability to access this information via multiple delivery systems will give organizations a strategic edge. HR will continue to move toward providing managers and employees with information so they can manage their own HR issues using web-based systems.[75] Future technology will transform information into knowledge that can be used by the organization as a decision-making tool, and it will require HR and IT to work together to leverage this technology.[76] A study by the Hackett Group, a business process advisory firm, found that high-performing organizations spend 25 percent less on HR compared to their peers because they use technology effectively to improve effectiveness and efficiency.[77] Companies will need to develop a comprehensive HR technology strategy for the acquisition and use of technology to ensure future success in this area. An **HR technology strategy** is a plan that is aimed at "increasing the effectiveness of the HR programs, processes, and service delivery by shortening cycle times, increasing customer service levels, reducing costs, and adding new service capabilities." It is a document that will guide future technology investments.[78]

HR technology strategy A plan that is aimed at increasing the effectiveness of HR programs, processes, and service delivery by shortening cycle times, increasing customer service levels, reducing costs, and adding new service capabilities.

Watson Wyatt consultants have identified several major technology trends that will influence HR management in the future:[79]

1. *The increased use of portals and intranets and a greater focus on the use of virtual tools.* A survey of over 182 companies by Watson Wyatt found that one in five expect to change their HR service delivery systems. The most commonly planned changes are implementing a healthcare portal that provides employees with health improvement information (73 percent) and offering total compensation information to employees via the web (65 percent).[80] Training and education will be required to ease the transition for employees to learn to access their own information as opposed to going to HR.[81]

2. *Greater access to technology.* This will require HR to ensure that the appropriate security measures are in place and to be highly diligent in terms of access protocols.

3. *Continued optimization of current systems.* This will mean that HR must continue to be "technologically educated."

4. *Enhanced focus on workforce analytics.* This will require HR to continue its evolution with respect to providing managers with valuable information for decision-making.

5. *Increased focus on reducing costs.* This will require HR to optimize the functionality of HR technology.

6. *Increased use of standards for data exchange and processes (XML).* Companies who operate globally will need to find ways to streamline wide variations in HR processes. Developing a standard global architecture for HR data will be important, as will ensuring that the vendor they work with is capable of complying with this global standard.

7. *Contingency planning.* This will require HR to ensure that plans are in place to deal with disasters, helping organizations get employees back to work, and providing them with the appropriate emotional support.

8. *Heightened awareness of HR data privacy.* Government legislation will continue to increase and require organizations to comply.[82] Currently, Canada has two federal privacy acts, the Privacy Information Act and the Personal Information Protection and Electronic Documents Act (PIPEDA). This will require HR to stay current with respect to legislation and to use their information systems to ensure compliance.

9. *Continued use of outsourcing of non-core HR-related work.* The main strategies behind outsourcing are cost reduction and the ability to focus on core business objectives. The growth in HR outsourcing has been in areas relating to basic

HR transactions and those services that focus on managing the employee life cycle, such as recruiting. Studies have shown that 96 percent of large companies currently outsource some portion of their HR-related activities.[83] The outsourcing of Unilever's administrative HR functions is highlighted in the Global HRM box.

GLOBAL HRM

Outsourcing HR Functions

Accenture, a global management consulting, technology, and outsourcing company, has recently entered into an agreement with Unilever Corporation. Unilever is a multinational marketing organization with familiar products such as Dove soap, Becel margarine, and Lipton soup that employs 206 000 people in 100 countries worldwide. To optimize its HR services to its employees, Unilever has decided to outsource its administrative HR functions to Accenture. The agreement will cover three geographic regions—Europe, the Americas, and Asia—and provide services to approximately 200 000 employees in more than 20 languages. Accenture will manage critical HR software applications. Some of the services it will provide are recruitment, payroll administration, total rewards administration, performance management workforce reporting, and core HR administration.

This arrangement will change the way Unilever manages and delivers its HR services across the company. Once these functions are outsourced, the remaining HR activities will be redesigned to focus more on the customer and establish a targeted service delivery model.

Source: J. Finlaw, "Accenture to Help Unilever Transform Human Resources Operations in 100 Countries with a Seven-Year Outsourcing Agreement," Press Release, June 6, 2006. Used with permission of Accenture.

Today's HR professionals must be technically savvy and be able to "speak the language of business." They must understand the business environment and the major drivers relating to workforce productivity as determined by management. The use of HR metrics will be increasingly important to assess whether HR is providing services that provide value to the organization.

HR departments today are faced with significant challenges if they are going to contribute to organizational effectiveness. How HR uses technology to evaluate its own effectiveness and leverages emerging technologies to drive productivity and the management of human capital will make the difference between an HR department that just plays a supporting role and one that is truly a business partner.

Chapter SUMMARY

1. Technology has the potential to reduce the administrative burden on the HR department so they are able to focus on more meaningful HR activities, such as providing managers with the appropriate decision-making tools that will enable them to make more effective HR-related decisions. Companies who use technology appropriately to manage their HR functions will be more effective than those that do not. Enhancing the relationship between HR and technology will enable HR to achieve three key objectives: (1) strategic alignment with the business objectives, (2) business intelligence—providing users with relevant data, and (3) effectiveness and efficiency—changing how the work is performed by reducing lead times and costs and increasing service levels.

2. The role of the HR professional has changed fundamentally as a result of technology. It has enabled HR to decrease its involvement in transactional (administrative) activities and to increase its focus on how to increase its delivery of strategic services. The core competencies that have developed are mastery of HR technology, strategic contribution, business knowledge, personal credibility, data management, HR delivery, and financial management.

3. An HRIS is a group of integrated systems used to gather, store, and analyze information regarding an organization's human resources. Its main components are administration, recruitment, compensation and benefit administration, payroll, time and attendance, employment equity, performance evaluation, and health and safety.

4. The key functions of an HRIS are to create and maintain employee records, ensure legal compliance, enable managers to forecast and plan their staffing requirements, enable managers and HR to manage knowledge and talent through career and succession planning, ensure the organization is aligned more effectively with its strategic plan, and assist managers with decision making by providing the relevant data required to make effective and informed decisions. The key stakeholders include employees, managers, and HR/payroll professionals.

5. Electronic HR (e-HR) refers to a form of technology that enables HR professionals to integrate an organization's HR strategies, processes, and human capital to improve overall HR service delivery. Examples include the migration of HRIS applications onto an intranet, the use of web-based HR portals that provide users with a single Internet access point for customized and personalized HR services, and the use of web-based applications such as employee self-service (ESS) and management self-service (MSS) to enhance HR services.

6. The three steps in the process of selecting and implementing an HRIS are (1) the adoption phase, where organizations carry out a needs analysis to determine requirements; (2) the implementation phase, where project teams are created, the software is tested, and privacy and security concerns are addressed; and (3) the institutionalization phase, where training and change management activities are highlighted.

7. HR technology has evolved from paper and pencil systems to PCs, then to relational databases, and finally to web-based technology platforms and integration with enterprise-wide systems.

8. Current technology trends that will impact HR are the use of HR portals, outsourcing, a focus on talent management, the need to develop an HR technology strategy, and a continued focus on measuring the value that HR brings to the organization.

MyManagementLab

Visit MyManagementLab to access a personalized Study Plan and additional study tools for this chapter.

Key TERMS

data warehouse *(p. 61)*
electronic HR (e-HR) *(p. 73)*
employee self-service (ESS) *(p. 74)*
enterprise-wide system/enterprise resource planning (ERP) system *(p. 70)*
HR portal *(p. 74)*
HR technology *(p. 57)*
HR technology strategy *(p. 80)*

human resources information system (HRIS) *(p. 61)*
intranet *(p. 73)*
management self-service (MSS) *(p. 75)*
metrics (workforce analytics) *(p. 68)*
relational database *(p. 79)*
request for proposal (RFP) *(p. 72)*
stand-alone system *(p. 70)*
web-based application *(p. 74)*

Review and Discussion QUESTIONS

1. Enhancing the strategic relationship between HR and technology will necessitate the achievement of three key objectives. What are these objectives?

2. Discuss the seven key competencies of an HR professional in an IT-enabled world.

3. Describe two web-based service delivery applications that are popular today.

4. Describe several technological trends that HR must be aware of in order to offer value-added technology solutions.

5. Explain what an HR technology strategy plan is and why it is important.

6. What are the eight generic subsystem components that reside in an HRIS?

7. Discuss the six key functions of an HRIS system.

8. Describe the three steps involved in selecting and implementing an HRIS system.

9. Explain the four stages in the evolution of HR technology.

Critical Thinking QUESTIONS

1. In order for HR to demonstrate that it is a strategic partner with the business, it must be aware of its customer requirements. In terms of technology, what actions and initiatives would HR have to take to demonstrate this awareness?

2. The role of HR has fundamentally changed as a result of technology. How will HR deliver service in the future? What delivery mechanisms will work best?

3. Do you think that it is important for all types of organizations to have an HRIS? Why or why not?

4. Compare and contrast the costs and benefits of being a member of an HRIS implementation team.

5. Do you think that maintaining the security of an HRIS is a major concern for HR technology professionals? What security issues are most important today?

6. How does HR technology help organizations deliver transactional HR activities in a more efficient way?

7. In today's economic climate, organizations are concerned with talent management. How can HR technology be used to ease these concerns?

Experiential EXERCISES

1. Explore two vendors who offer technology-related solutions for talent management such as Taleo (www.taleo.com) and Halogen Software (www.halogensoftware.com). Consider how these programs can contribute to organizational effectiveness. How will they help managers manage more effectively? How will they aid HR in delivering strategic services?

2. Go to www.workopolis.com or www.monster.ca. Find a job posting for an HRIS manager and HRIS

analyst/administrator. How are the jobs different? What types of activities does each role carry out?

3. Investigate what workers are saying about how the web has helped them work more effectively. Go to www.GigaOM.com/collaboration. What types of issues are being discussed there? Are there some trends?

4. To accommodate a diverse workforce, HR must consider various types of delivery methods to communicate HR information. Explore the difference

between video and audio podcasts, interactive voice response (IVR), and a company intranet. Describe these methods of delivery and how they can be used to deliver HR information. (Some interesting HR-related podcasts—such as the Harvard Business Review Idea Cast—can be found at www.apple.com by accessing the iTunes store.)

Running CASE

Does LearnInMotion Need an HRIS?

Jennifer was getting frustrated. With only a few employees, the company kept a paper-based file for each employee with personal information, benefits forms, and so on. She and Pierre had decided to outsource payroll, but she still had to spend several hours every two weeks gathering payroll information, such as regular hours, overtime hours, vacation time and sick time that had been taken, and so on to send to the payroll company. The benefits information and calculations were supposed to be carried out by the payroll company, but there had been several instances where mistakes had been made.

Jennifer and Pierre discussed the issue and decided that, as a high-tech company, they should investigate the possibility of computerizing their employee files and information. Even with a very small number of employees, they both thought it might be easier for them to use some sort of HRIS. They have asked you, their management consultant, to provide answers to the following questions.

QUESTIONS

1   What data should be stored for each employee? How would the company use these data?

2   Conduct an HRIS needs analysis for the company. What are the results?

3   Would you recommend an HRIS to Jennifer and Pierre? If so, what kind of system?

Case INCIDENT

Integration and Transfer of HR Functions Using HRIS

Jack Newman had recently been appointed regional director of Boomerang Water Corporation, a major service utility in Australia. Jack's previous appointment was with a large manufacturing company in the United States, where he had made a reputation for himself as a visionary specializing in customer service and performance management. Jack was the youngest person and only non-Australian ever to be appointed as a director at Boomerang Water Corporation. This particular region of the utility employed approximately 2000 workers engaged in the customer service and maintenance provision side of the business. These employees operated in groups of about 30 workers. One supervisor managed each work group. These groups were located in five departments across the region, with each department specializing in a particular customer service or maintenance function. The region serviced about 500 000 customers.

A central division controlled the human resource management functions for the region. This division was located in the region's main town. Elaine MacVain headed the HR division. Elaine had been with the utility for nearly 25 years and over these years had developed a reputation for running a strong, controlled division that provided the customer service and maintenance department with a diversity of HR services. Elaine considered the main focus of the division to be to process day-to-day HR transactions and maintain employee records. Elaine managed a staff of 10 HR professionals who processed employee data that included workers' pay, leave entitlements and requests, and shift work entitlements. The HR department was responsible for recruitment and selection, the performance management system, occupational health and safety records, and career planning. Ron Locat, a member of Elaine's division, had developed a stand-alone HRIS to maintain the HR department's records. Ron had little formal IT training but had undergone in-house training in the use of Microsoft Access and had used Access to create the division's database system. Elaine and the other members of the HR division did not have a high level of IT literacy, but they could operate the Access system that Ron had developed. Elaine was grateful for the work Ron had put into the database system and felt indebted to him for the support that he gave to the HR staff.

A major focus of the utility was training the customer service and maintenance employees. The utility had a promotion system based on the employee's level of technical skills. Employees were promoted to higher levels of competency and pay scales on completion of skills training. Peter Noall, who had been with the utility for about four years, headed the training division, which had three staff in addition to Peter. One staff member was an ex-technical college teacher, and two had been technical supervisors in the organization. Due to the small size of the training division, Peter was forced to outsource much of the organization's training needs. Work safety was a major responsibility of Peter's, and he was very proud of the organization's safety record. Peter had contracted the purchase of an expensive, dedicated training database system to support the organization's training function. The system provided the training division with a powerful tool with which to profile the total skills base of the organization, identify present and future training needs, track employees' competency levels, and evaluate training outcomes in relation to productivity gains. The training division was proud of its use of high-level technology to support strategic training initiatives.

On commencing his appointment, Jack Newman decided his immediate focus was on improving the organization's customer service. He engaged the Fast Track–Immediate Success consultancy group to run a number of focus groups and conduct a strategic analysis related to the delivery of customer service. Eddie Wanton from Fast Track organized focus groups within the HR division and the training division and ran three focus groups of 20 randomly selected supervisors. Eddie's report to Jack Newman included the following concerns and recommendations aimed to improve customer service.

Report from Fast Track

Concern 1: At present, customer complaints are directed to work group supervisors.

Recommendation: Introduce a new division dedicated to customer service quality.

Concern 2: Customer service is not supported by an integration of customer feedback, work group practices, training, and HR strategies.

Recommendation: Link the new customer service quality division to HR, training, and work group supervision.

Concern 3: At present, the HR division has sole responsibility for performance management, not the training division or work group supervisors.

Recommendation: Link performance management responsibilities to work group supervisors via training plans and HR recruitment strategies.

Concern 4: Communications among the HR division, training division, and work group supervisors are low level and infrequent.

Recommendation: Introduce an organization structure that seamlessly integrates and promotes strategic communication between HR, training, and work group supervision.

Concern 5: The HR division and the training division have created tightly controlled centres of knowledge that do not directly inform work group supervisors.

Recommendation: Introduce the transfer of targeted HR and training responsibilities directly to work group supervisors.

Eddie Wanton's Recommended Strategy

Introduce a database information system that will seamlessly integrate HR functions, training functions, and customer service functions. Use the information system to develop strategic links between these functions. Use the new information system to break down information channel barriers between the HR and training divisions. Use the system to devolve appropriate HR and training operations to work group supervisors. Create a new customer service quality division and use the new IT system to integrate it with the other divisions and work group supervisors. In short, change the organization's communication and information architecture to promote the integration of cross-divisional information sharing, decision making, and control.

Jack Newman's Response

Jack Newman's response to Fast Track's recommendations was to target changes to the organization's structure and design to promote the improvement of customer service. Jack immediately decided to act as champion of the cause and constituted a taskforce with the responsibility of implementing Fast Tack's recommendations. Jack appointed to the change taskforce Elaine, Peter, Bobby Bea (a work group supervisor who was a union official and had been with the utility for nearly 30 years), and two consultants from IT Now, a company marketing an integrated HRIS. Jack decided to act as chairperson of the taskforce. The objectives of the taskforce were to assist the consultants in identifying the organization's needs and to inform the consultants as to the type of configuration necessary for the off-the-shelf HRIS to meet those needs. Jack expected the consultants to have the new system up and running within six months.

At the very first meeting of the taskforce it was apparent that, while Peter shared Jack's vision for change, Elaine was very concerned about the implication of these proposed changes for her division. Jack told Elaine that the HR staff would have to significantly upgrade their IT skills, or the organization might have to offer HR division staff redeployment or redundancy packages. Peter quickly pointed out that greater integration between HR and training should place all occupational health and safety responsibilities within the training division. Peter also emphasized that the need to train employees in the new system would entail increasing the number of training division staff. Bobby Bea was concerned that any transfer of HR transactions, such as employees' leave applications or performance management responsibilities, onto work group supervisors would cut down on their time to oversee service or maintenance operations. Bobby also pointed out that any changes to supervisors' job descriptions would need

to be approved by the union and would involve pay raises. The consultant drew the taskforce's attention to the fact that if the organization required the new system to be functional within six months, they would most likely be forced to implement the off-the-shelf version with little specific tailoring to meet organizational needs. Both Elaine and Peter were concerned about who would head the new customer service quality division and the implications of the creation of this new division for their divisional budgets.

QUESTIONS

1   How can the assignment of a champion facilitate the introduction of the new HRIS? Is Jack Newman the best person to act as champion?

2   Why have the HR and training divisions built quite different database systems? What are the difficulties involved in integrating the functions of these divisions?

3   What are the advantages of integrating the functions of the HR division, training division, and those of the work group supervisors?

4   What are the advantages and disadvantages of the Boomerang Water Corporation buying an off-the-shelf integrated HR database system?

5   In what ways may the transfer of some HR functions to work group supervisors improve the efficiency of the HR division? In what ways may work group supervisors be advantaged or disadvantaged by the transfer of HR functions?

Source: G. Dessler, J. Griffiths, and B. Lloyd-Walker, *Human Resources Management*, 2nd ed. (Frenchs Forest, New South Wales: Pearson Education Australia, 2004), pp. 97–99. Reprinted with permission of the publisher.

MyManagementLab

Visit MyManagementLab to access a personalized Study Plan and additional study tools for this chapter.

 To view the CBC videos, read a summary, and answer discussion questions, go to MyManagementLab

CHAPTER

4 Designing and Analyzing Jobs

LEARNING OUTCOMES

AFTER STUDYING THIS CHAPTER, YOU SHOULD BE ABLE TO

EXPLAIN the steps in job analysis.

DEFINE job design and explain the difference between a job and a position.

DESCRIBE the evolution of job design and how organizational structure influences job design.

EXPLAIN the three reasons why competency-based job analysis has become more common.

DESCRIBE and evaluate multiple methods of collecting job analysis information.

EXPLAIN the difference between a job description and a job specification.

REQUIRED PROFESSIONAL CAPABILITIES (RPC)

- Provides the information necessary for the organization to effectively manage its people practices

- Identifies the data required to support HR planning

- Gathers and analyzes employee feedback to assist with decision making

FUNDAMENTALS OF JOB ANALYSIS

job A group of related activities and duties, held by a single employee or a number of incumbents.

position The collection of tasks and responsibilities performed by one person.

job analysis The procedure for determining the tasks, duties, and responsibilities of each job, and the human attributes (in terms of knowledge, skills, and abilities) required to perform it.

Job analysis is a process by which information about jobs is systematically gathered and organized. Job analysis is sometimes called the cornerstone of HRM.

A **job** consists of a group of related activities and duties. Ideally, the duties of a job should be clear and distinct from those of other jobs, and they should involve natural units of work that are similar and related. This approach helps to minimize conflict and enhance employee performance. A job may be held by a single employee or may have a number of incumbents. The collection of tasks and responsibilities performed by one person is known as a **position**. To clarify, in a department with 1 supervisor, 1 clerk, 40 assemblers, and 3 tow-motor operators, there are 45 positions and 4 jobs.

Uses of Job Analysis Information

Job analysis is the procedure firms use to determine the tasks, duties, and responsibilities of each job, and the human attributes (in terms of knowledge, skills, and abilities) required to perform it. Once this information has been gathered it is used for developing job descriptions (what the job entails) and job specifications (what the human requirements are). As illustrated in **Figure 4.1**, the information gathered, evaluated, and summarized through job analysis is the basis for a number of interrelated HRM activities.

Human Resources Planning

Knowing the actual requirements of an organization's various jobs is essential for planning future staffing needs. When this information is combined with knowledge about the skills and qualifications of current employees, it is possible to determine which jobs can be filled internally and which will require external recruitment.

FIGURE **4.1**   Uses of Job Analysis Information

Recruitment and Selection

The job description and job specification information should be used to decide what sort of person to recruit and hire. Identifying bona fide occupational requirements and ensuring that all activities related to recruitment and selection (such as advertising, screening, and testing) are based on these requirements is necessary for legal compliance in all Canadian jurisdictions.

Compensation

Job analysis information is also essential for determining the relative value of and appropriate compensation for each job. Job evaluation should be based on the required skills, physical and mental demands, responsibilities, and working conditions—all assessed through job analysis. The relative value of jobs is one of the key factors used to determine appropriate compensation and justify pay differences if challenged under human rights or pay equity legislation. Information about the actual job duties is also necessary to determine whether a job qualifies for overtime pay and for maximum-hours purposes, as specified in employment standards legislation.

Performance Management

To be legally defensible, the criteria used to assess employee performance must be directly related to the duties and responsibilities identified through job analysis. For many jobs involving routine tasks, especially those of a quantifiable nature, performance standards are determined through job analysis. For more complex jobs, performance standards are often jointly established by employees and their supervisors. To be realistic and achievable, such standards should be based on actual job requirements as identified through job analysis.

Labour Relations

In unionized environments, the job descriptions developed from the job analysis information are generally subject to union approval before being finalized. Such union-approved job descriptions then become the basis for classifying jobs and bargaining over wages, performance criteria, and working conditions. Once approved, significant changes to job descriptions may have to be negotiated.

Training, Development, and Career Management

By comparing the knowledge, skills, and abilities (KSAs) that employees bring to the job with those that are identified by job analysis, managers can determine gaps that require training programs. Having accurate information about jobs also means that employees can prepare for future advancement by identifying gaps between their current KSAs and those specified for the jobs to which they aspire.

Restructuring

Job analysis is useful for ensuring that all of the duties that need to be done have actually been assigned and for identifying areas of overlap within duties. Also, having an accurate description of each job may lead to the identification of unnecessary requirements, areas of conflict or dissatisfaction, or health and safety concerns that can be eliminated through job redesign or restructuring.

Steps in Job Analysis

There are six critical steps involved in analyzing jobs. Organizations collect details about jobs on a relatively continuous basis for many uses, such as the ones outlined above (planning, recruitment and selection, performance management, compensation, and so on). Traditionally, organizations would first determine the intended use of job analysis information, since this determined the types of data that should be collected and the techniques used. However, this preliminary step has been largely abolished in practice given the diverse uses of job analysis information and the continual need for such information.

The six steps involved in job analysis are as follows:

1. Relevant organizational information is reviewed.
2. Jobs are selected to be analyzed.
3. Using one or more job analysis techniques, data are collected on job activities.
4. The information collected in Step 3 is then verified and modified, if required.
5. Job descriptions and specifications are developed based on the verified information.
6. The information is then communicated and updated on an as-needed basis.

The structure of this chapter aligns with the six steps of job analysis.

STEP 1: REVIEW RELEVANT BACKGROUND INFORMATION

An organization consists of one or more employees who perform various tasks. The relationships between people and tasks must be structured so that the organization achieves its strategic goals in an efficient and effective manner through a motivated and engaged workforce. There are many ways to distribute work among employees, and careful consideration of how this is done can provide a strategic advantage over competitors.

STRATEGIC HR

IKEA Canada doesn't just want to fill jobs; it wants to partner with people. It recruits unique individuals who share the corporate values of togetherness, cost consciousness, respect, and simplicity. IKEA listens and supports each employee to identify his or her needs, ambitions, and capabilities. Employees are expected not to ask others what they should be doing but to ask themselves and then get on with it. It is important for IKEA employees to have a strong desire to learn and the motivation to continually do things better, because the IKEA way of working is less structured than that of many other organizations.

IKEA Canada employee Ingeborg, a sales co-worker who is 71 years young, says, "Everyone asks me why I am still working. I tell them I love my job. There is always a great atmosphere in the store; I really enjoy the company of my managers and co-workers. We work together very well."

Source: Adapted from IKEA Canada, www.ikea.com/ms/en_CA/jobs/simply_ikea/index.html and www.ikea.com/ms/en_JP/jobs/true_stories/ingeborg/index.html. (Accessed April 6, 2009). Used with permission from IKEA Canada.

organizational structure The formal relationships among jobs in an organization.

organization chart A "snapshot" of the firm, depicting the organization's structure in chart form at a particular point in time.

Online Organization Charts
www.nakisa.com

Example of Online Organization Charts
www.forces.gc.ca/site/ about-notresujet/org-eng. asp or http://office.microsoft. com/en-us/templates/ business-organizational-chart- TC006088976.aspx

Organizational structure refers to the formal relationships among jobs in an organization. An **organization chart** is often used to depict the structure. As illustrated in **Figure 4.2**, the chart indicates the types of departments established and the title of each manager's job. By means of connecting lines, it clarifies the chain of command and shows who is accountable to whom. An organization chart presents a "snapshot" of the firm at a particular point in time, but it does not provide details about actual communication patterns, degree of supervision, amount of power and authority, or specific duties and responsibilities. In the example provided in Figure 4.2, there may be the expectation that Auditor Plant A will have to report some information to Manager Plant A. Often an organizational chart will exclude this information or identify secondary reporting responsibilities using a dotted line.

Designing an organization involves choosing a structure that is appropriate given the company's strategic goals. **Figure 4.3** depicts three common types of organizational structure: bureaucratic, flat, and matrix. In flatter organizations, managers have increased spans of control (the number of employees reporting to them) and thus less time to manage each one. Therefore, employees' jobs involve more responsibility. In organizations using self-managed work teams, employees' jobs change daily, so management intentionally avoids having employees view their jobs as a specific, narrow set of responsibilities. The focus is on defining the job at hand in terms of the overall best interests of the organization, as is the case at IKEA, described in the Strategic HR box.

FIGURE 4.2 A Sample Organization Chart

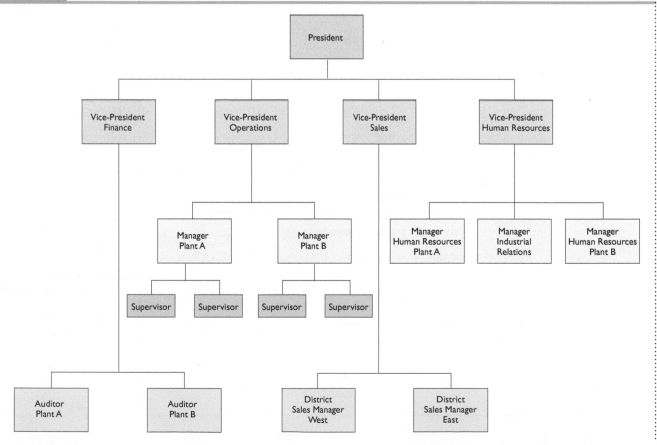

FIGURE 4.3   Bureaucratic, Flat, and Matrix Organizational Structures

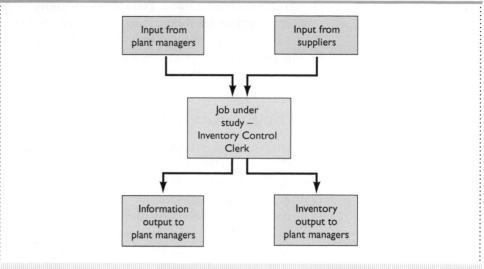

Source: Henderson, Richard I. (ed.), *Compensation Management in a Knowledge-based World*, 10th ed. (Upper Saddle River, NJ: Pearson Education, Inc., 2006), p. 114. Reprinted by permission of the publisher.

process chart A diagram showing the flow of inputs to and outputs from the job under study.

Step 1 includes the review of relevant background information, such as organization charts, process charts, and existing job descriptions.[1] A **process chart** (like the one in **Figure 4.4**) shows the flow of inputs to and outputs from the job under study. (In Figure 4.4, the inventory control clerk is expected to receive inventory from suppliers, take requests for inventory from the two plant managers, provide requested inventory to these managers, and give information to the plant accountant on the status of in-stock inventories.)

STEP 2: SELECT JOBS TO BE ANALYZED

The next step involves the selection of representative positions and jobs to be analyzed. This selection is necessary when there are many incumbents in a single job and when a number of similar jobs are to be analyzed because it would be too time-consuming to analyze every position and job.

job design The process of systematically organizing work into tasks that are required to perform a specific job.

Job design is the process of systematically organizing work into the tasks that are required to perform a specific job. An organization's strategy and structure influence the ways in which jobs are designed. In bureaucratic organizations, for example, because a hierarchical division of labour exists, jobs are generally highly specialized. In addition, effective job design also takes into consideration human and technological factors.

In the twenty-first century, the traditional meaning of a "job" as a set of well-defined and clearly delineated responsibilities has changed. Companies are grappling with challenges such as rapid product and technological change, global competition, deregulation, political instability, demographic changes, and a shift to a service economy. This has increased the need for firms to be responsive, flexible, and much more competitive. In turn, the organizational methods managers use to accomplish this have helped weaken this traditional definition of a "job." Requiring employees to limit themselves to narrow jobs runs counter to the need to have them willingly switch from task to task as jobs and team assignments change.

All these changes have led to work becoming more cognitively complex, more team-based and collaborative, more dependent on social skills, more dependent on technological competence, more time pressured, more mobile, and less dependent on geography.[2] This situation has led some organizations to focus on personal competencies and skills in job analysis, hiring, and compensation management, rather than on specific duties and tasks.

The Evolution of Jobs and Job Design

In most organizations, work is divided into manageable units and, ultimately, into jobs that can be performed by employees. The term "job" as it is known today is largely an outgrowth of the efficiency demands of the Industrial Revolution. As the substitution of machine power for people power became more widespread, experts wrote glowingly about the positive correlation between (1) job specialization and (2) productivity and efficiency.[3] The popularity of specialized, short-cycle jobs soared—at least among management experts and managers.

work simplification An approach to job design that involves assigning most of the administrative aspects of work (such as planning and organizing) to supervisors and managers, while giving lower-level employees narrowly defined tasks to perform according to methods established and specified by management.

Work simplification evolved from scientific management theory. It is based on the premise that work can be broken down into clearly defined, highly specialized, repetitive tasks to maximize efficiency. This approach to job design involves assigning most of the administrative aspects of work (such as planning and organizing) to supervisors and managers, while giving lower-level employees narrowly defined tasks to perform according to methods established and specified by management.

Work simplification can increase operating efficiency in a stable environment and may be very appropriate in settings employing individuals with intellectual disabilities or those lacking education and training (as in some operations in the developing world); it is not effective, however, in a changing environment in which customers/clients demand custom-designed products and/or high-quality services, or one in which employees want challenging work. Moreover, among educated employees, simplified jobs often lead to lower satisfaction, higher rates of absenteeism and turnover, and sometimes to a demand for premium pay to compensate for the repetitive nature of the work.

Another important contribution of scientific management was the study of work. **Industrial engineering**, which evolved with this movement, is concerned with analyzing work methods and establishing time standards to improve efficiency. Industrial engineers systematically identify, analyze, and time the elements of each job's work cycle and determine which, if any, elements can be modified, combined, rearranged, or eliminated to reduce the time needed to complete the cycle.

industrial engineering A field of study concerned with analyzing work methods; making work cycles more efficient by modifying, combining, rearranging, or eliminating tasks; and establishing time standards.

Too much emphasis on the concerns of industrial engineering—improving efficiency and simplifying work methods—may result in human considerations being neglected or downplayed. For example, an assembly line, with its simplified and repetitive tasks, embodies the principles of industrial engineering but may lead to repetitive strain injuries, high turnover, and low satisfaction because of the lack of psychological fulfillment. Thus, to be effective, job design must also satisfy human psychological and physiological needs.

job enlargement (horizontal loading) A technique to relieve monotony and boredom that involves assigning workers additional tasks at the same level of responsibility to increase the number of tasks they have to perform.

By the mid-1900s, reacting to what they viewed as the "dehumanizing" aspects of highly repetitive and specialized jobs, various management theorists proposed ways of broadening the activities employees engaged in. **Job enlargement**, also known as **horizontal loading**, involves assigning workers additional tasks at the same level of responsibility to increase the number of tasks they have to perform. Thus, if the work was assembling chairs, the worker who previously only bolted the

job rotation A technique to relieve monotony and employee boredom that involves systematically moving employees from one job to another.

job enrichment (vertical loading) Any effort that makes an employee's job more rewarding or satisfying by adding more meaningful tasks and duties.

Tips FOR THE FRONT LINE

ergonomics An interdisciplinary approach that seeks to integrate and accommodate the physical needs of workers into the design of jobs. It aims to adapt the entire job system—the work, environment, machines, equipment, and processes—to match human characteristics.

seat to the legs might take on the additional tasks of assembling the legs and attaching the back as well. Job enlargement reduces monotony and fatigue by expanding the job cycle and drawing on a wider range of employee skills.

Another technique to relieve monotony and employee boredom is **job rotation**. This involves systematically moving employees from one job to another. Although the jobs themselves don't change, workers experience more task variety, motivation, and productivity. The company gains by having more versatile, multiskilled employees who can cover for one another efficiently.

It has also been suggested that the best way to motivate workers is to build opportunities for challenge and achievement into jobs through **job enrichment**, also known as **vertical loading**.[4] This is defined as any effort that makes an employee's job more rewarding or satisfying by adding more meaningful tasks and duties. Job enrichment involves increasing autonomy and responsibility by allowing employees to assume a greater role in the decision-making process.

Enriching jobs can be accomplished through activities such as

- increasing the level of difficulty and responsibility of the job;
- assigning workers more authority and control over outcomes;
- providing feedback about individual or unit job performance directly to employees;
- adding new tasks requiring training, thereby providing an opportunity for growth; and
- assigning individuals entire tasks or responsibility for performing a whole job rather than only parts of it, such as conducting an entire background check rather than just checking educational credentials.

Job enrichment is not always the best approach. It is more successful in some jobs and settings than in others; for example, not all employees want additional responsibilities and challenges. Some people prefer routine jobs and may resist job redesign efforts. In addition, job redesign efforts almost always fail when employees lack the physical or mental skills, abilities, or education needed to perform the job.

By the late twentieth century, it became apparent that in addition to considering psychological needs, effective job design also required taking physiological needs and health and safety issues into account. **Ergonomics** seeks to integrate and accommodate the physical needs of workers into the design of jobs. It aims to adapt the entire job system—the work, environment, machines, equipment, and processes—to match human characteristics. Doing so results in eliminating or minimizing product defects, damage to equipment, and worker injuries or illnesses caused by poor work design.

Competency-Based Job Analysis

Not coincidentally, many employers and job analysis experts say traditional job analysis procedures can't go on playing a central role in HR management.[5] Their basic concern is this: In high-performance work environments in which employers need workers to seamlessly move from job to job and exercise self-control, job descriptions based on lists of job-specific duties may actually inhibit (or fail to encourage) the flexible behaviour companies need. Employers are therefore shifting toward newer approaches for describing jobs, such as competency-based analysis.

Competency-based job analysis basically means writing job descriptions based on competencies rather than job duties. It emphasizes what the employee must be capable of doing, rather than a list of the duties he or she must perform.

competencies Demonstrable characteristics of a person that enable performance of a job.

Competencies are demonstrable characteristics of a person that enable performance. Job competencies are always observable and measurable behaviours that comprise part of a job. The job's required competencies can be identified by simply completing this sentence: "In order to perform this job competently, the employee should be able to . . ."

competency-based job analysis Describing a job in terms of the measurable, observable behavioural competencies an employee must exhibit to do a job well.

Competency-based job analysis means describing the job in terms of the measurable, observable behavioural competencies (knowledge, skills, or behaviours) that an employee doing that job must exhibit to do the job well. This contrasts with the traditional way of describing a job in terms of job duties and responsibilities. Traditional job analysis focuses on "what" is accomplished—on duties and responsibilities. Competency-based analysis focuses more on "how" the worker meets the job's objectives or actually accomplishes the work. Traditional job analysis is thus job focused; competency-based analysis is worker focused—specifically, what must he or she be competent to do?

Three Reasons to Use Competency Analysis

There are three reasons to describe jobs in terms of competencies rather than duties. First, as mentioned earlier, traditional job descriptions (with their lists of specific duties) may actually backfire if a *high-performance work system* is the goal. The whole thrust of these systems is to encourage employees to work in a self-motivated way: by organizing the work around teams, by encouraging team members to rotate freely among jobs (each with its own skill set), by pushing more responsibility for things like day-to-day supervision down to the workers, and by organizing work around projects or processes in which jobs may blend or overlap. Employees here must be enthusiastic about learning and moving among jobs. Giving someone a job description with a list of specific duties may simply breed a "that's-not-my-job" attitude by pigeonholing workers too narrowly.

Second, describing the job in terms of the skills, knowledge, and competencies the worker needs is *more strategic*. For example, a company with a strategic emphasis on miniaturization and precision manufacturing should encourage some employees to develop their expertise in these two strategically crucial areas.

Third, measurable skills, knowledge, and competencies support the employer's *performance management process*. Training, appraisals, and rewards should be based on fostering and rewarding the skills and competencies required to achieve work goals. Describing the job in terms of skills and competencies facilitates understanding of those required competencies.

Examples of Competencies

In practice, managers often write paragraph-length competencies for jobs and organize these into two or three clusters. For example, the job's required competencies might include *general or core competencies* (such as reading, writing, and mathematical reasoning), *leadership competencies* (such as leadership, strategic thinking, and teaching others), and *technical/task/functional competencies* (which focus on the specific technical competencies required for specific types of jobs or occupations).

So, some technical competencies for the job of systems engineer might include the following:

- Design complex software applications, establish protocols, and create prototypes.
- Establish the necessary platform requirements to efficiently and completely coordinate data transfer.

- Prepare comprehensive and complete documentation including specifications, flow diagrams, process patrols, and budgets.[6]

Similarly, for a corporate treasurer, technical competencies might include the following:

- Formulate trade recommendations by studying several computer models for currency trends and using various quantitative techniques to determine the financial impact of certain financial trades.
- Recommend specific trades and when to make them.
- Present recommendations and persuade others to follow the recommended course of action.[7] (Note: Exhibiting this competency presumes the treasurer has certain knowledge and skills that one could measure.)

Research INSIGHT

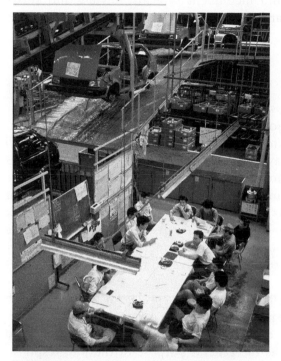

At a Nissan factory in Tokyo, Japan, workers meet at a productivity session, surrounded by unfinished car frames hanging along the assembly line. Work teams like this are part of the trend toward a multiskilled, cross-functional, self-directed team organization that allows workers greater autonomy in meeting goals. In plants like these, broadly described jobs that emphasize employees' required competencies are replacing narrowly defined jobs.

Comparing Traditional versus Competency-Based Job Analysis

In practice, in almost any job description today some of the job's listed duties and responsibilities are competency-based, while most are not. For example, consider the typical duties you might find in a marketing manager's job description. Which of the duties would complete this phrase: "In order to perform this job competently, the employee should be able to . . ."?

Some familiar duties and responsibilities would not easily fit these requirements. For example, "works with writers and artists and oversees copywriting, design, layout, and production of promotional materials" is not particularly measurable. How can the extent to which the employee "works with writers and artists" or "oversees copywriting, design, and layout" be measured? Put another way, in analyzing this job, how would one determine whether the person had been adequately trained to work with writers and artists? In fact, what sort of training would that duty and responsibility even imply? It's not clear at all.

On the other hand, some of the job's typical duties and responsibilities are more easily expressed as competencies. For example, the phrase "to perform this job competently, the employee should be able to . . ." could easily be completed with "conduct marketing surveys on current and new-product concepts; prepare marketing activity reports; and develop and execute marketing plans and programs."

team-based job designs Job designs that focus on giving a team, rather than an individual, a whole and meaningful piece of work to do and empowering team members to decide among themselves how to accomplish the work.

team A small group of people with complementary skills who work toward common goals for which they hold joint responsibility and accountability.

Team-Based Job Designs

A logical outgrowth of job enrichment and the job characteristics model has been the increasing use of **team-based job designs**, which focus on giving a **team**, rather than an individual, a whole and meaningful piece of work to do. Team members are empowered to decide among themselves how to accomplish the work.[8] Often they are cross-trained and then rotated through different tasks. Team-based designs are best suited to flat and matrix organization structures. Increasingly, organizations are using "virtual teams"—people working together effectively and efficiently across boundaries of time and space and using software to make team meetings more productive.[9]

STEP 3: COLLECTING JOB ANALYSIS INFORMATION

Various qualitative and quantitative techniques are used to collect information about the duties, responsibilities, and requirements of the job; the most important ones will be discussed in this section. In practice, when the information is being used for multiple purposes, ranging from developing recruitment criteria to compensation decisions, several techniques may be used in combination.

Collecting job analysis data usually involves a joint effort by an HR specialist, the incumbent, and the jobholder's supervisor. The HR specialist (an HR manager, job analyst, or consultant) might observe and analyze the work being done and then develop a job description and specification. The supervisor and incumbent generally also get involved, perhaps by filling out questionnaires. The supervisor and incumbent typically review and verify the job analyst's conclusions regarding the job's duties, responsibilities, and requirements.

The Interview

The interview is probably the most widely used method for determining the duties and responsibilities of a job. Three types of interviews are used to collect job analysis data: *individual interviews* with each employee; *group interviews* with employees who have the same job; and *supervisory interviews* with one or more supervisors who are thoroughly knowledgeable about the job being analyzed. The group interview is used when a large number of employees are performing similar or identical work, and it can be a quick and inexpensive way of learning about the job. As a rule, the immediate supervisor attends the group session; if not, the supervisor should be interviewed separately to get that person's perspective on the duties and responsibilities of the job.

The most fruitful interviews follow a structured or checklist format. A job analysis questionnaire, like the one presented in **Figure 4.5**, may be used to interview job incumbents or may be filled out by them. It includes a series of detailed questions regarding such matters as the general purpose of the job; responsibilities and duties; the education, experience, and skills required; physical and mental demands; and working conditions.

Interview Guidelines

When conducting a job analysis interview, supervisors and job analysts should keep several things in mind:

1. The job analyst and supervisor should work together to identify the employees who know the job best as well as those who might be expected to be the most objective in describing their duties and responsibilities.

2. Rapport should be established quickly with the interviewee by using the individual's name, speaking in easily understood language, briefly reviewing the purpose of the interview (job analysis, not performance appraisal), and explaining how the person came to be chosen.

3. A structured guide or checklist that lists questions and provides spaces for answers should be used. Using a form ensures that crucial questions are identified ahead of time, that complete and accurate information is gathered, and

Tips FOR THE FRONT LINE

Job title: _____   Job grade: _____
Department: _____   Location: _____
Prepared by: _____   Date: _____

1. Purpose of job
- What is the purpose of the job? Why does the job exist?

_____
_____
_____

2. Major responsibilities and essential functions (list in order of importance)
- What are the responsibilities?
- How are they done?
- Percentage of time?
- Why is the activity performed?
- What is the measure of success?
- What direction of others is involved?

_____
_____
_____
_____

3. Knowledge
- What techniques and/or practices are necessary? Why?

_____
_____

- List specific education requirement(s).

_____
_____

- List experience requirement(s) and number of years required in each.

_____
_____

- List required licences or certificates.

_____
_____

4. Problem solving and decision making
- List how the jobholder solves problems (i.e., planning, scheduling, creativity techniques, complexity of procedures, degree of independent thinking, and resourcefulness or ingenuity required). List examples of required development of new methods. What are the consequences if problems are not solved?

_____
_____
_____
_____
_____

5. Resource responsibility
- List annual pay of personnel who report to jobholder: _____
- List annual operating budget (include pay): _____

continued

- List any other financial resources (i.e., annual project value/cost, shop order value, total sales, total unit payroll, gross sales booked, purchasing/contracts volume, transportation costs, facilities budget, assets, investment income, program development costs, gross sales billed):

  _____

  _____

- What is the jobholder's role in planning, organizing, acquiring, or monitoring these resources?

  _____

  _____

- What is the jobholder's impact in planning, organizing, acquiring, or monitoring these resources?

  _____

  _____

6. Skills of persuasion
- Describe the communication skills required in the job (e.g., explaining, convincing, selling).
- Are contacts inside or outside?
- What are the levels of contacts?
- What type of oral or written communications are involved?
- Who is communicated with and why?

  _____

  _____

  _____

  _____

  _____

  _____

7. Working conditions
Read the list of working conditions below and put a check mark if they impact on your job.

Condition	Amount of Exposure		
	Occasional	Regular	Frequent
Dust, dirt, fumes	_____	_____	_____
Heat, cold	_____	_____	_____
Noise	_____	_____	_____
Vibration	_____	_____	_____
Inclement weather	_____	_____	_____
Lighting	_____	_____	_____

Describe any health or safety hazards related to the job.

_____

_____

_____

Source: Carswell's Compensation Guide, ed. D.E. Tyson, CHRP, Tab 3 Job Analysis and Evaluation, Chapter 9, "Job Analysis and Job Descriptions," by T.J. Hackett and E.G. Vogeley, adapted by S. Weeks, P. Drouillard and D.E. Tyson, pages 9–21 and 9–23. Reprinted by permission of Carswell, a division of Thomson Reuters Canada Limited.

that all interviewers (if there is more than one) glean the same types of data, thereby helping to ensure comparability of results. However, leeway should also be permitted by including some open-ended questions, such as "Is there anything that we didn't cover with our questions?"

4. When duties are not performed in a regular manner—for instance, when the incumbent doesn't perform the same tasks or jobs over and over again many times a day—the incumbent should be asked to list his or her duties *in order of importance and frequency of occurrence*. This will ensure that crucial activities that occur infrequently—like a nurse's occasional emergency room duties—aren't overlooked.

5. The data should be reviewed and verified by both the interviewee and his or her immediate supervisor.

Questionnaire

Having employees or supervisors fill out questionnaires to describe job-related duties and responsibilities is another good method of obtaining job analysis information. There are two major decisions around questionnaires.

The first is determining how structured the questionnaire should be and what questions to include. Some questionnaires involve structured checklists: Each employee is presented with a long list of specific duties or tasks (such as "change and splice wire") and is asked to indicate whether or not he or she performs each and, if so, how much time is normally spent on the task. At the other extreme, the questionnaire can be open-ended and simply ask the employee to describe the major duties of his or her job. In practice, a typical job analysis questionnaire often falls between the two extremes.

The second major decision is determining who will complete the questionnaire. Employees may inflate requirements and supervisors may be unaware of all components of the job. Technology often assists with overcoming this challenge in that questionnaires can be relatively easily and affordably posted online to allow for multiple respondents.

One of the most popular pre-developed, structured job analysis questionnaires is the **Position Analysis Questionnaire (PAQ)**, a portion of which is shown in **Figure 4.6**.[10] The PAQ itself is filled in by a job analyst, who should already be acquainted with the particular job to be analyzed. The PAQ contains 194 items, each of which represents a basic element that may or may not play an important role in the job. The job analyst decides whether each item plays a role in the job and, if so, to what extent (using a five-point scale). If, for example, "written materials" received a rating of four, this would indicate that materials such as books, reports, and office notes play a considerable role in this job.

The advantage of the PAQ is that it provides a quantitative score or profile of the job in terms of how that job rates on six basic dimensions: (1) information input, (2) mental processes, (3) work output (physical activities and tools), (4) relationships with others, (5) job context (the physical and social environment), and (6) other job characteristics (such as pace and structure). Because it allows for the assignment of a quantitative score to each job based on these six dimensions, the PAQ's real strength is in classifying jobs. Results can be used to compare jobs with one another; this information can then be used to determine appropriate pay levels.[11]

Position Analysis Questionnaire (PAQ) A questionnaire used to collect quantifiable data concerning the duties and responsibilities of various jobs.

PAQ Services Inc.
www.paq.com

FIGURE 4.6 Position Analysis Questionnaire (Excerpt)

A1. Visual Sources of Job Information

Using the response scale at the left, rate each of the following items on the basis of the extent to which it is used by the worker as a source of information in performing the job.

1. **Written materials**
   E.g., books, reports, office notes, articles, job instructions, or signs

2. **Quantitative materials**
   Materials that deal with quantities or amounts, e.g., graphs, accounts, specifications, or tables of numbers

3. **Pictorial materials**
   Pictures or picturelike materials used as sources of information, e.g., drawings, blueprints, diagrams, maps, tracings, photographic films, x-ray films, or TV pictures

4. **Patterns or related devices**
   E.g., templates, stencils, or patterns used as sources of information when observed during use (Do not include materials described in item 3.)

5. **Visual displays**
   E.g., dials, gauges, signal lights, radarscopes, speedometers, or clocks

6. **Measuring devices**
   E.g., rules, calipers, tire pressure gauges, scales, thickness gauges, pipettes, thermometers, or protractors used to obtain visual information about physical measurements (Do not include devices described in item 5.)

7. **Mechanical devices**
   E.g., tools, equipment, or machinery that are sources of information when observed during use or operation

8. **Materials in process**
   E.g., parts, materials, or objects which are sources of information when being modified, worked on, or otherwise processed, such as bread dough being mixed, a workpiece being turned in a lathe, fabric being cut, or a shoe being resoled

9. **Materials not in process**
   E.g., parts, materials, or objects not in the process of being changed or modified, which are sources of information when being inspected, handled, packaged, distributed, or selected, such as items or materials in inventory, storage, or distribution channels, or items being inspected

10. **Features of nature**
    E.g., landscapes, fields, geological samples, vegetation, cloud formations, and other natural features that are observed or inspected to provide information

11. **Constructed features of environment**
    E.g., structures, buildings, dams, highways, bridges, docks, railroads, and other "constructed" or altered aspects of the indoor or outdoor environment which are observed or inspected to provide job information (Do not consider equipment, machines, etc., that individuals use in their work, as covered by item 7.)

12. **Behaviour**
    Observing the actions of people or animals, e.g., in teaching, supervising, or sports officiating, where the behaviour is a source of job information

13. **Events or circumstances**
    Events the worker observed and may participate in, such as flow of traffic, movement of materials, or airport control tower operations

14. **Art or décor**
    Artistic or decorative objects or arrangements used as *sources* of job information, e.g., paintings, sculpture, jewellery, window displays, or interior design

Note: The 194 PAQ elements are grouped into six dimensions. This figure exhibits 14 of the "information input" questions or elements. Other PAQ pages contain questions regarding mental processes, work output, relationships with others, job context, and other job characteristics.

Source: E.J. McCormick, P.R. Jeanneret, and R.D. Mecham, *Position Analysis Questionnaire.* West Lafayette, IN: Purdue Research Foundation, 1989. Copyright © 1989 by Purdue Research Foundation. Reprinted with permission.

Functional Job Analysis (FJA) A quantitative method for classifying jobs based on types and amounts of responsibility for data, people, and things. Performance standards and training requirements are also identified.

Functional Job Analysis (FJA) is also a regularly used pre-established questionnaire that rates a job on responsibilities for data, people, and things from simple to complex. For example, working with "things" literally means the physical interaction with tangibles such as desktop equipment (pencils, paper clips, telephone), groceries, luggage, or a bus. Physical involvement with tangibles such as a telephone may not seem very important in tasks primarily concerned with data (such as data analysis) or people (such as nursing), but its importance is quickly apparent for a worker with a disability. This technique also identifies performance standards and training requirements. Thus, FJA allows the analyst to answer the question: "To do this task and meet these standards, what training does the worker require?"[12]

Observations

Observation involves watching employees perform their work and recording the frequency of behaviours or the nature of performance. This can be done using information that is prepared in advance (structured), or in real time with no advance information provided to the observer (unstructured), or a combination of the two.

Direct observation is especially useful when jobs consist mainly of observable physical activities. Jobs like those of a janitor, assembly-line worker, and accounting clerk are examples. Third-party observation focuses more on reality than perception. As a result, third-party observation is often viewed as having more credibility, since there is minimal incentive to distort the results.

A challenge is that observations can influence job behaviour. Additionally, observation is usually not appropriate when the job entails a lot of immeasurable mental activity (e.g., lawyers or design engineers). Nor is it useful if the employee engages in important activities that might occur only occasionally, such as compiling year-end reports. Often, direct observation and interviewing are used together.

Participant Diary/Log

diary/log Daily listings made by employees of every activity in which they engage, along with the time each activity takes.

Another technique involves asking employees to keep a **diary/log** or list of what they do during the day. Each employee records every activity in which he or she is involved (along with the time spent) in a log. This can produce a very complete picture of the job, especially when supplemented with subsequent interviews with the employee and his or her supervisor. The employee might, of course, try to exaggerate some activities and underplay others. However, the detailed, chronological nature of the log tends to minimize this problem.

The National Occupational Classification

National Occupational Classification (NOC) A reference tool for writing job descriptions and job specifications. Compiled by the federal government, it contains comprehensive, standardized descriptions of about 40 000 occupations and the requirements for each.

The **National Occupational Classification (NOC)**, the product of systematic, field-based research by Human Resources and Skills Development Canada (HRSDC), is an excellent source of standardized job information. It was updated and revised in 2011 and contains comprehensive descriptions of approximately 40 000 occupations and the requirements for each. To illustrate the types of information included, the NOC listing for specialists in human resources is shown in **Figure 4.7**.

FIGURE 4.7   NOC Job Description for Specialists in Human Resources

Specialists in Human Resources develop, implement, and evaluate human resources and labour relations policies, programs, and procedures and advise managers and employees on personnel matters. Specialists in Human Resources are employed throughout the private and public sectors, or may be self-employed.

Examples of titles classified in this unit group

Business Agent, Labour Organization
Classification Officer—human resources
Classification Specialist
Compensation Research Analyst
Conciliator
Consultant, Human Resources
Employee Relations Officer
Employment Equity Officer
Human Resources Research Officer
Job Analyst
Labour Relations Officer
Mediator
Union Representative
Wage Analyst

Main duties
Specialists in Human Resources perform some or all of the following duties:

- Plan, develop, implement, and evaluate personnel and labour relations policies, programs, and procedures to address an organization's human resource requirements
- Advise managers and employees on the interpretation of personnel policies, compensation and benefit programs, and collective agreements
- Negotiate collective agreements on behalf of employers or workers, mediate labour disputes and grievances, and provide advice on employee and labour relations
- Research and prepare occupational classifications, job descriptions, salary scales, and competency appraisal measures and systems
- Plan and administer staffing, total compensation, training and career development, employee assistance, employment equity, and affirmative action programs
- Manage programs and maintain human resources information and related records systems
- Hire and oversee training of staff
- Coordinate employee performance and appraisal programs
- Research employee benefit and health and safety practices and recommend changes or modifications to existing policies

Employment requirements
- A university degree or college diploma in a field related to personnel management, such as business administration, industrial relations, commerce, or psychology
  or
  Completion of a professional development program in personnel administration is required.
- Some experience in a clerical or administrative position related to personnel administration is required.

Additional information
- Progression to management positions is possible with experience.

Classified elsewhere
- *Human Resources Managers* (0112)
- *Personnel and Recruitment Officers* (1223)
- *Personnel Clerks* (1442)
- *Professional Occupations in Business Services to Management* (1122)
- Training officers and instructors (in 4131 *College and Other Vocational Instructors*)

Source: Adapted from Human Resources and Skills Development Canada, *National Occupational Classification*, 2001. Reproduced with the permission of Her Majesty The Queen in Right of Canada 2009. http://www5.hrsdc.gc.ca/noc/English/NOC/2006/QuickSearch.aspx?val65=1121 (Accessed March 29, 2009).

Organizations can readily access information regarding the activities, requirements, competencies, and so on required by job title. However, it is highly recommended that companies who use external sources such as the NOC:

1. adjust information based on their organizational strategy and structure;

2. update information as required (for example, in Figure 4.7 the term "personnel" is used in reference to educational attainment. While this was an appropriate term in the late 1990s when the data was collected, the evolution of HR has made this term obsolete); and

3. engage in the verification techniques in detail as per Step 4 (which we will discuss shortly).

occupation A collection of jobs that share some or all of a set of main duties.

The NOC and its counselling component, the *Career Handbook* (2nd ed.), both focus on occupations rather than jobs. An **occupation** is defined as a collection of jobs that share some or all of a set of main duties. The list of examples of job titles within each of the 520 Unit Groups in the NOC provides a frame of reference for the boundaries of that occupational group. The jobs within each group are characterized by similar skills.

Occupational Information Network
www.job-analysis.net

To provide a complete representation of work in the Canadian economy, the NOC classifies occupations into Major Groups based on two key dimensions—skill level and skill type. The Major Groups, which are identified by two-digit numbers, are then broken down further into Minor Groups, with a third digit added, and Unit Groups, at which level a fourth digit is added. Within these three levels of classification, a Unit Group provides the actual profile of an occupation.[13] For example:

Major Group 31—Professional Occupations in Health
Minor Group 311—Physicians, Dentists, and Veterinarians
Unit Group 3113—Dentists

Using Multiple Sources of Job Analysis Information

An Ethical : Dilemma

If a job analyst is on the other side of the world from an employee who completed a web-based job analysis questionnaire, should another method of job analysis also be used to confirm the accuracy of the information?

Job analysis information can be obtained from individual workers, groups, supervisors, or observers. Interviews, observations, or questionnaires can be used. Some firms use a single approach, but one study suggests that using just one source is not wise because each approach has drawbacks. For example, in a group interview, some group members may feel pressure to go along with the group's consensus, or an individual employee may be careless about how he or she completes a questionnaire. Thus, collecting job analysis data from only one source may lead to inaccurate conclusions, so when possible, job analysis data should be collected from several sources.

STEP 4: VERIFYING INFORMATION

RPC

Gathers and analyzes employee feedback to assist with decision making

The job analysis information should be verified with any workers performing the job and with the immediate supervisor. This corroboration will help to confirm that the information is factually correct and complete, and it can also help gain the employees' acceptance of the job analysis data.

The knowledge that information will be verified increases the reliability and validity of the results in two ways. First, areas of inconsistency or concern can be further probed to develop awareness as to why the inconsistency exists and what should be done about it. Second, participants in the data collection techniques will be more honest and consistent knowing that they may later be held accountable for their contributions.

STEP 5: WRITING JOB DESCRIPTIONS AND JOB SPECIFICATIONS

Job Descriptions

job description A list of the duties, responsibilities, reporting relationships, and working conditions of a job—one product of a job analysis.

A **job description** is a written statement of *what* the jobholder actually does, *how* he or she does it, and *under what conditions* the job is performed. The description in **Figure 4.8**—in this case for a vice-president of human resources, Asia-Pacific region—provides an example. As can be seen, the description is quite comprehensive and includes such essential elements as job identification, summary, and duties and responsibilities, as well as the human qualifications for the job.

No standard format is used in writing job descriptions, but most include the following types of information: job identification, job summary, relationships, duties and responsibilities, authority of incumbent, performance standards, and working conditions. As mentioned previously, job specifications (human qualifications) may also be included, as is the case in Figure 4.8.

Job Identification

As in Figure 4.8, the job identification section generally contains several categories of information. The *position title* specifies the title of the job, such as vice-president, marketing manager, recruiter, or inventory control clerk. The *department* and *location* are also indicated, along with the title of the immediate supervisor—in this case under the heading *reports to*.

Job Summary

The *job summary* should describe the general nature of the job, listing only its major functions or activities. Thus (as in Figure 4.8), the vice-president of human resources, Asia-Pacific region, will "develop, recommend, and implement approved HRM strategies, policies, and practices that will facilitate the achievement of the company's stated business and HRM objectives." For the job of materials manager, the summary might state that he or she will "purchase economically, regulate deliveries of, store, and distribute all materials necessary on the production line," while the summary for a mailroom supervisor might indicate that he or she will "receive, sort, and deliver all incoming mail properly, and he or she will handle all outgoing mail, including the accurate and timely posting of such mail."[14]

Relationships

The *relationships* section indicates the jobholder's relationships with others inside and outside the organization, as shown in Figure 4.8. Others directly and indirectly supervised are included, along with peers, superiors, and outsiders relevant to the job.

FIGURE **4.8**   Sample Job Description

Sample Job Description

Position:	Vice-President, Human Resources, Asia-Pacific
Location:	Hong Kong
Division:	Asia-Pacific
Department:	Human Resources
Reports to:	President Asia-Pacific (administrative), Vice-President, Human Resources—Corporate (functional)
Date:	April 2, 2013

Job Summary

Under the administrative direction of the President, Asia-Pacific, and the functional guidance of the Vice-President, Human Resources—Corporate, develop, recommend, and implement approved HRM strategies, policies, and practices that will facilitate the achievement of the company's stated business and HRM objectives.

Duties and Responsibilities

- Develop and recommend HRM strategies, policies and practices that promote employee commitment, competence, motivation, and performance, and that facilitate the achievement of the Asia-Pacific region's business objectives.
- Provide policy guidance to senior management regarding the acquisition, development, reward, maintenance, and existence of the division's human resources so as to promote the status of the company as an ethical and preferred employer of choice.
- Identify, analyze, and interpret for Asia-Pacific regional senior management and corporate HR management influences and changes in the division's internal and external environment and their impact on HRM and divisional business objectives, strategies, policies, and practices.

Relationships

Internally, relate with senior line and functional managers within the Asia-Pacific region and corporate headquarters in Vancouver. Externally, successfully relate with senior academic, business, government, and trade union personnel. Directly supervise the following positions: Manager, Compensation and Benefits, Asia-Pacific and Manager, Training and Development, Asia-Pacific. Functionally supervise the HR managers in 13 geographic locations within the Asia-Pacific region.

Problem Solving

Diverse cultures and varying stages of economic development within the Asia-Pacific region create a unique and tough business environment. The incumbent will often face complex HR and business problems demanding solutions that need to be creative and, at the same time, sensitive to local and company requirements.

Authority

This position has the authority to:

- approve expenditures on budgeted capital items up to a total value of $100 000 in any one financial year
- hire and fire subordinate personnel in accordance with company policies and procedures
- approve expense accounts for subordinate personnel in accordance with company policies and procedures

continued

- authorize all non-capital item expenditures within approved budgetary limit
- exercise line authority over all direct reporting positions

Accountability

Employees: 3000. Sales: $4 billion. Direct budget responsibility: $2.7 million. Assets controlled: $780 000. Locations: Australia, China, Hong Kong, India, Indonesia, Japan, South Korea, Malaysia, New Zealand, the Philippines, Singapore, Taiwan, Thailand.

Special Circumstances

Successful performance requires the incumbent to work long hours, to travel extensively (50–60 percent of the time), to quickly adapt to different cultures and business conditions, to successfully handle high-stress situations, and to constantly work under pressure in a complex and very competitive business environment.

Performance Indicators

Performance indicators will include both quantitative and qualitative measures as agreed by the President, Asia-Pacific Division, and Vice-President, Human Resources—Corporate and the incumbent. Indicators may be market based (e.g., share price improvement), business based (e.g., division profitability, budget control, days lost through industrial unrest, positive changes in employee commitment, job satisfaction, and motivation), and individual based (e.g., performance as a leader and manager as assessed by superiors, peers, and subordinates). Performance expectations and performance indicators generally will be defined on an annual basis. A formal performance appraisal will be conducted at least once a year.

Source: Adapted from R.J. Stone, *Human Resource Management*, 4th ed. Milton, Queensland: John Wiley & Sons, 2002, pp. 131–132. Reprinted with permission of the author.

Duties and Responsibilities

This section presents a detailed list of the job's major duties and responsibilities. As in Figure 4.8, each of the job's major duties should be listed separately and described in a few sentences. In the figure, for instance, the duties of the vice-president of human resources, Asia-Pacific region, include developing and recommending HRM strategies, policies, and practices; providing policy guidance; and identifying, analyzing, and interpreting internal and external environmental changes. Typical duties of other jobs might include maintaining balanced and controlled inventories, making accurate postings to accounts payable, maintaining favourable purchase price variances, or repairing production line tools and equipment.

Most experts state unequivocally that "one item frequently found that should *never* be included in a job description is a 'cop-out clause' like 'other duties, as assigned.'" This phrase leaves open the nature of the job and the people needed to staff it, and it can be subject to abuse.[15]

Authority

This section of a job description should define the limits of the jobholder's authority, including his or her decision-making authority, direct supervision of other employees, and budgetary limitations. For example, the vice-president of

An Ethical | Dilemma

In view of the fact that job descriptions are not required by law and that some organizations have found them no longer relevant, would abolishing job descriptions raise any moral or legal concerns?

human resources, Asia-Pacific region (in Figure 4.8) has the authority to approve all budgeted non-capital expenditures and budgeted capital expenditures up to $100 000; approve expense accounts for subordinates; hire and fire subordinates; and exercise line authority over direct reporting positions.

Performance Standards/Indicators

Some job descriptions also contain a performance standards/indicators section, which indicates the standards the employee is expected to achieve in each of the job description's main duties and responsibilities.

Setting standards is never easy. Most managers soon learn, however, that just telling employees to "do their best" doesn't provide enough guidance to ensure top performance. One straightforward way of setting standards is to finish the statement: "I will be completely satisfied with your work when . . ." This sentence, if completed for each duty listed in the job description, should result in a usable set of performance standards.[16] Some examples would include the following:

Duty: Accurately Posting Accounts Payable

- All invoices received are posted within the same working day.
- All invoices are routed to the proper department managers for approval no later than the day following receipt.
- No more than three posting errors per month occur, on average.
- The posting ledger is balanced by the end of the third working day of each month.

Duty: Meeting Daily Production Schedule

- Work group produces no fewer than 426 units per working day.
- No more than 2 percent of units are rejected at the next workstation, on average.
- Work is completed with no more than 5 percent overtime per week, on average.

Working Conditions and Physical Environment

The job description should also list the general working conditions involved in the job. This section generally includes information about noise level, temperature, lighting, degree of privacy, frequency of interruptions, hours of work, amount of travel, and hazards to which the incumbent may be exposed.

Special guidelines for entrepreneurial and small businesses are provided in the Entrepreneurs and HR box.

Job Descriptions and Human Rights Legislation

Human rights legislation requires employers to ensure that there is no discrimination on any of the prohibited grounds in any aspect of the terms and conditions of employment. To ensure that job descriptions comply with this legislation, a few key points should be kept in mind:

Hints | TO ENSURE LEGAL COMPLIANCE

- Job descriptions are not legally required but are highly advisable.
- Essential job duties should be clearly identified in the job description. Indicating the percentage of time spent on each duty or listing duties in

ENTREPRENEURS and HR

A Practical Approach to Job Analysis and Job Descriptions

Without their own job analysts or even their own HR managers, many small-business owners need a more streamlined approach to job analysis. A resource that includes all of the possible positions that they might encounter, with a detailed listing of the duties normally assigned to these positions, exists in the National Occupational Classification (NOC) mentioned earlier. The practical approach to job analysis for small-business owners presented next is built around this invaluable reference tool.

Step 1: Develop an Organization Chart

Drawing up the organization chart of the present structure comes first. Then, depending on how far in advance planning is being done, a chart can be produced that shows how the organization should look in the immediate future (say, in two months), as well as two or three other charts showing how the organization is likely to evolve over the next two or three years.

Step 2: Use a Job Analysis Questionnaire

Next, a job analysis questionnaire can be used to determine what each job entails. A shorter version of one of the more comprehensive job analysis questionnaires, such as that in Figure 4.5, may be useful for collecting job analysis data. An example of a job summary for a customer service clerk follows:

> Answers inquiries and gives directions to customers, authorizes cashing of customers' cheques, records and returns lost credit cards, sorts and reviews new credit applications, and works at the customer service desk.

Step 3: Obtain a Copy of the National Occupational Classification (NOC) and Related Publications for Reference

Next, standardized examples of the job descriptions needed should be obtained from the NOC website at www.hrsdc.gc.ca/eng/workplaceskills/noc/index.shtml. A related publication entitled *Job Descriptions: An Employers' Handbook* is also available for downloading from the NOC website at www.hrsdc.gc.ca/eng/workplaceskills/noc/employers/emplr_handbooks.shtml.

Step 4: Choose Appropriate Job Titles and Job Descriptions and Copy Them for Reference

For each department, the NOC job titles and job descriptions that are believed to be appropriate should be chosen. The NOC definition will provide a firm foundation for the job description being created. It will provide a standardized list and constant reminder of the specific duties that should be included.

Step 5: Complete the Job Description

An appropriate job description for the job under consideration can then be written. The job analysis information, together with the information from the NOC, can be used to create a complete listing of the tasks and duties of each of the jobs. The working conditions section can be completed once all of the tasks and duties have been specified.

---

order of importance are strategies used to differentiate between essential and non-essential tasks and responsibilities.

- When assessing suitability for employment, training program enrollment, and transfers or promotions, and when appraising performance, the only criteria examined should be the knowledge, skills, and abilities (KSAs) required for the essential duties of the job.

- When an employee cannot perform one or more of the essential duties because of reasons related to a prohibited ground, such as a physical disability or religion, reasonable accommodation to the point of undue hardship is required.

job specification A list of the "human requirements," that is, the requisite knowledge, skills, and abilities needed to perform the job—another product of a job analysis.

Job Specifications

Writing the **job specification** involves examining the duties and responsibilities of the job and answering the question, "What human traits and experience are required to do this job?" Much of this information can be obtained from the job analysis questionnaire. The job specification clarifies what kind of person to recruit and which qualities that person should be tested for. It is sometimes included with the job description.

Complying with human rights legislation means keeping a few pointers in mind:

- All listed qualifications are bona fide occupational requirements (BFORs) based on the current job duties and responsibilities.

- Unjustifiably high educational or lengthy experience requirements can lead to systemic discrimination.

- The qualifications of the current incumbent should not be confused with the minimum requirements, since he or she might be underqualified or overqualified.

- For entry-level jobs, identifying the actual physical and mental demands is critical. For example, if the job requires detailed manipulation on a circuit-board assembly line, finger dexterity is extremely important and is something for which candidates should be tested. A **physical demands analysis**—which identifies the senses used and the type, frequency, and amount of physical effort involved in the job—is often used to supplement the job specification. A sample form is included in **Figure 4.9**. Having such detailed information is particularly beneficial when determining accommodation requirements. The mental and emotional demands of a job are typically missing from job analysis information. They should be specified so that the mental and emotional competencies of job applicants can be assessed and any need for accommodation can be identified.

physical demands analysis
Identification of the senses used and the type, frequency, and amount of physical effort involved in a job.

Identifying the human requirements for a job can be accomplished through a judgmental approach (based on educated guesses of job incumbents, supervisors, and HR managers) or statistical analysis (based on the relationship between some human trait or skill and some criterion of job effectiveness). Basing job specifications on statistical analysis is more legally defensible. For example, the Personality-Related Position Requirements Form (PPRF) is a survey instrument designed to assist managers in identifying potential personality-related traits that may be important in a job. Identifying personality dimensions is difficult when using most job analysis techniques, because they tend to be much better suited to unearthing human aptitudes and skills—like manual dexterity. The PPRF uses questionnaire items to assess the relevance of such basic personality dimensions as agreeableness, conscientiousness, and emotional stability to the job under study. The relevance of these personality traits can then be assessed through statistical analysis.[17]

An Ethical Dilemma

Are personality traits really part of the KSAs and bona fide occupational requirements/essential duties of a job?

Completing the Job Specification Form

Once the required human characteristics have been determined, whether using statistical analysis or a judgmental approach, a job specification form should be completed. To illustrate the types of information and amount of detail that should be provided in a well-written job specification, a sample has been included in **Figure 4.10**.

Writing Competency-Based Job Descriptions

Defining the job's competencies and writing them up involves a process that is similar in most respects to traditional job analysis. In other words, the manager will

FIGURE 4.9   Physical Demands Analysis

Division:		Job Title:	
Job Code:		Level:	
Date:		Date of Last Revision:	

Physical Requirements
Review the chart below. Indicate which of the following are essential to perform the functions of this job, with or without accommodation. Check one box in each section.

Section I					Section 2		Section 3			Section 4	
Incumbent Uses:	NA	Right	Left	Both	Repetitive motion		The job requires the use of the first category up to 2 hours per day	The job requires the use of the first category up to 4 hours per day	The job requires the use of the first category up to 8 hours per day	Frequent breaks: Normal breaks plus those caused by performing jobs outside of the area.	Limited breaks: Two short breaks and one lunch break.
					Y	N					
Hands: (requires manual manipulation)											
Feet: (functions requiring foot pedals and the like)											

Lifting capacity: Indicate, by checking the appropriate box, the amount of lifting necessary for this job, with or without accommodation.

	NA	Occasionally (As Needed)	Often (Up to 4 Hours Per Day)	Frequently (Up to 8 Hours Per Day)
5 kg				
5–10 kg				
10–25 kg				
25–50 kg				
50+ kg				

Mobility: Indicate which category the job functions fall under by placing a check next to those that apply.
☐ Sits constantly (6 hours or more with two breaks and one lunch break)
☐ Sits intermittently (6 hours or more with frequent change, due to breaks and getting up to perform jobs outside of the area)
☐ Stands intermittently (6 hours or more with frequent changes, due to breaks and getting up to perform jobs outside of the area)
☐ Bending constantly (4 hours or more with two breaks and one lunch break)
☐ Bending intermittently (4 hours or more with frequent changes, due to breaks and getting up to perform jobs outside of the area)
☐ Walks constantly (6 hours or more with two breaks and one lunch break)
☐ Walks intermittently (6 hours or more with frequent changes, due to breaks and getting up to perform jobs outside of the area)

continued

Visual acuity: Indicate the minimum acceptable level, with or without accommodation, necessary for the job
☐ Excellent visual acuity
☐ Good visual acuity
☐ Not relevant to the job

Auditory acuity: Indicate the minimum acceptable level, with or without accommodation, necessary for the job.
☐ Excellent auditory acuity
☐ Good auditory acuity
☐ Not relevant to the job

Source: M. Rock and D.R. Berger, eds., *The Compensation Handbook: A State-of-the-Art Guide to Compensation Strategy and Design*, 4th ed. Columbus, OH: McGraw-Hill, 2000, pp. 69–70. © 2000 The McGraw-Hill Companies, Inc.

interview job incumbents and their supervisors, ask open-ended questions regarding job responsibilities and activities, and perhaps identify critical incidents that pinpoint success on the job. These job descriptions can be particularly useful in organizations that use competency-based pay, as discussed in Chapter 11.

FIGURE 4.10   Job Specification

Job Title: Lifeguard
Job Code: LG1
Department: Recreation
Date: May 1, 2013

Location: Lethbridge Community Pool
Supervisor: Head Lifeguard
Division: Parks and Recreation

Job Summary
The incumbent is required to safeguard the health of pool users by patrolling the pool, rescuing swimmers in difficulty, treating injuries, advising pool users of safety rules, and enforcing safety rules.

Skill
Formal Qualifications: Royal Life Saving Society Bronze Medallion or equivalent
Experience: No prior experience required but would be an asset.
Communication Skills: Good oral communication skills are required. Proficiency in one or more foreign languages would be an asset. The incumbent must be able to communicate courteously and effectively. Strong interpersonal skills are required. All interaction with the public must be handled with tact and diplomacy.

Effort
Physical Effort: The incumbent is required to stand during the majority of working hours. In the event of an emergency where a swimmer is in distress, the incumbent must initiate rescue procedures immediately, which may involve strenuous physical exertion.
Mental Effort: Continuous mental attention to pool users. Must remain vigilant despite many simultaneous demands on his or her attention.
Emotional Effort: Enforcement of safety rules and water rescue can be stressful. Must maintain a professional demeanour when dealing with serious injuries or death.

Working Conditions
Job is performed in humid indoor environment, temperature-controlled. No privacy. Shift work to cover pool hours from 7 A.M. to 11 P.M., seven days a week. Some overtime and split shifts may be required.

Approval Signatures
Incumbent: _____
Supervisor: _____ Date: _____

STEP 6: COMMUNICATION AND PREPARATIONS FOR REVISIONS

Organizations are often affected by internal and external factors, as described in Chapter 1, that influence organizational strategy, structure, or processes. Most organizations adopt strategies with a three- to five-year target, and many are forced to adjust according to environmental factors much sooner. Significant organizational changes like restructuring, new product development, technological changes, and competition modify the nature of how work is done, resulting in a need for revisions to the existing job descriptions and specifications.

Job analysis must be structured enough to allow for modifications as required while still providing current and future employees with an understanding of what they are expected to do. Once a system is developed to collect data, an organization may choose to (1) regularly update the data collected in a proactive manner, (2) develop systems to collect data on an ongoing basis, or (3) adjust job analysis activities in a reactive manner after a significant organizational change is initiated.

Information provided from the job analysis must be communicated to all relevant stakeholders. For example, employees must be aware of the core job requirements to help drive desired performance. Line managers must be aware of information provided in the job analysis to help align expectations of various jobs, manage performance, and manage HR planning activities. Recruiters use this information to determine and assess the desired knowledge, skills, abilities, and other characteristics (KSAO's) of potential candidates and to develop job ads. Compensation specialists can use this information to develop or modify pay scales according to job-related act ivities. Overall, the job analysis process is a fundamental component of HRM and a cornerstone that is critical to other organizational activities related to labour and work processes.

Chapter SUMMARY

1. In any organization, work has to be divided into manageable units and ultimately into jobs that can be performed by employees. The process of organizing work into tasks that are required to perform a specific job is known as job design. The term "job" means a group of tasks and duties, and several employees may have the same job. The collection of tasks and responsibilities performed by one person is known as a "position."

2. Job analysis involves six steps: (1) collect background information, (2) select the representative positions and jobs to be analyzed, (3) collect data, (4) review the information collected with the incumbents and their supervisors, (5) develop job descriptions and job specifications, and (6) communicate and review on an ongoing basis.

3. Techniques used to gather job analysis data include interviews, questionnaires (including the PAQ and FJA), direct observation, participant diaries/logs, and the National Occupational Classification (NOC), to list just a few.

4. Competency-based job analysis, focusing on how the job is done (the behaviours required) more than on task requirements, has become more common for three reasons. First, traditional job descriptions may not be appropriate in organizations with flexible jobs. Second, describing the job in terms of the skills, knowledge, and competencies the worker needs is more strategic. Third, competency-based job analysis supports the employer's performance management process.

5. A job description is a written statement of what the jobholder actually does, how he or she does it, and under what conditions the job is performed. The job specification involves examining the duties and responsibilities and answering this question: "What human traits and experience are required to do this job?"

MyManagementLab

Visit MyManagementLab to access a personalized Study Plan and additional study tools for this chapter.

Key TERMS

competencies (p. 96)
competency-based job analysis (p. 96)
diary/log (p. 103)
ergonomics (p. 95)
Functional Job Analysis (FJA) (p. 103)
industrial engineering (p. 94)
job (p. 88)
job analysis (p. 88)
job description (p. 106)
job design (p. 93)
job enlargement (horizontal loading) (p. 94)
job enrichment (vertical loading) (p. 95)
job rotation (p. 95)

job specification (p. 110)
National Occupational Classification (NOC) (p. 103)
occupation (p. 105)
organization chart (p. 91)
organizational structure (p. 91)
physical demands analysis (p. 111)
position (p. 88)
Position Analysis Questionnaire (PAQ) (p. 101)
process chart (p. 93)
team (p. 97)
team-based job design (p. 97)
work simplification (p. 94)

Review and Discussion QUESTIONS

1. Explain how job analysis provides important information that is required for at least three different functions of HRM.

2. Differentiate among job enlargement, job rotation, and job enrichment, and provide an example of each.

3. Why is ergonomic job design becoming increasingly important?

4. Several methods for collecting job analysis data are available—interviews, the Position Analysis Questionnaire, and so on. Compare and

contrast four of these methods, explaining what each is useful for and listing the pros and cons of each.

5. Although not legally required, having job descriptions is highly advisable. Why? How can firms ensure that their job specifications are legally defensible?

6. What are competencies? Why are companies starting to use competency-based job analysis? How is this approach different from the traditional approach?

Critical Thinking QUESTIONS

1. Why isn't it always desirable or appropriate to use job enrichment when designing jobs? How would you determine how enriched an individual employee's job should be?

2. Assume that you are the job analyst at a bicycle manufacturing company in British Columbia and have been assigned responsibility for preparing job descriptions (including specifications) for all

the supervisory and managerial positions. One of the production managers has just indicated that he will not complete the job analysis questionnaire you have developed.

a. How would you handle this situation?

b. What arguments would you use to attempt to persuade him to change his mind?

c. If your persuasion efforts failed, how would you go about obtaining the job analysis information you need to develop the job description for his position?

3. Because the top job in a firm (such as president, executive director, or CEO) is by nature more strategic and broader in scope than any other job, is competency-based job analysis more appropriate? Is there less need for a job description for the president? Why or why not?

4. If you were designing a job for a new marketing and sales representative for a small entrepreneurial company that is experiencing rapid growth, what approach would you take? Explain why you would take this approach. How would you go about determining job specifications?

5. If a supervisor reviews the job analysis information provided by an employee and says that the job duties and responsibilities have been inflated, but the employee says that the supervisor does not really know what the job entails, how can a decision be made about what information is accurate?

Experiential EXERCISES

1. Use organization chart software to draw an organization chart that accurately depicts the structure of the organization in which you are currently employed or one with which you are thoroughly familiar. Once you have completed this task, form a group with several of your classmates. Taking turns, have each member show his or her organization chart to the group, briefly describe the structure depicted, explain whether or not the structure seems to be appropriate, and identify several advantages and disadvantages he or she experienced working within this structure.

2. Working individually or in groups and using the HRSDC website, find the National Occupational Classification (NOC) job descriptions for both a university professor and a college professor. Compare the two descriptions, noting similarities and differences. Using the NOC descriptions and your own observations of people in this role, create a competency profile for each job.

How similar are they? Why do you think this is so? Compare and discuss your results with other individual students or groups.

3. Working individually, prepare a job description (including job specifications) for a position that you know well, using the job analysis questionnaire in this chapter. Once you have done so, exchange job descriptions with someone else in the class. Critique your colleague's job description and provide specific suggestions regarding any additions/deletions/revisions that you would recommend to ensure that the job description accurately reflects the job and is legally defensible.

4. Working in groups of three or four, identify the jobs that have been or are held by students in your group. Select one job to analyze. Use the job analysis questionnaire provided in the chapter to conduct a job analysis interview and document a job description and specifications. Compare and critique your work with the work done by another group.

Running CASE

Who Do We Have to Hire?

As the excitement surrounding the move into their new offices wound down, the two principal owners of LearnInMotion.com, Pierre and Jennifer, turned to the task of hiring new employees. In their business plan they'd specified several basic goals for the venture capital funds they'd just received, and hiring a team topped the list. They knew their other goals—boosting sales and expanding the website, for instance—would be unreachable without the right team.

They were just about to place their ads when Pierre asked a question that brought them to a stop: "What kind of people do we want to hire?" It seemed they hadn't really considered this. They knew the answer in general terms, of course. For example, they knew they needed at least two salespeople, a programmer, a web designer, and several content management people to transform the incoming material into content they could post on their site. But it was obvious that job titles alone really didn't provide enough guidance. For example, if they couldn't specify the exact duties of these positions, how could they decide whether they needed experienced employees? How could they decide exactly what sorts of experiences and skills they had to look for in their candidates if they didn't know exactly what these candidates would have to do? They wouldn't even know what questions to ask.

And that wasn't all. For example, there were other tasks to do that weren't necessarily included in the sorts of things that salespeople, programmers, web designers, or content management people typically do. Who was going to answer the phones? (Jennifer and Pierre had originally assumed they'd put in one of those fancy automated call directory and voicemail systems—until they found out it would cost close to $10 000.) As a practical matter, they knew they had to have someone answering the phones and directing callers to the proper extensions. Who was going to keep track of the monthly expenses and compile them for the accountants, who'd then produce monthly reports for the venture capitalist? Would the salespeople generate their own leads? Or would LearnInMotion.com have to hire web surfers to search and find the names of people for the sales staff to call or email? What would happen when the company had to purchase supplies, such as fax paper or printer ink? Would the owners have to do this themselves, or should they have someone in-house do it for them? The list, it seemed, went on and on.

It was obvious, in other words, that the owners had to get their managerial act together and draw up the sorts of documents they'd read about as business majors—job descriptions, job specifications, and so forth. The trouble was, it had all seemed a lot easier when they read the textbook. Now they want you, their management consultant, to help them actually do it.

QUESTIONS

1 To assist Pierre and Jennifer in developing much-needed job descriptions, follow the steps outlined in the job analysis process and design a job description for the positions of web designer, salesperson, and receptionist.

2 As part of the job analysis process you will follow in question 1, evaluate the methods of collecting job analysis information and discuss which ones you would recommend (including why) to Pierre and Jennifer as part of developing the job descriptions.

3 As their management consultant, would you recommend they use quantitative or qualitative methods, or both? Why?

Case INCIDENT

What Is a Human Resources Consultant to Do?

Anthony LePage is the owner of a local recruitment agency that has an established presence in the northern Ontario market. He is looking to expand its service offerings to include consulting services to small businesses. A recent marketing blitz advertising this new service has led to a new partnership with a large local manufacturing business.

After the meeting with the owner of the manufacturing business, the mandate is clear that the owner is seeking the agency's assistance in creating and writing job descriptions for all of the positions within the company. Some of these positions include administrative assistants, sales, engineering, and skilled trades, along with many others. There are more than 100 descriptions to write. The owner would like to see a sample job description within one week before he signs the contract to complete the remainder of the job descriptions.

Anthony LePage has just hired you as the human resources consultant in charge of producing this job description sample for his new client and has asked you to answer the following questions.

QUESTIONS

1   Outline what the crucial differences are between a job description and a job specification.

2   The owner of the business has heard that qualitative methods produce the best job descriptions. Would you attempt to persuade him otherwise?

3   Develop a sample job description for the position of administrative assistant for the owner and explain why you included the various sections that you did.

4   The owner has heard from some of his colleagues about the use of competencies. He wants to know what they are and if these should be incorporated into the job descriptions he requires.

MyManagementLab

Visit MyManagementLab to access a personalized Study Plan and additional study tools for this chapter.

CBC ⊛   To view the CBC videos, read a summary, and answer discussion questions, go to to MyManagementLab

CHAPTER 5

Human Resources Planning

LEARNING OUTCOMES

AFTER STUDYING THIS CHAPTER, YOU SHOULD BE ABLE TO

DEFINE human resources planning (HRP) and **DISCUSS** its strategic importance.

DESCRIBE four quantitative and two qualitative techniques used to forecast human resources demand.

DISCUSS briefly the four strategies used to forecast internal human resources supply and four types of market conditions assessed when forecasting external human resources supply.

DESCRIBE the ways in which a surplus of human resources can be handled.

EXPLAIN how organizations deal with a shortage of human resources.

REQUIRED PROFESSIONAL CAPABILITIES (RPC)

- Maintains an inventory of HR talent for use within the organization

- Identifies the organization's staffing needs

- Researches, analyzes, and reports on potential people issues affecting the organization

- Forecasts HR supply and demand conditions

- Plans for and manages the HR aspects of organizational change

THE STRATEGIC IMPORTANCE OF HUMAN RESOURCES PLANNING

human resources planning (HRP)
The process of forecasting future human resources requirements to ensure that the organization will have the required number of employees with the necessary skills to meet its strategic objectives.

Human resources planning (HRP) is the process of forecasting future human resources requirements to ensure that the organization will have the required number of employees with the necessary skills to meet its strategic objectives. HRP is a proactive process, which both anticipates and influences an organization's future by systematically forecasting the supply of and demand for employees under changing conditions and by developing plans and activities to satisfy these needs. Effective HRP helps an organization achieve its strategic goals and objectives, achieve economies in hiring new workers, make major labour market demands more successfully, anticipate and avoid shortages and surpluses of human resources, as well as control or reduce labour costs.

HRP has recently become a key strategic priority not just for HR departments but for strategic business planners as well. The existing labour shortage in Canada is forecast to increase to 1 million workers over the next 15 years.[1] Currently, Canada is in the beginning stages of a major labour

FIGURE 5.1   Occupations Currently Showing or Expected to Show Labour Shortages

Occupation	Normalized future labour market situation (NFLMS)	The increase in the number of school leavers and immigrants needed to restore balance between expected supply and demand (annually)
Contractors & Supervisors, Trades & Related	4.2	509%
Contractors / Operators / Supervisors: Agriculture	4.1	305%
Facility Operation & Maintenance Managers	3.9	335%
Health / Education / Social & Community Services Managers	5.0	156%
Legislators & Senior Management	5.5	250%
Managers in Communication (Except Broadcasting)	3.6	217%
Managers in Construction & Transportation	4.5	521%
Managers in Protective Service	5.2	226%
Managers in Public Administration	6.6	355%
Optometrists / Chiropractors / Other Health Professions	3.5	124%
Supervisors, Railway & Motor Transportation	5.5	1090%
Supervisors, Assembly & Fabrication	4.3	294%
Supervisors, Mining / Oil / Gas	3.2	338%
Supervisors, Processing Occupations	4.8	403%
Train Crew Operating Occupations	4.0	1062%

Source: Looking-Ahead: A 10-Year Outlook for the Canadian Labour Market (2006–2015), http://www.hrsdc.gc.ca/eng/publications_resources/research/categories/labour_market_e/sp_615_10_06/la06-shortages-29jan07.pdf, Human Resources and Social Development in Canada, 2007. Reproduced with the permission of the Minister of Public Works and Government Services Canada, 2012.

shortage. As the baby boom generation begins to retire, there are not enough candidates to fill vacant positions.[2] On average, two out of every three job openings over the next decade will be focused on replacing retiring workers. In addition, fertility rates in Canada continue to decline, resulting in fewer possible workers for the future labour force. Combined, these conditions create a situation of fierce labour competition, further increasing the importance of effective HRP. **Figure 5.1** highlights occupations that are currently facing a labour shortage or ones that are expected to face a labour shortage by 2015. HRP will be absolutely essential for successful strategy implementation.[3]

As illustrated in **Figure 5.2,** key steps in the HRP process include analyzing forecasted labour supply, forecasting labour demands, and then planning and implementing HR programs to balance supply and demand.

Lack of or inadequate human resources planning within an organization can result in significant costs when unstaffed positions create costly inefficiencies and when severance pay is required for large numbers of employees being laid off. It can also create situations in which one department is laying off employees while another is hiring individuals with similar skills, which can reduce morale or productivity and can often result in turnover. The greater concern is that ineffective HRP can lead to an organization's inability to accomplish short-term operational plans or long-range strategic plans.

FIGURE 5.2 Human Resources Planning Model

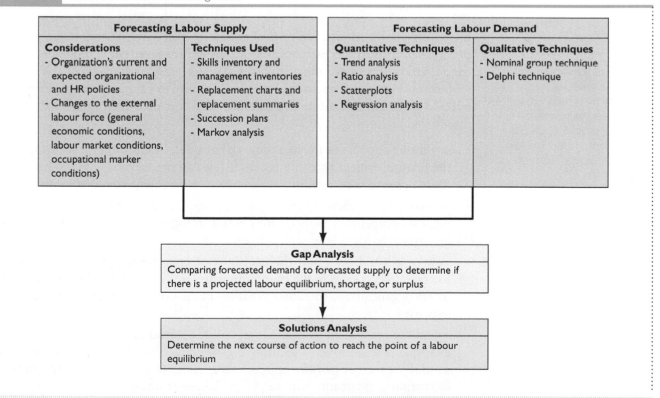

The Relationship between HRP and Strategic Planning

An HR plan (HRP) does not occur independently of the other departments within an organization (such as finance, marketing, research and development). The HRP must align with the overall goals of the organization as well as both the long-term and short-term strategic plans set by the organization. Fundamental to the business planning process is the impact and alignment of HRP (as discussed in detail in Chapter 1). An organization's strategic decision to expand, redirect, diverge, divest, partner, or merge will have an associated effect on the HR expectations and plans of the organization.

Failure to integrate HRP and strategic planning can have very serious consequences. For example, in Ontario, a fifth year of high school called the Ontario Academic Credit (OAC) year (often referred to as Grade 13) was abolished in 2003 as an effort to cut provincial government costs. As a result, there was a double cohort of students (from both Grade 12 and Grade 13) graduating and wanting to attend postsecondary institutions. Most universities and colleges adopted a strategic decision to significantly increase admissions in 2003 to accommodate for the double cohort. Postsecondary institutions that aligned their HRP with the strategy of increased admissions benefited from an associated increase in labour. Organizations that did not link their strategic decision with HRP struggled with supporting the increased number of students inside the classroom (professors and teaching assistants) and outside of the classroom (libraries, career and learning centres, cafeterias, and so on). Thus, alignment of HR planning to strategic decisions is essential to an organization's success.

The Importance of Environmental Scanning

Environmental scanning is a critical component of HRP and strategic planning processes; the most successful organizations are prepared for changes before they occur. **Environment scanning** involves assessing factors that affect the external labour market as well as an organization's ability to find and secure talent from outside of the organization. The external environmental factors most frequently monitored include

environment scanning An assessment of external factors influencing the organizations ability to find and secure talent from the external labour market including economic, competitive, legislative, social, technological and demographic trends.

- economic conditions (local, regional, national, international); for example, if the unemployment rate in a region is low, an organization would have to be more aggressive in recruiting talent, as selection may be more scarce

- market and competitive trends; for example, compensation policies that lag behind competitors' policies may result in higher turnover or more difficulties in attracting talent

- new or revised laws and the decisions of courts and quasi-judicial bodies; for example, a raise in the minimum wage rate can inflate the cost of labour in an organization, therefore creating budgetary pressure to reduce labour expenses

- social concerns such as healthcare, childcare, and educational priorities; for example, a trend toward securing higher education can reduce the size of the available external workforce in the short run, but in the longer run can result in retaining applicants with more specialized training

- technological changes affecting processes, products, and people; for example, a new technology developed at a local university can be implemented in the organization and significantly reduce labour demands through automation of a previously labour-intensive process
- demographic trends of an internal and external labour force; for example, if an organization is situated in a community largely inhabited by senior citizens, it may face difficulties securing a diverse or full-time workforce from the local area

Steps in Human Resources Planning

HRP is critical to an organization's success as it aligns forecasted labour supply (provided by the human resources department) with the predicted labour demands of the organization (such as the number of employees needed and the skill sets required). An element of HR planning that is often taken for granted is the availability and accuracy of information regarding the current HR situation. Understanding the internal labour force in the present is the basis for a number of demand and supply estimates. Therefore, before embarking on an HR planning exercise, current HR levels must be assessed.

There are numerous sources of information for identifying existing talent and human resources in an organization. An organization chart can provide HR planners and managers with an understanding of the organizational structure, business units, and possible career paths. This macro-level information can be linked to more micro-level information, such as how many employees the company currently has at each level, what existing skill sets the employees have, as well as the demographic information and job-related information about the existing employee base.

An organization must forecast future HR demand (the number of employees and the skill sets needed in the future) and forecast future HR supply (internal availability of workers). These two forecasts can occur simultaneously or one after the other depending on the resources available (time, money, people, and so on). Only after demand and supply is forecast can an organization identify potential labour imbalance issues, which leads to the development and implementation of plans to balance HR.

RPC

Researches, analyzes, and reports on potential people issues affecting the organization

FORECASTING THE AVAILABILITY OF CANDIDATES (SUPPLY)

Short-term and long-range HR demand forecasts only provide half of the staffing equation by answering the question, "How many employees will we need?" The next major concern is how projected openings will be filled. There are two sources of supply:

1. *Internal*—present employees who can be trained, transferred, or promoted to meet anticipated needs
2. *External*—people in the labour market not currently working for the organization, including those who are employed elsewhere and those who are unemployed who can be expected to join the organization to meet anticipated needs

While internal forecasting identifies which members of the internal workforce will remain within the organization and where, an awareness of the external labour force can aid organizations in identifying challenges that may occur with expected recruitment of candidates into the internal labour force, such as the number of graduates in a specific program that acts as a significant source of talent, the literacy levels of the local or target population, as well as general economic trends. These external factors can impact how much compensation an organization must provide to secure top talent. As well, in times of low unemployment the internal workforce may be more inclined to seek employment elsewhere, if there is a general labour shortage for employees with their specific skill set. Therefore, trends in the external labour force have a direct impact on projections of the internal labour force.

Forecasting the Supply of Internal Candidates

Before estimating how many external candidates will need to be recruited and hired, management must determine how many candidates for projected openings will likely come from within the firm. This is the purpose of forecasting the supply of internal candidates.

Skills Inventories and Management Inventories

skills inventories Manual or computerized records summarizing employees' education, experience, interests, skills, and so on, which are used to identify internal candidates eligible for transfer or promotion.

Skills inventories contain comprehensive information about the capabilities of current employees. Data gathered for each employee include name, age, date of employment, current position, present duties and responsibilities, educational background, previous work history, skills, abilities, and interests. Information about current performance and readiness for promotion is generally included as well. Data pertaining to managerial staff are compiled in **management inventories**. Records summarizing the background, qualifications, interests, and skills of management employees, as well as information about managerial responsibilities and management training, are used to identify internal candidates eligible for promotion or transfer opportunities.

management inventories Records summarizing the qualifications, interests, and skills of management employees, along with the number and types of employees supervised, duties of such employees, total budget managed, previous managerial duties and responsibilities, and managerial training received.

To be useful, skills and management inventories must be updated regularly. Failure to do so can lead to present employees being overlooked for job openings. Updating every two years is generally adequate if employees are encouraged to report significant qualifications changes (such as new skills learned or courses completed) to the HR department as they occur.

Replacement Charts and Replacement Summaries

replacement charts Visual representations of who will replace whom in the event of a job opening. Likely internal candidates are listed, along with their age, present performance rating, and promotability status.

Replacement charts are typically used to keep track of potential internal candidates for the firm's most critical positions. It assumes that the organization chart will remain static for a long period of time and usually identifies three potential candidates for a top-level position, should it become vacant. As can be seen in **Figure 5.3**, such charts typically indicate the age of potential internal candidates (which cannot be used as a criterion in making selection or promotion decisions but is necessary to project retirement dates), the current performance level of the employee, and his or her promotion potential. The latter is based on the employee's future career aspirations and a supervisory assessment of readiness for promotion.

FIGURE **5.3**   Management Replacement Chart

Cenera **www.cenera.ca**

replacement summaries Lists of likely replacements for each position and their relative strengths and weaknesses, as well as information about current position, performance, promotability, age, and experience.

To provide a more objective estimate of future potential this information may be supplemented by results of psychological tests, interviews with HR specialists, and other selection techniques.

Although replacement charts provide an excellent quick reference tool, they contain very little information. For that reason, many firms prefer to use **replacement summaries.** Such summaries list likely replacements for each position and their relative strengths and weaknesses, as well as information about current position, performance, promotability, age, and experience. These additional data can be extremely helpful to decision makers, although caution must be taken to ensure that no discrimination occurs on the basis of age, sex, and so on.

succession planning The process of ensuring a suitable supply of successors for current and future senior or key jobs so that the careers of individuals can be effectively planned and managed.

Succession Plans

Forecasting the availability of inside candidates is particularly important in succession planning. In a nutshell, **succession planning** refers to the plans a company makes to fill its most important executive positions. It extends beyond the replacement chart by focusing on developing people rather than simply identifying potential replacements. As a result, there is a stronger focus on skills development for a specific list of potential successors within an organization.

In the days when companies were hierarchical and employees tended to remain with a firm for years, executive succession was often straightforward: Staff climbed the ladder one rung at a time, and it wasn't unusual for someone to start on the shop floor and end up in the president's office. Although that kind of ascent is still possible, employee turnover and flatter structures mean that the lines of succession are no longer as direct. For example, potential successors for top positions might be routed through the top jobs at several key divisions, as well as overseas, and sent through a university graduate-level, advanced management program.

Succession planning is extremely important today, affecting both large and small organizations. The Entrepreneurs and HR box highlights some of the challenges that entrepreneurial organizations often face with succession planning. Because succession planning requires balancing the organization's top management needs with the potential career aspirations of available candidates, succession should include these activities:

- analysis of the demand for managers and professionals in the company
- audit of existing executives and projection of likely future supply
- planning of individual career paths based on objective estimates of future needs, performance appraisal data, and assessments of potential
- career counselling and performance-related training and development to prepare individuals for future roles
- accelerated promotions, with development targeted at future business needs
- planned strategic recruitment aimed at obtaining people with the potential to meet future needs as well as filling current openings[4]

It should be noted that replacement charts, replacement summaries, and succession plans are considered highly confidential in most organizations.

An Ethical : Dilemma

You were recently asked to identify one employee you manage as a top performer to align with a new company program offering top performers intensive management skills training. The employee you identified for this role is unaware of the program. This morning, she confided in you that she just applied for graduate school and will find out if she has been accepted five months from now, with the intent to start the program one month after that. Would you change the identification of who was the top performer in your team based on this information? Why or why not?

Tips FOR THE FRONT LINE

Markov Analysis

Markov analysis A method of forecasting internal labour supply that involves tracking the pattern of employee movements through various jobs and developing a transitional probability matrix.

Estimating internal supply involves much more than simply calculating the number of employees. Some firms use the **Markov analysis** technique to track the pattern of employee movements through various jobs and develop a transitional probability matrix for forecasting internal supply by specific categories, such as position and gender. As illustrated in **Figure 5.4**, such an analysis shows the actual number (and percentage) of employees who remain in each job from one year to the next, as well as the proportions promoted, demoted, transferred, and leaving the organization. These proportions (probabilities) are used to forecast human resources supply.

| FIGURE 5.4 | Hypothetical Markov Analysis for a Manufacturing Operation |

2013 → 2014	Plant Manager	Foreperson	Team Leader	Production Worker	Exit
Plant Manager (n = 5)	80% / 4				20% / 1
Foreperson (n = 35)	8% / 3	82% / 28			10% / 4
Team Leader (n = 110)		11% / 12	70% / 77	7% / 8	12% / 13
Production Worker (n = 861)			6% / 52	72% / 620	22% / 189
Projected Supply	7	40	129	628	

Percentages represent transitions (previous year's actuals).
Actual numbers of employees are shown as whole numbers in each block (projections for 2014 based on current staffing).

ENTREPRENEURS and HR

Succession Planning and Family Businesses

In the second quarter of 2010, small businesses created 35 549 jobs, while large firms created only 728 jobs. During that period, small businesses in the construction sector alone accounted for 23 014 new jobs, while healthcare and social assistance small businesses introduced 9 755 new jobs. Needless to say, the impact of small businesses in Canada is paramount to economic success and job creation.

Multigenerational family-controlled businesses often struggle with succession planning. Only one-third of family-owned businesses survive the transition to the second generation. And of these, only one-third survive the transition to the third generation.[5]

There are many reasons for these failures. First, the topic of potential retirement planning or planning for the eventual death of the business owner is a topic that is difficult to address. The tough decision of determining who will inherit the business and how ownership will be determined among children can be a source of immense stress for family business owners. Therefore, many choose to ignore the issue of succession planning altogether.

Second, a family business is a great source of pride for the business owner and is often their single largest asset. The concept of retirement or walking away can be incomprehensible to those who built the business. Likewise, the notion that another person will be given full decision-making authority includes the risk that the strategic agenda, long-term plans, or business approach of the successor will not align with the visions of the current business owner.

Third, within a family there may not be a qualified or interested successor. Successors themselves may be hesitant to take the reins in a family business because of the perception that the person who left the business may continue to stay involved in decision making, which can act as a disincentive to the potential successor(s).

While these are difficult issues to deal with, family businesses must begin to take an informed and strategic approach to these issues. Objectivity in decision making and honesty in discussing various approaches to the business can help start the dialogue of succession planning in a small business.

In the example provided, there were 35 employees in the foreperson occupation in 2013. Out of these, 82 percent (28 employees) are expected to remain in that position next year (based on past levels of activity). The organization can anticipate that 8 percent of the foreperson population (which would be 3 out of the 35 employees in 2013) would be promotable to the role of plant manager. In addition, the past trends show that 10 percent of employees at this level are lost to turnover (representing four employees who are expected to leave the organization before the start of next year). In addition, out of the 110 team leaders (the level below), 11 percent (12 employees) would be eligible for promotion to a foreperson position. Therefore, next year's projected supply of forepersons would be the 28 from this year who are projected to stay in that role plus the 12 team leaders who are projected to be eligible for promotion over the year, for a total supply of 40 forepersons.

In addition to such quantitative data, the skills and capabilities of current employees must be assessed and skills inventories prepared. From this information, replacement charts or summaries and succession plans can be developed.

Forecasting the Supply of External Candidates

Some jobs cannot be filled with internal candidates because no current employees are qualified (such as entry-level jobs) or they are jobs that experience significant growth. In these situations, the firm looks for external candidates. Employer growth is primarily responsible for the number of entry-level openings. A key factor in determining the number of positions that must be filled externally is the effectiveness of the organization's training, development, and career-planning initiatives. If employees are not encouraged to expand their capabilities, they may not be ready to fill vacancies as they arise, and external sources must be tapped.

To project the supply of outside candidates, employers assess general economic conditions, labour market conditions, and occupational market conditions.

General Economic Conditions

General economic conditions refer to the impact of natural fluctuations in economic activity, which impacts all businesses. These include factors such as interest rates, wage rates, rate of inflation, and unemployment rates. In general terms, the lower the rate of unemployment, the smaller the labour supply and the more difficult it will be to recruit employees. It is important to note that unemployment rates vary by occupation and geographic location and can result in an organization's inability to fill certain positions.

Labour Market Conditions

Labour market conditions refer to the demographics of those in the population, such as education levels, age, gender, marital status, and so on. Demographic conditions remain stable and can be forecast with a relatively high degree of accuracy. Fortunately, a wealth of national labour market information is available from Statistics Canada and other government or private sources. Regional chambers of commerce and provincial/local development and planning agencies can be excellent sources of local labour market information.

Statistics Canada
www.statcan.gc.ca

A crucial reality is that a large portion of the population is expected to retire over the next decade, significantly decreasing the size of the labour force. Graduating students (from any level of education) who are just joining the workforce are projected to account for 550 000 new entrants to the labour market a year.[6] In contrast, new immigrants are expected to account for 131 500 new entrants to the labour market a year. An example of a company that has come to realize the benefits of new immigrants as a major source of talent is provided in the Strategic HR box.

STRATEGIC HR

Pumping Up People Supply

Building an aortic pericardial heart valve is no easy task. The intricate medical device, measuring mere millimetres, requires highly specialized skills in its production and engineering. Therefore, there is a very small talent pool available to Burnaby, BC–based Sorin Group Canada. They hire engineers who focus on custom-engineered machinery and equipment, quality assurance experts who ensure that regulations are followed, and production technicians who hand-sew and hand-suture the heart valves.

According to Judith Thompson, senior manager of HR at Sorin Group, "Canada isn't well-known for its biomedical engineers so even when we hire now, to ask for medical device experience, we wouldn't get it. So we hire an engineer or scientist and train on the rest of it." The company has come to realize the benefits, and necessity, of new immigrants as a major source of talent. "Our culture is very diverse. About 90 percent of our staff speak English as a second language, from production people to vice-presidents, so we don't look for Canadian-born, Canadian-educated, Canadian experience because in these economic times that would set us back," she says. "I would never have filled 60 positions last year with those criteria."

Training is extensive, as it takes three or four months before workers, wearing gowns and gloves in a super-clean environment, can make a product that is usable. And even then they can only make a certain number of valves or components per week—it takes another six months to ramp up to regular production, says Thompson.

Sorin supports its employees with in-house English-language training, through a partnership with immigration services, and provides subsidies to foreign-trained engineers who want to pursue an engineering degree in British Columbia.

"We just can't speak enough about the program and the return on investment we've gotten," says Thompson. "We're getting better feedback on problems on the floor because the employees are more comfortable speaking to the researchers and scientists and surgeons who come in on tours. The confidence level of the group has gone up and they are very devoted to the company and the product they make."

Source: Adapted from S. Dobson, "Pumping Up People Supply at Sorin Group Canada to Build Heart Valves," *Canadian HR Reporter*, February 23, 2009. Reprinted by permission of Canadian HR Reporter. © Copyright Thomson Reuters Canada Ltd., (2012) Toronto, Ontario, 1-800-387-5164. Web: www.hrreporter.com

In recent years, the information, communication, and technology sectors (ICT) have suffered from a significant skills shortage, where the demand for ICT workers exceeds the supply. This shortage is expected to continue until 2016.

Occupational Market Conditions

In addition to looking at the overall labour market, organizations also generally want to forecast the availability of potential candidates in specific occupations (engineers, drill press operators, accountants, and so on) for which they will be recruiting. Alberta has recently faced a severe labour shortage of workers in the oil and gas sector.[7] Furthermore, the mining industry, the construction industry, the electricity industry, the manufacturing industry, as well as the non-profit sector are also experiencing significant labour shortages.[8] A shortage of information technology workers is projected to cost the Canadian economy $10 billion per year until it is resolved.[9] Shortages of civil service workers, accountants, lawyers, engineers, meteorologists, funeral directors (to bury the baby boomers), and hospitality industry workers are also expected.[10]

FORECASTING FUTURE HUMAN RESOURCES NEEDS (DEMAND)

RPC

Identifies the organization's staffing needs

A key component of HRP is forecasting the number and type of people needed to meet organizational objectives. Managers should consider several factors when forecasting such requirements. From a practical point of view, the demand for the organization's product or service is paramount. Thus, in a manufacturing firm, sales are projected first. Then the volume of production required to meet these sales requirements is determined. Finally, the staff needed to maintain this volume of output is estimated. In addition to this "basic requirement" for staff, several other factors should be considered, including

1. *projected turnover* as a result of resignations or terminations
2. *quality and nature of employees* in relation to what management sees as the changing needs of the organization
3. *decisions to upgrade* the quality of products or services *or enter into new markets,* which might change the required employee skill mix
4. *planned technological and administrative changes* aimed at increasing productivity and reducing employee head count, such as the installation of new equipment or introduction of a financial incentive plan
5. the *financial resources* available to each department; for example, a budget increase may enable managers to pay higher wages or hire more people; conversely, a budget crunch might result in wage freezes or layoffs

In large organizations, needs forecasting is primarily quantitative in nature and is the responsibility of highly trained specialists. *Quantitative techniques* for determining human resources requirements include trend analysis, ratio analysis, scatter plot analysis, and regression analysis. These are often viewed as numerically or mathematically grounded, and therefore more objective in nature. *Qualitative approaches* to forecasting range from sophisticated analytical models to informal expert opinions about future needs, often involving subjective interpretations or estimates, such as the nominal group technique or the Delphi technique.

Quantitative Approaches

Trend Analysis

trend analysis The study of a firm's past employment levels over a period of years to predict future needs.

Trend analysis involves studying the firm's employment levels over the last three to five years to predict future needs. The purpose is to identify employment trends that might continue into the future, assuming that the past is a strong predictor of the future. Trend analysis is valuable as an initial estimate only, since employment levels rarely depend solely on the passage of time. Other factors (like changes in sales volume and productivity) will also affect future staffing needs.

Ratio Analysis

ratio analysis A forecasting technique for determining future staff needs by using ratios between some causal factor (such as sales volume) and the number of employees needed.

Ratio analysis involves making forecasts based on the ratio between some causal factor (such as sales volume) and the number of employees required (for example, the number of salespeople). Ratio analysis can also be used to help forecast other employee requirements. Like trend analysis, ratio analysis assumes that productivity remains about the same. For example, suppose a salesperson traditionally generates $500 000 in sales and that plans call for increasing the firm's sales by $3 million next year. Then, if the sales revenue–salespeople ratio remains the same, six new salespeople would be required (each of whom produces an extra $500 000 in sales).

The Scatter Plot

scatter plot A graphical method used to help identify the relationship between two variables.

Scatter plots can be used to determine whether two factors—a measure of business activity and staffing levels—are related. If they are, then when the measure of business activity is forecast, HR requirements can also be estimated.

An example to illustrate follows. Legislative changes to the healthcare system require that two 500-bed Canadian hospitals be amalgamated. Both previously had responsibility for acute, chronic, and long-term care. The government's plan is for Hospital A to specialize in acute care while Hospital B assumes responsibility for chronic and long-term care. In general, providing acute care requires staffing with registered nurses (RNs), while chronic and long-term care facilities can be staffed primarily with registered practical nurses (RPNs).

By the end of the calendar year, 200 beds at Hospital A must be converted from chronic and long-term care beds to facilities for acute patients. At the same time, Hospital A's 200 chronic and long-term patients must be transferred to Hospital B. In a joint meeting, the directors of nursing and HR decide that a good starting point in the planning process would be to calculate the relationship between hospital size (in terms of number of acute beds) and the number of RNs required. After placing telephone calls to their counterparts at eight hospitals in larger centres across the country, they obtain the following information:

Size of Hospital (Number of Acute Beds)	Number of Registered Nurses
200	240
300	260
400	470
500	500
600	620
700	660
800	820
900	860

To determine how many RNs would be needed, they use the data obtained to draw the scatter plot shown in **Figure 5.5**, in which hospital size is shown on the horizontal axis and number of RNs is shown on the vertical axis. If the two factors are related, then the points will tend to fall along a straight line, as they do in this case. Carefully drawing a line that minimizes the distances between the line and each of the plotted points (the line of best fit) permits an estimate of the number of nurses required for hospitals of various sizes. Thus, since Hospital A will now have 500 acute-care beds, the estimated number of RNs needed is 500.

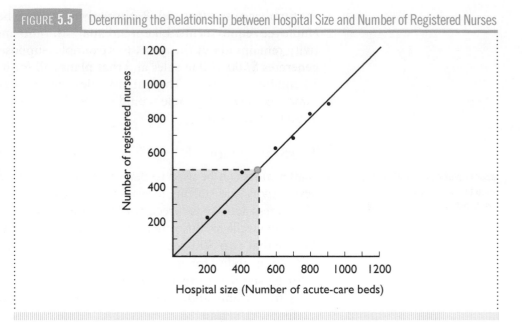

FIGURE **5.5**   Determining the Relationship between Hospital Size and Number of Registered Nurses

Note: After fitting the line, the number of employees needed, given the projected volume, can be extrapolated (projected).

Regression Analysis

regression analysis A statistical technique involving the use of a mathematical formula to project future demands based on an established relationship between an organization's employment level (dependent variable) and some measurable factor of output (independent variable).

Regression analysis is a more sophisticated statistical technique to determine the line of best fit, often involving multiple variables (rather than just two, as per the example above). As a statistical tool used to investigate the effect of one variable on another, the investigator is able to determine the magnitude and direction of the relationship between variables to develop future predictions. In the context of HRP, it involves the use of a mathematical formula to project future demands based on an established relationship between an organization's employment level (dependent variable) and some measurable factors of output (independent variables), such as revenue, sales, or production level.

Qualitative Approaches

In contrast to quantitative approaches, which use statistical formulas, qualitative techniques rely solely on expert judgments. Two approaches used to forecast human resources demand (or supply) are the nominal group and Delphi techniques. Although managerial judgment is central to qualitative forecasting, it also plays a key role when quantitative techniques are used. It's rare that any historical trend, ratio, or relationship will continue unchanged into the future. Judgment is therefore needed to modify the forecast based on anticipated changes.

Nominal Group Technique

nominal group technique A decision-making technique that involves a group of experts meeting face to face. Steps include independent idea generation, clarification and open discussion, and private assessment.

The **nominal group technique** involves a group of experts (such as first-line supervisors and managers) meeting face to face. Although one of its uses is human resources demand forecasting, this technique is used to deal with issues and problems ranging from identifying training needs to determining safety program incentives. The steps involved are as follows:[11]

1. Each member of the group independently writes down his or her ideas on the problem or issue (in this case, estimates of demand).

2. Going around the table, each member then presents one idea. This process continues until all ideas have been presented and recorded, typically on a flipchart or chalkboard. No discussion is permitted during this step.

3. Clarification is then sought, as necessary, followed by group discussion and evaluation.

4. Finally, each member is asked to rank the ideas. This is done independently and in silence.

The advantages of this technique include involvement of key decision makers, a future focus, and the fact that the group discussion involved in the third step can facilitate the exchange of ideas and greater acceptance of results. Drawbacks include subjectivity and the potential for group pressure to lead to a less accurate assessment than could be obtained through other means.

Delphi Technique

Delphi technique A judgmental forecasting method used to arrive at a group decision, typically involving outside experts as well as organizational employees. Ideas are exchanged without face-to-face interaction and feedback is provided and used to fine-tune independent judgments until a consensus is reached.

Although short-term forecasting is generally handled by managers, the **Delphi technique** is useful for long-range forecasting and other strategic planning issues. It typically involves outside experts as well as company employees, based on the premise that outsiders may be able to assess changes in economic, demographic, governmental, technological, and social conditions, and their potential impact more objectively. The Delphi technique involves the following steps:[12]

1. The problem is identified (in this case, estimates of demand) and each group member is requested to submit a potential solution by completing a carefully designed questionnaire. Direct face-to-face contact is not permitted.

2. After each member independently and anonymously completes the initial questionnaire, the results are compiled at a centralized location.

3. Each group member is then given a copy of the results.

4. If there are differences in opinion, each individual uses the feedback from other experts to fine-tune his or her independent assessment.

5. The third and fourth steps are repeated as often as necessary until a consensus is reached.

As with the nominal group technique, the advantages of the Delphi technique include involvement of key decision makers and a future focus; in addition, though, it permits the group to critically evaluate a wider range of views. Drawbacks include the fact that judgments may not efficiently use objective data, the time and costs involved, and the potential difficulty in integrating diverse opinions.

Gap Analysis: Summarizing Human Resources Requirements

The end result of the forecasting process is an estimate of short-term and long-range HR requirements. Long-range plans are general statements of potential staffing needs and may not include specific numbers.

staffing table A pictorial representation of all jobs within the organization, along with the number of current incumbents and future employment requirements (monthly or yearly) for each.

Short-term plans—although still approximations—are more specific and are often depicted in a **staffing table**. As illustrated in **Figure 5.6**, a staffing table is a pictorial representation of all jobs within the organization, along with the number of current incumbents and future employment requirements (monthly or yearly) for each.

FIGURE **5.6**   A Sample Staffing Table

Springbrook Utilities Commission Staffing Table														
Date compiled:_____														
Job Title (As on Job Description)	**Department**	**Anticipated Openings**												
		Total	Jan.	Feb.	Mar.	Apr.	May	June	July	Aug.	Sept.	Oct.	Nov.	Dec.
General Manager	Administration	1					1							
Director of Finance	Administration	1												1
Human Resources Officer	Administration	2	1					1						
Collection Clerk	Administration	1		1										
Groundskeeper	Maintenance	4						1	1					2
Service and Maintenance Technician	Maintenance	5	1			2					2			
Water Utility Engineer	Operations	3									2			1
Apprentice Lineperson	Operations	10	6						4					
Water Meter Technician	Operations	1												1
Engineering Technician	Operations	3			2							1		
Field Technician	Operations	8						8						
Senior Programmer/ Analyst	Systems	2				1				1				
Programmer/Operator	Systems	4		2						1			1	
Systems Operator	Systems	5					2						3	
Customer Service Representative	Sales	8	4					3				1		

PLANNING AND IMPLEMENTING HR PROGRAMS TO BALANCE SUPPLY AND DEMAND

Once the supply and demand of human resources have been estimated, program planning and implementation begin. To successfully fill positions internally, organizations must manage performance and careers. Performance is managed through effectively designing jobs and quality-of-working-life initiatives; establishing performance standards and goals; coaching, measuring, and evaluating; and implementing a suitable reward structure (compensation and benefits).

To manage careers effectively, policies and systems must be established for recruitment, selection and placement (including transfer, promotion, retirement, and termination), and training and development. Policies and systems are also required for job analysis, individual employee assessment, replacement and succession planning, and career tracking, as well as career planning and development.

Specific strategies must be formulated to balance supply and demand considerations. As illustrated in **Figure 5.7**, there are three possible scenarios:

1. projected labour demand matches projected labour supply (equilibrium)
2. projected labour supply exceeds projected demand (surplus)
3. projected labour demand exceeds projected supply (shortage)

FIGURE **5.7** Balancing Supply and Demand Considerations

Conditions	Possible Solutions
Labour Equilibrium (when labour demand equals labour supply)	• Vacancies are filled internally through training, transfers, or promotions or externally through hiring
Labour Surplus (when labour demand is less than labour supply)	• Hiring freeze: reassign current workers to job openings • Attrition: standard employee resignation, retirement, or death • Early retirement buyout programs: entice those close to retirement to retire early with a buyout program, access to full or reduced pension, and/or continuation of benefits • Job sharing, work sharing, or reduced workweek programs: reducing work from the standard full-time workload to a less than full-time work • Layoff: temporary or permanent withdrawal of employment due to business or economic reasons • Termination: permanent separation from the organization because of job performance reasons • Leave of absence: voluntary, temporary withdrawal of employment with guaranteed job upon return
Labour Shortage (when labour demand is greater than labour supply)	• Scheduling overtime hours • Hiring temporary workers • Subcontracting work • External recruitment • Internal promotions or transfers

Labour Equilibrium

Although it is extremely rare to have a labour equilibrium, when the expected supply matches the actual demand organizations do not need to change their course of action. Existing plans to replace outgoing employees should be maintained by promoting or transferring internal members of the organization as well as recruiting external labourers.

Labour Surplus

A labour surplus exists when the internal supply of employees exceeds the organization's demand. Most employers respond initially by instituting a **hiring freeze**, which means that openings are filled by reassigning current employees and no outsiders are hired. The surplus is slowly reduced through **attrition**, which is the normal separation of employees because of resignation, retirement, or death. When employees leave, the ensuing vacancies are not filled and the staffing level decreases gradually without any involuntary terminations. In addition to the time it takes, a major drawback of this approach is that the firm has no control over who stays and who leaves.

Some organizations attempt to accelerate attrition by offering incentives to employees to leave, such as **early retirement buyout programs.** Staffing levels

hiring freeze A common initial response to an employee surplus; openings are filled by reassigning current employees and no outsiders are hired.

attrition The normal separation of employees from an organization because of resignation, retirement, or death.

early retirement buyout programs Strategies used to accelerate attrition that involve offering attractive buyout packages or the opportunity to retire on full pension with an attractive benefits package.

Hints TO ENSURE LEGAL COMPLIANCE

job sharing A strategy that involves dividing the duties of a single position between two or more employees.

work sharing Employees work three or four days a week and receive EI benefits on their non-workday(s).

reduced workweek Employees work fewer hours and receive less pay.

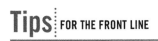

Tips FOR THE FRONT LINE

layoff The temporary or permanent withdrawal of employment to workers for economic or business reasons.

termination Permanent separation from the organization for any reason.

leave of absence Allows those who may be interested in taking time away from work for a variety of reasons (e.g. personal, educational, etc.) to have a set period of time aware from their position without pay, but with a guarantee that their job will be available upon their return.

are reduced and internal job openings created by offering attractive buyout packages or the opportunity to retire on full pension with an attractive benefits package at a relatively early age (often 50 or 55). To be successful, buyouts must be handled carefully. Selection criteria should be established to ensure that key people who cannot be easily replaced do not leave the firm. A drawback of buyouts and early retirement packages is that they often require a great deal of money upfront. Care must also be taken to ensure that early retirement is voluntary, since forced early retirement is a contravention of human rights legislation.

Another strategy used to deal with an employee surplus involves reducing the total number of hours worked. **Job sharing** involves dividing the duties of a single position between two or more employees. Reducing full-time positions to *part-time work* is sometimes more effective, especially if there are peak demand periods. Creating a job-share position or offering part-time employment can be win–win strategies, since layoffs can be avoided. Although the employees involved work fewer hours and thus have less pay, they are still employed, and they may enjoy having more free time at their disposal; the organization benefits by retaining good employees.

Twenty-five years ago, the federal government introduced a **work-sharing** scheme, a layoff-avoidance strategy that involves employees working three or four days a week and receiving employment insurance (EI) benefits on their non-workday(s). The program was temporarily extended to provide 52 weeks of benefits from February 1, 2009, to April 3, 2010, during the recent economic slowdown.[13] Similar to work sharing, but without a formal arrangement with the government regarding EI benefits, is a **reduced workweek**. Employees simply work fewer hours and receive less pay. The organization retains a skilled workforce, lessens the financial and emotional impact of a full layoff, and reduces production costs. One potential drawback is that it is sometimes difficult to predict in advance, with any degree of accuracy, how many hours of work should be scheduled each week.

Another strategy used to manage employee surplus is a **layoff**; the temporary withdrawal of employment to workers for economic or business reasons. Layoffs may be short in duration (for example, when a plant closes for brief periods in order to adjust inventory levels or to retool for a new product line), but can last months or even years at a time if the organization is negatively affected by a major change in the business cycle. However, layoffs are often permanent in nature. Layoffs are not easy for managers, who have to reduce the number of employees to the required level, or for workers, but are usually necessary to ultimately reduce the impact of the organization's economic downturn. Layoffs and terminations are discussed in depth in Chapter 15.

Termination is a broad term that encompasses permanent separation of the worker from the organization. Termination is often triggered by a management decision to sever the employment relationship due to reasons that are related to job performance. Purging poorly performing employees is often an ongoing activity in any organization, regardless of any projected labour surpluses; however, the rate of termination may increase if there is a projected surplus of labour.

The option of a voluntary **leave of absence** can also be used if the labour surplus is temporary in nature. A leave of absence allows those who may be interested in time off for personal, educational, or other reasons to have a set period of time away from their position, with a guarantee that their job will be available upon their return. A leave of absence can be paid or unpaid, but often seniority and benefits remain intact. Terms of the leave and expected return must be clearly outlined, including potential conflicts of interest and mutual expectations from each party.

Easing the Pain of Labour Surplus Management

survivor syndrome A range of negative emotions experienced by employees remaining after a major restructuring initiative, which can include feelings of betrayal or violation, guilt, or detachment, and can result in stress symptoms, including depression, increased errors, and reduced performance.

Although restructuring initiatives, ranging from layoffs to mergers and acquisitions, were prevalent in the last two decades, organizations that engaged in layoffs were not consistently achieving the desired goals or financial benefits of their decisions. In a study of 6418 workforce reductions in Fortune 500 firms over 18 years, researchers found no consistent evidence that downsizing led to improved financial performance.[14]

A primary reason for this is the high cost associated with **survivor syndrome**, a range of emotions that can include feelings of betrayal or violation, guilt, or detachment. The remaining employees, anxious about the next round of terminations, often suffer stress symptoms, including depression, increased errors, and reduced performance.

An Ethical Dilemma

How much time, effort, and money should firms devote to helping "surviving" employees deal with downsizing? With mergers and acquisitions?

To ease the financial burden of layoffs, some organizations offer **supplemental unemployment benefits (SUBs)**, which are a top-up of EI benefits to bring income levels of temporarily laid-off workers closer to their regular, on-the-job pay. SUB programs are generally negotiated through collective bargaining between the employee and employer. Benefits are payable until the pool of funds set aside has been exhausted.

supplemental unemployment benefits (SUBs) A top-up of EI benefits to bring income levels closer to what an employee would receive if on the job.

severance package A lump-sum payment, continuation of benefits for a specified period of time, and other benefits that are provided to employees who are being terminated.

A **severance package** is typically provided when employees are being terminated through no fault of their own in order to avoid wrongful dismissal lawsuits. Severance pay is legally required in certain situations, such as mass layoffs.

In addition to pay, severance packages often include the continuation of benefits for a specified period. In determining the appropriate package, employers should take salary, years of service, the employee's age, and his or her likelihood of obtaining another job into consideration.[15] Executives may be protected by a *golden parachute clause* in their contract of employment, which is a guarantee by the employer to pay specified compensation and benefits in the case of termination because of downsizing or restructuring. To soften the blow of termination, *outplacement assistance,* generally offered by an outside agency, can assist affected employees in finding employment elsewhere. The issues and processes related to managing a labour surplus legally and fairly are provided in significant detail in Chapter 15 (managing employee terminations).

Labour Shortage

A labour shortage exists when the internal supply of human resources cannot meet the organization's needs. Scheduling overtime hours is often the initial response. Employers may also subcontract work on a temporary or permanent basis. Another short-term solution is to hire temporary employees.

As vacancies are created within the firm, opportunities are generally provided for employee transfers and promotions, which necessitate performance management, training (and retraining), and career development. Of course, internal movement does not eliminate a shortage, which means that recruitment will be required. It is hoped, though, that resultant vacancies will be for entry-level jobs, which can be filled more easily externally.

Internal Solutions to a Labour Shortage

transfer Movement of an employee from one job to another that is relatively equal in pay, responsibility, or organizational level.

A **transfer** involves a lateral movement from one job to another that is relatively equal in pay, responsibility, or organizational level. Transfers can lead to more effective use of human resources, broaden an employee's skills and perspectives, and help make him or her a better candidate for future promotions. Transfers also offer additional technical and interpersonal challenges and increased variety of work, which may enhance job satisfaction and motivation.

promotion Movement of an employee from one job to another that is higher in pay, responsibility, or organizational level, usually based on merit, seniority, or a combination of both.

A **promotion** involves the movement of an employee from one job to another that is higher in pay, responsibility, or organizational level. Such a move may be based on merit, seniority, or a combination of both. Merit-based promotions are awarded in recognition of a person's outstanding performance in his or her present job or as an assessment of his or her future potential.

A focus on employee retention initiatives can also mitigate potential labour shortages. The HRP process often highlights challenges the organization is having with turnover or retention at specific levels. This may warrant further investigation into why employees are leaving and which types of employees are leaving. Rather than a broad focus on retention, organizations can benefit from focusing on retaining key employees or employees with strong job performance. A discussion of career planning to assist with internal solutions regarding a labour shortage are provided in Chapters 9 and 10 (career development and performance management).

External Solutions to a Labour Shortage

External solutions to managing a labour shortage involve recruiting the right quality and quantity of talent needed in an organization to meet the long-term goals and strategy of the company. The next chapter (Chapter 6) extensively discusses the recruitment process, methods of recruitment, and strategies of determining recruitment targets. Options for recruitment and selection related to managing a labour shortage are provided in Chapters 6 and 7 (recruitment and selection).

Chapter SUMMARY

1. Human resources planning (HRP) is the process of reviewing HR requirements to ensure that the organization has the required number of employees with the necessary skills to meet its strategic goals. Forecasting future labour demand and supply is a critical element of the strategic planning process. HRP and strategic planning become effective when a reciprocal and interdependent relationship exists between them.

2. Four quantitative techniques for forecasting future HR demand are trend analysis, ratio analysis, scatter plots, and regression analysis. Two qualitative techniques used to forecast demand are the nominal group technique and the Delphi technique.

3. Four strategies used to forecast internal HR supply are Markov analysis, skills and management inventories, replacement charts and summaries, and succession planning. Forecasting external HR supply requires an assessment of general economic conditions,

labour market conditions, and occupational labour conditions.

4. Strategies to manage a labour surplus include a hiring freeze; downsizing through attrition; early retirement buyout programs; reduced hours through job sharing, part-time work, work sharing, or reduced workweeks; leaves of absence; and termination of employment.

5. Strategies to manage a human resources shortage include internal and external solutions, such as hiring employees, employee transfers and promotions, and retention programs.

MyManagementLab

Visit MyManagementLab to access a personalized Study Plan and additional study tools for this chapter.

Key TERMS

attrition *(p. 135)*
Delphi technique *(p. 133)*
early retirement buyout programs *(p. 135)*
environment scanning *(p. 122)*
hiring freeze *(p. 135)*
human resources planning (HRP) *(p. 120)*
job sharing *(p. 136)*
layoff *(p. 136)*
leave of absence *(p. 136)*
management inventories *(p. 124)*
Markov analysis *(p. 126)*
nominal group technique *(p. 132)*
promotion *(p. 138)*
ratio analysis *(p. 130)*
reduced workweek *(p. 136)*

regression analysis *(p. 132)*
replacement charts *(p. 124)*
replacement summaries *(p. 125)*
scatter plot *(p. 131)*
severance package *(p. 137)*
skills inventories *(p. 124)*
staffing table *(p. 133)*
succession planning *(p. 126)*
supplemental unemployment benefits (SUBs) *(p. 137)*
survivor syndrome *(p. 137)*
termination *(p. 136)*
transfer *(p. 138)*
trend analysis *(p. 130)*
work sharing *(p. 136)*

Review and Discussion QUESTIONS

1. Describe the costs associated with a lack of or inadequate HRP.
2. After analyzing the human resources implications of an organization's strategic plans, what are the three subsequent processes involved in HRP?
3. Discuss the pros and cons of five of the approaches to dealing with a labour surplus from both the organization and employee perspective.
4. Differentiate between replacement charts and succession plans, and explain in which situation each is preferred.
5. Discuss various methods of easing the burden of a layoff or termination.

Critical Thinking QUESTIONS

1. A number of quantitative and qualitative techniques for forecasting human resources demand were discussed in this chapter. Working in groups, identify which strategies would be most appropriate for (a) small versus large companies, (b) industries undergoing rapid change, and (c) businesses/industries in which there are seasonal variations in HR requirements.
2. Suppose that it has just been projected that, because of a number of technological innovations, your firm will need 20 percent fewer clerical employees within the next three years. There are currently 122 clerical positions in the company, split between three departments of equal size. Retirements at this level are projected to be roughly 2 percent per year. Annual voluntary turnover and involuntary turnover for Department A is 2 percent and 5 percent, respectively; Department B is 3 percent and 3 percent; and Department C is 5 percent and 0 percent. Do you project a labour shortage or surplus in the next three years for clerical positions? What actions would you take in this situation?
3. Suppose that you are the HR manager at a firm at which a hiring freeze has just been declared. The plan is to downsize through attrition. What steps would you take to ensure that you reap the advantages of this strategy while minimizing the disadvantages?

Experiential EXERCISES

1. Develop a realistic, hypothetical staffing table for a department or organization that you are familiar with.
2. Contact the HR manager at a firm in your area and find out whether the firm uses any of the following: (a) skills/management inventories, (b) replacement charts or summaries, and (c) a succession plan. Prepare a brief summary of the information gathered. Once you have completed these tasks, form a group with several of your classmates. Share your findings with the group members. Were there similarities across firms? Did company size seem to make a difference in terms of strategies used for forecasting the supply of internal candidates? Can you identify any other factors that seem to play a role in the choice of forecasting techniques used?

3. This assignment requires working in teams of five or six. Half of each team is to assume the role of management at a firm that is about to undergo major downsizing. The other half of each team is to assume the role of employees—some who will be affected and others who will remain. Each management team is paired with an employee team and must prepare and role-play a realistic meeting of the two parties. Managers should work toward minimizing the negative impact on those who will be affected as well as on those who will remain. Individuals in employee roles should envision what their thoughts and feelings would be (if they have never actually been in this situation, that is) and to portray them as realistically as possible.

4. Form teams of three or four people. Your instructor will assign you a position on the following statement: "All employees in an organization should be aware of their personal standing with respect to replacement charts and succession planning." Formulate your arguments to support your assigned position and then debate the statement with an opposing team, as instructed.

5. With a partner, research "survivor syndrome" and what specific companies have done to successfully mitigate this response and regain full employee commitment. Prepare a brief (two to three minute, maximum) oral presentation to share what you have learned.

Running CASE

Running Case: LearnInMotion.com

To Plan or Not to Plan?

One aspect of HRM that Jennifer and Pierre studied at university was HR planning. Their professor emphasized its importance, especially for large organizations. Although LearnInMotion.com as certainly small at this point, with only a few employees, they were planning to expand, and it seemed that detailed HRP should be an essential part of their plans. There was no succession plan—after all, they have just started the business! But they both knew that the market for technology workers, in general, was competitive. Jennifer and Pierre have asked for some assistance with the following questions.

QUESTIONS

1 What is human resources planning and how will it help LearnInMotion's strategic plans?

2 Describe the steps in the human resources planning process and discuss the important elements within each that will benefit LearnInMotion.

Case INCIDENT

How to Downsize Successfully While Using HRP Fundamentals

A successful franchise owner of a prestigious sporting goods chain is feeling the effects of technology, with more and more online sales and less and less customers in the shops. Locally there are three stores, and typically each store needs the following positions staffed for optimum profitability and success: a store manager, an assistant manager, five department managers, and 20 customer service representatives, averaging $1 200 000 in annual revenue. However, there has been a trend of 20 percent sales decline in stores, with an increase of 30 percent sales online (last year the online revenue stream was $300 000). The franchise owner was able to handle all of the online sales with a team of five full-time remote workers (working from home) last year.

The owner wants each store to maintain their productivity, which he measures as the revenue per employee. He also thinks that there is potential to grow the online business.

Please help the owner by answering the following questions.

QUESTIONS

1   Using your HR planning expertise, forecast the demand of labour in the stores and the online environment over the next three years.

2   Assuming an annual 15 percent turnover level of in-store workers and a 30 percent turnover level of online-focused employees, determine HR supply estimates over the next three years.

3   Do you forecast a labour shortage or surplus? Develop a clear plan to help address the forecast labour shortage or surplus.

MyManagementLab

Visit MyManagementLab to access a personalized Study Plan and additional study tools for this chapter.

 To view the CBC videos, read a summary, and answer discussion questions, go to MyManagementLab

Recruitment

LEARNING OUTCOMES

AFTER STUDYING THIS CHAPTER, YOU SHOULD BE ABLE TO

DEFINE recruitment and discuss the increasing use of employer branding.

EXPLAIN the recruitment process.

ANALYZE the role of job posting, human resources records, and skills inventories in recruiting from within.

IDENTIFY at least 10 methods used for external recruitment

EXPLAIN two strategies used to recruit non-permanent staff.

DISCUSS strategies for recruiting a more diverse workforce.

EXPLAIN the importance of application forms.

REQUIRED PROFESSIONAL CAPABILITIES (RPC)

- Develops, implements, and monitors processes for attracting qualified candidates

- Evaluates recruiting effectiveness

- Identifies the potential sources of internal and external qualified candidates

- Evaluates the relevance of alternatives to recruitment (developing, outsourcing, contingent workers, agencies, and so on)

- Implements and monitors processes for attracting qualified candidates

THE STRATEGIC IMPORTANCE OF RECRUITMENT

recruitment The process of searching out and attracting qualified job applicants, which begins with the identification of a position that requires staffing and is completed when résumés or completed application forms are received from an adequate number of applicants.

Human talent is beginning to be referred to as the world's most sought-after commodity.[1] The quality of an organization's human resources begins with a strategic perspective in the management of recruitment. **Recruitment** is the process of searching out and attracting qualified job applicants. It begins with the identification of a position that requires staffing and is completed when résumés or completed application forms are received from an adequate number of applicants. A Watson Wyatt study found that organizations with superior recruiting practices financially outperform those with less effective programs and that successful recruiting is a strong indicator of higher shareholder value.[2]

Authority for recruitment is generally delegated to HR staff members, except in small businesses where line managers usually recruit their own staff. In large organizations where recruiting is done on a continual basis, the HR team typically includes specialists, known as **recruiters**, whose job is to find and attract qualified applicants. Recruiters are becoming increasingly critical to achieving an organization's strategic objectives as competition for the employees necessary for strategy implementation increases due to the growing talent shortage.

recruiter A specialist in recruitment whose job is to find and attract capable candidates.

Recruiters Café
www.recruiterscafe.com

Great Place to Work Institute Canada
www.greatplacetowork.ca

Organizations are increasingly seeking the high profile given to an "employer of choice," such as those included in lists such as Mediacorp's "Top 100 Employers," the Hewitt Associates "50 Best Employers," and the *Financial Post*'s "Ten Best Companies to Work for." Employers such as Scotiabank, Purolator, Tim Hortons, and many others are also applying the marketing concept of branding to strengthen their recruitment activities.[3]

Employer Branding

Gabriel Bouchard, founder of the Monster Canada online job board, says, "In an increasingly tight job market, employers must remain permanently visible to potential employees, establishing and maintaining relationships with potential candidates before they even begin pursuing a new job. This is particularly crucial when it comes to hard-to-fill or mission-critical positions."[4] Proactive employers are trying to obtain a competitive advantage in recruitment by establishing themselves as employers of choice through employer branding. The purpose of an employer brand is to attract people to apply to work at the organization and to earn the loyalty of current employees.

employer branding The image or impression of an organization as an employer based on the benefits of being employed by the organization.

Employer branding is the image or impression of an organization as an employer based on the perceived benefits of being employed by the organization. It is the experience of an employee when working for a company, based on feelings, emotions, senses, realities, and benefits (functional benefits such as personal development, economic benefits such as monetary rewards, and psychological benefits such as feelings of purpose, belonging, and recognition). It is essentially a promise made to employees and their perception of how well that promise is delivered.[5]

Employer branding is particularly important during the recruitment process, not just for applicants who are eventually hired but also for those not hired who are out in the marketplace communicating their experience as an applicant to other job seekers.[6] Inconsiderate recruiting practices can be brand suicide for companies. Branding includes the experiences a candidate goes through while interacting with a company throughout the recruitment process, including[7]

- what candidates experience when they go to the company's website,
- whether HR sends an acknowledgement letter or email thanking each candidate who sends in a résumé,
- how candidates are greeted by the receptionist when they make initial contact by phone or in person, and
- whether the HR person who interviews candidates is a good spokesperson who can articulate the organization's values and culture.

RPC

Implements and monitors processes for attracting qualified candidates

Employer branding involves three steps.[8] Step 1 is to define the target audience, where to find them, and what they want from an employer. The target group may be one of the four generations in today's workforce, the underemployed, or the four employment equity groups. McDonald's may target potential Generation Y employees who are seeking career development. At Southland Transportation, a school bus service provider in Alberta, the target audience is retired police officers, recent retirees, and parents with young children.[9]

Step 2 is to develop the employee value proposition—the specific reasons why the organization is a unique place to work and a more attractive employer for the target audience compared to other organizations. The use of concrete facts, programs, policies, survey results, and information will clearly portray the organization as an employer of choice. It is also important to ensure that current managers are prepared to deliver the value proposition by guiding and mentoring employees.[10] Loblaw and Fairmont Hotels offer potential employees the opportunity to participate in "green" environmental initiatives.[11] At PCL Construction of Alberta, 80 percent of employees own stock in the company.[12]

Step 3 is to communicate the brand by incorporating the value proposition into all recruitment efforts. The communication should reinforce and remind current and potential employees of promises in the employee value proposition and of the organization's ability to deliver it through their managers. An integrated marketing approach to internal and external communication should use various channels, such as television, radio, print, websites, social media, and so on.[13]

McDonald's Recruiting
www.worksforme.ca/mcd

McDonald's used focus groups to identify the interests of one of their target markets for recruitment (young people). The results of the focus groups suggest that this target market is interested in balancing their own freedom and goals with making money. As a result, McDonald's offered flexible hours, uniform choices, scholarships, and discount cards to support its value proposition slogan "We take care of our employees." This value proposition was also communicated through television ads and a recruiting website. Following the introduction of this branding initiative, McDonald's saw a surge in the number of young people who recognized McDonald's as a great place to work.[14] With the right branding strategy, job seekers line up to apply for jobs. A successful brand results in job seekers saying "I'd like to work there."[15]

THE RECRUITMENT PROCESS

RPC

Develops, implements, and monitors processes for attracting qualified candidates

As illustrated in **Figure 6.1**, the recruitment process has a number of steps:

1. Job openings are identified through HR planning (based on the organization's strategic plan) or manager request. HR plans play a vital role in the identification process, because they indicate present and future openings and specify which should be filled internally and which externally. Openings do arise unexpectedly, though, when managers request that a new employee be hired.

2. The job requirements are determined. This step involves reviewing the job description and the job specifications and updating them, if necessary. Chapter 4 included a discussion of job analysis, which outlined how to collect and interpret job descriptions and specifications.

3. Appropriate recruiting source(s) and method(s) are chosen. The major decision here is whether to start with internal or external recruiting. There is no single, best recruiting technique, and the most appropriate for any given position depends on a number of factors, which will be discussed in the next section.

4. A pool of qualified recruits is generated. The requirements of employment equity legislation (if any) and the organization's diversity goals should be reflected in the applicant pool.

A recruiter must be aware of constraints affecting the recruitment process to be successful in his or her job. Constraints arise from organizational policies, such as promote-from-within policies, which mean that a recruiter cannot start recruiting externally for a specified period, even if he or she is aware that there are no suitable internal candidates. Constraints also arise from compensation policies, since they influence the attractiveness of the job to potential applicants. If there is an employment equity plan, it will specify goals for increasing recruitment from the designated groups. Monetary and non-monetary inducements offered by competitors impose a constraint, since recruiters must try to meet the prevailing standards of the company or use alternative inducements.

Perhaps the biggest constraint on recruiting activity at this time is the current labour shortage, which makes recruiting more difficult. One survey by Hewitt Associates found that recruitment practices will have to undergo "enormous change" over the next several years.[16] Some initiatives are already underway to attract foreign recruits, as explained in the Global HRM box.

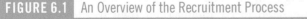

FIGURE 6.1 An Overview of the Recruitment Process

GLOBAL HRM

Recruiting European Candidates

An often overlooked option for managing the talent shortage is to recruit more candidates from Europe. Canada has strong ties to the European Union, and Europeans have a lot to offer the Canadian marketplace, including global business perspectives.

"An important value-added Europeans can bring to the Canadian market is their ability to interact and negotiate within a multicultural environment and context. This aptitude strengthens Canadian companies' ability to function better in Canada's increasingly multicultural environment," says David Delfini, head of business development at Volareweb/Alitalia.

For Europeans, Canada offers an opportunity for advancement they might not get at home. In Italy, for example, it is almost impossible to move up the ranks if you haven't dedicated at least 20 years to the company. A 2007 study by BlueSteps.com polled over 933 senior executives worldwide and revealed that traditional values about job tenure and loyalty remain well-ingrained with executives. The research also highlighted that 76 percent of European executives cited a lack of career advancement opportunities as the number one motivator to leave a company.

The borders have changed with the crisis of retiring Baby Boomers and impending talent shortages.

Countries are opening their doors. The world is building broader intellectual capacity and perspectives and better preparation for the global market. Europeans can offer Canadian organizations needed experience and a global perspective in a tightening labour market.

One company pursuing this strategy is EBA Engineering Consultants of Edmonton. They have successfully recruited people in the UK to relocate to western Canada by using a high-tech/high-touch promotional tool that communicates EBA's employment brand in a powerful way. A leather-bound album features stunning photographs of western Canada, testimonials from EBA employees who had been previously recruited from overseas, and a USB key that links candidates to a comprehensive website. At the back of the album, a leather luggage tag is mounted as a call to action, inviting candidates to pack their bags and join the EBA family in Canada.

Source: Adapted from A. Mirza, "Recruiting International Candidates," *HR Professional* (December 2008/January 2009), p. 27; and from K. Peters, "Public Image Ltd.," *HR Professional* (December 2007/January 2008), pp. 24–30. Reprinted with permission of *HR Professional.*

DEVELOPING AND USING APPLICATION FORMS

For most employers, completion of an application form is the last step in the recruitment process. An application form provides an efficient means of collecting verifiable historical data from each candidate in a standardized format; it usually includes information about education, prior work history, and other job-related skills.

A completed application form can provide the recruiter with information on the applicant's education and experience, a brief overview of the applicant's career progress and growth, and information that can be used to predict whether or not the candidate will succeed on the job. Even when detailed résumés have been submitted, most firms also request that a standardized company application form be completed. There are many reasons for this practice:

• Candidate comparison is facilitated because information is collected in a uniform manner.

- The information that the company requires is specifically requested, rather than just what the candidate wants to reveal.
- Candidates are typically asked to complete an application form while on the company premises, and thus it is a sample of the candidate's own work (obtaining assistance with résumés is common, given that many job boards offer online résumé building options).
- Application forms typically ask the candidate to provide written authorization for reference checking.
- Candidates are asked to acknowledge that the information provided is true and accurate, which protects the company from applicants who falsify their credentials.
- Many application forms today have an optional section regarding designated group member status. An example is provided in Figure 6.2. The data collected are used for employment equity tracking purposes.

biographical information blank (BIB) A detailed job application form requesting biographical data found to be predictive of success on the job, pertaining to background, experiences, and preferences. Responses are scored.

One type of application form that can be used to predict performance is a **biographical information blank (BIB)**, also known as a biodata form. Essentially, it is a more detailed version of an application form, focusing on biographical data found to be predictive of job success. Questions relating to age, gender, race, or other grounds prohibited under human rights legislation cannot be used. Candidates respond to a series of questions about their background, experiences, and preferences, including willingness to travel and leisure activities. Because biographical questions rarely have right or wrong answers, BIBs are difficult to fake. The development of a BIB requires that the items that are valid predictors of job success be identified and that scores be established for different responses to these items. By totalling the scores for each item, it is possible to obtain a composite score for each applicant.

There has been a shift in the format of the forms from the traditional pen and paper methods to online applications given the exposure to the World Wide Web and the advances in human resource information systems. **Figure 6.3** provides an example of an online application used by Canadian Tire to collect the same information that was traditionally collected in pen and paper format. Online applications significantly reduce the risk of lost applications, increase the exposure level of the job ad (global reach), and can reduce the likelihood of biases associated with other forms of face-to-face recruitment.

However, online application forms can result in a large number of applicants (for example, Google receives over 3000 applications per day[18]), therefore putting pressure on staff to manage the high volume of applicants. HRIS can be extremely useful here in automatically coding and storing applications, allowing HR professionals to search through the applications using specified search functions. The HRIS can also pre-screen applicants against predetermined criteria, providing an automated shortlist of qualified candidates. This significantly reduces the need for HR staff to screen résumés, but increases the importance of the content of the résumés and the validity of the pre-screening criteria. Due to the convenience and ubiquity of web browsers, application forms are increasingly being used online to allow applicants to build a profile and submit information directly or indirectly to potential employers. This offers around-the-clock convenience since applicants can create and submit applications or résumés on an ongoing and continuous real-time basis.

FIGURE **6.2** Self-Identification for Employment Equity Purposes

---

Employee Self-Identification Form

(Confidential when completed)

- This form is designed to collect information on the composition of the Public Service workforce to comply with legislation on employment equity and to facilitate the planning and implementation of employment equity activities. Your response is **voluntary** and you may identify in more than one designated group.

- The information you provide will be used in compiling statistics on employment equity in the federal Public Service. With your consent (see Box E), it may also be used by the employment equity coordinator of your department for human resource management purposes. This includes referral for training and developmental assignments and, in the case of persons with disabilities, facilitating appropriate accommodation in the workplace.

- Employment equity information will be retained in the Employment Equity Data Bank (EEDB) of the Treasury Board Secretariat and its confidentiality is protected under the *Privacy Act*. You have the right to review and correct information about yourself and can be assured that it will not be used for unauthorized purposes.

Step 1: Complete boxes A to E. In boxes B, C and D, refer to the definitions provided.

Step 2: Sign and date the form and return it to your department's EE coordinator.

Thank you for your cooperation.

TBS/PPB 300-02432
TBS/SCT 330-78 (Rev. 1999–02)

A.

Family Name	Given Name and Initial

Department or Agency/Branch

( )	
Telephone # (office)	Personal Record Identifier (PRI)

○ Female   ○ Male

B. A person with a disability . . . (i) . . . has a long-term or recurring physical, mental, sensory, psychiatric, or learning impairment and

1. considers himself/herself to be disadvantaged in employment by reason of that impairement, or,

2. believes that an employer or potential employer is likely to consider him/her to be disadvantaged in employment by reason of that impairment,
   and includes persons whose functional limitations owing to their impairment have been accommodated in their current job or workplace.

ARE YOU A PERSON WITH A DISABILITY?

○ No

○ Yes, check all that apply

11 ○ **Co-ordination or dexterity** *(difficulty using hands or arms, for example, grasping or handling a stapler or using a keyboard)*

12 ○ **Mobility** *(difficulty moving around, for example, from one office to another or up and down stairs)*

16 ○ **Blind or visual impairment** *(unable to see or difficulty seeing)*

19 ○ **Deaf or hard of hearing** *(unable to hear or difficulty hearing)*

13 ○ **Speech impairment** *(unable to speak or difficulty speaking and being understood)*

continued

FIGURE **6.2**   *(Continued)*

23 ○ **Other disability** *(including learning disabilities, developmental disabilities and all other types of disabilities)*

(Please specify) _____

C. An Aboriginal person . . .
. . . is a North American Indian or a member of a First Nation or who is Métis or Inuit. North American Indians or members of a First Nation include status, treaty or registered Indians, as well as non-status and non-registered Indians.

ARE YOU AN ABORIGINAL PERSON

○ No

○ Yes, check the appropriate circle

03 ○ North American Indian/First Nation

02 ○ Métis

01 ○ Inuit

D. A person in a visible minority . . .
. . . in Canada is someone (other than an Aboriginal person as defined in C above) who is non-white in colour/race, regardless of place of birth.

ARE YOU IN A VISIBLE MINORITY GROUP

○ No

○ Yes, check the circle which best describes your visible minority group or origin

41 ○ Black

45 ○ Chinese

51 ○ Filipino

47 ○ Japanese

48 ○ Korean

56 ○ South Asian/East Indian *(including Indian from India; Bangladeshi; Pakistani; East Indian from Guyana; Trinidad; East Africa; etc.)*

58 ○ Southeast Asian *(including Burmese; Cambodian; Laotian; Thai; Vietnamese; etc.)*

57 ○ Non-White West Asian, North African and Arab *(including Egyptian; Libyan; Lebanese; Iranian; etc.)*

42 ○ Non-White Latin American *(including indigenous persons from Central and South America, etc.)*

44 ○ Persons of Mixed Origin *(with one parent in one of the visible minority groups listed above)*

59 ○ Other Visible Minority Group

(Please specify) _____

E. 99○ The information in this form may be used for human resources management

_____   _____
Signature   Date (DD/MM/YY)

Source: Employee Self-Identification Form, www.tbs-sct.gc.ca/gui/iden2-eng.asp, Treasury Board of Canada Secretariat, 2002. Reproduced with the permission of the Minister of Public Works and Government Services Canada, 2012.

| FIGURE **6.3** | Sample Online Application Form—Canadian Tire |

Source: Reproduced with permission of Canadian Tire.

RECRUITING FROM WITHIN THE ORGANIZATION

Although recruiting often brings job boards and employment agencies to mind, current employees are generally the largest source of recruits. Filling open positions with inside candidates has several advantages. According to human capital theory, the accumulation of firm-specific knowledge and experience involves a joint investment by both the employee and employer, therefore, both parties benefit from maintaining a long-term relationship. Employees see that competence is rewarded, thus enhancing their commitment, morale, and performance. Having already been with the firm for some time, insiders may be more committed to the company's goals and less likely to leave. Managers (as agents of the organization) are provided with a longer-term perspective when making business decisions. It is generally safer to promote from within, because the firm is likely to have a more accurate assessment of the person's skills and performance level than would otherwise be the case. In addition, inside candidates require less orientation than outsiders do.

Recruiting from within also has a number of drawbacks. Employees who apply for jobs and don't get them may become discontented (informing unsuccessful applicants as to why they were rejected and what remedial action they might take to be more successful in the future is thus essential).[19] Managers may be required to post all job openings and interview all inside candidates, even when they already know whom they want to hire, thus wasting considerable time and creating false hope on the part of those employees not genuinely being considered. Employees may be less satisfied with and accepting of a boss appointed from within their own ranks than they would be with a newcomer; it is sometimes difficult for a newly chosen leader to adjust to no longer being "one of the gang."[20] There is also a possibility of "inbreeding." When an entire management team has been brought up through the ranks, they may have a tendency to make decisions "by the book" and to maintain the status quo when a new and innovative direction is needed.

Internal Recruitment Methods

Recruiting from within can be accomplished by using job posting, human resources records, and skills inventories.

Job Posting

job posting The process of notifying current employees about vacant positions.

Job posting is a process of notifying current employees about vacant positions. Most companies now use computerized job-posting systems, where information about job vacancies can be found on the company's intranet. This involves a notice outlining the job title, duties (as listed in the job description), qualifications (taken from the job specification), hours of work, pay range, posting date, and closing date, as shown in **Figure 6.4**. Not all firms use intranets. Some post jobs on bulletin boards or in employee publications. As illustrated in **Figure 6.5**, there are advantages and disadvantages to using job postings to facilitate the transfer and promotion of qualified internal candidates.

An Ethical Dilemma

Suppose a manager has already made up his or her mind about who will be selected for an internal position. But an internal job posting and subsequent interviews have shown another equally qualified candidate. Who should be offered the position?

Human Resources Records

Human resources records are often consulted to ensure that qualified individuals are notified, in person, of vacant positions. An examination of employee files, including résumés and application forms, may uncover employees who are working in jobs below their education or skill levels, people who already have the requisite KSAs, or individuals with the potential to move into the vacant position if given some additional training.

Skills Inventories

Skills inventories are an even better recruitment tool. Although such inventories may be used instead of job postings, they are more often used as a supplement. Whether computerized or manual, referring to such inventories ensures that qualified internal candidates are identified and considered for transfer or promotion when opportunities arise.

Limitations of Recruiting from Within

It is rarely possible to fill all non-entry-level jobs with current employees. Middle- and upper-level jobs may be vacated unexpectedly, with no internal replacements yet qualified or ready for transfer or promotion; or the jobs may require such specialized training and experience that there are no potential internal replacements. Even in firms with a policy of promoting from within, potential external candidates are increasingly being considered to meet strategic objectives. Hiring someone from outside may be preferable in order to acquire the latest knowledge and expertise or to gain new ideas and revitalize the department or organization.[21]

FIGURE **6.4** Sample Job Posting: University of Alberta

Faculty of Physical Education and Recreation—Academic Programs

Competition No.: A103814421

Closing Date: June 3, 2011

The Academic Programs area of the Faculty of Physical Education and Recreation oversees and manages the academic programs of approximately 920 undergraduates in four undergraduate degree programs and 135 graduate students at the master's and doctoral level. The goal of this unit is to provide an optimal learning experience for our students. It is also responsible for the appointment and management of Sessional Instructors for the Fall and Winter courses and a combination of Graduate Teaching Assistants (GTAs) and Sessional staff for the Spring and Summer courses.

In order to aid in the overall strategic direction and planning of this unit, as well as undertaking necessary day-to-day service functions, this unit is seeking an Academic Programs Administrative Professional Officer (APO) who will lead important administrative aspects in a collegial working environment. Out of the 11 continuing staff members who work in the Academic Programs Unit, this position is one of two that reports directly to the Vice Dean. The APO is accountable for establishing/coordinating an efficient and effective administrative support system for the teaching and service functions of the Academic Programs Unit.

Responsibilities:

- Identifies, recruits, conducts preliminary interviews and makes final decision on appointments regarding the hiring of Sessional Academic Staff (Contract Academic Staff: Teaching (CAST)); prepares all data for the production of the CAST contracts for Fall and Winter terms and advises the Vice Dean on these appointments
- Manages and supervises the Faculty's Sessional teaching instructors including preparing and monitoring the Faculty's CAST budget
- Responsible for all human resource functions for seven full-time support staff including supervision and performance evaluations
- Responsible for the administrative support of the Faculty Evaluation Committee (FEC) process within the Faculty; for this activity the position is responsible to the Dean, as Chair of FEC within the Faculty
- Responsible for the preparation of the annual Academic Programs operating budget
- Advises the Academic Planning Committee on the relevant Faculty and University policies in all areas of operation
- Contributes to the development of policies and procedures for the Academic Unit and represents the best interests of the unit through membership on Faculty ad hoc task forces, committees, etc.
- Responsible for the Faculty of Physical Education and Recreation's section of the UofA calendar
- Schedules academic courses, final exams, course restrictions, and Management & Balancing Lab/Seminar sections
- Maintains and upgrades the functionality of the Faculty's Teaching Assignment database

Qualifications

- Bachelor's degree in Physical Education, Recreation, Kinesiology, or a related allied health field preferred; undergraduate degrees in other disciplines may be considered
- Excellent interpersonal, communication and written skills
- Ability to work effectively both in a team environment and independently
- Ability to work under tight timelines and make decisions involving the recruitment and appointment of CAST instructional staff
- Excellent PeopleSoft skills with both Campus Solutions and Human Capital Management
- Superior information systems skills including: MS Office Suite, WWW, etc.
- Superior analytical, problem-solving and critical-thinking skills
- Demonstrated ability to provide precise and concise information/advice to all areas in the unit
- Demonstrated strong leadership capabilities and organizational skills
- Strong financial analysis/reporting skills and attention to detail; ability to develop and monitor operating budgets in the Academic Programs Unit
- Well-developed planning and organization skills
- Extensive knowledge of University and Faculty Policies & Procedures

In accordance with the Administrative Professional Officer agreement, this full-time continuing position offers a comprehensive benefits package and annual salary range of $55,388–$92,316 (subject to current negotiations).

How to Apply

Apply Online

Note: Online applications are accepted until midnight Mountain Standard Time of the closing date.

Mail

Dr. Dan Syrotuik, Vice Dean
Academic Programs Office
Faculty of Physical Education and Recreation
University of Alberta
E407 Van Vliet Centre
EDMONTON, Alberta, T6G 2H9

Email
Dan.Syrotuik@ualberta.ca

Fax
(780) 492-6583

The University of Alberta hires on the basis of merit. We are committed to the principle of equity in employment. We welcome diversity and encourage applications from all qualified women and men, including persons with disabilities, members of visible minorities and Aboriginal persons.)

Source: Reprinted by permission of Recruitment Services, Human Resources, University of Alberta.

FIGURE **6.5**   Advantages and Disadvantages of Job Posting

Advantages

- Provides every qualified employee with a chance for a transfer or promotion.
- Reduces the likelihood of special deals and favouritism.
- Demonstrates the organization's commitment to career growth and development.
- Communicates to employees the organization's policies and guidelines regarding promotions and transfers.
- Provides equal opportunity to all qualified employees.

Disadvantages

- Unsuccessful job candidates may become demotivated, demoralized, discontented, and unhappy if feedback is not communicated in a timely and sensitive manner.
- Tensions may rise if it appears that a qualified internal candidate was passed over for an equally qualified or less qualified external candidate.
- The decision about which candidate to select may be more difficult if there are two or more equally qualified candidates.

RECRUITING FROM OUTSIDE THE ORGANIZATION

RPC

Identifies the potential sources of internal and external qualified candidates

Unless there is a workforce reduction, even in firms with a promote from within policy, a replacement from outside must eventually be found to fill the job left vacant once all eligible employees have been given the opportunity for transfer or promotion. In addition, most entry-level positions must be filled by external candidates. The advantages of external recruitment include the following:

- the generation of a larger pool of qualified candidates, which may have a positive impact on the quality of the selection decision
- the availability of a more diverse applicant pool, which can assist in meeting employment equity goals and timetables
- the acquisition of skills or knowledge not currently available within the organization or the introduction of new ideas and creative problem-solving techniques
- the elimination of rivalry and competition caused by employees jockeying for transfers and promotions, which can hinder interpersonal and interdepartmental cooperation
- the potential cost savings resulting from hiring individuals who already have the required skills, rather than providing extensive training

Planning External Recruitment

When choosing the external recruitment method(s), several factors should be considered in addition to the constraints mentioned earlier. The type of job to be filled has a major impact on the recruitment method selected. For example, most firms normally rely on professional search firms for recruiting executive-level employees. In contrast, Internet advertising is commonly used for recruiting other salaried employees.

Yield ratios help to indicate which recruitment methods are the most effective at producing qualified job candidates. A **yield ratio** is the percentage of applicants that proceed to the next stage of the selection process. A recruiting yield pyramid, such as that shown in **Figure 6.6**, can be devised for each method by calculating the yield ratio for each step in the selection process.

The hypothetical firm in Figure 6.6 typically hires 50 entry-level accountants each year. As the figure illustrates, this company knows that if they recruit 1 200 potential new hires only 200 will be invited for interviews (a 6:1 ratio of leads generation to candidates interviewed). In other words, of six leads generated through college/university recruiting efforts, one applicant is invited to attend an interview. Of those, only 150 will actually make it to the interview process with a mere 100 being offered a position, and of those only 50 will accept and eventually be hired. The firm calculates that this method leads to a ratio of offers made to actual new hires of two to one (about half of the candidates to whom offers are made accept). The firm also knows that the ratio of candidates interviewed to offers made is three to two, while the ratio of candidates invited for interviews to candidates actually interviewed is generally four to three. Finally, the firm knows that the ratio between leads generated and candidates selected for interviews is six to one. Given these ratios, the firm knows that using this particular recruitment method, 1 200 leads must be generated to hire 50 new accountants. While this example identifies how yields are calculated and used, each organization typically determines their own desired yields based on industry, position, size, and resources of the organization to determine their own internal yield targets.

The average number of days from when the company initiates a recruitment method to when the successful candidate begins to work is called *time-lapse data*. Assume that the accounting company in the above example found the following scenario: Six days elapsed between submission of application forms and résumés to invitation for an interview; five days then passed from invitation to actual interview; five days from interview to job offer; six days from job offer to acceptance; and 23 days from acceptance of job offer to commencement of work. These data indicate that, using on-campus recruiting, the firm must initiate recruitment efforts at least 45 days before the anticipated job opening date.

yield ratio The percentage of applicants that proceed to the next stage of the selection process.

RPC

Evaluates recruiting effectiveness

FIGURE **6.6**   Recruiting Yield Pyramid

Calculating time-lapse data for each recruitment method means that the amount of lead time available can be taken into account when deciding which strategy or strategies would be most appropriate.

External Recruitment Methods

Many methods of recruiting from the external labour market are in use. A 2010 study by Right Management of 5 858 job seekers found that the most successful way to find a job was through traditional networking, followed by online job boards. The results of the study are highlighted in **Figure 6.7**. Traditional networking includes employee referrals, former employees who have remained in contact with the organization, concentrated job fairs based on relationships formed with educational institutes, professional and trade associations, labour organizations, and military personnel. Online job boards include traditional online job boards, corporate websites, and government-initiated job boards.

Employee Referrals

Some organizations encourage applications from friends and relatives of current employees by mounting an employee referral campaign. Openings are announced in the company's intranet or newsletter along with a request for referrals. Cash awards or prizes may be offered for referrals that culminate in a new hire. Because no advertising or agency fees are involved, paying bonuses still represents a low recruiting cost.

The disadvantages associated with employee referrals include the potential for inbreeding and **nepotism** to cause morale problems and dissatisfaction among employees whose referrals are not hired. Perhaps the biggest drawback, however, is that this method may result in systemic discrimination.

nepotism A preference for hiring relatives of current employees.

FIGURE **6.7** Most Successful Ways to Find a Job in Canada, 2010

Note: Often candidates rely on more than one method (for example, networking leads to an awareness about a job posted online in a colleague's company). The above survey forced respondents to identify only one tool that they used to find their most recent job.

Source: Survey by Right Management, published in "Networking Gets the Job Done," *Canadian HR Reporter* (August 15, 2011), p. 4.

Former Employees

In these times of talent shortage and diminishing employee loyalty, some organizations are making efforts to keep in touch with former employees who may be interested in rejoining the organization in future. Organizations such as Microsoft, Ernst & Young, and Procter & Gamble are establishing alumni networks that offer benefits such as healthcare, job boards, and alumni parties. About 25 percent of hires at the manager level and above at Microsoft are returning employees, known as "boomerangs."[22]

Educational Institutions

Recruiting at educational institutions is extremely effective when candidates require formal training but need relatively little full-time work experience. High schools can provide recruits for clerical and some blue-collar jobs. For example, Encana, an oil and gas company headquartered in Calgary, is facing an ongoing shortage of skilled workers. It has started a program called "Oil and Gas Production Field Operator Career Pathway," which offers high school students an opportunity to earn credits while learning about field production work. Beginning in Grade 10, students in participating high schools can sign up for a distance-learning course supplied by Calgary-based Southern Alberta Institute of Technology (SAIT). Students who progress through the course in all three years will graduate with a production field operation certificate from SAIT. Students will have a chance of getting one of at least six paid 8-week summer internship positions with Encana following each year.[23]

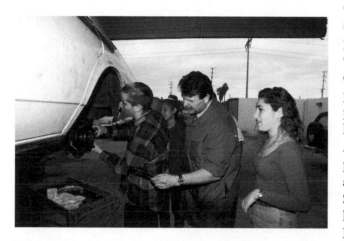

Many companies take recruitment campaigns into high schools to sell careers to a younger generation. This type of recruitment helps a variety of industries meet future recruitment demands. Here, students learn how to work on a car.

Most high schools, colleges, and universities have counselling centres that provide job-search assistance to students through such activities as skills assessment testing and workshops on résumé preparation and interview strategies. Sometimes they arrange for onsite job fairs, at which employers set up displays outlining the types of job opportunities available. The Halifax Career Fair, a partnership among Nova Scotia's universities and colleges, is the foremost recruiting event in Atlantic Canada. Every year the event attracts about 100 companies from across the country and 1 200 students.[24]

Cooperative (co-op) education and field placement programs have become increasingly popular in Canada. These programs require students to spend a specified amount of time working in organizations as an integral part of the academic program, thereby gaining some hands-on skills in an actual work setting. Co-op programs are offered in some high schools, as well as in colleges and universities.

Career Edge
www.careeredge.ca

Job Postings (Student Job Magazine)
www.jobpostings.ca

Halifax Career Fair
www.halifaxcareerfair.com

Summer internship programs hire college or university students to complete summer projects between their second-last and final year of study. Their performance is assessed, and those who are judged to be superior are offered permanent positions following graduation. Other firms offer internship opportunities to graduates, thereby enabling them to acquire hands-on skills to supplement their education. As with student internships, outstanding performers are often offered full-time employment at the end of the program. It is now possible for firms to recruit graduate interns online through Career Edge, an organization committed to helping university, college, and high school graduates gain essential career-related experience through internships. Career Edge uses the Internet as its sole means of bringing companies and youth together. More than 8 000 young Canadians have started their careers through the program in more than 1 000 organizations. Within a few months of completing their internship, nearly 80 percent of interns have found permanent employment with competitive salaries, and nearly 60 percent of the interns are hired by host organizations on a full-time basis.[25]

Internship, co-op, and field placement programs can produce a win–win result. The employer is provided with an inexpensive opportunity to assess potential employees while benefiting from the current knowledge and enthusiasm of bright, talented individuals. Because co-op students and interns have been exposed to the organization, they are less likely to leave shortly after permanent hire than recruits with no previous exposure to the firm.[26] Recognizing these benefits has made such programs a major recruitment method in many organizations.

Open Houses and Job Fairs

Another popular recruitment method involves holding an open house. Common in retail firms looking to staff a new store from the ground up, open houses have also been the choice of corporations trying to draw out scarce talent in an ultra-tight job market. A similar recruitment method involves holding a job fair onsite. At such events, recruiters share information about the organization and job opportunities with those attending in an informal, relaxed setting. Some organizations are now holding job fairs online (known as virtual job fairs) to connect with a wider geographical audience. Top prospects are invited to visit the firm or to return at a later date for a more in-depth assessment.

Professional and Trade Associations

CA Source
www.casource.com

Hire Authority
www.hireauthoritycanada.com

Professional and trade associations can be extremely helpful when recruiters are seeking individuals with specialized skills in such fields as IT, engineering, HR, and accounting, particularly if experience is a job requirement. Many such associations conduct ongoing placement activities on behalf of their members, and most regularly send their members newsletters or magazines in which organizations can place job advertisements. Such advertising may attract individuals who hadn't previously thought about changing jobs, as well as those actively seeking employment. For example, the Human Resources Professionals Association (HRPA) in Ontario has an employment service called the Hire Authority. For a nominal fee, employers can post HR-related employment opportunities on the HRPA website, where they can be viewed by HRPA members. Additionally, employers can pay for access to an online database of member résumés and can search, sort, and pre-screen qualified candidates for vacant positions.[27]

Labour Organizations

Some firms, particularly in the construction industry, obtain recruits through union hiring halls. The union maintains a roster of members (typically skilled trades people, such as carpenters, pipe fitters, welders, plumbers, and electricians), whom it sends out on assignment as requests from employers are received. Once the union members have completed their contracted work at one firm, they notify the union of their availability for another assignment.

Military Personnel

Military reservists are also potential recruits. The Canadian Forces Liaison Council (CFLC) is responsible for promoting the hiring of reservists by civilian employers. The CFLC also encourages civilian employers to give reservists time off for military training. Reserve force training develops skills and attributes sought after in the civilian workforce, such as leadership, planning, coordination, and teamwork.[28] Many organizations—such as Home Depot Canada and Énergie New Brunswick Power—have recognized the value of such leave and have joined the 4 700 organizations in Canada that have signed a statement of support for the reserve forces with the CFLC.[29] The CFLC's Reserve Employment Assistance Program (REAP) allows employers to place job postings for skilled personnel at more than 300 military units across the country at no charge.[30]

Online Recruiting

The majority of companies now use *online recruitment*, and a majority of Canadian workers use the Internet to research prospective employers, review job postings, complete online applications, and post their résumés. The Internet provides recruiters with a large audience for job postings and a vast talent pool. Online recruiting can involve accessing one or more Internet job boards, using a corporate website, or using social networking sites.

Internet Job Boards Online job boards are fast, easy, and convenient and allow recruiters to search for candidates for positions in two ways. First, companies can post a job opening online (often for a fee) and customize it by using corporate logos and adding details about the company benefits and culture. Job seekers can search through the job postings, often by job type, region, or other criterion, and apply for the position online through the job board. The popularity of Internet job boards among job seekers is high because of the number of job postings available on one site.

Second, job seekers can post their résumés on job boards, and firms can search the database. Canada has hundreds of job boards, ranging from the two largest, Workopolis and Monster, to many smaller job boards serving specific fields from tourism to medicine.[31] Job board meta-crawlers such as simplyhired. ca enable job seekers to search multiple job boards with one query.

The advantages of job boards include candidate assistance with self-assessment and résumé writing, and pre-screening assistance for recruiters. One problem with Internet job boards is their vulnerability to privacy breaches. Fake job postings can lead to identity theft from submitted résumés, and résumés are sometimes copied onto competing job boards or other sites.[32] As a result, job boards are now providing tips for job seekers on maintaining privacy and confidentiality.[33]

Corporate Websites With the overabundance of applicants found on most online job boards, employers are now using their own corporate websites to recruit.

Career pages provide a single platform for recruitment that promotes the employer brand, educates the applicant about the company, captures data about the applicant, and provides an important link to job boards where a company's positions may be advertised.[34] Virtual workplace tours using video can be provided to attract top talent aligned with the employer brand.[35] Corporate websites also help the company create a pool of candidates who have already expressed interest in the organization.[36]

Using pre-screening strategies is essential, however. The volume of résumés definitely does not diminish when the firm accepts them online. At Hewlett-Packard, for example, more than 1 million online applications are received each year.[37] One way of coping with this volume is to generate automatic replies acknowledging receipt of applications.[38] Applicant tracking software is available to help recruiters track individual candidates through the recruitment and selection processes and to enable candidates to keep their profiles up to date.

Active job seekers are not the only potential future employees who visit corporate websites. Customers, investors, and competitors also visit them.[39] Many of those visiting career websites are "happily employed" individuals (known as "passive" job seekers) who are likely to arrive at the career site after browsing the company's main pages for other reasons, such as research into products or services. Therefore, it is important that a firm have a prominently positioned link on the homepage leading directly to the careers section to make it easy for passive job seekers to pursue job opportunities within the company.[40]

Best practices for career websites include the following:

- Include candid information about company culture, career paths, and business prospects.

- Include third-party sources of information on your company, such as articles, rankings, and awards.

- Design separate sections for different types of job seekers, such as students and part-timers.

- Have a direct link from the homepage to the career page.

- Have a job search tool that allows applicants to search open job positions by location and job category.

- Have a standardized application or résumé builder to allow for easy applicant screening.

- Use "email to a friend" options for visitor referrals.[41]

Tips FOR THE FRONT LINE

Human Resources and Skills Development Canada (HRSDC)

Job Bank
www.jobbank.gc.ca

Training and Careers
www.jobsetc.gc.ca

Through various programs, including those for youth, Aboriginals, and persons with disabilities, HRSDC helps unemployed individuals find suitable jobs and helps employers locate qualified candidates to meet their needs—at no cost to either party. The Job Bank is the largest web-based network of job postings available to Canadian employers free of charge, and it provides access to 700 000 new jobs each year, with more than 40 000 jobs at any given time and up to 2 000 new jobs posted every day. HRSDC also operates Job Match, a web-based recruitment tool that can match employers' skill requirements with individuals' skill sets. Job seekers receive a list of employers with a matching job vacancy and employers receive a list of qualified candidates.[42]

Executive Search Firms

Employers use executive search firms to fill critical positions in a firm, usually middle- to senior-level professional and managerial positions. Such firms often specialize in a particular type of talent, such as executives, sales, scientific, or middle-management employees. They typically know and understand the marketplace, have many contacts, and are especially adept at contacting qualified candidates who are employed and not actively looking to change jobs (which is why they have been given the nickname "headhunters"). Generally, one-third of the fee is payable as a retainer at the outset. Compared with the value of the time savings realized by the client firm's executive team, however, such a fee often turns out to be insignificant.

Using this recruitment method has some potential pitfalls.[43] Executive search firms cannot do an effective job if they are given inaccurate or incomplete information about the job or the firm. It is therefore essential for employers to explain in detail the type of candidate required—and why. A few headhunters are more salespeople than professionals, and they are more interested in persuading the employer to hire a candidate rather than in finding one who really meets the job specifications. Some firms have also been known to present an unpromising candidate to a client simply to make their one or two other prospects look that much better. The Association of Canadian Search, Employment, and Staffing Services (ACSESS) sponsors the Certified Personnel Consultant (CPC) designation, which signifies that recruiters have met specific educational and testing requirements and confirms an individual's commitment to best industry practices.[44]

Private Employment Agencies

Private employment agencies are often called on to provide assistance to employers seeking clerical staff, functional specialists, and technical employees. The "staffing" business has grown into a $6 billion industry that places hundreds of thousands of job seekers each year.[45] Generally, it is the employer who pays the agency fee. It is not uncommon for employers to be charged a fee equal to 15 to 30 percent of the first year's salary of the individual hired through agency referral. This percentage may vary depending on the volume of business provided by the client and the type of employee sought.

These agencies take an employer's request for recruits and then solicit job seekers, relying primarily on Internet job boards, advertising, and walk-ins/write-ins. Employment agencies serve two basic functions: (1) expanding the applicant pool and (2) performing preliminary interviewing and screening. Specific situations in which an employment agency might be used for recruiting include the following:

- The organization does not have an HR department or does not have anyone with the requisite time and/or expertise.
- The firm has experienced difficulty in generating a pool of qualified candidates for the position or a similar type of position in the past.

Association of Canadian Search, Employment, and Staffing Services (ACSESS)
www.acsess.org

- A particular opening must be filled quickly.
- There is a desire to recruit a greater number of designated group members than the firm has been able to attract on its own.
- The recruitment effort is aimed at reaching individuals who are currently employed and might therefore feel more comfortable answering ads placed by and dealing with an employment agency.

Tips FOR THE FRONT LINE

It should be noted, however, that the amount of service provided varies widely, as does the level of professionalism and the calibre of staff. Although most agencies carefully screen applicants, some simply provide a stream of applicants and let the client's HR department staff do the screening. Agency staff is usually paid on a commission basis, and their desire to earn a commission may occasionally compromise their professionalism (for example, encouraging job seekers to accept jobs for which they are neither qualified nor suited).

Cold Calls: Walk-Ins and Write-Ins

Individuals who go to organizations in person to apply for jobs without referral or invitation are called walk-ins. People who submit unsolicited résumés to organizations are known as write-ins. Walk-ins and write-ins are an inexpensive recruitment method. Their résumés are generally screened by the HR department and if an applicant is considered suitable, his or her résumé is retained on file for three to six months or passed on to the relevant department manager if there is an immediate or upcoming opening for which the applicant is qualified. Some organizations, such as RBC Financial Group, are using computer databases to store the information found on the résumés and application forms of walk-in and write-in candidates. Whether the original document is paper based or submitted online, it can be scanned and stored in databases for fast, easy access using a few key words.[46]

Online Networking Sites

Many organizations are turning to social networking sites like Facebook to find young, tech-savvy recruits. Some create virtual recruitment booths and others create a company profile where they can post jobs and publicize their employer brand. Other users seeking jobs can become "friends" of potential employers and upload their profiles, which contain more information than résumés. Ernst & Young is one firm that has used this approach—it has even established its own company social networking site for employees and alumni.[47]

An Ethical Dilemma

Is it ethical to use personal information on social networking sites to assess job candidates?

The advantage of using social networking for recruitment purposes is the opportunity to connect with millions of other users at little or no cost. One disadvantage is the possibility of unhappy employees or customers posting negative comments on the site.[48]

Print Advertising

Despite the advent of online recruiting, traditional advertising in newspapers and other print media is still a very common method of recruiting.[49] For advertising to bring the desired results, two issues must be addressed: the media to be used and the construction of the ad.[50] The selection of the best medium—whether it is the local newspaper, a national newspaper, a technical journal, or even a billboard—depends on the types of positions for which the organization is recruiting. Reaching individuals who are already employed and not actively seeking alternative employment requires a different medium than is appropriate to attract those who are unemployed.

To achieve optimum results from an advertisement, the following four-point guide, called AIDA, should be kept in mind as the ad is being constructed:

1. The ad should *attract attention*. The ads that stand out have borders, a company logo or picture, and effective use of empty white space. To attract attention, key positions should be advertised in display ads, rather than classified ads.

2. The ad should develop *interest* in the job. Interest can be created by the nature of the job itself, by pointing out the range of duties or the amount of challenge or responsibility involved. Sometimes other aspects of the job, such as its location or working conditions, are useful in attracting interest. To ensure that the individuals attracted are qualified, the job specifications should always be included.

3. The ad should create a *desire* for the job. This may be done by capitalizing on the interesting aspects of the job itself or by pointing out any unique benefits or opportunities associated with it, such as the opportunity for career development or travel. Desire may also be created by stressing the employer's commitment to employment equity. The target audience should be kept in mind as the ad is being created.

4. The ad should instigate *action*. To prompt action, ads often include a closing date and a statement such as "Call today," "Send your résumé today," "Check out our website for more information," or "Go to the site of our next job fair."

When properly constructed, advertisements can be an effective instrument for recruiting, as well as for communicating the organization's corporate image to the general public.

There are two general types of newspaper advertisements: want ads and blind ads. **Want ads** describe the job and its specifications, the compensation package, and the hiring employer. Although the content pertaining to the job, specifications, and compensation is identical in **blind ads**, such ads omit the identity and address of the hiring employer. Although many job seekers do not like responding to blind ads because there is always the danger of unknowingly sending a résumé to the firm at which they are currently employed, such ads do result in the opening remaining confidential (which may be necessary if the position is still staffed).

Many factors make advertising a useful recruiting method. Employers can use advertisements to reach and attract potential job applicants from a diverse labour market in as wide or narrow a geographical area as desired. To meet employment equity goals and timetables, ads can be placed in publications read by designated group members, such as a minority-language newspaper or the newsletter of a not-for-profit agency assisting individuals who have a particular mental or physical disability.

want ad A recruitment ad describing the job and its specifications, the compensation package, and the hiring employer. The address to which applications or résumés should be submitted is also provided.

blind ad A recruitment ad in which the identity and address of the employer are omitted.

Recruiting Non-Permanent Staff

In recent years, many companies have increased their use of contingent workers to attain labour flexibility and acquire employees with special skills on an as needed basis. In these firms, recruiters are spending more time seeking temporary (term, seasonal, casual) and contract workers and less time recruiting permanent staff.[51] Two common sources of non-permanent staff are temporary help agencies and contract workers.

Temporary Help Agencies

Temporary help agencies, such as Kelly Services and Office Overload, exist in major cities in Canada. They specialize in providing temporary workers to cover for employees who are ill, on vacation, or on a leave of absence. Firms also use temporary employees to handle seasonal work, peak workloads, and special projects for which no current employees have the time or expertise. Temporary workers (temps) are agency employees and are reassigned to another employer when their services are no longer required.

Temps provide employers with three major benefits:

1. They cost much less than permanent employees, as they generally receive less compensation than permanent staff. There are also savings related to the hiring and training costs associated with permanent employees. In fact, training has become the central investment in the business strategy of many temporary employment agencies. For example, Accountemps invests in the skills and training of employees after they have worked for a specified amount of time. This training includes online tutoring in software they may use on the job and tuition reimbursement for skills training.[52]

2. If a temp performs unsatisfactorily, a substitute can be requested immediately. Generally, a suitable replacement is sent to the firm within one business day.

3. Individuals working as temps who are seeking full-time employment are often highly motivated, knowing that many firms choose full-time employees from the ranks of their top-performing temps.

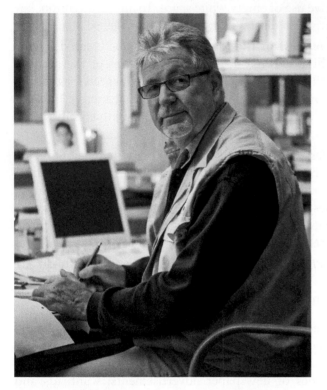

The number of temporary and freelance workers is increasing all over the world. Freelancing allows employers to match their job needs to independent workers who complete tasks on an as needed basis.

Contract Workers

contract workers Employees who develop work relationships directly with the employer for a specific type of work or period of time.

Contract workers are employees who develop work relationships directly with the employer for a specific type of work or period of time.[53] For example, Parc Aviation is a major supplier of contract workers to the airline industry. Airline organizations benefit from the services of contract engineers by having them cover seasonal or unplanned peaks in business, carry out special tasks or projects, and reduce the necessity for airlines to downsize permanent staff during cyclical downturns.[54]

An Ethical : **Dilemma**

Is it ethical to keep extending the contracts of contract workers rather than hiring them as permanent employees to avoid the cost of employee benefits?

Many professionals with specialized skills become contract workers, including project managers, accountants, and lawyers. Some have consciously made a decision to work for themselves; others have been unable to obtain full-time employment in their field of expertise or have found themselves out of a full-time job because of cutbacks. Thus, some want to remain self-employed; others work a contract while hoping to obtain a full-time position eventually. Some firms hire former employees (such as retirees) on a contract basis.

RECRUITING A MORE DIVERSE WORKFORCE

Recruiting a diverse workforce is not just socially responsible—it's a necessity. As noted previously, the composition of Canada's workforce is changing dramatically. Trends of particular significance include the increasing necessity of hiring older employees, a decrease in the availability of young workers, and an increase in the number of women, visible minorities, Aboriginal people, and persons with disabilities in the workforce.

Attracting Older Workers

Prime50
www.prime50.com

Many employers, recognizing the fact that the workforce is aging, are encouraging retirement-age employees to stay with the company or are actively recruiting employees who are at or beyond retirement age. For example, 20 percent of Home Depot Canada's workforce is over the age of 50.[55] Hiring and retaining older employees has significant benefits. These workers typically have high job satisfaction, a strong sense of loyalty and organizational commitment, a strong work ethic, good people skills, and a willingness to work in a variety of roles, including part time.[56]

To make a company attractive to older workers, it is important to deal with stereotypical attitudes toward older workers through education, ensure that HR policies do not discourage recruitment of older workers, develop flexible work arrangements, and redesign jobs to accommodate decreased dexterity and strength. Canadian employers have been encouraged to take action to retain and recruit older workers as they represent a large, underutilized, skilled labour pool, but so far little effort has been made to attract these people.[57] A 2008 Conference Board of Canada study found that the most common recruitment strategy for older workers was rehiring former employees and retirees. Less than 20 percent were using recruitment campaigns directed specifically at mature workers.[58]

Attracting Younger Employees

Many firms are recognizing the benefits of a multigenerational workforce and are not only trying to attract older workers, but are also taking steps to address the pending shortage of younger employees. Although older employees have comparatively wider experience and wisdom, the young bring energy, enthusiasm, and physical strength to their positions.

Successful organizations balance these different kinds of experience. McDonald's Restaurants of Canada (one of the largest employers of youth in the country and an active recruiter of seniors) feels that it is critical for organizations in the service industry to have employees who mirror their customer base. Its experience is that each member of the multi-age teams brings a particular strength, which leads to synergy, respect, and team building.[59]

Younger members of the workforce are part of the Generation X and Generation Y cohorts. To appeal to Generation Xers, it is important to stress that they will be able to work independently and that work–life balance is supported. Potential employees from Generation Y will want to know that they will be working with experts from across the organization and that the will have a variety of experiences, as described in the Strategic HR box. They will be attracted by organizations that value social responsibility, diversity, and creativity.[60] Accounting firm Meyers Norris Penny built an award-winning student recruiting campaign around the question "What do you want?" which resulted in continuously improving the quality of the students hired.[61]

STRATEGIC HR

Attracting the Younger Generation

The authors of the book *Bridging the Generation Gap* asked 500 Gen Ys this question: "What's important to you on the job?" The top three responses were quality of friendships, feeling they can make a contribution on the job, and a feeling of safety. These young workers want an organization where they can create friendships, much as they did in school. In other words, the organization must have a social flair to catch their eye. Some examples include a company sports league and company social events like movie nights or meeting after work for a drink. But these quality relationships must go along with a feeling that what they do adds value to the organization.

The Gen Ys said that the top three ways an organization can entice their generation to want employment with the organization are offering a competitive salary, a casual work environment, and growth/development opportunities such as mentoring and training. Other benefits that organizations can offer to entice younger workers include state-of-the-art technology, opportunities to volunteer in the community (on company time), regular feedback, tuition reimbursement programs, strong reward and recognition programs, and a connection to the mission and vision of the organization.

The younger generation aims to take advantage of every form of technology to make their job search successful and easier. Organizations need to advertise jobs on multiple online job boards, including local, national, and trade related. Organizations should also create a job board on the company's website that should be regularly updated and provide an easy and responsive way for candidates to apply online. The posting should include an email address for the HR department or an online application process. For the process to succeed, organizations must regularly check the applications and follow-up with candidates.

The actual copy of the ads is critical. Certain key words attract these individuals to an organization's ads when they do online searches. The younger generation likes short, snappy copy that gets right to the point of what they will be doing. But of equal or more importance, the ad needs to advertise the culture of the organization as it relates to the values of this generation. The ads should include statements such as "fast-paced environment," "individual contribution," "work–life balance," "do it your way," "opportunity to grow," "no rules," and "state-of-the-art technology." Of course, organizations should only list these kinds of features in the ads if they truly offer them. Otherwise, the organization will see just how fast these workers will leave a company that doesn't fulfill its promises.

Source: Adapted from R. Throckmorton and L. Gravett, "Attracting the Younger Generation," *Canadian HR Reporter* (April 23, 2007).

Recruiting Designated Group Members

Most of the recruitment methods already discussed can be used to attract members of designated groups (Aboriginal people, women, visible minorities, and persons with disabilities), provided that the employer's commitment to

After struggling to restart his career in Canada, Sibaway Issah found the assistance he needed with Career Edge, a not-for-profit agency that links qualified immigrants with possible employers.

Aboriginal Human Resource Council
http://aboriginalhr.ca

Canadian Council on Rehabilitation and Work
www.ccrw.org

WORKink
www.workink.com

HireImmigrants.ca
www.hireimmigrants.ca

equality and diversity is made clear to all involved in the recruitment process—whether it is employees who are asked for referrals or private employment agencies. This can also be stressed in all recruitment advertising. Alternative publications targeted at designated group members should be considered for advertising, and linkages can be formed with organizations and agencies specializing in assisting designated group members. Specific examples follow.

The Aboriginal Human Resource Council, headquartered in Saskatoon, Saskatchewan, sponsors the Aboriginal Inclusion Network, which offers a job board, résumé database, and other tools to hire, retain, and promote Aboriginal talent. The Inclusion Network is linked to 350 Aboriginal employment centres across Canada, and the number of job seekers on the network increased 70 percent from 2009 to 2011.[62]

The Society for Canadian Women in Science and Technology (SCWIST) is a not-for-profit, volunteer organization aimed at improving attitudes and stereotypes about and assisting women in scientific, technological, and engineering careers. Employers can access valuable resources such as websites, employment agencies, and publications to attract professional women for employment opportunities in industries where they generally have a low representation.[63]

WORKink is Canada's most powerful online career development and employment portal for Canadians with disabilities. The WORKink site offers a full complement of employment and recruitment resources and services for job seekers with disabilities and for employers looking to create an inclusive workplace. WORKink is sponsored by the Canadian Council on Rehabilitation and Work. Employers can post job openings free of charge, browse résumés of people with disabilities, or access information on how to adapt the work environment to accommodate people with disabilities in their region.[64]

The Ontario Ministry of Community and Social Services sponsors a program called Paths to Equal Opportunity intended to provide links to information on removing and preventing barriers so that people with disabilities can work, learn, and play to their fullest potential. In conjunction with the Canadian Abilities Foundation, the program publishes a resource booklet called *Abilities @ Work*, which provides specific information to employers who want to find out about recruiting, interviewing, hiring, and working with people with disabilities. It also provides information to employees and job seekers with disabilities who want information on looking for work, accommodation in the workplace, and maintaining employment.

Another useful tool is the guidebook *Tapping the Talents of People with Disabilities: A Guidebook for Employers*, which is available through the Conference Board of Canada. More information on hiring people with disabilities is provided in the Workforce Diversity box.

WORKFORCE DIVERSITY

The Disconnect in Recruiting People with Disabilities

The good news is that employers want to hire people with disabilities, and qualified candidates are available. But putting employers and job seekers together needs improved coordination to create more success stories. Employers have bottom-line reasons for building workforce diversity. Inclusiveness is a competitive advantage that lets an organization better connect with a diverse community and customer base. Inclusiveness provides access to a larger pool of strong job candidates in a time of skills shortages and enhances an organization's reputation as an employer of choice.

So why aren't more employers tapping into the wealth of human potential in people with disabilities? After all, as a group they make up roughly 13 percent of the working-age population. That is precisely what the Canadian Abilities Foundation set out to determine in its recently completed Neglected or Hidden study, the findings of which may surprise employers.

Likely the most revealing finding that illustrates the need for a new employment strategy for people with disabilities is the disconnect that exists among employers, people with disabilities, and the service providers who help these individuals enter the workforce.

With few exceptions, these stakeholders just don't seem to know how to communicate with one another,

if they are fortunate enough to find one another in the first place. The commitment and passion of workers with disabilities and those assisting them is sound. Meanwhile, hundreds of disability-related organizations across Canada provide some level of employment support to their clients. The Neglected or Hidden study suggests that the number of Canadian employers willing to hire people with disabilities should be more than adequate to meet the availability of disabled job seekers.

The good news is that a small number of disability organizations have made significant inroads in their regions by using employer partnerships. One example is the Dartmouth Work Activity Society in Nova Scotia, which started its new approach with just a single employer "partner" who was highly satisfied with the services provided. EmployAbilities, a full-time service agency serving Edmonton and northern Alberta for more than 35 years, has also launched a partnership-building strategy. A unique feature of the agency's approach is its partnership with the local chamber of commerce through which it offers advice on disability issues to employers.

Source: Adapted from A. Prost, "Successful Recruiting from an Untapped Source," *Canadian HR Reporter* (January 16, 2006), pp. 11–12.

Chapter SUMMARY

1. Recruitment is the process of searching out and attracting qualified job applicants. It begins with the identification of a position that requires staffing and is completed when résumés or completed application forms are received. In order to manage the increasing talent shortage, proactive employers are trying to obtain a competitive advantage in recruitment by establishing themselves as employers of choice through employer branding.

2. The recruitment process has four steps. First, job openings are identified through HR planning or manager request. Second, the job description and job specifications are reviewed to determine the job requirements. Third, appropriate recruiting source(s) and method(s) are chosen. Fourth, using these strategies, a pool of qualified candidates is generated.

3. Application forms have been largely replaced by online applications, where candidates provide information on education and experience, a brief overview of past career progress, and other information that can be used to predict whether an applicant will succeed on the job.

4. Job posting is the process of notifying existing employees about vacant positions. Human resources records may indicate appropriate applicants for vacant positions. Skills inventories may provide even better information.

5. External recruitment methods include traditional networking, online job boards, agencies, recruiters, cold calls, online networks, and print ads.

6. Two strategies for obtaining non-permanent staff include using temporary help agencies and hiring contract workers.

7. Recruiting a diverse workforce is a necessity, given the shrinking labour force. In particular, recruiters are trying to attract older workers, younger workers, women, visible minorities, Aboriginal people, and people with disabilities.

MyManagementLab

Visit MyManagementLab to access a personalized Study Plan and additional study tools for this chapter.

Key TERMS

biographical information blank (BIB) *(p. 148)*
blind ad *(p. 163)*
contract workers *(p. 164)*
employer branding *(p. 144)*
job posting *(p. 152)*

nepotism *(p. 156)*
recruiter *(p. 144)*
recruitment *(p. 144)*
want ad *(p. 163)*
yield ratio *(p. 155)*

Review and Discussion QUESTIONS

1. Discuss the advantages and disadvantages of recruiting from within the organization. Identify and describe the three tools that are used in this process.

2. Brainstorm the advantages of external recruitment. Discuss the risks associated with external recruiting.

3. Explain the difference between an Internet job board and a corporate career website.

4. Under what circumstances should a private employment agency be used?

5. Describe the advantages of using online application forms or résumé repositories as part of the recruitment process.

Critical Thinking QUESTIONS

1. What potential problems may result if the employer branding value proposition presented during the recruitment process is not reinforced once the new recruit is working for the organization? What could organizations do to avoid this situation?

2. What potential problems could be created by offering referral bonuses to existing employees?

3. Compare and contrast the advantages and disadvantages of traditional and virtual career fairs.

4. As the labour supply gets tighter and tighter, would you be in favour of loosening requirements for foreign-trained professionals (for example, doctors, professors, accountants, engineers) to become immediately qualified in Canada? Why or why not? Identify the underlying assumptions in the position you took.

5. What are some of the specific reservations that a 30-year-old candidate might have about applying for a job that requires managing a workforce that is on average 10 years older than he or she is?

6. Assume you are the HR manager in a highly homogenous company that now wants to better reflect the diversity of the target client group in its employee population. What must you consider as you think about implementing your new recruitment strategy?

Experiential EXERCISES

1. Go to your university's or college's career centre and gather information on all the services they provide. How many companies come to recruit students through the centre each year? What services does the centre provide to employers seeking to hire graduating students? Employers seeking to hire summer students? Employers seeking to hire students for internships?

2. Given the importance of networking to recruitment success, organize the class around core jobs that students would like to have. In each group, brainstorm sources of networking. Poll the group to determine how many people in the group are taking advantage of each available network. Highlight reasons for low involvement and brainstorm ideas about how these challenges can be overcome.

3. Considering the current economic situation and using the following list of jobs, identify all of the sources that could be used to recruit qualified applicants:

- Registered nurses to work in the critical care unit of a new regional hospital
- Carpenters to work on a new home building project
- Chief financial officer for an international engineering firm with a head office located in Vancouver
- Retail sales associates to work in an urban clothing chain
- Customer service representatives to work in a bank branch
- Bilingual administrative assistants for a Canadian financial services company operating internationally

Running CASE

Getting Better Applicants

If Jennifer and Pierre were asked what the main problem was in running their business, their answer would be quick and short: hiring good people. They were simply astonished at how hard it was to attract and hire good candidates. After much debate, they decided to post openings for seven positions: two salespeople, one web designer, two content management people, one office manager, and one web surfer.

Their first approach was to design and place a large display ad in two local newspapers. The display ad listed all the positions available. Jennifer and Pierre assumed that by placing a large ad with the name of the company prominently displayed and a bold border around the ad, it would draw attention and therefore generate applicants. For two consecutive weekends, the ad cost the fledgling company close to $1000, but it produced only a handful of applicants. After speaking with them by phone, Jennifer and Pierre rejected three outright, two said they weren't interested, and two scheduled interviews but never showed up.

The owners therefore decided to change their approach. They used different recruiting methods for each position. In the paper, they placed ads for the salespeople under "Sales" and for the office manager under "Administrative."

They advertised for a web designer by placing an ad on Monster.ca. And for the content managers and web surfer they placed neatly typed help wanted ads in the career placement offices of a technical college and a community college about 10 minutes away from their office. They also used this job posting approach to find independent contractors they could use to physically deliver courses to users' homes or offices.

The results were disappointing. Over a typical weekend, literally dozens of want ads for experienced salespeople appear, as well as almost as many for office managers. The ad for salespeople generated three calls, one of whom Jennifer and Pierre felt might be a viable candidate, although the person wanted a much higher salary than they had planned to pay. One possible candidate emerged for the office manager position.

They decided to change the positioning of the sales ad in the newspaper from "Salespersons Wanted" to "Phone Sales," which is a separate category (since the job involved entirely inside phone sales). Many of the calls they got (not all of them, but many) were from salespeople who were used to working in what some people called "boiler-room" operations. In other words, they sit at the phone all day making cold calls from lists provided by their employers, selling anything from burglar alarms to investments, all under very high-pressure conditions. They weren't interested in LearnInMotion, nor was LearnInMotion interested in them.

They fared a little better with the web designer ad, which produced four possible applicants. They got no phone calls from the local college job postings; when they called to ask the placement offices why, they were told that their posted salary of $8 per hour was "much too low." They went back and replaced the job postings with $10 hourly rates.

"I just don't understand it," Jennifer finally said. Especially for the sales job, Jennifer and Pierre felt that they were offering perfectly acceptable compensation packages, so the lack of applicants surprised them. "Maybe a lot of people just don't want to work for dot-coms anymore," said Pierre, thinking out loud. "When the bottom fell out of the dot-com market, a lot of good people were hurt by working for a series of two or three failed dot-coms. Maybe they've just had enough of the wired world."

QUESTIONS

1 Describe how the recruitment process (including all of the steps) outlined in Figure 6.1 will be of assistance to Jennifer and Pierre to solve their recruitment problems.

2 Draft a new job posting for each of the seven positions discussed in the case. Then discuss how you put the job postings together and why, using Figure 6.2 and Figure 6.3 as examples.

Case INCIDENT

Solving a Potential Recruitment Dilemma

Rachel Lucas is the human resources manager of a prestigious accounting firm. Rachel recently attended a local human resources professionals' association meeting where recruitment was the topic up for discussion. At this meeting all aspects of the recruitment process, including recruitment methods and how to increase diversity through the use of application forms, were to be discussed. Rachel couldn't wait to apply what she learned at this meeting to her job.

While listening to the scheduled speaker for the evening, Rachel started to think about the current recruitment initiatives she was dealing with at work. The firm was entering its traditional busy season where many clients would need tax returns completed. This time every year she needed to source and hire quality, qualified candidates to fill 50 tax preparer positions. The partners were relying heavily on her this year to get higher quality candidates because of the complex returns that would have to be completed, and to have them in place within three weeks.

As the speaker was finishing his presentation, Rachel wondered what recruitment process and techniques she should use. What would be the best decisions for the firm?

QUESTIONS

1   Should Rachel use internal or external recruitment techniques to staff these 50 positions?

2   Rachel is hoping to recruit qualified candidates from a variety of diverse demographics. Will she have to use different recruitment techniques to do this? If so, what ones are the most effective to attract these candidates (older workers, designated group members, and so on)?

3   Rachel plans on hiring recruiters to assist her in staffing these 50 positions. Knowing the company will require the recruiters to adhere to the concept of employer branding, describe what steps Rachel should take to orient the new recruiters to the branding process.

MyManagementLab

Visit MyManagementLab to access a personalized Study Plan and additional study tools for this chapter.

 To view the CBC videos, read a summary, and answer discussion questions, go to MyManagementLab

CHAPTER

Selection

LEARNING OUTCOMES

AFTER STUDYING THIS CHAPTER, YOU SHOULD BE ABLE TO

DEFINE selection and **DISCUSS** its strategic importance.

DEFINE reliability and validity and **EXPLAIN** their importance in selection techniques.

DESCRIBE at least four types of testing used in selection and **ANALYZE** the conflicting legal concerns related to alcohol and drug testing.

DESCRIBE the major types of selection interviews by degree of structure, type of content, and manner of administration.

EXPLAIN the importance of reference checking, **DESCRIBE** strategies to make such checking effective, and **ANALYZE** the legal issues involved.

REQUIRED PROFESSIONAL CAPABILITIES (RPC)

- Analyzes position and competency requirements to establish selection criteria

- Establishes screening and assessment procedures

- Determines the appropriate selection tools and develops new tools as required

- Administers a variety of selection tools, including tests, interviews, reference checks, and so on

- Supports managers in the selection of candidates

- Evaluates the effectiveness of selection processes, tools, and outcomes

- Establishes appointment procedures for candidates selected through the recruitment process, ensuring that conditions of employment are documented and consistent with established policies

- Supports managers in the negotiation of terms and conditions of employment

THE STRATEGIC IMPORTANCE OF EMPLOYEE SELECTION

. . . .

selection The process of choosing among individuals who have been recruited to fill existing or projected job openings.

Selection is the process of choosing among individuals who have been recruited to fill existing or projected job openings. Whether considering current employees for a transfer or promotion or outside candidates for a first-time position with the firm, information about the applicants must be collected and evaluated. Selection begins when a pool of applicants has submitted their résumés or completed application forms as a result of the recruiting process.

The selection process has important strategic significance. More and more managers have realized that the quality of the company's human resources is often the single most important factor in determining whether the firm is going to survive and be successful in reaching the objectives specified in its strategic plan. Those individuals selected will be implementing strategic decisions and, in some cases, creating strategic plans. Thus, successful candidates must fit with the strategic direction of the organization. For example, if the organization is planning to expand internationally, language skills and international experience will become important selection criteria.

When a poor selection decision is made and the individual selected for the job is not capable of acceptable performance in the job, strategic objectives will not be met. In addition, when an unsuccessful employee must be terminated, the recruitment and selection process must begin all over again, and the successor must be properly oriented and trained. The "hidden" costs are frequently even higher, including internal disorganization and disruption and customer alienation. For example, the City of Waterloo was forced to fire its new chief administrative officer after three weeks on the job when it was found that he had provided inaccurate and misleading information to city council in a previous job.[1]

There are also legal implications associated with ineffective selection. Human rights legislation in every Canadian jurisdiction prohibits discrimination in all aspects, terms, and conditions of employment on such grounds as race, religion or creed, colour, marital status, gender, age, and disability. Firms must ensure that all their selection procedures are free of both intentional and systemic discrimination (see **Appendix 7.1**, which provides the Canadian Human Rights Commission's *Guide to Screening and Selection in Employment*). Organizations required by law to implement an employment equity plan must ensure that all their employment systems, including selection, are bias-free and do not have an adverse impact on members of the four designated groups—women, visible minorities, Aboriginal people, and persons with disabilities.

An Ethical : Dilemma

As the company recruiter, how would you handle a request from the CEO that you hire her son for a summer job, knowing that, given current hiring constraints, the sons and daughters of other employees will not be able to obtain such positions?

Another legal implication is employer liability for negligent or wrongful hiring. Courts are increasingly finding employers liable when employees with unsuitable backgrounds are hired and subsequently engage in criminal activities falling within the scope of their employment. British Columbia has a law that requires schools, hospitals, and employers of childcare workers to conduct criminal record checks for all new employees.[2]

Suggested guidelines for avoiding negative legal consequences, such as human rights complaints, liability for negligent hiring, and wrongful dismissal suits, include the following:

Hints TO ENSURE LEGAL COMPLIANCE

1. Ensure that all selection criteria and strategies are based on the job description and the job specifications.
2. Adequately assess the applicant's ability to meet performance standards or expectations.
3. Carefully scrutinize all information supplied on application forms and résumés.
4. Obtain written authorization for reference checking from prospective employees, and check references carefully.
5. Save all records and information obtained about the applicant during each stage of the selection process.
6. Reject applicants who make false statements on their application forms or résumés.

Supply Challenges

Although it is desirable to have a large, qualified pool of recruits from which to select applicants, this is not always possible. Certain vacant positions may be subject to a labour shortage (based on job requirements, location, work environment, and so on), while other simultaneous vacant positions may be subject to a labour surplus (due to external environment factors, training and education levels, immigration patterns, and so on). A **selection ratio** is the ratio of the number of applicants hired to the total number of applicants available, as follows:

selection ratio The ratio of the number of applicants hired to the total number of applicants.

Number of Applicants Hired ÷ Total Number of Applicants = Selection Ratio

A small selection ratio, such as 1:2, may be indicative of a limited number of applicants from which to select, and it may also mean low-quality recruits. If this is the case, it is generally better to start the recruitment process over again, even if it means a hiring delay, rather than taking the risk of hiring an employee who will be a marginal performer at best.

A large selection ratio, such as 1:400, may be indicative that the job ad is too vague, that the organization's HR team may need to automate the screening process, or that there is a need for more resources to find the right job candidate amongst the high number of applicants.

The Selection Process

Most firms use a sequential selection system involving a series of successive steps— a **multiple-hurdle strategy**. Only candidates clearing a "hurdle" (selection techniques including pre-screening, testing, interviewing, and background/reference checking) are permitted to move on to the next step. Clearing the hurdle requires meeting or exceeding the minimum requirements established for that hurdle. Thus, only candidates who have cleared all of the previous hurdles remain in contention for the position at the time that the hiring decision is being made.

multiple-hurdle strategy An approach to selection involving a series of successive steps or hurdles. Only candidates clearing the hurdle are permitted to move on to the next step.

RPC

Analyzes position and competency requirements to establish selection criteria

To assess each applicant's potential for success on the job, organizations typically rely on a number of sources of information. The number of steps in the selection process and their sequence vary with the organization. An abbreviated selection process for entrepreneurs and small business owners is provided in the Entrepreneurs and HR box. The types of selection instruments

ENTREPRENEURS and HR

Employment Testing and Interviewing

For the small business, one or two hiring mistakes could be disastrous, so a formal testing program is advisable. Some tests are so easy to use that they are particularly good for smaller firms. Several examples follow.

- The Wonderlic Personnel Test measures general mental ability. It takes less than 15 minutes to administer the four-page booklet. The tester reads the instructions and then keeps time as the candidate works through the 50 problems on the two inside sheets. The tester scores the test by adding up the number of correct answers. Comparing the candidate's score with the minimum scores recommended for various occupations shows whether the candidate achieved the minimally acceptable score for the type of job in question.

- The Predictive Index measures work-related personality traits, drives, and behaviours—in particular, dominance, extroversion, patience, and blame avoidance—on a two-sided sheet. A template makes scoring simple. The Predictive Index program includes 15 standard personality patterns. For example, there is the "social interest" pattern for a person who is generally unselfish, congenial, persuasive, patient, and unassuming. This person would be good with people and a good personnel interviewer, for instance.

- Computerized testing programs are especially useful for small employers. For example, many employers rely on informal typing tests when hiring office help. A better approach is to use a program like the Minnesota Clerical Assessment Battery published by Assessment Systems Corporation. It runs on a PC and includes a typing test, proofreading test, filing test, business vocabulary test, business math test, and clerical knowledge test.

Interviewing

A practical, streamlined employment interview process would proceed as follows:

- Preparing for the interview: Even a busy entrepreneur or small business manager can quickly specify the kind of person who would be best for the job. One way to do so is to focus on four basic required factors—knowledge and experience, motivation, intellectual capacity, and personality—and to ask the following questions:

  - Knowledge and experience: What must the candidate know to perform the job? What experience is absolutely necessary to perform the job?

  - Motivation: What should the person like doing to enjoy this job? Is there anything the person should not dislike? Are there any essential goals or aspirations the person should have? Are there any unusual energy demands on the job?

  - Intellectual capacity: Are there any specific intellectual aptitudes required (mathematical, mechanical, and so on)? How complex are the problems the person must solve? What must a person be able to demonstrate he or she can do intellectually? How should the person solve problems (cautiously, deductively, and so on)?

  - Personality: What are the critical personality qualities needed for success on the job (ability to withstand boredom, decisiveness, stability, and so on)? How must the job incumbent handle stress, pressure, and criticism? What kind of interpersonal behaviour is required in the job up the line, at peer level, down the line, and outside the firm with customers?

- Specific factors to probe in the interview: A combination of situational questions and open-ended questions like those in **Figure 7.6** on page 195 should be asked to probe the candidate's suitability for the job. For example:

  - Knowledge and experience factor: Situational questions such as "How would you organize such a sales effort?" or "How would you design that kind of website?" can probe for information on this factor.

  - Intellectual factor: Here, such things as complexity of tasks the person has performed, grades in school, test results (including scholastic aptitude tests and so on), and how the person organizes his or her thoughts and communicates are assessed.

  - Motivation factor: The person's likes and dislikes (for each task, what he or she liked or disliked about it), aspirations (including the validity of each goal in terms of the person's reasoning about why he or she chose it), and energy level should be probed, perhaps by asking what he or she does on, say, a "typical Tuesday."

  - Personality factor: Questions probing for selfdefeating behaviours (aggressiveness, compulsive fidgeting, and so on) and exploring the person's past interpersonal relationships should be asked. Additional questions about the person's

continued

past interactions (working in a group at school, working with fraternity brothers or sorority sisters, leading the work team on the last job, and so on) should also be asked. A judgment about the person's behaviour in the interview itself can also be made—is the candidate personable? Shy? Outgoing?

- Conducting the interview. Devise and use a plan to guide the interview. According to interviewing expert John Drake, significant areas to cover include the candidate's

  - college or university experiences

  - work experiences—summer, part time

  - work experience—full time

  - goals and ambitions

  - reactions to the job you are interviewing for

  - self-assessments (by the candidate of his or her strengths and weaknesses)

  - military experiences

  - present outside activities

  - Follow the plan: Begin with an open-ended question for each topic, such as, "Could you tell me about what you did when you were in high school?"

Keep in mind that information must be elicited regarding four main traits—intelligence, motivation, personality, and knowledge and experience. The information in each of these four areas can then be accumulated as the person answers. Follow-up questions on particular areas such as "Could you elaborate on that, please?" can then be used.

- Match the candidate to the job: After following the interview plan and probing for the four factors, conclusions can be drawn about the person's intellectual capacity, knowledge and experience, motivation, and personality, and the candidate's general strengths and limitations can be summarized using an interview evaluation form (for instance, see **Figure 7.7** on page 196). The conclusions can then be compared to both the job description and the list of behavioural requirements developed when preparing for the interview. This should provide a rational basis for matching the candidate to the job based on an analysis of the traits and aptitudes the job actually requires.

Source: Based on John Drake, *Interviewing for Managers: A Complete Guide to Employment Interviewing* (New York, NY: AMCOM, 1982). Reprinted with permission.

and screening devices used are also not standardized across organizations. Even within a firm, the number and sequence of steps often vary with the type and level of the job, as well as the source and method of recruitment. **Figure 7.1** illustrates the steps commonly involved.

At each step in the selection process, carefully chosen selection criteria must be used to determine which applicants will move on to the next step. It is through job analysis that the duties, responsibilities, and human requirements for each job are identified. By basing selection criteria on these requirements, firms can create a legally defensible hiring system.[3] Individuals hired after thorough screening against these carefully developed selection criteria (based directly on the job description and job specifications) learn their jobs readily, are productive, and generally adjust to their jobs with a minimum of difficulty.

Designing an effective selection process involves composing a series of job-related questions to be asked of all applicants for a particular job. There are also a few job-related, candidate-specific questions. Doing so involves the following five steps, the first two of which should occur before recruitment:[4]

1. *Decide who will be involved in the selection process and develop selection criteria.* Specifying selection criteria involves clarifying and weighting the information in the job description and job specifications and holding discussions among the interview-team members, especially those most familiar with the job and co-workers.

FIGURE **7.1** Typical Steps in the Selection Process

6. Hiring decision and candidate notification

5. Supervisory interview and realistic job preview

4. Background investigation/reference checking

3. Selection interview

2. Selection testing

1. Preliminary applicant screening

must criteria Requirements that are absolutely essential for the job, include a measurable standard of acceptability, or are absolute and can be screened initially on paper.

want criteria Those criteria that represent qualifications that cannot be screened on paper or are not readily measurable, as well as those that are highly desirable but not critical.

RPC

Supports managers in the selection of candidates

2. *Specify musts and wants and weight the wants.* Once agreed on, the selection criteria should be divided into the two categories: musts and wants.[5] **Must criteria** are those that are absolutely essential for the job, include a measurable standard of acceptability, or are absolute. There are often only two musts: a specific level of education (or equivalent combination of education and work experience) and a minimum amount of prior work experience. These criteria can be initially screened, based on the applicants' résumés or applications. The **want criteria** include skills and abilities that cannot be screened on paper (such as verbal skills) or are not readily measurable (such as leadership ability, teamwork skills, and enthusiasm), as well as qualifications that are desirable but not critical.

3. Determine assessment strategies and *develop an evaluation form.* Once the must and want criteria have been identified, appropriate strategies for learning about each should be specified. For some qualifications, especially those that are critically important, the team may decide to use several assessment strategies. For example, leadership skills might be assessed through behavioural questions, situational questions, a written test, and an assessment centre. Once all want criteria have been agreed on and weighted, it becomes the basis for candidate comparison and evaluation, as illustrated in **Figure 7.2.**

4. *Develop interview questions* to be asked of all candidates. Questions should be developed for each KSA to be assessed during the interview. *Job-knowledge questions* and *worker-requirements questions* to gauge the applicants' motivation and willingness to perform under prevailing working conditions, such as shift work or travel, should also be included.

5. *Develop candidate-specific questions.* A few open-ended, job-related questions that are candidate specific should be planned, based on each candidate's résumé and application form.

FIGURE 7.2 Worksheet—Comparison of Candidates for an Administrative Assistant Position

Alternatives

Criteria — Must	A Smith Info	A Go/No	B Brown Info	B Go/No	C Yuill Info	C Go/No
Education — Office Admin. diploma or equivalent experience (3 years' clerical/secretarial experience)	Office admin. diploma	Go	Office admin. diploma	Go	No diploma, 1 year related experience	No Go
Experience — At least 2 years' secretarial/clerical experience	3 years' experience	Go	2 years' experience	Go		Go

Wants	Wt.	A Smith Info	A Sc.	A Wt. Sc.	B Brown Info	B Sc.	B Wt. Sc.	C Yuill Info	C Sc.	C Wt. Sc.
Keyboarding/word processing	10	Word processing test			Word processing test	9	90	Word processing test	10	100
Good oral communication	9	Interview assessment			Interview assessment	9	81	Interview assessment	9	81
Good spelling/grammar	9	Test results			Test results	8	72	Test results	9	81
Organizational ability	9	Interview questions/simulation/ reference checking			Interview questions/simulation/ reference checking	8	72	Interview questions/simulation/ reference checking	9	81
Initiative	8	Interview questions/simulation/ reference checking			Interview questions/simulation/ reference checking	7	56	Interview questions/simulation/ reference checking	8	64
High ethical standards	7	Interview questions/simulation/ reference checking			Interview questions/simulation/ reference checking	7	49	Interview questions/simulation/ reference checking	7	49
Shorthand skills (or speed writing)	4	Interview question and test results			Interview question and test results	4	16	Interview question and test results	0	0
Designated group member, other than white female	2	Application form			Application form	2	4	Application form	0	0
							440			456 TOP CANDIDATE

Acquiring Employees and the Law

The entire recruitment and selection procedure must comply with human rights legislation. All information collected from the time an ad is posted to the time that the selection decision is made must be free from questions that would directly or indirectly classify candidates on the basis of any of the prohibited grounds under human rights legislation; potential employers cannot ask for a photograph, information about illnesses, disabilities or workers' compensation claims, or information that could lead to direct, intentional discrimination, such as age, gender, sexual orientation, marital status, maiden name, date of birth, place of origin, number of dependents, and so on.

If the process collects any information that is considered a prohibited ground for discrimination, an unsuccessful candidate may challenge the legality of the entire recruitment and selection processes. In such cases, the burden of proof is on the employer. Thus, taking human rights legislation requirements into consideration when designing effective recruitment and selection procedures is imperative. *A Guide to Screening and Selection in Employment* in **Appendix 7.1** provides helpful hints. Specific guidelines regarding questions that can and cannot be asked on application forms are available through the human rights commissions in each jurisdiction.

Managing the process in a legally defensible way involves keeping the following guidelines in mind:

1. Selection personnel cannot ask questions that would violate human rights legislation, either directly or indirectly. Questions cannot be asked about candidates' marital status, childcare arrangements, ethnic background, or workers' compensation history, for example.

2. All candidates must be treated in the same manner. Any agent of the organization cannot ask only female factory position applicants to demonstrate their lifting abilities, for example, or question female sales applicants about their willingness to travel but not ask male candidates. However, accommodation must be provided to applicants with disabilities (see the Workforce Diversity box).

3. Cutting short an interview based on preconceived notions about the gender or race of the "ideal" candidate must also be avoided, because this is another example of illegal differential treatment.

4. A helpful phrase to keep in mind when designing selection criteria is "This job requires . . ." Organization representatives who focus on the job description and job specifications can gather all the information required to assess applicants without infringing on the candidates' legal rights.

STEP 1: PRELIMINARY APPLICANT SCREENING

Initial applicant screening is generally performed by members of the HR department. Application forms and résumés are reviewed, and those candidates not meeting the essential selection criteria are eliminated first. Then, the remaining applications are examined and those candidates who most closely match the remaining job specifications are identified and given further consideration.

The use of technology is becoming increasingly popular to help HR professionals improve the initial screening process. Almost all large firms or firms with high turnover use technological applications to help screen large numbers of candidates and generate short lists of individuals who will move on to the next step in the selection process.

WORKFORCE DIVERSITY

Principles for Assessment Accommodations

There are four principles those responsible for assessment should be guided by in determining accommodations when assessing persons with disabilities.

Principle 1: Provide all applicants with an equal opportunity to fully demonstrate their qualifications.
A disability may hinder a person from fully demonstrating his or her qualifications using a particular assessment instrument. Therefore, adjustments need to be made to the administration procedures or to the assessment instrument itself so that the person is in a position to fully demonstrate his or her qualifications.

Principle 2: Determine assessment accommodations on a case-by-case basis.
Three key elements must be considered when determining appropriate accommodations:

- The nature and the extent of the individual's functional limitation
- The type of assessment instrument being used
- The nature and level of the qualification being assessed

Principle 3: Do not alter the nature or level of the qualification being assessed.
For example, although providing additional time to complete a test could be appropriate when the qualification "knowledge of the organization's mandate and its business" is assessed, providing additional time could be inappropriate for a test assessing the qualification "verify information rapidly and accurately." In the latter case, the obtained result may not be representative of the applicant's true ability to do the task rapidly, considering the additional time given.

Principle 4: Base assessment accommodations on complete information.
To make appropriate decisions when determining assessment accommodations, there is a need to rely on complete information on the three elements mentioned earlier, justifying the case-by-case approach:

1. The nature and the extent of the individual's functional limitations: For example, the appropriate accommodation for one person who is partially sighted may require a large print format of a test; while for another person who is also partially sighted, the appropriate accommodation may require special lighting. These differences arise because the nature and extent of the functional limitations vary from one individual to another.

2. Type of assessment instrument: For example, someone who has functional limitations that affect his or her manual writing speed may need some additional time to write an essay-style exam, while the same person may not need additional time for a multiple-choice exam that does not require written responses beyond filling in circles on a response sheet.

3. Nature of the qualification being assessed: For example, allowing the use of a calculator for a test assessing "ability to perform financial calculations" could be appropriate. However, allowing the use of a calculator when the "ability to do mental calculations" is assessed would be inappropriate. In the latter case, the provision of the calculator would invalidate the result, as it would not be representative of the applicant's ability to do the task mentally.

Source: Guide for Assessing Persons with Disabilities, http://www.psc-cfp.gc.ca/plcy-pltq/guides/assessment-evaluation/apwd-eph/pdf/apwd-eph-eng.pdf (pp. 10–12), Public Service Commission of Canada, Policy Development Directorate, July 2007. Reproduced with the permission of the Minister of Public Works and Government Services Canada, 2012.

STEP 2: SELECTION TESTING

Selection testing is a common screening device used by approximately two-thirds of Canadian organizations to assess specific job-related skills as well as general intelligence, personality characteristics, mental abilities, interests, and preferences.[6] Testing techniques provide efficient, standardized procedures for screening large numbers of applicants. Several thousand psychological and personality tests are on the market.[7]

The Importance of Reliability and Validity

Tests and other selection techniques are only useful if they provide reliable and valid measures.[8] All reputable tests will provide information to users about the reliability and validity of the test.

Reliability

reliability The degree to which interviews, tests, and other selection procedures yield comparable data over time; in other words, the degree of dependability, consistency, or stability of the measures used.

The degree to which interviews, tests, and other selection procedures yield comparable data over time is known as **reliability**. Reliability is the degree of dependability, consistency, or stability of the measures used. For example, a test that results in widely variable scores (for example, if the same candidate completes the test three times and secures scores of 60 percent, 82 percent, and 71 percent) when it is administered on different occasions to the same individual is unreliable. Reliability also refers to the extent to which two or more methods yield the same results or are consistent. For example, applicants with high scores on personality tests for impulsivity or lack of self-control are correlated with the likelihood of failing background checks due to criminal behaviour.[9] Reliability also means the extent to which there is agreement between two or more raters (inter-rater reliability).

When dealing with tests, another measure of reliability that is taken into account is internal consistency. For example, suppose a vocational interest test has 10 items, all of which were supposed to measure, in one way or another, the person's interest in working outdoors. To assess internal reliability, the degree to which responses to those 10 items vary together would be statistically analyzed (which is one reason that tests often include questions that appear rather repetitive). Reliability can be diminished when questions are answered randomly, when the test setting is noisy or uncomfortable, and when the applicant is tired or unwell.

Validity

validity The accuracy with which a predictor measures what it is intended to measure.

Validity, in the context of selection, is an indicator of the extent to which data from a selection technique, such as a test or interview, are related to or predictive of subsequent performance on the job. For example, high impulsivity is correlated with low productivity.[10] Separate validation studies of selection techniques should be conducted for different subgroups, such as visible minorities and women, to assess **differential validity**. In some cases, the technique may be a valid predictor of job success for one group (such as white males) but not for other applicants, thereby leading to systemic discrimination.

differential validity Confirmation that the selection tool accurately predicts the performance of all possible employee subgroups, including white males, women, visible minorities, persons with disabilities, and Aboriginal people.

Three types of validity are particularly relevant to selection: criterion-related, content, and construct validity.

criterion-related validity The extent to which a selection tool predicts or significantly correlates with important elements of work behaviour.

Criterion-Related Validity The extent to which a selection tool predicts or significantly correlates with important elements of work behaviour is known as **criterion-related validity**. Demonstrating criterion-related validity requires proving that those who exhibit strong sales ability on a test or in an interview, for example, also have high sales on the job, and that those individuals who do poorly on the test or in the interview have poor sales results.

content validity The extent to which a selection instrument, such as a test, adequately samples the knowledge and skills needed to perform the job.

Content Validity When a selection instrument, such as a test, adequately samples the knowledge and skills needed to perform the job, **content validity** is assumed to exist. The closer the content of the selection instrument is to actual samples of work or work behaviour, the greater the content validity. For example, asking a candidate for a secretarial position to demonstrate word processing skills, as required on the job, has high content validity.

construct validity The extent to which a selection tool measures a theoretical construct or trait deemed necessary to perform the job successfully.

Construct Validity The extent to which a selection tool measures a theoretical construct or trait deemed necessary to perform the job successfully is known as **construct validity**. Intelligence, verbal skills, analytical ability, and leadership skills are all examples of constructs. Measuring construct validity requires demonstrating that the psychological trait or attribute is related to satisfactory job performance, as well as showing that the test or other selection tool used accurately measures the psychological trait or attribute. As an example of poor construct validity, an accounting firm was selecting applicants for auditor positions based on a test for high extroversion, when the job in fact required working alone with data. A test to select applicants with high introversion would have had higher construct validity and would have helped to avoid the high turnover rate the firm was experiencing.[11]

Professional standards for psychologists require that tests be used as supplements to other techniques, such as interviews and background checks; that tests be validated in the organization where they will be used; that a certified psychologist be used to choose, validate, administer, and interpret tests; and that private, quiet, well-lit, and well-ventilated settings be provided to all applicants taking the tests.[12]

RPC

Evaluates the effectiveness of selection processes, tools, and outcomes

Tests of Cognitive Abilities

Ensuring validity of selection tools when assessing candidates with disabilities may require accommodation of the disability. Some guidelines are provided in the Workforce Diversity box on page 181. Included in the category of tests of cognitive abilities are tests of general reasoning ability (intelligence), tests of emotional intelligence, and tests of specific cognitive abilities, like memory and inductive reasoning.

RPC

Determines the appropriate selection tools and develops new tools as required

Intelligence Tests

intelligence (IQ) tests Tests that measure general intellectual abilities, such as verbal comprehension, inductive reasoning, memory, numerical ability, speed of perception, spatial visualization, and word fluency.

Intelligence (IQ) tests are tests of general intellectual abilities (also referred to as general mental abilities) and have been used since the end of World War I.[13] They measure not a single "intelligence" trait, but rather a number of abilities, including memory, vocabulary, verbal fluency, and numerical ability. An IQ score is actually a *derived* score, reflecting the extent to which the person is above or below the "average" adult's intelligence score. Empirical research suggests that general mental ability is the strongest general predictor of job performance at one's chosen occupation.[14] Intelligence is often measured with individually administered tests, such as the Stanford-Binet test or the Wechsler test. Other IQ tests, such as the Wonderlic Personnel Test, can be administered to groups of people. These are relatively quick pen and paper or online tests that can be accessed for a nominal fee.

Emotional Intelligence Tests

emotional intelligence (EI) tests Tests that measure a person's ability to monitor his or her own emotions and the emotions of others and to use that knowledge to guide thoughts and actions.

Emotional intelligence (EI) tests measure a person's ability to monitor his or her own emotions and the emotions of others and to use that knowledge to guide thoughts and actions. Someone with a high emotional quotient (EQ) is self-aware, can control his or her impulses, is self-motivated, and demonstrates empathy and social awareness. Many people believe that EQ, which can be modified through conscious effort and practice, is actually a more important determinant of success than a high IQ. However, there is extremely limited and somewhat highly controversial empirical evidence to support the importance of EI in the workplace.[15] Self-assessment EI tests include the Emotional Quotient Inventory (EQ-i), the EQ Map, the Mayer-Salovey-Caruso Emotional Intelligence Test (MSCEIT), and the Emotional Intelligence Questionnaire (EIQ). The Emotional Competence Inventory (ECI) is a 360-degree assessment in which several individuals evaluate one person to get a more complete picture of the individual's emotional competencies.[16]

Emotional Intelligence Consortium
www.eiconsortium.org

Specific Cognitive Abilities

There are also measures of specific thinking skills, such as inductive and deductive reasoning, verbal comprehension, memory, and numerical ability. Tests in this category are often called **aptitude tests**, since they purport to measure the applicant's aptitude for the job in question, that is, the applicant's potential to perform the job once given proper training. An example is the test of mechanical comprehension illustrated in **Figure 7.3**. It tests the applicant's understanding of basic mechanical principles. It may therefore reflect a person's aptitude for

aptitude tests Tests that measure an individual's aptitude or potential to perform a job, provided he or she is given proper training.

FIGURE 7.3 Two Problems from the Test of Mechanical Comprehension

Source: Sample Items from the Bennet Mechanical Comprehension Test. Copyright 1942, 1967–1970, and 1980 by NCS Pearson, Inc. Reproduced with permission. All rights reserved. "Bennet Mechanical Comprehension Test" and "BMCT" are trademarks in the US and/or other countries, of Pearson Education, Inc. or its affiliates(s).

jobs—like that of machinist or engineer—that require mechanical comprehension. Multidimensional aptitude tests commonly used in applicant selection include the General Aptitude Test Battery (GATB).

Tests of Motor and Physical Abilities

There are many *motor abilities* that a firm might want to measure. These include finger dexterity, manual dexterity, speed of arm movement, and reaction time. The Crawford Small Parts Dexterity Test, as illustrated in **Figure 7.4**, is an example. It measures the speed and accuracy of simple judgment, as well as the speed of finger, hand, and arm movements. Other tests include the Stromberg Dexterity Test, the Minnesota Rate of Manipulation Test, and the Purdue Pegboard.

Tests of physical abilities may also be required.[17] For example, some firms are now using functional abilities evaluations (FAE) to assist with placement decisions. An FAE, which measures a whole series of physical abilities—ranging from lifting, to pulling and pushing, sitting, squatting, climbing, and carrying—is particularly useful for positions with a multitude of physical demands, such as a firefighter or police officer.[18] Ensuring that physical abilities tests do not violate human rights legislation requires basing such tests on job duties identified through job analysis and a physical demands analysis, ensuring that the tests duplicate the actual physical requirements of the job, developing and imposing such tests honestly and in good faith, ensuring that those administering the tests are properly trained and administer the tests in a consistent manner, and ensuring that testing standards are objectively related to job performance.[19]

FIGURE 7.4   Crawford Small Parts Dexterity Test

Measuring Personality and Interests

A person's mental and physical abilities are seldom sufficient to explain his or her job performance. Other factors, such as the person's motivation and interpersonal skills, are important too. Personality and interest inventories are sometimes used as predictors of such intangibles.

personality tests Instruments used to measure basic aspects of personality, such as introversion, stability, motivation, neurotic tendency, self-confidence, self-sufficiency, and sociability.

Personality tests can measure basic aspects of an applicant's personality, such as introversion, stability, and motivation. The use of such tests for selection assumes that it is possible to find a relationship between a measurable personality trait (such as conscientiousness) and success on the job.[20] Many of these tests are *projective*. In the Thematic Apperception Test, an ambiguous stimulus (like an inkblot or clouded picture) is presented to the test taker, and he or she is asked to interpret or react to it. Because the pictures are ambiguous, the person's interpretation must come from within—the viewer supposedly *projects* into the picture his or her own emotional attitudes about life. Thus, a security-oriented person might have a very different description of what he or she sees compared to someone who is not.

Psychometric Assessments
www.psychometrics.com

The Myers-Briggs Type Indicator instrument, which has been in use for more than 50 years, is believed to be the most widely used personality inventory in the world. More than 2 million assessments are administered annually in the United States alone.[21] Another example of a common personality test is the Minnesota Multiphasic Personality Inventory (MMPI), which measures traits like hypochondria and paranoia.

Research **INSIGHT**

Research studies confirm that personality tests can help companies hire more effective workers. For example, industrial psychologists often talk in terms of the "Big Five" personality dimensions as they apply to employment testing: *extroversion, emotional stability, agreeableness, conscientiousness,* and *openness to experience.*[22] These dimensions can be measured using the NEO Five-Factor Inventory (NEO-FFI) and similar tests. One study focused on the extent to which these dimensions predicted performance (in terms of job and training proficiency, for example) for professionals, police officers, managers, sales workers, and skilled/semi-skilled workers. Conscientiousness showed a consistent relationship with all performance criteria for every occupation.

FIGURE **7.5** Sample Picture from Thematic Apperception Test: How Do You Interpret It?

Extroversion was a valid predictor of performance for managers and sales employees—the two occupations involving the most social interaction. Both openness to experience and extroversion predicted training proficiency for all occupations.[23]

There has been an ongoing debate in the research world on whether personality can be faked. In a test of 77 experienced assessors, over 70 percent agreed that "faking is a serious threat to the validity of personality inventory in the assessment process."[24] Evidence supports two specific trends in personality tests and faking: (1) people can fake personality inventories when they are motivated to do so, and (2) individual differences exist in the ability to fake.[25]

Interest inventories compare a candidate's interests with those of people in various occupations. Thus, a person taking the Strong-Campbell Interest Inventory would receive a report comparing his or her interests with those of people already in occupations such as accountant, engineer, manager, or medical technologist. Interest inventories have many uses. One is career planning, since people generally do better in jobs involving activities in which they have an interest. Another is selection. If the firm can select people whose interests are roughly the same as those of high-performing incumbents in the jobs for which it is hiring, the new employees are more likely to be successful.[26]

Achievement Tests

An **achievement test** is basically a measure of what a person has learned. Most of the tests taken in school are achievement tests. They measure knowledge or proficiency in such areas as economics, marketing, or HRM. Achievement tests are also widely used in selection. For example, the Purdue Test for Machinists and Machine Operators tests the job knowledge of experienced machinists with such questions as "What is meant by 'tolerance'?" Other tests are available for electricians, welders, carpenters, and so forth. In addition to job knowledge, achievement tests measure the applicant's abilities; a keyboarding test is one example.

Work Sampling

Work samples focus on measuring job performance directly and thus are among the best predictors of job performance. In developing a work-sampling test, experts first list all the possible tasks that jobholders would be required to perform. Then, by listing the frequency of performance and relative importance of each task, key tasks are identified. Each applicant then performs the key tasks, and his or her work is monitored by the test administrator, who records the approach taken. Finally, the work-sampling test is validated by determining the relationship between the applicants' scores on the work samples and their actual performance on the job. Once it is shown that the work sample is a valid predictor of job success, the employer can begin using it for selection.[27]

Management Assessment Centres

In a two- to three-day **management assessment centre**, the management potential of 10 or 12 candidates is assessed by expert appraisers who observe them performing realistic management tasks. The centre may be a plain conference room, but it is often a special room with a one-way mirror to facilitate unobtrusive

---

Research Psychologists Press
www.rpp.on.ca

interest inventories Tests that compare a candidate's interests with those of people in various occupations.

achievement tests Tests used to measure knowledge or proficiency acquired through education, training, or experience.

management assessment centre A comprehensive, systematic procedure used to assess candidates' management potential that uses a combination of realistic exercises, management games, objective testing, presentations, and interviews.

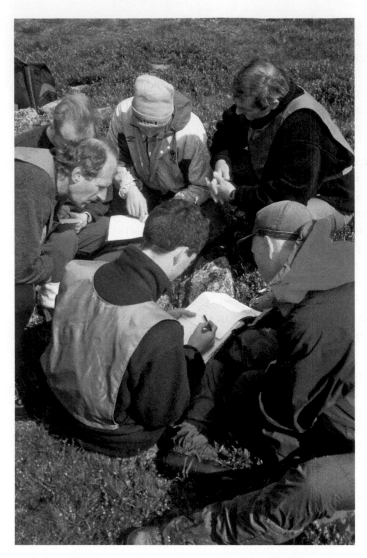

A management game or simulation is a typical component in a management assessment centre.

observations. Examples of the types of activities and exercises involved include the following:

1. *An in-basket exercise.* Each candidate is faced with an accumulation of reports, memos, messages from incoming phone calls, letters, and other materials collected in the in-basket of the simulated job that he or she is to take over and is required to take appropriate action. For example, he or she must write letters, return phone calls, and prepare meeting agendas. The trained evaluators then review the results.

2. *A leaderless group discussion.* A leaderless group is given a discussion question and told to arrive at a group decision. The raters evaluate each candidate's interpersonal skills, acceptance by the group, leadership ability, and individual influence.

3. *Management games.* Participants engage in realistic problem solving, usually as members of two or more simulated companies that are competing in the marketplace. Decisions might have to be made about issues such as how to advertise and manufacture and how much inventory to keep in stock.

4. *Individual presentations.* During oral presentations on an assigned topic, each participant's communication skills and persuasiveness are evaluated.

5. *Objective tests.* Candidates may be asked to complete paper and pencil or computer-based personality, aptitude, interest, or achievement tests.

6. *An interview.* Most centres also require an interview between at least one of the expert assessors and each participant to evaluate interests, background, past performance, and motivation.

Situational Testing

situational tests Tests in which candidates are presented with hypothetical situations representative of the job for which they are applying and are evaluated on their responses.

In **situational tests,** candidates are presented with hypothetical situations representative of the job for which they are applying (often on video) and are evaluated on their responses.[28] Several of the assessment centre exercises described above are examples of situational tests. In a typical test, a number of realistic scenarios are presented and each is followed by a multiple-choice question with several possible courses of action, from which candidates are asked to select the "best" response, in their opinion.[29] The level of each candidate's skills is then evaluated, and an assessment report can be easily generated, making the simulation easier and less expensive to administer than other screening tools. Simulations also provide a realistic job preview by exposing candidates to the types of activities they will encounter on the job.

Research **INSIGHT**

A research study of situational testing on 160 civil service employees demonstrated the validity of the situational test in predicting overall job performance as well as three performance dimensions: core technical proficiency, job dedication, and interpersonal facilitation. The situational test provided valid predictive information over and above cognitive ability tests, personality tests, and job experience.[30]

Micro-Assessments

micro-assessment A series of verbal, paper-based, or computer-based questions and exercises that a candidate is required to complete, covering the range of activities required on the job for which he or she is applying.

An entirely performance-based testing strategy that focuses on individual performance is a **micro-assessment**. In a micro-assessment, each applicant completes a series of verbal, paper-based, or computer-based questions and exercises that cover the range of activities required on the job for which he or she is applying. In addition to technical exercises, participants are required to solve a set of work-related problems that demonstrate their ability to perform well within the confines of a certain department or corporate culture. Exercises are simple to develop because they are taken directly from the job.

Physical Examination, Substance Abuse Testing, and Polygraph Tests

Interactive employment tests administered on the computer are becoming popular as screening devices at many firms.

The use of medical examinations in selection has decreased, in part because of the loss of physically demanding manufacturing and natural resource jobs. Before 1980, 25 percent of new hires underwent a medical exam, but by 2001, only 11 percent were required to do so.[31] Three main reasons that firms may include a medical examination as a step in the selection process are (1) to determine that the applicant *qualifies for the physical requirements* of the position and, if not, to document any *accommodation requirements*; (2) to establish a *record and baseline* of the applicant's health for the purpose of future insurance or compensation claims; and (3) to *reduce absenteeism and accidents* by identifying any health issues or concerns that need to be addressed, including communicable diseases of which the applicant may have been unaware. Medical exams are only permitted after a written offer of employment has been extended (except in the case of bona fide occupational requirements, as for food handlers).

The purpose of pre-employment substance abuse testing is to avoid hiring employees who would pose unnecessary risks to themselves and others or perform below expectations. However, in Canada, employers are not permitted to screen candidates for substance abuse. Alcohol and drug addiction is considered to be a disability under human rights codes (see Chapter 2), and an employee cannot be discriminated against during the selection process based on a disability.[32]

A polygraph test (also referred to as a lie detector test) involves using a series of controlled questions while simultaneously assessing physiological conditions of individuals such as blood pressure, pulse, respiration, and skin conductivity, with the assumption that deceptive responses produce different physiological responses than truthful responses. Such tests have been widely rejected by the scientific community since they have failed to produce valid or reliable results. In Ontario, the Employment Standards Act specifically prohibits use of polygraphs in pre-employment selection. Validated tests of honesty or integrity are more useful and reliable in the selection process.

STEP 3: THE SELECTION INTERVIEW

selection interview A procedure designed to predict future job performance on the basis of applicants' oral responses to oral inquiries.

The interview is used by virtually all organizations for selecting job applicants. The **selection interview**, which involves a process of two-way communication between the interviewee and the interviewer, can be defined as "a procedure designed to predict future job performance on the basis of applicants' oral responses to oral inquiries."[33]

Interviews are considered to be one of the most important aspects of the selection process and generally have a major impact on both applicants and interviewers. Interviews significantly influence applicants' views about the job and organization, enable employers to fill in any gaps in the information provided on application forms and résumés, and supplement the results of any tests administered. They may also reveal entirely new types of information.

RPC

Administers a variety of selection tools, including tests, interviews, reference checks, and so on

A major reason for the popularity of selection interviews is that they meet a number of the objectives of both the interviewer and interviewee. Interviewer objectives include assessing applicants' qualifications and observing relevant aspects of applicants' behaviour, such as verbal communication skills, degree of self-confidence, and interpersonal skills; providing candidates with information about the job and expected duties and responsibilities; promoting the organization and highlighting its attractiveness; and determining how well the applicants would fit into the organization. Typical objectives of job applicants include presenting a positive image of themselves, selling their skills and marketing their positive attributes to the interviewer(s), and gathering information about the job and the organization so that they can make an informed decision about the job, career opportunities in the firm, and the work environment.[34]

Types of Interviews

Selection interviews can be classified according to the degree of structure, their content, and the way in which the interview is administered.

The Structure of the Interview

unstructured interview An unstructured, conversational-style interview. The interviewer pursues points of interest as they come up in response to questions.

First, interviews can be classified according to the degree to which they are structured. In an **unstructured interview**, questions are asked as they come to mind. Thus, interviewees for the same job may or may not be asked the same or similar questions, and the interview's unstructured nature allows the interviewer to ask questions based on the candidate's last statements and to pursue points of interest as they develop. Unstructured interviews generally have low reliability and validity.[35]

structured interview An interview following a set sequence of questions.

The interview can also be structured. In the classical **structured interview**, the questions and acceptable responses are specified in advance and the responses are rated for appropriateness of content.[36] In practice, however, most structured interviews do not involve specifying and rating responses in advance. Instead, each candidate is asked a series of predetermined, job-related questions based on the job description and specifications. Such interviews are generally high in validity and reliability. However, a totally structured interview does not provide the flexibility to pursue points of interest as they develop, which may result in an interview that seems quite mechanical to all concerned.

mixed (semi-structured) interview An interview format that combines the structured and unstructured techniques.

Between these two extremes is the **mixed (semi-structured) interview**, which involves a combination of pre-set, structured questions based on the job description and specification, and a series of candidate-specific, job-related questions based on information provided on the application form or résumé. The questions asked of all candidates facilitate candidate comparison, while the job-related, candidate-specific questions make the interview more conversational. A realistic approach that yields comparable answers and indepth insights, the mixed interview format is extremely popular.

Research INSIGHT

A study of 92 real employment interviews found that the interviewers using high levels of structure in the interview process evaluated applicants less favourably than those who used semi-structured or unstructured interviews, and those applicants who were evaluated using a semi-structured interview were rated slightly higher than those evaluated by unstructured interviews. Additionally, the study found that significant differences occur in the way that female and male interviewers evaluate their applicants. Although male interviewers' ratings were unaffected by the interview structure, female interviewers' ratings were substantially higher in unstructured and semi-structured interviews than in highly structured interviews.[37]

The Content of the Interview

situational interview A series of job-related questions that focus on how the candidate would behave in a given situation.

Interviews can also be classified according to the content of their questions. A **situational interview** is one in which the questions focus on the individual's ability to project what his or her *future* behaviour would be in a given situation.[38] The underlying premise is that intentions predict behaviour. For example, a candidate for a supervisory position might be asked how he or she would respond to an employee coming to work late three days in a row. The interview can be both *structured* and *situational*, with predetermined questions requiring the candidate to project what his or her behaviour would be. In a structured situational interview, the applicant could be evaluated, say, on whether he or she would try to determine if the employee was experiencing some difficulty in getting to work on time or would simply issue a verbal or written warning to the employee.

behavioural interview or behaviour description interview (BDI) A series of job-related questions that focus on relevant past job-related behaviours.

The **behavioural interview**, also known as a **behaviour description interview (BDI)**, involves describing various situations and asking interviewees how they behaved *in the past* in such situations.[39] The underlying assumption is that the best predictor of future performance is past performance in similar circumstances.

Administering the Interview

Interviews can also be classified based on how they are administered:

- One-on-one or by a panel of interviewers
- Sequentially or all at once
- Face-to-face or technology aided (such as videoconferencing or by phone)

The majority of interviews are sequential, face-to-face, and one-on-one. In a *sequential* interview the applicant is interviewed by several persons in sequence before a selection decision is made. In an *unstructured sequential* interview each interviewer may look at the applicant from his or her own point of view, ask different questions, and form an independent opinion of the candidate. Conversely, in a *structured sequential* (or serialized) interview, each interviewer rates the candidate on a standard evaluation form, and the ratings are compared before the hiring decision is made.[40]

panel interview An interview in which a group of interviewers questions the applicant.

A panel interview is an efficient and cost-effective way of permitting a number of qualified persons to assess a candidate's KSAs.

A **panel interview** involves the candidate being interviewed simultaneously by a group (or panel) of interviewers, including an HR representative, the hiring manager, and potential co-workers, superiors, or reporting employees. The key advantages associated with this technique are the increased likelihood that the information provided will be heard and recorded accurately; varied questions pertaining to each interviewer's area of expertise; minimized time and travel/accommodation expenses as each interviewee only attends one interview; reduced likelihood of human rights/employment equity violations since an HR representative is present; and less likelihood of interviewer error, because of advanced planning and preparation.

A more stressful variant of the panel interview is the *mass interview*, which involves a panel simultaneously interviewing several candidates. The panel poses a problem to be solved and then sits back and watches which candidate takes the lead in formulating an answer.

Common Interviewing Mistakes

Several common interviewing errors that can undermine the usefulness of interviews are discussed in the following pages. These interviewer errors can be reduced by properly planning and training interviewers on the process, as well as educating interviewers about these risks.

Poor Planning

Many selection interviews are simply not carefully planned and may be conducted without having prepared written questions in advance. Lack of planning often leads to a relatively unstructured interview, in which whatever comes up is discussed. The end result may be little or no cross-candidate job-related information. The less structured the interview is, the less reliable and valid the evaluation of each candidate will be.[41]

Snap Judgments

One of the most consistent literature findings is that interviewers tend to jump to conclusions—make snap judgments—during the first few minutes of the interview or even before the interview begins based on the candidates' test scores or résumé data. Thus, candidates feel pressure to start off on the right foot with the interviewer. However, snap judgments are not accurate or reliable in the selection process and should be avoided.

Negative Emphasis

Many interviewers seem to have a consistent negative bias. They are generally more influenced by unfavourable than favourable information about the candidate. Also, their impressions are much more likely to change from favourable to unfavourable than vice versa. Providing information about the value or weight of criteria in the selection process can ensure that the interviewer assesses the criteria accordingly.

Halo Effect

It is also possible for a positive initial impression to distort an interviewer's rating of a candidate, because subsequent information is judged with a positive bias. This is known as the **halo effect**. Having gained a positive impression of the candidate on one or more factors, the interviewer may not seek contradictory information when listening to the candidate's answers to the questions posed or may interpret/frame all responses positively.

Poor Knowledge of the Job

Interviewers who do not know precisely what the job entails and what sort of candidate is best suited for it usually make their decisions based on incorrect stereotypes about what a good applicant is. Interviewers who have a clear understanding of what the job entails conduct more effective interviews.

Contrast (Candidate-Order) Error

Contrast or candidate-order error means that the order in which applicants are seen can affect how they are rated. In one study, managers were asked to evaluate a candidate who was "just average" after first evaluating several "unfavourable" candidates. The average candidate was evaluated more favourably than he or she might otherwise have been because, in contrast to the unfavourable candidates, the average one looked better than he or she actually was.

Influence of Nonverbal Behaviour

Interviewers are also influenced by the applicant's nonverbal behaviour, and the more eye contact, head moving, smiling, and other similar nonverbal behaviours, the higher the ratings. These nonverbal behaviours often account for more than 80 percent of the applicant's rating. This finding is of particular concern since nonverbal behaviour is tied to ethnicity and cultural background. An applicant's attractiveness and gender also play a role. Research has shown that those rated as being more physically attractive are also rated as more suitable for employment, well ahead of those rated average looking and those regarded as physically unattractive. Although this bias is considered to be unconscious, it may have serious implications for aging employees.[42]

Leading

Some interviewers are so anxious to fill a job that they help the applicants to respond correctly to their questions by asking leading questions or guiding the candidate to the expected answer. An obvious example might be a question like: "This job calls for handling a lot of stress. You can do that, right?" The leading is not always so obvious. Subtle cues regarding the preferred response, such as a smile or nod, are also forms of leading.[43]

Too Much/Too Little Talking

If the applicant is permitted to dominate the interview, the interviewer may not have a chance to ask his or her prepared questions and often learns very little about the candidate's job-related skills. At the other extreme, some interviewers talk so much that the interviewee is not given enough time to answer questions. One expert suggests using the 30/70 rule: During a selection interview, encourage the candidate to speak 70 percent of the time, and restrict the interviewer speaking to just 30 percent of the time.[44]

Similar-to-Me Bias

Interviewers tend to provide more favourable ratings to candidates who possess demographic, personality, and attitudinal characteristics similar to their own, regardless of the value of those characteristics to the job.[45] The result can be a lack of diversity in the organization and a poor fit with the job if secured.

Designing an Effective Interview

Problems like those just described can be avoided by designing and conducting an effective interview. Combining several of the interview formats previously discussed enables interviewers to capitalize on the advantages of each.[46] To allow for probing and to prevent the interview from becoming too mechanical in nature, a semi-structured format is recommended. Given their higher validity in predicting job performance, the focus should be on situational and behavioural questions.

Conducting an Effective Interview

Although the following discussion focuses on a semi-structured panel interview, the steps described apply to all selection interviews.[47]

Planning the Interview

Before the first interview, agreement should be reached on the procedure that will be followed. Sometimes all members of the team ask a question in turn; in other situations, only one member of the team asks questions and the others serve as observers. Sitting around a large table in a conference room is much more appropriate and far less stressful than having all panel members seated across from the candidate behind a table or desk, which forms both a physical and a psychological barrier. As noted earlier, special planning is required when assessing candidates with disabilities.

Establishing Rapport

The main purpose of an interview is to find out as much as possible about the candidate's fit with the job specifications, something that is difficult to do if the individual is tense and nervous. The candidate should be greeted in a friendly manner and put at ease.

Asking Questions

The questions written in advance should then be asked in order. Interviewers should listen carefully, encourage the candidate to express his or her thoughts and ideas fully, and record the candidate's answers briefly but thoroughly. Taking notes increases the validity of the interview process, since doing so (1) reduces the likelihood of

The rapport established with a job applicant not only puts the person at ease but also reflects the company's attitude toward its public.

forgetting job-relevant information and subsequently reconstructing forgotten information in accordance with biases and stereotypes; (2) reduces the likelihood of making a snap judgment and helps to prevent the halo effect, negative emphasis, and candidate-order errors; and (3) helps to ensure that all candidates are assessed on the same criteria.[48] Some examples of appropriate interview questions are shown in **Figure 7.6**.

Closing the Interview

Toward the end of the interview, time should be allocated to answer any questions that the candidate may have and, if appropriate, to advocate for the firm and position. It is useful to also inform the candidate about the next steps and timelines that the organization will follow at this point.

Evaluating the Candidate

Immediately following each interview, the applicant's interview performance should be rated by each panel member independently, based on a review of his or her notes or an observation form like the one shown in **Figure 7.7**. Since interviews are only one step in the process, and since a final decision cannot be reached until all assessments (including reference checking) have been completed, these evaluations should not be shared at this time.

FIGURE 7.6   Suggested Supplementary Questions for Interviewing Applicants

1. How did you choose this profession?
2. What did you enjoy most about your previous job?
3. What did you like least about your previous job?
4. Why did you leave your last job? What were the circumstances?
5. What has been your greatest frustration on your current job? Why?
6. Why should we be hiring you?
7. What do you expect from us?
8. What are three things you will not do in your next job?
9. What would your last employer say your three weaknesses are?
10. What would your last employer say your three major strengths are?
11. How can your manager best help you obtain your goals?
12. How did your manager rate your job performance?
13. Would you change your last supervisor? How?
14. What are your career goals during the next 1–3 years? 5–10 years?
15. How will working for this company help you reach those goals?
16. What did you do the last time you received instructions with which you disagreed?
17. What are some of the disagreements between you and your manager? What did you do?
18. Which do you prefer, working alone or working with teams?
19. What motivated you to do better at your last job?
20. Do you consider your progress on that job representative of your ability? Why?
21. Do you have any questions about the duties of the job for which you have applied?
22. How do you think you can perform the essential functions of the job for which you have applied?

Source: Based on www.HR.BLR.com

FIGURE **7.7** Interview Evaluation Form

Name of candidate:

Date interviewed:

Position:

Completed by:

Date:

Instructions: Circle one number for each criterion, then add them together for a total.

KNOWLEDGE OF SPECIFIC JOB AND JOB-RELATED TOPICS

0. No knowledge evident.
1. Less than we would prefer.
2. Meets requirements for hiring.
3. Exceeds our expectations of average candidates.
4. Thoroughly versed in job and very strong in associated areas.

EXPERIENCE

0. None for this job; no related experience either.
1. Would prefer more for this job. Adequate for job applied for.
2. More than sufficient for job.
3. Totally experienced in job.
4. Strong experience in all related areas.

COMMUNICATION

0. Could not communicate. Will be severely impaired in most jobs.
1. Some difficulties. Will detract from job performance.
2. Sufficient for adequate job performance.
3. More than sufficient for job.
4. Outstanding ability to communicate.

INTEREST IN POSITION AND ORGANIZATION

0. Showed no interest.
1. Some lack of interest.
2. Appeared genuinely interested.
3. Very interested. Seems to prefer type of work applied for.
4. Totally absorbed with job content. Conveys feeling only this job will do.

OVERALL MOTIVATION TO SUCCEED

0. None exhibited.
1. Showed little interest in advancement.
2. Average interest in advancement.
3. Highly motivated. Strong desire to advance.
4. Extremely motivated. Very strong desire to succeed and advance.

POISE AND CONFIDENCE

0. Extremely distracted and confused. Displayed uneven temper.
1. Sufficient display of confusion or loss of temper to interfere with job performance.
2. Sufficient poise and confidence to perform job.
3. No loss of poise during interview. Confidence in ability to handle pressure.
4. Displayed impressive poise under stress. Appears unusually confident and secure.

COMPREHENSION

0. Did not understand many points and concepts.
1. Missed some ideas or concepts.
2. Understood most new ideas and skills discussed.
3. Grasped all new points and concepts quickly.
4. Extremely sharp. Understood subtle points and underlying motives.

_____ **TOTAL POINTS**

ADDITIONAL REMARKS:

Source: Reprinted with permission of the publisher, Business & Legal Reports, Inc. Copyright Business & Legal Reports, Inc., 2011. www.HR.BLR.com

STEP 4: BACKGROUND INVESTIGATION/ REFERENCE CHECKING

Background investigation and reference checking are used to verify the accuracy of the information provided by candidates on their application forms and résumés. In an ideal world, every applicant's story would be completely accurate, but in real life this is often not the case, as illustrated in **Figure 7.8**. At least one-third of applicants lie—overstating qualifications or achievements, attempting to hide negative information, or being deliberately evasive or untruthful.[49]

Unfortunately, some employers do not check references, which can have grave consequences. Background checks are thus necessary to avoid negligent hiring lawsuits when others are placed in situations of unnecessary and avoidable risk.[50] Cases in Canada have included a nurse who practised in a Toronto hospital for almost two years without a registered nurse qualification, a manufacturing plant payroll officer who embezzled almost $2 million, and a teacher arrested for possessing child pornography.[51] Other problems can also be addressed through background checks. Loblaw recently took action to reduce its $1 billion disappearing goods problem by making criminal record checks mandatory for all prospective employees. As a result, 7.5 percent of prospective hires have been eliminated because of criminal records.[52]

Surveys indicate that at least 90 percent of Canadian organizations conduct background checks.[53] Many firms use reference-checking services or hire a consultant to perform this task. Obtaining such assistance may be a small price to pay to avoid the time and legal costs associated with the consequences of failing to do a thorough background check.

Whether requesting reference information in writing or asking for such information over the telephone, questions should be written down in advance. If enough time is taken and the proper questions are asked, such checking is an inexpensive and straightforward way of verifying factual information about the applicant. This may include current and previous job titles, salary, dates of employment, and reasons for leaving, as well as information about the applicant's fit with the prospective job and organizational culture.

CKR Global
www.ckrglobal.com

BackCheck
www.backcheck.ca

Investigative Research Group
www.irgcanada.com

FIGURE **7.8**   Top Seven Résumé Lies

1   Dates of employment

2   Job title (inflated rank)

3   Salary level

4   Criminal records

5   Education (bogus degrees, diploma mills)

6   Professional licence (MD, RN, etc.)

7   "Ghost" company (self-owned business)

Source: AccuScreen Inc., www.accuscreen.com/TOP7 (accessed May 24, 2009). Used with permission.

Information to Be Verified

A basic background check includes a criminal record check, independent verification of educational qualifications, and verification of at least five years' employment, together with checks of three performance-related references from past supervisors. For financially sensitive positions, a credit check may also be included.

Obtaining Written Permission

As a legal protection for all concerned, applicants should be asked to indicate, in writing, their willingness for the firm to check with current or former employers and other references. There is generally a section on the application form for this purpose. Many employers will not give out any reference information until they have received a copy of such written authorization. Because background checks may provide information on age or other prohibited grounds for discrimination, some employers do not conduct background checks until a conditional offer of employment has been extended.[54]

However, other employers do not hesitate to seek out information in the public domain at any time, without permission. A recent survey found that almost one-quarter of employers are using social networking sites like Facebook to gather information on job applicants. A third of those employers find enough negative information (such as the items listed in **Figure 7.9**) to eliminate a candidate from further consideration, and one-quarter of them find favourable content that supports the candidate's application.[55]

Providing References

In providing reference information, the concept of *qualified privilege* is important. Generally speaking, if comments are made in confidence for a public purpose, without malice, and are honestly believed, the defence of qualified privilege exists.

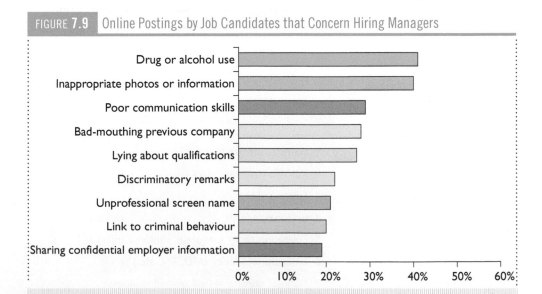

FIGURE 7.9 Online Postings by Job Candidates that Concern Hiring Managers

Thus, if honest, fair, and candid references are given by an individual who is asked to provide confidential information about the performance of a job applicant, then the doctrine of qualified privilege generally protects the reference giver, even if negative information is imparted about the candidate.[56] An overly positive reference, however, describing an employee dismissed for theft as "trustworthy," for example, can be considered *negligent misrepresentation* if the former employee steals from a new employer.[57] Due to concerns about the possibility of civil litigation, some Canadian companies have adopted a "no reference" policy regarding previous employees or are only willing to confirm the position held and dates of employment—especially in the case of discharged employees.[58]

STEP 5: SUPERVISORY INTERVIEW AND REALISTIC JOB PREVIEW

The two or three top candidates typically return for an interview with the immediate supervisor, who usually makes the final selection decision. The supervisory interview is important because the supervisor knows the technical aspects of the job, is most qualified to assess the applicants' job knowledge and skills, and is best equipped to answer any job-specific questions from the candidate. Also, the immediate supervisor generally has to work closely with the selected individual and must feel comfortable with that person. The selected individual must fit with the current members of the hiring department, something that the supervisor is often best able to assess. When a supervisor makes a hiring recommendation, he or she is usually committed to the new employee's success and will try to provide assistance and guidance. If the new hire is not successful, the supervisor is more likely to accept some of the responsibility.

realistic job preview (RJP)
A strategy used to provide applicants with realistic information—both positive and negative—about the job demands, the organization's expectations, and the work environment.

A **realistic job preview (RJP)** should be provided at the time of the supervisory interview. The purpose of an RJP is to create appropriate expectations about the job by presenting realistic information about the job demands, the organization's expectations, and the work environment.[59] Studies have reported that RJPs lead to improved employee job satisfaction, reduced voluntary turnover, and enhanced communication.[60] Although some candidates may choose not to accept employment with the firm after an RJP, those individuals probably would not have remained with the firm long had they accepted the job offer.[61]

STEP 6: HIRING DECISION AND CANDIDATE NOTIFICATION

RPC

Establishes appointment procedures for candidates selected through the recruitment process, ensuring that conditions of employment are documented and consistent with established policies

To make the hiring decision, information from the multiple selection techniques used must be combined, and the applicant who is the best fit with the selection criteria must be identified. HR department staff members generally play a major role in compiling all the data. It is the immediate supervisor who is usually responsible for making the final hiring decision, though. Firms generally make a subjective evaluation of all the information gleaned about each candidate and arrive at an overall judgment. The validity and reliability of these judgments can be improved by using tests that are objectively scored and by devising a candidate-rating sheet based on the weighted want criteria.

Another approach involves combining all the pieces of information according to a formula and giving the job to the candidate with the highest score. Research studies have indicated that this approach, called a **statistical strategy**, is generally more reliable and valid than is a subjective evaluation.[62]

statistical strategy A more objective technique used to determine whom the job should be offered to; involves identifying the most valid predictors and weighting them through statistical methods, such as multiple regression.

Regardless of collection methodology, all information used in making the selection decision should be kept in a file, including interview notes, test results, reference-checking information, and so on. In the event of a human rights challenge, negligent hiring charge, or union grievance about the selection decision, such data are critical.

Once the selection decision has been made, a job offer is extended to the successful candidate. Often, the initial offer is made by telephone, but it should be followed up with a written employment offer that clearly specifies important terms and conditions of employment, such as starting date, starting salary, probation period, and so on.

RPC

Supports managers in the negotiation of terms and conditions of employment

Candidates should be given a reasonable length of time in which to think about the offer and not be pressured into making an immediate decision. If there are two candidates who are both excellent and the first-choice candidate declines the offer, the runner-up can then be offered the job.

An Ethical : **Dilemma**

As the HR manager, how much feedback should you provide to those individuals not selected for a position?

Chapter SUMMARY

1. Selection is the process of choosing among individuals who have been recruited to fill existing or projected job openings. The purpose of selection is to find the "best" candidate. Because the quality of the company's human resources is often a competitive advantage in achieving the company's strategic objectives, selection of employees has considerable strategic importance. Those individuals selected will be implementing strategic decisions and, in some cases, creating strategic plans. Thus, the successful candidates must fit with the strategic direction of the organization.

2. Reliability (the degree to which selection techniques are dependable, consistent, and stable) and validity (which relates to accuracy) of selection tests and interviews are critically important for effective selection of the best candidate and to satisfy legal requirements.

3. The different types of tests used for selection include intelligence tests, emotional intelligence tests, aptitude tests, tests of motor and physical

abilities, personality tests, interest inventories, achievement tests, the work-sampling technique, management assessment centres, situational testing, micro-assessments, and medical examinations. Pre-employment substance abuse testing is not permitted under human rights legislation in Canada.

4. Selection interviewing can be unstructured, structured, or semi-structured. The content varies between situational interviews (focus on future behaviour) and behavioural interviews (focus on past behaviour). Interviews can be administered on a one-on-one basis, sequentially, or by using a panel.

5. Reference checking is an important source of information about job candidates. Failure to check references can lead to negligent or wrongful-hiring lawsuits. When providing references, the legal concept of qualified privilege means that if honest, fair, and candid references are given, the reference-giver is protected from litigation, even if negative information is

imparted about the candidate. Providing falsely positive references can lead to charges of negligent misrepresentation by subsequent employers. Fear of civil litigation has led some Canadian companies to adopt a policy of "no references" or to only confirm a former employee's position and dates of employment.

MyManagementLab

Visit MyManagementLab to access a personalized Study Plan and additional study tools for this chapter.

Key TERMS

achievement tests *(p. 187)*
aptitude tests *(p. 184)*
behavioural interview or behaviour description interview (BDI) *(p. 191)*
construct validity *(p. 183)*
content validity *(p. 182)*
contrast or candidate-order error *(p. 193)*
criterion-related validity *(p. 182)*
differential validity *(p. 182)*
emotional intelligence (EI) tests *(p. 183)*
halo effect *(p. 193)*
intelligence (IQ) tests *(p. 183)*
interest inventories *(p. 187)*
management assessment centre *(p. 187)*
micro-assessment *(p. 189)*
mixed (semi-structured) interview *(p. 190)*

multiple-hurdle strategy *(p. 175)*
must criteria *(p. 178)*
panel interview *(p. 192)*
personality tests *(p. 186)*
realistic job preview (RJP) *(p. 199)*
reliability *(p. 182)*
selection *(p. 174)*
selection interview *(p. 190)*
selection ratio *(p. 175)*
situational interview *(p. 191)*
situational tests *(p. 188)*
statistical strategy *(p. 200)*
structured interview *(p. 190)*
unstructured interview *(p. 190)*
validity *(p. 182)*
want criteria *(p. 178)*

Review and Discussion QUESTIONS

1. Explain the differences among criterion-related validity, content validity, and construct validity.

2. Describe five different types of testing that may be used in the selection process and give an example of each.

3. Describe any four activities involved in a management assessment centre.

4. Name and describe the pros and cons of the three different types of interview structures.

5. Explain the difference between situational and behavioural interviews. Give examples of situational and behavioural interview questions.

6. Briefly discuss any five common interviewing mistakes and explain how such errors can be avoided.

7. Why is the supervisory interview so important in the selection process?

Critical Thinking QUESTIONS

1. If you were asked to design an effective selection process for retail sales representatives working on a 100 percent commission basis, which of the steps described in this chapter would you include and why? Justify the omission of any steps and explain why the quality of the selection decision will not be compromised by their elimination.

2. Assume that you have just been hired as the employment manager in a small manufacturing firm that has never done any selection testing. Write a memorandum to the CEO describing the types of tests that you would recommend the firm consider using in the future. Also list some of the legal and ethical concerns pertaining to such testing and how such concerns can be overcome, and the benefits to the firm for using the recommended testing.

3. Describe strategies that you could use to (a) establish rapport with an extremely nervous candidate, (b) get an interviewee who is rambling "back on track," (c) clarify a statement made by an applicant during an interview, and (d) obtain detailed reference information from an individual who seems reluctant to say much.

4. Alberta oil and gas companies are using pre-employment substance abuse testing even though it is prohibited. Their argument is that, because they have multibillion-dollar projects underway with a lot of potential for accidents, environmental damage, and so on, they want to be sure that they are not hiring employees who have substance abuse problems. They know that their young, transient, and relatively wealthy oil sands workforce commonly abuses drugs and alcohol. How could this situation be resolved in the spirit of the law on accommodating disabilities?

Experiential EXERCISES

1. Design a semi-structured interview questionnaire for a position with which you are extremely familiar, basing the candidate-specific questions on your own résumé. Ensure that behavioural, situational, job-knowledge, and worker-requirements questions are included. Once you have done so, select a partner. Role-play two selection interviews—one based on your questionnaire and the other based on your partner's questionnaire. The individual who wrote the questions is to play the role of interviewee, with his or her partner serving as the interviewer. Do not forget to build rapport, ask the questions in order, take effective notes, and bring the interview to a close. Once you have completed the two role-plays, critically evaluate each interview questionnaire.

2. Create an offer of employment for a successful customer service representative at a call centre, outlining the terms and conditions of employment. Keep in mind that a copy of the letter should be signed and returned by the new hire and that a signed letter of offer becomes an employment contract.

3. Using the NOC job description and the competency job analysis you created earlier in the course for either a university or college professor, Develop two situational and two behavioural interview questions along with an outline of a "good" answer for each that you expect from the interviewees. Share and critique both questions and answers. Discuss how taking the time to complete this activity can help in candidate selection.

Running CASE

Running Case: LearnInMotion.com

The Better Interview

Like virtually all the other HR-related activities at LearnInMotion.com, the company has no organized approach to interviewing job candidates. Three people, Jennifer, Pierre, and Greg (from the board of directors), interview each candidate, and the three then get together for a discussion. Unfortunately, they usually reach strikingly different conclusions. For example, Greg thought a particular candidate was "stellar" and would not only be able to sell but also eventually assume various administrative responsibilities to take the load off Jennifer and Pierre. Pierre thought this particular candidate was hopeless: "I've been selling for eight years and have hired many salespeople, and there's no way this person's going to be a closer," he said. Jennifer, noting that a friend of her mother had recommended this particular candidate, was willing to take a wait-and-see attitude: "Let's hire her and see how she does," she said. Pierre replied that this was no way to hire a salesperson, and, in any case, hiring another administrator was pretty far down their priority list. "I wish Greg would stick to the problem at hand, namely hiring a 100-percent salesperson."

Jennifer was sure that inadequate formal interviewing practices, procedures, and training accounted for at least some of the problems they were having in hiring and keeping good salespeople. They did hire one salesperson whom they thought was going to be terrific, based on the praise provided by her references and on what they understood her previous sales experience had been; she stayed for a month and a half, sold hardly anything, cost the company almost $10 000 of its precious cash, and then left for another job.

The problem wasn't just with the salespeople. They also hired a programmer largely based on his assertion that he was expert in various web-related programming languages, including HTML, XML, and JavaScript. They followed up with one of his references, who was neutral regarding the candidate's programming abilities. But, being desperate, Jennifer and Pierre hired him anyway—only to have him leave three weeks later, more or less by mutual consent.

"This is a total disaster," said Jennifer, and Pierre could only agree. It was obvious that in some respects their interviews were worse than not interviewing at all. For example, if they didn't have interviews, perhaps they would have used more caution in following up with the candidates' references. In any case, they now want you, their management consultant, to tell them what to do.

QUESTIONS

1 How would you restructure LearnInMotion's selection process?

2 Should Pierre and Jennifer use the multiple-hurdle strategy? Why or why not?

3 What are some of the legal implications of a new selection process that Jennifer and Pierre need to be aware of?

Case INCIDENT

The Case of What Should Have Been Known

Sunrise Academy, a privately run technical college, has been operating now for four successful years. Executive Director Ron Phillips is responsible for overseeing the college. He has just been reviewing the latest enrollment figures and is pleasantly surprised again by the projected number for the upcoming school year. This will mean that a new professor will be needed in the business administration program. Ron picks up the phone and calls the director of human resources to start the process for drafting a job posting to advertise the position both internally and externally.

A week goes by and HR calls Ron to indicate that they have many applications available to be reviewed for potential interviews. Ron reviews the applicants and a short list is developed and called for interviews. After a round of four "okay, but not spectacular" interviews, Ron was beginning to think they would never find a good candidate. However, the last interviewee, Rita Miller, turned out to be the successful choice and was subsequently offered the position. HR checked two references prior to offering Rita the position in writing. HR also asked Rita to bring an original copy of her Masters of Business Administration degree once it was received, as this degree was a requirement in the professor posting.

Rita brought a copy of her degree to HR within a week of being offered the position. HR's policy is also to call the issuing institution to verify degrees. Things became busy in the department so it was nearly two months later when someone finally checked Rita's degree. The results indicated Rita's degree was forged. HR called Ron with the news, and Ron has asked you to come in to help him decide what to do next.

QUESTIONS

1 Are there any legal implications to be aware of as a result of this selection decision?

2 What should have been done differently in the selection process?

3 How should the background-checking process be improved at Sunrise Academy?

MyManagementLab

Visit MyManagementLab to access a personalized Study Plan and additional study tools for this chapter.

CBC To view the CBC videos, read a summary, and answer discussion questions, go to MyManagementLab

Subject	Avoid Asking	Preferred	Comment
Name	about name change: whether it was changed by court order, marriage, or other reason maiden name		ask after selection if needed to check on previously held jobs or educational credentials
Address	for addresses outside Canada	ask place and duration of current or recent address	
Age	for birth certificates, baptismal records, or about age in general	ask applicants whether they are eligible to work under Canadian laws regarding age restrictions	if precise age is required for benefits plans or other legitimate purposes, it can be determined after selection
Sex	males or females to fill in different applications about pregnancy, childbearing plans, or childcare arrangements	ask applicant if the attendance requirements can be met	during the interview or after selection, the applicant, for purposes of courtesy, may be asked which of Dr., Mr., Mrs., Miss, or Ms. is preferred
Marital Status	whether the applicant is single, married, divorced, engaged, separated, widowed, or living common law whether an applicant's spouse may be transferred about spouse's employment	if transfer or travel is part of the job, the applicant can be asked if he or she can meet these requirements ask whether there are any circumstances that might prevent completion of a minimum service commitment	information on dependants can be determined after selection if necessary
Family Status	number of children or dependants about childcare arrangements	if the applicant would be able to work the required hours and, where applicable, overtime	contacts for emergencies and/or details on dependants can be determined after selection
National or Ethnic Origin	about birthplace, nationality of ancestors, spouse, or other relatives whether born in Canada for proof of citizenship	since those who are entitled to work in Canada must be citizens, permanent residents, or holders of valid work permits, applicants can be asked if they are legally entitled to work in Canada	documentation of eligibility to work (papers, visas, etc.) can be requested after selection
Military Service	about military service in other countries	inquire about Canadian military service where employment preference is given to veterans by law	
Language	mother tongue where language skills obtained	ask whether applicant understands, reads, writes, or speaks languages required for the job	testing or scoring applicants for language proficiency is not permitted unless it is job related
Race or Colour	about race or colour, including colour of eyes, skin, or hair		*continued*

Subject	Avoid Asking	Preferred	Comment
Photographs	for photo to be attached to applications or sent to interviewer before interview		photos for security passes or company files can be taken after selection
Religion	whether applicant will work a specific religious holiday about religious affiliation, church membership, frequency of church attendance for references from clergy or religious leader	explain the required work shift, asking whether such a schedule poses problems for the applicant	reasonable accommodation of an employee's religious beliefs is the employer's duty
Height and Weight			no inquiry unless there is evidence that they are genuine occupational requirements
Disability	for list of all disabilities, limitations, or health problems whether applicant drinks or uses drugs whether applicant has ever received psychiatric care or been hospitalized for emotional problems whether applicant has received workers' compensation		the employer should: – disclose any information on medically related requirements or standards early in the application process – then ask whether the applicant has any condition that could affect his or her ability to do the job, preferably during a pre-employment medical examination a disability is only relevant to job ability if it: – threatens the safety or property of others – prevents the applicant from safe and adequate job performance even when reasonable efforts are made to accommodate the disability
Medical Information	whether currently under a physician's care name of family doctor whether receiving counselling or therapy		medical exams should be conducted after selection and only if an employee's condition is related to job duties offers of employment can be made conditional on successful completion of a medical exam
Pardoned Conviction	whether applicant has ever been convicted whether applicant has ever been arrested whether applicant has a criminal record	if bonding is a job requirement, ask whether the applicant is eligible	inquiries about criminal records or convictions are discouraged unless related to job duties

continued

Subject	Avoid Asking	Preferred	Comment
Sexual Orientation	about the applicant's sexual orientation		contacts for emergencies and/or details on dependants can be determined after selection
References			the same restrictions that apply to questions asked of applicants apply when asking for employment references

Source: A Guide to Screening and Selection in Employment, Canadian Human Rights Commission. www.chrc-ccdp.ca/publications/screening_employment-en.asp. Reprinted with permission of the Minister of Public Works and Government Services Canada, 2009.

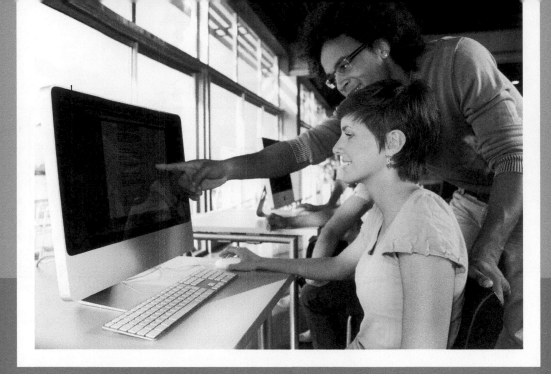

PART THREE

Developing Effective
Human Resources

CHAPTER

8

Orientation and Training

LEARNING OUTCOMES

AFTER STUDYING THIS CHAPTER, YOU SHOULD BE ABLE TO

EXPLAIN how to develop an orientation program.

DESCRIBE the five-step training process.

DISCUSS two techniques used for assessing training needs.

EVALUATE at least five traditional training techniques.

DESCRIBE the three types of e-learning.

DESCRIBE how to evaluate the training effort.

EXPLAIN several common types of training for special purposes.

REQUIRED PROFESSIONAL CAPABILITIES (RPC)

- Develops orientation policies and procedures for new employees

- Ensures compliance with legislated training obligations

- Conducts training needs assessments

- Recommends the most appropriate way to meet identified learning needs

- Facilitates post-training support activities to ensure transfer of learning to the workplace

- Identifies and accesses external sources of training funding available to employees

- Recommends the selection of external training providers

- Participates in course design and selection and delivery of learning materials

- Ensures arrangements are made for training schedules, facilities, trainers, participants, and equipment and course material

The terms "orientation" and "training" are associated, but actually represent slightly different variations of employee assimilation efforts. Orientation refers to a long-term, continuous socialization process in which employee and employer expectations or obligations are considered. With a focus on organization-specific topics, orientation attempts to transfer learning into behaviour using disciplined, consistent efforts.[1] In comparison, training refers to short-term, discrete efforts in which organizations impart information and instructions in an effort to help the recipient gain the required skills or knowledge to perform the job at adequate levels. Given that training often occurs after the orientation process, this chapter first reviews the process of orienting employees, followed by a review of the training process.

ORIENTING EMPLOYEES

Once employees have been recruited and selected, the next step is orienting them to their new company and their new job. A strategic approach to recruitment and retention of employees includes a well-integrated orientation program, both before and after hiring.[2] New employees need a clear understanding of company policies, expectations regarding their performance, and operating procedures. In the long term, a comprehensive orientation (also called onboarding) program can lead to reductions in turnover, increased morale, fewer instances of corrective discipline, and fewer employee grievances. It can also reduce the number of workplace injuries, particularly for young workers.[3] The bottom-line implications of successful orientation can be dramatic, as described in the Strategic HR box.

Purpose of Orientation Programs

employee orientation (onboarding)
A procedure for providing new employees with basic background information about the firm and the job.

Employee orientation (onboarding) provides new employees with basic background information about the employer and specific information that they need to perform their jobs satisfactorily. At the Law Society of Upper Canada, any time a new employee walks through the door the organization acts quickly to help the person get started on the right foot. The Law Society views orientation as an investment in the retention of talent. The essence of the orientation program is to introduce people to the culture, give them a common bond, teach the importance of teamwork in the workplace, and provide the tools and information to be successful at the Law Society.[4]

socialization The ongoing process of instilling in all employees the prevailing attitudes, standards, values, and patterns of behaviour that are expected by the organization.

Orientation is actually one component of the employer's new-employee socialization process. **Socialization** is the ongoing process of instilling in all employees the prevailing attitudes, standards, values, and patterns of behaviour that are expected by the organization.[5] During the time required for socialization to occur, a new employee is less than fully productive. A strong onboarding program can speed up the socialization process and result in the new employee achieving full productivity as quickly as possible.

reality shock (cognitive dissonance)
The state that results from the discrepancy between what the new employee expected from his or her new job and the realities of it.

Orientation helps the employee to perform better by providing necessary information about company rules and practices. It helps to clarify the organization's expectations of an employee regarding his or her job, thus helping to reduce the new employee's first-day jitters and **reality shock** (also referred to as **cognitive dissonance**)—the discrepancy between what the new employee expected from his or her new job and its realities.

STRATEGIC HR

Onboarding: The First Step in Motivation and Retention

Professor Jerry Newman is one of the authors of a best-selling book on compensation. He worked undercover as a crew member in seven fast-food restaurants during a 14-month period to research total rewards. One of his findings was that the onboarding (also known as employee orientation) process played a significant role in long-term perceptions of management's leadership abilities and the quality of non-monetary rewards.

In the best restaurant he worked for, he walked in and asked a counter worker for an application. She handed it to him, suggested that he fill out the application in the lobby, and in one simple gesture, created a positive first impression by asking "Would you like a soda?" Although it may seem trivial, it was one of the few times anyone went to any lengths, however minor, to satisfy the needs of a future employee.

The first days and weeks of employment are crucial in the turnover reduction process as reality begins to converge or diverge with an employee's needs and aspirations. Making good first impressions goes a long way toward shaping a future view of non-monetary rewards.

In recent years, the fast-food industry has made concerted efforts to reduce turnover. Many chains have cut turnover in half during the past five years. Why? Because when they start to analyze costs, the results of successful onboarding are dramatic.

Assume a typical store does $1 million in sales and profits are 10 percent ($100 000). A typical turnover, according to most brands, costs between $1 500 and $2 000. If turnover is 150 percent and the typical store has 40 employees, then 60 employees turn over during the course of the year. Taking the midpoint of the replacement cost, 60 employees at $1750 each equals $105 000. With profits at $100 000, the turnover costs eat up a store's profitability. This is why fast food has made reducing turnover a high priority. And the cost of turnover in, say, high-tech industries is much higher than $1 500 or $2 000. It quickly becomes apparent that reducing turnover, partially accomplished through a positive and successful onboarding experience, can have very positive payoffs.

An important part of any effective orientation program is sitting down and deciding on work-related goals with the new employee. These goals provide the basis for early feedback and establish a foundation for ongoing performance management.[6] Orientation is the first step in helping the new employee manage the learning curve; it helps new employees become productive more quickly than they might otherwise.

Some organizations commence orientation activity before the first day of employment. At Ernst & Young, the firm keeps in touch with people who have been hired but have not yet started work by sending them internal newsletters, inviting them to drop by for chats, and hosting dinners for them.[7] Others use orientation as an ongoing "new-hire development process" and extend it in stages throughout the first year of employment to improve retention levels and reduce the overall costs of recruitment.[8]

Online onboarding systems that can be provided to new employees as soon as they accept the job offer are increasingly being used to engage employees more quickly and accelerate employee performance.[9] Online onboarding provides strategic benefits starting with building the brand as an employer of choice. This approach engages new hires in a personalized way and accelerates their time-to-productivity by completing benefits decisions, payroll forms, new-hire data, introduction of policies and procedures, and preliminary socialization using videos and graphics before the first day on the job, leading to a productive day one.[10]

Content of Orientation Programs

Orientation programs range from brief, informal introductions to lengthy, formal programs. In the latter, the new employee is usually given (over an extended period of time) the following:

- Internal publications, including employee handbooks that cover matters such as company history, current mission, activities, products, and people
- Facility tour and staff introductions
- Job-related documents, including an explanation of job procedures, duties and responsibilities, working hours, and attendance expectations; vacations and holidays; payroll, employee benefits, and pensions; and work regulations and policies such as personal use of company technology
- Expected training to be received (when and why)
- Performance appraisal criteria, including the estimated time to achieve full productivity.

Hints TO ENSURE LEGAL COMPLIANCE

Note that some courts have found employee handbook contents to represent a contract with the employee. Therefore, disclaimers should be included that make it clear that statements of company policies, benefits, and regulations do not constitute the terms and conditions of an employment contract, either express or implied. Firms should think twice before including such statements in the handbook as "No employee will be terminated without just cause," or statements that imply or state that employees have tenure; these could be viewed as legal and binding commitments.

In an orientation, the supervisor explains the exact nature of the job, introduces new colleagues, and familiarizes new employees with the workplace.

Responsibility for Orientation

The first day of the orientation usually starts with the HR specialist, who explains such matters as working hours and vacation. The employee is then introduced to his or her new supervisor, who continues the orientation by explaining the exact nature of the job, introducing the person to his or her new colleagues, and familiarizing the new employee with the workplace. Sometimes, another employee at a peer level will be assigned as a "buddy" or mentor for the newly hired employee for the first few weeks or months of employment.[11] It is a good idea for the HR department to follow up with each new employee about three months after the initial orientation to address any remaining questions.

Special Orientation Situations

Diverse Workforce

In an organization that has not had a diverse workforce in the past, orienting new employees from different backgrounds poses a special challenge. The values of the organization may be new to the new employees if these values were not part of their past experience. New employees should be advised to expect a variety of reactions from current employees to someone from a different background and be given some tips on how to deal with these reactions. In particular, they need to know which reactions are prohibited under human rights legislation and how to report these, should they occur. In addition, as diversity of the internal workforce increases, existing employees can be oriented toward a broader range of employee perceptions and effective communication techniques.

Mergers and Acquisitions

Employees of a newly merged company need to receive information about the details of the merger or acquisition as part of the information on company history. They also need to be made aware of any ongoing, as-yet-unresolved difficulties regarding day-to-day operational issues related to their work. A further orientation issue arises with respect to the existing employees at the time of the merger or acquisition: A new company culture will evolve in the merged organization, and everyone will experience a resocialization process. This presents an opportunity for the merged organization to emphasize the new organizational values and beliefs, thereby reinforcing corporate culture and furthering the new organization's business objectives.[12]

Union versus Non-Union Employees

New employees in unionized positions need to be provided with a copy of the collective bargaining agreement and be told which information relates specifically to their particular job. They also need to be introduced to their union steward, have payroll deduction of union dues explained, and be informed of the names of union executive members. New employees, both unionized and non-unionized, need to be made aware of which jobs are unionized and which ones are not.

Multi-Location Organizations

New employees in a multi-location company need to be made aware of where the other locations are and what business functions are performed in each location. The Ontario Ministry of Education is one such organization, and it uses a web-based, online orientation to deliver corporate-level information.[13] All employees have equal access regardless of their location, and the same message is delivered to each one. Updates can be made instantaneously, and employees can view the information at their own pace.

IBM has been piloting two virtual onboarding programs for interns in China and India. In the Chinese pilot, US-based HR staff and Chinese interns create individual avatars to build relationships, learn about their functions, and hold meetings within Second Life (an online artificial 3-D world). In India, IBM is using another virtual tool called Plane Shift to allow virtual teams to simulate project work.[14]

Problems with Orientation Programs

A number of potential problems can arise with orientation programs. Often, *too much information* is provided in a short time (usually one day) and the new employee is overwhelmed. New employees commonly find themselves inundated with forms to fill out for payroll, benefits, pensions, and so on. Another problem is that *little or no orientation* is provided, which means that new employees must personally seek answers to each question that arises and work without a good understanding of what is expected of them. This is a common problem for part-time and contract workers. Finally, the orientation information provided by the HR department can be *too broad* to be meaningful to a new employee, especially on the first day; whereas the orientation information provided by the immediate supervisor may be *too detailed* to realistically be remembered by the new employee.

Evaluation of Orientation Programs

Orientation programs should be evaluated to assess whether they are providing timely, useful information to new employees in a timely and cost-effective manner. Three approaches to evaluating orientation programs are as follows:

1. *Employee reaction.* Interview or survey new employees for their opinion on the usefulness of the orientation program. Also, evaluate job performance within specified time periods to assess transference of learning and behaviours where possible.

2. *Socialization effects.* Review new employees at regular intervals to assess progress toward understanding and acceptance of the beliefs, values, and norms of the organization.

3. *Cost/benefit analysis.* Compare (1) orientation costs, such as printing handbooks and time spent orienting new employees by HR staff and immediate supervisors, with (2) benefits of orientation, including reduction in errors, rate of productivity, efficiency levels, and so on.

Executive Integration

The orientation process is a continuous, long-term process aimed at moulding desired behaviours and aligning values of the employee and the organization. As such, there is a formal component of orientation that often occurs when a new employee first joins the organization. There is also an ongoing informal orientation process, with the aim to build a strong employee bond with organizational values, history, and tradition. This can include staff involvement such as mentoring, management guidance (by using high level staff, firms communicate the importance of messages and experiences in a more meaningful way), and through employee empowerment (indoctrination of values and information to guide workplace behaviour).

Additionally, newly hired or promoted executives typically do not participate in formal orientation activities, and there is little planning regarding how they will be integrated into their new position and company. The common assumption is that the new executive is a professional and will know what to do, but full executive integration can take up to 18 months. [15] To make things even more difficult, executives are often brought in as change agents, in which case they can expect to face considerable resistance. Thus, a lack of attention to executive integration can result in serious problems with assimilation and work effectiveness. It is common to perceive executive integration as an orientation issue, but integration at senior levels in the

An Ethical **Dilemma**

Is it ethical to withhold information from an incoming executive about critical problems that he or she will face?

organization requires an ongoing process that can continue for months as the new executive learns about the unspoken dynamics of the organization that are not covered in orientation programs, such as how decisions are really made and who holds what type of power.[16]

Executive integration is of critical importance to a productive relationship between a new executive and his or her organization, and it is important to review previous successes and failures at executive integration on an ongoing basis. Key aspects of the integration process include the following:

- Identifying position specifications (particularly the ability to deal with and overcome jealousy)
- Providing realistic information to job candidates and providing support regarding reality shock
- Assessing each candidate's previous record at making organizational transitions
- Announcing the hiring with enthusiasm
- Stressing the importance of listening as well as demonstrating competency, and promoting more time spent talking with the boss
- Assisting new executives who are balancing their work to change cultural norms while they themselves are part of the culture itself.[17]

THE TRAINING PROCESS

training The process of teaching employees the basic skills/competencies that they need to perform their jobs.

Canadian Society for Training and Development (CSTD)
www.cstd.ca

Training employees involves a learning process in which workers are provided with the information and skills that they need to successfully perform their jobs. Training might mean showing a production worker how to operate a new machine, a new salesperson how to sell the firm's product, or a new supervisor how to interview and appraise employees. Whereas *training* focuses on skills and competencies needed to perform employees' current jobs, *development* is training of a long-term nature. Its aim is to prepare current employees for future jobs within the organization.

It is important to ensure that business and training goals are aligned and that training is part of an organization's strategic plan.[18] A training professional in today's business world has to understand the organization's business, speak its language, and demonstrate the business value of training investment.[19] Purolator, one of Canada's largest courier services, has 12 500 employees in Canada, and Stephen Gould, senior vice-president of HR, says it's critical to the success of the business that the company's trainers understand the business strategy.[20]

In today's service-based economy, highly knowledgeable workers can be the company's most important assets. Thus, it is important to treat training as a strategic investment in human capital.[21] For example, Vancouver's Sierra Systems, an information technology consulting company, offers ongoing in-house training and more than 2 000 online courses for its employees. Their senior HR manager explains: "Training and development is critical to our business. We're a professional services firm and our people are how we deliver our business."[22] Unfortunately, formal training levels have been reducing over the last few years, as discussed in the Strategic HR box.

STRATEGIC HR

The Role of Training and Orientation in a Tough Economy

In 2008, Canadian organizations dedicated roughly 1.5 percent of their payroll to training and orientation activities, resulting in more than 11 million working Canadians experiencing some form of workplace-related training. A Conference Board of Canada survey of Canadian organizations provides detailed information about the status of training and orientation in recent years.

Canada's lagging productivity is partially attributed to the skills shortage in Canada, as well as the inability to create new products and successfully commercialize them. In addition, the pressures of an increasingly diverse and aging workforce, demand for more knowledge-based activities in the workplace, and economic globalization present challenges that an organization can only meet by renewing, developing, and upgrading workers' skills.

Yet, organizations have been rapidly reducing investments in training and development. According to a 2009 Learning and Development Outlook survey, the amount of training each employee received annually was the equivalent of 20 hours, compared to 28.5 hours just four years earlier. Also, the real term expenditure on training and orientation activities averaged $787 per employee, representing a 40 percent decrease from levels 15 years ago.

There are a number of possible explanations for this, including the move to more informal training (which increased 56 percent over four years); the use of more cost-effective, immediate, and relevant training; and a lack of monitoring of training and orientation activities of the organization.

In addition, it may be possible that the responsibility for training and development shifted from the organization to the employee as the economy contracted. In a tight labour market, unemployed persons and those who are looking to change jobs are pressured to make themselves more enticing to potential employers. As a result, individuals often engage in initiatives such as licensing, education, training, and professional certifications outside of the workplace environment, which can have a depressionary effect on workplace training metrics (including cost and time).

Source: Learning and Development Outlook 2009: Learning in Tough Times, by P. Derek Hughes and Alison Campbell. Used with permission from the Conference Board of Canada.

A federal government report concluded that:

> To remain competitive and keep up with the accelerating pace of technological change, Canada must continuously renew and upgrade the skills of its workforce. We can no longer assume that the skills acquired in youth will carry workers through their active lives. Rather, the working life of most adults must be a period of continuous learning.[23]

Already, a skills crisis has arisen in the manufacturing sector, where lack of qualified personnel is a major problem. Skills in greatest need of improvement are problem solving, communications, and teamwork.[24] Training is therefore moving to centre stage as a necessity for improving employers' competitiveness. The federal government has called for businesses to increase spending on training, and business has asked the government to expand programs for professional immigrants to get Canadian qualifications in their fields. In response, the Canadian Council on Learning was created by the federal government to promote best practices in workplace learning. The Quebec government has legislated that all firms with a payroll of more than $250 000 must spend 1 percent of payroll on employee training (or else pay a tax in the same amount).[25]

Another benefit of increased training is the fact that training can strengthen employee commitment. It implies faith in the future of the company and of the individual employee. Few things can better illustrate a firm's commitment to its employees than continuing developmental opportunities to improve themselves, and such commitment is usually reciprocated.[26] This loyalty is one reason that a high-commitment firm like the Bank of Montreal provides seven days of training per year for all employees at a cost of $1 800 per employee—more than double the national average.[27] Today's young employees view learning and growth as the pathway to a successful and secure future and are attracted to organizations that have a commitment to keeping and growing their talent.[28]

Training and Learning

Training is essentially a learning process. To train employees, therefore, it is useful to know something about how people learn. For example, people have three main learning styles: *auditory*, learning through talking and listening; *visual*, learning through pictures and print; and *kinesthetic*, tactile learning through a whole-body experience. Training effectiveness can be enhanced by identifying learning styles and personalizing the training accordingly.[29]

First, it is easier for trainees to understand and remember material that is meaningful. At the start of training, provide the trainees with an overall picture of the material to be presented. When presenting material, use as many visual aids as possible and a variety of familiar examples. Organize the material so that it is presented in a logical manner and in meaningful units. Try to use terms and concepts that are already familiar to trainees.

Second, make sure that it is easy to transfer new skills and behaviours from the training site to the job site. Maximize the similarity between the training situation and the work situation and provide adequate training practice. Give trainees the chance to use their new skills immediately on their return to work. Train managers first and employees second to send a message about the importance of the training, and control contingencies by planning rewards for trainees who successfully complete and integrate the new training.[30]

Third, motivate the trainee. Motivation affects training outcomes independently of any increase in cognitive ability. Training motivation is affected by individual characteristics like conscientiousness and by the training climate.[31] Therefore, it is important to try to provide as much realistic practice as possible. Trainees learn best at their own pace and when correct responses are immediately reinforced, perhaps with a quick "Well done." For many younger employees, the use of technology can motivate learning. Simulations, games, virtual worlds, and online networking are revolutionizing how people learn and how learning experiences are designed and delivered. Learners who are immersed in deep experiential learning in highly visual and interactive environments become intellectually engaged in the experience.[32]

Fourth, effectively prepare the trainee. Research evidence shows that the trainee's pre-training preparation is a crucial step in the training process. It is important to create a perceived need for training in the minds of participants.[33] Also, provide preparatory information that will help to set the trainees' expectations about the events and consequences of actions that are likely to occur in the training environment (and, eventually, on the job). For example, trainees learning to become first-line supervisors might face stressful conditions, high workload, and difficult employees. Studies suggest that the negative impact of such events can be reduced by letting trainees know ahead of time what might occur.[34]

Legal Aspects of Training

Hints : **TO ENSURE LEGAL**
      : **COMPLIANCE**

RPC

Ensures compliance with legislated training obligations

Under human rights and employment equity legislation, several aspects of employee training programs must be assessed with an eye toward the program's impact on designated group members.[35] For example, if relatively few women or visible minorities are selected for the training program, there may be a requirement to show that the admissions procedures are valid—that they predict performance on the job for which the person is being trained. It could turn out that the reading level of the training manuals is too advanced for many trainees for whom English is not their first language, which results in their doing poorly in the program, quite aside from their aptitude for the jobs for which they are being trained. The training program might then be found to be unfairly discriminatory. On the other hand, employees who refuse a lawful and reasonable order to attend a training program may be considered to have abandoned their position.[36]

negligent training Occurs when an employer fails to adequately train an employee who subsequently harms a third party.

Negligent training is another potential problem. **Negligent training** occurs when an employer fails to train adequately, and an employee subsequently harms a third party. Also, employees who are dismissed for poor performance or disciplined for safety infractions may claim that the employer was negligent in that the employee's training was inadequate.

The Five-Step Training Process

International Personnel Assessment Council
www.ipacweb.org

A typical training program consists of five steps, as summarized in **Figure 8.1**. The purpose of the *needs analysis* step is to identify the specific job performance skills needed, to analyze the skills and needs of the prospective trainees, and to develop specific, measurable knowledge and performance objectives. Managers must make sure that the performance deficiency is amenable to training rather than caused by, say, poor morale because of low salaries. In the second step, *instructional design*, the actual content of the training program is compiled and produced, including workbooks, exercises, and activities. The third step is *validation*, in which the bugs are worked out of the training program by presenting it to a small, representative audience. Fourth, the training program is *implemented*, using techniques like those discussed in this chapter and the next (such as on-the-job training and programmed learning). Fifth, there should be an *evaluation* and follow-up step in which the program's successes or failures are assessed.

FIGURE **8.1**   The Five Steps in the Training and Development Process

1. NEEDS ANALYSIS

- Identify specific job performance skills needed to improve performance and productivity.
- Analyze the audience to ensure that the program will be suited to their specific levels of education, experience, and skills, as well as their attitudes and personal motivations.
- Use research to develop specific measurable knowledge and performance objectives.

2. INSTRUCTIONAL DESIGN

- Gather instructional objectives, methods, media, description of and sequence of content, examples, exercises, and activities. Organize them into a curriculum that supports adult learning theory and provides a blueprint for program development.
- Make sure all materials (such as video scripts, leaders' guides, and participants' workbooks) complement each other, are written clearly, and blend into unified training geared directly to the stated learning objectives.
- Carefully and professionally handle all program elements—whether reproduced on paper, film, or tape—to guarantee quality and effectiveness.

3. VALIDATION

- Introduce and validate the training before a representative audience. Base final revisions on pilot results to ensure program effectiveness.

4. IMPLEMENTATION

- When applicable, boost success with a train-the-trainer workshop that focuses on presentation knowledge and skills in addition to training content.

5. EVALUATION AND FOLLOW-UP

- Assess program success according to

    REACTION—Document the learners' immediate reactions to the training.

    LEARNING—Use feedback devices or pre- and post-tests to measure what learners have actually learned.

    BEHAVIOUR—Note supervisors' reactions to learners' performance following completion of the training. This is one way to measure the degree to which learners apply new skills and knowledge to their jobs.

    RESULTS—Determine the level of improvement in job performance and assess needed maintenance.

Source: This article was originally published in IOMA's monthly newsletter *HRFocus*® and is republished here with the express written permission of IOMA. © 2009. Further use of, electronic distribution, or reproduction of this material requires the permission of IOMA. www.ioma.com

STEP 1: TRAINING NEEDS ANALYSIS

RPC

Conducts training needs assessments

The first step in training is to determine what training is required, if any. The main task in assessing the training needs of new employees is to determine what the job entails and to break it down into subtasks, each of which is then taught to the new employee. Assessing the training needs of current employees can be more complex, because it involves the added task of deciding whether or not training is the solution. For example, performance may be down not because of lack of training but because the standards are not clear or because the person is not motivated.

task analysis A detailed study of a job to identify the skills and competencies it requires so that an appropriate training program can be instituted.

performance analysis Verifying that there is a performance deficiency and determining whether that deficiency should be rectified through training or through some other means (such as transferring the employee).

Task analysis and performance analysis are the two main techniques for identifying training needs. **Task analysis**—an analysis of the job's requirements—is especially appropriate for determining the training needs of employees who are *new* to their jobs. **Performance analysis** appraises the performance of *current* employees to determine whether training could reduce performance problems (such as excess scrap or low output). Other techniques used to identify training needs include supervisors' reports, HR records, management requests, observations, tests of job knowledge, and questionnaire surveys.[37]

Whichever technique is used—task analysis, performance analysis, or some other—employee input is essential. It is often true that no one knows as much about the job as the people actually doing it, so soliciting employee input is usually wise.[38]

Task Analysis: Assessing the Training Needs of New Employees

Task analysis—identifying the broad competencies and specific skills required to perform job-related tasks—is used for determining the training needs of employees who are new to their jobs. Particularly with entry-level workers, it is common to hire inexperienced people and train them.[39] Thus, the aim is to develop the skills and knowledge required for effective performance—like soldering (in the case of an assembly worker) or interviewing (in the case of a supervisor).

The job description and job specifications are helpful here. These list the specific duties and skills required on the job and become the basic reference point in determining the training required to perform the job.

Task Analysis Record Form

Some employers supplement the current job description and specification with a task analysis record form. This consolidates information regarding the job's required tasks and skills in a form that is especially helpful for determining training requirements. As illustrated in **Table 8.1**, a task analysis record form contains six types of information:

1. *Column 1, Task List.* Here, the job's main tasks and subtasks are listed.
2. *Column 2, When and How Often Performed.* Here, the frequency with which the tasks and subtasks are performed is indicated.
3. *Column 3, Quantity and Quality of Performance.* Here, the standards of performance for each task and subtask are described in measurable terms, like "tolerance of 0.007 inches," or "within two days of receiving the order," for instance.

TABLE 8.1   Task Analysis Record Form

Task List	When and How Often Performed	Quantity and Quality of Performance	Conditions Under Which Performed	Competencies and Specific Knowledge Required	Where Best Learned
1. Operate paper cutter	4 times per day		Noisy press room:		
1.1 Start motor			distractions		
1.2 Set cutting distance		± tolerance of 0.007 in.		Read gauge	On the job
1.3 Place paper on cutting table		Must be completely even to prevent uneven cut		Lift paper correctly	On the job
1.4 Push paper up to cutter				Must be even	On the job
1.5 Grasp safety release with left hand	100% of time, for safety			Essential for safety	On the job but practise first with no distractions
1.6 Grasp cutter release with right hand				Must keep both hands on releases	On the job but practise first with no distractions
1.7 Simultaneously pull safety release with left hand and cutter release with right hand					
1.8 Wait for cutter to retract	100% of time, for safety			Must keep both hands on releases	On the job but practise first with no distractions
1.9 Retract paper				Wait till cutter retracts	On the job but practise first with no distractions
1.10 Shut off	100% of time, for safety				On the job but practise first with no distractions
2. Operate printing press					
2.1 Start motor					
.					
.					
.					

Note: Task analysis record form showing some of the tasks and subtasks performed by a right-handed printing press operator.

4. *Column 4, Conditions Under Which Performed*. This column indicates the conditions under which the tasks and subtasks are to be performed.

5. *Column 5, Competencies and Specific Knowledge Required*. This is the heart of the task analysis form. Here, the competencies and specific skills or knowledge required for each task and subtask are listed, specifying exactly what knowledge or skills must be taught. Thus, for the subtask "Set cutting distance," the trainee must be taught how to read the gauge.

6. *Column 6, Where Best Learned*. The decision as to whether the task is learned best on or off the job is based on several considerations. Safety is one: For example, prospective jet pilots must learn something about the plane off the job in a simulator before actually getting behind the controls.

Once the essential skills involved in doing the job are determined, new employees' proficiency in these skills can be assessed and training needs identified for each individual.

Performance Analysis: Determining the Training Needs of Current Employees

Performance analysis means verifying whether there is a significant performance deficiency and, if so, determining whether that deficiency should be rectified through training or some other means (such as transferring the employee). The first step is to appraise the employee's performance because, to improve it, the firm must first compare the person's current performance with what it should be. Examples of specific performance deficiencies follow:

> "Salespeople are expected to make ten new contacts per week, but John averages only six."

> "Other plants our size average no more than two serious accidents per month; we are averaging five."

Tips FOR THE FRONT LINE

Distinguishing between *can't do* and *won't do* problems is at the heart of performance analysis. First, the firm must determine whether it is a *can't do* problem and, if so, its specific causes. For example, the employees do not know what to do or what the standards are; there are obstacles in the system (such as a lack of tools or supplies); job aids are needed; poor selection has resulted in hiring people who do not have the skills to do the job; or training is inadequate. Conversely, it might be a *won't do* problem. In this case, employees *could* do a good job if they wanted to. If so, the reward system might have to be changed, perhaps by implementing an incentive program.

Training Objectives

Once training needs have been identified, training objectives can be established, which should be concrete and measurable. Objectives specify what the trainee should be able to accomplish after successfully completing the training program. They thus provide a focus for the efforts of both the trainee and the trainer and provide a benchmark for evaluating the success of the training program. A training program can then be developed and implemented with the intent to achieve these objectives. These objectives must be accomplished within the organization's training budget.

STEP 2: INSTRUCTIONAL DESIGN

RPC

Recommends the most appropriate way to meet identified learning needs

After the employees' training needs have been determined and training objectives have been set, the training program can be designed. Descriptions of the most popular traditional training techniques and more recent e-learning techniques follow.

Traditional Training Techniques

On-the-Job Training

On-the-job training (OJT) involves having a person learn a job by actually performing it. Virtually every employee—from mailroom clerk to company president—gets some on-the-job training when he or she joins a firm. In many companies, OJT is the only type of training available. It usually involves assigning new employees to experienced workers or supervisors who then do the actual training.[40]

OJT has several advantages: it is relatively inexpensive, trainees learn while producing, and there is no need for expensive off-job facilities, like classrooms or manuals. The method also facilitates learning, since trainees learn by actually doing the job and get quick feedback about the quality of their performance.

Apprenticeship Training

More employers are going "back to the future" by implementing apprenticeship training programs, an approach that began in the Middle Ages. Apprenticeship training basically involves having the learner/apprentice study under the tutelage of a master craftsperson.

Apprentices become skilled workers through a combination of classroom instruction and on-the-job training. Apprenticeships are widely used to train individuals for many occupations, including those of electrician and plumber. In Canada, close to 170 established trades have recognized apprenticeship programs.[41]

Apprenticeship training is critical today as more than half of skilled trades workers are expecting to retire by 2020. Federal, provincial, and territorial governments are increasing their funding of apprenticeship training programs to meet this growing need for more trades people.[42]

On-the-job training is structured and concrete. Here, a supervisor teaches an employee to use a drum-forming machine.

Informal Learning

About two-thirds of industrial training is not "formal" at all but rather results from day-to-day unplanned interactions between the new worker and his or her colleagues. Informal learning may be defined as "any learning that occurs in which the learning process is not determined or designed by the organization."[43]

Job Instruction Training

Many jobs consist of a logical sequence of steps and are best taught step by step. This step-by-step process is called **job instruction training (JIT)**. To begin, all necessary steps in the job are listed, each in its proper sequence. Alongside each step, a corresponding "key point" (if any) should be noted. The steps show *what* is to be done, while the key points show *how* it is to be done and *why*. Here is an example of a job instruction training sheet for teaching a right-handed trainee how to operate a large, motorized paper cutter:

Steps	Key Points
1. Start motor	None
2. Set cutting distance	Carefully read scale to prevent wrong-sized cut
3. Place paper on cutting table	Make sure paper is even to prevent uneven cut
4. Push paper up to cutter	Make sure paper is tight to prevent uneven cut
5. Grasp safety release with left hand	Do not release left hand to prevent hand from being caught in cutter
6. Grasp cutter release with right hand	Do not release right hand to prevent hand from being caught in cutter
7. Simultaneously pull cutter and safety releases	Keep both hands on corresponding releases to avoid hands being on cutting table
8. Wait for cutter to retract	Keep both hands on releases to avoid having hands on cutting table
9. Retract paper	Make sure cutter is retracted; keep both hands away from releases
10. Shut off motor	None

In today's service economy, job instruction training for step-by-step manual work is being superseded by behaviour modelling for service workers. Behaviour modelling is discussed in the next chapter.

Classroom Training

Classroom training continues to be the primary method of providing corporate training in Canada, and lectures are a widely used method of classroom training delivery. Lecturing has several advantages. It is a quick and simple way of providing knowledge to large groups of trainees, as when the sales force must be taught the special features of a new product.

Classroom learning has evolved to maintain its relevance in the technological age. For Generation Y employees familiar with Web 2.0 features such as wikis, blogs, and podcasts, learning opportunities must reflect their new abilities and needs. Blended learning, using a combination of instructor-led training and online e-learning, has been found to provide better learning results and higher learner engagement and enthusiasm than expected. In blended learning, the in-class training becomes tightly integrated with the online experience, and the relevance to the learner is vastly improved. Thus the classroom has evolved to include interactions with remote colleagues and instructors, e-learning in many forms, coaching, assessment, and feedback.[44]

Audiovisual Techniques

Audiovisual techniques (CDs or DVDs) can be very effective and are widely used. Audiovisuals can be more expensive than conventional lectures to develop, but offer some advantages. Trainers should consider using them in the following situations:

1. *When there is a need to illustrate how a certain sequence should be followed over time*, such as when teaching wire soldering or telephone repair. The stop-action, instant-replay, or fast- or slow-motion capabilities of audiovisuals can be useful.

2. *When there is a need to expose trainees to events not easily demonstrable in live lectures*, such as a visual tour of a factory or open-heart surgery.

3. *When the training is going to be used organization-wide* and it is too costly to move the trainers from place to place.

There are three options when it comes to audiovisual material: buying an existing product, making one, or using a production company. Dozens of businesses issue catalogues that list audiovisual programs on topics ranging from applicant interviewing to zoo management.

videoconferencing Connecting two or more distant groups by using audiovisual equipment.

Videoconferencing, in which an instructor is televised live to multiple locations, is now a common method for training employees. It has been defined as "a means of joining two or more distant groups using a combination of audio and visual equipment."[45] Videoconferencing allows people in one location to communicate live with people in another city or country or with groups in several places at once. It is particularly important to prepare a training guide ahead of time, as most or all of the learners will not be in the same location as the trainer. It is also important for the trainer to arrive early and test all equipment that will be used.

Programmed Learning

programmed learning A systematic method for teaching job skills that involves presenting questions or facts, allowing the person to respond, and giving the learner immediate feedback on the accuracy of his or her answers.

Whether the programmed instruction device is a textbook or a computer, **programmed learning** consists of three functions:

1. Presenting questions, facts, or problems to the learner
2. Allowing the person to respond
3. Providing feedback on the accuracy of his or her answers

The main advantage of programmed learning is that it reduces training time by about one-third.[46] Programmed instruction can also facilitate learning because it lets trainees learn at their own pace, provides immediate feedback, and (from the learner's point of view) reduces the risk of error. However, trainees do not learn much more from programmed learning than they would from a traditional textbook. Therefore, the cost of developing the manuals or software for programmed instruction has to be weighed against the accelerated but not improved learning that should occur.

Vestibule or Simulated Training

vestibule or simulated training Training employees on special off-the-job equipment, as in airplane pilot training, whereby training costs and hazards can be reduced.

Vestibule or simulated training is a technique by which trainees learn on the actual or simulated equipment that they will use on the job, but they are trained off the job. Therefore, it aims to obtain the advantages of on-the-job training without actually putting the trainee on the job. Vestibule training is virtually a necessity when it is too costly or dangerous to train employees on the job. Putting new assembly-line workers right to work could slow production, for instance, and when safety is a concern—as with pilots—vestibule training may be the only practical alternative.

Vestibule training may just place a trainee in a separate room with the equipment that he or she will actually be using on the job; however, it often involves the use of equipment simulators. In pilot training, for instance, the main advantages of flight simulators are safety, learning efficiency, and cost savings (on maintenance costs, pilot cost, fuel cost, and the cost of not having the aircraft in regular service).[47]

E-Learning

Electronic training techniques have been developed that allow trainers to provide learning in a more flexible, personalized, and cost-effective manner. **E-learning** is the delivery and administration of learning opportunities and support via computer, networked, and web-based technology to enhance employee performance and development. Canadian employers are using e-learning to become more productive and innovative and to make self-directed, lifelong learners of their employees.[48]

Effective e-learning requires good instructional design. It is critical to motivate learners by describing the benefits they will gain from the training, providing content designed to the learner's specific needs, and offering interactivity, such as application of the material to common problems in the context of the learner's workplace and intrinsic feedback.[49]

The Canadian Society for Training and Development has found that e-learning is generally as effective as other forms of learning, but at a reduced cost. The primary users of e-learning in Canada are professional and technical employees; clerical, service, and support employees; and managers. Interestingly, learners are more satisfied when web-based learning involves high levels of human interaction.[50] Mobile technologies are growing in influence in training and development. Short videos, instant messages, podcasts, and email are examples of smartphone features that can be used for training.[51]

There are three major types of e-learning: computer-based training, online training, and electronic performance support systems (EPSS).

Computer-Based Training

In computer-based training (CBT), the trainee uses a computer-based system to interactively increase his or her knowledge or skills. Computer-based training almost always involves presenting trainees with integrated computerized simulations and using multimedia (including video, audio, text, and graphics) to help the trainee learn how to do the job.[52] Cisco Systems developed a binary math game intended to improve the effectiveness of network engineers and made it available for free on its website and for use on mobile devices. This simple game solved a key training problem and also turned out to be an effective corporate marketing tool.[53]

A new generation of simulations has been developed to simulate role-play situations designed to teach behavioural skills and emotional intelligence. Body language, facial expressions, and subtle nuances are programmed in. These new

Vestibule training simulates flight conditions at NASA headquarters.

e-learning Delivery and administration of learning opportunities and support via computer, networked, and web-based technology to enhance employee performance and development.

RPC

Participates in course design and selection and delivery of learning materials

RPC

Recommends the selection of external training providers

simulations offer authentic and relevant scenarios involving pressure situations that tap users' emotions and force them to act.[54] At L'Oréal Canada, new product managers participate in a training program that combines e-learning and a virtual simulation where they apply their new skills. Teams of trainees compete as virtual companies in the marketplace and continue to learn when they see their results compared to the others.[55]

A higher percentage of Canadian firms use CBT compared with American firms, primarily because of Canada's geography. CBT is often more cost-effective than traditional training methods, which require instructors or trainees to travel long distances to training sites.[56] Alberta Pacific Forest Industries (Al-Pac) had such good results from using CBT as a staple of its training program that it launched a new component to enable employees to learn the skills of another trade. Employees benefit from having training that is accessible 24 hours a day, which addresses shift work and different learning styles. This training program also helps to keep non-union staff members satisfied, as the multi-skilling resulting from CBT enables many employees to rotate jobs.[57]

CBT programs can be very beneficial. Advantages include instructional consistency (computers, unlike human trainers, do not have good days and bad days), mastery of learning (if the trainee does not learn it, he or she generally cannot move on to the next step in the CBT), flexibility for the trainee, and increased trainee motivation (resulting from the responsive feedback of the CBT program).

Online Training

Web-based training is now commonly used by Canadian organizations. It is generally estimated that online training costs about 50 percent less than traditional classroom-based training. Also, online learning is ideal for adults, who learn what they want, when they want, and where they want. Online training is often the best solution for highly specialized business professionals who have little time available for ongoing education. Students (the workers of tomorrow) thrive in online learning environments. They do not find it to be an isolated or lonely experience, and they find that they have more time to reflect on the learning material, which leads to livelier interaction.[58] Further, online training is ideal for global organizations that want consistent training for all employees worldwide. Alcan Inc. is using this approach to standardize its training programs for 72 000 employees in 55 countries.[59]

However, critics point out that content management, sound educational strategy, learner support, and system administration should receive more attention, as they are often the critical determining factors in successful training outcomes. In the last few years, "learner content management systems" have been developed to deliver personalized content in small "chunks" or "nuggets" of learning. These systems complement "learning management systems" that are focused on the logistics of managing learning. Together, they form a powerful combination for an e-learning platform. This development is considered part of the "second wave" of e-learning, involving greater standardization and the emergence of norms. Another problem is that the freedom of online learning means that unless learners are highly motivated, they may not complete the training. It is estimated that learners don't complete 50 to 90 percent of online courses. In general, it is important to seek "blended learning," including both personal interaction and online training tools.[60]

Electronic Performance Support Systems (EPSS)

electronic performance support systems (EPSS) Computer-based job aids, or sets of computerized tools and displays, that automate training, documentation, and phone support.

Electronic performance support systems (EPSS) are computer-based job aids, or sets of computerized tools and displays, that automate training, documentation, and phone support. EPSS provides support that is faster, cheaper, and more effective than traditional paper-based job aids, such as manuals. When a customer calls a Dell Computer service representative about a problem with a new computer, for example, the representative is probably asking questions prompted by an EPSS, which takes the service representative and the customer through an analytical sequence, step by step. Without the EPSS, Dell would have to train its service representatives to memorize an unrealistically large number of solutions. Learners say that an EPSS provides significant value in maximizing the impact of training. If a skill is taught but the trainees don't need to use it until several weeks or months later, the learning material is always available through the EPSS.[61]

STEPS 3 AND 4: VALIDATION AND IMPLEMENTATION

RPC

Ensures arrangements are made for training schedules, facilities, trainers, participants, equipment, and course materials

Validation of the training program that has been designed is an often-overlooked step in the training process. In order to ensure that the program will accomplish its objectives, it is necessary to conduct a pilot study, or "run through," with a representative group of trainees. The results of the pilot study are used to assess the effectiveness of the training.

Revisions to the program can be made to address any problems encountered by the pilot group of trainees in using the training material and experiences provided to them. Testing at the end of the pilot study can measure whether or not the program is producing the desired improvement in skill level. If the results fall below the level of the training objectives, then more work must be undertaken to strengthen the instructional design.

Once the program has been validated, it is ready to be implemented by professional trainers. In some cases, a train-the-trainer workshop may be required to familiarize trainers with unfamiliar content or with unique and innovative new methods for presenting the training content.

STEP 5: EVALUATION OF TRAINING

transfer of training Application of the skills acquired during the training program into the work environment and the maintenance of these skills over time.

It is important to assess the return on investment in human capital made through training by determining whether the training actually achieved the objectives. **Transfer of training** is the application of the skills acquired during the training program into the work environment and the maintenance of these skills over time. A number of actions can be taken before, during, and after a training program to enhance transfer of training.[62]

Before training, potential trainees can be assessed on their level of ability, aptitude, and motivation regarding the skill to be taught, and those with higher levels can be selected for the training program. Trainees can be involved in designing the training, and management should provide active support at this stage.

During the training, it is important to provide frequent feedback, opportunities for practice, and positive reinforcement. After the training program, trainees can use goal-setting and relapse-prevention techniques to increase the likelihood of applying what they have learned. Management can enhance transfer of training by providing opportunities to apply new skills and by continuing to provide positive reinforcement of the new skills while being tolerant of errors.

After trainees complete their training (or at planned intervals during the training), the program should be evaluated to see how well its objectives have been met and the extent to which transfer of training has occurred. Thus, if assemblers should be able to solder a junction in 30 seconds, or a photocopier technician repair a machine in 30 minutes, then the program's effectiveness should be measured based on whether these objectives are attained. For example, are trainees learning as *much* as they can? Are they learning as *fast* as they can? Is there a *better method* for training them? These are some of the questions that are answered by properly evaluating training efforts.

Overall, there is little doubt that training and development can be effective. Formal studies of training programs substantiate the potential positive impact of such programs. Profitable companies spend the most on training, and those rated as being among the 100 best companies to work for in Canada spend the most per employee on training.[63]

There are two basic issues to address when evaluating a training program. The first is the design of the evaluation study and, in particular, whether controlled experimentation will be used. The second is the training effect to be measured.

Controlled experimentation is the best method to use in evaluating a training program. A controlled experiment uses both a training group and a control group (that receives no training). Data (for example, on quantity of production or quality of soldered junctions) should be obtained both before and after the training effort in the training group, and before and after a corresponding work period in the control group. In this way, it is possible to determine the extent to which any change in performance in the training group resulted from the training itself, rather than from some organization-wide change like a raise in pay, which would likely have affected employees in both groups equally.

Training Effects to Measure

Four basic categories of training outcomes can be measured:[64]

1. *Reaction.* First, evaluate trainees' reactions to the program. Did they like the program? Did they think it worthwhile? One expert suggests using an evaluation form like the one shown in **Figure 8.2** to evaluate employee reaction to the training program.[65]

2. *Learning.* Second, test the trainees to determine whether they learned the principles, skills, and facts that they were supposed to learn.

3. *Behaviour.* Next, ask whether the trainees' behaviour on the job changed because of the training program. For example, are employees in the store's complaint department more courteous toward disgruntled customers than they were previously? These measures determine the degree of transfer of training.

Facilitates post-training support activities to ensure transfer of learning to the workplace

controlled experimentation Formal methods for testing the effectiveness of a training program, preferably with a control group and with tests before and after training.

FIGURE **8.2** Sample Training Evaluation Form

PROGRAM NAME: _____ DATE: _____

YOUR NAME (Optional): _____ FACILITATOR(S): _____

OVERALL PROGRAM RATING	Poor		Fair		Good		Excellent
	1	2	3	4	5	6	7

What did you like **best** about the program?	What did you like **least** about the program?	What would you like to have spent **more** time on?

Please complete this form to help us assess how well this program met your needs and our objectives. Your feedback is important to us and will be used in our continuous efforts to improve the quality and usefulness of this program. Circle the number that best expresses your reaction to each item.

	Strongly Disagree		Disagree		Agree		Strongly Agree
1. The program was well-organized	1	2	3	4	5	6	7
2. The sequence of material presented was logical	1	2	3	4	5	6	7
3. The content of the program was understandable	1	2	3	4	5	6	7
4. The program activities were effective in helping me learn the concepts and skills presented	1	2	3	4	5	6	7
5. The objectives of the program were clear	1	2	3	4	5	6	7
6. The program met its stated objectives	1	2	3	4	5	6	7
7. The facilitator(s) grasped the material and activities they presented	1	2	3	4	5	6	7
8. The knowledge and skills learned in this program will help me do my job better	1	2	3	4	5	6	7
9. The length of the program	was appropriate		should be shorter		should be longer		

Thank you for your participation and feedback!

Source: Reproduced, with permission, from the *Ultimate HR Manual*, published by and copyright CCH Canadian Limited, Toronto, Ontario.

4. *Results.* Last, but probably most important, ask questions such as these: "Did the number of customer complaints about employees drop?" "Did the rejection rate improve?" "Was turnover reduced?" "Are production quotas now being met?" and so on. Improvements in these "metrics"— specific measures of workplace results—are especially important. The training program may succeed in terms of the reactions from trainees, increased learning, and even changes in behaviour, but if the results are not achieved, then in the final analysis the training has not achieved its goals. If so, the

problem may be related to inappropriate use of a training program. For example, training is ineffective when environmental factors are the cause of poor performance.

Although the four basic categories are understandable and widely used, there are several things to keep in mind when using them to measure training effects. First, there are usually only modest correlations among the four types of training criteria (that is, scoring "high" on learning does not necessarily mean that behaviour or results will also score "high," and the converse is true as well). Similarly, studies show that "reaction" measures (for example, asking trainees "How well did you like the program?") may provide some insight into how trainees felt about the program, but probably will not provide much insight into what they learned or how they will behave once they are back on the job.

TRAINING FOR SPECIAL PURPOSES

Training increasingly does more than just prepare employees to perform their jobs effectively. Training for special purposes—increasing literacy and adjusting to diversity, for instance—is required too. The following is a sampling of such special-purpose training programs.

Literacy and Essential Skills Training

National Adult Literacy Database
www.nald.ca

Functional illiteracy is a serious problem for many employers. As the Canadian economy shifts from goods to services, there is a corresponding need for workers who are more skilled, more literate, and better able to perform at least basic arithmetic. Not only does enhanced literacy give employees a better chance for success in their careers, but it also improves bottom-line performance of the employer—through time savings, lower costs, and improved quality of work.[66]

In 2008, the Canadian Council on Learning reported that almost half of Canadian adults are below the internationally accepted literacy standard for coping in a modern society.[67] A 2010 update of this research suggests that Canada's largest cities (like Toronto, Vancouver, and Ottawa) will see a substantial increase in the illiteracy rate of the workforce, largely due to the spike in the number of seniors and the growing number of immigrants.[68] Research by University of Ottawa economists for Statistics Canada has shown that investments in essential skills training to improve literacy and numeracy pay off. For every increase of 1 percent in national literacy scores relative to the international average, a country will realize a 2.5 percent gain in productivity and a 1.5 percent increase in per capita GDP over the long term.[69]

Employers are responding to this issue in two main ways. Organizations such as diamond mining company BHP Billiton, steel giant Dofasco, the Construction Sector Council, and the Canadian Trucking Human Resources Council have implemented a training strategy with the objective of raising the essential skills of their workforce. Essential skills of workers can be measured with the Test of Workplace Essential Skills (TOWES), developed by Bow Valley College in Calgary. In 2005, the federal government made funding available for

RPC

Identifies and accesses external sources of training funding available to employees training professionals to develop enhanced language training (ELT) to provide job-specific English instruction to help immigrants gain employment in their area of expertise.[70]

Training for Global Business and Diverse Workforces

With increasingly diverse workforces and customers, there is a strong business case for implementing global business and diversity training programs. Research by Healthy Companies International has found that success in the global marketplace is predicted by developing leaders at all levels of business and by placing a high value on multicultural experience and competencies. The research identified four global literacies, or critical competencies, required to succeed in the global economy:

- personal literacy—understanding and valuing oneself
- social literacy—engaging and challenging other people
- business literacy—focusing and mobilizing the business
- cultural literacy—understanding and leveraging cultural differences[71]

Diversity training enhances cross-cultural sensitivity among supervisors and non-supervisors, with the aim of creating more harmonious working relationships among a firm's employees. It also enhances the abilities of salespeople to provide effective customer service.[72]

Two broad approaches to diversity training are cross-cultural communication training and cultural sensitivity training. *Cross-cultural communication training* focuses on workplace cultural etiquette and interpersonal skills. *Cultural sensitivity training* focuses on sensitizing employees to the views of different cultural groups toward work so that employees from diverse backgrounds can work together more effectively. All employees should be involved in managing diversity, and diversity initiatives should be planned and supported as any other business opportunity would be.[73]

Diversity Training
www.diversityatwork.org
www.diversitytraining.com

Customer Service Training

More and more retailers are finding it necessary to compete based on the quality of their service, and many are therefore implementing customer service training programs. The basic aim is to train all employees to (1) have excellent product knowledge and (2) treat the company's customers in a courteous and hospitable manner. The saying "The customer is always right" is emphasized by countless service companies today. However, putting the customer first requires employee customer service training.

The Canadian retail industry has struggled in the past with poorly trained workers who were not equipped to provide quality customer service. Retailers now understand that they need to make a serious investment in their employees.[74] The Retail Council of Canada offers a national customer service certification program for retail sales associates and retail first-level managers, based on national occupational standards and essential skills profiles for each group. Certification requires the completion of a workbook, a multiple-choice exam, an in-store evaluation-of-performance interview, and experience (600 hours for sales associates, one year for first-level managers). The certification program for sales associates includes the topics of professionalism, customer service and sales, inventory, store appearance, security and safety, and communication. Topics for first-level managers include professionalism, communication, leadership, human resources, operations, marketing, sales, customer service, administration, and planning.[75]

Training for Teamwork

An increasing number of firms today use work teams to improve their effectiveness. However, many firms find that teamwork does not just happen and that employees must be trained to be good team members.

Some firms use outdoor training—such as Outward Bound programs—to build teamwork. Outdoor training usually involves taking a group of employees out into rugged terrain, where, by overcoming physical obstacles, they learn team spirit, cooperation, and the need to trust and rely on each other.[76]

An example of one activity is the "trust fall." Here, an employee has to slowly lean back and fall backward from a height of, say, three metres into the waiting arms of five or ten team members. The idea is to build trust in one's colleagues.

Not all employees are eager to participate in such activities. Firms like Outward Bound have prospective participants fill out extensive medical evaluations to make sure that participants can safely engage in risky outdoor activities. Others feel that the outdoor activities are too contrived to be applicable back at work. However, they do illustrate the lengths to which employers will go to build teamwork.

An Ethical Dilemma

Is it ethical to require employees to participate in weekend and evening training programs if they do not want to because it is going to take time that they would otherwise be spending on personal and family responsibilities?

Training for First-Time Supervisors/Managers

As Baby Boomers head into retirement, young employees are rising to positions of authority quickly and in large numbers. They are assuming supervisory and managerial roles at much younger ages than their counterparts were only 10 to 15 years ago, with some university graduates being hired into management training programs right after graduation. Along with the steep learning curve that all first-time supervisors/managers face, the latest group faces the challenges of managing employees from previous generations who are still present in the workforce.

New supervisors/managers are often chosen for their technical ability, and their interpersonal and communication skills get overlooked. But it is precisely these skills that will determine success as a manager, which requires networking and the ability to get work done through other people. New managers also need to learn to define their personal management style, how to give and receive feedback, how to motivate others, and how to manage conflict.[77]

The transition demands crucial training because first-time supervisors/managers need to learn a new set of skills. Formal training is required, and higher-level managers need to coach, mentor, and provide performance feedback to new young supervisors.[78] This type of training can be provided by external organizations like the Canadian Management Centre.

Canadian Management Centre
www.cmctraining.org

Chapter SUMMARY

1. A strategic approach to recruitment and retention of employees includes a well-integrated orientation (onboarding) program both before and after hiring. New employees need a clear understanding of company policies, expectations regarding their performance, and operating procedures. Orientation is part of the socialization process that instills in new employees the prevailing attitudes, standards, values, and patterns of behaviour that are expected by the organization. Onboarding helps to reduce reality shock—the discrepancy between what the new employee expected from his or her job and its realities.

2. The basic training process consists of five steps: needs analysis, instructional design, validation, implementation, and evaluation.

3. Two techniques for assessing training needs are (1) task analysis to determine the training needs of employees who are new to their jobs, and (2) performance analysis to appraise the performance of current employees to determine whether training could reduce performance problems.

4. Traditional training techniques include on-the-job-training, apprenticeship training, informal learning, job instruction training, classroom training, audiovisual techniques, programmed learning, and vestibule or simulated training.

5. Three types of e-learning are computer-based training, online training, and electronic performance support systems.

6. In evaluating the effectiveness of a training program, four categories of outcomes can be measured: reaction, learning, behaviour, and results.

7. Today's organizations often provide training for special purposes, including literacy training, diversity training, customer service training, training for teamwork, and training for first-time supervisors/managers.

MyManagementLab

Visit MyManagementLab to access a personalized Study Plan and additional study tools for this chapter.

Key TERMS

controlled experimentation *(p. 228)*
electronic performance support systems (EPSS) *(p. 227)*
e-learning *(p. 225)*
employee orientation (onboarding) *(p. 209)*
job instruction training (JIT) *(p. 223)*
negligent training *(p. 217)*
performance analysis *(p. 219)*

programmed learning *(p. 224)*
reality shock (cognitive dissonance) *(p. 209)*
socialization *(p. 209)*
task analysis *(p. 219)*
training *(p. 214)*
transfer of training *(p. 227)*
vestibule or simulated training *(p. 224)*
videoconferencing *(p. 224)*

Review and Discussion QUESTIONS

1. Prepare an orientation program checklist for your current or most recent job.
2. Identify and describe three special orientation situations that may be encountered.
3. Choose a task you are familiar with—such as mowing the lawn or using a chat room—and develop a job instruction training sheet for it.
4. Ali Khan is an undergraduate business student majoring in accounting. He has just failed the first accounting course, Accounting 101, and is understandably upset. Explain how you would use performance analysis to identify what, if any, are Ali's training needs.
5. Describe how you would go about determining the best way to train a group of newly hired managers on how to conduct selection interviews.
6. Think about a job you have had in the past. For this job, identify which training technique was used and reflect on reasons why you think that system was used. Next, select a different training technique from the chapter that you think would have been good to use, providing a justification as to why this would be a suitable technique.

Critical Thinking QUESTIONS

1. "A well-thought-out onboarding program is especially important for employees (like many recent graduates) who have had little or no work experience." Explain why you agree or disagree with this statement.
2. What do you think are some of the main drawbacks of relying on informal on-the-job training for teaching new employees their jobs?
3. This chapter points out that one reason for implementing special global training programs is to avoid business loss because of cultural insensitivity. What sort of cultural insensitivity do you think is meant, and how might that translate into lost business? What sort of training programs would you recommend to avoid such cultural insensitivity?
4. Most training programs are not formally evaluated beyond a reaction measure. Why do you think employers do not measure the impact of training on learning, behaviour, and results more often?
5. Assume that your company president wants to develop a more customer-focused organization. For the past 10 years, the company has focused on cost containment while growing the business. Write a memo to your company president that supports the investment in customer service training as part of the strategic plan.

Experiential EXERCISES

1. Obtain a copy of an employee handbook from your employer or from some other organization. Review it and make recommendations for improvement.
2. Working individually or in groups, follow the steps in **Figure 8.1** and prepare a training program for a job that you currently hold or have had in the past.
3. In small groups of four to six students, complete the following exercise:

   WestJet has asked you to quickly develop the outline of a training program for its new reservation clerks. Airline reservation clerks obviously need numerous skills to perform their jobs. (You may want to start by listing the job's main duties, using the information provided below.)

Produce the requested training outline, making sure to be very specific about what you want to teach the new clerks and what methods and aids you suggest using to train them.

Duties of Airline Reservation Clerks:

Customers contact airline reservation clerks to obtain flight schedules, prices, and itineraries. The reservation clerks look up the requested information on the airline's flight schedule systems, which are updated continuously. The reservation clerk must deal courteously and expeditiously with the customer and be able to quickly find alternative flight arrangements to provide the customer with the itinerary that fits his or her needs. Alternative flights and prices must be found quickly so that the customer is not kept waiting and so that the reservation operations group maintains its efficiency standards. It is often necessary to look under various routings, since there may be a dozen or more alternative routes between the customer's starting point and destination.

4. Working in groups of four to six students, complete the following exercise:

Determine who in your group knows how to make paper objects such as cranes, boxes, balloons, ninja darts, fortunes, boats, and so on. Select one person who is willing to be a subject matter expert (SME) to assist your group in developing an on-the-job training program to make one product.

Using the expertise of your SME, develop, document (refer to the sample job instruction template earlier in the chapter), and validate a training plan to make the chosen product. Modify the documented plan as required after your pilot. Ensure that everyone in your group has a copy of the plan and can reliably make the product to standards. Once this is accomplished, each group member will pair up with a member of another group that made a different product. Each person in the resulting pairs will train his or her partner on how to make the products using the training plan and sample he or she created.

Debrief the exercise as instructed.

Running CASE

Running Case: LearnInMotion.com

The New Training Program

"I just don't understand it," said Pierre. "No one here seems to follow instructions, and no matter how many times I've told them how to do things, they seem to do them their own way." At present, LearnInMotion.com has no formal onboarding or training policies or procedures. Jennifer believes this is one reason why employees generally ignore the standards that she and Pierre would like them to adopt.

Several examples illustrate this problem. One job of the web designer (her name is Maureen) is to take customer copy for banner ads and adapt it for placement on LearnInMotion.com. She has been told several times not to tinker in any way with a customer's logo: Most companies put considerable

thought and resources into logo design, and as Pierre has said, "Whether or not Maureen thinks the logo is perfect, it's the customer's logo, and she's to leave it as it is." Yet just a week ago, they almost lost a big customer when Maureen, to "clarify" the customer's logo, modified its design before posting it on LearnInMotion.com.

That's just the tip of the iceberg. As far as Jennifer and Pierre are concerned, it is the sales effort that is completely out of control. For one thing, even after several months on the job, it still seems as if the salespeople don't know what they're talking about. For example, LearnInMotion has several co-brand arrangements with websites like Yahoo! This setup allows users on other sites to easily click through to LearnInMotion.com if they are interested in ordering educational courses or CDs. Jennifer has noticed that, during conversations with customers, the two salespeople have no idea which sites co-brand with LearnInMotion, or how to get to the LearnInMotion site from the partner website. The salespeople also need to know a lot more about the products themselves. For example, one salesperson was trying to sell someone who produces programs on managing call centres on the idea of listing its products under LearnInMotion's "communications" community. In fact, the "communications" community is for courses on topics like interpersonal communications and how to be a better listener; it has nothing to do with managing the sorts of call centres that, for instance, airlines use for handling customer inquiries.

As another example, the web surfer is supposed to get a specific email address with a specific person's name for the salespeople to use; instead he often just comes back with an "information" email address from a website. The list goes on and on.

Jennifer feels the company has had other problems because of the lack of adequate employee training and orientation. For example, a question came up recently when employees found out they weren't paid for the Canada Day holiday. They assumed they would be paid, but they were not. Similarly, when a salesperson left after barely a month on the job, there was considerable debate about whether the person should receive severance pay and accumulated vacation pay. Other matters to cover during an orientation, says

Jennifer, include company policy regarding lateness and absences; health and hospitalization benefits (there are none, other than workers' compensation); and matters like maintaining a safe and healthy workplace, personal appearance and cleanliness, personal telephone calls and email, substance abuse, and eating on the job.

Jennifer believes that implementing orientation and training programs would help ensure that employees know how to do their jobs. She and Pierre further believe that it is only when employees understand the right way to do their jobs that there is any hope those jobs will in fact be carried out in the way the owners want them to be. Now they want you, their management consultant, to help them.

QUESTIONS

1 How would you change LearnInMotion's orientation program? Should this company rename this process to an onboarding program instead?

2 Should Pierre and Jennifer be involved in the onboarding program to emphasize the importance of this process to their staff?

3 Should management of each department assist in the development and subsequent enforcement of the new onboarding program? Why or why not?

Case INCIDENT

A Case of Too Little Training Too Late!

It's late Friday afternoon in Thunder Bay, Ontario, and Jeff Hartley, a returning summer student, is looking forward to the end of the workday so that he can join his team from the paint department at the baseball game tonight. At the same time, in the office area adjacent to the plant, Julie Adler is working on the finishing touches to a new training program she will be requiring all new employees to take prior to being hired at Simplas Inc. Julie just completed hiring back all of the summer students who were on staff last year and is anxious to have them attend this required training/onboarding program scheduled for Monday morning.

The company has never had a formal onboarding program before, including no Workplace Hazardous Materials Information System (WHMIS) training regarding chemicals and their affects in the workplace. Julie has been noticing some unsafe behaviours lately and wants to take this opportunity to put appropriate training in place. Another part of Julie's plan for this training is to emphasize the supervisor's role in each department with regard to promoting safe behaviours, especially in the area of proper handling of chemicals in the workplace.

An hour later Julie has put the finishing touches on her new orientation/training program, has confirmed the trainer scheduled to certify everyone in WHMIS on Monday, and has received top management support for her program when she hears screams coming from the paint department. Running down the stairs to the paint department, she sees Jeff Hartley unconscious on the floor. The sound of the arrival of the ambulance erupts into the air. After Jeff is taken to the hospital, Julie is desperate to investigate what happened. She turns to his supervisor and demands to know all the details. Apparently, in his hurry to be done for the day, Jeff did not wear his face mask while he was painting a final part and must have passed out from the paint fumes collecting in the area. Julie sighs and realizes just how much more training will be needed at this company; onboarding is just a start. Please assist Julie by answering the following questions.

QUESTIONS

1   What legal aspects regarding the obvious lack of training in this case will Julie, as HR manager, and the company have to deal with?

2   How can the five-step training process assist in this scenario?

3   Should Julie put together specific training for all summer students?

MyManagementLab

Visit MyManagementLab to access a personalized Study Plan and additional study tools for this chapter.

   To view the CBC videos, read a summary, and answer discussion questions, go to MyManagementLab

CHAPTER

9

Career Development

LEARNING OUTCOMES

AFTER STUDYING THIS CHAPTER, YOU SHOULD BE ABLE TO

EXPLAIN the strategic importance of career planning and development in the context of today's talent shortage.

ANALYZE the factors that affect career choices.

EXPLAIN the evolution of career development and the impact of that on employers and employees.

RECOMMEND how to manage transfers and promotions more effectively.

EXPLAIN what management development is and why it is important.

DESCRIBE on-the-job and off-the-job management-development techniques.

REQUIRED PROFESSIONAL CAPABILITIES (RPC)

- Assesses and recommends internal and external suppliers of development programs

- Applies general principles of adult learning to ensure appropriate development methods and techniques

- Uses a variety of methods to deliver development programs

- Helps supervisors/managers identify career options for employees that align with business needs

- Provides assessment tools for career development

- Ensures performance management information is an integral component of employee development

- Assists employees in identifying career paths, establishing learning plans and activities required for achieving personal and organizational success

- Facilitates the implementation of developmental work assignments

- Monitors, documents, and reports on career development activities

- Implements deployment procedures ensuring that necessary compensation and benefits changes and education plans are addressed

CAREER PLANNING AND DEVELOPMENT

career planning and development
The deliberate process through which a person becomes aware of personal career-related attributes and the lifelong series of activities that contribute to his or her career fulfillment.

Career Planning Exercises
www.careerstorm.com

Career Networking
www.careerkey.com

career A series of work-related positions, paid or unpaid, that help a person to grow in job skills, success, and fulfillment.

Career planning has become a critical strategic issue for CEOs and boards of directors, as well as HR executives.[1] The aging workforce and shifts in occupations and employment patterns have created a sense of urgency regarding the development of careers for the next generation of managers and executives. Increasing competition for talent is expected to create a serious challenge for retaining high-potential employees. Proactive organizations have already started to take action to manage the need for more managerial talent.

At the same time, there is an increasing need for employees who are interested in global careers, in virtual work as a key aspect of their careers, in careers that involve continuously changing technology, and many other variations on traditional career paths. HRM activities play an important role in **career planning and development**. Career-related programs help HR professionals maintain employee commitment—an employee's identification with and agreement to pursue the company's or the unit's strategic goals. Most employees appreciate and respond well to having their skills and potential enhanced, and to knowing that they will be more marketable. Developmental activities, such as providing the educational and training resources required to help employees identify and develop their promotion and career potential, are extremely important to younger employees today. Career-oriented firms also stress career-oriented appraisals that link the employee's past performance, career preferences, and developmental needs in a formal career plan.

Career planning can play a significant role in retaining employees in the organization and reducing turnover of valued workers. The key factors in employee retention today are an organizational culture that values and nurtures talented employees, fair processes in "people" decisions, and managers who understand what motivates employees.[2] Employers and employees also recognize the need for lifelong learning. Retention can be strengthened by providing extensive continuing training—from basic remedial skills to advanced decision-making techniques—throughout employees' careers.

Before proceeding, it would be useful to clarify some of the terms that will be used throughout this chapter.[3] A **career** is a series of work-related positions, paid or unpaid, that help a person to grow in job skills, success, and fulfillment. *Career development* is the lifelong series of activities (such as workshops) that contribute to a person's career exploration, establishment, success, and fulfillment. And, as the Workforce Diversity box illustrates, career development for older workers is just as important as it is for younger employees. *Career planning* is the deliberate process through which someone becomes aware of personal skills, interests, knowledge, motivations, and other characteristics; acquires information about opportunities and choices; identifies career-related goals; and establishes action plans to attain specific goals.

WORKFORCE DIVERSITY

Career Development for Older Workers

If an employer doesn't pay attention to the career development of staff as they approach age 60, it won't have the benefit of their productivity during their second middle age. The "second middle age" is a term coined by Helen Harkness in the book *Don't Stop the Career Clock*. It refers to the 20-year period when an individual is between ages 60 and 80. It ought to be viewed as a time of potential and valuable contribution rather than as "the retirement years" or, worse, "old age."

Here are practical career development strategies that will help keep employees fully engaged during their second middle age:

- *Adopt a new attitude:* Discard the stereotypes. Older workers are not necessarily closed-minded, reluctant to embrace change, risk averse, or focused on the past. Their views are grounded in years of hard-earned experience and many of them are open-minded, flexible, forward-thinking, and willing to take calculated risks.

- *Provide career counselling:* People want to do work that interests them, takes advantage of their knowledge, honours their values, and uses their key skills. These factors change for the individual over time, and often a person's career path takes him or her away from work that is truly enjoyed. Returning to an earlier role could be rejuvenating in second middle age or it might be feasible to launch into a completely new endeavour as an alternative to retirement. To help employees stay on a productive career track, it is crucial to provide good career counselling.

- *Invest in training and development:* Recent research debunks the myth of the inevitable decline of mental ability with age. Although slower processing and some memory loss are typical of aging, these are not necessarily signs of diminishing capacity in primary mental functions, such as verbal meaning, spatial orientation, inductive reasoning, numerical ability, or word fluency. These important mental competencies, which can remain intact well into someone's 90s in the absence of illness, make second middle-agers worthy candidates for training and development. It is easy to compensate for a slower mental pace and occasional memory lapse when intellectual capability is respected.

- *Honour the need for work–life balance:* After decades of commuting, working long hours, and taking short holidays, many people look forward to retirement as a welcome break from the unrelenting routine. The prospect of sleeping in seven days a week, taking an extended trip, or spending the winter in Florida can have a lot of appeal. Creative work arrangements could offer some of these perks to second middle-agers.

Second middle-agers could be organizational gold. Research has shown that they have lower rates of absenteeism, fewer accidents, higher levels of job satisfaction, and a stronger work ethic. Why wouldn't employers encourage them to develop their careers and remain productive in the workforce as long as possible?

Source: Adapted from M. Watters of Optimum Talent/KWA Partners, "Career Development for Employees Heading into Their 'Second Middle Age,'" *Canadian HR Reporter* (February 13, 2006), p. 13. Reprinted by permission of Canadian HR Reporter. © Copyright Thomson Reuters Canada Ltd., (2012) Toronto, Ontario, 1-800-387-5164. Web: www.hrreporter.com

THE EVOLUTION OF CAREER DEVELOPMENT

occupational orientation The theory, that there are six basic personal orientations that determine the sorts of careers to which people are drawn.

In the early stages of career development research, career patterns were assumed to be stable, predictable, linear, and based on hierarchies. Career stages were seen as influential on the employee's knowledge of and preference for various occupations, and were often associated to the concept that based on an employee's age, their career stage could be established. Later studies, like the Vocational Preference Test (VPT) by John Holland suggested that a person's personality (including values, motives, and needs) determines his or her **occupational orientation**, which is another important factor in career choices.

Based on research with the Vocational Preference Test (VPT), six basic personality types or orientations were identified:

1. *Realistic orientation.* These people are attracted to occupations that involve physical activities requiring skill, strength, and coordination. Examples include forestry, farming, and agriculture.

2. *Investigative orientation.* Investigative people are attracted to careers that involve cognitive activities (thinking, organizing, and understanding) rather than affective activities (feeling, acting, or interpersonal and emotional tasks). Examples include biologists, chemists, and university professors.

3. *Social orientation.* These people are attracted to careers that involve interpersonal rather than intellectual or physical activities. Examples include clinical psychology, foreign service, and social work.

4. *Conventional orientation.* A conventional orientation favours careers that involve structured, rule-regulated activities, as well as careers in which it is expected that the employee subordinate his or her personal needs to those of the organization. Examples include accountants and bankers.

5. *Enterprising orientation.* Verbal activities aimed at influencing others are attractive to enterprising personalities. Examples include managers, lawyers, and public relations executives.

6. *Artistic orientation.* People here are attracted to careers that involve self-expression, artistic creation, expression of emotions, and individualistic activities. Examples include artists, advertising executives, and musicians.

Most people have more than one orientation (they might be social, realistic, and investigative, for example). Holland believes that the more similar or compatible these orientations are, the less internal conflict or indecision a person will face in making a career choice.

New Approaches to Career Development

The beginning of the twenty-first century was marked by a new social arrangement and diversification of approaches to work, which have begun to challenge traditional theories of career development. Job transitions are more frequent, therefore occupational prospects and linear career patterns lose definability and predictability.

As a result, a new concept of career development emerged, in which the primary stakeholder of a career is the person, not the organization.[4] Therefore, a more dynamic and holistic approach to career development is emerging, with a focus on lifelong learning, flexibility, and adaptability. As such, a number of individual and organizational considerations need to be made.

Identify Skills and Aptitudes

Successful performance depends not just on motivation, but also on ability. Someone may have a conventional orientation, but whether he or she has the skills to be an accountant, banker, or credit manager will largely determine the specific occupation ultimately chosen. Therefore, each individual's skills must be identified based on his or her education and experience. In organizations using competency- or skill-based pay, a formal system for evaluating skills will already be in place.

For career-planning purposes, a person's aptitudes are usually measured with a test battery, such as the general aptitude test battery (GATB). This instrument measures various aptitudes, including intelligence and mathematical ability.

Considerable work has been done to relate aptitudes, such as those measured by the GATB, to specific occupations.

Identify Career Anchors

career anchor A concern or value that a person will not give up if a choice has to be made.

Edgar Schein says that career planning is a continuing process of self-discovery. As a person learns more about him- or herself, a dominant **career anchor** may become apparent. Career anchors, as their name implies, are concerns or values that a person will not give up if a choice has to be made. Schein identified eight career anchors:

1. *Technical/functional:* People who have a strong technical/functional career anchor tend to avoid decisions that would drive them toward general management. Instead, they make decisions that will enable them to remain and grow in their chosen technical or functional fields.

2. *Managerial competence:* Other people show a strong motivation to become managers, and their career experience convinces them that they have the skills and values required to rise to general management positions. A management position of high responsibility is their ultimate goal.

3. *Creativity:* People who become successful entrepreneurs have a need to build or create something that is entirely their own product—a product or process that bears their name, a company of their own, or a personal fortune that reflects their accomplishments.

4. *Autonomy and independence:* Some people seem driven to be on their own, free of the dependence that can arise when a person works in a large organization where promotions, transfers, and salary decisions make them subordinate to others.

5. *Security:* Some people are mostly concerned with long-run career stability and job security. A stable future with one organization that offers a good retirement program and benefits or maintaining similar geographic surroundings may be important.

6. *Service/dedication:* More and more people feel a need to do something meaningful in a larger context. Information technology has made global problems, such as the environment, overpopulation, and poverty, highly visible.

7. *Pure challenge:* A small group of people define their career in terms of overcoming impossible odds, solving unsolved problems, and winning out over competitors.

8. *Lifestyle:* A growing number of people, particularly dual-career couples, define their careers as part of a larger lifestyle, integrating two careers and two sets of personal and family concerns.

RPC

Assists employees in identifying career paths and establishing learning plans and activities required for achieving personal and organizational success

Focus on Life Trajectories

Issues of work–life balance are becoming more significant in a person's reflections about their career aspirations. In addition, the growth in the number of people employed in the contingent workforce (temporary, part time, contractual, freelance, casual, and so on) makes managing interactions between work and life domains more critical in career planning.

As a result, career development can be envisioned as a *life trajectory*, in which a person designs and builds his or her career and life simultaneously. This increases the importance of ensuring that employees are empowered decision makers when an organization engages in career planning. As well, the value of career development initiatives must extend beyond adding value to the employer to also include an explicit discussion of the transferability and value of the initiatives to the employee.[5]

The focus on life trajectories requires a shift in thinking about career development, as outlined below:

1. *From traits and states to context:* Research on personality traits and ability factors to guide occupation-driven careers relied on stability and predictability. In the new economy, career patterns should be viewed as professional identities that are dynamic. Understanding the range of factors that are outside of the organization's control is critical to the new approach of career development.

2. *From prescriptive to process:* On average, people up to the age of 36 change their jobs every 2 years. Traditional career paths involving a single, committed occupational choice are no longer a reality. Instead, career planners must stay informed about all of the job-specific requirements and offer a best fit of career patterns, focusing on adding information and content to enable employees to achieve a range of career ambitions.

3. *From linear to non-linear:* Traditional career development was very deductive in that it assumed past employment patterns were valid predictors of future career ambitions. Thus, there is a necessary shift to a more holistic life design for career development, with an awareness of non-linear, often mutually dependant, causalities. Career plans must be frequently reevaluated and updated involving an iterative strategy between organizational agents and employees.

4. *From scientific facts to narrative evaluations:* The old path of completing all desired education, securing a job, then establishing a family is no longer a reality for many Canadians; there is growing diversity of individual realities. Career development must empower employees to self-assess and interpret their own life experiences (often in the form of a narrative) and assist employees in making sense of their distinct perspective and implementing co-evolution.

5. *From describing to modelling:* Career development must adapt to individual experiences, ambitions, abilities, opportunities, and perspectives. Thus, the use of simple descriptive or scientific statistics alone undermines the complexity of career development. Career forecasting in this sense should develop a number of possible configurations and continuously monitor interacting variables to increase the success of career development.

Become a Learning Organization

learning organization An organization skilled at creating, acquiring, and transferring knowledge and at modifying its behaviour to reflect new knowledge and insights.

Learning is a survival technique for both individuals and organizations. Today, employees at all levels know that they must engage in lifelong learning to remain employable and have a satisfying career. A **learning organization** is an organization skilled at creating, acquiring, and transferring knowledge and at modifying its behaviour to reflect new knowledge and insights. The HR department is often the driving force behind ensuring that the training and development opportunities necessary to create a learning organization are in place, particularly in transferring knowledge, learning from experience, experimentation through searching for and testing new knowledge, learning from others, and systematic problem solving.

Roles in Career Development

The individual, the manager, and the employer all have roles in the individual's career development. Ultimately, however, it is the *individual* who must accept responsibility for his or her own career, since workers are often seen as collaborators in the organizations that employ them.[6] This requires an entrepreneurial, goal-oriented approach that uses four key skills: self-motivation, independent learning, effective time and money management, and self-promotion.[7] Younger workers today are increasingly expecting to develop these skills by pursuing a career path that involves moving through multiple organizations.[8] **Networking** is the foundation of active career management and is essential for accessing the most valuable career resource—people. Networking is an organized process whereby the individual arranges and conducts a series of face-to-face meetings with his or her colleagues and contacts, plus individuals that they recommend. Networking does not involve asking for a job and it is not a one-sided encounter where only one individual benefits, but rather is a mutual sharing process. Its objectives are to let people know about background and career goals, and to exchange information, advice, and referrals.[9] A personal networking chart is shown in **Figure 9.1**.

Within the organization, the individual's *manager* plays a role in career development, too. The manager should provide timely and objective performance feedback, offer developmental assignments and support, and participate in career development discussions. The manager acts as a coach, an appraiser, an adviser, and a referral agent by listening to and clarifying the individual's career

networking An organized process whereby the individual arranges and conducts a series of face-to-face meetings with his or her colleagues and contacts, plus individuals that they recommend.

FIGURE 9.1   Personal Networking Chart

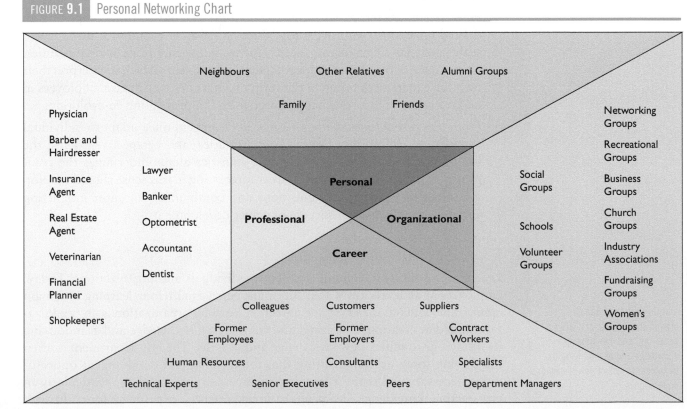

Source: Personal Network Chart From *It's Your Move.* Copyright © 2001, 2004 by Marge Watters. Published by HarperCollins Publishers Ltd. All rights reserved.

plans, giving feedback, generating career options, and linking the employee to organizational resources and career options.

Finally, the *employer* also plays a career development role. For example, an organization wanting to retain good employees should provide career-oriented training and development opportunities, offer career information and career programs, and give employees a variety of career options. Most employees will ultimately assess their employers on the extent to which the organization allowed them to excel and to become the people they believed they had the potential to become. How well an employer fulfills this career development role will help determine an employee's overall job satisfaction and commitment to his or her employer.[10]

MANAGING TRANSFERS AND PROMOTIONS

Transfers and promotions are significant career-related decisions that managers make on an ongoing basis. These decisions have important career development implications for the transferred or promoted employee and substantial benefits for the organization in terms of creating a pool of potential future managers with broad experience throughout the firm.

Managing Transfers

Employees may seek transfers into jobs that offer greater possibility for career advancement or opportunities for personal enrichment, or into those that are more interesting or more convenient—better hours, location of work, and so on.[11]

Employers may transfer a worker to fill a vacant position or, more generally, to find a better fit for the employee within the firm. Transfers are thus increasingly used as a way to give employees opportunities for diversity of job assignment and, therefore, personal and career growth. Many organizations are recognizing that future leaders will need international experience to effectively manage their organizations in the increasingly globalized world of business, and they are providing international assignments as a career development experience.

Policies of routinely transferring employees from locale to locale, either to give their employees more exposure to a wider range of jobs or to fill open positions with trained employees, have fallen into disfavour, partly because of the cost of relocating employees and partly because of the assumption that frequent transfers have a bad effect on an employee's family life. Companies are facing a record number of rejections of their relocation offers. About two-thirds of all transfer refusals are due to family or spousal concerns. Providing reassurances that relocation costs will be covered is often no longer enough to persuade employees to upset their lifestyles, their spouses' careers, and their children's activities. To overcome this problem, companies are offering spousal support in the form of career transition programs to encourage employees to accept transfers.[12]

Making Promotion Decisions

Employers must decide on the criteria on which to promote employees, and the way that these decisions are made will affect the employees' motivation, performance, and commitment.

RPC

Implements deployment procedures ensuring that necessary compensation and benefit changes and education plans are addressed

Hints : TO ENSURE LEGAL
            : COMPLIANCE

Decision 1: Is Seniority or Competence the Rule?

From the point of view of motivation, promotion based on competence is best. However, union agreements often contain a clause that emphasizes seniority in promotions, meaning that only *substantial differences in abilities* can be taken into account in such situations.[13]

Decision 2: How Is Competence Measured?

If promotion is to be based on competence, how will competence be defined and measured? Defining and measuring *past* performance are relatively straightforward matters, but promotion also requires predicting the person's *potential*; thus, there must be a valid procedure for predicting a candidate's future performance. Tests and assessment centres can be used to evaluate employees and identify those with executive potential.[14]

Decision 3: Is the Process Formal or Informal?

Many employers still depend on an informal system where the availability and requirements of open positions are kept secret. Key managers make promotion decisions among employees whom they know personally and who have impressed them.[15] The problem is that when employees are not made aware of the jobs that are available, the criteria for promotion, and how promotion decisions are made, the link between performance and promotion is severed, thereby diminishing the effectiveness of promotion as a reward. For this reason, many employers establish formal, published promotion policies and procedures that describe the criteria by which promotions are awarded. Skills inventories, replacement charts, and replacement summaries (like those discussed in Chapter 5) can be used to compile detailed information about the qualifications of hundreds or even thousands of employees. The net effect of such actions is twofold: (1) an employer ensures that all qualified employees are considered for openings, and (2) promotion becomes more closely linked with performance in the minds of employees, which also increases the legal defensibility of the decision.

MANAGEMENT DEVELOPMENT

management development Any attempt to improve current or future management performance by imparting knowledge, changing attitudes, or increasing skills.

Management development is any attempt to improve managerial performance by imparting knowledge, changing attitudes, or increasing skills. Management development is particularly important as Baby Boomers enter retirement and the next generation of managers assumes senior management responsibilities. It can also help attract top talent or achieve employer-of-choice status. The ultimate aim of management development programs is to achieve business strategy. For this reason, the management development process consists of (1) assessing the company's human resources needs to achieve its strategic objectives, (2) creating a talent pool, and (3) developing the managers themselves.[16]

Another critical issue in management development is training local managers in other parts of the world to take over from the original expatriate managers first sent out to initiate operations. Many organizations are focusing on management development in the Asia-Pacific region, as outlined in the Global HRM box.

GLOBAL HRM

Leadership Development in the Asia-Pacific Region

The Asia-Pacific region represents the major source of growth within the local market and internationally for many corporations over the next ten years. It is forecast that by 2015 the region will account for 45 percent of world GDP, compared to 20 percent for the United States and 17 percent for Western Europe. Inherent within such rapid growth projections are both opportunities and challenges that organizations will need to surmount.

The growth opportunities are often in locations where there is currently a limited supply of leadership capability, so it has been necessary for organizations to import excellence from their home base rather than to source locally. While this solution is effective over the short term, only the development of local leadership competence, in terms of quantity and quality, over the long term will ensure the achievement of future growth targets.

The Asia-Pacific region embodies wide socio-economic and cultural diversity and has examples of both the most and least developed countries in the world. The primary focus of leadership development for most organizations is on people who are native to Asia-Pacific and who, over the long term, will keep their home base there. This is because the localization of leadership has been found to have a positive impact on performance and because the cost of expatriate assignments is high.

In Asia-Pacific, the current limitations of local leadership supply are serious, creating severe competition for talent. As well, the planned reduction in the number of expatriates has taken longer than expected due to job fulfillment and interest in career development (on the part of expatriates), and due to the efficiency and familiarity of working within established networks and behaviours and preservation of common cultural characteristics and behaviours (on the part of organizations).

A Conference Board survey of 55 companies in the region found that these companies have a genuine interest in changing the balance between expatriate and local leadership, and they are looking to attract, inspire, and retain their best local and regional talent by offering challenging career opportunities and improved leadership development programs, and by recruiting the best new talent from all available sources. Almost 80 percent are trying to accelerate talent development in the Asia-Pacific region. More than half have developed competency models that take a consistent global view of what makes global leadership effective. A clear majority of 83 percent said that global skills and competencies are transferable across geographies and cultures; however, they also said that other competencies need to be developed and learned, or re-learned, for different locations.

Although these companies found that experiential activities, such as challenging assignments, were the most effective in developing leaders, they were actually using formal training and learning activities more often. Therefore, organizations may get a better return on investment if they rebalance their resources and processes more toward experiential development opportunities/responsibilities than formal learning interventions.

Source: Excerpt from A. Bell, *Leadership in Asia-Pacific: Identifying and Developing Leaders for Growth*, Research Report #R-1387-06-RR (New York, NY: The Conference Board, 2006). Reprinted with permission.

Succession Planning

succession planning A process through which senior-level and critical strategic job openings are planned for and eventually filled.

Most organizations take special measures to plan ahead to develop replacements for senior executives because of their key strategic role. This process is called **succession planning**. Succession planning provides "a significant competitive advantage to companies that take it seriously—and serious risks to those that do not."[17] Although succession planning has traditionally been focused only on management jobs, many organizations today include other strategic positions as well. When an organization loses a top salesperson or a talented engineer, the loss will not make headlines but the impact on the bottom line could still be significant. A vacant position can mean that important decisions are delayed or made by other employees with less knowledge and expertise.[18]

Successful succession planning begins with the following steps:[19]

1. Establishing a strategic direction for the organization and jobs that are critical to achieving that strategic direction

2. Identifying core skills and competencies needed in jobs that are critical to achieve the strategy

3. Identifying people inside the organization who have, or can acquire, those skills and providing them with developmental opportunities (being prepared to recruit externally as well)

Succession planning for senior managers needs to be overseen by the CEO, as it can easily become an emotional issue for ambitious managers and can evoke political behaviour that can only be dealt with at the highest level.[20] HR staff ensure that all the required information for effective succession planning (such as skills inventories) is available, help to ensure objectivity in the process, and provide the development activities required for employees identified in the succession plan.[21]

Once potential successors have been identified, a *replacement chart* is often prepared. As shown in **Figure 9.2**, this chart summarizes potential candidates and their development needs for each job in the succession management plan.[22] It is important to ensure that these plans are implemented and carefully managed. A recent survey showed that half of North American companies with succession plans did not actively manage them.[23]

Employees should be encouraged to be proactive and accept responsibility for their own careers, including seeking out opportunities for leadership training. Employees who feel empowered and motivated to be the initiators

FIGURE **9.2**   Replacement Chart Showing Development Needs of Future Divisional Vice-President of their own management development process may already be demonstrating leadership potential. Empowering employees in the organization to be part of a mutual succession-planning process increases the potential for its success.[24]

Management Development Techniques

Management development can include both on-the-job and off-the-job techniques. On-the-job development techniques are very popular, including developmental job rotation, the coaching/understudy approach, and action learning approach.

Developmental Job Rotation

developmental job rotation
A management training technique that involves moving a trainee from department to department to broaden his or her experience and identify strong and weak points.

Developmental job rotation involves moving management trainees from department to department to broaden their understanding of all parts of the business.[25] The trainee—often a recent college or university graduate—may work for several months in each department; this not only helps to broaden his or her experience, but it also helps the trainee discover which jobs he or she prefers. For example, Labatt Breweries' global management trainee program is helping to ensure a supply of future leaders, as described in the Strategic HR box.

In addition to providing a well-rounded training experience for each person, job rotation helps to prevent stagnation through the constant introduction of new points of view in each department. It also tests the trainee and helps to identify the person's strong and weak points.[26] Job rotation is more appropriate for developing general line managers than functional staff experts.

Coaching/Understudy Approach

In the *coaching/understudy approach*, the trainee works directly with the person that he or she is to replace; the latter is, in turn, responsible for the trainee's coaching. Normally, the trainee relieves the executive of certain responsibilities and learns the job by doing it.[27] This helps to ensure that the employer will have trained managers to assume key positions.

To be effective, the executive has to be a good coach and mentor. His or her motivation to train the replacement will depend on the quality of the relationship between them.

Action Learning

action learning A training technique by which management trainees are allowed to work full time, analyzing and solving problems in other departments.

Action learning releases managers from their regular duties so that they can work full time on projects, analyzing and solving problems in departments other than their own. The trainees meet periodically with a project group of four or five people with whom their findings and progress are discussed and debated. TD Bank Group and TELUS use this method.[28]

The idea of developing managers in this way has pros and cons. It gives trainees real experience with actual problems, and to that extent it can develop skills like problem analysis and planning. Furthermore, working with the others in the group, the trainees can and do find solutions to major problems. The main

STRATEGIC HR

Brewing Up Management Trainee Programs

For the past two months, Luca Lorenzoni has gone to work every day in a lab coat and goggles—not exactly where the University of Waterloo business major expected to find himself after graduating. "If you'd told me that I'd be in the quality control lab analyzing chemicals in beer, I would have laughed at you," he says. "But that's the opportunity we're given here."

Lorenzoni is in the midst of Labatt Breweries of Canada's global management trainee program, a cross-sectional program aimed at building leaders who understand the beer business from start to finish. Having learned about brewing, Lorenzoni is now going on the road with sales reps to learn how to sell beer. Later he'll move to the head office, where he'll train in the HR, information technology, and the legal and corporate affairs side of the business. Then he'll be assigned to a five-month project before moving into his first management role with the company. In all, Lorenzoni will spend 10 months in the program, where he'll learn every aspect of the business and travel across the country—all while receiving a full salary.

The program has helped Labatt entice the best and the brightest as future leaders, says Amy Secord, manager of people development. Roughly 3000 students and recent graduates (within two years of graduating) apply for the 15 position available in the program. The selection process involves five rigorous rounds of interviews, including a business simulation that resembles the game of Risk, says Secord. Applicants are divided into teams and assigned a continent where they manage a beer company. "We go through different rounds to represent different years. We throw in factors such as another entry into the market, or perhaps they had a bad year with weather," she says. "It's not so much to see what their results are but how they interact as a team and who steps up as a natural leader."

Lorenzoni jokes that he still has nightmares about the intense selection process, but says that's what attracted him to the program in the first place. It also gives him the time and experience to decide whether Labatt is the right fit for him and vice versa. "Any time you spend that much time and dedicate that many resources to actually finding candidates, you know that the company has got a lot behind the program," he says. "You get to see, round through round, who's staying on and to see if you really fit with them."

Before applying for the program, Lorenzoni did consulting work in Toronto with little vision for the future. The management training program has opened up more opportunities than he could have imagined, he says. "You see a path. It's something that at every step you have to earn, but, at the same time, there is a lot of opportunity here," he says.

"The program is already paying off for Labatt," says Secord. Several trainees from the first intake have shot straight up the corporate ranks, landing roles just below the director level—roles that have traditionally taken 10 to 15 years to achieve. "These are people two to three years out of school," she says. "[The program] is imperative. We have to make sure we have the right people in the right places."

Some components of the program have been modified along the way and, more significantly, Labatt has condensed the interview process to have candidates in the door by November instead of December. "We've had to speed up the recruitment process quite a bit," says Secord. "Even in this tough market, more and more companies are trying to get the best talent. Last year, in Luca's year, we actually lost a lot of candidates because we were only offering to them at the beginning of December."

Labatt is also trying to reach a broader audience through a Facebook group and trainees' blogs. Secord declines to say how much the program costs per trainee but will say it's one of the company's more expensive—and valued—programs. "If we don't take the time to make sure that we have the right people, who are trained the right way, we're in a lot of trouble further down the line. We need them now."

Source: Adapted from D. Harder, "Brewing up Management Trainee Programs," *Canadian HR Reporter* (December 15, 2008).

drawback is that, in releasing trainees to work on outside projects, the employer loses the full-time services of a competent manager.

There are many techniques that are used to develop managers off the job, perhaps in a conference room at headquarters or off the premises entirely at a university or special seminar. These options are addressed next.

Adventure learning participants enhance their leadership skills, team skills, and risk-taking behaviour.

Niagara Institute
www.niagarainstitute.com

RPC

Assesses and recommends internal and external suppliers of development programs

in-house development centre
A company-based method for exposing prospective managers to realistic exercises to develop improved management skills.

BMO Financial Group
www.bmo.com/home

Outside Seminars

Many organizations offer special seminars and conferences aimed at providing skill-building training for managers. For example, the Niagara Institute in Niagara-on-the-Lake, Ontario, offers programs that develop skills essential for strong leadership; and the Canadian Management Professionals Association offers a professional accreditation program leading to the Canadian Management Professional (CMP) designation.[29] Outdoor experiential expeditions, or adventure learning experiences, are sometimes used to enhance leadership skills, team skills, and risk-taking behaviour.[30]

College/University-Related Programs

Colleges and universities provide three types of management development activities. First, many schools provide *executive development programs* in leadership, marketing, HRM, operations management, and so on. The programs use cases and lectures to provide senior-level managers with the latest management skills, as well as practice in analyzing complex organizational problems. Most of these programs take the executives away from their jobs, putting them in university-run learning environments for their entire stay.

Second, many colleges and universities also offer *individualized courses* in areas like business, management, and healthcare administration. Managers can take these courses to fill gaps in their backgrounds. Thus, a prospective division manager with a gap in experience with accounting controls might sign up for a two-course sequence in managerial accounting.

Finally, many schools also offer *degree programs*, such as the MBA or Executive MBA. The latter is a Master of Business Administration degree program geared especially to middle managers and above, who generally take the courses on weekends and proceed through the program with the same group of colleagues.

The employer usually plays a role in university-related programs.[31] First, many employers offer *tuition refunds* as an incentive for employees to develop job-related skills. Thus, engineers may be encouraged to enroll in technical courses aimed at keeping them abreast of changes in their field. Supervisors may be encouraged to enroll in programs to develop them for higher-level management jobs. Employers are also increasingly granting technical and professional employees extended *sabbaticals*—periods of time off—to attend a college or university to pursue a higher degree or to upgrade skills.

In-House Development Centres

Some employers have **in-house development centres**, also called "corporate universities." These centres usually combine classroom learning (lectures and seminars, for instance) with other techniques, like assessment centres, in-basket exercises, and role-playing, to help develop employees and other managers. The number of corporate universities in North America has grown exponentially over the last several years because of their effectiveness in recruiting and retaining the brightest minds and in developing employee loyalty.[32] In Canada, BMO Financial Group, Canada Post, the City of Richmond, and many others all find that corporate universities can create a competitive advantage.[33]

Behaviour Modelling

From the career development perspective, learning techniques can assist in the short-term or long-term career development of employees using behaviour modelling.

Behaviour modelling involves (1) showing employees the right (or "model") way of doing something, (2) letting each person practice the right way to do it, and (3) providing feedback regarding each employee's performance.[34] It has been used to train first-line supervisors to better handle common supervisor–employee interactions; this includes giving recognition, disciplining, introducing changes, and improving poor performance. It has also been used to train middle managers to better handle interpersonal situations, such as performance problems and undesirable work habits. Finally, it has been used to train employees and their supervisors to take and give criticism, give and ask for help, and establish mutual trust and respect.

The basic behaviour-modelling procedure can be outlined as follows:

1. *Modelling:* First, trainees watch films that show model persons behaving effectively in a problem situation. In other words, trainees are shown the right way to behave in a simulated but realistic situation. The film or video might thus show a supervisor effectively disciplining an employee, if teaching how to discipline is the aim of the training program.

2. *Role-playing:* Next, the trainees are given roles to play in a simulated situation; here they practice and rehearse the effective behaviours demonstrated by the models.

3. *Social reinforcement:* The trainer provides reinforcement in the form of praise and constructive feedback based on how the trainee performs in the role-playing situation.

4. *Transfer of training:* Finally, trainees are encouraged to apply their new skills when they are back on their jobs.

Critical elements of behaviour modelling include case studies, role-playing, management games, and simulations. The **case study method** presents a trainee with a written description of an organizational problem. The person then analyzes the case in private, diagnoses the problem, and presents his or her findings and solutions in a discussion with other trainees.[35] The case study method is aimed at giving trainees realistic experience in identifying and analyzing complex problems in an environment in which their progress can be subtly guided by a trained discussion leader. Through the class discussion of the case, trainees learn that there are usually many ways to approach and solve complex organizational problems. Trainees also learn that their own needs and values often influence their solutions.

The aim of **role-playing** is to create a realistic situation and then have the trainees assume the parts (or roles) of specific people in that situation.[36] When combined with the general instructions for the role-playing exercise, roles like these for all of the participants can trigger a spirited discussion among the role-players, particularly when they all throw themselves into the roles. The idea of the exercise is to solve the problem at hand and thereby develop trainees' skills in areas like leadership and delegation.

management game A computerized development technique in which teams of managers compete with one another by making decisions regarding realistic but simulated companies.

Development Dimensions International
www.ddiworld.com

In a computerized **management game**, trainees are divided into five- or six-person companies, each of which has to compete with the others in a simulated marketplace. Each company sets a goal (for example, "maximize sales") and is told that it can make several decisions, such as (1) how much to spend on advertising, (2) how much to produce, (3) how much inventory to maintain, and (4) how many of which product to produce. As in the real world, each company usually cannot see what decisions the other firms have made, although these decisions do affect their own sales. Management games can be good development tools. People learn best by getting involved in the activity itself, and the games can be useful for gaining such involvement. They help trainees develop their problem-solving and leadership skills, as well as foster cooperation and teamwork.

Several things can be done to increase the effectiveness of behaviour modelling approaches. If possible, the cases should be actual scenarios from the trainees' own firms; this will help ensure that trainees understand the background of the situation, as well as make it easier for trainees to transfer what they learn to their own jobs and situations. Instructors have to guard against dominating the behaviour modelling sessions and make sure that they remain no more than a catalyst or coach. Finally, they must carefully debrief employees about the intended versus actual behaviour as part of the learning process.[37]

Trainees participating in a case study discussion

Mentoring

mentoring The use of an experienced individual (the mentor) to teach and train someone (the protégé) with less knowledge in a given area.

RPC

Helps supervisors/managers identify career options for employees that align with business needs

Another approach to behaviour modelling includes mentoring. **Mentoring** has traditionally been defined as the use of an experienced individual (the mentor) to teach and train someone (the protégé) with less knowledge in a given area. Through individualized attention, "the mentor transfers needed information, feedback, and encouragement to the protégé," and in that way, the opportunities for the protégé to optimize his or her career success are improved. Effective mentoring builds trust both ways in the mentor–protégé relationship. Mentoring provides benefits to mentors, who demonstrate enhanced attitudes and job performance, and protégés, who become more self-confident and productive and experience greater career satisfaction and faster career growth.[38]

Organizational mentoring may be formal or informal. Informally, of course, middle- and senior-level managers will often voluntarily take up-and-coming employees under their wings, not only to train them but also to give career advice and to help them steer around political pitfalls. However, many employers also establish formal mentoring programs. Here, employers actively encourage mentoring relationships to take place and may pair protégés with potential mentors.[39] Training may be provided to facilitate the mentoring process and, in particular, to aid both mentor and protégé in understanding their respective responsibilities in the mentoring relationship.

Through reverse mentoring, a younger employee can provide an older one with guidance in using modern technology.

A new development in mentoring is *reverse mentoring* programs, where younger employees provide guidance to senior executives on how to use technology for messaging, buying products and services, finding new business opportunities, and so forth. Procter & Gamble, General Electric, and the Wharton Business School are all using reverse mentoring. The relationship that develops often provides benefits to the young mentor as well when the technology-challenged older manager reciprocates in the form of career advice and guidance. Younger employees can also contribute toward understanding the ever-changing consumer marketplace.[40]

LEADERSHIP DEVELOPMENT

Canada is facing a shortage of leadership talent. At the same time, leadership values are evolving. The traditional command-and-control leadership style is losing its effectiveness, and there is a growing need for leaders who can listen to others and tolerate mistakes made in good faith as part of a learning process. Organizations can gain competitive advantage by addressing this leadership gap.[41]

Bob Hedley, vice-president of people and leadership at Maple Leaf Foods, says, "Where I lose sleep right now is we still don't have enough bench strength. One of the challenges is to acquire enough talent within the company and grow them fast enough so that we are ready to grow ourselves."[42] Maple Leaf Foods believes that employees' success guarantees the success of the company. They call it the "Leadership Edge"—thousands of high-performing people thriving in a high-performance culture. Employees are provided with ongoing feedback about their performance through a state-of-the-art performance assessment and development process. Employees receive recognition for both their accomplishments and their potential. This feedback is followed up with well-targeted developmental activities to ensure continued growth and development.[43]

At the executive level, 70 percent of learning comes from job experience, 20 percent comes from other individuals such as mentors and coaches, and 10 percent comes from formal training.[44] Many companies are trying to enhance learning from others by providing one-on-one executive coaching by independent coaches as part of the executive development process. In some cases, company managers are being provided with training in coaching skills, indicating the growing interest in developing coaching competencies throughout the management ranks.[45] For example, SaskEnergy created a long-term coaching program for 200 managers from all levels to help them develop successful leadership behaviours and provide skills they could apply to their teams. Coaching goals were tied to organizational strategy and succession planning, and senior management actively supported the program. The success of the program is helping to build leaders and position SaskEnergy for future success.[46]

The leadership development programs at the Banff Centre in Alberta focus on building leadership capability in five crucial areas that make up the leadership system: self, team, business unit, organization, and community/society. Leading in increasingly complex situations requires a systematic approach to successfully understand and navigate the interdependencies and linkages among all parts of the system, from the self through to the greater community. For this reason, the Banff Centre uses an integrated approach to develop leaders.[47] The Banff Centre believes that the three basic requirements of successful leadership are knowledge, competency, and character. **Figure 9.3** illustrates the Banff Centre Competency Matrix Model, which is based on

FIGURE 9.3 Banff Centre Competency Matrix Model

Source: Banff Centre Competency Matrix Model. © 2006. Banff AB: The Banff Centre, www.banffcentre.com/departments/leadership/ assessment_tools/competency_matrix (accessed May 8, 2009). Reproduced with permission of The Banff Centre.

six categories of competencies—self-mastery, futuring (vision), sense making (thinking), design of intelligent action, aligning people to action (leading), and adaptive learning.

Today it is critical that leadership development be a strategic priority for organizations to successfully cope with the coming exodus of Boomer executives. Without new executive talent that is trained and ready to assume senior-level responsibilities, Canadian companies will find it difficult to continue to compete successfully in the global economy.

Chapter SUMMARY

1. Career planning and development is a critical strategic issue in ensuring that the supply of necessary talent is available. It involves the deliberate process through which a person becomes aware of personal career-related attributes, and the lifelong series of activities that contribute to his or her career fulfillment.

2. The evolution of career development involved identifying occupational orientation: realistic, investigative, social, conventional, enterprising, and artistic. In addition, skills and aptitudes can be identified, as can career anchors: technical/functional, managerial competence, creativity, autonomy, security, service/dedication, pure challenge, or lifestyle.

3. The focus on life trajectories involves reframing career development from traits and states to context, from prescriptive to process, from linear to non-linear, from scientific to narrative, and from descriptive to modelling. In this evolution, organizations can benefit from becoming learning organizations that use behaviour modelling, including role-playing, simulations, management games, and mentoring opportunities.

4. Transfers offer an opportunity for personal and career development, but they have become more difficult to manage because of spousal and family concerns. Thus, career-transition programs for spouses are often provided. In making promotion decisions, firms have to (1) decide to promote based on seniority or competence, (2) decide how to measure competence, and (3) choose between a formal or informal promotion system.

5. Management development is any attempt to improve managerial performance and is aimed at preparing employees for future jobs with the organization. When an executive position needs to be filled, succession planning is often involved. Management development is important because the majority of Canadian companies are facing a leadership shortage at all levels.

6. Managerial on-the-job training methods include developmental job rotation, coaching, and action learning. Basic off-the-job techniques include case studies, management games, outside seminars, college/university-related programs, and in-house development centres.

MyManagementLab

Visit MyManagementLab to access a personalized Study Plan and additional study tools for this chapter.

Key TERMS

action learning *(p. 249)*
behaviour modelling *(p. 252)*
career *(p. 239)*
career anchor *(p. 242)*
career planning and development *(p. 239)*
case study method *(p. 252)*
developmental job rotation *(p. 249)*
in-house development centre *(p. 251)*

learning organization *(p. 243)*
management development *(p. 246)*
management game *(p. 253)*
mentoring *(p. 253)*
networking *(p. 244)*
occupational orientation *(p. 240)*
role-playing *(p. 252)*
succession planning *(p. 247)*

Review and Discussion QUESTIONS

1. Describe why career planning and development has become more strategically important. Give a brief outline of what organizations are doing to take a more strategic approach in this area.

2. Briefly describe each of the five aspects of the new approach to career development.

3. What are the six main types of occupational orientation?

4. What is a career anchor? For each of the five career anchors, explain why you think each is important today?

5. Explain three different ways in which managers can assist in the career development of their employees.

6. Explain the four important decisions to be made in establishing a promotion policy.

7. Explain the three major on-the-job management development techniques.

Critical Thinking QUESTIONS

1. Do you think developmental job rotation is a good method to use for developing management trainees? Why or why not?

2. Would you tell high-potential employees that they are on the "fast track"? How might this knowledge affect their behaviour? How might the behaviour of employees who are

disappointed at not being included in management development activities be affected?

3. How do you think employees are going to respond to the new focus on career planning, given the emphasis in recent years on "being in charge of your own career"?

4. What steps could a company take to reduce political behaviour in the succession planning process?

5. Discuss the six competencies in the Competency Matrix Model used at the Banff Centre. Do you think that any one of these is more important than the others? Why or why not? If you were asked to list them in order of importance, what order would you put them in and why?

Experiential EXERCISES

1. Review the website of a provider of management development seminars, such as the Canadian Institute of Management. Obtain copies of recent listings of seminar offerings. At what levels of management are the seminar offerings aimed? What seem to be the most popular types of development programs? Why do you think that is the case?

2. Find a person who is web-challenged (perhaps a family friend or one of your professors who is having trouble setting up a website or getting full use of the email system). Offer to reverse mentor him or her on using the web for a short time (a few weeks) in return for some career mentoring for you. Prepare a short report on the benefits of this experience for both of you.

3. Review all positions you have ever held. Below each position, identify core knowledge, skills, and abilities that you learned in each position. Next, identify a career you would like to be actively engaged in over the next three years. Under the future career, outline core knowledge, skills, and abilities the position would require. Now reflect on your own career trajectory to highlight your history of skill development and identify any gaps that may exist for you to advance to your desired career in the future.

4. Using both the Strategic HR box and the Workforce Diversity box in this chapter, compare and contrast the approaches that firms are taking with respect to career development for younger and older workers. Based on your comparison, develop a career development policy statement for a financial institution that reflects the diverse needs of different groups of employees.

Running CASE

Running Case: LearnInMotion.com

What to Do about Succession?
In the second year of operation of LearnInMotion.com, Jennifer was involved in a serious car accident and spent two months in the hospital and another four months in rehabilitation before she was able to return to work. During this six-month period, Pierre had to manage the entire business on his own. It proved to be next to impossible. Despite some new training, the sales effort continued to falter and sales revenues declined by 25 percent.

Staff turnover at LearnInMotion increased, as employees found it frustrating that it was so difficult to have even a brief conversation with Pierre. Employees who left were not replaced, as the decline in sales meant that costs had to be reduced. Thus, Pierre was spared the difficult job of downsizing—at least for now.

The first day that Jennifer returned to work, Pierre said, "We have to have a succession plan. This business will not survive unless we have other employees who can take over from us temporarily now and permanently in the long term."

Jennifer agreed. "Yes, it was difficult for me being unable to work and knowing that you were overwhelmed with every problem in every part of the company," she said. "And maybe our employees' performance in their current jobs would be enhanced if they knew they had been identified as having management potential and were provided with specific development opportunities. We'll have to establish a management development program as well."

"I agree," said Pierre, "but we can't afford to spend much money on this." So Pierre and Jennifer would like your help in establishing a succession plan and a management development plan.

QUESTIONS

1 Would the process of career and development planning assist Pierre and Jennifer?

2 If Jennifer and Pierre decide to use succession planning, what steps of this process should they follow to put such a program in place? Who should be involved in the process?

3 If they decide to promote from within, how should promotions or transfers be handled?

4 What management development techniques should be developed?

Case INCIDENT

What Should Wilma and Frank Do?

Frank and Wilma Rogers live in the Toronto area. Frank is a product engineer in the automotive industry and Wilma is a professor for a local community college. Wilma has been working on her doctorate for the last five years and is scheduled to graduate with her Ph.D. in Business Administration shortly. Wilma has just received an interesting telephone call and can't wait to talk to Frank about it.

Over dinner that night Wilma tells Frank about the phone call: a past boss of hers called to tell her about an open position at a university in Nunavut. As Wilma excitedly discusses the associate professor of business position and the opportunities it will bring, Frank is thinking to himself what a great opportunity it is, but that he doesn't find the location appealing. He subsequently tells her this and nothing more is discussed.

A week goes by and Wilma still finds herself yearning to know more about this position and wanting to apply. She calls Frank and explains this to him and he encourages her to apply. Wilma calls her former boss and applies for the position. Eventually she gets a offer. Wilma gives her notice at the college and within the next six months starts her new position. Wilma moves to Nunavut, but Frank stays in Toronto until he can find a job in

Nunavut. A few more months go by and Frank has not been able to find a comparable job, so he pressures Wilma to consider moving back to Toronto and leaving her new position. Wilma is torn about what to do as she loves her new job but understands why Frank is frustrated.

QUESTIONS

1 According to Edgar Schein, what career anchors are driving Wilma's and Frank's careers at this point?

2 If Wilma wishes to stay in her new job, how could her employer assist her with this dilemma?

3 Is there anything Frank and Wilma should have done differently in your opinion? If so, what?

MyManagementLab

Visit MyManagementLab to access a personalized Study Plan and additional study tools for this chapter.

To view the CBC videos, read a summary, and answer discussion questions, go to MyManagementLab

CHAPTER 10

Performance Management

LEARNING OUTCOMES

AFTER STUDYING THIS CHAPTER, YOU SHOULD BE ABLE TO

EXPLAIN the five steps in the performance management process.

DESCRIBE five performance appraisal methods and the pros and cons of each.

DISCUSS the major problems inhibiting effective performance appraisals.

DISCUSS 360-degree appraisal from multiple sources.

DESCRIBE the three types of appraisal interviews.

DISCUSS the future of performance management.

REQUIRED PROFESSIONAL CAPABILITIES (RPC)

- Provides development information, support activities, and procedures for learners, supervisors, and managers to assist in achieving performance improvement

- Assists and coaches supervisors to help employees achieve required performance levels

THE STRATEGIC IMPORTANCE OF PERFORMANCE MANAGEMENT

In any organization, achieving strategic objectives requires employee productivity above all else as organizations strive to create a high-performance culture by using a minimum number of employees. Thus, it has been suggested that better performance management represents a largely untapped opportunity to improve company profitability.[1] Many companies are still dealing with the reality that their performance management systems are ineffective—for example, they need to downsize poor performers, but performance appraisal records indicate that all employees are performing adequately.

performance management The process encompassing all activities related to improving employee performance, productivity, and effectiveness.

Performance management is a process encompassing all activities related to improving employee performance, productivity, and effectiveness. It includes *goal setting*, *pay for performance*, *training and development*, *career management*, and *disciplinary action*. The performance management system must provide an integrated network of procedures across the organization that will influence all work behaviour.[2] There are three major purposes of performance management: it aligns employee actions with strategic goals, it is a vehicle for culture change, and it provides input into other HR systems such as development and remuneration.[3]

THE PERFORMANCE MANAGEMENT PROCESS

Performance management is of considerable strategic importance to today's organizations because the most effective way for firms to differentiate themselves in a highly competitive, service-oriented, global marketplace is through the quality of its employees.[4] The performance management process contains five steps:[5]

1. Defining performance expectations and goals
2. Providing ongoing feedback and coaching
3. Conducting performance appraisal and evaluation discussions
4. Determining performance rewards/consequences
5. Conducting development and career opportunities discussions

Robert Thorndike researched performance management processes and suggests that employment decisions (such as a performance appraisal system) must be valid, practical, reliable, and free from bias.[6] Failure to measure and use appraisal results effectively in human resource decision making and career development negates the primary purpose of performance evaluations. Effective performance management thus begins with defining the job and its performance standards, which will now be discussed.

STEP 1: DEFINING PERFORMANCE EXPECTATIONS

Defining performance expectations and goals is a critical step in employees' understanding of how their work makes a contribution to achieving business results. Over the last 30 years there has been more recognition that job performance is a multidimensional construct which can be split into what has become widely acknowledged as *task* versus *contextual* performance.[7]

task performance An individual's direct contribution to their job related processes.

Task performance reflects an individual's direct contribution to their job-related processes. Focusing on tasks means that performance expectations are grounded in realistic job demands and align with the organization's strategic objectives and implementation plans. They may also be partially based on previous performance evaluations.

However, as part of the movement toward more corporate social responsibility, expectations are beginning to extend beyond job skills and skills required for promotion to addressing the concept of whole person development (aligned with the direction, attitudes, motivation, and advancement opportunities of the employee). In addition to task performance, contextual performance is often evaluated as a second factor contributing to an employee's overall work-related performance. **Contextual performance** reflects an individual's indirect contribution to the organization by improving the organizational, social, and psychological behaviours that contribute to organizational effectiveness beyond those specified for the job. This includes extra-role behaviours and contextual factors like "demonstrates a positive attitude" and "pitches in to help others when needed," which have surfaced as contextual performance expectations.[8] These goals may be informally known, but not formally defined, which can become problematic in performance management. Employees also need to be aware of which behaviours are expected and which are discretionary to maintain the legitimacy of the performance management system.

contextual performance An individual's indirect contribution to the organization by improving the organizational, social, and psychological behaviours that contribute to organizational effectiveness beyond those specified for the job.

Research finds that most employees require much more clarification of their performance expectations and how these contribute to the organization's overall results.[9] For example, the sales associate job description may list such duties as "supervise support staff" and "be responsible for all customer liaisons." However, one particular sales associate may be expected to personally sell at least $600 000 worth of products per year by handling the division's two largest accounts, to keep the sales assistants happy, and to keep customers away from company executives.[10]

Ultimately, the performance management process cannot be separated from performance measurement. Performance expectations need to be developed in a legally defensible (correlated with job activities), clear, and measurable way. In addition, they must be communicated and supported as such by the organization. Aligned with the sales associate example, a "personal selling" activity can be measured in terms of how many dollars of sales the associate is to generate personally. "Keeping customers away from executives" can be measured with a standard of no more than 10 customer complaints per year being the sales associate's target. In general, employees should always know ahead of time how and on what basis they will be appraised. It is important to note that expectations cannot discriminate directly or indirectly against anyone on protected grounds (gender, age, disability, and so on).

Hints TO ENSURE LEGAL COMPLIANCE

In global companies, performance appraisal criteria may need to be modified to be consistent with cultural norms and values. An interesting study found that some criteria are acceptable in many cultures, as discussed in the Global HRM box.

GLOBAL HRM

Performance Appraisal Criteria in China

Performance appraisal gradually has become more widely used in Chinese enterprises since 1978, when Deng Xiaoping's "open-door" policy began. The appraisal criteria used then were "good moral practice" (*de*), which refers to virtue or moral integrity; "adequate competence" (*neng*), which relates to one's educational background, physical condition, and ability to lead and manage; "positive working attitude" (*qing*), which covers diligence, attendance, and sense of responsibility; and "strong performance record" (*jie*), which refers mainly to work effectiveness, including work quality and quantity.

In the west, where individuals have an inalienable right to choose their own lifestyles and moralities, performance criteria cannot be based on personal character, but instead need to focus on more objective criteria, such as job competence, abilities, and achievements. In China, however, the attitudes and moral character of a person have been regarded as highly relevant to performance. The Confucian view stresses that the most important aspect of an individual is the moral base of his or her character. Chinese culture tends to ascribe achievement more to effort (that is, diligence, which reflects one's morality) than to ability (which, conceived as an inborn trait, requires no moral effort). For the Chinese, hard work reflects admirably on one's character, and achievement is thought to be closely related to moral character. These deeply rooted Confucian values in China thus lead to an emphasis on appraisals that are based upon personal attitudes and moral characteristics (a practice that is clearly antithetical to the appraisal practices in western societies) that appear to reflect traditional Chinese values, such as working hard and being loyal and respectful toward senior staff. Some specific examples are accepting overtime work; being punctual, careful, helpful, loyal, and respectful toward senior staff; as well as being persistent, adaptable, dedicated, and hard working.

Researchers Robert Taormina and Jennifer Gao from the University of Macau gave Chinese workers a list of appraisal items from both western and Chinese sources and asked which ones would be acceptable. They found three performance appraisal factors that were very acceptable to Chinese employees: work dedication, work efficiency, and teamwork. Work dedication behaviours, such as punctuality, loyalty, working hard, and dedication toward one's work, exist in both eastern and western cultures. Employee efficiency has long been considered important to good job performance, as it is considered to be a means to achieve organizational goals. Chinese employees appear to recognize this managerial objective since they were willing to be evaluated on criteria that assess the efficiency of their work. Teamwork is a behavioural manifestation of the group orientation in eastern cultures.

These findings indicate that relevant and carefully selected appraisal criteria can be applicable across cultures.

Source: Robert J. Taormina and Jennifer H. Gao (2009). Identifying Acceptable Performance Appraisal Criteria: An International Perspective. *Asia Pacific Journal of Human Resources* 47(1), pp. 102–125. Copyright © 2009, Australian Human Resources Institute. Used with permission from John Wiley and Sons.

STEP 2: PROVIDING ONGOING COACHING AND FEEDBACK

Throughout the performance management process, managers and their reports should continue to discuss progress. **Figure 10.1** provides an example of a performance improvement plan (often referred to as a PIP) that can be used to focus such discussions and facilitate ongoing performance improvement. It is important to have open two-way communication, and both the employee and the manager need to check in frequently throughout the performance management process to talk about progression toward goals.

In some organizations, strategies and objectives change quickly. In such cases, managers and employees may need to change their goals to be consistent. Employees are responsible for monitoring their own performance and asking for help. This promotes employee ownership and control over the process.

FIGURE **10.1**   Example of a Performance Improvement Plan

Sample Performance Improvement Plan

TO: [Employee's Name]

FROM: [   ]

SUBJECT: [30/60/90] Day Performance Improvement Plan

DATE: [   ]

This memorandum is written as a [30/60/90] Day Performance Improvement Plan designed to focus your attention on substantially improving your performance in several key areas.

[As was discussed in your most recent performance review dated _____ , you received several "1's" in key areas and an overall rating of "1" meaning you did not meet expectations.]

[Since your performance review on _____, your performance has been unsatisfactory in several respects. For example, _____ .]

This being the case, I have outlined the following Performance Improvement Plan which sets forth objectives that you must accomplish in order to bring your performance up to minimal acceptable standards. The plan is as follows:

1.

2.

3. [list fair objectives – they can be both objective and subjective – in clear terms that could reasonably be accomplished within the required time frame]

4.

5.

You have [30/60/90] days from today to meet these objectives. I will meet with you twice over the next [30/60/90] days to discuss your progress. Our first meeting will be on _____ at _____ and the second meeting will be on _____ at _____ . Both meetings will be in my office.

It is your responsibility to contact me at anytime during this time period regarding your performance and to seek assistance in removing roadblock(s) you may come up against which may impede your progress.

MILW_513764.1

Source: Docstoc, Documents & Resources for Small Businesses & Professionals, www.docstoc.com/docs/4960973/ Sample-Performance-Improvement-Plan-TO-FROM-SUBJECT-DATE-Employee.

STEP 3: PERFORMANCE APPRAISAL AND EVALUATION DISCUSSION

The appraisal itself is generally conducted with the aid of a predetermined and formal method, like one or more of those described in this section.

Formal Appraisal Methods

Graphic Rating Scale

graphic rating scale A scale that lists a number of traits and a range of performance for each. The employee is then rated by identifying the score that best describes his or her level of performance for each trait.

The **graphic rating scale** is the simplest and most popular technique for appraising performance. **Figure 10.2** shows a typical rating scale. It lists traits (such as reliability) and a range of performance values (from unsatisfactory to outstanding) for each one. The supervisor rates each employee by circling or checking the score that best describes his or her performance for each trait. The assigned values are then totalled.

Instead of appraising generic traits or factors, many firms specify the duties to be appraised. For a payroll coordinator, these might include being the liaison with accounting and benefits staff, continually updating knowledge regarding relevant legislation, maintenance of payroll records, data entry and payroll calculations, and ongoing responses to employee inquiries regarding payroll issues.

Alternation Ranking Method

alternation ranking method Ranking employees from best to worst on a particular trait.

Ranking employees from best to worst on a trait or traits is another method for evaluating employees. Because it is usually easier to distinguish between the worst and best employees than to rank them, an **alternation ranking method** is popular. First, list all employees to be rated, and then cross out the names of any not known well enough to rank. Then, on a form such as that shown in **Figure 10.3**, indicate the employee who is the highest on the characteristic being measured and also the one who is the lowest. Then choose the next highest and the next lowest, alternating between highest and lowest until all the employees to be rated have been ranked.

Paired Comparison Method

paired comparison method Ranking employees by making a chart of all possible pairs of employees for each trait and indicating the better employee of the pair.

The **paired comparison method** helps to make the ranking method more precise. For every trait (quantity of work, quality of work, and so on), every employee is paired with and compared with every other employee.

Suppose that five employees are to be rated. In the paired comparison method, a chart is prepared, as in **Figure 10.4**, of all possible pairs of employees for each trait. Then, for each trait, indicate (with a + or −) who is the better employee of the pair. Next, the number of times that an employee is rated as better is added up. In Figure 10.4, employee Maria was ranked highest (she has the most + marks) for quality of work, while Art was ranked highest for creativity.

Forced Distribution Method

forced distribution method Predetermined percentages of ratees are placed in various performance categories.

Jack Welch, retired chief executive officer of General Electric (GE), is most often associated with the **forced distribution method**, which places predetermined percentages of ratees in performance categories. At GE, the bell curve was used to identify the top 10–20% of the workforce (which are then identified as those exceeding

FIGURE 10.2   Sample Graphic Rating Scale Form

Sample Performance Rating Form

Employee's Name _____   Level: Entry-level employee

Manager's Name _____

Key Work Responsibilities   Results/Goals to be Achieved
1. _____   1. _____
2. _____   2. _____
3. _____   3. _____
4. _____   4. _____

Communication

	1		2		3		4		5	

Below Expectations	Meets Expectations	Role Model
Even with guidance, fails to prepare straight-forward communications, including forms, paperwork, and records, in a timely and accurate manner; products require extensive corrections.	With guidance, prepares straightforward communications, including forms, paperwork, and records, in a timely and accurate manner; products require minimal corrections.	Independently prepares communications, such as forms, paperwork, and records, in a timely, clear, and accurate manner; products require few, if any, corrections.
Even with guidance, fails to adapt style and materials to communicate straightforward information.	With guidance, adapts style and materials to communicate straightforward information.	Independently adapts style and materials to communicate information.

Organizational Know-How

	1		2		3		4		5	

Below Expectations	Meets Expectations	Role Model
<performance standards appear here>	<performance standards appear here>	<performance standards appear here>

Personal Effectiveness

	1		2		3		4		5	

Below Expectations	Meets Expectations	Role Model
<performance standards appear here>	<performance standards appear here>	<performance standards appear here>

Teamwork

	1		2		3		4		5	

Below Expectations	Meets Expectations	Role Model
<performance standards appear here>	<performance standards appear here>	<performance standards appear here>

Achieving Business Results

	1		2		3		4		5	

Below Expectations	Meets Expectations	Role Model
<performance standards appear here>	<performance standards appear here>	<performance standards appear here>

continued

Results Assessment

Accomplishment 1: _____

1	2	3	4	5

Low Impact	Moderate Impact	High Impact
The efficiency or effectiveness of operations remained the same or improved only minimally. The quality of products remained the same or improved only minimally.	The efficiency or effectiveness of operations improved quite a lot. The quality of products improved quite a lot.	The efficiency or effectiveness of operations improved tremendously. The quality of products improved tremendously.

Accomplishment 2: _____

1	2	3	4	5

Low Impact	Moderate Impact	High Impact
The efficiency or effectiveness of operations remained the same or improved only minimally. The quality of products remained the same or improved only minimally.	The efficiency or effectiveness of operations improved quite a lot. The quality of products improved quite a lot.	The efficiency or effectiveness of operations improved tremendously. The quality of products improved tremendously.

Narrative

_____

_____

_____

_____

_____

Areas to Be Developed	Actions	Completion Date

Manager's Signature _____ Date _____

Employee's Signature _____ Date _____

The above employee signature indicates receipt of, but not necessarily concurrence with, the evaluation herein.

Source: Adapted from Elaine Pulakos, *Performance Management* (SHRM Foundation, 2004) pp. 16–17. Reprinted by permission of Society for Human Resource Management Foundation.

FIGURE **10.3** Alternation Ranking Scale

ALTERNATION RANKING SCALE

For the Trait: _____

For the trait you are measuring, list all the employees you want to rank. Put the highest-ranking employee's name on line 1. Put the lowest-ranking employee's name on line 20. Then list the next highest ranking on line 2, the next lowest ranking on line 19, and so on. Continue until all names are on the scale.

Highest-ranking employee

1. _____	11. _____
2. _____	12. _____
3. _____	13. _____
4. _____	14. _____
5. _____	15. _____
6. _____	16. _____
7. _____	17. _____
8. _____	18. _____
9. _____	19. _____
10. _____	20. _____

Lowest-ranking employee

FIGURE **10.4**   Ranking Employees by the Paired Comparison Method

FOR THE TRAIT "QUALITY OF WORK"						*FOR THE TRAIT "CREATIVITY"*					
Employee Rated:						Employee Rated:					
As Compared with:	A Art	B Maria	C Chuck	D Diane	E José	As Compared with:	A Art	B Maria	C Chuck	D Diane	E José
A Art		+	+	−	−	A Art		−	−	−	−
B Maria	−		−	−	−	B Maria	+		−	+	+
C Chuck	−	+		+	−	C Chuck	+	+		−	+
D Diane	+	+	−		+	D Diane	+	−	+		−
E José	+	+	+	−		E José	+	−	−	+	
		↑ Maria Ranks Highest Here						↑ Art Ranks Highest Here			

Note: "+" means "better than" and "−" means "worse than." For each chart, add up the number of + signs in each column to get the highest-ranked employee.

expectations, with a focus on receiving the highest compensation increases and advancement opportunities), the bottom 10% (which are identified as those not meeting expectations, with a focus on coaching for improvement or possible termination). The remaining employees, by default, are considered the backbone of the workforce and receive moderate compensation increases and development opportunities. While the method allows for a concentration of effort and resources on those deemed to be top performers, this method has been criticized as being demotivating since the majority of the workforce are classified as at or below average.[11]

Critical Incident Method

critical incident method Keeping a record of uncommonly good or undesirable examples of an employee's work-related behaviour and reviewing the list with the employee at predetermined times.

With the **critical incident method**, the supervisor keeps a log of desirable or undesirable examples or incidents of each employee's work-related behaviour. Then, every six months or so, the supervisor and employee meet to discuss the latter's performance by using the specific incidents as examples.

This method has several advantages. It provides specific hard facts for explaining the appraisal. It also ensures that a manager thinks about the employee's appraisal throughout the year, because the incidents must be accumulated; therefore, the rating does not just reflect the employee's most recent performance. Keeping a running list of critical incidents should also provide concrete examples of what an employee can do to eliminate any performance deficiencies.

The critical incident method can be adapted to the specific job expectations laid out for the employee at the beginning of the year. Thus, in the example presented in **Table 10.1**, one of the assistant plant manager's continuing duties is to supervise procurement and to minimize inventory costs. The critical incident shows that the assistant plant manager let inventory storage costs rise 15 percent; this provides a specific example of what performance must be improved in the future.

The critical incident method is often used to supplement another appraisal technique, like a ranking system. It is useful for identifying specific examples of good and poor performance and for planning how deficiencies can be corrected. It is not as useful by itself for comparing employees nor, therefore, for making salary decisions.

Narrative Forms

Some employers use narrative forms to evaluate employees. For example, the form in Figure 10.1 presented a suggested format for identifying a performance issue and presenting a *performance improvement plan* (PIP). The performance problem is described in specific detail, and its organizational impact is specified. The improvement plan identifies measurable improvement goals, provides directions regarding training and any other suggested activities to address the performance issue, and encourages the employee to add ideas about steps to be taken to improve performance. Therefore, a PIP essentially facilitates a constructive discussion between an employee and his or her manager, and provides

TABLE 10.1 Examples of Critical Incidents for an Assistant Plant Manager

Continuing Duties	Targets	Critical Incidents
Schedule production for plant	Full utilization of employees and machinery in plant; orders delivered on time	Instituted new production scheduling system; decreased late orders by 10 percent last month; increased machine utilization in plant by 20 percent last month
Supervise procurement of raw materials and inventory control	Minimize inventory costs while keeping adequate supplies on hand	Let inventory storage costs rise 15 percent last month; overordered parts "A" and "B" by 20 percent; underordered part "C" by 30 percent
Supervise machinery maintenance	No shutdowns because of faulty machinery	Instituted new preventative maintenance system for plant; prevented a machine breakdown by discovering faulty part

clarity as to how to improve work performance. Finally, the outcomes and consequences, both positive and negative, are explicitly stated. A summary performance appraisal discussion then focuses on problem solving.[12]

Behaviourally Anchored Rating Scales

behaviourally anchored rating scale (BARS) An appraisal method that aims to combine the benefits of narratives, critical incidents, and quantified ratings by anchoring a quantified scale with specific narrative examples of good and poor performance.

A **behaviourally anchored rating scale (BARS)** combines the benefits of narratives, critical incidents, and quantified ratings by anchoring a series of quantified scales, one for each performance dimension, with specific behavioural examples of good or poor performance. The guiding principle to BARS is that by elaboration of the dimension and rating scale, it gives raters a uniform interpretation as to the types of behaviour being measured.[13] BARS usually involves a scale of nine anchors, although seven and five anchors have also been used.[14]

The midpoint scales are more difficult to develop in a standardized format than the scale extremes. Recent efforts have focused on addressing midpoint scale development to influence inter-rater reliability and inter-rater agreement.[15] The research suggests that all levels of the scale be anchored with statements reflecting how users are to interpret them to increase uniform use of the scale. As well, developers of the scales should be involved in the training of users to increase the consistency in how the scale is used, which increases the effectiveness and legal defensibility of the performance appraisal. **Figure 10.5** provides an example of a BARS for one performance dimension: "sales skills."

FIGURE 10.5   Behaviourally Anchored Rating Scale

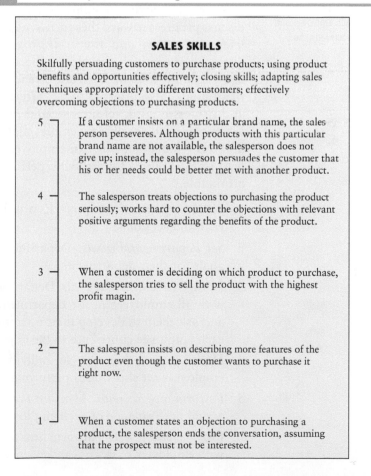

Developing a BARS can be more time-consuming than developing other appraisal tools, like graphic rating scales. But BARS may also have important advantages:[16]

1. *A more accurate measure*. People who know the job and its requirements better than anyone else does develop BARS. The result should therefore be a good measure of performance on that job.

2. *Clearer standards*. The critical incidents along the scale help to clarify what is meant by extremely good performance, average performance, and so forth.

3. *Feedback*. The critical incidents may be more useful in providing feedback to appraisees than simply informing them of their performance rating without providing specific behavioural examples.

4. *Independent dimensions*. Systematically clustering the critical incidents into five or six performance dimensions (such as "knowledge and judgment") should help to make the dimensions more independent of one another. For example, a rater should be less likely to rate an employee high on all dimensions simply because he or she was rated high in "conscientiousness."

5. *Consistency*. BARS evaluations also seem to be relatively consistent and reliable in that different raters' appraisals of the same person tend to be similar.[17]

Management by Objectives (MBO)

management by objectives (MBO)
Involves setting specific measurable goals with each employee and then periodically reviewing the progress made.

Stripped to its essentials, **management by objectives (MBO)** requires the manager and employee to jointly set specific measurable goals and periodically discuss progress toward these goals, aligned with a comprehensive, *organization-wide goal-setting and appraisal program*. When managers and employees set goals collaboratively, employees become more engaged and committed to the goal, leading to a higher rate of success.[18] While there is a notion that difficult goals (also referred to as "stretch goals") can increase personal growth and professional development, and improve organizational effectiveness,[19] it is important to set objectives that match the job description and the person's abilities. Goals that push an employee too far beyond his or her abilities may lead to burnout.[20] To motivate performance, the objectives must be fair and attainable.

1. *Set the organization's goals*. Establish an organization-wide plan for the next year and set goals.

2. *Set departmental goals*. Department heads and their superiors jointly set goals for their departments.

3. *Discuss departmental goals*. Department heads discuss the department's goals with all employees in the department (often at a department-wide meeting) and ask them to develop their own individual goals; in other words, how can each employee contribute to the department's attainment of its goals?

4. *Define expected results* (set individual goals). Here, department heads and employees set short-term performance targets.

5. *Performance reviews: Measure the results*. Department heads compare the actual performance of each employee with the expected results.

6. *Provide feedback*. Department heads hold periodic performance review meetings with employees to discuss and evaluate progress in achieving expected results.

Problems to Avoid Using MBO has three potential problems. *Setting unclear, unmeasurable objectives* is the main one. Such an objective as "will do a better job of training" is useless. Conversely, "will have four employees promoted during the year" is a measurable objective. Second, MBO is *time-consuming*. Taking the time to set objectives, measure progress, and provide feedback can take several hours per employee per year, over and above the time already spent doing each person's appraisal. Third, setting objectives with an employee sometimes turns into a *tug of war*; managers push for higher goals and employees push for lower ones. It is thus important to know the job and the person's ability. To motivate performance, the objectives must be fair and attainable.

Mixing the Methods

Most firms combine several appraisal techniques. The form shown in Figure 10.2 is a graphic rating scale with behavioural incidents included to define values for the traits being measured. The quantifiable ranking method permits comparisons of employees and is therefore useful for making salary, transfer, and promotion decisions. The critical incidents provide specific examples of performance relative to expectations and can be used to develop the high and low anchors for the BARS technique.[21] Ultimately, no one single solution is best for all performance management systems. Instead, resource constraints (time, money, people) and organizational factors (budget, turnover, strategy) will help determine which of the options is best for each organization.

The Use of Technology in Performance Appraisals

Over the past few years, web-based performance management has moved from being a leading-edge approach adopted by only large companies to a mainstream practice that is quickly becoming an industry standard among medium and small organizations.[22] It enables managers to keep computerized notes on employees, combine these with ratings on several performance traits, and then generate written text to support each part of the appraisal.

But the true value in web-based performance management goes beyond simply automating time-consuming, tedious tasks like tracking down paper-based appraisal forms. They ultimately improve the overall performance management process, starting with higher completion rates, which can dramatically increase the value of performance management within organizations of all sizes. Performance management systems provide employees with a clear development path and a better understanding of how their goals are aligned with those of the organization, which in turn increases their support of the process. Managers have the information they need to ensure development plans are relevant and executed. Executives have a clear picture of the organization's talent strategy and how it ties into the bottom line.

Most web-based performance management systems provide advanced reporting capabilities, which allow managers to track the status of performance management initiatives easily. Goal management functions enable organizations to link individual goals to strategic corporate goals, meaning that executives have insight into the progress being made on corporate objectives. Succession planning tools provide executives with a clear plan to build a talent pool to meet the organization's business needs and address potential attrition.

In a relatively short time, employee performance management has undergone a rapid evolution with the development of powerful, web-based tools. HR professionals are no longer mired in paperwork and other mundane administrative tasks. They have more time to focus on meeting strategic objectives, better tools to implement best practices programs, and access to critical workforce metrics they can share with their executive team.

Electronic performance monitoring (EPM) is in some respects the ultimate in computerized appraising. Electronic performance monitoring means having supervisors electronically observe the employee's output or whereabouts. This typically involves using computer networks and wireless audio or video links to monitor and record employees' work activities. It includes, for instance, monitoring a data clerk's hourly keystrokes, tracking via GPS the whereabouts of delivery drivers, and monitoring the calls of customer service clerks.

electronic performance monitoring (EPM) Having supervisors electronically monitor the amount of computerized data an employee is processing per day and thereby his or her performance.

Performance Appraisal Problems and Solutions

Few of the things a manager does are fraught with more peril than appraising employees' performance. Employees in general tend to be overly optimistic about what their ratings will be, and they also know that their raises, career progress, and peace of mind may well hinge on how they are rated. Thus, an honest appraisal inevitably involves an emotional component, which is particularly difficult when managers are not trained on formal appraisal discussion skills. The result is often dishonest appraisals or avoidance of appraisals.[23]

Even more problematic, however, are the numerous structural problems that can cast serious doubt on just how fair the whole process is. Fortunately, research shows that action by management to implement a more acceptable performance appraisal system can increase employee trust in management.[24] According to several studies, the majority of organizations view their performance management systems as ineffective. More focus on the execution of performance appraisal is required instead of searching for new techniques and methods.[25] Some of the main appraisal problems and how to solve them, as well as several other pertinent appraisal issues, will now be reviewed.

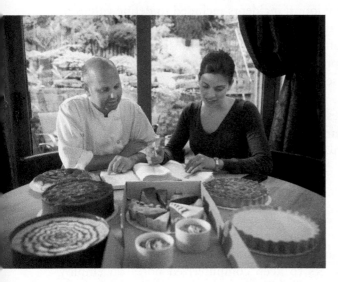

This food service supervisor is conducting a feedback session about an employee's performance during a major banquet to keep communications open and build employee commitment.

Research INSIGHT

Validity and Reliability

Appraisal systems must be based on performance criteria that are valid for the position being rated and must be reliable, in that their application must produce consistent ratings for the same performance. Employee concerns about appraisal fairness are influenced by these characteristics of the performance appraisal system.

Criteria used in performance appraisal must be accurate, or valid, to produce useful results. Criteria must be (1) relevant to the job being appraised, (2) broad enough to cover all aspects of the job requirements, and (3) specific. For example, including a broad criterion, such as "leadership," may not be relevant to non-management jobs and may be so vague that it can be interpreted in many different ways.

Effective appraisal criteria are precise enough to result in consistent measures of performance when applied across many employees by many different raters. This is difficult to achieve without quantifiable and measurable criteria.

Rating Scale Problems

Seven main problems can undermine appraisal tools like graphic rating scales: unclear standards, the halo effect, central tendency, leniency or strictness, appraisal bias, the recency effect, and the similar-to-me bias.

unclear performance standards An appraisal scale that is too open to interpretation of traits and standards.

The problem of **unclear performance standards** is illustrated in **Table 10.2**. Although the graphic rating scale seems objective, it would probably result in unfair appraisals because the traits and degrees of merit are open to interpretation. For example, different supervisors would probably differently define "good" performance, "fair" performance, and so on. The same is true of traits, such as "quality of work" or "creativity." There are several ways in which to rectify this problem. The best way is to develop and include descriptive phrases that define each trait, as in Figure 10.2. There, the form specified what was meant by "outstanding," "very good," and "good" quality of work. This specificity results in appraisals that are more consistent and more easily explained.

halo effect In performance appraisal, the problem that occurs when a supervisor's rating of an employee on one trait biases the rating of that person on other traits.

The **halo effect** means that the rating of an employee on one trait (such as "gets along with others") biases the way that person is rated on other traits (such as "reliability"). This problem often occurs with employees who are especially friendly (or unfriendly) toward the supervisor. For example, an unfriendly employee will often be rated unsatisfactory for all traits rather than just for the trait "gets along well with others." Being aware of this problem is a major step toward avoiding it. Supervisory training can also alleviate the problem.[26]

central tendency A tendency to rate all employees in the middle of the scale.

Many supervisors have a **central tendency** when filling in rating scales. For example, if the rating scale ranges from one to seven, they tend to avoid the highs (six and seven) and lows (one and two) and rate most of their employees between three and five. If a graphic rating scale is used, this central tendency could mean that all employees are simply rated "average." Such a restriction can distort the evaluations, making them less useful for promotion, salary, or counselling purposes. Ranking employees instead of using a graphic rating scale can avoid this central tendency problem, because all employees must be ranked and thus cannot all be rated average.

Some supervisors tend to rate all of their employees consistently high (or low), just as some instructors are notoriously high graders and others are not. Fear of interpersonal conflict is often the reason for leniency.[27] Conversely, evaluators

TABLE 10.2   A Graphic Rating Scale with Unclear Standards

	Excellent	Good	Fair	Poor
Quality of work				
Quantity of work				
Creativity				
Integrity				

Note: For example, what exactly is meant by "good," "quantity of work," and so forth?

strictness/leniency The problem that occurs when a supervisor has a tendency to rate all employees either low or high.

appraisal bias The tendency to allow individual differences, such as age, race, and sex, to affect the appraisal ratings that these employees receive.

Canadian Human Rights Commission **www.chrc-ccdp.ca**

tend to give more weight to negative attributes than to positive ones.[28] This **strictness/leniency** problem is especially serious with graphic rating scales, since supervisors are not necessarily required to avoid giving all of their employees low (or high) ratings. However, when ranking employees, a manager is forced to distinguish between high and low performers. Thus, strictness/leniency is not a problem with the ranking or forced distribution approaches.

Individual differences among ratees in terms of a wide variety of characteristics, such as age, race, and sex, can affect their ratings, often quite apart from their actual performance.[29] In fact, research shows that less than half of performance evaluation ratings are actually related to employee performance and that most of the rating is based on idiosyncratic factors.[30] This is known as **appraisal bias**. Not only does this bias result in inaccurate feedback, but it is also illegal under human rights legislation. Although age-related bias is typically thought of as affecting older workers, one study found a negative relationship between age and performance evaluation for entry-level jobs in public accounting firms.[31] A related issue is described in the Workforce Diversity box.

Interestingly, the friendliness and likeability of an employee have been found to have little effect on that person's performance ratings.[32] However, an employee's previous performance can affect the evaluation of his or her current performance.[33] The actual error can take several forms. Sometimes the rater may systematically overestimate improvement by a poor worker or decline by a good worker, for instance. In some situations—especially when the change in behaviour is more gradual—the rater may simply be insensitive to improvement or decline. In any case, it is important to rate performance objectively. Such factors as previous performance, age, or race should not be allowed to influence results.

WORKFORCE DIVERSITY

Watch for Cultural Biases in Assessing Employees

Canadian organizations are increasingly turning to immigrants as the supply of workers dries up in Canada. This demographic shift poses some unique challenges for organizations in integrating these new Canadians into the workplace, particularly when it comes to performance management.

Values, beliefs, and perspectives vary by culture. Typical group and individual behaviours in Canada may not be the norm for people from other cultures. The performance appraisal, with its goal-setting procedures and inherent feedback process, is a western concept that can be a cultural disconnect for employees with different cultural roots. In eastern cultures, appraisals are as likely to deal with attributes such as cooperation and sociability as they are with achievement of results. And because status is so important in eastern cultures (it is crucial to an individual's sense of worth and contribution), it is important to ensure that the employee does not become insulted or lose face.

In some cultures, managers provide explicit directions and employees are more deferential to their superiors. Technical expertise is the proven path to promotion rather than taking initiative and seeking new responsibilities. Also, performance is more often assessed on a group basis, with recognition and rewards being assigned for strong group performance; the individual is expected to work for the good of the group. Typical performance criteria used in Canada are more individual-focused and may not value group-oriented performance.

Cultural diversity in the workplace provides an opportunity to maximize sales and profits while creating a work atmosphere appropriate for all cultures. Managers and executives in an economy becoming more dependent on the successful integration of highly skilled internationally trained professionals owe it to their organizations—and their futures as business leaders—to successfully manage the entire diverse workforce.

Source: Adapted from R. Singer, "Watch for Cultural Biases in Assessing Employees," *Canadian HR Reporter* (June 19, 2006). Reprinted by permission of Canadian HR Reporter. © Copyright Thomson Reuters Canada Ltd., (2012) Toronto, Ontario, 1-800-387-5164. Web: www.hrreporter.com

recency effect The rating error that occurs when ratings are based on the employee's most recent performance rather than on performance throughout the appraisal period.

similar-to-me bias The tendency to give higher performance ratings to employees who are perceived to be similar to the rater in some way.

The **recency effect** occurs when ratings are based on the employee's most recent performance, whether good or bad. To the extent that this recent performance does not exemplify the employee's average performance over the appraisal period, the appraisal is biased.

If a supervisor tends to give higher ratings to employees with whom he or she has something in common, the **similar-to-me bias** is occurring. This bias can be discriminatory if it is based on similarity in race, gender, or other prohibited grounds.

How to Avoid Appraisal Problems

There are at least four ways in which managers can minimize the impact of appraisal problems, such as bias and central tendency. First, raters must be familiar with the problems just discussed. Understanding the problem can help to prevent it.

Second, training supervisors on how to eliminate rating errors, such as the halo effect, leniency, and central tendency, can help them avoid these problems.[34] In a typical training program, raters are shown videos of jobs being performed and are asked to rate the worker. Ratings made by each participant are then placed on a flip chart and the various errors (such as leniency and halo) are explained. For example, if a trainee rated all criteria (such as quality, quantity, and so on) about the same, the trainer might explain that a halo error had occurred. Typically, the trainer gives the correct rating and then illustrates the rating errors made by the participants.[35] According to one study, computer-assisted appraisal training improved managers' ability to conduct performance appraisal discussions with their employees.[36]

Rater training will not eliminate all rating errors or ensure absolute accuracy. In practice, several factors—including the extent to which pay is tied to performance ratings, union pressure, employee turnover, time constraints, and the need to justify ratings—may be more important than training. This means that improving appraisal accuracy calls not only for training but also for reducing outside factors, such as union pressure and time constraints.[37] It has also been found that employee reaction to current performance reviews is affected by past appraisal feedback, which is beyond the control of the current manager.[38]

Third, raters must choose the right appraisal tool. Each tool, such as the graphic rating scale or critical incident method, has its own advantages and disadvantages. For example, the ranking method avoids central tendency but can cause ill feelings when employees' performances are, in fact, all "high" (see **Table 10.3**).

Fourth, errors in performance appraisals can be reduced by using multiple raters in the evaluation. Multiple raters increase the validity and accuracy of the rating by controlling for individual biases or idiosyncrasies. Also, responsibility for poor appraisals is diffused; therefore, raters are more comfortable giving a poor rating. When raters are accountable for their rating, reliability also increases.[39] As an additional benefit, multiple ratings may be more legally defensible.

Who Should Do the Appraising?

Who should actually rate an employee's performance? Several options exist as to who can be involved in the performance management appraisal process.

TABLE 10.3   Important Advantages and Disadvantages of Appraisal Tools

	Advantages	Disadvantages
Graphic rating scale	Simple to use; provides a quantitative rating for each employee.	Standards may be unclear; halo effect, central tendency, leniency, and bias can also be problems.
Alternation ranking	Simple to use (but not as simple as graphic rating scale); avoids central tendency and other problems of rating scales.	Can cause disagreements among employees and may be unfair if all employees are, in fact, excellent.
Paired comparison method	A more precise ranking method that involves multiple traits.	Difficult to use as employee numbers increase; differences may not be noticeable enough to rank.
Forced distribution method	End up with a predetermined number of people in each group.	Appraisal results depend on the adequacy of the original choice of cutoff points.
Critical incident method	Helps specify what is "right" and "wrong" about the employee's performance; forces the supervisor to evaluate employees on an ongoing basis.	Difficult to rate or rank employees relative to one another; cannot be used to defend salary decisions.
Narrative form	Explicitly states improvement goals and associated outcomes or consequences.	Employees may take these too personally.
Behaviourally anchored rating scale (BARS)	Provides behavioural "anchors"; very accurate; high inter-rater reliability.	Difficult to develop.
Management by objectives	Tied to jointly agreed-upon performance objectives.	Risk of unclear performance measures, time-consuming, and inflated/deflated goals due to tug of war.

The best performance appraisal systems are those in which the supervisor or manager makes an ongoing effort to coach and monitor employees instead of leaving evaluation to the last minute.

Supervisors

Supervisors' ratings are still the heart of most appraisal systems. Getting a supervisor's appraisal is relatively easy and also makes a great deal of sense. The supervisor should be—and usually is—in the best position to observe and evaluate the performance of employees reporting to him or her and is responsible for their performance.

Self

Employees' self-ratings of performance are sometimes used, generally in conjunction with supervisors' ratings. Employees value the opportunity to participate in performance appraisal more for the opportunity to be heard than for the opportunity to influence the end result.[40] Nevertheless, the basic problem with self-ratings is that employees usually rate themselves higher than they are rated by supervisors or peers.[41] In one study, for example, it was found that when asked to rate their own job performance, 40 percent of the employees in jobs of all types placed themselves in the top 10 percent ("one of the best"), while virtually all remaining employees rated themselves either in the top 25 percent ("well above average") or at least in the top 50 percent ("above average"). Usually no more than 1 percent or 2 percent will place themselves in a below-average category, and then almost invariably in the top below-average category. However, self-ratings have been found to correlate more highly with performance measures if employees know that this comparison will be made and if they are instructed to compare themselves with others.[42]

Supervisors requesting self-appraisals should know that their appraisals and their employees' self-appraisals may accentuate appraiser–appraisee differences, and rigidify positions.[43] Furthermore, even if self-appraisals are not formally requested, each employee will enter the performance review meeting with his or her own self-appraisal in mind, and this will usually be higher than the supervisor's rating.

Peers

The appraisal of an employee by his or her peers can be effective in predicting future management success. Peers may have more opportunity to observe ratees and to observe them at more revealing times than supervisors do. One potential problem is *logrolling*; here, all the peers simply get together to rate each other highly.

With more firms using self-managing teams, peer or team appraisals are becoming more popular. One study found that peer ratings had an immediate positive impact on perceptions of open communication, motivation, group cohesion, and satisfaction, and these were not dependent on the ratio of positive to negative feedback.[44] Thus, peer appraisals would appear to have great potential for work teams.

Committees

Many employers use rating committees to evaluate employees. These committees usually comprise the employee's immediate supervisor and three or four other supervisors. Using multiple raters can be advantageous. Although there may be a discrepancy in the ratings made by individual supervisors, the composite ratings tend to be more reliable, fair, and valid.[45] Using several raters can help cancel out problems like bias and the halo effect on the part of individual raters. Furthermore, when there are variations in raters' ratings, they usually stem from the fact that raters often observe different facets of an employee's performance and the appraisal ought to reflect these differences.[46] Even when a committee is not used, it is common to have the appraisal reviewed by the manager immediately above the one who makes the appraisal.

Subordinates

Traditionally, supervisors feared that being appraised by their employees would undermine their management authority. However, with today's flatter organizations and empowered workers, much managerial authority is a thing of the past, and employees are in a good position to observe managerial performance.[47] Thus, more firms today are letting employees anonymously evaluate their supervisors' performance, a process many call *upward feedback*.[48] When conducted throughout the firm, the process helps top managers diagnose management styles, identify potential "people" problems, and take corrective action with individual managers as required. Such employee ratings are especially valuable when used for developmental rather than evaluative purposes.[49] Managers who receive feedback from employees who identify themselves view the upward appraisal process more positively than do managers who receive anonymous feedback; however, employees (not surprisingly) are more comfortable giving anonymous responses, and those who have to identify themselves tend to provide inflated ratings.[50] Research comparing employee and peer ratings of managers found them to be comparable. [51]

Upward feedback from reporting employees is quite effective in terms of improving the supervisor's behaviour, according to the research evidence. One study examined data for 92 managers who were rated by one or more reporting employees in each of four administrations of an upward feedback survey over two and a half years. The reporting employees were asked to rate themselves and their managers in surveys that consisted of 33 behavioural statements. The feedback to the managers also contained results from previous administrations of the survey so that they could track their performance over time.

According to the researchers, managers whose initial performance level was lower than the average employee performance level improved performance by the next performance assessment and sustained this improvement two years later. Interestingly, the results also suggest that it is not necessarily the specific feedback that caused the performance improvement, because low-performing managers seemed to improve over time even if they did not receive any feedback. Instead, learning what the critical supervisory behaviours were (as a result of themselves filling out the appraisal surveys) and knowing that they might be appraised may have been enough to result in the improved supervisory behaviours. In a sense, therefore, it is the existence of the formal upward feedback program rather than the actual feedback itself that may signal and motivate supervisors to get their behaviours in line with what they should be.[52]

360-Degree Appraisal

360-degree appraisal A performance appraisal technique that uses multiple raters including peers, employees reporting to the appraisee, supervisors, and customers.

Many Canadian firms are now using what is called **360-degree appraisal,** or "multisource feedback." Here, as shown in **Figure 10.6**, performance information is collected "all around" an employee—from his or her supervisors, subordinates, peers, and internal or external customers.[53] This feedback was originally used only for training and development purposes, but it has rapidly

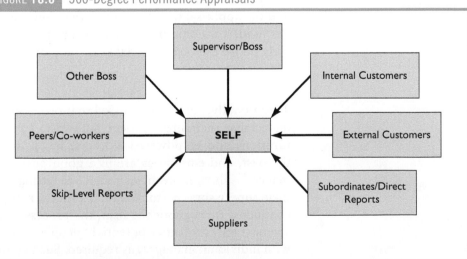

FIGURE **10.6** 360-Degree Performance Appraisals

Source: Alma M. McCarthy, Thomas N. Garavan, "360° Feedback Process: Performance, Improvement and Employee Career Development," *Journal of European Industrial Training*, 25, no. 1 (2001), pp. 5–32.
© Emerald Group Publishing Limited all rights reserved.

spread to the management of performance and pay.[54] The 360-degree approach supports the activities of performance feedback, coaching, leadership development, succession planning, and rewards and recognition.[55]

There are a number of reasons for the rapid growth of 360-degree appraisal, despite the significant investment of time required for it to function successfully. Today's flatter organizations employ a more open communicative climate conducive to such an approach, and 360-degree appraisal fits closely with the goals of organizations committed to continuous learning. A multiple-rater system is also more meaningful in today's reality of complex jobs, with matrix and team reporting relationships. A 360-degree appraisal can be perceived as a jury of peers, rather than the supervisor as a single judge, which enhances perceptions of fairness.[56]

Most 360-degree appraisal systems contain several common features (including Internet-based 360-degree feedback systems, as described in Chapter 3). They are usually applied in a confidential and anonymous manner. Appropriate parties—peers, superiors, employees, and customers, for instance—complete survey questionnaires about an individual. The questionnaires must be custom-designed and linked to the organization's strategic direction, vision, and values.[57] All this information is then compiled into individualized reports. When the information is being used for self-development purposes only, the report is presented to the person being rated, who then meets with his or her own supervisor and information pertinent for the purpose of developing a self-improvement plan is shared. When the information is being used for management of performance or pay, the information is also provided to the ratee's supervisor, and a supportive and facilitative process to follow up is required to ensure that the behavioural change required for performance improvement is made.[58]

Research INSIGHT

There is a limited amount of research data on the effectiveness of 360-degree feedback. Some organizations have abandoned it for appraisal purposes because of negative attitudes from employees and inflated ratings.[59] Some studies have found that the different raters often disagree on performance ratings.[60]

A recent study by researchers at Concordia University in Montreal found that 360-degree feedback is popular among Canadian employers, despite such problems as the amount of time and effort involved, lack of trust in the system by employees, and lack of fit with strategic goals and other HR practices. The results showed that organizations that successfully implemented 360-degree feedback were those that had the most clarity on what their initial objectives were. Organizations that rely exclusively on external consultants to establish 360-degree appraisal have less success than organizations that are more sensitive to contextual factors, such as the readiness of employees and the culture of the organization.[61]

An Ethical Dilemma

Is it fair to factor in employee self-ratings in 360-degree performance appraisal, when we know that these appraisals tend to be inflated?

Some experts suggest that 360-degree feedback be used for developmental purposes only.[62] In general, it is advisable to use 360-degree feedback for developmental/career-planning purposes initially, and then to determine whether the organization is ready to use it for evaluative appraisal purposes. A pilot test in one department is often recommended. Once a decision to use 360-degree appraisal has been made, organizations should consider the following advice:[63]

Tips FOR THE FRONT LINE

- Have the performance criteria developed by a representative group that is familiar with each job.

- Be clear about who will have access to reports.
- Provide training for all supervisors, raters, and ratees.
- Assure all raters that their comments will be kept anonymous.
- Plan to evaluate the 360-degree feedback system for fine-tuning.

Formal Appraisal Discussions

formal appraisal discussion An interview in which the supervisor and employee review the appraisal and make plans to remedy deficiencies and reinforce strengths.

The essence of a performance appraisal is the feedback provided in a one-on-one conversation called the **formal appraisal discussion.** This is an interview in which the supervisor and employee review the appraisal and make plans to remedy deficiencies and reinforce strengths. Unfortunately, surveys show that less than half of companies describe their performance appraisal systems as effective or very effective because of weak execution due to managers abdicating their responsibility for screening out poor performers.[64] This discussion is often avoided by supervisors and managers who have not been trained to provide constructive feedback and to deal with defensive employees. Ultimately, feedback should be ongoing, making the formal appraisal discussion one of many performance discussions.

Types of Interviews

There are three basic types of formal appraisal discussions, each with its own objectives:[65]

Formal Appraisal Discussion Type	Formal Appraisal Discussion Objective
(1) Satisfactory performance—Promotable employee	(1) Make development plans
(2) Satisfactory performance—Nonpromotable employee	(2) Maintain performance
(3) Unsatisfactory performance—Correctable	(3) Plan correction

If the employee's performance is unsatisfactory and the situation uncorrectable, there is usually no need for any formal appraisal discussion because the person's performance is not correctable anyway. Either the person's poor performance is tolerated for now, or he or she is dismissed.

Satisfactory—Promotable

Here, the person's performance is satisfactory and there is a promotion ahead. This is the easiest of the three formal appraisal discussions. The objective is to discuss the person's career plans and to develop a specific action plan for the educational and professional development that the person needs to move to the next job.

Satisfactory—Not Promotable

This interview is for employees whose performance is satisfactory but for whom promotion is not possible. Perhaps there is no more room in the company; some employees are happy where they are and do not want a promotion.[66] The objective here is not to improve or develop the person but to maintain satisfactory performance.

This situation is not easy. The best option is usually to find incentives that are important to the person and are enough to maintain satisfactory performance. These might include extra time off, a small bonus, additional authority to handle a slightly enlarged job, and verbal reinforcement in the form of "Well done!"

Unsatisfactory—Correctable

When the person's performance is unsatisfactory but correctable, the interview objective is to lay out an *action plan* (as explained later) for correcting the unsatisfactory performance.

Preparing for the Formal Appraisal Discussion

An important component of the performance management process is the effective use of feedback. This often happens in a formal appraisal discussion after the performance has been evaluated. There are three things to do in preparation for the interview.[67] First, assemble the data. Study the person's job description, compare the employee's performance to the standards, and review the files of the employee's previous appraisals. Next, prepare the employee. Give the employee at least a week's notice to review his or her own work, read over his or her job description, analyze problems he or she may be dealing with, and gather questions and comments for the interview. Finally, find a mutually agreeable time and place and allow plenty of time for the interview. Interviews with non-supervisory staff should take no more than an hour. Appraising management employees often takes two or three hours. Be sure that the interview is conducted in a private place where there will be no interruptions. It is important to keep in mind what is said and how it is said. The Strategic HR box provides an example of how management teams in a global company were guided on managing the formal appraisal discussion.

How to Conduct the Interview

Constructive feedback is considered a positive and motivating experience.[68] There are four things to keep in mind when conducting a formal appraisal discussion to ensure the feedback is constructive.[69]

1. *Be direct and specific.* Talk in terms of objective work data. Use examples, such as absences, tardiness, quality records, inspection reports, scrap or waste, orders processed, productivity records, material used or consumed, timeliness of tasks or projects, control or reduction of costs, numbers of errors, costs compared with budgets, customers' comments, product returns, order processing time, inventory level and accuracy, accident reports, and so on.

2. *Do not get personal.* Do not say, "You are too slow in producing those reports." Instead, try to compare the person's performance with a standard ("These reports should normally be done within 10 days"). Similarly, do not compare the person's performance with that of other people ("He is quicker than you are").

3. *Encourage the person to talk.* Stop and listen to what the person is saying; ask open-ended questions, such as, "What do you think we can do to improve the situation?" Use phrases such as, "Go on," or "Tell me more." Restate the person's last point as a question, such as, "You do not think that you can get the job done?"

Tips FOR THE FRONT LINE

STRATEGIC HR

Jaguar Land Rover Formal Appraisal Discussion Training

In 2008, an Indian conglomerate (Tata) took over the Jaguar Land Rover carmaker. This triggered a new set of management behaviours, including the redesign of the performance management process. The contract to develop a companywide performance management system for the 1500 managers (from line level to board level) went to learning and development specialist Ashorne Hill.

As part of this process, management was educated on a standardized approach to performance evaluation. Management was coached on techniques for managing behaviour during the formal appraisal discussion, including the following suggestions:

- Say what you see—acknowledging signposting by reflecting behaviour back to the individual in words
- Empathy—demonstrating genuine understanding and concern, even when challenging specific behaviours or questioning performance standards
- Broken record—interrupting without creating confrontation

- Active listening—focusing on what is being said and responding directly
- Questioning—using open, closed, and probing questions, as required, to elicit information
- Reassurance—being supportive of the other person's point of view, where appropriate
- Nonverbal communication—adopting body language that encourages communication
- Calm, even tone and pace—bringing the conversation back to a considered, mutual exchange of views whenever emotion threatens to disrupt the discussion or lead it into a dead end.

The training program is viewed as a success by management and participants alike. Jaguar Land Rover believes that managers are now equipped with the skills to implement the performance management system successfully.

Source: J. Hicks, "Jaguar Land Rover Bosses Get to Grips with Performance Management: Program Teaches Practical Skills for the Workplace," *Human Resource Management International Digest* (2011), volume 19, issue 4, pp. 10–12. © Emerald Group Publishing Limited all rights reserved.

4. *Develop an action plan.* Do not get personal, but do make sure that by the end of the interview you have (a) provided specific examples of performance that does and does not need attention or improvement, (b) made sure the person understands how he or she should improve his or her performance, (c) obtained an agreement from the person that he or she understands the reasons for the appraisal, and (d) developed an action plan that shows steps to achieving specified goals and the results expected. Be sure that a timeline is included in the plan.

How to Handle Criticism and Defensive Employees

When criticism is required, it should be done in a manner that lets the person maintain his or her dignity and sense of worth. Specifically, criticism should be provided constructively, in private, and immediately following poor performance. Provide examples of critical incidents and specific suggestions of what could be done and why. Finally, ensure that criticism is objective and free of any personal biases.

When poor performance by an employee is described, the first reaction will often be denial. By denying the fault, the person avoids having to question his or her own competence. Others react to criticism with anger and aggression. This helps them let off steam and postpones confronting the immediate problem until they are able to cope with it. Still others react to criticism by retreating into a shell.

Tips FOR THE FRONT LINE

Understanding and dealing with defensiveness is an important appraisal skill that requires the following:[70]

1. Recognize that defensive behaviour is normal.

2. Never attack a person's defences. Do not try to "explain someone" to himself or herself by saying things like, "You know the real reason you are using that excuse is that you cannot bear to be blamed for anything." Instead, try to concentrate on the act itself ("sales are down") rather than on the person ("you are not selling enough").

3. Postpone action. Sometimes it is best to do nothing at all. People frequently react to sudden threats by instinctively hiding behind their "masks." Given sufficient time, however, a more rational reaction usually takes over.

4. Recognize human limitations. Do not expect to be able to solve every problem that comes up, especially the human ones. More importantly, remember that a supervisor should not try to be a psychologist. Offering employees understanding is one thing; trying to deal with deep psychological problems is another matter entirely.

Ensuring That the Formal Appraisal Discussion Leads to Improved Performance

It is important to clear up performance problems by setting goals and a schedule for achieving them. However, even if you have obtained agreement from your employees about the areas for performance improvement, they may or may not be satisfied with their appraisal. In one study, researchers found that whether or not employees expressed satisfaction with their formal appraisal discussion depended mostly on three factors: (1) not feeling threatened during the interview, (2) having an opportunity to present their ideas and feelings and to influence the course of the interview, and (3) having a helpful and constructive supervisor conduct the interview.[71]

Ultimately, the main objective of performance apprasials is to improve employee performance, keeping performance expectations clear and targeted on activities that build value for the organization. In dealing with employee performance issues, legal experts suggest that management follow seven steps to ensure that performance appraisals have the desired effect and are legally defensible:

Hints TO ENSURE LEGAL COMPLIANCE

1. Let the employee know that his or her performance is unacceptable and explain your minimum expectations.

2. Ensure that your expectations are reasonable.

3. Let employees know that warnings play a significant role in the process of establishing just cause; employees must be warned and told that discharge will result if they continue to fail to meet minimum standards.

4. Ensure that you take prompt corrective measures when required; failure to do so could lead to a finding that you condoned your employee's conduct.

5. Avoid sending mixed messages, such as a warning letter together with a "satisfactory" performance review.

6. Provide the employee with a reasonable amount of time to improve performance.

7. Be prepared to provide your employees with the necessary support to facilitate improvement.[72]

How to Handle a Formal Written Warning

There will be times when an employee's performance is so poor that a formal written warning is required. Such written warnings serve two purposes: (1) They may serve to shake the employee out of his or her bad habits, and (2) they can help the manager defend his or her rating of the employee, both to his or her boss and (if needed) to a court or human rights commission.

Written warnings should identify the standards under which the employee is judged, make it clear that the employee was aware of the standard, specify any violation of the standard, indicate that the employee has had an opportunity to correct his or her behaviour, and specify what the employee must now do to correct his or her behaviour.

STEP 4: DETERMINE PERFORMANCE REWARDS/ CONSEQUENCES

Some time after the performance review has taken place, the manager should use the salary planning guidelines to determine the appropriate rewards or consequences, comparing actual performance against the defined levels. Performance rewards are given through merit pay or extra payment such as a cash bonus. The two most important aspects used to determine the appropriate reward/consequence are achievement of goals and how the employee meets the defined standards. Further detail on compensation and rewards is provided in Chapters 11 and 12.

STEP 5: CAREER DEVELOPMENT DISCUSSION

During this discussion, the manager and employee discuss opportunities for development to strengthen or improve the employee's knowledge, skills, and abilities. Business needs must be balanced with the employee's preferences. These opportunities may focus on actions to boost performance in the area of current goals or to develop new knowledge aimed at a future career plan. Further detail on career planning and development is provided in Chapter 9.

LEGAL AND ETHICAL ISSUES IN PERFORMANCE MANAGEMENT

Ethics should be the bedrock of performance management. Accurate, well-documented performance records and performance appraisal feedback are necessary to avoid legal penalties and to defend against charges of bias based on grounds prohibited under human rights legislation, such as age, sex, and so on. As one commentator puts it,

> The overall objective of high-ethics performance reviews should be to provide an honest assessment of performance and to mutually develop a plan to improve the individual's effectiveness. That requires that we tell people where they stand and that we be straight with them.[73]

Ashland Canada Ltd., an automotive products marketing company in British Columbia, was fined $20 000 for dismissing a sales employee based on an "unacceptable" performance rating even though the employee had exceeded his sales goals. The British Columbia Supreme Court found that the performance rating was unwarranted and undeserved, and criticized Ashland's human resources department for a "reprehensible and substantial departure" from good faith dealings with the employee.[74] In another case, a worker in a government mental health facility was terminated for unsatisfactory performance after 10 years of work with no performance evaluations and no disciplinary record. An adjudicator determined that the employer had failed to establish that the worker's job performance was unsatisfactory, that she had not been given a chance to improve, and that the employer did not have just cause for termination. The employer was required to pay compensation in lieu of reinstatement.[75]

Hints TO ENSURE LEGAL COMPLIANCE

Guidelines for developing an effective appraisal process include the following:[76]

1. Conduct a job analysis to ascertain characteristics (such as "timely project completion") required for successful job performance. Use this information to create job performance standards.

2. Incorporate these characteristics into a rating instrument. (The professional literature recommends rating instruments that are tied to specific job behaviours, that is, BARS.)

3. Make sure that definitive performance standards are provided to all raters and ratees.

4. Use clearly defined individual dimensions of job performance (like "quantity" or "quality") rather than undefined, global measures of job performance (like "overall performance").

5. When using a graphic rating scale, avoid abstract trait names (such as "loyalty," "honesty") unless they can be defined in terms of observable behaviours.

6. Employ subjective supervisory ratings (essays, for instance) as only one component of the overall appraisal process.

7. Train supervisors to use the rating instrument properly. Give instructions on how to apply performance appraisal standards ("outstanding," "satisfactory," and so on) when making judgments. Ensure that subjective standards are not subject to bias.

8. Allow appraisers regular contact with the employee being evaluated.

9. Whenever possible, have more than one appraiser conduct the appraisal, and conduct all such appraisals independently. This process can help to cancel out individual errors and biases.

10. Use formal appeal mechanisms and a review of ratings by upper-level managers.

11. Document evaluations and reasons for any termination decision.

12. Where appropriate, provide corrective guidance to assist poor performers in improving their performance.

THE FUTURE OF PERFORMANCE MANAGEMENT

Effective appraisals are the basis for successful performance management. Although performance appraisal is a difficult interpersonal task for managers, it cannot be eliminated.

Managers need some way to review employees' work-related behaviour, and no one has offered any concrete alternative. Despite the difficulties involved, performance management is still the basis for fostering and managing employee skills and talents, and it can be a key component of improved organizational effectiveness. Performance management techniques in high- and low-performing organizations are essentially the same, but managers in high-performing organizations tend to conduct and implement appraisals and manage performance on a daily basis more effectively.[77]

Recent research indicates that effective performance management involves

- linking individual goals and business strategy,
- showing leadership and accountability at all levels of the organization,
- ensuring close ties among appraisal results, rewards, and recognition outcomes,
- investing in employee development planning, and
- having an administratively efficient system with sufficient communication support. [78]

The key success factor for effective performance appraisal that will lead to optimum employee performance is the quality of the performance appraisal dialogue between a manager and an employee.[79] Managers need to engage in training on an ongoing basis to ensure that they are in a position to engage in high-quality formal appraisal discussions.

Overall, the solution is to create more effective appraisals, as described in this chapter. Effective appraisals are essential to managing the performance required of an organization's employees to achieve that organization's strategic objectives.

Chapter SUMMARY

1. The five steps in the performance management process are (1) defining performance expectations and goals, (2) providing ongoing feedback and coaching, (3) conducting performance appraisal and evaluation discussions, (4) determining performance rewards/consequences, and (5) conducting development and career opportunities discussions.

2. There are a number of performance appraisal methods. Graphic rating scales are simple to use

and facilitate comparison of employees, but the performance standards are often unclear and bias can be a problem. Alternation ranking is a simple method that avoids central tendency, but it can be unfair if most employees are doing well. Paired comparison ensures that all employees are compared with each other, but it can also be unfair if most employees are performing similarly. Narrative forms provide concrete information to the employee but are time-consuming and can be subjective. The forced distribution method ensures differentiation of performance ratings but can be demotivating for employees classified as less than average. The critical incident method is very specific about the employee's strengths and weaknesses and forces the supervisor to evaluate employees on an ongoing basis, but it makes it difficult to compare employees. BARS is very accurate, but is difficult and time-consuming to develop. MBO ties performance ratings to jointly agreed-upon performance objectives, but it is time-consuming to administer.

3. Appraisal problems to be aware of include unclear standards, the halo effect, central tendency, leniency or strictness, appraisal bias, the recency effect, and the similar-to-me bias.

4. The use of 360-degree feedback has grown rapidly. Performance information is collected from the individual being appraised, his or her supervisor, other employees reporting to the person being appraised, and customers. This approach supports the activities of performance appraisal, coaching, leadership development, succession planning, and employee rewards and recognition.

5. There are three types of formal appraisal discussion. When performance is unsatisfactory but correctable, the objective of the interview is to set out an action plan for correcting

performance. For employees whose performance is satisfactory but for whom promotion is not possible, the objective of the interview is to maintain satisfactory performance. Finally, the satisfactory-and-promotable interview has the main objective of discussing the person's career plans and developing a specific action plan for the educational and professional development that the person needs to move on to the next job.

6. Although appraisals can be a difficult interpersonal task for managers, they cannot be eliminated. There is no alternative method for assessing employee performance, which is essential for talent management and improved organizational effectiveness. The key success factor is the quality of the performance appraisal dialogue between managers and employees. More training on how to effectively conduct these discussions is required.

MyManagementLab

Visit MyManagementLab to access a personalized Study Plan and additional study tools for this chapter.

Key TERMS

360-degree appraisal *(p. 280)*
alternation ranking method *(p. 266)*
appraisal bias *(p. 276)*
behaviourally anchored rating scale (BARS) *(p. 271)*
central tendency *(p. 275)*
contextual performance *(p. 263)*
critical incident method *(p. 270)*
electronic performance monitoring (EPM) *(p. 274)*
forced distribution method *(p. 266)*
formal appraisal discussion *(p. 282)*

graphic rating scale *(p. 266)*
halo effect *(p. 275)*
management by objectives (MBO) *(p. 272)*
paired comparison method *(p. 266)*
performance management *(p. 262)*
recency effect *(p. 277)*
similar-to-me bias *(p. 277)*
strictness/leniency *(p. 276)*
task performance *(p. 263)*
unclear performance standards *(p. 275)*

Review and Discussion QUESTIONS

1. Describe the five steps in the performance appraisal process.

2. Explain how to ensure that the performance appraisal process is carried out ethically and without violating human rights laws.

3. Discuss the pros and cons of using different potential raters to appraise a person's performance.

4. What are the four key actions in conducting a formal appraisal discussion?

5. Explain how to handle a defensive employee in a formal appraisal discussion.

Critical Thinking QUESTIONS

1. Assume you are presenting to an upper-year group of business students and one student asks the question, "Which performance appraisal system is the best?" How would you respond to that question?

2. How can the problem of inconsistency between managers who are rating workers be solved or at least diminished? Make two or more suggestions.

3. Given the difficulty with providing traditional performance standards for jobs that are quite flexible, what sort of "standards" could be developed for these flexible jobs?

4. Some HR professionals avoid using BARS given that it is so time-consuming to develop. How could the development steps be streamlined?

5. Do you agree with the use of forced distribution methods to rate employees? Why or why not?

6. How might a supervisor handle a situation in which negative appraisals in the past have caused an employee to undervalue his or her performance?

7. Discuss how employees might respond to the proposed implementation of electronic performance management systems, such as call monitoring, and so on. How might an organization deal with employees' reactions?

8. How might a supervisor deal with an extremely defensive yet productive member of his or her team in the event of having to deliver the "improvement portion" of the employee's performance appraisal? What techniques would the supervisor need to use to maximize the efficacy of the appraisal and reduce the defensibility of the employee?

Experiential EXERCISES

1. Working individually or in groups, develop a graphic rating scale for a retail sales associate and a fast-food restaurant manager.

2. Working individually or in groups, develop, over a week, a set of critical incidents covering the classroom performance of one of your instructors. Categorize the critical incidents to identify themes within activities that are viewed positively and negatively. Expand on this identification by assessing how the one-week period may be affecting the results and what differences you would have expected had you selected a different week within the year to conduct the assessment.

3. Working in groups, using the NOC job description for cafeteria staff at a local university or college and the example of a performance rating form in Figure 10.2, develop a graphic rating scale with behavioural incidents for a job of a chef within the cafeteria. You may also want to consider your own experience when constructing your form.

Once you have drafted your form, exchange forms with another student or group. Critique and suggest possible improvements to the forms. Then with your revised form in hand, develop statements of behavioural incidents for two of your rating scale items to address the following circumstances:

- The employee has achieved outstanding results.
- The employee meets acceptable standards.
- The employee has performed very poorly in this aspect of the job.

Be prepared to share and critique statements developed by other students. Debrief the exercise as directed.

Running CASE

Running Case: LearnInMotion.com

The Performance Appraisal

Jennifer and Pierre disagree over the importance of having performance appraisals. Pierre says it's quite clear whether any particular LearnInMotion.com employee is doing his or her job. It's obvious, for instance, if the salespeople are selling, if the web designer is designing, if the web surfer is surfing, and if the content management people are managing to get the customers' content up on the website in a timely fashion. Pierre's position, like that of many small-business managers, is that "we have 1000 higher-priority things to attend to," such as boosting sales and creating the calendar. And in any case, he says, the employees already get plenty of day-to-day feedback from him or Jennifer regarding what they're doing right and what they're doing wrong.

This informal feedback notwithstanding, Jennifer believes that a more formal appraisal approach is required. For one thing, they're approaching the end of the 90-day "introductory" period for many of these employees, and the owners need to make decisions about whether they should go or stay. And from a practical point of view, Jennifer simply believes that sitting down and providing formal, written feedback is more likely to reinforce what employees are doing right and get them to modify things they may be doing wrong. "Maybe this is one reason we're not getting enough sales," she says. They've been debating this for about an hour. Now, they want you, their management consultant, to advise them on what to do.

QUESTIONS

1 What performance appraisal problems will LearnInMotion encounter if they continue on the course of not using formalized performance appraisals?

2 What guidelines would you recommend to Pierre and Jennifer for developing an effective appraisal system?

Case INCIDENT

A Performance Dilemma

Brenda Jackson, a newly hired human resources manager, has been on the job for approximately six months and is in the process of trying to create a new performance appraisal system for her employer, Starbrite Manufacturing Systems. Brenda has reviewed the company's current employee files and has noted that no formal performance appraisals exist in the files. This situation is of great concern to Brenda.

In response, Brenda schedules a meeting with the CEO to discuss her concerns and to gain his support to ultimately recommend the designing of a new performance appraisal system. After the meeting, Brenda is happy at gaining the CEO's approval but starts to feel overwhelmed at the large task she has in pulling the new performance management system together. This is where you come in to help Brenda by answering the following questions.

QUESTIONS

1 Discuss the performance management process highlighted in the chapter and how it will aid Brenda in creating this new performance appraisal system for her employer.

2 Discuss and suggest the type of appraisal methods that Brenda should recommend the company use.

3 Discuss the rating errors that Brenda must be aware of and how these can be avoided.

MyManagementLab

Visit MyManagementLab to access a personalized Study Plan and additional study tools for this chapter.

 To view the CBC videos, read a summary, and answer discussion questions, go to MyManagementLab

CHAPTER

11

Strategic Pay Plans

LEARNING OUTCOMES

AFTER STUDYING THIS CHAPTER, YOU SHOULD BE ABLE TO

EXPLAIN the strategic importance of total rewards.

EXPLAIN in detail each of the three stages in establishing pay rates.

DISCUSS competency-based pay.

DESCRIBE the five basic elements of compensation for managers.

DEFINE pay equity and **EXPLAIN** its importance today.

REQUIRED PROFESSIONAL CAPABILITIES (RPC)

- Monitors the competitiveness of the total compensation strategy on an ongoing basis
- Monitors the competitiveness of the compensation program relative to comparable organizations
- Provides for delivery of payroll services in compliance with applicable legislation and company policy and advises the organization on related matters
- Ensures compliance with legally required programs
- Ensures accurate and timely delivery of pay
- Ensures pay records are accurate and complete
- Recommends job price and pay ranges based on relevant internal and external factors

THE STRATEGIC IMPORTANCE OF TOTAL EMPLOYMENT REWARDS

total employment rewards An integrated package of all rewards (monetary and non-monetary, extrinsic and intrinsic) gained by employees arising from their employment.

Compensation and rewards management is extremely important to every employee. **Total employment rewards** refer to an integrated package of all rewards gained by employees arising from their employment. These rewards encompass everything that employees value in the employment relationship.

There are a variety of models that attempt to define the elements of total employee rewards. Some models segment rewards based on the monetary (extrinsic), non monetary (intrinsic) divide, with further differentiation between bash payments and benefits that have are a cash expense for the organization, but are not paid as cash to the employees, as illustrated in **Figure 11.1**.[1]

Alternatively, WorldatWork conceptualized the total rewards model within three broad categories:

Compensation (extrinsic), *benefits (extrinsic)*, and *non-monetary rewards (intrinsic)*. Recently, the work experience category was further refined by splitting it into three parts—work–life programs, performance and recognition, and development and career opportunities—resulting in five categories of total rewards, as shown in **Figure 11.2**.

The total rewards approach, as opposed to the previous approach of managing different elements of compensation in isolation, has arisen from the changing business environment of the last several decades. The economies of developed nations like Canada have evolved from a largely industrialized base to become far more virtual, knowledge-based, and service-based, where employees are increasingly regarded as drivers of productivity. A total rewards approach considers individual reward components as part of an integrated whole to determine the best mix of rewards that are aligned with

RPC

Monitors the competitiveness of the total compensation strategy on an ongoing basis

FIGURE 11.1   Employment Rewards: An Integrated Package of Rewards

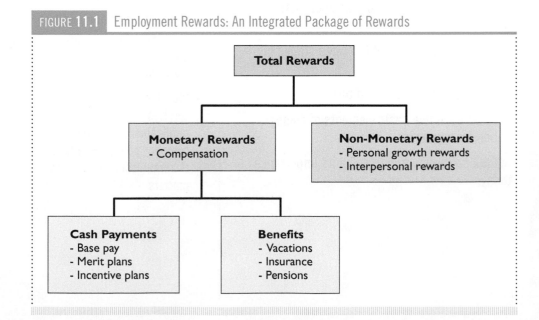

FIGURE **11.2**   The Total Rewards Model

Source: Total Rewards: WorldatWork Introduces a New View 2006. Reprinted with permission of WorldatWork, Scottsdale, AZ. www.worldatwork.org.

business strategy and that provide employee value, all within the cost constraints of the organization. Alignment is the extent to which rewards support outcomes that are important to achieving the organization's strategic objectives. For example, when competitive advantage relies on relentless customer service, this behaviour should be reinforced. Employee value is created when rewards are meaningful to employees and influence their affiliation with the organization.[2]

The Five Components of Total Rewards

1. *Compensation.* This category includes direct financial payments in the form of wages, salaries, incentives, commissions, and bonuses. Wages and salaries are discussed in this chapter, and other direct financial payments are discussed in Chapter 12.

2. *Benefits.* This category includes indirect payments in the form of financial benefits, like employer-paid insurance and vacations. It also includes employee services, as discussed in Chapter 13.

3. *Work–life programs.* This category of rewards relates to programs that help employees do their jobs effectively, such as flexible scheduling, telecommuting, childcare, and so on. Work–life programs are discussed in Chapter 13.

4. *Performance and recognition.* This category includes pay-for-performance and recognition programs. These programs are discussed in Chapter 12.

5. *Development and career opportunities.* This category of rewards focuses on planning for the advancement or change in responsibilities to best suit individual skills, talents, and desires. Tuition assistance, professional development, sabbaticals, coaching and mentoring opportunities, succession planning, and apprenticeships are all examples of career-enhancing programs.

The world's most admired companies excel at taking a total rewards approach, as discussed in the Strategic HR box.

STRATEGIC HR

Rewards Program Effectiveness at the World's Most Admired Companies

Every year, the world's most admired companies (MACs) are featured in *Fortune* magazine. In 2009, these companies excelled in six key areas related to reward program effectiveness:

1. focusing on excellence in the execution of rewards programs

2. ensuring their rewards programs are aligned with organizational goals, strategy, and culture

3. promoting a total rewards view across the organization and effectively leveraging intangible rewards

4. having stronger programs for developing talent from within, resulting in lower base salaries than that of their peers

5. better leveraging their managers' skills in rewards program implementation

6. reinforcing HR's role in helping managers succeed at putting reward programs into action

One key reason MACs are more successful at aligning their rewards programs with their organizational goals is that they tend to take a more global, centralized approach to managing rewards strategy, compensation structures, and performance management programs. They also excel at communicating their business strategies to managers and employees. The emphasis on communication also extends to the rewards arena.

MACs understand that employees are motivated by much more than money. They are more likely to take a total rewards approach, covering not just tangible rewards like base salary, incentives, and other monetary benefits, but also intangible rewards such as career-growth opportunities, quality of work, recognition, and work climate.

MACs generally pay lower base salaries than their peers. On average, MACs pay approximately 5 percent less in base pay for management and professional roles than other organizations. This is most likely the result of the emphasis that MACs place on intangible rewards like career development. They have a stronger pool of homegrown talent to choose from when job vacancies arise, so they are less reliant on hiring expensive external talent.

Organizations tend to fuss and fret about the design of their rewards programs, but these companies exemplify what research has indicated: Impressive design is not why rewards programs generally work well. It is the way they are put into action and then sustained by the organization that drives their effectiveness.

Source: Adapted from T. McMullen, M. Royal, and M. Stark, "Rewards-Program Effectiveness: What Makes the World's Most Admired Companies Great?" *WorldatWork Journal*, 18, no. 1, pp. 65–74. Contents © 2009. Reprinted with permission from WorldatWork. Content is licensed for use by purchaser only. No part of this article may be reproduced, excerpted, or redistributed in any form without express written permission from WorldatWork.

Impact of Rewards

Towers Perrin (now known as Towers Watson)
www.towerswatson.com

The purposes of rewards are to attract, retain, motivate, and engage employees. *Engagement* refers to a positive emotional connection to the employer and a clear understanding of the strategic significance of the job, which results in discretionary effort on the part of the employee. The *2007–2008 Global*

Workforce Study by Towers Perrin (now known as Towers Watson) consultants found that, for Canadians, competitive base pay was the number one factor in attracting employees to an organization, having excellent career opportunities was the most important factor in retaining employees, and senior management's interest in employee well-being was the top factor influencing employee engagement.[3] Similarly, a study of 446 organizations across Canada by Western Compensation and Benefits Consultants found that the most effective attraction strategy was offering competitive base salaries, and the top reason for turnover among employees was dissatisfaction with cash compensation. Opportunities for advancement, work–life balance programs, and competitive benefits programs are also used by over 70 percent of Canadian companies to attract talent.[4]

BASIC CONSIDERATIONS IN DETERMINING PAY RATES

Four basic considerations influence the formulation of any pay plan: legal requirements, union issues, compensation policy, and equity.

Legal Considerations in Compensation

Hints TO ENSURE LEGAL COMPLIANCE

All of the 14 jurisdictions regulating employment in Canada (ten provinces, three territories, and the federal jurisdiction) have laws regulating compensation. Thus, HR managers must pay careful attention to which legislation affects their employees. Further, these laws are constantly changing and require continual monitoring to ensure compliance. Legislation affecting compensation administration is discussed below.

Employment/Labour Standards Acts (Canada Labour Code)

Employment/labour laws set minimum standards regarding pay, including minimum wage, maximum hours of work, overtime pay, paid vacation, paid statutory holidays, termination pay, record keeping of pay information, and more. There are variations in some of the minimum standards for students, trainees, domestics, nannies, seasonal agricultural workers, and others. Executive, administrative, and professional employees are generally exempt from the overtime pay requirements.

Pay Equity Acts

Pay equity laws were enacted to address the historical undervaluation of "women's work" by providing equal pay for work of equal (or comparable) value performed by men and women. Employers are required to identify male- and female-dominated jobs, and then use a gender-neutral job evaluation system based on specific compensable factors (such as skill, effort, responsibility, and working conditions) to evaluate the jobs. Pay for female-dominated jobs that are equivalent in value to male-dominated jobs must be increased to the pay level of the comparable male-dominated job. Not all Canadian jurisdictions have pay equity laws, as will be discussed later in this chapter.

Human Rights Acts

All jurisdictions have enacted human rights laws to protect Canadians from discrimination on a number of grounds in employment and other areas. These grounds differ somewhat among jurisdictions, but most prohibit discrimination in employment (such as in compensation and promotion) on the basis of age, sex, colour, race/ancestry/place of origin, religion/creed, marital/family status, and physical or mental disability.

Canada/Quebec Pension Plan

All employees and their employers must contribute to the Canada/Quebec Pension Plan throughout the employee's working life. Pension benefits based on the employee's average earnings are paid during retirement. Details of these and other benefits are provided in Chapter 13.

Association of Workers'
Compensation Boards of Canada
www.awcbc.org

Other Legislation Affecting Compensation

Each province and territory, as well as the federal government, has its own *workers' compensation laws*. The objective of these laws is to provide a prompt, sure, and reasonable income to victims of work-related accidents and illnesses. The Employment Insurance Act is aimed at protecting Canadian workers from total economic destitution in the event of employment termination that is beyond their control. Employers and employees both contribute to the benefits provided by this act. This act also provides up to 45 weeks of compensation for workers unemployed through no fault of their own (depending on the unemployment rate in the claimant's region and other factors). Maternity leave, parental leave, and compassionate care leave benefits are also provided under the Employment Insurance Act.[5]

Work stoppages may reflect employee dissatisfaction with pay plans and other forms of compensation, such as pensions.

Union Influences on Compensation Decisions

Unions and labour relations laws also influence how pay plans are designed. Historically, wage rates have been the main issue in collective bargaining. However, other issues—including time off with pay, income security (for those in industries with periodic layoffs), cost-of-living adjustments, and pensions—are also important.[6]

The Canada Industrial Relations Board and similar bodies in each province and territory oversee employer practices and ensure that employees are treated in accordance with their legal rights. Their decisions underscore the need to involve union officials in developing the compensation package.

Union Attitudes toward Compensation Decisions

Research INSIGHT

Several classic studies shed light on union attitudes toward compensation plans and on commonly held union fears.[7] Many union leaders fear that any system used to evaluate the worth of a job can become a tool for management malpractice. They tend to believe that no one can judge the relative value of jobs better than the workers themselves. In addition, they believe that management's usual method of using several compensable factors (like "degree of responsibility") to evaluate and rank the worth of jobs can be a manipulative device for restricting or lowering the pay of workers. One implication is that the best way in which to gain the cooperation of union members in evaluating the worth of jobs is to get their active involvement in this process and in assigning fair rates of pay to these jobs. However, management has to ensure that its prerogatives—such as the right to use the appropriate job evaluation technique to assess the relative worth of jobs—are not surrendered.

Compensation Policies

An employer's compensation policies provide important guidelines regarding the wages and benefits that it pays. A number of factors are taken into account when developing a compensation policy, including whether the organization wants to be a leader or a follower regarding pay, business strategy, and the cost of different types of compensation. Important policies include the basis for salary increases, promotion and demotion policies, overtime pay policy, and policies regarding probationary pay and leaves for military service, jury duty, and holidays. Compensation policies are usually written by the HR or compensation manager in conjunction with senior management.[8]

Equity and Its Impact on Pay Rates

external equity Employees perceives his or her pay as fair given the pay rates in other organizations.

internal equity Employees perceives his or her pay as fair given the pay rates of others in the organization.

A crucial factor in determining pay rates is the need for equity, specifically **external equity** and **internal equity**. Research has indicated that employee perceptions of fairness are one of the two key conditions for effective reward programs.[9] Externally, pay must compare favourably with rates in other organizations or an employer will find it hard to attract and retain qualified employees. Pay rates must also be equitable internally: Each employee should view his or her pay as equitable given other pay rates in the organization.

ESTABLISHING PAY RATES

In practice, the process of establishing pay rates that are both externally and internally equitable requires three stages:

1. Determine the worth of jobs within the organization through job evaluation (to ensure internal equity), and group jobs with similar worth into pay grades.
2. Conduct a wage/salary survey of what other employers are paying for comparable jobs (to ensure external equity).
3. Combine the job evaluation (internal) and salary survey (external) information to determine pay rates for the jobs in the organization.

Each of these stages will be explained in turn.

Stage 1: Job Evaluation

job evaluation A systematic comparison to determine the relative worth of jobs within a firm.

Job evaluation is aimed at determining a job's relative worth. It is a formal and systematic comparison of jobs within a firm to determine the worth of one job relative to another, and it eventually results in a job hierarchy.

benchmark job A job that is critical to the firm's operations or that is commonly found in other organizations.

The basic procedure is to compare the content of jobs in relation to one another, for example, in terms of their effort, responsibility, skills, and working conditions. Job evaluation usually focuses on **benchmark jobs** that are critical to the firm's operations or that are commonly found in other organizations. Rohm and Haas, a multinational chemical company, ensures that its benchmark jobs represent all the various business units and departments in the organization, are drawn from all levels of the organization, have large numbers of incumbents, are clear and well known in the industry, are stable and easily understood in terms of purpose and work content, and are visible and well understood by all employees.[10] The resulting evaluations of benchmark jobs are used as reference points around which other jobs are arranged in order of relative worth.

Compensable Factors

Jobs can be compared intuitively by deciding that one job is "more important" or "of greater value or worth" than another without digging any deeper into why in terms of specific job-related factors. This approach, called the *ranking method*, is hard to defend to employees or others who may not agree with the resulting job hierarchy. As an alternative, jobs can be compared by focusing on certain basic factors that they have in common. In compensation management, these basic factors are called **compensable factors**. They are the factors that determine the definition of job content, establish how the jobs compare with one another, and set the compensation paid for each job.

compensable factor A fundamental, compensable element of a job, such as skill, effort, responsibility, and working conditions.

Some employers develop their own compensable factors. However, most use factors that have been popularized by packaged job evaluation systems or by legislation. For example, most of the pay equity acts in Canada focus on four compensable factors: *skill, effort, responsibility*, and *working conditions*. As another example, the job evaluation method popularized by the Hay Group consulting firm focuses on four compensable factors: *know-how, problem solving, accountability*, and *working conditions*. Often, different job evaluation systems are used for different departments, employee groups, or business units.

Identifying compensable factors plays a pivotal role in job evaluation. All jobs in each employee group, department, or business unit are evaluated *using the same compensable factors*. An employer thus evaluates the same elemental components for each job within the work group and is then better able to compare jobs—for example, in terms of the degree of skill, effort, responsibility, and working conditions present in each.[11]

Job Evaluation Committee

Job evaluation is largely a judgmental process and one that demands close cooperation among supervisors, compensation specialists, and the employees and their union representatives. The main steps involved include identifying the need for the program, getting cooperation, and choosing an evaluation committee; the committee then carries out the actual job evaluation.[12]

job evaluation committee A diverse group (including employees, HR staff, managers, and union representatives) established to ensure the fair and comprehensive representation of the nature and requirements of the jobs in question.

A **job evaluation committee** is established to ensure the representation of the points of view of various people who are familiar with the jobs in question, each of whom may have a different perspective regarding the nature of the jobs. The committee may include employees, HR staff, managers, and union representatives.

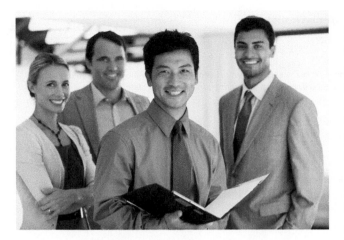

The job evaluation committee typically includes several employees and has the important task of evaluating the worth of each job using compensable factors.

Tips FOR THE FRONT LINE

classification/grading method A method for categorizing jobs into groups.

classes Groups of jobs based on a set of rules for each class, such as amount of independent judgment, skill, physical effort, and so forth. Classes usually contain similar jobs—such as all secretaries.

grades Groups of jobs based on a set of rules for each grade, where jobs are similar in difficulty but otherwise different. Grades often contain dissimilar jobs, such as secretaries, mechanics, and firefighters.

grade/group description A written description of the level of compensable factors required by jobs in each grade; sed to combine similar jobs into grades or classes.

point method A job evaluation method in which a number of compensable factors are identified, the degree to which each of these factors is present in the job is determined, and an overall point value is calculated.

The evaluation committee first identifies 10 or 15 key benchmark jobs. These will be the first jobs to be evaluated and will serve as the anchors or benchmarks against which the relative importance or value of all other jobs can be compared. Then the committee turns to its most important function—actually evaluating the worth of each job. For this, the committee will probably use either the job classification method or the point method.

Classification Method

The **classification/grading method** involves categorizing jobs into groups. The groups are called **classes** if they contain similar jobs or **grades** if they contain jobs that are similar in difficulty but otherwise different.

This method is widely used in the public sector. The federal government's UT (University Teaching) job group is an example of a job class because it contains similar jobs involving teaching, research, and consulting. Conversely, the AV (Audit, Commerce, and Purchasing) job group is an example of a job grade because it contains dissimilar jobs, involving auditing, economic development consulting, and purchasing.

There are several ways in which to categorize jobs. One is to draw up class descriptions (similar to job descriptions) and place jobs into classes based on their correspondence to these descriptions. Another is to draw up a set of classifying rules for each class (for instance, the amount of independent judgment, skill, physical effort, and so on that the class of jobs requires). Then the jobs are categorized according to these rules.

The usual procedure is to choose compensable factors and then develop class or grade descriptions that describe each class in terms of the amount or level of compensable factor(s) in jobs. The federal government's classification system, for example, employs different compensable factors for various job groups. Based on these compensable factors, a **grade/group description** (like that in **Figure 11.3**) is written. Then, the evaluation committee reviews all job descriptions and slots each job into its appropriate class or grade.

The job classification method has several advantages. The main one is that most employers usually end up classifying jobs anyway, regardless of the job evaluation method that they use. They do this to avoid having to work with and develop pay rates for an unmanageable number of jobs; with the job classification method, all jobs are already grouped into several classes. The disadvantages are that it is difficult to write the class or grade descriptions and that considerable judgment is required in applying them. Yet many employers use this method with success.

Point Method

The **point method** is widely used in the private sector and requires identifying several compensable factors. The extent or degree to which each factor is present in the job is evaluated, a corresponding number of points is assigned for each factor, and the number of points for each factor is summed to arrive at an overall point value for the job.

FIGURE **11.3**   Example of a Group Definition in the Federal Government

Correctional Services (CX) Group Definition

The Correctional Services Group comprises positions that are primarily involved in the custody, control and correctional influence of inmates in the institutions of Correctional Service Canada and the training of staff engaged in custodial and correctional work at a Staff College of Correctional Service Canada.

Inclusions

Notwithstanding the generality of the foregoing, for greater certainty, it includes positions that have as their primary purpose, responsibility for one or more of the following activities:

1. the custody and control of inmates and the security of the institution;
2. the custody and control of detainees being held under Immigration and Refugee Protection Act (IRPA) Security Certificates;
3. the correctional influence of inmates with the continuing responsibility to relate actively and effectively to inmates;
4. the admission and discharge of inmates, and the control of inmate visits and correspondence;
5. the organization and implementation of recreational activities, the surveillance and control of inmates engaged in these activities and the custody and issue of recreational equipment;
6. the training of staff in custodial and correctional procedures and techniques; and
7. the leadership of any of the above activities.

Exclusions

Positions excluded from the Correctional Services Group are those whose primary purpose is included in the definition of any other group or those in which one or more of the following activities is of primary importance:

1. the operation of heating plant, sewage facilities and water supplies and the provision of maintenance services;
2. the provision of patient care that requires the application of a comprehensive knowledge of or specialized expertise in physical and mental health care;
3. the provision of services and supplies to inmates; and
4. the instruction of inmates in workshops, crafts and training programs.

Source: Correctional Services (CX) Classification Standard. www.tbs-sct.gc.ca/cla/def/cx-eng.asp, Treasury Board of Canada Secretariat, 2004. Reproduced with the permission of the Minister of Public Works and Government Services Canada, 2012.

1. *Preliminary steps.* To use the point method, it is necessary to have current job descriptions and job specifications based on a thorough job analysis. The foundation of the job evaluation plan is a number of compensable factors that must be agreed upon. In Canada, four compensable factors are commonly used: skill, effort, responsibility, and working conditions. These factors are general and can mean different things in different workplaces. Therefore subfactors of each one may also be determined to clarify the specific meaning of each factor, as shown below.

Factor	Sub-Factors
Skill	Education and Experience Interpersonal Skill
Effort	Physical Effort Mental Effort
Responsibility	Supervision of Others Planning
Working Conditions	Physical Environment Travel

Each sub-factor must be carefully defined to ensure that the evaluation committee members will apply them consistently. An example of a sub-factor definition is presented in **Figure 11.4**.

| FIGURE 11.4 | Sub-Factor Definition |

Responsibility for Others

This sub-factor is used to measure the responsibility that the incumbent of the position assumes for the direction and/or supervision of volunteers, external suppliers/contractors and staff. The following characteristics of the work are to be considered in selecting a level: the nature of supervision given, based either on accountability for results or functional guidance (how-to), and the number of employees or others directed/supervised. Occasional supervision, such as that performed during the absence of the supervisor on vacation or sick leaves, is not to be considered. **This sub-factor does NOT include the academic supervision of students or the activities of others outside of an employee-type relationship.**

Source: Based on McMaster University CAW Local 555 Job Evaluation Plan, www.workingatmcmaster.ca/jjesc (accessed March 23, 2009).

2. *Determine factor weights and degrees.* The next step is to decide on the maximum number of points (called "weight") to assign to each factor. Assigning factor weights is generally done by the evaluation committee. The committee members carefully study each factor and determine the relative value of the factors. For example:

Skill	30 percent
Effort	30 percent
Responsibility	30 percent
Working conditions	10 percent
	100 percent

Then definitions of varying amounts (called "degrees" or "levels") of each sub-factor (or overall factor if no sub-factors are used) are prepared so that raters can judge the degree of a sub-factor/factor existing in a job. Thus, sub-factor "physical environment" for the factor "working conditions" might have three degrees—occasional, frequent, continuous—defined as follows:

Degree 1: Occasional—less than 30 percent of the time on an annual basis. Typically occurs once in a while, but not every day, or every day for less than 30 percent of the day.

Degree 2: Frequent—30 percent to 60 percent of the time on an annual basis. A regular feature of the job that occurs during any given day, week, or season.

Degree 3: Continuous—More than 60 percent of the time on an annual basis. Typically occurs for most of the regular work day, all year round (on average).

The number of degrees usually does not exceed five or six, and the actual number depends mostly on judgment. It is not necessary to have the same number of degrees for each factor, and degrees should be limited to the number necessary to distinguish among jobs.

3. *Assign points for each degree of each sub-factor.* Points are then assigned to each factor, as in **Table 11.1**. For example, suppose that it is decided to use a total number of 1 000 points in the point plan. Then, since the factor "skill" had a weight of 30 percent, it would be assigned a total of 30 percent of

TABLE 11.1   Point Method Job Evaluation Plan

Factor	Sub-Factors	Degrees					Maximum Weight Points	
		1	2	3	4			
Skill	Education and Experience	50	100	150	200	200		
	Interpersonal Skill	25	50	75	100	100		
							300	30%
Effort	Physical Effort	25	50	75	100	100		
	Mental Effort	50	100	150	200	200		
							300	30%
Responsibility	Supervision of Others	50	100	150		150		
	Planning	50	100	150		150		
							300	30%
Working Conditions	Physical Environment	20	40	60		60		
	Travel	10	20	30	40	40		
							100	10%
							1000	100%

1 000 = 300 points. This automatically means that the highest degree for each sub-factor of the skill factor would be 300 points. Points are then assigned to the other degrees for this factor, in equal amounts from the lowest to the highest degree. This step is repeated for each factor and its sub-factors, resulting in the final job evaluation plan, as shown in Table 11.1. All these decisions are recorded in a job evaluation manual to be used by the job evaluation committee.

4. *Evaluate the jobs.* Once the manual is complete, the actual evaluations can begin. Each job is evaluated factor by factor to determine the number of points that should be assigned to it. First, committee members determine the degree (first degree, second degree, and so on) to which each factor is present in the job. Then they note the corresponding points (see Table 11.1) that were assigned to each of these degrees. Finally, they add up the points for all factors, arriving at a total point value for the job. Raters generally start by rating benchmark jobs and obtaining consensus on these, and then they rate the rest of the jobs.

Point systems involve a quantitative technique that is easily explained to and used by employees. However, it can be difficult and time-consuming to develop a point plan and to effectively train the job evaluation user group. This is one reason why many organizations adopt a point plan developed and marketed by a consulting firm. In fact, the availability of a number of ready-made plans probably accounts in part for the wide use of point plans in job evaluation.

If the committee assigned pay rates to each individual job, it would be difficult to administer since there might be different pay rates for hundreds or even thousands of jobs. Even in smaller organizations there is a tendency to try to simplify wage and salary structures as much as possible. Therefore, the committee will probably want to group similar jobs (in terms of their number of points, for instance) into grades for pay purposes. Then, instead of having to deal with pay rates for hundreds of jobs, it might only have to focus on pay rates for 10 or 12 groupings of jobs.

A **pay grade** comprises jobs of approximately equal value or importance, as determined by job evaluation. If the point method was used, the pay grade consists of jobs falling within a range of points. If the classification system was used, then the jobs are already categorized into classes or grades. The next stage is to obtain information on market pay rates by conducting a wage/salary survey.

pay grade Comprises jobs of approximately equal value.

Stage 2: Conduct a Wage/Salary Survey

Compensation or **wage/salary surveys** play a central role in determining pay rates for jobs.[13] An employer may use wage/salary surveys in three ways. First, survey data are used to determine pay rates for benchmark jobs that serve as reference points or anchors for the employer's pay scale, meaning that other jobs are then paid based on their relative worth compared to the benchmark jobs. Second, an increasing number of positions are paid solely based on the marketplace (rather than relative to the firm's benchmark jobs).[14]

wage/salary survey A survey aimed at determining prevailing wage rates. A good salary survey provides specific wage rates for comparable jobs. Formal written questionnaire surveys are the most comprehensive.

As a result of the current shift away from long-term employment, compensation is increasingly shaped by market wages and less by how it fits into the hierarchy of jobs in one organization. Finally, surveys also collect data on employee benefits, work–life programs, pay-for-performance plans, recognition plans, and so on to provide a basis on which to make decisions regarding other types of rewards.

Formal and Informal Surveys by the Employer

Most employers rely heavily on formal or informal surveys of what other employers are paying.[15] Informal telephone surveys are good for collecting data on a relatively small number of easily identified and quickly recognized jobs, such as when a bank's HR director wants to determine the salary at which a newly opened customer service representative's job should be advertised. Informal discussions among human resources specialists at regular professional association meetings are other occasions for informal salary surveys. Some employers use formal questionnaire surveys to collect compensation information from other employers, including things like number of employees, overtime policies, starting salaries, and paid vacations.

Commercial, Professional, and Government Salary Surveys

Many employers also rely on surveys published by various commercial firms, professional associations, or government agencies. For example, Statistics Canada provides monthly data on earnings by geographic area, by industry, and by occupation. **Table 11.2** provides an example of earnings data by industry and occupation.

The Toronto Board of Trade conducts five compensation surveys annually, covering executive; management; professional, supervisory, and sales; information technology; and administrative and support positions. The surveys include information from small, medium, and large employers in the Greater Toronto Area. A separate survey of employee benefits and employment practices is also conducted.

TABLE 11.2 Average Weekly Earnings by Industry 2004–2009

Geography=Canada
Type of employees=All employees
Overtime=Including overtime

North American Industry Classification System (NAICS)	2004	2005	2006	2007	2008	2009
Industrial aggregate excluding unclassified businesses	709.41	737.29	755.48	788.06	810.52	823.53
Mining, quarrying, and oil and gas extraction	1,278.11	1,296.35	1,325.73	1,437.44	1,527.90	1,594.04
Utilities	1,261.08	1,298.32	1,350.66	1,421.49	1,424.73	1,500.79
Construction	846.38	877.34	900.32	961.16	1,014.51	1,048.42
Manufacturing	862.60	896.35	904.69	940.67	949.54	917.73
Wholesale trade	826.89	865.92	905.24	937.14	956.59	988.89
Retail trade	425.65	441.18	449.86	458.80	475.17	486.70
Transportation and warehousing	807.78	828.07	834.40	864.51	883.28	874.69
Information and cultural industries	916.99	952.30	955.52	1,003.44	1,003.54	1,077.16
Finance and insurance	887.00	921.01	951.17	998.93	1,002.03	1,036.81
Real estate and rental and leasing	654.56	698.06	710.73	756.11	772.87	771.83
Professional, scientific and technical services	937.42	989.94	1,016.41	1,060.36	1,093.67	1,129.10
Management of companies and enterprises	1,012.41	1,005.19	1,050.28	1,086.16	1,087.91	1,144.86
Admistrative and support, waste management and remediation services	546.15	583.67	600.98	648.97	673.97	671.44

Source: Statistics Canada, CANSIM database, Table 281-0027, 2011. Available for free at www.statcan.gc.ca/pub/72-002-x/72-002-x2011002-eng.pdf.

Private consulting or executive recruiting companies, such as Towers Watson, Mercer, and Hewitt Associates, annually publish data covering the compensation of senior and middle managers and members of boards of directors. Professional organizations, such as the Certified General Accountants and Professional Engineers Ontario, conduct surveys of compensation practices among members of their associations.

For some jobs, salaries are determined directly based on formal or informal salary surveys like those available from Monster.ca. In most cases, though, surveys are used to price benchmark jobs around which other jobs are then slotted based on their relative worth as determined through job evaluation.

Monster.ca Salary & Benefits Centre
http://career-advice.monster.ca/Salary-Benefits/careers.aspx

Salary Survey Interpretation and Use

Data from the Hay Group consulting firm indicate that large organizations participate in an average of 11 compensation surveys and use information from seven of them to administer their own compensation practices.[16]

Upward bias can be a problem regardless of the type of compensation survey used. At least one compensation expert argues that the way in which most surveys are constructed, interpreted, and used leads almost invariably to a situation in which firms set higher wages than they otherwise might. For example, "companies like to compare themselves against well-regarded, high-paying, and high-performing companies," so baseline salaries tend to be biased upward.

RPC

Monitors the competitiveness of the compensation program relative to comparable organizations

Similarly, "companies that sponsor surveys often do so with an implicit (albeit unstated) objective: to show the company [is] paying either competitively or somewhat below the market, so as to justify positive corrective action." For these and similar reasons, it is probably wise to review survey results with a skeptical eye and to acknowledge that upward bias may exist and should perhaps be considered when making decisions.[17]

Whatever the source of the survey, the data must be carefully assessed for accuracy before they are used to make compensation decisions. Problems can arise when the organization's job descriptions only partially match the descriptions contained in the survey, the survey data were collected several months before the time of use, the participants in the survey do not represent the appropriate labour market for the jobs being matched, and so on.[18]

Now all the information necessary to move to the next stage—determining pay for jobs—has been obtained.

Stage 3: Combine the Job Evaluation and Salary Survey Information to Determine Pay for Jobs

The final stage is to assign pay rates to each pay grade. (Of course, if jobs were not grouped into pay grades, individual pay rates would have to be assigned to each job.) Assigning pay rates to each pay grade (or to each job) is usually accomplished with a **wage curve**.

The wage curve graphically depicts the market pay rates currently being paid for jobs in each pay grade, relative to the job evaluation points for each job or grade. An example of a wage curve is presented in **Figure 11.5**. Note that pay rates are shown on the vertical axis, while the points for pay grades are shown along the horizontal axis. The purpose of the wage curve is to show the relationship between the value of the job as determined by one of the job evaluation methods and the current average pay rates for each job or grade.

RPC

Recommends job price and pay ranges based on relevant internal and external factors

wage curve A graphic description of the relationship between the value of the job and the average wage paid for this job.

FIGURE **11.5**   Plotting a Wage Curve

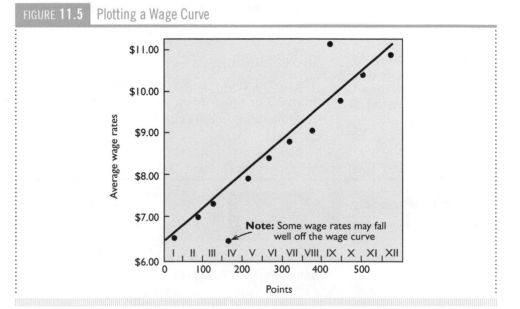

Note: The average market pay rate for jobs in each grade (Grade I, Grade II, Grade III, etc.) is plotted, and the wage curve is fitted to the resulting points.

An Ethical : Dilemma

What should employers do when there is a shortage of a certain type of skill and they cannot attract any workers unless they pay a market rate above the maximum of their salary range for that job? How should other jobs (without a skills shortage) in the same company in the same salary range be paid?

There are several steps in determining pay for pay grades using a wage curve. First, find the average pay for each pay grade, since each of the pay grades consists of several jobs. Next, plot the pay rates for each pay grade, as was done in Figure 11.5. Then fit a line (called a "wage line") through the points just plotted. This can be done either freehand or by using a statistical method known as regression analysis. Finally, determine pay for jobs. Wages along the wage line are the target wages or salary rates for the jobs in each pay grade.

Developing Rate Ranges

pay ranges A series of steps or levels within a pay grade, usually based on years of service.

Most employers do not just pay one rate for all jobs in a particular pay grade. Instead, they develop **pay ranges** for each grade so that there might, for instance, be 10 levels or "steps" and 10 corresponding pay rates within each pay grade. This approach is illustrated in **Table 11.3**, which shows the pay rates and levels for some of the federal government pay grades. As of the time of this pay schedule, for instance, employees in positions that were classified in grade CX-1 could be paid annual salaries between $52 604 and $66 413, depending on the level at which they were hired into the grade, the amount of time they were in the grade, and their merit increases (if any). Another way to depict the rate ranges for each grade is with a wage structure, as in **Figure 11.6**. The wage structure graphically depicts the range of pay rates (in this case, per hour) to be paid for each grade.

The use of pay ranges for each pay grade has several benefits. First, the employer can take a more flexible stance with respect to the labour market; for example, some flexibility makes it easier to attract experienced, higher-paid employees into a pay grade where the starting salary for the lowest step may be too low to attract such experienced people. Pay ranges also allow employers to provide for performance differences between employees within the same grade or between those with differing seniority. As in Figure 11.6, most employers structure their pay ranges to overlap a bit so that an employee with greater experience or seniority may earn more than an entry-level person in the next higher pay grade.

Broadbanding

broadbanding Reducing the number of salary grades and ranges into just a few wide levels or "bands," each of which then contains a relatively wide range of jobs and salary levels.

The trend today is for employers to reduce their salary grades and ranges from 10 or more down to three to five, a process that is called **broadbanding**. Broadbanding means combining salary grades and ranges into just a few wide

TABLE 11.3 Federal Government Pay Schedules CX-1 and CX-2

| Rate Levels within Grade | | | | | |
Grade	1	2	3	4	5
CX-1	$52 604	55 761	59 107	62 652	66 413
CX-2	$55 826	59 176	62 726	66 489	70 477

Source: CX - Correctional Services Group Annual Rates of Pay, www.tbs-sct.gc.ca/pubs_pol/hrpubs/coll_agre/cx/cx08-eng.asp, Treasury Board of Canada Secretariat, 2006. Reproduced with the permission of the Minister of Public Works and Government Services Canada, 2012.

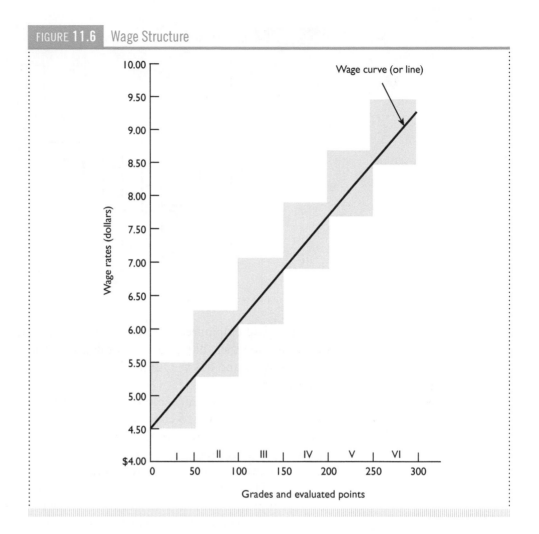

FIGURE 11.6 Wage Structure

levels or "bands," each of which then contains a relatively wide range of jobs and salary levels (see **Figure 11.7**).

Broadbanding a pay system involves several steps. First, the number of bands is decided on and each is assigned a salary range. The bands usually have wide salary ranges and also overlap substantially. As a result, there is much more flexibility to move employees from job to job within bands and less need to "promote" them to new grades just to give them higher salaries.

Broadbanding's basic advantage is that it injects greater flexibility into employee compensation.[19] The new, broad salary bands can include both supervisors and those reporting to them. Broadbanding also facilitates less specialized, boundaryless jobs and organizations. Less specialization and more participation in cross-departmental processes generally mean enlarged duties or capabilities and more possibilities for alternative career tracks.

Correcting Out-of-Line Rates

The actual wage rate for a job may fall well off the wage line or well outside the rate range for its grade. This means that the average pay for that job is currently too high or too low relative to other jobs in the firm. If a point falls well below the line, a pay raise for the job may be required. If the plot falls well above the wage line, pay cuts or a pay freeze may be required.

FIGURE **11.7** Broadbanding

red circle pay rate A rate of pay that is above the pay range maximum.

Underpaid employees should have their wages raised to the minimum of the rate range for their pay grade, assuming that the organization wants to retain the employees and has the funds. This can be done either immediately or in one or two steps.

Pay rates of overpaid employees are often called **red circle pay rates**, and there are several ways to cope with this problem. One is to freeze the rate paid to employees in this grade until general salary increases bring the other jobs into line with it. A second alternative is to transfer or promote some or all of the employees involved to jobs for which they can legitimately be paid their current pay rates. The third alternative is to freeze the rate for six months, during which time attempts are made to transfer or promote the overpaid employees. If this is not possible, then the rate at which these employees are paid is cut to the maximum in the pay range for their grade.

PAY FOR KNOWLEDGE

Pay-for-knowledge systems are known as *competency-based pay* (for management and professional employees) and *skill-based pay* (for manufacturing employees). These plans pay employees for the range, depth, and types of knowledge that they are capable of using, rather than for the job that they currently hold. Competencies are individual knowledge, skills, and behaviours that are critical to successful individual or corporate performance based on their relation to the organization's visions, values, and business strategy.[20]

Core competencies describe knowledge and behaviours that employees throughout the organization must exhibit for the organization to succeed, such as "customer service orientation" for all hotel employees. *Functional competencies* are associated with a particular organizational function, such as "negotiation skills" for salespeople, or "safety orientation" for pilots. *Behavioural competencies* are expected behaviours, such as "always walking a customer to the product they are looking for rather than pointing."[21] A pay-for-knowledge program should include the following:

- Competencies and skills—directly important to job performance—that can be defined in measurable and objective terms. Skills tend to be easier to define and measure than competencies.

- New and different competencies that replace obsolete competencies or competencies that are no longer important to job performance. If additional competencies are needed, the obsolete competency should be removed from the program.

- On-the-job training, not "in the classroom" training. Those who possess the competencies or skills should teach them. Also include on-the-job assessment, which can be supplemented by paper-and-pencil exams administered on the job.[22]

As an example, in a manufacturing plant setting, workers would be paid based on their attained skill levels. In a three-level plan:

1. Level 1 would indicate limited ability, such as knowledge of basic facts and ability to perform simple tasks without direction.

2. Level 2 would mean that the employee has attained partial proficiency and could, for instance, apply technical principles on the job.

3. Level 3 would mean that the employee is fully competent in the area and could, for example, analyze and solve production problems.

Construction workers today are often compensated for their work through the method of skill-based pay.

Increased workforce flexibility is one of the most significant advantages of pay for knowledge. Employees rotate between different jobs or production areas to encourage the learning of new competencies and skills. This process fosters flexibility by encouraging workers to learn multiple competencies and skills and to willingly switch tasks.[23]

Experience has shown that competency-based pay is more efficient in the first years of its existence. The greatest challenge is measurement of competencies. As time goes on, employees often become dissatisfied if these measurements are not valid or if the people responsible for assessing competencies are considered incompetent or biased.[24]

Another major employee concern is that pay be linked sufficiently to performance as well as competencies. Some compensation consultants suggest that firms should not pay for competencies at the exclusion of rewards for high performance results. For example, competencies could be linked to the determination of base salary combined with bonuses that are based on performance.[25] One final issue for many Canadian companies is that pay-for-knowledge systems do not meet pay equity requirements.[26]

Although only about 15 to 20 percent of workplaces use pay for knowledge at present, experts predict that the viewpoint that people, rather than jobs, provide advantages to organizations will continue to grow in popularity. They foresee the emergence of new pay systems combining competencies and market values.[27]

PAY FOR EXECUTIVE, MANAGERIAL, AND PROFESSIONAL JOBS

Developing a compensation plan to pay executive, managerial, and professional employees is similar in many respects to developing a plan for other employees.[28] The basic aims of the plan are the same in that the goal is to attract good employees and maintain their commitment. Yet for executive, managerial, and professional jobs, job evaluation provides only a partial answer to the question of how to pay these employees. Executives, managers, and professionals are almost always paid based on their performance as well as on the basis of static job demands, like working conditions.

Compensating Executives and Managers

There are five elements in an executive/managerial compensation package: salary, benefits, short-term incentives, long-term incentives, and perquisites.[29] The amount of salary paid usually depends on the value of the person's work to the organization and how well the person is honouring his or her responsibilities. Salary is the cornerstone of executive compensation, because it is the element on which the others are layered, with benefits, incentives, and perquisites often awarded in some proportion to base pay.

Executive compensation tends to emphasize performance incentives more than other employee pay plans do, since organizational results are likely to reflect the contributions of executives more directly than those of other employees. The heavy incentive component of executive compensation can be illustrated by using some of Canada's best-paid executives as an example.[30] The highest paid executive in Canada in 2010 was Hank Swartout, CEO of Precision Drilling Corporation, who earned a total compensation of $74 824 331, of which $840 000 was base salary. Hunter Harrison, CEO of Canadian National Railway, received total compensation of $56 219 494, which included his base salary of $1 665 950. A study on CEO pay determined that firm size accounts for 40 percent of the variance of total CEO pay, while firm performance accounts for less than 5 percent of the variance.[31]

There has been considerable debate regarding whether top executives are worth what they are paid. Some argue that the job of an executive is increasingly difficult. The stakes are high, and job tenure is often short. Expectations are getting higher, the questions from shareholders are more direct, and the challenge of navigating an organization through difficult economic times has never been so great. However, shareholder activism regarding executive pay has attempted to tighten the restrictions on what firms pay their top executives.

Some believe that pay for performance is taking hold, with companies now making stronger links between company performance and CEO total compensation. Others believe that linking pay to performance is still inadequate in the majority of companies. Most agree that better disclosure of executive pay is required, and groups such as the Canadian Securities Administrators and the Canadian Coalition for Good Governance are pressing for dramatic changes in executive compensation disclosure.[32]

An Ethical Dilemma

Is it right that CEOs earn enormous amounts of money when most employees are getting small increases each year (sometimes even less than inflation)?

Research INSIGHT

Compensating Professional Employees

Compensating non-supervisory professional employees, like engineers and scientists, presents unique problems. Analytical jobs require creativity and problem solving, compensable factors not easily compared or measured. Furthermore, the professional's economic impact on the firm is often related only indirectly to the person's actual efforts; for example, the success of an engineer's invention depends on many factors, like how well it is produced and marketed.

In theory, the job evaluation methods explained previously can be used for evaluating professional jobs.[33] The compensable factors here tend to focus on problem solving, creativity, job scope, and technical knowledge and expertise. The job classification method is commonly used—a series of grade descriptions are written, and each position is slotted into the grade having the most appropriate definition.

In practice, traditional methods of job evaluation are rarely used for professional jobs since it is so difficult to identify compensable factors and degrees of factors that meaningfully capture the value of professional work. "Knowledge and the skill of applying it," as one expert notes, "are extremely difficult to quantify and measure."[34]

As a result, most employers use a *market-pricing approach* in evaluating professional jobs. They price professional jobs in the marketplace to the best of their ability to establish the values for benchmark jobs. These benchmark jobs and the employer's other professional jobs are then slotted into a salary structure. Specifically, each professional discipline (like mechanical engineering or electrical engineering) usually ends up having four to six grade levels, each of which requires a fairly broad salary range. This approach helps ensure that the employer remains competitive when bidding for professionals whose attainments vary widely and whose potential employers are found literally worldwide.[35]

PAY EQUITY

Historically, the average pay for Canadian women has been considerably lower than that for men. In 1967, women's average wages were 46.1 percent of men's average wages. **Table 11.4** shows the most recent wage gap statistics. Some of this gap is due to the fact that women do more part-time work than men, but even when full-year, full-time workers are compared, the gap has stalled at approximately 30 percent since 1998 (see Workforce Diversity box). The wage gap is narrower for single women over those who are married, and for younger women when compared to those who are older.[36]

Moreover, the gap persists even when women have the same qualifications and do the same type of work as men. A 2004 study showed that, two years after graduation, female university graduates in the Maritime provinces working full time earned 78 percent of the weekly wage of males, even after accounting for differences in field of study, occupation, location, and hours worked.[37]

Although such factors as differences in hours worked, experience levels, education levels, and level of unionization contribute to the wage gap, systemic discrimination is also present.[38] The purpose of pay equity legislation is to redress systemic gender discrimination in compensation for work performed by employees in female-dominated job classes. **Pay equity** requires that equal wages be paid for jobs of equal value or "worth" to the employer, as determined by gender-neutral (i.e., free of any bias based on gender) job evaluation techniques.

pay equity Providing equal pay to male-dominated job classes and female-dominated job classes of equal value to the employer.

The legal process involved can be lengthy. A final decision is still pending in a pay equity complaint filed against Canada Post in 1983 claiming that 6 000 clerical workers had been subjected to systemic discrimination.[39] In 2006,

TABLE 11.4 Male–Female Average Earnings Ratio* for Full-Year, Full-Time Workers, 1998–2008

Geography=Canada

Work activity=Full-year full-time workers

Earnings	Average earnings, females (dollars)	Average earnings, males (dollars)	Female-to-male average earnings ratio (percent)
1998	40,500	56,300	71.9
1999	38,900	56,900	68.4
2000	40,200	56,900	70.6
2001	40,600	58,100	69.9
2002	40,800	58,200	70.2
2003	40,700	57,900	70.2
2004	42,000	59,900	70.1
2005	41,800	59,400	70.5
2006	43,200	60,000	71.9
2007	44,100	61,700	71.4
2008	44,700	62,600	71.3

*Earnings stated in constant year 2006 dollars.

Source: Statistics Canada, CANSIM Table 202-0102, http://estat.statcan.gc.ca/cgi-win/CNSMCGI.EXE (accessed August 20, 2011).

WORKFORCE DIVERSITY

Women Work for Free as of September 17

For women in Ontario, the middle of September means more than the end of summer. It is a stark reminder of the gender pay gap that persists in the province. As of September 17, the year is 71 percent of the way through, and with women in Ontario earning an average of 71 cents for every dollar men earn, it also marks the day women start working for free, according to the Equal Pay Coalition.

With an overall 29 percent gender pay gap, women are effectively denied their fair pay from September 17 until the end of the year while men get their full pay, states the coalition. Ontario's Pay Equity Act, which turned 20 years old in 2008, was supposed to end this devaluation by requiring employers to pay women's and men's jobs the same when they were of comparable value. The pay gap has decreased from 38 percent in 1988 to 29 percent today, but that is still too high, according to the coalition.

Canada ranks seventeenth among 22 Organisation for Economic Co-operation and Development countries and is behind the United States, which has a 23 percent wage gap. The World Economic Forum's *2007 Global Gender Gap Report* highlighted the key role gender "remuneration gaps" play in preventing economies from realizing their full potential. Businesses, communities, and governments all benefit from pay equity enforcement.

Discriminatory pay affects women throughout their lives, beginning with their first jobs and continuing into retirement. Young women graduating from high school earn 27 percent less than male high school graduates; young women graduating from university earn 16 percent less than male graduates. But this pay gap widens as their careers progress. The median income of retired women is almost half that of retired men. Over a lifetime these pay gaps add up to enormous financial losses for working women, estimating the total for each woman to be between US$700 000 and US$2 million, depending on education level.

Source: Adapted from "Women Work for Free as of Sept. 17," *Canadian HR Reporter* (September 18, 2008); and M. Cornish, "Much Work to Be Done on Pay Equity," *Canadian HR Reporter* (February 28, 2008). Reprinted by permission of Canadian HR Reporter. © Copyright Thomson Reuters Canada Ltd., (2012) Toronto, Ontario, 1-800-387-5164. Web: www.hrreporter.com

Saskatchewan workers demonstrate for pay equity.

the Supreme Court of Canada ruled against a Canadian Human Rights Tribunal decision that female Air Canada flight attendants' jobs could not be compared with those of mainly male mechanics and pilots and sent the case back to the tribunal. The court condemned Air Canada's use of legal technicalities to delay the case, which began in 1991.[40]

Six provinces (Ontario, Quebec, Manitoba, Nova Scotia, New Brunswick, and Prince Edward Island) have created separate proactive legislation that specifically requires that pay equity be achieved. Ontario and Quebec require pay equity in both the public and the private sectors, whereas the legislation in the other four provinces applies only to the public sector. In the federal jurisdiction and the Yukon (public sector only), human rights legislation requires equal pay for work of equal value.

The wage gap has narrowed since the introduction of pay equity legislation, but there is still no explanation other than systemic discrimination for much of the 30 percent gap that still persists.[41] In the long term, the best way to remove the portion of the wage gap resulting from systemic discrimination is to eliminate male- and female-dominated jobs by ensuring that women have equal access to and are equally represented in all jobs.

Chapter SUMMARY

1. A total rewards approach considers individual reward components as part of an integrated whole to determine the best mix of rewards that are aligned with business strategy and provide employee value, all within the cost constraints of the organization. Alignment is the extent to which rewards support outcomes that are important to achieving the organization's strategic objectives. For example, when competitive advantage relies on relentless customer service, this behaviour should be reinforced. Employee value is created when rewards are meaningful to employees and influence their affiliation with the organization.

2. Establishing pay rates involves three stages: job evaluation (to ensure internal equity), conducting wage/salary surveys (to ensure external equity), and combining job evaluation and salary survey results to determine pay rates. Job evaluation is aimed at determining the relative worth of jobs within a firm. It compares jobs with one another based on their content, which is usually defined in terms of compensable factors, such as skill, effort, responsibility, and working conditions. Jobs of approximately equal value are combined into pay grades for pay purposes. Salary surveys collect data from other employers in the marketplace who are competing for employees in similar kinds of positions. The wage curve shows the average market wage for each pay grade (or job). It illustrates what the average wage for each grade should be and whether any present wages or salaries are out of line.

3. Competency-based pay plans provide employee compensation based on the skills and knowledge that they are capable of using, rather than the job that they currently hold.

4. The five basic elements of compensation for managers are salary, benefits, short-term incentives, long-term incentives, and perquisites.

5. Pay equity is intended to redress systemic gender discrimination as measured by the wage gap, which indicates that full-time working women in Canada make about 71 cents for every dollar made by full-time working men. Pay equity requires equal pay for female-dominated jobs of equal value to male-dominated jobs (where value is determined through job evaluation).

MyManagementLab

Visit MyManagementLab to access a personalized Study Plan and additional study tools for this chapter.

Key TERMS

benchmark job *(p. 300)*
broadbanding *(p. 308)*
classes *(p. 301)*
classification/grading method *(p. 301)*
compensable factor *(p. 300)*
external equity *(p. 299)*
grade/group description *(p. 301)*
grades *(p. 301)*
internal equity *(p.299)*
job evaluation *(p. 299)*

job evaluation committee *(p. 300)*
pay equity *(p. 313)*
pay grade *(p. 305)*
pay ranges *(p. 308)*
point method *(p. 301)*
red circle pay rate *(p. 310)*
total employment rewards *(p. 294)*
wage curve *(p. 307)*
wage/salary survey *(p. 305)*

Review and Discussion QUESTIONS

1. What are the five components of total rewards?
2. Describe what is meant by the term "benchmark job."
3. Identify and briefly describe the three stages in establishing pay rates.
4. What are the pros and cons of the following methods of job evaluation: ranking, classification, factor comparison, point method?
5. Explain the term "competencies" and explain the differences among core, functional, and behavioural competencies.
6. Explain what is meant by the market-pricing approach in evaluating professional jobs.
7. Explain what pay equity legislation is intended to accomplish, what action is required by the legislation to accomplish it, and how effective the legislation has been in accomplishing its objectives.

Critical Thinking QUESTIONS

1. Do you think that transactional or relational rewards have more impact on overall organizational performance?
2. Why do companies pay for compensation surveys where job matching may be difficult rather than conducting their own surveys?
3. It was recently reported in the news that the base pay for Canadian bank CEOs range in the millions of dollars, and the pay for the governor of the Bank of Canada is less than half of that of the lowest paid bank CEO. How do you account for this difference? Should anything be done about this? Why or why not?
4. Do you agree with paying people for competencies and skills that they are rarely required to use on the job?
5. What are some of the potential reasons that gender-based pay discrimination is so hard to eradicate?
6. Why do you think there is such a discrepancy between the pay rates of executives and employees? Is this fair? Why or why not?

Experiential EXERCISES

1. Working individually or in groups, conduct salary surveys for the positions of entry-level accountant and entry-level chemical engineer. What sources did you use, and what conclusions did you reach? If you were the HR manager for a local engineering firm, what would you recommend that each job be paid?

2. Obtain information on the pay grades and rate ranges for each pay grade at your college or university. Do they appear to be broadbands? If not, propose specific broadbands that could be implemented.

3. You have been asked by the owner of your medium-sized import and export company (200+ people) to develop a way to standardize pay ranges for different jobs in the company. He says he is tired of employees complaining about the pay they get compared to others and is concerned that if he does nothing someone will complain about inequitable pay practices. Outline the steps you will follow to do this. Make sure to give a rationale for the type of job evaluation system you propose as well as for the method you suggest to obtain comparable salary data. The jobs he is most concerned about are

   - sales representative
   - shipping and receiving manager
   - multilingual contract negotiator
   - accounts receivable clerk
   - shipping clerk.

4. You are the HR manager at a large construction firm headquartered in Edmonton. Most of the company's administrative staff are also in Edmonton. You have regional and local site offices across the country. Draft a memo to employees about your company's new pay-for-knowledge and skills policy. Make sure to document at least one fully complete section on how this policy will be administered. Your professor may give you some ideas on what might be considered or you may create your own circumstances under which pay for knowledge and skills will be applied.

Running CASE

The New Pay Plan

LearnInMotion.com does not have a formal wage structure, nor does it have rate ranges or use compensable factors. Jennifer and Pierre base wage rates almost exclusively on those prevailing in the surrounding community, and they temper these by trying to maintain some semblance of equity among what workers with different responsibilities are paid. As Jennifer says, "Deciding what to pay dot-com employees is an adventure: Wages for jobs like web designer and online salesperson are always climbing dramatically, and there's not an awful lot of loyalty involved when someone else offers you 30 percent or 40 percent more than you're currently making." Jennifer and Pierre are therefore continually scanning various sources to see what others are paying for positions like theirs. They peruse the want ads almost every day and conduct informal surveys among their friends at other dot-coms. Once or twice a week, they also check compensation websites like Monster.ca.

Although the company has taken a somewhat unstructured, informal approach to establishing its compensation plan, the firm's actual salary schedule is guided by several basic pay policies. For one thing, the difficulty they had recruiting and hiring employees caused them to pay salaries 10 to 20 percent above what the market would seem to indicate. Jennifer and Pierre write this off to the need to get and keep good employees. As Jennifer says,

"If you've got 10 web designers working for you, you can afford to go a few extra weeks without hiring another one, but when you need one designer and you have none, you've got to do whatever you can to get that one designer hired." Their somewhat informal approach has also led to some potential inequities. For example, the two salespeople—one a man, the other a woman—are earning different salaries, and the man is making about 30 percent more. If everything was going fine—for instance, if sales were up and the calendar was functional—perhaps they wouldn't be worried. However, the fact is that the two owners are wondering if a more structured pay plan would be a good idea. Now they want you, their management consultant, to help them decide what to do.

QUESTIONS

1. Describe the total rewards model and its five components and whether it would benefit LearnInMotion.

2. What are some basic considerations in determining pay rates that LearnInMotion must be aware of?

3. Using the three stages of establishing pay rates, provide recommendations to LearnInMotion in regard to job evaluation, wage/salary surveys, and how to combine the first two steps to determine pay rates for LearnInMotion's jobs.

Case INCIDENT

Salary Inequities at Acme Manufacturing

Joe Blackenship was trying to figure out what to do about a problem salary situation that he had in his plant. Blackenship recently took over as president of Acme Manufacturing. The founder, Bill George, had been president for 35 years. The company is family-owned and located in a small eastern Manitoba town. It has approximately 250 employees and is the largest employer in the community. Blackenship is a member of the family that owns Acme, but he had never worked for the company prior to becoming president. He has an MBA and a law degree, plus 15 years of management experience with a large manufacturing organization where he was senior vice-president of human resources when he made his move to Acme.

A short time after joining Acme, Blackenship started to notice that there was considerable inequity in the pay structure for salaried employees. A discussion with the HR director led him to believe that salaried employees' pay was very much a matter of individual bargaining with the past president. Hourly paid factory workers were not part of the problem because they were unionized and their wages were set by collective bargaining. An examination of the salaried payroll showed that there were 25 employees, whose pay ranged from that of the president to that of the receptionist. A closer examination showed that 14 of the salaried employees were female. Three of these were front-line factory supervisors, and one was the HR director. The rest were non-management employees.

This examination also showed that the HR director appeared to be underpaid and that the three female supervisors were paid somewhat less than any of the male supervisors. However, there were no similar supervisory jobs in which there were both male and female incumbents. When asked, the HR director said that she thought the female supervisors may have been paid at a lower rate mainly because they were women, and perhaps George did not think that women needed as much money because they had working husbands. However, she added the thought that they might be paid less because they supervised lesser-skilled employees than did male supervisors. Blackenship was not sure that this was true.

The company from which Blackenship had moved had a good job evaluation system. Although he was thoroughly familiar and capable with this compensation tool, Blackenship did not have time to create a job evaluation study at Acme. Therefore, he decided to hire a compensation consultant from a nearby university to help him. Together, they decided that all 25 salaried jobs should be in the same job evaluation cluster, that a modified ranking system of job evaluation should be used, and that the job descriptions recently completed by the HR director were current, accurate, and usable in the study.

The job evaluation showed that there was no evidence of serious inequities or discrimination in the non-management jobs, but that the HR director and the three female supervisors were being underpaid relative to comparable male salaried employees.

Blackenship was not sure what to do. He knew that if the underpaid supervisors took their case to the local pay equity commission, the company could be found guilty of sex discrimination and then have to pay considerable back wages. He was afraid that if he gave these women an immediate salary increase large enough to bring them up to where they should be, the male supervisors would be upset and the female supervisors might comprehend the total situation and want back pay. The HR director told Blackenship that the female supervisors had never complained about pay differences, and they probably did not know the law to any extent.

The HR director agreed to take a sizable salary increase with no back pay, so this part of the problem was solved. Blackenship believed that he had four choices relative to the female supervisors:

- Do nothing.
- Increase the female supervisors' salaries gradually.
- Increase their salaries immediately.
- Call the three supervisors into his office, discuss the situation with them, and jointly decide what to do.

QUESTIONS

1 What would you do if you were Blackenship?
2 How do you think the company got into a situation like this in the first place?

3 Why would you suggest that Blackenship pursue your suggested alternative?

Source: Based on a case prepared by Professor James C. Hodgetts of the Fogelman College of Business and Economics at the University of Memphis. All names are disguised. Used with permission.

MyManagementLab

Visit MyManagementLab to access a personalized Study Plan and additional study tools for this chapter.

 To view the CBC videos, read a summary, and answer discussion questions, go to MyManagementLab

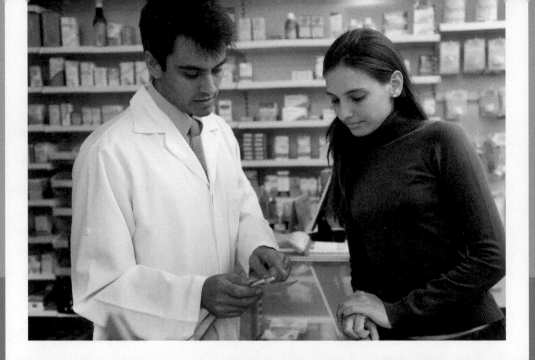

CHAPTER

12

Pay-for-Performance and Financial Incentives

|||||||||||||||||||||||||||||||||||||||||||||||

LEARNING OUTCOMES

AFTER STUDYING THIS CHAPTER, YOU SHOULD BE ABLE TO

DISCUSS how piecework and team or group incentive plans are used.

EXPLAIN how to use short-term and long-term incentives for managers and executives.

ANALYZE the main advantages and disadvantages of salary plans and commission plans for salespeople.

EXPLAIN why money is somewhat less important as an incentive for professional employees than it is for other employees.

COMPARE the three types of organization-wide incentive plans.

EXPLAIN under what conditions it is best to use an incentive plan.

ANALYZE the emerging emphasis on employee recognition.

|||||||||||||||||||||||||||||||||||||||||||||||||||||||||||||||||||||||

REQUIRED PROFESSIONAL CAPABILITIES (RPC)

- Monitors the competitiveness of the total compensation strategy on an ongoing basis

- Recommends the appropriate mix of base and variable compensation

- Recommends benefit plans most suited to organizational needs

MONEY AND MOTIVATION

fixed pay Compensation that is independent of the performance level of the individual, group, or organization.

variable pay Any plan that ties pay to productivity or profitability.

The use of financial incentives—financial rewards paid to workers whose production exceeds some predetermined standard—is not new; it was popularized by Frederick Taylor in the late 1800s. As a supervisory employee of the Midvale Steel Company, Taylor had become concerned with the tendency of employees to work at the slowest pace possible and produce at the minimum acceptable level. What especially intrigued him was the fact that some of these same workers still had the energy to run home and work on their cabins, even after a 12-hour day. Taylor knew that if he could find some way to harness this energy during the workday, huge productivity gains would be achieved.

Today's efforts to achieve the organization's strategy through motivated employees include fixed and variable compensation plans. **Fixed pay** represents compensation that is independent of the performance level of the individual, group, or organization. Fixed compensation includes base pay and other forms of relatively consistent compensation (for example, allowances) that satisfy the need for income stability. In contrast, **variable pay** represents any plan that links pay with productivity, profitability, or some other measure of organizational performance. Employers continue to increase their use of variable pay plans while holding salary increases or fixed compensation at modest levels. On average, organizations spend roughly 11 percent of total pay-related spending on variable pay-related expenses. More than 84 percent of Canadian employers have one or more types of variable pay plans in place.[1] As shown in **Figure 12.1**, cash bonuses or incentives are the most common form of short-term incentives, used in 87 percent of organizations that have short-term incentive plans in place.

Variable pay facilitates management of total compensation by keeping base pay inflation controlled. The fundamental premise of variable pay plans is that top performers must get top pay to secure their commitment to the organization. Thus, accurate performance appraisal or measurable outcomes is a precondition of effective pay-for-performance plans. Another important prerequisite for effective variable pay plans is "line of sight", or the extent to

FIGURE 12.1   Variable Pay Programs, 2011

Note: n = 323; percent based on organizations with at least one annual variable pay plan in place.

Figures do not add to 100 because some respondents have more than one plan.

Source: A. Cowan, *Compensation Planning Outlook 2011* (Ottawa, ON: Conference Board of Canada, 2010), p. 7. Reprinted by permission of The Conference Board of Canada, Ottawa.

which an employee can relate his or her daily work to the achievement of overall corporate goals. Employees need to understand corporate strategy and how their work as individual employees is important to the achievement of strategic objectives.[2]

The entire thrust of such programs is to treat workers like partners and get them to think of the business and its goals as their own. It is thus reasonable to pay them more like partners, too, by linking their pay more directly to performance. For example, the owners of a Surrey, British Columbia–based trucking company handed out bonus cheques totalling more than $400 000 to more than 400 employees in August 2005. Over the preceding five years, the owners had grown Coastal Pacific Xpress (CPX) by 500 percent and decided to reward their employees for their hard work.[3]

Types of Incentive Plans

There are several types of incentive plans. Individual incentive programs give income over and above base salary to individual employees who meet a specific individual performance standard. Informal incentives may be awarded, generally to individual employees, for accomplishments that are not readily measured by a standard, such as "to recognize the long hours that this employee put in last month," or "to recognize exemplary customer service this week." Group incentive programs are like individual incentive plans, but they provide payments over and above base salary to all team members when the group or team collectively meets a specified standard for performance, productivity, or other work-related behaviour. Organization-wide incentive plans provide monetary incentives to all employees of the organization. Examples are profit-sharing plans that provide employees with a share of the organization's profits in a specified period, and gainsharing programs designed to reward employees for improvements in organizational productivity. Finally, non-monetary recognition programs motivate employees through praise and expressions of appreciation for their work.

It is important to ensure that whatever incentive is being provided is appealing to the individual receiving it. Demographic factors can have an impact on what is appealing, as discussed in the Workforce Diversity box.

For simplicity, these plans will be discussed as follows: incentives for operations employees; incentives for senior managers and executives; incentives for salespeople; incentives primarily for other managers and professional employees (merit pay); and organization-wide incentives.

INCENTIVES FOR OPERATIONS EMPLOYEES

Piecework Plans

piecework A system of pay based on the number of items processed by each individual worker in a unit of time, such as items per hour or items per day.

Several incentive plans are particularly well suited for use with operations employees, such as those doing production work.[4] **Piecework** is the oldest incentive plan and still the most commonly used. Earnings are tied directly to what the worker produces—the person is paid a piece rate for each unit that he or she produces. Thus, if Tom Smith gets $0.40 per piece for stamping out door jambs, then he would make $40 for stamping out 100 a day and $80 for stamping out 200.

WORKFORCE DIVERSITY

Targeting Incentives for Life Stage

In developing incentive programs, which are targeted to job function and performance level, employers should also consider the demographics of their workforce. For instance, what motivates a Generation X employee may not have an impact on a Baby Boomer in the same company. Understanding each employee's life stage will help employers determine the most effective incentive program approach, which results in a workforce that is satisfied, engaged, and more likely to perform better and remain with the company.

Traditionalists (1922–1945): Rewards that work for traditionalists include flexible schedules that allow them to work seasonally or as time permits; health and fitness rewards that help them enjoy this life stage; and entertainment rewards that they would not purchase for themselves, such as computers and cell phones.

Boomers (1946–1964): Rewards that work for boomers include recognition and being appreciated for their work; travel rewards, such as adventure travel; and luxury and health-related awards, such as spas, high-end fitness equipment, and personal chefs.

Generation X (1965–1980): Rewards that work for this generation include gadgets and high-tech rewards that are state-of-the-art technology; work–life balance rewards, such as extra vacation days and onsite childcare; and flexibility to allow time for family, friends, and meaningful life experiences.

Generation Y (1981–2000): Rewards that work for this group (sometimes referred to as the millennium generation) include relationship enhancers, such as electronic communications equipment, home entertainment items, and dining experiences; personalized rewards where they can choose colours and accessories; and charitable rewards, like time off to volunteer for not-for-profit organizations and charitable donations made in their names.

Motivation is highly personal. Companies that provide rewards and recognition that are meaningful to employees based on their stage in the life cycle will be more successful in creating the right environment for maximum performance.

Source: Adapted from R. Stotz, "Targeting Employee Incentives for Maximum Performance," *Workspan* (June 2006), pp. 46–48. Reprinted with permission of WorldatWork, Scottsdale, AZ. www.worldatwork.org.

Developing a workable piece-rate plan requires both job evaluation and (usually) industrial engineering. Job evaluation enables firms to assign an hourly wage rate to the job in question. The crucial issue in piece-rate planning is the production standard, however, and this standard is usually developed by industrial engineers. Production standards are stated in terms of a standard number of minutes per unit or a standard number of units per hour. In Tom Smith's case, the job evaluation indicated that his door-jamb stamping job was worth $10 per hour. The industrial engineer determined that 20 jambs per hour was the standard production rate. Therefore, the piece rate (for each door jamb) was $10 ÷ 20 = $0.50 per door jamb.

straight piecework plan A set payment for each piece produced or processed in a factory or shop.

With a **straight piecework plan**, Tom Smith would be paid on the basis of the number of door jambs that he produced; there would be no guaranteed minimum wage. However, after passage of employment/labour standards legislation, it became necessary for most employers to guarantee their workers a minimum wage. With a **guaranteed piecework plan**, Tom Smith would be paid the minimum wage whether or not he stamped out the number of door jambs required to make minimum wage—for example, 18 pieces if minimum wage is $9 per hour. As an incentive he would, however, also be paid at the piece rate of $0.50 for each unit that he produced over the number required to make minimum wage.

guaranteed piecework plan The minimum hourly wage plus an incentive for each piece produced above a set number of pieces per hour.

"Piecework" generally implies straight piecework, a strict proportionality between results and rewards regardless of the level of output. Thus, in Smith's case, he continues to get $0.50 apiece for stamping out door jambs, even if he stamps out many more than planned (say, 500 per day). Other types of piecework incentive plans call for a sharing of productivity gains between worker and employer such that the worker does not receive full credit for all production above normal.[5]

differential piece-rate plan A plan by which a worker is paid a basic hourly rate plus an extra percentage of his or her base rate for production exceeding the standard per hour or per day. It is similar to piecework payment but is based on a percentage premium.

The **differential piece-rate plan** is like the standard piece-rate plan with one major difference: With a piece-rate plan, the worker is paid a particular rate for each piece that he or she produces; with the differential piece rate plan, the worker is rewarded by a *premium that equals the percentage by which his or her performance exceeds the standard*. The plan assumes the worker has a guaranteed base rate.

As an example, suppose that the base rate for Smith's job is $10 per hour. (The base rate may, but need not, equal the hourly rate determined by the job evaluation; however, it must meet or exceed the minimums established in the applicable Employment Standards Act.) Assume also that the production standard for Smith's job is 20 units per hour, or three minutes per unit. Suppose that in one day (eight hours) Smith produces 200 door jambs. According to the production standard, this should have taken Smith 10 hours (200 ÷ 20 per hour); instead it took him eight hours. He produced at a rate that was 25 percent higher than the standard rate. The standard rate would be eight hours × 20 (units per hour) = 160: Smith actually produced 40 more, for a total of 200. He will, therefore, be paid at a differential piece rate of 25 percent (40/160) above his base rate for the day. His base rate was $10 per hour times eight hours, which equals $80, so he will be paid 1.25 times $80, or $100 for the day.

Advantages and Disadvantages

Piecework incentive plans have several advantages. They are simple to calculate and easily understood by employees. Piece-rate plans appear equitable in principle, and their incentive value can be powerful since rewards are directly tied to performance.

Piecework also has some disadvantages. A main one is its somewhat unsavoury reputation among many employees, based on some employers' habits of arbitrarily raising production standards whenever they found their workers earning "excessive" wages. In addition, piece rates are stated in monetary terms (like $0.50 per piece). Thus, when a new job evaluation results in a new hourly wage rate, the piece rate must also be revised; this can be a big clerical chore. Another disadvantage is more subtle: Since the piece rate is quoted on a per-piece basis, in workers' minds production standards become tied inseparably to the amount of money earned. When an attempt is made to revise production standards it meets considerable worker resistance, even if the revision is fully justified.[6]

In fact, the industrial-engineered specificity of piecework plans represents the seeds of piecework's biggest disadvantage these days. Piecework plans tend to be tailor-made for relatively specialized jobs in which employees do basically the same narrow set of tasks over and over again many times a day. This, in turn, fosters a certain rigidity—employees become preoccupied with producing the number of units needed and are less willing to concern themselves with meeting quality standards or switching from job to job (since doing so could reduce the person's productivity).[7] Employees tend to be trained to perform only a limited number of tasks. Similarly, attempts to introduce new technology or innovative processes may be more likely to fail, insofar as they require major adjustments to engineered standards and negotiations with employees. Equipment tends not to be as well maintained, since employees are focusing on maximizing each machine's output.

The differential piece-rate plan has most of the advantages of the piecework plan and is fairly simple to compute and easy to understand. The incentive is expressed in units of time instead of in monetary terms (as it is with the standard piece-rate system). Therefore, there is less of a tendency on the part of workers to link their production standard with their pay. Furthermore, the clerical job of recomputing piece rates whenever hourly wage rates are re-evaluated is avoided.

Such problems as these have led some firms to drop their piecework plans and to substitute team-based incentive plans or programs, like gainsharing, which will be discussed later in this chapter.

Team or Group Incentive Plans

team or group incentive plan
A plan in which a production standard is set for a specific work group and its members are paid incentives if the group exceeds the production standard.

There are several ways in which to implement **team or group incentive plans**.[8] One is to set work standards for each member of the group and maintain a count of the output of each member. Members are then paid based on one of three formulas: (1) All members receive the pay earned by the highest producer; (2) all members receive the pay earned by the lowest producer; or (3) all members receive payment equal to the average pay earned by the group.

The second approach is to set a production standard based on the final output of the group as a whole; all members then receive the same pay, based on the piece rate that exists for the group's job. The group incentive can be based on either the piece rate or standard hour plan, but the latter is somewhat more prevalent.

A third option is to choose a measurable definition of group performance or productivity that the group can control. For instance, broad criteria, such as total labour hours per final product, could be used; piecework's engineered standards are thus not necessarily required here.[9]

There are several reasons to use team incentive plans. Sometimes, several jobs are interrelated, as they are on project teams. Here, one worker's performance reflects not only his or her own effort but that of co-workers as well; thus, team incentives make sense. Team plans also reinforce group planning and problem solving and help to ensure that collaboration takes place. In Japan, employees are rewarded as a group to reduce jealousy, make group members indebted to one another (as they would be to the group), and encourage a sense of cooperation. There tends to be less bickering among group members over who has "tight" production standards and who has "loose" ones. Group incentive plans also facilitate on-the-job training, since each member of the group has an interest in getting new members trained as quickly as possible.[10]

A group incentive plan's chief disadvantage is that each worker's rewards are no longer based solely on his or her own effort. To the extent that the person does not see his or her effort leading to the desired reward, a group plan may be less effective at motivating employees than an individual plan is.

Group incentive plans have been found to be more effective when there are high levels of communication with employees about the specifics of the plan, when there is strong worker involvement in the plan's design and implementation, and when group members perceive the plan as fair.[11]

INCENTIVES FOR SENIOR MANAGERS AND EXECUTIVES

Most employers award their senior managers and executives a bonus or an incentive because of the role they play in determining divisional and corporate profitability.[12]

Short-Term Incentives: The Annual Bonus

More than 90 percent of firms in Canada with variable pay plans provide an *annual bonus*.[13] Unlike salaries, which rarely decline with reduced performance, short-term incentive bonuses can easily result in an increase or decrease of up to 70 percent or more in total pay relative to the previous year. Three basic issues should be considered when awarding short-term incentives: eligibility, fund-size determination, and individual awards.

Jim Balsillie, former co-CEO of Research In Motion, received very high bonuses in addition to his regular compensation.

Eligibility

Eligibility is usually decided in one of three ways. The first criterion is *key position*. Here, a job-by-job review is conducted to identify the key jobs (typically only line jobs) that have a measurable impact on profitability. The second approach to determining eligibility is to set a *salary-level* cut-off point; all employees earning over that threshold amount are automatically eligible for consideration for short-term incentives. Finally, eligibility can be determined by *salary grade*. This is a refinement of the salary cut-off approach and assumes that all employees at a certain grade or above should be eligible for the short-term incentive program. The simplest approach is just to use salary level as a cut-off.[14]

The size of the bonus is usually greater for top-level executives. Thus, an executive earning $150 000 in salary may be able to earn another 80 percent of his or her salary as a bonus, while a manager in the same firm earning $80 000 can earn only another 30 percent. Similarly, a supervisor might be able to earn up to 15 percent of his or her base salary in bonuses. Average bonuses range from a low of 10 percent to a high of 80 percent or more: A typical company might establish a plan whereby executives could earn 45 percent of base salary, managers 25 percent, and supervisors 12 percent.

How Much to Pay Out (Fund Size)

Next, a decision must be made regarding the fund size—the total amount of bonus money that will be available—and there are several formulas to do this. Some companies use a *non-deductible formula*. Here a straight percentage (usually of the company's net income) is used to create the short-term incentive fund. Others use a *deductible formula* on the assumption that the short-term incentive fund should begin to accumulate only after the firm has met a specified level of earnings.

In practice, what proportion of profits is usually paid out as bonuses? In fact, there are no hard-and-fast rules about what an ideal payout size would be, and some firms do not even have a formula for developing the bonus fund. One alternative is to reserve a minimum amount of the profits, say 10 percent, for safeguarding shareholders' investments, and then to establish a fund for bonuses equal to 20 percent of the corporate operating profit before taxes in excess of this base amount. Thus, if the operating profits were $100 000, then the management bonus fund might be 20 percent of $90 000, or $18 000.

Determining Individual Awards

The third issue is determining the *individual awards* to be paid. In some cases, the amount is determined on a discretionary basis (usually by the employee's boss), but typically a target bonus is set for each eligible position and adjustments are then made for greater or less than targeted performance. A maximum amount, perhaps double the target bonus, may be set. Performance ratings are obtained for each manager, and preliminary bonus estimates are computed. Estimates for the total amount of money to be spent on short-term incentives are thereby made and compared with the bonus fund available. If necessary, the individual estimates are then adjusted.

A related question is whether managers will receive bonuses based on individual performance, team performance, corporate performance, or some combination of these. Keep in mind that there is a difference between a profit-sharing plan and a true individual incentive bonus. In a profit-sharing plan, each person gets a bonus based on the company's results, regardless of the person's actual effort. With a true individual incentive, it is the manager's individual effort and performance that are rewarded with a bonus.

Here, again, there are no hard-and-fast rules. Top-level executive bonuses are generally tied to overall corporate results (or divisional results if the executive is, say, the vice-president of a major division). The assumption is that corporate results reflect the person's individual performance. However, as one moves further down the chain of command, corporate profits become a less accurate gauge of a manager's contribution. For supervisory staff or the heads of functional departments, the person's individual performance, rather than corporate results, is a more logical determinant of his or her bonus.

Many experts argue that, in most organizations, managerial and executive-level bonuses should be tied to both organizational and individual performance, and there are several ways to do this.[15] Perhaps the simplest is the *split-award method*, which breaks the bonus into two parts. Here, the manager actually gets two separate bonuses, one based on his or her individual effort and one based on the organization's overall performance. Thus, a manager might be eligible for an individual performance bonus of up to $10 000 but receive an individual performance bonus of only $8 000 at the end of the year, based on his or her individual performance evaluation.

An Ethical ⋮ Dilemma

Is it ethical to provide potentially large bonuses to managers and executives on a purely discretionary basis, not necessarily related to performance?

RPC

Recommends benefit plans most suited to organizational needs

In addition, though, the person might also receive a second bonus of $8 000 based on the company's profits for the year. Thus, even if there were no company profits, the high-performing manager would still get an individual performance bonus.

One drawback to this approach is that it pays too much to the marginal performer, who, even if his or her own performance is mediocre, at least gets that second, company-based bonus. One way to get around this problem is to use the *multiplier method*. For example, a manager whose individual performance was "poor" might not even receive a company-performance-based bonus, on the assumption that the bonus should be a *product* of individual *and* corporate performance. When either is very poor, the product is zero.

Whichever approach is used, outstanding performers should get substantially larger awards than do other managers. They are people that the company cannot afford to lose, and their performance should always be adequately rewarded by the organization's incentive system. Conversely, marginal or below-average performers should never receive awards that are normal or average, and poor performers should be awarded nothing. The money saved on those people should be given to above-average performers.[16]

Long-Term Incentives

The Conference Board of Canada
www.conferenceboard.ca

Long-term incentives are intended to motivate and reward top management for the firm's long-term growth and prosperity and to inject a long-term perspective into executive decisions. If only short-term criteria are used, a manager could, for instance, increase profitability in one year by reducing plant maintenance; this tactic might, however, reduce profits over the next two or three years. This issue of long- versus short-term perspective has received considerable attention in the past several years as shareholders have become increasingly critical of management focus on short-term returns at the expense of long-term increase in share price. The deep economic recession that began in late 2008 following the sub-prime mortgage lending crisis resulted in increasing regulatory focus on this type of compensation.

capital accumulation programs
Long-term incentives most often reserved for senior executives.

Long-term incentives are also intended to encourage executives to stay with the company by giving them the opportunity to accumulate capital (in the form of company shares) based on the firm's long-term success. Long-term incentives, or **capital accumulation programs**, are most often reserved for senior executives but have more recently begun to be extended to employees at lower organizational levels.[17] Approximately 60 percent of Canadian private sector organizations provide long-term incentives. They are rarely provided to public sector employees.[18]

Some of the most common long-term incentive plans (for capital accumulation) in Canada are stock options, performance share unit plans, restricted share unit plans, and deferred share unit plans.[19] The popularity of these plans changes over time because of economic conditions and trends, internal company financial pressures, changing attitudes toward long-term incentives, and changes in tax law, as well as other factors. **Figure 12.2** illustrates the popularity of various long-term incentive plans.

stock option The right to purchase a stated number of shares of a company stock at today's price at some time in the future.

Stock Options

The **stock option** is the most popular long-term incentive in Canada, but its use is decreasing. Forty-six percent of organizations using long-term incentives provided

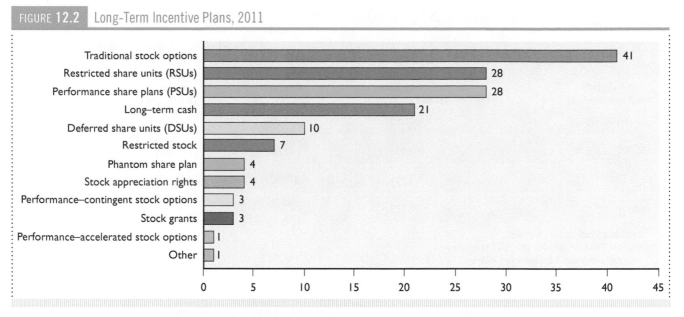

FIGURE 12.2   Long-Term Incentive Plans, 2011

Notes: n = 170; percent based on organizations with at least one LTIP in place.

Figures do not add to 100 because some respondents have more than one plan.

Source: A. Cowan, *Compensation Planning Outlook 2011* (Ottawa, ON: Conference Board of Canada, 2010), p. 11. Reprinted by permission of The Conference Board of Canada, Ottawa.

stock options in 2011, compared with 57 percent in 2005 and 72 percent in 2002.[20] A stock option is the right to purchase a specific number of shares of company stock at a specific price at some point in the future.

Often a vesting (waiting) period is required to ensure that the employee has contributed to any increase in stock price, which also aligns the stock option with the goal of long-term retention of talent. The executive thus hopes to profit by exercising his or her option to buy the shares in the future but at today's price. The assumption is that the price of the stock will go up rather than going down or staying the same. For example, if shares provided at an option price of $20 per share are exercised (bought) later for $20 when the market price is $60 per share and sold on the stock market when the market price is $80 per share, a cash gain of $60 per share results. The difference between fair market value of the stock at the time the option is sold and the amount paid by the employee to acquire it is treated as a taxable benefit. Often, the employee benefits since they are only required to pay capital gains tax on 50 percent of the gain. In comparison, from the employer's perspective, capital gains from cash incentive plans and stock purchase plans are taxed at full income inclusion levels. Thus, stock option plans are often seen as a cash windfall with no downside risk but unlimited upside potential.[21]

Unfortunately, stock price depends to a significant extent on considerations outside the executive's control, such as general economic conditions and investor sentiment. An executive performing valiantly in a declining market or troubled industry may receive nothing, since stock options are worthless if share prices don't rise. This is a particularly important concern in today's volatile stock market.[22] However, stock price is affected relative to the overall stock market by the firm's profitability and growth, and to the extent that the executive can affect these factors, the stock option can be an incentive.

FIGURE **12.3**   Distribution of Stock Option Deduction by Income, 2007

Individual's total income[1] ($)	Number of individuals claiming a stock option deduction	Stock option deduction claimed		
		Average amount ($)	Aggregate amount ($ millions)	% of total
Under 100,000	32,483	3,000	100	2%
100,000 to 500,000	38,034	23,000	890	22%
Over 500,000	7,985	393,000	3,140	75%
Total	78,502	53,000	4,130	100%

[1] Including stock option benefits
Source: Tax filer data for the 2007 taxation year.
Numbers may not add due to rounding.

Source: Archived - Annex 5: Tax Measures: Supplementary Information and Notices of Ways and Means Motions, http://www.budget.gc.ca/2010/plan/anx5-eng.html#a20, Department of Finance Canada, 2010. Reproduced with the permission of the Minister of Public Works and Government Services Canada, 2012.

As shown in **Figure 12.3**, stock options have traditionally been treated as a tool to attract and retain highly skilled workers. In 2007, the average stock option deduction was $53 000, with only 2 percent of claimants earning less than $100 000 per year and more than three-quarters of claimants earning more than $500 000 per year. One of the interesting trends in stock options as long-term incentives is that, increasingly, they are being used for non-managers and non-executives. PepsiCo, Starbucks, TELUS, and many other companies have broad-based stock option plans that include employees below the executive level. The trend toward broad-based plans is aimed at providing support for the competitive strategies being pursued by many firms today. Such companies have been asking more from employees than ever before, but employees often feel that they are corporate "partners" in name only, working harder but receiving little in return. In response,

> [c]ompanies are increasingly interested in drawing employees into the new deal by implementing broad-based stock option plans. By giving stock options to non-executives, companies make good the promise of letting employees share in the company's success.[23]

Proposals have been made to require that stock options be shown as an expense on company financial statements because the excessive issuing of options dilutes share values for shareholders and creates a distorted impression of the true value of a company. Guidelines used by the Canada Pension Plan Investment Board state the following:

> Stock options are a less effective and less efficient form of compensation than direct share ownership in aligning the interests of directors with those of shareholders, [and] it does not motivate the executive to enhance long-term corporate performance. Stock-based compensation is superior to option-based compensation plans for three broad reasons:
> - It provides better alignment of interest of employees with shareholders (across a wide range of future share prices);

- It is a more efficient form of compensation (in terms of the perceived value received by the executive); and

- It alters the capital structure in a more predictable way (with less potential dilution and more straightforward accounting treatment).[24]

Plans Providing Share "Units"

Although the use of stock options persists, a new approach based on providing "units" instead of stock has become increasingly common.[25] Executives are granted a specified number of units whose value is equal to (and fluctuates with) a company's share price, subject to certain conditions. A *performance share unit plan* provides units subject to the achievement of predetermined financial targets, such as profit or growth in earnings per share (often over a multiyear period). If the performance goals are met, then the value of the units is paid to the executive in cash or stock. The units have no value if the pre-established performance criteria are not met. In a *restricted share unit plan*, units are promised to the executive but will be forfeited if an executive leaves the company before a vesting period (typically three years). If the executive is still employed at the company after the vesting period, the full value of the units based on the current stock price is payable in cash or stock. In a *deferred share unit plan*, units are promised to the executive but are only payable when the executive leaves the company.

Relating Strategy to Executive Compensation

Executive compensation is more likely to be effective if it is appropriately linked to corporate strategy.[26] Few HR practices have as much connection to strategy as does how the company crafts its long-term incentives. Whether expanding sales through joint ventures abroad, consolidating operations and downsizing the workforce, or some other tactic, few strategies can be accomplished in just one or two years. As a result, the long-term signals that are sent to executives regarding the results and activities that will (or will not) be rewarded can have an impact on whether or not the firm's strategy is implemented effectively. For example, a strategy to boost sales by expanding abroad might suggest linking incentives to increased sales abroad. A cost-reduction strategy might instead emphasize linking incentives to improved profit margins.

Therefore, compensation experts suggest defining the strategic context for the executive compensation plan before creating the compensation package itself, as follows:[27]

1. Define the internal and external issues that face the company and its business objectives—boosting sales abroad, downsizing, and so on.

2. Based on the strategic aims, shape each component of the executive compensation package and then group the components into a balanced whole. Include a stock option plan to give the executive compensation package the special character it needs to meet the unique needs of the executives and the company.

3. Check the executive compensation plan for compliance with all legal and regulatory requirements and for tax effectiveness.

4. Install a process for reviewing and evaluating the executive compensation plan whenever a major business change occurs.

The Strategic HR box illustrates changes made in executive compensation at three of Canada's major banks as a result of the unexpected economic recession that began in late 2008.

STRATEGIC HR

Bank CEOs Take a Pay Cut

During the last recession, top executives at some of Canada's biggest banks took pay cuts in the face of falling stock prices and profits. In 2008, RBC CEO Gordon Nixon voluntarily turned down nearly $5 million in deferred shares and stock options. Before giving up these rewards, Nixon would have taken home $8.75 million in salary, bonus, and equity-based rewards. This was down from $10.9 million in 2007. RBC failed to meet most of its 2008 financial goals, and its annual profits dropped by 17 percent.

Scotiabank slashed CEO Rick Waugh's compensation package by 20 percent from $10.1 million in 2007 to $7.5 million in 2008. His base salary remained the same at $1 million, but his bonus was cut by nearly 70 percent to $500 000, which he took in deferred stock units. The bank's earnings per share fell by nearly one-quarter, and revenue dropped by 5.6 percent in 2008.

BMO Financial Group CEO William Downe received $6.38 million in total compensation in 2008, a 9.4 percent increase from 2007, but announced on February 2 that he was giving up both mid-term and long-term compensation worth $4.1 million.

The three banks are facing a proposal that would give shareholders a vote on executive compensation and a separate resolution calling for a comprehensive review of executive pay.

Source: Adapted from "Bank CEOs Take a Pay Cut," *Canadian HR Reporter* (February 3, 2009).

INCENTIVES FOR SALESPEOPLE

Sales compensation plans have typically relied heavily on incentives (sales commissions), although this varies by industry. In the real estate industry, for instance, salespeople are paid entirely via commissions, while in the pharmaceutical industry, salespeople tend to be paid a salary. However, the most prevalent approach is to use a combination of salary and commissions to compensate salespeople.[28]

Sales Compensation
www.davekahle.com/article/getem.html

The widespread use of incentives for salespeople is due to three factors: tradition, the unsupervised nature of most sales work, and the assumption that incentives are needed to motivate salespeople. The pros and cons of salary, commission, and combination plans follow.

Salary Plan

In a salary plan, salespeople are paid a fixed salary, although there may be occasional incentives in the form of bonuses, sales contest prizes, and the like. There are several reasons to use straight salary. It works well when the main sales objective is prospecting (finding new clients) or when the salesperson is mostly involved in account servicing, such as developing and executing product training programs for a distributor's sales force or participating in national and local trade shows.[29] Jobs like these are often found in industries that sell technical products. This is one reason why the aerospace and transportation equipment industries have a relatively heavy emphasis on salary plans for their salespeople.

There are advantages to paying salespeople on a straight salary basis. Salespeople know in advance what their income will be, and the employer also has fixed, predictable sales force expenses. Straight salary makes it simple to switch territories or quotas or to reassign salespeople, and it can develop a high degree of loyalty among the sales staff. Commissions tend to shift the salesperson's emphasis to making the sale rather than to prospecting and cultivating long-term customers. A long-term perspective is encouraged by straight salary compensation.

The main disadvantage is that salary plans do not depend on results.[30] In fact, salaries are often tied to seniority rather than to performance, which can be demotivating to potentially high-performing salespeople who see seniority—not performance—being rewarded.

Commission Plan

Commission plans pay salespeople in direct proportion to their sales—they pay for results and only for results. The commission plan has several advantages. Salespeople have the greatest possible incentive, and there is a tendency to attract high-performing salespeople who see that effort will clearly lead to rewards. Sales costs are proportional to sales rather than fixed, and the company's selling investment is reduced. The commission basis is also easy to understand and compute.

The commission plan also has drawbacks, however. Salespeople focus on making a sale and on high-volume items; cultivating dedicated customers and working to push hard-to-sell items may be neglected. Wide variances in income between salespeople may occur and this can lead to a feeling that the plan is inequitable. More serious is the fact that salespeople are encouraged to neglect other duties, like servicing small accounts. In addition, pay is often excessive in boom times and very low in recessions.

An Ethical Dilemma

Is it fair to compensate sales employees on a 100 percent commission basis with no financial security?

Research INSIGHT

Recent research evidence presents further insights into the impact of sales commissions. One study addressed whether paying salespeople on commission "without a financial net" might induce more salespeople to leave. The participants in this study were 225 field sales representatives from a telecommunications company. Results showed that paying salespeople a commission accounting for 100 percent of pay was the situation that resulted in the highest turnover of salespersons by far. Turnover was much lower in the situation in which salespeople are paid a combination of a base salary plus commissions.[31] These findings suggest that although 100 percent commissions can drive higher sales by focusing the attention of strong-willed salespeople on maximizing sales, without a financial safety net it can also undermine the desire of salespeople to stay.

The effects on the salesperson of a commission pay plan could also depend on that person's personality. A second study investigated 154 sales representatives who were responsible for contacting and renewing existing members and for identifying and adding new members. A number of the sales reps in this study were more extroverted than were the others—they were more sociable, outgoing, talkative, aggressive, energetic, and enthusiastic.[32] It might be expected that extroverted salespeople would usually generate higher sales than less extroverted ones, but in this study extroversion was positively associated with higher performance (in terms of percentage of existing members renewing their memberships and the count of new members paying membership fees) *only when the salespeople were explicitly rewarded for accomplishing these tasks.* Thus, being extroverted did not always lead to higher sales; extroverts only sold more than those less extroverted when their rewards were contingent on their performance.

Combination Plan

RPC

Recommends the appropriate mix of base and variable compensation

There has been a definite movement away from the extremes of straight commission or fixed salary to combination plans for salespeople. Combination plans provide some of the advantages of both straight salary and straight commission plans and also some of their disadvantages. Salespeople have a floor to their earnings. Furthermore, the company can direct its salespeople's activities by detailing what services the salary component is being paid for, while the commission component provides a built-in incentive for superior performance.

However, the salary component is not tied to performance, and the employer is therefore trading away some incentive value. Combination plans also tend to become complicated, and misunderstandings can result. This might not be a problem with a simple "salary plus commission" plan, but most plans are not so simple. For example, there is a "commission plus drawing account" plan, whereby a salesperson is paid basically on commissions but can draw on future earnings to get through low sales periods. Similarly, in the "commission plus bonus" plan, salespeople are again paid primarily on the basis of commissions, but they are also given a small bonus for directed activities, like selling slow-moving items.

An example can help to illustrate the complexities of the typical combination plan. In one company, the following three-step formula is applied:

- Step 1: Sales volume up to $18 000 a month—Base salary plus 7 percent of gross profits plus 0.5 percent of gross sales.
- Step 2: Sales volume from $18 000 to $25 000 a month—Base salary plus 9 percent of gross profits plus 0.5 percent of gross sales.
- Step 3: Sales volume more than $25 000 a month—Base salary plus 10 percent of gross profits plus 0.5 percent of gross sales.

In all cases, base salary is paid every two weeks, while the earned percentage of gross profits and gross sales is paid monthly. It should be remembered that setting sales goals or targets is complex and requires careful planning and analysis. Answers to such questions as why $18 000 and $25 000 were chosen as break points must be available.[33]

Tips :**FOR THE FRONT LINE**

The sales force also may get various special awards.[34] Trips and high-tech items such as BlackBerrys and iPhones are commonly used as sales prizes.

Sales Compensation in the E-commerce Era

Traditional product-based sales compensation focuses on the amount of product sold. In the Internet age, an integrated team of individuals works together to position the company with prospects, make sales, and service accounts. All sales team members work to deepen customer relationships. This new approach is due to the fact that, for customers who know what they want, rapid low-cost purchases can be made over the Internet. Face-to-face sales are now reserved for high-volume customers and higher-margin services.

Sales incentive plans now need to encourage the sales force to focus on the customer, integrate with e-commerce, and support rapid change. Cross-selling incentives (making multiple sales of different product lines to the same customer) are more important, along with incentives for relationship management and customer satisfaction. Experts recommend setting sales salaries at 50 to 75 percent of total expected compensation, plus incentives. A portion of the incentive should be tied to team-based sales results to encourage sharing, hand-offs, and peer pressure.[35]

INCENTIVES FOR OTHER MANAGERS AND PROFESSIONALS

merit pay (merit raise) Any salary increase awarded to an employee based on his or her individual performance.

Merit pay or a **merit raise** is any salary increase that is awarded to an employee based on his or her individual performance. It is different from a bonus in that it usually represents a continuing increment, whereas the bonus represents a one-time payment. Although the term "merit pay" can apply to the incentive raises given to any employees—office or factory, management or non-management—the term is more often used with respect to white-collar employees, and particularly professional, office, and clerical employees.

Merit pay has both advocates and detractors and is the subject of much debate.[36] Advocates argue that only pay or other rewards tied directly to performance can motivate improved performance. They contend that the effect of awarding identical pay raises to all employees (without regard to individual performance) may actually detract from performance by showing employees that they will be rewarded the same regardless of how they perform.

Conversely, merit pay detractors present good reasons why merit pay can backfire. One is that the usefulness of the merit pay plan depends on the validity of the performance appraisal system, because if performance appraisals are viewed as unfair, so too will the merit pay that is based on them. Second, supervisors often tend to minimize differences in employee performance when computing merit raises. They give most employees about the same raise, either because of a reluctance to alienate some employees or a desire to give everyone a raise that will at least help them to stay even with the cost of living. A third problem is that almost every employee thinks that he or she is an above-average performer; being paid a below-average merit increase can thus be demoralizing. Finally, some believe that merit pay pits employees against each other and harms team spirit.[37]

However, although problems like these can undermine a merit pay plan, the consensus of opinion is that merit pay can and does improve performance. It is critical, however, that performance appraisals be carried out effectively.[38]

Traditional merit pay plans have two basic characteristics: (1) Merit increases are usually granted to employees at a designated time of the year in the form of a higher base salary (or *raise*); and (2) the merit raise is usually based exclusively on individual performance, although the overall level of company profits may affect the total sum available for merit raises.[39] In some cases, merit raises are awarded in a single lump sum once a year, without changing base salary. Occasionally, awards are tied to both individual and organizational performance.

Incentives for Professional Employees

Professional employees are those whose work involves the application of learned knowledge to the solution of the employer's problems. They include lawyers, doctors, economists, and engineers. Professionals almost always reach their positions through prolonged periods of formal study.[40]

Pay decisions regarding professional employees involve unique problems. One is that, for most professionals, money has historically been somewhat less important as an incentive than it has been for other employees. This is true partly because professionals tend to be paid well anyway and partly because they are already driven by the desire to produce high-calibre work and receive recognition from colleagues.

However, that is not to say that professionals do not want financial incentives. For example, studies in industries like pharmaceuticals and aerospace consistently show that firms with the most productive research and development groups have incentive pay plans for their professionals, usually in the form of bonuses. However, professionals' bonuses tend to represent a relatively small portion of their total pay. The time cycle of the professionals' incentive plans also tends to be longer than a year, reflecting the long time spent in designing, developing, and marketing a new product.

There are also many non-salary items that professionals must have to do their best work. Not strictly incentives, these items range from better equipment and facilities and a supportive management style to support for professional journal publications.

ORGANIZATION-WIDE INCENTIVE PLANS

Many employers have incentive plans in which virtually all employees can participate. These include profit-sharing, employee stock ownership, and gain-sharing plans.

Profit-Sharing Plans

profit-sharing plan A plan whereby most or all employees share in the company's profits.

In a **profit-sharing plan,** most or all employees receive a share of the company's profits. Fewer than 15 percent of Canadian organizations offer profit-sharing plans.[41] These plans are easy to administer and have a broad appeal to employees and other company stakeholders. In addition to helping attract, retain, and motivate workers, profit-sharing plans have tax advantages for employees, including tax deferrals and income splitting. The main weakness of profit-sharing plans is "line of sight." It is unlikely that most employees perceive that they personally have the ability to influence overall company profit. It has been found that these plans produce a one-time productivity improvement but no change thereafter. Another weakness of these plans is that they typically provide an annual payout, which is not as effective as more frequent payouts.[42]

There are several types of profit-sharing plans. In *cash plans*, the most popular, a percentage of profits (usually 15 to 20 percent) is distributed as profit shares at regular intervals. One example is Atlas-Graham Industries in Winnipeg. There, a profit-sharing pool is calculated by deducting 2 percent of sales from pre-tax profit and then taking 30 percent of the result. The pool is distributed equally among all employees. Other plans provide cash and deferred benefits. Fisheries Products International in St. John's, Newfoundland, contributes 10 percent of pre-tax income to a profit-sharing pool that is divided up, just before Christmas, based on each employee's earnings. The first 75 percent of each employee's share is paid in cash, and the remaining 25 percent is allocated to pension plan improvements.[43]

Employee Share Purchase/Stock Ownership Plan

employee share purchase/stock ownership plan (ESOP) A plan whereby a trust is established to hold shares of company stock purchased for or issued to employees. The trust distributes the stock to employees on retirement, separation from service, or as otherwise prescribed by the plan.

Employee share purchase/stock ownership plans (ESOPs) are in place at approximately 60 percent of Canadian organizations with publicly traded stock.[44] A trust is established to purchase shares of the firm's stock for employees by using cash from employee (and sometimes employer) contributions. Employers may also issue treasury shares to the trust instead of paying cash for a purchase on the open market. The trust holds the stock in individual employee accounts and distributes it to employees, often on retirement or other separation from service. Some plans distribute the stock to employees once a year.

The corporation receives a tax deduction equal to the fair market value of the shares that are purchased by the trustee by using employer contributions, but not for any treasury shares issued. The value of the shares purchased with employer contributions, and of any treasury shares issued, is a taxable benefit to the employees in the year of purchase of the shares. This tax treatment can create two problems. First, if the plan requires employees to complete a certain period of service before taking ownership of the shares and the employee leaves before being eligible for ownership, the employee has paid tax on the value of shares that he or she never owns. Therefore, most plans have immediate vesting.[45] Second, if the value of the shares drops, employees may have paid tax on a greater amount than they will receive when they eventually sell the shares.

Hints : TO ENSURE LEGAL COMPLIANCE

National Center for Employee Ownership **www.nceo.org**

ESOPs can encourage employees to develop a sense of ownership in and commitment to the firm, particularly when combined with good communication, employee involvement in decision making, and employee understanding of the business and the economic environment.[46] For example, one employee at Creo, a digital products company in Burnaby, British Columbia, that offers an ESOP said, "It's not just the shares. It's the way of thinking. I'm extremely happy here."[47]

Gainsharing Plans

gainsharing plan An incentive plan that engages employees in a common effort to achieve productivity objectives and share the gains.

A **gainsharing plan** is an incentive plan that engages many or all employees in a common effort to achieve a company's productivity objectives; any resulting incremental cost-saving gains are shared among employees and the company.[48] Popular types of gainsharing plans include the Rucker and improshare plans.

The basic difference between these plans is in the formula used to determine employee bonuses.[49] The Rucker formula uses sales value minus materials and supplies, all divided into payroll expenses. It includes participative management systems that use committees. The improshare plan creates production standards for each department. It does not include a participative management component but instead considers participation an outcome of the bonus plan.

The financial aspects of a gainsharing program can be quite straightforward. Assume that a supplier wants to boost quality. Doing so would translate into fewer customer returns, less scrap and rework, and therefore higher profits. Historically, $1 million in output results in $20 000 (2 percent) scrap, returns, and rework. The company tells its employees that if next month's production results in only 1 percent scrap, returns, and rework, the 1 percent saved would be a gain to be split 50/50 with the workforce, less a small amount reserved for months in which scrap exceeds 2 percent. Awards are often posted monthly but allocated quarterly.[50]

Gainsharing works well in stable organizations with predictable goals and measures of performance, but is less flexible and useful in dynamic industries that require rapid business adjustment. In general, most of their cost savings are generated in the early years.[51] For example, in 2011, US Airways announced that its employees would receive profit-sharing payouts totalling more than $47 million associated with the previous year's financial performance success. US Airways' chair and chief executive officer, Doug Parker, said, "Thank you and congratulations to our professional team members on an outstanding 2010. Our team ran a safe, reliable airline in 2010, completing more scheduled flights and delivering baggage more reliably than our network peers. Our customers have noticed the turnaround and our financial results reflect these positive results." Individual employee payouts vary by the employee's base salary and collective bargaining agreement. In addition, US Airways' employees also received more than $25 million in operational incentive bonuses and individual employee recognition rewards in 2010.[52]

DEVELOPING EFFECTIVE INCENTIVE PLANS

There are two major practical considerations in developing an effective incentive plan: when to use it and how to implement it.

When to Use Incentives

Before deciding to implement an incentive plan, it is important to remember several points:

1. *Performance pay cannot replace good management.* Performance pay is supposed to motivate workers, but lack of motivation is not always the culprit. Ambiguous instructions, lack of clear goals, inadequate employee selection and training, unavailability of tools, and a hostile workforce (or management) are just a few of the factors that impede performance.

2. *Firms get what they pay for.* Psychologists know that people often put their effort where they know they will be rewarded. However, this can backfire. An incentive plan that rewards a group based on how many pieces are produced could lead to rushed production and lower quality. Awarding a plant-wide incentive for reducing accidents may simply reduce the number of reported accidents.

3. *"Pay is not a motivator."*[53] Psychologist Frederick Herzberg makes the point that money only buys temporary compliance; as soon as the incentive is removed, the "motivation" disappears too. Instead, Herzberg says, employers should provide adequate financial rewards and then build other motivators, like opportunities for achievement and psychological success, into their jobs.

4. *Rewards rupture relationships.* Incentive plans have the potential for reducing teamwork by encouraging individuals (or individual groups) to blindly pursue financial rewards for themselves.

5. *Rewards may undermine responsiveness.* Since the employees' primary focus is on achieving some specific goal, like cutting costs, any changes or extraneous distractions mean that achieving that goal will be harder. Incentive plans can, therefore, mediate against change and responsiveness.

Research by two professors at the University of Alberta focused on resolving a longstanding debate about whether extrinsic rewards can backfire by reducing intrinsic motivation, or whether extrinsic rewards boost performance and enhance intrinsic motivation. The authors concluded that *careful* management of rewards does enhance performance. Common problem areas to be avoided include not tying rewards to performance, not delivering on all rewards initially promised, and delivering rewards in an authoritarian style or manner.[54]

Potential pitfalls like these do not mean that financial incentive plans cannot be useful or should not be used. They do suggest, however, that goals need to be reasonable and achievable, but not so easily attained that employees view incentives as entitlements.[55] In general, any incentive plan is more apt to succeed if implemented with management support, employee acceptance, and a supportive culture characterized by teamwork, trust, and involvement at all levels.[56] This probably helps to explain why some of the longest-lasting incentive plans, like the improshare and Rucker plans, depend heavily on two-way communication and employee involvement in addition to incentive pay.

Therefore, in general, it makes more sense to use an incentive plan when units of output can be measured, the job is standardized, the workflow is regular, and delays are few or consistent. It is also important that there be a clear relationship between employee effort and quantity of output and that quality is less important than quantity, or, if quality is important, that it is easily measured and controlled.

How to Implement Incentive Plans

There are several specific common-sense considerations in establishing any incentive plan. Of primary importance is "line of sight." The employee or group must be able to see their own impact on the goals or objectives for which incentives are being provided.[57]

Research indicates that there are seven principles that support effective implementation of incentive plans that lead to superior business results:

Tips : **FOR THE FRONT LINE**

1. Pay for performance—and make sure that performance is tied to the successful achievement of critical business goals.

2. Link incentives to other activities that engage employees in the business, such as career development and challenging opportunities.

3. Link incentives to measurable competencies that are valued by the organization.

4. Match incentives to the culture of the organization—its vision, mission, and operation principles.

5. Keep group incentives clear and simple—employee understanding is the most important factor differentiating effective from ineffective group incentive plans.

6. Overcommunicate—employees become engaged when they hear the message that they are neither faceless nor expendable.

7. Remember that the greatest incentive is the work itself. For example, highly skilled engineers at MacDonald Dettwiler and Associates Ltd. in Richmond, British Columbia, feel valued and appreciated when they are chosen by their peers to work on project teams, to work on the Canada space arm, or to work on a project to save the rainforest, and they don't require large financial incentives to work hard.

EMPLOYEE RECOGNITION PROGRAMS

In today's fast-changing environment, recognition is emerging as a critical component of the total rewards mix.[59] Why? Because lack of recognition and praise is the number one reason that employees leave an organization. The traditional role of recognition plans has been to reward employees for long service, but today's employees value being appreciated by an employer throughout their career. In fact, recent Japanese research has shown that people get as excited about receiving a compliment as they do about receiving a cash reward because both activate the same reward centre in the brain (the striatum).[60]

An employee's introduction to a corporate recognition culture needs to start on the day he or she is hired. For example, the employee could receive a welcome note, a nameplate, and a personalized gift pack that includes a company T-shirt and coffee mug. These things are all very easy to do, and they send a clear message to a new employee.[61] Recognition and other simple incentives are particularly effective in smaller entrepreneurial companies, as explained in the Entrepreneurs and HR box.

Employees consistently say that they receive little recognition. One study found that only 50 percent of managers give recognition for high performance, and that up to 40 percent of workers feel that they never get recognized for outstanding performance. Nurses are one group of employees that has long suffered from lack of respect. They feel ignored and undervalued as subservient assistants to doctors. The shortage of nurses in Canada has forced employers to consider treating nurses with the respect and recognition they deserve as invaluable contributors of knowledge and skills to the healthcare system.[62]

ENTREPRENEURS and HR

Recognition and Incentives for Entrepreneurs

Entrepreneurs may not have the time or money to provide many formal incentive programs. But there are many other approaches they can use to motivate employees toward achieving the strategic objectives of the organization. There are three guides to follow.

First, the best option for motivating employees is also the simplest—make sure the employee has a doable goal and that he or she agrees with it. It makes little sense to try to motivate employees in other ways (such as with financial incentives) if they don't know their goals or don't agree with them. Psychologist Edwin Locke and his colleagues have consistently found that specific, challenging goals lead to higher task performance than specific, unchallenging goals or vague goals or no goals. The best goals are SMART goals—specific, measurable, attainable, relevant, and timely.

Second, recognizing an employee's contribution is a simple and powerful motivational tool. Studies show that recognition has a positive impact on performance, either alone or in combination with financial rewards. For example, in one study, combining financial rewards with recognition produced a 30 percent performance increase in service firms, almost twice the effect of using each reward alone.

Third, there are numerous positive reinforcement rewards that can be used on a day-to-day basis,

independent of formal incentive plans. A short list would include the following:

- challenging work assignments
- freedom to choose own work activity
- having fun built into work
- more of a preferred task
- role as boss' stand-in when he or she is away
- role in presentations to top management
- job rotation
- encouragement of learning and continuous improvement
- being provided with ample encouragement
- being allowed to set own goals
- compliments
- expression of appreciation in front of others
- note of thanks
- employee-of-the-month award
- special commendation
- bigger desk
- bigger office or cubicle

Source: E.A. Locke & G.P. Latham, *A Theory of Goal Setting and Task Performance* (Englewood Cliffs NJ: Prentice Hall, 1990); R. Nelson, *1001 Ways to Reward Employees* (New York, NY: Workmen Publishing, 1994), p. 19; S.J. Peterson & F. Luthans, "The Impact of Financial and Nonfinancial Incentives on Business Unit Outcomes Over Time," *Journal of Applied Psychology*, 91, no. 1 (2006) pp. 156–165.

Recognition Plus, Inc.
www.recognitionplusinc.com

Recognition Professionals International
www.recognition.org

O.C. Tanner Recognition Co.
www.octanner.ca

Some believe that this lack of recognition occurs because expressing generous appreciation means talking about feelings in public, which may make managers feel vulnerable. However, when lack of recognition and praise is resulting in the loss of valued employees, managers need to confront such apprehension and start recognizing their employees for their achievements. Why? Because employees favour recognition from supervisors and managers by a margin of two-to-one over recognition from other sources.[63] Thus, line managers are critical to the success of recognition programs.

Recognition is also cost-effective. It takes 5 to 15 percent of pay to have an impact on behaviour when a cash reward is provided, but only 3 to 5 percent when a non-cash form of reward is used (such as recognition and modest gifts).[64] Company DNA, an incentives provider, offers an online points system where recognition points can be spent on merchandise with merchant partners, such as Eddie Bauer, La Senza, Canadian Tire, and Future Shop.[65] There appears to be a growing interest by employees in having recognition awards linked to "green" or charitable causes, such as time off for volunteering.[66] The most common recognition awards are shown in **Figure 12.4.**

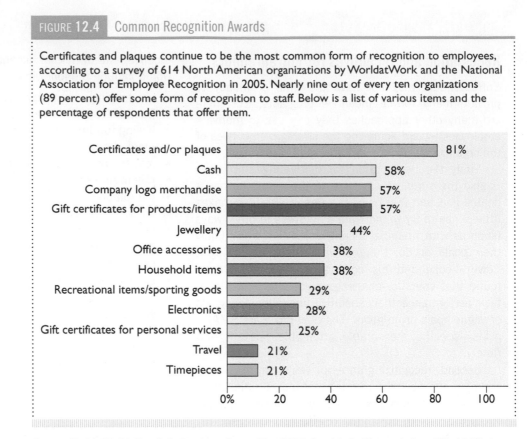

FIGURE **12.4**   Common Recognition Awards

Certificates and plaques continue to be the most common form of recognition to employees, according to a survey of 614 North American organizations by WorldatWork and the National Association for Employee Recognition in 2005. Nearly nine out of every ten organizations (89 percent) offer some form of recognition to staff. Below is a list of various items and the percentage of respondents that offer them.

Item	Percentage
Certificates and/or plaques	81%
Cash	58%
Company logo merchandise	57%
Gift certificates for products/items	57%
Jewellery	44%
Office accessories	38%
Household items	38%
Recreational items/sporting goods	29%
Electronics	28%
Gift certificates for personal services	25%
Travel	21%
Timepieces	21%

Source: WorldatWork's Trends in Employee Recognition 2005. Reprinted with permission of WorldatWork, Scottsdale, AZ. www.worldatwork.org.

Effective recognition is specific, immediate, personal, and spontaneous. Making time to recognize the individual in front of his or her colleagues is critical to the success of the program. Personal attention and public celebration create recognition that is personal in nature and that addresses the deep needs that we all have for belonging and contributing to something worthwhile. By making it memorable, the recognition experience will continue to evoke emotion and make the employee feel that his or her individual effort made a difference.

Recognition programs are more effective than cash in achieving improved employee attitudes, increased workloads and hours of work, and improved productivity (speed of work/intensity of work). They can build confidence, create a positive and supportive environment, build a sense of pride in accomplishments, inspire people to increase their efforts, and help people feel valued. Recognition can act as a strategic change effort if recognition criteria are aligned with business strategy, employee input is solicited regarding program design and implementation, and a recognition culture is created.[67]

Recognition is also important for high performers, who focus on what needs to be done to exceed expectations. These employees are driven by internal motivation and look to reward programs to add fuel to their achievements. Recognition satisfies "wants" rather than "needs" (where cash bonuses often go); such programs eliminate guilt about owning luxury items, provide bragging rights, and create a lasting impression in the employee's memory.[68]

Finally, recognition programs are key corporate communication tools that can achieve several goals—saying thank you, encouraging good workers, and encouraging behaviour that supports strategic objectives.[69] RBC Financial Group, Fairmont Hotels and Resorts, Research In Motion, Procor Limited, Montana's Cookhouse, Minto Developments Inc., Alberta Milk, Southland Transportation, and Snow Valley Edmonton are just some of the Canadian companies that are reaping the benefits of employee recognition programs.[70]

Chapter SUMMARY

1. Piecework is the oldest type of incentive plan. Here, a worker is paid a piece rate for each unit that he or she produces. The differential piece-rate plan rewards workers by a premium that equals the percentage by which their performance is above standard. Group incentive plans are useful when the workers' jobs are highly interrelated.

2. Most management employees receive a short-term incentive, usually in the form of an annual bonus linked to company or divisional profits. Long-term incentives are intended to motivate and reward top management for the firm's long-term growth and prosperity and to inject a long-term perspective into executive decisions.

3. Salary plans for salespeople are effective when the main sales objective is finding new clients or servicing accounts. The main disadvantage of salary plans is that pay is not tied to performance. Commission plans attract high-performing salespeople who see that performance will clearly lead to rewards. The problem with straight commission plans is that there is a tendency to focus on "big-ticket" or "quick-sell" items and to disregard long-term customer relationships.

4. Money is somewhat less important as an incentive for professional employees than it is for other employees; professionals are already driven by the desire to produce high-calibre work, and the time cycle of professionals' incentive plans tends to be longer than one year, reflecting time for research, design, and development of new products and services. Professionals seek recognition and support in the form of the latest equipment and support for journal publications.

5. Profit-sharing plans, employee share purchase/stock ownership plans, and gainsharing plans are examples of organization-wide incentive plans. Profit-sharing plans provide a share of company profits to all employees in the organization. The problem with such plans is that sometimes the link between a person's efforts and rewards is unclear. Stock purchase plans provide a vehicle for employees to purchase company stock with their own and sometimes employer contributions. Gainsharing plans engage employees in a common effort to achieve a company's productivity objectives in which incremental cost savings are shared among employees and the company. All these plans are intended to increase employee commitment toward the organization and are ultimately designed to motivate workers.

6. Incentive plans are particularly appropriate when units of output are easily measured, employees can control output, the effort–reward relationship is clear, work delays are under employees' control, and quality is not paramount.

7. Employee recognition plans are growing in popularity as a cost-effective method of retaining employees by praising their achievements. Recognition has the most impact when it is sincerely and meaningfully provided by the supervisor in a public presentation format.

MyManagementLab

Visit MyManagementLab to access a personalized Study Plan and additional study tools for this chapter.

Key TERMS

capital accumulation programs *(p. 330)*

differential piece-rate plan *(p. 326)*

employee share purchase/stock ownership plan (ESOP) *(p. 339)*

fixed pay *(p. 323)*

gainsharing plan *(p. 339)*

guaranteed piecework plan *(p. 325)*

merit pay (merit raise) *(p. 337)*

piecework *(p. 324)*

profit-sharing plan *(p. 338)*

stock option *(p. 330)*

straight piecework plan *(p. 325)*

team or group incentive plan *(p. 327)*

variable pay *(p. 323)*

Review and Discussion QUESTIONS

1. Describe why it is important to consider employee life stage when developing incentive plans.

2. Describe the three basic issues to be considered when awarding short-term management bonuses.

3. Explain how stock options work. What are some of the reasons that stock options have been criticized in recent years?

4. When and why should a salesperson be paid a salary? A commission? Salary and commission combined?

5. Explain five reasons why incentive plans fail.

6. Why are recognition plans useful for motivating high performers? Identify the possible reasons why the top forms of recognition shown in Figure 12.4 are the most frequently used.

Critical Thinking QUESTIONS

1. A major consulting firm recently launched a new "project managers' incentive" plan. Basically, senior managers in the company were told to award $5000 raises (not bonuses) to about 40 percent of the project managers in their team based on how good of a job they did in managing people on their projects, meeting deadlines, and the number of projects each project manager was responsible for that year. There were no additional criteria provided, given the wide variance in projects and teams that the consulting firm secures in a given year. What are the potential advantages and pitfalls of such an incentive program? What areas of support or concern do you think project managers might have with the incentives? What areas of support or concern do you think senior managers might have with the incentives?

2. Is it ethical for companies to offer incentive bonuses only to top managers? Why or why not? What are the pros and cons of making such bonuses available to all employees who meet performance criteria?

3. Do you think that it is a good idea to award employees with merit raises? Why or why not? If not, what approach would you take to incentive compensation?

4. In this chapter, we listed a number of reasons that experts give for not instituting a pay-for-performance plan in a vacuum (such as "rewards rupture relationships"). Do you think that these points (or any others) are valid? Why or why not?

5. Recognition can take many forms. Prepare a list of some forms of recognition that would be particularly motivational for Generation Y employees and explain why you have chosen them.

6. Think of organizations that have been in the news in the last few years because of scandals. Which of these involved incentives? What were the problems and how could they have been avoided?

Experiential EXERCISES

1. Working individually or in groups, develop an incentive plan for each of the following positions: web designer, hotel manager, and used-car salesperson. What factors had to be taken into consideration?

2. Employee recognition plans are growing in popularity. There has been some debate in research literature suggesting that once incentives are provided, they are viewed as entitlements by employees and therefore become non-removable. Assume that you are working for your local university or college in the HR department. Due to financial restraints, it has been suggested that the university eliminate a $5000 gift certificate award offered to professors who publish in specific top-tier journals (which cost the university $225 000 last year alone). Interview two professors in your university or college to understand their position on the incentive. Based on the information provided in this chapter and your interviews, draft a memo targeted to faculty assuming you were forced to adopt the cut and effectively communicate the change.

3. Express Automotive, an automobile mega-dealership with more than 600 employees that represents 22 brands, has just received a very discouraging set of survey results. It seems its customer satisfaction scores have fallen for the ninth straight quarter. Customer complaints included the following:

   - It was hard to get prompt feedback from mechanics by phone.
   - Salespeople often did not return phone calls.
   - The finance people seemed "pushy."
   - New cars were often not properly cleaned or had minor items that needed immediate repair or adjustment.
   - Cars often had to be returned to have repair work redone.

Team	Responsibility	Current Compensation Method
Sales force	Persuade buyers to purchase a car.	Very small salary (minimum wage) with commissions; commission rate increases with every 20 cars sold per month.
Finance office	Help close the sale; persuade customer to use company finance plan.	Salary, plus bonus for each $10 000 financed with the company.
Detailing	Inspect cars delivered from factory, clean them, and make minor adjustments.	Piecework paid on the number of cars detailed per day.
Mechanics	Provide factory warranty service, maintenance, and repair.	Small hourly wage, plus bonus based on (1) number of cars completed per day and (2) finishing each car faster than the standard estimated time to repair.
Receptionists/ phone service personnel	Act as primary liaison between customer and sales force, finance, and mechanics.	Minimum wage.

The table on the previous page describes Express Automotive's current compensation system.

The class is to be divided into five groups. Each group is assigned to one of the five teams in column one. Each group should analyze the compensation package for its team. Each group should be able to identify the ways in which the current compensation plan (1) helps company performance or (2) impedes company performance. Once the groups have completed their analyses, the following questions are to be discussed as a class:

a. In what ways might your group's compensation plan contribute to the customer service problems?

b. Do the rewards provided by your department impede the work of other departments?

c. What recommendations would you make to improve the compensation system in a way that would likely improve customer satisfaction?

4. Working in groups, brainstorm ways in which a company that previously provided generous incentive pay and bonuses might provide less costly incentives to encourage employee commitment and productivity in recessionary times when company revenues are falling. Create a communications plan to announce the changes to employees who may have come to expect and rely on these incentives. Critique your plan from the employee perspective.

Running CASE

Running Case: LearnInMotion.com

The Incentive Plan

Of all its HR programs, those relating to pay for performance and incentives are LearnInMotion's most fully developed. For one thing, the venture capital firm that funded it was very explicit about reserving at least 10 percent of the company's stock for employee incentives. The agreement with the venture capital firm also included very explicit terms and conditions regarding LearnInMotion's stock option plan. The venture fund agreement included among its 500 or so pages the specific written agreement that LearnInMotion.com would have to send to each of its employees, laying out the details of the company's stock option plan.

Although there was some flexibility, the stock option plan details came down to this:

1. Employees would get stock options (the right to buy shares of LearnInMotion stock) at a price equal to 15 percent less than the venture capital fund paid for those shares when it funded LearnInMotion.com.

2. The shares will have a vesting schedule of 36 months, with one-third of the shares vesting once the employee has completed 12 full months of employment with the company, and one-third vesting on successful completion of each of the following two full 12-month periods of employment.

3. If an employee leaves the company for any reason before his or her first full 12 months with the firm, the person is not eligible for stock options.

4. If the person has stock options and leaves the firm for any reason, he or she must exercise the options within 90 days of the date of leaving the firm or lose the right to exercise them.

5. The actual number of options an employee gets depends on the person's bargaining power and on how much Jennifer and Pierre think the person brings to the company. The options granted generally ranged from options to buy 10 000 shares for some employees up to 50 000 shares for others, but this has not raised any questions to date. When a new employee signs

on, he or she receives a letter of offer. This provides minimal details regarding the option plan; after the person has completed the 90-day introductory period, he or she receives the five-page document describing the stock option plan, which Jennifer or Pierre, as well as the employee, sign.

Beyond that, the only incentive plan is the one for the two salespeople. In addition to their respective salaries, both salespeople receive about 20 percent of any sales they bring in, whether those sales are from advertising banners or course listing fees. It's not clear to Jennifer and Pierre whether this incentive is effective. Each sales-person gets a base salary regardless of what he or she sells (one gets about $50 000, the other about $35 000). However, sales have simply not come up to the levels anticipated.

Jennifer and Pierre are not sure why. It could be that Internet advertising has dried up. It could be that their own business model is no good or there's not enough demand for their company's services. They may be charging too much or too little.

It could be that the salespeople can't do the job because of inadequate skills or inadequate training. Or, of course, it could be the incentive plan. ("Or it could be all of the above," as Pierre somewhat dejectedly said late one Friday evening.) They want to try to figure out what the problem is. They want you, their management consultant, to help them figure out what to do.

QUESTIONS

1   Is LearnInMotion's current compensation program motivating their staff? Or is it hindering employee performance?

2   Should LearnInMotion use a mix of individual, team, and organizational incentives? If so, recommend specific incentives that the company should use and discuss why you recommended each.

3   Do you think changing the compensation strategy will positively affect this firm? If so, how specifically?

Case INCIDENT

A New Compensation Program to Motivate Performance

Marilyn Brown started her chain of 10 wedding boutiques approximately five years ago. She presently operates within southwestern Ontario and has been enjoying record profits. Marilyn's wedding boutiques provide full-service amenities to future brides, including wedding planning services, custom fittings, and locating hard-to-find wedding dresses.

Marilyn's customer service philosophy is that customers are number one and must be satisfied with their purchases. However, recently, there has been a rise in complaints regarding the lack of friendly service being provided, and three long-standing employees have threatened to leave unless

their compensation is adjusted in response to servicing Marilyn's very demanding clients. Currently, Marilyn pays all of her staff the same base salary of $14 per hour without any benefits. Marilyn feels that this approach promotes equity and eliminates any perceptions of favouritism between employees regarding compensation.

Since receiving the negative complaints and the threats of some of her staff leaving, Marilyn has decided she needs to rethink her compensation philosophy and needs your help.

QUESTIONS

1   What are the specific problems with Marilyn's current compensation program?

2   Discuss the types of compensation programs and plans available to Marilyn to motivate and retain her existing staff.

3   Should Marilyn use only one type of compensation plan, or a combination plan for her employees? Discuss your recommendation in detail.

MyManagementLab

Visit MyManagementLab to access a personalized Study Plan and additional study tools for this chapter.

To view the CBC videos, read a summary, and answer discussion questions, go to MyManagementLab

CHAPTER

13

Employee Benefits and Services

LEARNING OUTCOMES

AFTER STUDYING THIS CHAPTER, YOU SHOULD BE ABLE TO

EXPLAIN the strategic role of employee benefits.

DESCRIBE six government-sponsored benefits.

EXPLAIN why the cost of health insurance benefits is increasing and how employers can reduce these costs.

DESCRIBE the two categories of pension plans and the shift that is occurring in their relative popularity.

DISCUSS three types of personal employee services and six types of job-related services offered to employees.

EXPLAIN how to set up a flexible benefits program.

REQUIRED PROFESSIONAL CAPABILITIES (RPC)

- Integrates the basic benefits program with disability management

- Performs an analysis of organizational and employee needs related to benefit plans

- Develops specifications for the acquisition or redesign of pension plans and their administration

- Administers the reporting, funding, and fiduciary aspects of the plan

- Provides information and counselling to pension plan participants

- Ensures the effectiveness and efficiency of benefit programs

THE STRATEGIC ROLE OF EMPLOYEE BENEFITS

employee benefits Indirect financial payments given to employees. They may include supplementary health and life insurance, vacation, pension plans, education plans, and discounts on company products.

Employee benefits and services can be defined as all the indirect financial payments that an employee receives during his or her employment with an employer.[1] Benefits are generally provided to all of a firm's employees and include such things as time off with pay, supplementary health and life insurance, and employee assistance plans. Employee services, traditionally a minor aspect of compensation, are becoming more sought after by today's employees in the post-job-security era. Research indicates that benefits do matter to employees and that, if they are aligned with business strategy, they can help to attract and retain the right people to achieve business objectives.[2] Alberta's AltaGas Ltd. uses benefits to help them compete for talented workers in the ultra-competitive Alberta labour market, as described in the Strategic HR box.

STRATEGIC HR

AltaGas Benefits Drive Successful Competition for Talent

Time off has been a big focus at AltaGas in the past year. The Calgary-based energy company changed its vacation policy for the third time in eight years and reduced its workday from 8 hours to 7.5. It also gives employees eight "corporate" days off, and workers enjoy provincial statutory holidays from outside their jurisdiction.

"We tried to listen to employees in terms of what's important and certainly time off stood out," says Kent Stout, vice-president of corporate resources at AltaGas. "Time off, quality of life, work–life balance are the issues we're taking to centre stage. And fun, we're trying to inject that as well."

AltaGas's range of generous benefits is typical of employers on Canada's Top 100 Employers list, published by Mediacorp Canada. To join the prestigious clan, organizations typically provide ample vacation, maternity leave top-ups, retirement savings options, bonuses, tuition subsidies, and health benefits, along with fitness incentives and flexible work arrangements. "We have a highly competitive, challenging labour market in Calgary, particularly in the industry we operate in, so there's lots of competition out there, lots of big oil and gas producers that have very attractive compensation packages, including benefits, so somehow—we're not that large—we have to distinguish ourselves and attract and retain employees."

AltaGas offers three weeks' vacation to new employees but decided to steer away from flex days and instead offers five pre-designated corporate days aligned with long weekends, so employees can take a four-day break. Three other corporate days are given at Christmas, usually making for a 10-day break. "employees really like it because they don't have to feel guilty, worrying about others working, because the office shuts down, so they can relax more," says Stout.

Employees also enjoy quarterly events, contingent on financial success, that include scavenger hunts, cross-country skiing, or dinners, with prizes such as WestJet certificates.

On the financial side, the 357-employee company provides signing bonuses, year-end bonuses up to $57 400, a share purchase plan, a pension plan with employer contributions up to 6 percent, life and disability insurance, and discounts on home computers.

AltaGas also pays 100 percent of health premiums, and employees receive full family coverage. Family-friendly benefits include maternity leave top-up to 100 percent of salary for six weeks, emergency short-term childcare, and compassionate top-up payments to 100 percent for one week.

"It's a very competitive marketplace, but we seem to be attracting good-quality employees," Stout says.

Source: S. Dobson, "Top Benefits Go Beyond Financials," *Canadian HR Reporter* (September 8, 2008).

Employee benefits are an important part of most employees' compensation, particularly given today's reality of modest salary increases.[3] For the aging workforce, healthcare benefits are becoming increasingly important. Employee benefits are in the midst of an evolution based on the aging population, the looming labour shortage in Canada, and advances in healthcare. Each of these factors is expected to increase the cost of benefits, which is already at an all-time high.[4]

Administering benefits today represents an increasingly specialized task, because workers are more financially sophisticated and demanding and because benefit plans must comply with a wide variety of laws. Providing and administering benefits is also an increasingly expensive task. Benefits as a percentage of payroll (for public and private sectors combined) are approximately 37 percent today (compared with about 15 percent in 1953). Most employees do not realize the market value and high cost to the employer of their benefits.

Certain benefits are mandated by law, and most Canadian companies voluntarily provide additional employee benefits such as group life insurance, health and dental care insurance, and retirement benefits. In the remainder of this chapter, government-sponsored benefits, voluntary employer-sponsored benefits, employee services, flexible benefits, and benefits administration will be discussed.

Benefits Interface
www.benefits.org

Employee Benefit Research Institute
www.ebri.org

BenefitsLink.com
www.benefitslink.com

Benefits Canada
www.benefitscanada.ca

GOVERNMENT-MANDATED BENEFITS

Canada has one of the world's finest collections of social programs to protect its citizens when they cannot earn income. Employers and employees provide funding for these plans, along with general tax revenues.

Employment Insurance (EI)

employment insurance (EI)
A federal program intended to provide temporary financial assistance to eligible persons who experience interruption to their work through no fault of their own.

Employment insurance (EI) is a federal program intended to provide temporary financial assistance to eligible persons who experience interruption to their work through no fault of their own. EI benefits are not payable when an employee is terminated for just cause—for example, for theft of company property—or when an employee quits for no good reason. EI is perceived to be a benefit, since it provides employees who are laid off, terminated without just cause, or who quit their job for a justifiable reason (such as harassment) with an alternative form of government income until they secure employment.

In addition to loss of employment through no fault of the employee, eligibility is also restricted to persons who have paid into the account (for example, a contractor who does not contribute to the EI account is ineligible for the benefit), have worked a minimum number of hours in a specified time, and are willing and able to work.

The EI benefit is generally 55 percent of average earnings during the last 14 to 45 weeks of the qualifying period or a maximum weekly rate (for example, as of January 1, 2012, in Ontario the maximum weekly rate was $485), depending on the regional unemployment rate. The benefit is payable for up to 45 weeks, depending on factors like the regional unemployment rate. To continue receiving EI benefits, individuals must demonstrate that they are actively seeking work. Claimants are encouraged to work part time, as they can earn up to 25 percent of their EI benefit amount before these earnings will be deducted from the benefit.

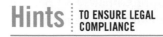

Ensures compliance with legally required programs

Hints TO ENSURE LEGAL COMPLIANCE

Income Security Programs
www.hrsdc.gc.ca/eng/corporate/ about_us/hrsdc_branches. shtml#issd

To receive benefits, an employee must first have worked a minimum number of hours during a minimum number of weeks called a *qualifying period* (the number of hours and weeks varies among regions of the country). Then there is a waiting period from the last day of work until benefits begin. The waiting period varies but is often two weeks. If the employee was provided with severance pay or holiday pay at the time of losing the job, these payments must run out before the waiting period begins.

The EI program is funded by contributions from eligible employees and their employers. Employee contributions are collected by payroll deduction, and employers pay 1.4 times the employee contribution. Employer contributions can be reduced if the employer provides a wage loss replacement plan for employee sick leave.

A supplemental unemployment benefit (SUB) plan is an agreement between an employer and the employees (often the result of collective bargaining) for a plan that enables employees who are eligible for EI benefits to receive additional benefits from a SUB fund created by the employer. SUB plans help employees maintain their standard of living during periods of unemployment (most often maternity leave) by receiving a combined benefit closer to their actual working wage. Most SUBs provide benefits of 90 percent of the working wage or greater.[5] Work-sharing programs are a related arrangement in which employees work a reduced workweek and receive EI benefits for the remainder of the week. The Canada Employment Insurance Commission must approve SUB plans and work-sharing programs.

Pay on Termination of Employment

Employment/labour standards legislation requires that employees whose employment is being terminated by the employer be provided with termination pay when they leave. The amount to be paid varies among jurisdictions and with the circumstances, as follows. Specifically, it should be noted that often employees confuse severance pay with reasonable advanced notice pay.

Reasonable Advance Notice Periods

An employee must be provided with advance written notice if the employer is going to terminate his or her employment, unless the employee is working on a short-term contract or is being fired for just cause (such as continued poor performance, theft, or if the employee initiated the termination of employment). The amount of advance notice that is required applies only to employees whose employment relationship is terminated through no cause of their own, increases with the length of employment of the employee (e.g. one week per year of employment to a specified maximum), and varies among jurisdictions. In practice, many employers do not provide advance written notice. Instead, they ask the employee to cease working immediately and provide the employee with a lump-sum equal to their pay for the notice period. This amount is called **pay in lieu of reasonable notice**.

pay in lieu of reasonable notice
A lump-sum equal to an employee's pay for the notice period provided to employees who cease working immediately.

Severance Pay

Employees only in Ontario and the federal jurisdiction may be eligible for severance pay in addition to pay in lieu of notice in certain termination situations (no other jurisdictions mandate severance pay). For example, in Ontario, employees with five or more years of service may be eligible for severance pay if (1) the employer's annual Ontario payroll is $2.5 million or more, or (2) the employer is closing down the business and 50 or more employees will be losing their jobs within a six-month period. The amount of the severance pay is one week's pay for each year of employment (maximum 26 weeks). In the federal jurisdiction system, employees who have been employed for 12 months or more receive the greater of either two days' worth of wages for every year employed with the company or a total of five days' wages (for example, an employee who has been with the company for one year would be entitled to five days' worth of severance, which is the greater of the two options above). Severance pay is an additional payout on top of the minimum notice period requirements and only applies if the specific conditions in the applicable jurisdiction are met.

Pay for Mass Layoffs

The provinces of British Columbia, Manitoba, Ontario, New Brunswick, and Newfoundland and Labrador require that additional pay be provided when a lay-off of 50 or more employees occurs. The rationale behind this regulation is that larger layoffs result in longer time to re-employment, so in cases of larger layoffs the employees are given longer reasonable notice periods. In Nova Scotia and Saskatchewan, additional pay is required if 10 or more employees are being laid off. The amount of additional pay ranges from 6 weeks to 18 weeks, depending on the province and the number of employees being laid off.

Leaves of Absence

All provinces and territories and the federal jurisdiction require unpaid leaves of absence to be provided to employees in certain circumstances. Maternity/parental leave is provided in every jurisdiction (usually after one year of service). The amount of maternity leave is 17 or 18 weeks in each jurisdiction (15 weeks in Alberta), but parental and adoption leaves range from 34 to 52 weeks. Employees who take these leaves of absence are guaranteed their old job or a similar job when they return to work. Parental leave benefits can be taken by one parent or split between both parents.

Bereavement leave on the death of a family member is provided for employees in some but not all jurisdictions. The amount of time off varies by jurisdiction and depends on the closeness of the relationship between the employee and the deceased. Bereavement leave is usually unpaid, but in some cases it can be partially or fully paid. All jurisdictions except Alberta provide compassionate care leave for employees who are caring for a critically or terminally ill relative (six weeks of EI is payable during these leaves).[6] Quebec has extended compassionate leave to cover situations where close family members are victims of criminal acts, commit suicide, or where a child disappears.[7]

Some employers provide full or partial pay for all or part of legally required unpaid leaves by "topping up" what employees receive from EI, such that the total amount they receive more closely matches their regular salary. For example, in some cases bereavement leave may be partially or fully paid by the employer.

Having a clear procedure for any leave of absence is essential. An application form, such as the one in **Figure 13.1**, should be the centrepiece of any such procedure. In general, no employee should be given a leave until it is clear what the leave is for. If the leave is for medical or family reasons, medical certification

FIGURE 13.1 Sample Application for Leave of Absence

APPLICATION FOR LEAVE
(SUPPORT STAFF)

UNB
UNIVERSITY OF
NEW BRUNSWICK

This form is used by all Support Staff employees to record applications for leave
of one-half day duration or longer.

HR USE ONLY

LAST NAME		FIRST NAME		DATATEL / EMPLOYEE ID#	

DEPARTMENT   ○ **UNBF**   ○ **UNBSJ**

TYPE OF LEAVE	DATES (use separate forms for each year) Specify first and last day of leave for those longer than 1 day. Show A.M. or P.M. for half days.	# OF WORK DAYS
VACATION		
SICK		

	START DATE	END DATE		
MATERNITY			HR USE ONLY	
PARENTAL				

	START DATE	END DATE	# of DAYS	
BEREAVEMENT				Relative:
EMERGENCY				Reason:
LEAVE WITHOUT PAY if over 30 days needs VP approval				Reason:
OTHER				Reason:

ADDITIONAL DETAILS:

EMPLOYEE SIGNS HERE _____   09-07-14 _____
DATE

APPROVAL

RECOMMENDED	POSITION	DATE
APPROVED	POSITION	DATE

FORWARD COMPLETED FORMS TO:

UNBF
HUMAN RESOURCES
ROOM 102
I.U.C. COMPLEX

UNBSJ
FINANCIAL & ADMINISTRATIVE SERVICES
ROOMS 114,115
OLAND HALL

HR USE ONLY   POSTED ON:

Source: Prepared by University of New Brunswick Human Resources. Used by permission.

should be obtained from the attending physician or medical practitioner. A form like this creates a record of the employee's expected return date and the fact that, without an authorized extension, his or her employment may be terminated.

Although these leaves are unpaid, it is incorrect to assume that the leave is costless to the employer. For example, one study concluded that the costs associated with recruiting new temporary workers, training replacement workers, and compensating for the lower level of productivity of these workers could represent a substantial expense over and above what employers would normally pay their full-time employees.[8]

Canada/Quebec Pension Plan (C/QPP)

Canada/Quebec Pension Plans (C/QPP) Programs that provide three types of benefits: retirement income; survivor or death benefits payable to the employee's dependants regardless of age at time of death; and disability benefits payable to employees with disabilities and their dependants. Benefits are payable only to those individuals who make contributions to the plans or to their family members.

The **Canada/Quebec Pension Plans (C/QPP)** were introduced in 1966 to provide working Canadians with a basic level of financial security on retirement or disability. Four decades later, these benefits do indeed provide a significant part of most Canadians' retirement income. Almost all employed Canadians between the ages of 18 and 65 are covered, including self-employed individuals. Casual and migrant workers are excluded, as are people who are not earning any employment income, such as homemakers or volunteers. The benefits are portable, meaning that pension rights are not affected by changes in job or residence within Canada. Both contributions and benefits are based only on earnings up to the "year's maximum pensionable earnings" (intended to approximate the average industrial wage), as defined in the legislation. Benefits are adjusted based on inflation each year in line with the consumer price index. Contributions made by employees (4.95 percent of pensionable earnings as of January 2012) are matched by employers.

Canada Pension Plan
www.hrsdc.gc.ca/eng/isp/cpp/cpptoc.shtml

Three types of benefits are provided: retirement pensions, disability pensions, and survivor benefits. The *retirement pension* is calculated as 25 percent of the average earnings (adjusted for inflation up to the average inflation level during the last five years before retirement) over the years during which contributions were made. Plan members can choose to begin receiving benefits at any time between the ages of 60 and 70. Benefits are reduced on early retirement before age 65 and are increased in the case of late retirement after age 65. *Disability benefits* are only paid for severe disabilities that are expected to be permanent or to last for an extended period. The disability benefit is 75 percent of the pension benefit earned at the date of disability, plus a flat-rate amount per child. *Survivor benefits* are paid on the death of a plan member. A lump-sum payment is made to the plan member's estate, and a monthly pension is also payable to the surviving spouse and each dependent child.

Workers' Compensation

workers' compensation Workers' compensation provides income and medical benefits to victims of work-related accidents or illnesses or their dependants, regardless of fault.

Workers' compensation laws are aimed at providing sure, prompt income and medical benefits to victims of work-related accidents or illnesses or their dependants, regardless of fault. Every province and territory and the federal jurisdiction has its own workers' compensation law. These laws impose compulsory collective liability for workplace accidents and work-related illnesses. This means that employees and employers cannot sue each other regarding the costs of workplace accidents or illnesses. Workers' compensation is, in effect, a "no fault" insurance plan designed to help injured or ill workers get well and return to work. For an injury or illness to be covered by workers' compensation, one must only prove that it arose while the employee was on the job. It does not matter that the employee may have been at fault; if he or she was on the job when the injury or illness occurred, he or she is entitled to workers' compensation. For example, suppose all employees are instructed to wear safety goggles when working at their machines, and one does not and is injured. Workers' compensation benefits will still be provided. The fact that the worker was at fault in no way waives his or her claim to benefits.

Employers collectively pay the full cost of the workers' compensation system, which can be an onerous financial burden for small businesses. The cost varies by industry and with actual employer costs; employer premiums are tax deductible. Workers' compensation boards (or equivalent bodies) exist in each jurisdiction to determine and collect payments from employers, determine rights to compensation, and pay workers the amount of benefit to which they are entitled under the legislation in their jurisdiction. Employers and employees have some representation on these boards, but usually both parties believe they should have more control.

Workers' compensation benefits include payment of expenses for medical treatment and rehabilitation, and income benefits during the time in which the worker is unable to work (temporarily or permanently) because of his or her disability (partial or total). Survivor benefits are payable if a work-related death occurs. All benefits are non-taxable.

Association of Workers'
Compensation Boards of Canada
www.awcbc.org

Controlling Workers' Compensation Costs

All parties agree that a renewed focus on accident prevention is the best way to manage workers' compensation costs over the long term. Minimizing the number of workers' compensation claims is an important goal for all employers. Although workers' compensation boards pay the claims, the premiums for most employers depend on the number and amount of claims that are paid. Minimizing such claims is thus important.

In practice, there are two basic approaches to reducing workers' compensation claims. First, firms try to reduce accident- or illness-causing conditions in facilities by instituting effective *safety and health programs* and complying with government safety standards. Second, since workers' compensation costs increase the longer an employee is unable to return to work, employers have become involved in instituting *rehabilitation programs* for injured or ill employees. These include physical therapy programs and career counselling to guide such employees into new, less strenuous or stressful positions. Workers are required to cooperate with return-to-work initiatives, such as modified work.[9] When Purolator's workers' compensation costs came to $13 million, it decided to use both of these approaches to reduce costs. The company hired occupational nurses, conducted physical demands analyses of many of its jobs, strengthened its return-to-work program, tied injury reduction to managers' bonuses, and increased its interaction with doctors.[10]

Vacations and Holidays

Labour/employment standards legislation sets out a minimum amount of paid vacation that must be provided to employees, usually two weeks per year, but the requirements vary by jurisdiction. The actual number of paid employee vacation days also varies considerably from employer to employer. Many employers provide additional paid holidays and paid vacation over and above the amount required by law. Thus, a typical vacation policy might call for

- two weeks for the first 5 years of service
- three weeks for 6 to 10 years of service
- four weeks for 11 to 15 years of service
- five weeks for 16 to 25 years of service
- six weeks after 25 years of service

The number of paid holidays similarly varies considerably from one jurisdiction to another, from a minimum of five to a maximum of nine. The most common paid holidays include New Year's Day, Good Friday, Canada Day, Labour Day, and Christmas and Boxing Day. Other common holidays include Victoria Day, Thanksgiving Day, and Remembrance Day. Additional holidays may be observed in each province, such as Saint-Jean-Baptiste Day in Quebec.

Paid Breaks

While vacation requirements mandate paid time off, in terms of full days of work off, there are also mandated paid and unpaid time off requirements within a work day at the provincial, territorial, or federal level. For example, in Nova Scotia, an employee shift of over five hours requires a minimum 30-minute uninterrupted break. If the employee is under direct control of the employer and expected to be available for work during this time, then the break must be paid. If not, then it can be unpaid. Similar conditions apply in Ontario. Contrary to popular belief, coffee or other rest breaks in addition to the eating period are often not government mandated. If the employee is free to leave the workplace, then the employer does not have to pay for the time.

VOLUNTARY EMPLOYER-SPONSORED BENEFITS

Although they are not required to do so, employers often provide many other employee benefits. Several of the most common types of employee benefits will now be described.

Life Insurance

group life insurance Life insurance provided at lower rates for all employees, including new employees, regardless of health or physical condition.

Virtually all employers provide **group life insurance** plans for their employees. As a group, employees can obtain lower rates than if they bought such insurance as individuals. In addition, group plans usually contain a provision for coverage of all employees—including new ones—regardless of health or physical condition.

In most cases, the employer pays 100 percent of the base premium, which usually provides life insurance equal to about two years' salary. Additional life insurance coverage is sometimes made available to employees on an optional, employee-paid basis. *Accidental death and dismemberment* coverage provides a fixed lump-sum benefit in addition to life insurance benefits when death is accidental. It also provides a range of benefits in case of accidental loss of limbs or sight and is often paid for by the employer.

Critical illness insurance provides a lump-sum benefit to an employee who is diagnosed with and survives a life-threatening illness. This benefit bridges the gap between life insurance and disability insurance by providing immediate funds to relieve some the financial burden associated with the illness (such as paying for out-of-country treatment or experimental treatment) or enabling employees to enjoy their remaining time by pursuing activities that would normally be beyond their financial means.[11]

Supplementary Healthcare/Medical Insurance

Most employers provide their employees with supplementary healthcare/medical insurance (over and above that provided by provincial healthcare plans). Along with life insurance and long-term disability, these benefits form the cornerstone of almost all benefits programs.[12] Supplementary healthcare insurance is aimed at providing protection against medical costs arising from off-the-job accidents or illness.

Most supplementary health insurance plans provide insurance at group rates, which are usually lower than individual rates and are generally available to all employees—including new ones—regardless of health or physical condition. Supplementary healthcare plans provide major medical coverage to meet medical expenses not covered by government healthcare plans, including prescription drugs, private or semi-private hospital rooms, private duty nursing, physiotherapy, medical supplies, ambulance services, and so on. In most employer-sponsored drug plans, employees must pay a specified amount of **deductible** expense (typically $25 or $50) per year before plan benefits begin. Many employers also sponsor health-related insurance plans that cover expenses like vision care, hearing aids, and dental services, often with deductibles. In a majority of cases, the participants in such plans have their premiums paid for entirely by their employers.[13]

Reducing Health Benefit Costs

Dramatic increases in healthcare costs are the biggest issue facing benefits managers in Canada today. **Figure 13.2** shows how increases in medical and dental plan costs have continued to escalate since 2006. The main reasons for these increases are increased use of expensive new drugs and rising drug use by an aging population.[14] Despite government healthcare plans, Canadian employers pay about 30 percent of all healthcare expenses in Canada, most of this for prescription drugs.[15]

Many Canadian managers now find controlling and reducing healthcare costs topping their to-do lists. The simplest approach to reducing health-benefit costs is to *increase the amount of healthcare costs paid by employees*. This can be accomplished by increasing employee premiums, increasing deductibles, reducing company **coinsurance** levels, instituting or lowering annual maximums on some services, or even eliminating coverage for spouses, private hospital rooms, and other benefits. An Angus Reid poll of 1 500 Canadians found that three-quarters of the respondents were willing to pay higher premiums to cover the high cost of prescription drugs.[16]

Another cost-reduction strategy is to publish a *restricted list of drugs* that will be paid for under the plan to encourage the use of generic rather than more expensive brand-name drugs. New drugs may not be covered if equally effective,

deductible The annual amount of health/dental expenses that an employee must pay before insurance benefits will be paid.

Tips : FOR THE FRONT LINE

coinsurance The percentage of expenses (in excess of the deductible) that are paid for by the insurance plan.

Public Health Agency of Canada
www.publichealth.gc.ca

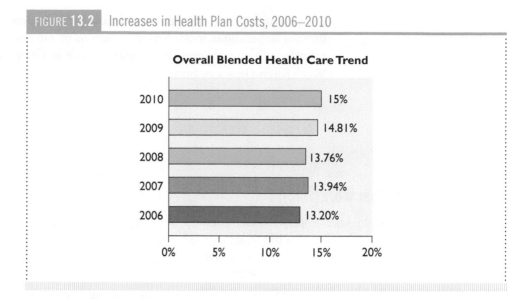

Source: *Canadian Health Care Trend Survey Results 2010* (Toronto ON: Buck Consultants, 2010), p. 2. Reprinted with permission of Buck Consultants, an ACS Company.

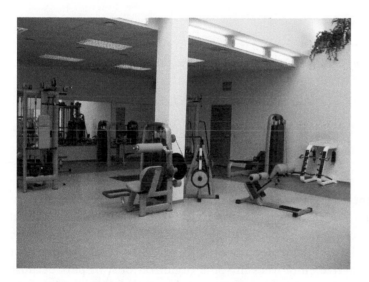

An onsite employee fitness centre

cheaper alternatives are available. This approach should be combined with employee education to effectively manage the demand for drugs.[17]

A third approach is *health promotion.* In-house newsletters can caution workers to take medication properly and advertise programs on weight management, smoking cessation, exercise classes, onsite massage therapy, nutrition counselling, and other wellness programs. After 10 years of providing an onsite exercise program for employees, Canada Life Assurance Company found that absenteeism dropped 24 percent for employees who exercised two to three times per week.[18] Employee assistance programs can help to combat alcohol and drug addiction and provide stress-management counselling.

A fourth approach is to implement *risk-assessment* programs. Such programs are being used by CIBC and other companies. A third party conducts a confidential survey of the health history and lifestyle choices of employees to identify common health risk factors, such as those associated with heart disease or mental health, so that problem-specific programs can be implemented.[19]

Finally, *healthcare spending accounts* (HCSA) are offered by more than 90 percent of Canadian employers, either alone or in combination with a standard healthcare plan.[20] The employer establishes an annual account for each employee containing a certain amount of money (determined by the employer to control costs). The employee can spend the money on healthcare costs as he or she wants. This provides flexibility for the employee. These accounts are governed by the Income Tax Act, which allows expenses not normally covered under employer-sponsored healthcare plans (such as laser eye surgery) and defines dependants more broadly than most employer plans.[21] HCSAs are very popular with employees, particularly those in Generation Y, as discussed in the Workforce Diversity box.

WORKFORCE DIVERSITY

Gen Y's Benefits That Work

Employers will need to take a different approach to their benefits plans to accommodate the latest generation in their workplace. In terms of plan design, Gen Ys will most likely want some kind of healthcare spending account (HCSA) in addition to a basic dental and medical plan so that they don't have to pay for what they won't use. And while Baby Boomers and Gen Xers will continue to work full time, this may not be the case for Gen Y. Many think they'll hold three part-time jobs, and thus employers may want to consider implementing benefits for part-time workers.

Unfortunately, the health picture for many Gen Ys isn't rosy. Twice as many young people are obese now as compared to 30 years ago. Roughly 15 percent suffer from at least one chronic disease such as diabetes, cancer, mental illness, and bone and joint disorders. In terms of prescription drugs, a study by Green Shield Canada found that, after oral contraceptives, the most-used drug type was antidepressants.

No matter what the composition of the benefits plan, online access is critical for this technologically savvy generation. Plan sponsors will want to ensure that benefits information is available online, accessible 24/7.

Source: Adapted from B. Smith, "Y's Benefits," *Benefits Canada* (July 2008), p. 9.

Retiree Health Benefits

Another concern is the cost of health benefits provided to retirees. These benefits typically include life insurance, drugs, and private/semi-private hospital coverage. Some continue coverage to a surviving spouse. Retiree benefit costs are already exceeding the costs for active employees in some organizations, in part because many early retirees between the ages of 50 and 65 are not yet eligible for government health benefits that start at age 65. Employers are required to disclose liabilities for retiree benefits in their financial statements. These liabilities are not required to be pre-funded and thus are at risk in the case of business failure.[22]

An Ethical Dilemma

Should it be the employer's responsibility to cover healthcare costs for early retirees until they become eligible for government healthcare benefits at age 65?

Employers can cut costs by increasing retiree contributions, increasing deductibles, tightening eligibility requirements, and reducing maximum payouts.[23] The last few years have seen a trend away from employer-provided retiree health benefits. This trend is expected to continue as a result of rising healthcare costs, growing retiree populations, uncertain business profitability, and federal regulations that provide only limited opportunities for funding retiree medical benefits.[24]

Short-Term Disability Plans and Sick Leave Plans

short-term disability and sick leave Plans that provide pay to an employee when he or she is unable to work because of a non-work-related illness or injury.

Short-term disability plans (also known as salary continuation plans) provide a continuation of all or part of an employee's earnings when the employee is absent from work because of non-work-related illness or injury. Usually a medical certificate is required if the absence extends beyond two or three days. These plans typically provide full pay for some period (often two or three weeks) and then gradually reduce the percentage of earnings paid as the period of absence lengthens. The benefits cease when the employee returns to work or when the employee qualifies for long-term disability. These plans are some-times provided through an insurance company.

Sick leave plans operate quite differently from short-term disability plans. Most sick leave policies grant full pay for a specified number of permissible sick days—usually up to about 12 per year (often accumulated at the rate of one day per month of service). Most jurisdictions require a few days of sick leave (unpaid) as a minimum standard. Sick leave pay creates difficulty for many employers. The problem is that, although many employees use their sick days only when they are legitimately sick, others simply use their sick leave as extensions to their vacations, whether they are sick or not. Also, seriously ill or injured employees get no pay once their sick days are used up.

Some employers now buy back unused sick leave at the end of the year by paying their employees a daily equivalent pay for each sick leave day not used. The drawback is that the policy can encourage legitimately sick employees to come to work despite their illness. Others have experimented with holding monthly lotteries in which only employees with perfect monthly attendance are able to participate; those who participate are eligible to win a cash prize. Still others aggressively investigate all absences, for instance by calling the absent employee at their home when they are off sick.

Long-Term Disability

National Institute of Disability Management and Research
www.nidmar.ca

Canadian Council on Rehabilitation and Work
www.ccrw.org

disability management A proactive, employer-centred process that coordinates the activities of the employer, the insurance company, and healthcare providers in an effort to minimize the impact of injury, disability, or disease on a worker's capacity to successfully perform his or her job.

Long-term disability insurance is aimed at providing income protection or compensation for loss of income because of long-term illness or injury that is not work related. The disability payments usually begin when normal short-term disability or sick leave is used up and may continue to provide income to age 65 or beyond. The disability benefits usually range from 50 to 75 percent of the employee's base pay.

The number of long-term disability claims in Canada is rising sharply. This trend is expected to accelerate as the average age of the workforce continues to increase because the likelihood of chronic illness, such as arthritis, heart disease, and diabetes, increases with age. Therefore, disability management programs with a goal of returning workers safely back to work are becoming a priority in many organizations.[25] For example, employers are beginning to put more effort into managing employees with episodic disabilities, which are chronic illnesses such as HIV, lupus, multiple sclerosis, arthritis, and some cancers and mental illnesses that are unpredictable. These employees may have long periods of good health followed by unpredicted episodes of poor health.[26]

Disability management is a proactive, employer-centred process that coordinates the activities of the employer, the insurance company, and healthcare providers in an effort to minimize the impact of injury, disability, or disease on a worker's capacity to successfully perform his or her job. Maintaining contact with a worker who is ill or injured is imperative in disability management so that the worker can be involved in the return-to-work process from the beginning. Ongoing contact also allows the employer to monitor the employee's emotional well-being, which is always affected by illness or injury.[27]

Effective disability management programs include prevention, early assessment and intervention regarding employee health problems, monitoring and management of employee absences, and early and safe return-to-work policies.[28] The three most common approaches to returning a worker with a disability to work are reduced work hours, reduced work duties, and workstation modification.[29] Evaluating the physical capabilities of the worker is an important step in designing work modifications to safely reintegrate injured workers. In many cases, the cost of accommodating an employee's disability can be quite modest.

Mental Health Benefits

World Federation for Mental Health
www.wfmh.org

Mental health issues continue to be the leading cause of short- and long-term disability claims in Canada. Psychiatric disabilities are the fastest growing of all occupational disabilities, with depression being the most common (even though only 32 percent of those afflicted seek treatment, as they do not want to admit it to their employer).[30]

For Canadian employers, the cost of mental health benefits is about $51 billion annually.[31] Despite the staggering costs, depression is not being addressed in a systematic way, and employers are unprepared to deal with stress, depression, and anxiety in the workplace. Some of the challenges involved in improving this situation are shown in **Figure 13.3**. Only one-third of employers have implemented return-to-work programs specific to mental health. Companies such as Bell Canada, Alcan, and Superior Propane are trying to help reduce costs with prevention and early intervention programs, including psychiatric counselling and peer-support groups.[32]

FIGURE 13.3   The Top Challenges in Improving How Mental Health Issues Are Addressed in the Workplace

1. Employee perceptions and stigma related to mental health issues	60%
2. Lack of front-line manager awareness	54%
3. Inability to identify suitable modified work	40%
4. Inability to introduce significant flexibility options	39%
5. Lack of tools and supports	29%
6. Lack of funds/budget for program enhancements	23%
7. Lack of senior management buy-in	20%
8. Don't know where to start	14%
9. Other	8%

Source: "What Are the Top Challenges You Face in Improving How Mental Health Issues Are Addressed in Your Workplace?" *2008 Mental Health in the Workplace National Survey* (Toronto, ON: Mercer and Canadian Alliance on Mental Illness and Mental Health, 2008), p. 22. Reprinted with permission of Mercer.

Sabbaticals

A few employers provide sabbatical leaves for employees who want time off to rejuvenate or to pursue a personal goal. Sabbatical leaves are usually unpaid, but some employers provide partial or full pay. Sabbaticals can help to retain employees and to avoid employee burnout, without the employee losing job security or seniority.

Retirement Benefits

pension plans Plans that provide income when employees reach a predetermined retirement age.

Employer-sponsored **pension plans** are intended to supplement an employee's government-sponsored retirement benefits, which, on average, makeup 50 percent of the average Canadian's retirement income.[33] Unlike government-provided retirement benefits, employer-sponsored pension plans are pre-funded. Money is set aside in a pension fund to accumulate with investment income until it is needed to pay benefits at retirement. Pension fund assets have grown rapidly over the past 40 years. Much of this money is invested in Canadian stocks and bonds because of laws restricting the investment of these assets in foreign securities.

Two Categories of Pension Plans

defined benefit pension plan A plan that contains a formula for determining retirement benefits.

defined contribution pension plan A plan in which the employer's contribution to the employees' retirement fund is specified.

Canadian Association for Retired Persons
www.carp.ca

Benefits and Pensions Monitor
www.bpmmagazine.com

Association of Canadian Pension Management
www.acpm.com

deferred profit-sharing plan (DPSP) A plan in which a certain amount of company profits is credited to each employee's account, payable at retirement, termination, or death.

Pension plans fall into two categories—defined benefit pension plans and defined contribution pension plans. A **defined benefit pension plan** contains a formula for determining retirement benefits so that the actual benefits to be received are defined ahead of time. For example, the plan might include a formula, such as 2 percent of final year's earnings for each year of service, which would provide a pension of 70 percent of final year's earnings to an employee with 35 years of service.

A **defined contribution pension plan** specifies what contribution the employer will make to a retirement fund set up for the employee. The defined contribution plan does not define the eventual benefit amount, only the periodic contribution to the plan. In a defined benefit plan, the employee knows ahead of time what his or her retirement benefits will be on retirement. With a defined contribution plan, the employee cannot be sure of his or her retirement benefits until retirement, when his or her share of the money in the pension fund is used to buy an annuity. Thus, benefits depend on both the amounts contributed to the fund and the retirement fund's investment earnings.

There are two other types of defined contribution arrangements. Under a *group registered retirement savings plan (group RRSP)*, employees can have a portion of their compensation (which would otherwise be paid in cash) put into an RRSP by the employer. The employee is not taxed on those set-aside dollars until after he or she retires (or removes the money from the plan). Most employers do not match all or a portion of what the employee contributes to the group RRSP because employer contributions are considered taxable income to employees. Instead, the employer often establishes a **deferred profit-sharing plan (DPSP)** and contributes a portion of company profits into the DPSP fund, where an account is set up for each employee. No employee contributions to a DPSP are allowed under Canadian tax law. Group RRSP/DPSP combinations are popular in Canada because no tax is paid until money is received from the plans at the time of the employee's death or termination of employment (at retirement or otherwise).

TABLE 13.1	Registered Pension Plans by Type, 2006–2010				
A	**B**	**C**	**D**	**E**	**F**
	2006	**2007**	**2008**	**2009**	**2010**
Defined benefit plans	50.30%	59.46%	60.15%	61.05%	61.40%
Defined contribution plans	47.56%	38.51%	37.35%	35.88%	35.47%
Composite or combination plans[1]	0.99%	0.77%	0.73%	0.71%	0.66%
Defined benefit and contribution plans	0.59%	0.78%	1.30%	2.03%	2.21%
Other types of plans[2]	1.14%	1.26%	1.78%	2.36%	2.47%

[1]In composite or combination plans, the pension has both defined benefit and defined contribution characteristics.

[2]These plans may be for different classes of employees or one benefit type may be for current employees and the other for new employees or these plans may be hybrid plans where the pension benefit is the better of that provided by defined benefit or defined contribution provisions.

Source: Adapted from Statistics Canada, CANSIM, table 280-0016, "Registered pension plans (RPPs) and members, by type of plan and sector," http://www.statcan.gc.ca/tables-tableaux/sum-som/l01/cst01/famil120a-eng.htm.

As shown in **Table 13.1,** both plans are quite popular, and a few companies use combination or other forms of pension plans.

The entire area of pension planning is complicated, a result of the laws governing pensions. For example, companies want to ensure that their pension contributions are tax deductible and must therefore adhere to the Income Tax Act. The provincial and federal jurisdictions also have laws governing employer-sponsored pension plans. In some cases, the complicated and overlapping federal and provincial legislation can make employers question whether or not to sponsor a pension plan.[34] Legislation regarding pension plans varies around the world, and Canada's regulators can learn important lessons from other countries' successes and failures, as described in the Global HRM box.

Employers must pay careful attention to their obligation to educate and inform (but not advise) plan members about pension investments. There have been cases where plan members who were unhappy with the information provided by the employer and surprised by small benefits have sued their employers and won. Conversely, the University of Western Ontario plan converted to defined contribution in 1970, and faculty members are retiring with incomes greater than their working salaries.[35]

The severe economic recession that began in late 2008 resulted in major shrinkage in the value of pension funds and highlighted issues with both types of plans. For defined benefit plans, the recession necessitated major increases in contributions to pension funds in order to maintain their required funding levels.[36] Although some jurisdictions eased the funding rules temporarily to allow more time to repay funding shortfalls, defined benefit plans began to be called an "endangered species."[37] For defined contribution

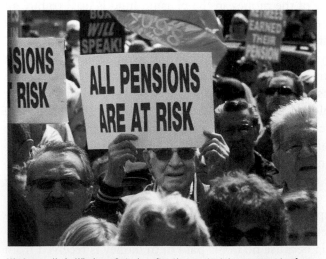

Workers rally in Windsor, Ontario, after the provincial government refuses to expand pension guarantees.

GLOBAL HRM

Defined Benefit Pension Problems and Solutions Around the World

Many countries designed generous defined benefit social security programs between 1950 and 1970 based on fertility rates that created a stable population. The actual experience of declining populations in many countries, particularly Japan, created serious intergenerational inequity as younger employees were subsidizing older ones. Solutions included increasing contribution rates (Belgium, Canada), raising the normal retirement age to 67 (European Union), both of these (Germany), moving to defined contribution plans (Australia, France, Switzerland, United Kingdom), and even more complex protective legislation (Netherlands). Japan first permitted defined contribution plans in 2001, and they have slowly become more prevalent.

Unfortunately, none of these national actions seem to be the optimal solution to the global defined benefits plan issue. The numerous retirement savings plans known as "provident funds" in Asia and defined contribution plans in Australia seem to be doing fairly well. The European Union encourages the creation of pan-European pension plans where an employer can create a plan in one location and cover all European employees under that single plan. This encourages employee mobility and reduces administrative costs. The plans must comply with the rules from the plan's home country while still respecting some of the pension laws of other countries where employees reside or have retired. Countries such as Luxembourg, Ireland, and Belgium have tried to create the best tax and legal environment to attract these plans, but it is too early to tell if a leader will emerge.

The European Union situation is very similar to our Canadian system with its patchwork of legislation. Given Canada's population of 33 million, versus 700 million in Europe, it is clear that our pension landscape should have been more straightforward from the outset and desperately needs to be simplified. There is some hope for the future as three expert commissions in Ontario, Nova Scotia, and, jointly, in Alberta and British Columbia are undertaking reviews of the pension legislation in those provinces. Perhaps they will find the right balance between regulation and governance, and perhaps other provinces will also align with their findings.

But until we find better ways to enhance and preserve defined benefit plans, employers will have to make some difficult decisions. Country by country, they must choose between assuming the risks and higher administrative costs of sponsoring defined benefit plans or moving to defined contribution plans, which typically do not produce the same retirement value to each dollar spent and are less flexible as an HR tool.

Source: Adapted from F. Letourneau, "Around the World in Six Pages," *BenefitsCanada* (August 2008), pp. 14–19. Reprinted with permission.

---

plans, many plan members nearing retirement saw no other option but to defer retirement and continue working until the markets recovered and their pension fund account balance recovered to an amount that would provide them with the retirement income they needed. These issues created considerable debate about the adequacy of retirement savings for future generations.

When designing a pension plan, there are several legal and policy issues to consider:[39]

Hints TO ENSURE LEGAL COMPLIANCE

- *Membership requirements.* For example, at what minimum number of years of service do employees become eligible to join the plan?
- *Benefit formula* (defined benefit plans only). This usually ties the pension to the employee's final earnings, or an average of his or her last three to five years' earnings.
- *Retirement age.* Traditionally, the normal retirement age in Canada has been 65. However, since mandatory retirement is now prohibited by human rights laws across the country, employees cannot be required to retire at age 65. Some plans call for "30 and out." This permits an employee to retire after 30 years of continuous service, regardless of the person's age.

vesting A provision that employer money placed in a pension fund cannot be forfeited for any reason.

- *Funding*. The question of how the plan is to be funded is another key issue. One aspect is whether the plan will be contributory or non-contributory. In the former, contributions to the pension fund are made by both employees and the employer. In a non-contributory fund, only the employer contributes.

- *Vesting*. Employee **vesting** rights is another critical issue in pension planning. Vesting refers to the money that the employer has placed in the pension fund that cannot be forfeited for any reason; the employees' contributions can never be forfeited. An employee is vested when he or she has met the requirements set out in the plan, whereby, on termination of employment, he or she will receive future benefits based on the contributions made to the plan by the *employer* on behalf of the employee. In most provinces, pension legislation requires that employer contributions be vested once the employee has completed two years of service. Plans may vest more quickly than required by law. If the employee terminates employment before being vested, he or she is only entitled to a refund of his or her own contributions plus interest (unless the employer has decided to be more generous). Once an employee is vested, all contributions are "locked in" and cannot be withdrawn by the employee on termination of employment; that is, employees must wait until retirement to receive a pension from the plan. Most plans permit the employee to transfer the amount into a locked-in RRSP (see the discussion on portability below), but the money cannot be accessed until retirement.

An Ethical ⋮ Dilemma

Should an employer with a pension plan that covers employees in several provinces give each group the minimum vesting and portability benefits for their province, or take the most generous of these and provide it to all employees?

portability A provision that employees who change jobs can transfer the lump-sum value of the pension they have earned to a locked-in RRSP or their new employer's pension plan.

- *Portability*. Canadian employers today are required by pension legislation to make their pensions more "portable" for employees on termination of employment. **Portability** means that employees in defined contribution plans can take the money in their company pension account to a new employer's plan or roll it over into a locked-in RRSP. For defined benefit plans, the lump-sum value of the benefit earned can be transferred.

Phased Retirement

phased retirement An arrangement whereby employees gradually ease into retirement by using reduced workdays or shortened workweeks.

The labour shortage is resulting in employers seeking to retain older employees. At the same time, many Canadians wishing to retire early are finding that they are not in a financial position to do so and that they need to continue working to age 60, 65, or even later.[40] The idea of **phased retirement**, whereby employees gradually ease into retirement using reduced workdays or shortened workweeks, has been increasing in Canada, as shown in **Figure 13.4**. Constraints under the Income Tax Act and pension legislation in some jurisdictions are slowly being loosened, and it is now possible for older workers to receive some benefits from their pension plan while they are being paid to continue to work.[41]

Supplemental Employee Retirement Plans (SERPs)

The Income Tax Act has not changed the maximum pension benefit permissible under the act (for tax deductibility of plan contributions) since 1976. Thus, many Canadians have their pension benefits capped at less than what their defined benefit plan formula would otherwise provide. Originally this situation only

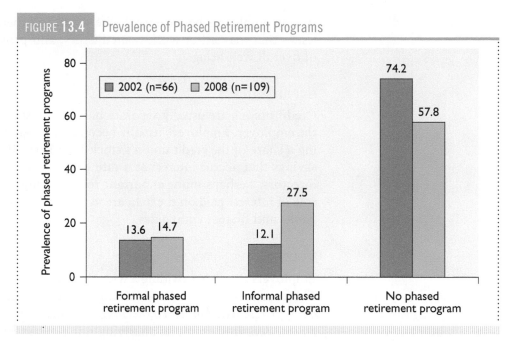

FIGURE **13.4**   Prevalence of Phased Retirement Programs

Source: K. Thorpe, *Harnessing the Power: Recruiting, Engaging, and Retaining Mature Workers* (Ottawa, ON: The Conference Board of Canada, October 2008), p. 23. Reprinted by permission of The Conference Board of Canada, Ottawa.

supplemental employee retirement plans (SERPs) Plans that provide the additional pension benefit required for employees to receive their full pension benefit in cases where their full pension benefit exceeds the maximum allowable benefit under the Income Tax Act.

created problems for highly paid executives, but in recent years more and more employees have been affected. **Supplemental employee retirement plans (SERPs)** are intended to provide the difference in pension benefit and thus restore pension adequacy for high earners.

A Towers Perrin survey found that nearly three-quarters of employers provide SERPs (including about two-thirds of small employers with fewer than 500 employees). The survey also found that 53 percent of SERP sponsors cover employees below the executive level in "broad-based" plans. Most SERPs are "pay-as-you-go" plans; that is, they do not have a fund established to accumulate money to pay the benefits (because contributions are not tax deductible). However, the security of SERP benefits has been improving, as 41 percent of plans are now secured in some manner.[42]

EMPLOYEE SERVICES

Although an employee's time off and insurance and retirement benefits account for the largest portion of an organization's benefits costs, many employers also provide a range of services, including personal services (such as counselling), job-related services (such as childcare facilities), and executive perquisites (such as company cars and planes for executives).

Personal Services

First, many companies provide personal services that most employees need at one time or another. These include credit unions, counselling, employee assistance plans, and social and recreational opportunities. The intent of these services is to help employees balance work–life issues, aid them in dealing with non-work issues that may affect work-related issues, and provide employees with a sense of overall well-being.

Credit Unions

Credit unions are usually separate businesses established with the assistance of the employer. Employees usually become members of a credit union by purchasing a share of the credit union's stock for $5 or $10. Members can then deposit savings that accrue interest at a rate determined by the credit union's board of directors. Perhaps more important to most employees, loan eligibility and the rate of interest paid on the loan are usually more favourable than those found in banks and finance companies.

Counselling Services

Employers are also providing a wider range of counselling services to employees. These include *financial counselling* (for example, how to overcome existing debt problems), *family counselling* (for marital problems and so on), *career counselling* (for example, analyzing one's aptitudes and deciding on a career), *job placement counselling* (for helping terminated or disenchanted employees find new jobs), and *pre-retirement counselling* (aimed at preparing retiring employees for what many find is the trauma of retiring). Many employers also make available to employees a full range of *legal counselling* services through legal insurance plans.[43]

Employee Assistance Plans (EAPs)

employee assistance plan (EAP)
A company-sponsored program to help employees cope with personal problems that are interfering with or have the potential to interfere with their job performance, as well as issues affecting their well-being or the well-being of their families.

Family Services Employee
Assistance Programs
www.familyserviceseap.com

Shepell.fgi
www.shepellfgi.com

An **employee assistance plan (EAP)** is a formal employer program that provides employees (and often their family members) with confidential counselling or treatment programs for problems such as mental health issues, marital/family problems, work–life balance issues, stress, legal problems, substance abuse, and other addictions such as gambling. They are particularly important for helping employees who suffer workplace trauma—ranging from harassment to physical assault. There was a significant increase in EAP usage during the economic recession that began in late 2008, particularly in the areas of financial problems and stress.[44]

The number of EAPs in Canada is growing because they are a proactive way for organizations to reduce absenteeism and disability costs. A general estimate is that 10 percent of employees use EAP services. With supervisory training in how to identify employees who may need an EAP referral, usage can be expanded to more employees who need help.[45]

EAP counsellors can be employed in-house, or the company can contract with an external EAP firm.[46] It is important to assess the services provided by external EAP providers before using them, as quality levels vary. Whatever the model, an EAP provider should be confidential, accessible to employees in all company locations, and timely in providing service, and should offer highly educated counsellors and provide communication material to publicize the plan to employees. They should also provide utilization reports on the number of employees using the service and the types of services being provided, without compromising confidentiality.[47]

Other Personal Services

Finally, some employers also provide various social and recreational opportunities for their employees, including company-sponsored athletic events, dances, annual summer picnics, craft activities, and parties. In practice, the benefits offered are limited only by creativity in thinking up new benefits. For example, pharmaceutical giant Pfizer Inc. provides employees with free drugs made by the company, including Viagra.[48]

Job-Related Services

Job-related services aimed directly at helping employees perform their jobs, such as educational subsidies and childcare centres, constitute a second group of services.

Subsidized Childcare

Eighty percent of Canadian families with young children have both parents working.[49] Subsidized childcare is offered to assist in balancing these work and life

Subsidizing childcare facilities for children of employees has many benefits for the employer, including lower employee absenteeism.

responsibilities. Many employers simply investigate the childcare facilities in their communities and recommend certain ones to interested employees, but more employers are setting up company-sponsored childcare facilities themselves, both to attract young parents to the payroll and to reduce absenteeism. In this case, the centre is a separate, privately run venture, paid for by the firm. IKEA, Husky Injection Molding Systems, IBM, and the Kanata Research Park have all chosen this option. Where successful, the hours of operation are structured around parents' schedules, the childcare facility is close to the workplace (often in the same building), and the employer provides 50 to 75 percent of the operating costs. Two emerging benefits are childcare for mildly ill children and emergency backup childcare.[50]

To date, the evidence regarding the actual effects of employer-sponsored childcare on employee absenteeism, turnover, productivity, recruitment, and job satisfaction is positive, particularly with respect to reducing obstacles to coming to work and improving workers' attitudes.[51]

Eldercare

With the average age of the Canadian population rising, eldercare is increasingly a concern for many employers and individuals. It is a complex, unpredictable, and exhausting process that creates stress for the caregiver, the family, and co-workers. Eldercare is expected to become a more common workplace issue than childcare as the twenty-first century progresses.[52]

Company eldercare programs are designed to assist employees who must help elderly parents or relatives who are not fully able to care for themselves, up to and including palliative care of the dying. Eldercare benefits include flexible hours, support groups, counselling, free pagers, and adult daycare programs. Referral services to help employees connect with the wide variety of services for the elderly are particularly helpful for employees with eldercare responsibilities.[53]

For example, BMO Financial Group's EAP can be used to find nursing homes by entering a postal code and using the list of questions provided to assist in selecting the best one. BMO employee Yasmin Meralli says, "It helped me with my work because it reduced the amount of time I had to spend outside of work doing other stuff... It really felt to me that I worked for a company that cared."[54]

Subsidized Employee Transportation

Some employers also provide subsidized employee transportation. An employer can negotiate with a transit system to provide free year-round transportation to its employees. Other employers facilitate employee carpooling, perhaps by acting as the central clearinghouse to identify employees from the same geographic areas who work the same hours.

Food Services

Food services are provided in some form by many employers; they allow employees to purchase meals, snacks, or coffee onsite, usually at relatively low prices. Even employers that do not provide full dining facilities generally make available food services, such as coffee wagons or vending machines, for the convenience of employees.

Educational Subsidies

Educational subsidies, such as tuition refunds, have long been a popular benefit for employees seeking to continue or complete their education. Payments range from all tuition and expenses to some percentage of expenses to a flat fee per year of, say, $500 to $600. Most companies pay for courses directly related to an employee's present job. Many also reimburse tuition for courses that are not job related (such as a secretary taking an accounting class) that pertain to the company business, and those that are part of a degree or diploma program. In-house educational programs include remedial work in basic literacy and training for improved supervisory skills.

Family-Friendly Benefits

Research INSIGHT

One of the top drivers of workforce commitment in Canada is management's recognition of personal and family life. Ninety percent of responding employees in one survey said work–life benefits were "important" or "very important" to them.[55] Recognition of the pressures of balancing work and family life has led many employers to bolster what they call their "family-friendly" benefits. Examples include flexible work hours, onsite childcare, and eldercare benefits.

Family-friendly benefits are intended to reduce the extent to which work–family conflicts spill over into the employee's job and undermine the person's job satisfaction and performance. Research has found that "the relationship between job satisfaction and various [work–family] conflict measures is strong and negative across all samples; people with high levels of [work–family] conflict tend to be less satisfied with their jobs."[56] Similarly, there was a strong negative

Boomers are the "Sandwich Generation," caring for both children and elderly parents.

correlation between work–family conflict and the extent to which the employees were satisfied with their lives in general. Managers should therefore understand that providing their employees with family-friendly benefits can have very positive effects on the employees, one of which is making them more satisfied with their work and their jobs.

Executive Perquisites

Perquisites (perks, for short) are usually given to only a few top executives. Perks can range from the substantial to the almost insignificant. A bank chairperson may have a chauffeur-driven limousine and use of a bank-owned property in the Caribbean. Executives of large companies often use a corporate jet for business travel. At the other extreme, perks may entail little more than the right to use a company car.[57]

A multitude of popular perks fall between these extremes. These include management loans (which typically enable senior officers to use their stock options); salary guarantees (also known as *golden parachutes*) to protect executives if their firms are the targets of acquisitions or mergers; financial counselling (to handle top executives' investment programs); and relocation benefits, often including subsidized mortgages, purchase of the executive's current house, and payment for the actual move. A potpourri of other executive perks include outplacement assistance, company cars, chauffeured

An Ethical : Dilemma

Is it ethical for executive perquisites to continue if the company is facing financial problems?

limousines, security systems, company planes and yachts, executive dining rooms, legal services, tax assistance, liberal expense accounts, club memberships, season tickets, credit cards, and subsidized education for their children. Perks related to wellness and quality of life (such as physical fitness programs) are highly valued in today's stressful environment. An increasingly popular new perk offered at KPMG, TELUS, and Ernst & Young is concierge service, intended to carry out errands, such as grocery shopping or organizing a vacation, for busy executives.[58]

FLEXIBLE BENEFITS PROGRAMS

flexible benefits programs
Individualized benefit plans to accommodate employee needs and preferences.

Research conducted more than 30 years ago found that an employee's age, marital status, and sex influenced his or her choice of benefits.[59] For example, preference for pensions increased significantly with employee age, and preference for the family dental plan increased sharply as the number of dependants increased. Thus, benefits that one worker finds attractive, may be unattractive to another. In the last 25 years in Canada, there has been a significant increase in **flexible benefits programs** that permit employees to develop individualized benefits packages for themselves by choosing the benefits options they prefer. In 1980, there were no flex plans in Canada, but by 2005, 41 percent of employers offered flex benefits plans. Benefit consultants Hewitt Associates report that 85 percent of Canadian employers either have a flex plan in place or expect to implement one at some point. Fifty-three percent either have a full flex plan now or are in the process of creating one.[60]

RPC

Performs an analysis of organizational and employee needs related to benefit plans

Benefits Design, Inc
www.benefitsdesign.com

International Foundation of Employee Benefit Plans
www.ifebp.org

Employers derive several advantages from offering flexible benefit plans: the two most important being cost containment and the ability to meet the needs of an increasingly diverse workforce. Hewitt Associates' surveys have found that, over the years, the most important advantage of implementing flexible benefits has been meeting diverse employee needs. However, in 2005, for the first time in survey history, the concern about containing benefit cost increases surpassed meeting diverse employee needs as the most significant reason to implement flexible plans. In the 2006 survey, 100 percent of respondents reported that their flex plans were meeting or exceeding their expectations regarding meeting employee needs, and the level of satisfaction with flex plans as a cost containment measure was 78 percent.[61]

Flexible benefits plans empower the employee to put together his or her own benefit package, subject to two constraints. First, the employer must carefully limit total cost for each total benefits package. Second, each benefit plan must include certain items that are not optional. These include, for example, Canada/Quebec Pension Plan, workers' compensation, and employment insurance. Subject to these two constraints, employees can pick and choose from the available options. Thus, a young parent might opt for the company's life and dental insurance plans, while an older employee opts for an improved pension plan. The list of possible options that the employer might offer can include many of the benefits discussed in this chapter—vacations, insurance benefits, pension plans, educational services, and so on.

Advantages and disadvantages of flexible benefit programs are summarized in **Figure 13.5**. The flexibility is, of course, the main advantage. Although most

FIGURE **13.5**   Advantages and Disadvantages of Flexible Benefit Programs

ADVANTAGES

1. Employees choose packages that best satisfy their unique needs.
2. Flexible benefits help firms meet the *changing* needs of a *changing* workforce.
3. Increased involvement of employees and families improves understanding of benefits.
4. Flexible plans make introduction of new benefits less costly. The new option is added merely as one among a wide variety of elements from which to choose.
5. Cost containment—the organization sets the dollar maximum. Employee chooses within that constraint.

DISADVANTAGES

1. Employees make bad choices and find themselves not covered for predictable emergencies.
2. Administrative burdens and expenses increase.
3. Adverse selection—employees pick only benefits they will use. The subsequent high benefit utilization increases its cost.

Source: G.T. Milkovich, J.M. Newman, N.D. Cole, *Compensation*, 3rd Canadian ed. (Toronto: McGraw Hill Ryerson). © 2010. Reprinted with permission of McGraw-Hill Ryerson Ltd.

employees favour flexible benefits, some do not like to spend time choosing among available options, and some choose inappropriate benefits. Communication regarding the choices available in a flexible plan is considered the biggest challenge for employers. A majority of flex plan sponsors provide a plan website. However, even with new technology employers still find face-to-face communication is the preferred method for providing initial information about a new flex plan.[62] The recent rapid increase in the number of flexible plans in Canada indicates that the pros outweigh the cons.

BENEFITS ADMINISTRATION

Whether it is a flexible benefits plan or a more traditional one, benefits administration is a challenge. Even in a relatively small company with 40 to 50 employees, the administrative problems of keeping track of the benefits status of each employee can be a time-consuming task as employees are hired and separated and as they use or want to change their benefits. However, software is available to assist with this challenge. Many companies make use of some sort of benefits spreadsheet software to facilitate tracking benefits and updating information. Another approach is outsourcing benefits administration to a third-party expert. The major advantages are greater efficiency and consistency, and enhanced service.[63]

Keeping Employees Informed

Benefits communication, particularly regarding pension plans and flexible benefits, is increasingly important as a large number of people are approaching retirement. Correct information must be provided in a timely, clear manner. Pension legislation across Canada specifies what information must be disclosed to plan members and their spouses. Court challenges concerning information on benefits plans are on the rise as people's awareness of their right to information grows.[64]

Increasingly, organizations are using new technology, such as intranets, to ensure that up-to-date information is provided in a consistent manner. Some companies are now using real-time e-statements. At Hewlett Packard (Canada), an electronic pension booklet is available on the company's intranet, and a pension-modelling tool can be accessed through the web. The modelling software allows employees to fill in their personal information to calculate various "what if" scenarios.[65]

Chapter SUMMARY

1. The strategic importance of employee benefits is increasing in the post-job-security era. When benefits are aligned with business strategy, they can help to attract and retain the right people to achieve business objectives.

2. Six major government-mandated benefits are employment insurance, Canada/Quebec Pension Plan, workers' compensation, vacations and holidays, leaves of absence, and pay on termination of employment.

3. Health insurance costs are rising because of expensive new drugs, rising drug use by an aging population, and reductions in coverage under provincial healthcare plans. These costs can be reduced by increasing the amount of healthcare costs paid by employees, publishing a restricted list of the drugs that will be paid for under the plan, implementing health and wellness promotion plans, using risk assessment programs, and offering health services spending accounts.

4. The two categories of pension plans are defined benefit plans and defined contribution plans. Defined benefit plans provide a benefit based on a formula related to years of service, and the employer assumes the investment risk associated with the pension fund assets. Defined contribution plans provide for specified contributions to a pension fund by the employer, and the benefit will vary depending on the rate of return on the pension fund assets (employees assume the investment risk).

5. Three types of personal employee services offered by many organizations include credit unions, counselling services, and employee assistance plans. Six types of job-related services offered by many employers include subsidized childcare, eldercare, subsidized employee transportation, food services, educational subsidies, and family-friendly benefits.

6. The flexible benefits approach allows the employee to put together his or her own benefit plan, subject to total cost limits and the inclusion of certain compulsory items. The employer first determines the total cost for the benefits package. Then a decision is made as to which benefits will be compulsory (such as Canada/Quebec Pension Plan, workers' compensation, and employment insurance). Then other benefits are selected for inclusion in the plan, such as life insurance, health and dental coverage, short- and long-term disability insurance, and retirement plans. Sometimes vacations and employee services are included as well. Then employees select the optional benefits they prefer with the money they have available to them under the total plan.

MyManagementLab

Visit MyManagementLab to access a personalized Study Plan and additional study tools for this chapter.

Key TERMS

Canada/Quebec Pension Plans (C/QPP) *(p. 357)*
coinsurance *(p. 360)*
deductible *(p. 360)*
deferred profit-sharing plan (DPSP) *(p. 365)*
defined benefit pension plan *(p. 365)*
defined contribution pension plan *(p. 365)*
disability management *(p. 363)*
employee assistance plan (EAP) *(p. 370)*
employee benefits *(p. 352)*
employment insurance (EI) *(p. 353)*
flexible benefits programs *(p. 373)*

group life insurance *(p. 359)*
pay in lieu of reasonable notice *(p. 354)*
pension plans *(p. 365)*
phased retirement *(p. 368)*
portability *(p. 368)*
short-term disability and sick leave *(p. 363)*
supplemental employee retirement plans (SERPs)
   (p. 369)
vesting *(p. 368)*
workers' compensation *(p. 357)*

Review and Discussion QUESTIONS

1. Explain two main approaches to reducing workers' compensation claims.

2. Explain what companies are doing to reduce health-benefit costs.

3. Explain the difference between sick leave plans and short-term disability plans.

4. Explain the difference between a defined benefit pension plan and a defined contribution pension plan.

5. Why are long-term disability claims increasing so rapidly in Canada?

6. Outline the kinds of services provided by EAPs.

7. Explain the pros and cons of flexible benefits from both an employer and employee perspective.

8. Answer or complete the following questions from the information in this chapter.

   • What company gives their employees a 10-day break at Christmas?

   • What are the six government-sponsored or legislated benefits?

   • A ____ _____ is the amount the employee must pay on a yearly basis before supplementary healthcare benefits begin.

   • _____ _____ includes such things as news-letters, fitness centres, and nutrition counselling.

   • Generation ____ wants their benefits information online.

   • The difference between a group pension plan and a group registered retirement savings plan is _____.

   • _____ rights mean that the employee with the required length of service has a non-for-feitable right to the money contributed to the pension plan by the employer.

   • There are two types of employee services, _____ and _____. One example of each are _____ and _____.

   • Tuition reimbursement is an example of a(n) _____ _____.

   • The preferred way to communicate initial flexible benefits plan information to employees is _____.

Critical Thinking QUESTIONS

1. You are applying for a job as a manager and are at the point of negotiating salary and benefits. What questions would you ask your prospective employer concerning benefits? Describe the benefits package that you would try to negotiate for yourself.

2. What are pension "vesting" and "portability"? Why do you think these are (or are not) important to a recent university or college graduate?

3. You are the HR consultant to a small business with about 40 employees. Currently, the business offers only the legal minimum number of days for vacation and paid holidays and the legally mandated benefits. Develop a list of other benefits that you believe should be offered, along with your reasons for suggesting them.

4. If you were designing a retirement benefit for a mid-sized organization that had not previously offered one, what type of plan would you recommend to them and why?

5. What questions might an employee who currently has no benefits or a minimal coverage standard benefits plan have about flexible benefits? How can an organization address these questions and concerns? List suggested topics for a new flexible benefits plan communication plan and include at least two suggestions about the appropriate media to be used.

Experiential EXERCISES

1. Working individually or in groups, compile a list of the perks available to the following individuals: the head of your local public utilities commission, the president of your college or university, and the president of a large company in your area. Do they all have certain perks in common? What do you think accounts for any differences?

2. Working individually or in groups, contact your provincial workers' compensation board (or equivalent regulatory body in your province/ territory) and compile a list of its suggestions for reducing workers' compensation costs. What seem to be the main recommendations?

Running CASE

The New Benefits Plan

LearnInMotion.com provides only legislatively required benefits for all its employees. These include participation in employment insurance, Canada Pension Plan, and workers' compensation. No employee services are provided.

Jennifer can see several things wrong with the company's policies regarding benefits and services. First, she wants to determine whether similar companies' experiences with providing health and life insurance benefits make hiring easier or reduces employee turnover. Jennifer is also concerned that the company has no policy regarding vacations or sick leave. Informally, at least, it is understood that employees get a one-week vacation after one year's work. However, the policy regarding pay for such days as New Year's and Thanksgiving has been inconsistent. Sometimes new employees, on the job only two or three weeks, are paid fully for one of these holidays; sometimes employees who have been with the firm for six months or more get paid for only half a day. No one really knows what the company's chosen "paid" holidays are. Jennifer knows these policies must be more consistent.

She also wonders about the wisdom of establishing some type of retirement plan for the firm. Although everyone working for the firm is still in their 20s, she believes a defined contribution plan in which employees contribute a portion of their pre-tax salary, to be matched up to some limit by a contribution from LearnInMotion, would contribute to the sense of commitment she and Pierre would like to create among their employees. However, Pierre isn't so sure. His position is that if they don't get sales up pretty soon, they're going to burn through their cash. Now they want you, their management consultant, to help them decide what to do.

QUESTIONS

1   Which benefit and services policy would you recommend LearnInMotion change first and why?

2   What changes would you recommend to Jennifer regarding their lack of a vacation policy?

3   As most of LearnInMotion's staff are in their 20s, what type of pension plan would appeal to this employee demographic? Why?

Case INCIDENT

Technology Plus's Benefit Dilemma

To stay competitive, many organizations today are choosing to restructure their benefit programs. Technology Plus is an example of such a company. Technology Plus has 150 employees, including upper management, skilled tradespersons, sales representatives, and customer service representatives. Five years ago this company was enjoying huge profits and could afford their current benefits program; however, times have changed and now they need to find cost savings without laying off any of the staff.

Up to this point, Technology Plus has offered all of their staff a premium benefits program, including much more than government-required benefits of employment insurance, Canada Pension Plan, worker's compensation, standard vacation of two weeks per year, and access to legislated leaves of absence. They offer group life insurance of three times salary, accidental death and dismemberment insurance of three times salary, extended healthcare benefits (with vision care, dental care, hearing aids, and more), long-term disability of 75 percent of salary (employer paid), and a defined benefit pension plan.

They also provide a wellness program, an employee assistance plan, and many other services such as subsidized childcare and assistance with eldercare. However, now they need your help in deciding how to restructure their benefit plan to find significant cost savings but still provide meaningful benefit coverage for their employees.

QUESTIONS

1 What voluntary employer-sponsored benefits should this company maintain and which ones should they not maintain in your opinion? Why?

2 Would a flexible benefit program save this organization money if administered properly?

MyManagementLab

Visit MyManagementLab to access a personalized Study Plan and additional study tools for this chapter.

To view the CBC videos, read a summary, and answer discussion questions, go to MyManagementLab

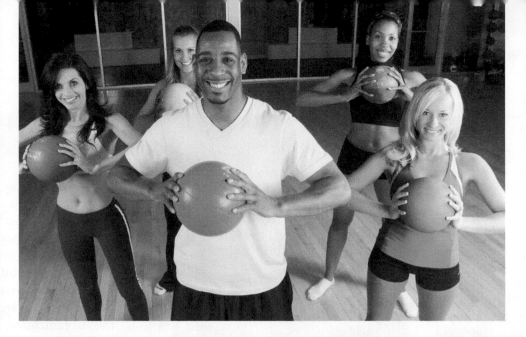

CHAPTER 14

Occupational Health and Safety

LEARNING OUTCOMES

AFTER STUDYING THIS CHAPTER, YOU SHOULD BE ABLE TO

ANALYZE the responsibilities and rights of employees and employers under occupational health and safety legislation.

EXPLAIN WHMIS legislation.

ANALYZE in detail three basic causes of accidents.

DESCRIBE how accidents at work can be prevented.

EXPLAIN why employee wellness programs are becoming increasingly popular.

DISCUSS six major employee health issues at work and **RECOMMEND** how they should be handled.

REQUIRED PROFESSIONAL CAPABILITIES (RPC)

- Prepares organizational health and safety files for investigation or for litigation

- Responds to any refusals to perform work believed to be unsafe

- Establishes a joint health and safety committee as required by law

- Provides information to employees and managers on available programs

- Ensures that policies for required medical testing fall within the limits of statute and contract

- Ensures compliance with legislated reporting requirements

- Ensures adequate accommodation, modified work, and graduated return-to-work programs are in place

- Ensures that modifications to the work environment are consistent with worker limitations

STRATEGIC IMPORTANCE OF OCCUPATIONAL HEALTH AND SAFETY

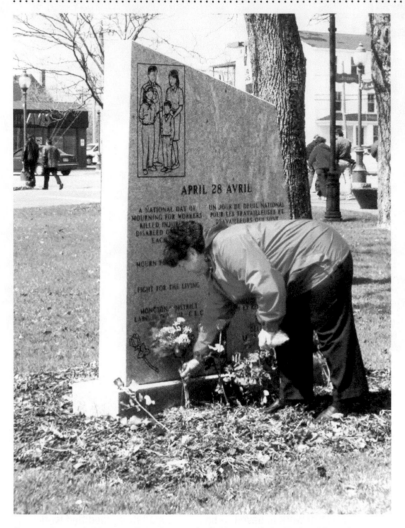

Ceremonies are held across Canada every April 28 to mark the National Day of Mourning for workers killed or injured on the job. In Moncton, New Brunswick, Pauline Farrell lays roses in memory of her late husband, Bill Kelly, who was killed more than 30 years ago.

Lost-time injury rate Measures any occupational injury or illness resulting in an employee being unable to fulfill the work full work assignments, not including any fatalities.

Health and safety initiatives are part of a strategic approach to human resources management. Service provided to clients and customers is a function of how employees are treated, and employee health, safety, and wellness management are important determinants of employee perceptions regarding fair treatment by the organization. Further, investment in disability management and proactive wellness programs create measurable bottom-line returns.[1]

Another reason that safety and accident prevention concerns managers is that the work-related accident figures are staggering. **Lost-time injury rate** measures any occupational injury or illness resulting in an employee being unable to fulfill the work full work assignments, not including any fatalities. According to the Association of Workers' Compensation Boards of Canada, in 2007 there were 1 055 deaths and 317 524 injuries resulting from accidents at work. Thus, on average, more than three Canadian workers died each working day.[2] These figures do not include minor injuries that do not involve time lost from work beyond the day of the accident. Moreover, these figures do not tell the full story. They do not reflect the human suffering incurred by injured or ill workers and their families. On April 28 each year, a day of mourning is observed for Canadian workers killed or injured on the job.

Workplace health concerns are also widespread. Surveys have shown that 61 percent of Canadians believe that workplace accidents are inevitable.[3] According to the Canadian Centre for Justice Statistics, 17 percent of all self-reported incidents of violent victimization, including sexual assault, robbery, and physical assault, occur at the respondents' place of work, representing over 356 000 violent workplace incidents in Canada in one year alone.[4] This statistic is particularly disturbing because workplace accidents are largely preventable.

BASIC FACTS ABOUT OCCUPATIONAL HEALTH AND SAFETY LEGISLATION

occupational health and safety legislation Laws intended to protect the health and safety of workers by minimizing work-related accidents and illnesses.

All provinces, territories, and the federal jurisdiction have **occupational health and safety legislation** based on the principle of joint responsibility. There is an implicit and explicit expectation that both workers and employers must maintain a hazard-free work environment and enhance the health and safety of workers.[5]

Purpose

These laws fall into three categories: general health and safety rules, rules for specific industries (for example, mining), and rules related to specific hazards (for example, asbestos). In some jurisdictions, these are combined into one overall law with regulations for specific industries and hazards, while in others they remain separate. The regulations are very complex and cover almost every conceivable hazard in great detail, as shown in **Figure 14.1**. Provisions of occupational health and safety legislation differ significantly across Canada but most have certain basic features in common.

Responsibilities and Rights of Employers and Employees

In all jurisdictions, employers are responsible for taking every reasonable precaution to ensure the health and safety of their workers. This is called the "due diligence" requirement. Specific duties of the employer include filing government accident reports, maintaining records, ensuring that safety rules are enforced,

---

FIGURE 14.1   Ontario Occupational Health and Safety Act—Construction Regulations

O.REG.213/91

68. A sign used to direct traffic,

(a) shall be diamond shaped, 450 millimetres wide and 450 millimetres long, with the diamond mounted at one corner on a pole 1.2 metres long; (b) shall be made of material that has at least the rigidity of six millimetres thick plywood; (c) shall be reflective fluorescent and coloured, (i) red-orange on one side with the corner areas coloured black, so that the red-orange area forms a regular eight-sided figure, with the word "STOP" written in legible white letters 150 millimetres high in a central position on the sign, and (ii) chartreuse on one side, with the word "SLOW" written in legible black letters 150 millimetres high in a central position on the sign; and (d) shall be maintained in a clean condition.

Source: Ontario Health and Safety Act © Queen's Printer for Ontario, 2011.

and posting safety notices and legislative information.[6] A recent Ontario court decision suggests that employers must enforce safe work procedures through a progressive discipline process to establish a defence of due diligence when workers do not follow safety rules and are injured on the job.[7]

Employees are responsible for taking reasonable care to protect their own health and safety and, in most cases, that of their co-workers. Specific requirements include wearing protective clothing and equipment and reporting any contravention of the law or regulations. Employees have three basic rights under the joint responsibility model: (1) the right to know about workplace safety hazards, (2) the right to participate in the occupational health and safety process, and (3) the right to refuse unsafe work if they have "reasonable cause" to believe that the work is dangerous. "Reasonable cause" usually means that a complaint about a workplace hazard has not been satisfactorily resolved, or a safety problem places employees in immediate danger. If performance of a task would adversely affect health and safety, a worker cannot be disciplined for refusing to do the job.

RPC

Responds to any refusals to perform work believed to be unsafe

Joint Health and Safety Committees

RPC

Establishes a joint health and safety committee as required by law

The function of joint health and safety committees is to provide a non-adversarial atmosphere where management and labour can work together to ensure a safe and healthy workplace. Most jurisdictions require a joint health and safety committee to be established in each workplace with a minimum number of workers (usually 10 or 20). In the other jurisdictions, the government has the power to require a committee to be formed. Committees are usually required to consist of between 2 and 12 members, at least half of whom must represent workers. In small workplaces, one health and safety representative may be required.

The committee is generally responsible for making regular inspections of the workplace to identify potential health and safety hazards, evaluate the hazards, and implement solutions. Hazard control can be achieved by addressing safety issues before an accident or injury happens, identifying ways in which a hazardous situation can be prevented from harming workers, and establishing procedures to ensure that a potential hazard will not recur. Health and safety committees are also responsible for investigating employee complaints, accident investigation, development and promotion of measures to protect health and safety, and dissemination of information about health and safety laws and regulations. In Ontario, at least one management and one labour representative must be certified in occupational health and safety through a provincial training program. Committees are often more effective if the company's health and safety manager acts as an independent expert rather than as a management representative.[8]

The Supervisor's Role in Safety

Most jurisdictions impose a personal duty on supervisors to ensure that workers comply with occupational health and safety regulations. They place a specific obligation on supervisors to advise and instruct workers about safety, to ensure that all reasonable precautions have been taken to provide for the safety of all employees, and to minimize risk of injuries or illness.

Safety-minded managers must aim to instill in their workers the desire to work safely. Minimizing hazards (by ensuring that spills are wiped up, machine guards are adequate, and so forth) is important, but no matter how safe the workplace is, there will be accidents unless workers want to and do act safely. Of course, supervisors try to watch each employee closely, but most managers know that this will not work. In the final analysis, the best (and perhaps only) alternative is to get workers to want to work safely. Then, when needed, safety rules should be enforced.[9]

Enforcement of Occupational Health and Safety Laws

In all Canadian jurisdictions, occupational health and safety law provides for government inspectors to periodically carry out safety inspections of workplaces. Health and safety inspectors have wide powers to conduct inspections in any workplace at any time without a warrant or prior notification and may engage in any examination and inquiry that they believe necessary to ascertain whether the workplace is in compliance with the law. Safety inspectors may order a variety of actions on the part of employers and employees, including orders to stop work or stop using tools, install first aid equipment, and stop emission of contaminants. Governments have been criticized for weak enforcement of health and safety laws, and several provinces have recently strengthened their inspection services.[10]

Penalties consist of fines and/or jail terms. Governments across Canada are increasingly turning to prosecutions as a means of enforcing health and safety standards. In 2008, Alberta imposed a record $5 million in penalties against companies for health and safety violations.[11] Other provinces are increasing the number of charges laid against both individual managers and organizations.[12]

Canadian corporate executives and directors may be held directly responsible for workplace injuries, and in some cases corporate officers have been convicted and received prison sentences for health and safety violations.[13] The Criminal Code includes a criminal offence (known as Bill C-45 amendments, and commonly referred to as "corporate killing") that imposes criminal liability on "all persons" who direct the work of other employees and fail to ensure an appropriate level of safety in the workplace. Criminal Code convictions can be penalized by incarceration up to life in prison, and financial fines can be imposed on guilty parties.

The first company to be charged with and plead guilty to criminal negligence causing death of a worker was Transpavé, a concrete block manufacturer in Quebec. The incident involved a young employee who was crushed by heavy machinery when he tried to remove debris jamming a stacking machine. The machine did have a safety guard device, but the device had been disabled almost two years prior to the accident. In addition, the court found that the company had inadequate programs to ensure safe operations of the machine, and there was a lack of training regarding safety and hazards in the workplace. As a result, the company was found to be negligent in its responsibility of safety in the workplace and the company was fined $110 000.[14]

Control of Toxic Substances

Most occupational health and safety laws require basic precautions with respect to toxic substances, including chemicals, biohazards (such as HIV/AIDS and SARS), and physical agents (such as radiation, heat, and noise). An accurate inventory of these substances must be maintained, maximum exposure limits for airborne concentrations of these agents adhered to, the substances tested, and their use carefully controlled.

The **Workplace Hazardous Materials Information System (WHMIS)** is a Canada-wide, legally mandated system designed to protect workers by providing crucial information about hazardous materials or substances in the workplace. WHMIS was the outcome of a cooperative effort among the federal, provincial, and territorial governments together with industry and organized labour. The WHMIS legislation has three components:[15]

Workplace Hazardous Materials Information System (WHMIS)
A Canada-wide, legally mandated system designed to protect workers by providing information about hazardous materials in the workplace.

1. Labelling of hazardous material containers to alert workers that there is a potentially hazardous product inside (see **Figure 14.2** for examples of hazard symbols).

2. Material safety data sheets (MSDS) to outline a product's potentially hazardous ingredients and the procedures for safe handling of the product (see **Figure 14.3** for a sample MSDS).

WHMIS Training
www.whmis.net

3. Employee training to ensure that employees can identify WHMIS hazard symbols, read WHMIS supplier and workplace labels, and read and apply the information on an MSDS.

Occupational Health and Safety and Other Legislation

Health and safety, human rights, labour relations, and employment standards laws are in force in every jurisdiction in Canada in an interlaced web of legislation. For example, Bill 168 came into effect in June 2010 as an amendment to the Ontario Occupational Health and Safety Act. The amendment has specific legislation requiring the employer to develop violence and harassment policies/ programs, report and investigate violence and harassment situations, develop violence-related emergency response procedures, and deal with complaints, incidents, and threats of violence through a formalized process. Such changes to legislation may be specific or vague, local or national, and short or long term, but the role of HR in addressing and responding to changing occupational health and safety legislation will remain critical.

In addition, situations arise in which it is difficult to know which law is applicable, or which one takes precedence over another. For example, are the human rights of one employee to wear a ceremonial knife related to his or her religion more important than the safety of other employees? How much discipline is acceptable to labour arbitrators for health and safety violations? Should fights in the workplace be considered a safety hazard? Is sexual harassment a safety hazard? And how long does an employer have to tolerate poor performance from an alcoholic employee whose attempts at treatment fail? In Saskatchewan, human rights and occupational health and safety legislation overlap because sexual harassment is considered to be a workplace hazard.[16]

FIGURE 14.2   WHMIS Symbols

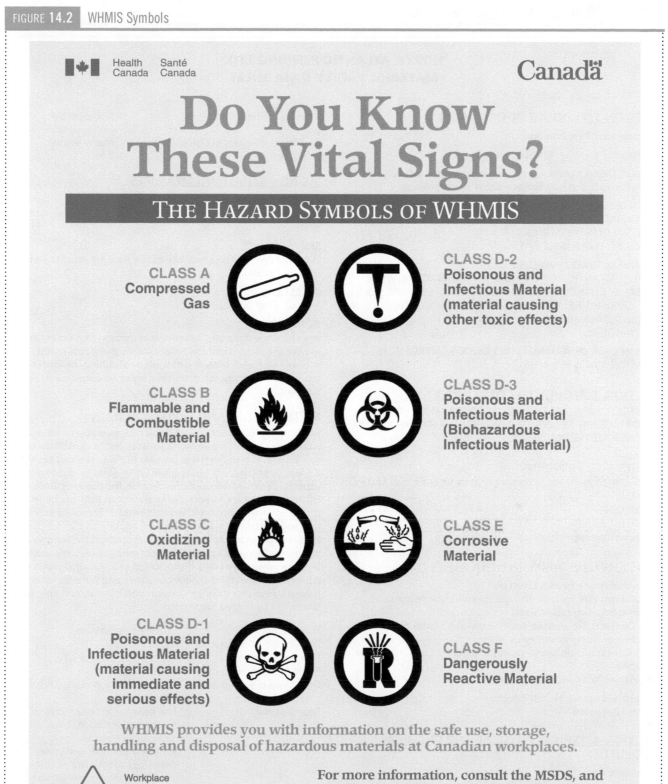

Source: The Hazard Symbols of WHMIS, http://www.hc-sc.gc.ca/ewh-semt/alt_formats/hecs-sesc/pdf/occup-travail/whmis-simdut/poster_symbols-eng.pdf, Health Canada 2011 ©. Adapted and reproduced with the permission of the Minister of Public Works and Government Services Canada, 2012.

FIGURE 14.3   Material Safety Data Sheet (MSDS)

NORTH ATLANTIC REFINING LTD.
MATERIAL SAFETY DATA SHEET

PREPARED: July 26, 2008

SECTION 1. PRODUCT INFORMATION

Product Identifier: **Propane**

Application and Use: Multiple use fuel gas.

Product Description: A colourless gas composed primarily of C3 hydrocarbons and handled as a liquid under pressure.

REGULATORY CLASSIFICATION
W.H.M.I.S.
CLASS A: COMPRESSED GAS
CLASS B1: FLAMMABLE GAS

MANUFACTURER/SUPPLIER:

NORTH ATLANTIC REFINING LTD.	CONTACT BETWEEN
COME BY CHANCE, NFLD. A0B 1N0	07:30–1600 HRS N.S.T.
TEL: (709) 463-8811 (24 hrs.)	Plant Industrial Hygienist
FAX: (709) 463-8076	
AFTER HOURS:	Plant Security

USE IN CASE OF A DANGEROUS GOODS EMERGENCY:
CANUTEC: (613) 996 6666

SECTION 2. REGULATED COMPONENT

THE FOLLOWING ARE DEFINED IN ACCORDANCE WITH SUBPARAGRAPH 13 (a)(I) TO (iv) OR PARAGRAPH 14(a) OF THE HAZARDOUS PRODUCTS ACT:

Name	%	CAS #
CONTROLLED INGREDIENTS		
PROPANE	90 to 95 v/v	74-98-6
ETHANE	0 to 5 v/v	74-84-0
PROPYLENE	0 to 5 v/v	115-07-1
BUTANE	1 to 2.5 v/v	106-97-8

Manufacturer recommended TWA: 1000 ppm

SECTION 3. HAZARDS IDENTIFICATION

Potential Acute Health Effects:
Inhalation: Low toxicity. This gas may displace oxygen and cause suffocation (asphyxiant)
Eye Contact: Exposure to rapidly expanding gases may cause frostbite and permanent eye injury.
Skin Contact: Exposure to rapidly expanding gases may cause frostbite.
Ingestion: Not considered a hazard.

Potential Chronic Health Effects:
None established

SECTION 4. TYPICAL PHYSICAL AND CHEMICAL PROPERTIES

Physical state:	Gas
Odour and appearance:	Colourless gas; may be odorized
Odour threshold:	Not available
Density:	0.51 g/cc @ 15 °C
Vapour pressure:	92000 kPa @ 16 °C
Vapour density:	1.52 (Air = 1)
Evaporation rate:	>1
Boiling point:	−42 °C
Freezing/melting point:	Not available
pH:	Not applicable
Coefficient of water/oil distribution:	Not available
Solubility in water:	0 %

SECTION 5. FIRST AID MEASURES

EYE CONTACT:
In case of cold burns or frostbite of the eye, get prompt medical attention.

SKIN CONTACT:
In case of cold burns or frostbite to the skin, get prompt seek medical attention.

INGESTION:
First aid is not applicable.

INHALATION:
In emergence situations, use proper respiratory protection to remove the victim from the hazard. Allow the victim to rest in a well-ventilated area. If victim is not breathing, perform mouth-to-mouth resuscitation. Seek immediate medical attention.

SECTION 6. FIRE AND EXPLOSION DATA

Fire Fighting Instructions: Flammable gas, insoluble in water. Use water spray to cool fire-exposed surfaces and to protect personnel. Shut off fuel to fire if it is possible to do so without hazard. If a leak or spill has not ignited, use water spray to disperse the vapours. Remotely disconnect or shut off the power sources. Either, allow the fire to burn out under controlled conditions or extinguish with foam, dry chemicals or other approved extinguishing medium. Try to cover spilled liquid with foam. Respiratory, eye and body protection is required for fire fighting personnel. Response to small fire with extinguishers will usually be done upwind and only if considered safe. Personal protective equipment is usually not required when using portable extinguishers. Response to larger (catastrophic) fires should only be attempted by trained fire fighters.

Flammability:	Extremely flammable
Auto-Ignition Temperature:	432 °C
Flammable Limits:	Approx. 2.4 LEL, 9.5 UEL
Products of Combustion:	CO_X, and Smoke
Conditions of Flammability:	Heat and ignition source, flame or electric spark.
Explosion Hazards:	Not believed to be sensitive to mechanical agitation. May accumulate static charge.
Auto-refrigerant:	Rapidly expanding gases may cause ice to form. Drains and valves may become inoperable due to ice formation.

SECTION 7. ACCIDENTAL RELEASE MEASURES

Small Spill: Eliminate sources of ignition. Keep people away. Prevent additional discharge. Warn downwind occupant of hazard.

continued

FIGURE **14.3** (Continued)

Large Spill: Eliminate sources of ignition. Keep people away. Prevent additional discharge. Warn downwind occupant of hazard. Seek advice from the appropriate authorities.

SECTION 8. REACTIVITY DATA

Stability:	Product is stable.
Conditions for instability:	Not available.
Conditions to avoid:	Avoid excessive heat, sources of ignition product extremely flammable
Incompatibility:	Highly reactive with oxidising agents such as peroxides, perchlorates.
Decomposition products:	CO_X, and Smoke.

SECTION 9. PREVENTATIVE MEASURES

Personal Protective Equipment: A full-face shield is recommended to protect eyes and face. Chemically resistant gloves (with a thermal liner) and impervious clothing should be worn at all times while handling the product. When eye or skin contact may occur during short and/or periodic events, long sleeves, chemical-resistant gloves (thermal liner) and a face shield are required. A full-face respirator may be necessary to prevent overexposure by inhalation.

Engineering Controls: Highly recommended for all indoor situations to control fugitive emissions. Electrical and mechanical equipment should be explosion proof Concentrations should be maintained below the lower explosion limit at all times or below the recommended threshold limit value if unprotected personnel are involved. For personnel entry into a confined space (i.e. bulk storage tanks), a proper confined space entry must be followed, including ventilation and testing of tank atmosphere. Make up air should always be supplied to balance air exhausted.

Land Spill: Allow gases to dissipate. Eliminate any sources of ignition. Keep the public away. Prevent additional discharge of material if possible to do so without hazard. Consult an expert on disposal of recovered material. Ensure disposal is performed in compliance with government regulations. Notify the appropriate authorities. For spills over 70L in Canada contact the Canadian Coast Guard, 1-800-563-2444. Take additional action to prevent and remedy the adverse effects of the spill.

Water Spill: Allow gases to dissipate. Eliminate all sources of ignition. Prevent additional discharge of material. Consult an expert on disposal of recovered material. Ensure disposal is performed in compliance with government regulations. Notify the appropriate authorities. For all spills in Canada contact the Canadian Coast Guard, 1-800-563-2444. Take additional action to prevent and remedy the adverse effects of the spill.

Storage and handling: Combustible, store in a cool, dry, well ventilated area away from heat sources.

Keep containers closed. Handle and open propane containers with care.

The information contained herein is based on the data available to us and is believed to be correct. However, North Atlantic Refining Limited makes no warranty, expressed or implied regarding the accuracy of these data or results to be obtained from the use thereof. North Atlantic Refining Limited assumes no responsibility for injury from the use of the product described herein.

Prepared by:
Paul Sullivan
North Atlantic Refining Limited
P.O. Box 40
Come By Chance, Newfoundland, Canada
A0B 1N0
Phone: 709-463-8811 ext 306
FAX: 709-463-3489

At DuPont, safety is the company's highest value, and its accident rate worldwide has been much lower than that of the chemical industry as a whole. As the DuPont safety philosophy states, "Safety management is an integral part of our business and is built on the belief that all injuries and occupational illnesses are preventable; that we are all responsible for our safety and also that of our fellow employees; and that managers are responsible for the safety of those in their organizations."[17]

Without full commitment at all levels of management, any attempts to reduce unsafe acts by workers will meet with little success. The first-line supervisor is a critical link in the chain of management. If the supervisor does not take safety seriously, it is likely that those under him or her will not either.

WHAT CAUSES ACCIDENTS?

Workplace accidents have three basic causes: (1) chance occurrences, (2) unsafe conditions, and (3) unsafe acts on the part of employees.

Chance Occurrences

Chance occurrences (such as walking past a plate-glass window just as someone hits a ball through it) contribute to accidents but are more or less beyond management's control. We will therefore focus on *unsafe conditions* and *unsafe acts*.

Unsafe Conditions

Unsafe conditions are one main cause of accidents. They include such factors as improperly guarded equipment; defective equipment; hazardous procedures in, on, or around machines or equipment; unsafe storage (congestion, overloading); improper illumination (glare, insufficient light); and improper ventilation (insufficient air change, impure air source).[18] In addition, a number of factors have been found to increase the risk of violence in the workplace. These are highlighted in **Figure 14.4**.

The basic remedy here is to eliminate or minimize the unsafe conditions. Government standards address the mechanical and physical conditions that cause accidents. Furthermore, a checklist of unsafe conditions can be used to conduct a job hazard analysis. Common indicators of job hazards include increased numbers of accidents, employee complaints, poor product quality, employee modifications to workstations, and higher levels of absenteeism and turnover.[19]

Tips FOR THE FRONT LINE

In addition to unsafe conditions, three other work-related factors contribute to accidents: the *job itself,* the *work schedule,* and the *psychological climate* of the workplace. Certain jobs are inherently more dangerous than others. According to one study, for example, the job of crane operator results in about three times more accident-related hospital visits than does the job of supervisor. Similarly, the work of some departments is inherently safer than that of others. An accounting department usually has fewer accidents than a shipping department.

FIGURE **14.4**   Who Is at Risk From Workplace Violence?

Violence can happen in any workplace. However, people whose jobs involve any of the following factors are at increased risk of workplace violence:

- Contact with the public
- Exchange of money
- Delivery of passengers, goods, or services
- Having a mobile workplace (such as a vehicle)
- Working with unstable or volatile people
- Working alone or in small numbers
- Working late at night or during early morning hours
- Guarding valuable property or possessions
- Working in community-based settings (e.g., home care)

Source: Workplace Safety and Insurance Board Ontario, "Who Is at Risk from Workplace Violence?" www.wsib.on.ca/en/community/WSIB/230/ArticleDetail/24338?vgnextoid=bb194c23529d7210VgnVCM1000 00449c710aRCRD (accessed July 10, 2012).

Work schedules and fatigue also affect accident rates. Accident rates usually do not increase too noticeably during the first five or six hours of the workday. Beyond that, however, the accident rate increases quickly as the number of hours worked increases. This is due partly to fatigue. It has also been found that accidents occur more often during night shifts.

Finally, many experts believe that the psychological climate of the workplace affects the accident rate. For example, accidents occur more frequently in plants with a high seasonal layoff rate and those where there is hostility among employees, many garnished wages, and blighted living conditions. Temporary stress factors, such as high workplace temperature, poor illumination, and a congested workplace, are also related to accident rates. It appears that workers who work under stress or who consider their jobs to be threatened or insecure have more accidents than those who do not work under these conditions.[20]

Unsafe Acts

Most safety experts and managers know that it is impossible to eliminate accidents just by improving unsafe conditions. People cause accidents, and no one has found a sure-fire way to eliminate *unsafe acts* by employees, such as

- throwing materials
- operating or working at unsafe speeds (either too fast or too slow)
- making safety devices inoperative by removing, adjusting, or disconnecting them
- using unsafe equipment or using equipment unsafely
- using unsafe procedures in loading, placing, mixing, and combining
- taking unsafe positions under suspended loads
- lifting improperly
- distracting, teasing, abusing, startling, quarrelling, and instigating horseplay

Such unsafe acts as these can undermine even the best attempts to minimize unsafe conditions, and the progressive discipline system should be used in such situations.

Personal Characteristics

A model summarizing how personal characteristics are linked to accidents is presented in **Figure 14.5**. Personal characteristics (personality, motivation, and so on) can serve as the basis for certain undesirable attitudes and behaviour tendencies, such as the tendency to take risks. These behaviour tendencies can, in turn, result in unsafe acts, such as inattention and failure to follow procedures. It follows that such unsafe acts increase the probability of someone having an accident.[21]

Years of research have failed to unearth any set of traits that accident repeaters seem to have in common. Instead, the consensus is that the person who is accident prone on one job may not be that way on a different job—that accident proneness is *situational*. For example, *personality traits* (such as emotional stability) may distinguish accident-prone workers on jobs involving

Research INSIGHT

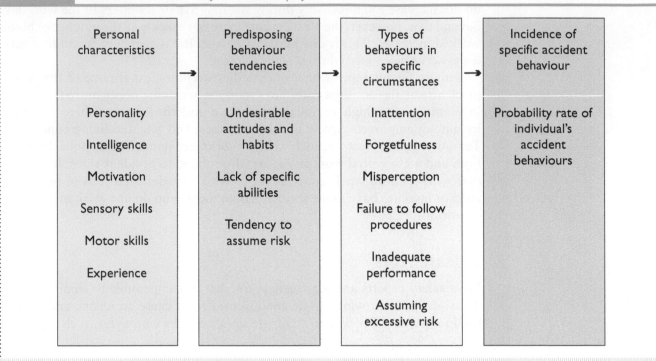

risk; and *lack of motor skills* may distinguish accident-prone workers on jobs involving coordination. In fact, many human traits have been found to be related to accident repetition in specific situations, as the following discussion illustrates.[22]

Vision

Vision is related to accident frequency for many jobs. For example, passenger car drivers, intercity bus drivers, and machine operators who have high visual skills have fewer injuries than those who do not.[23]

Literacy

The risk of accidents is higher for employees who cannot read and understand machinery operating instructions, safety precautions, equipment and repair manuals, first aid instructions, or organizational policies on workplace health and safety. Low literacy skills potentially put workers and their co-workers in harm's way and increase the likelihood of work stoppages due to accidents or errors.[24] This situation is complicated by the fact that most workers with low literacy skills believe that their skills are good or excellent.[25]

A report by the Conference Board of Canada concluded that employers can reduce accidents by improving employees' literacy skills. They found an inverse relationship between industries requiring a high level of health and safety and investment in literacy skills.[26] This finding, together with the reality that people with lower levels of literacy often end up in more dangerous occupations like trucking, manufacturing, or construction, where literacy requirements are low compared to more intellectual jobs, clearly indicates the need for action to heighten literacy skills of workers.

Age

Canadian LifeQuilt
www.youngworkerquilt.ca

Accidents are generally most frequent among people between the ages of 17 and 28, declining thereafter to reach a low in the late 50s and 60s. Although different patterns might be found with different jobs, this age factor repeats year after year.

Across Canada, young workers between the ages of 15 and 24 (often students in low-paying summer jobs) are over five times more likely to be injured during their first four weeks on the job than others, which raises questions about the supervision and training of young workers.[27] Suggestions regarding training of young workers are provided in the Workforce Diversity box.

Perceptual versus Motor Skills

If a worker's perceptual skill is greater than or equal to his or her motor skill, the employee is more likely to be a safe worker than another worker whose perceptual skill is lower than his or her motor skill.[28] In other words, a worker who reacts more quickly than he or she can perceive is more likely to have accidents.

Jessica DiSabatino, with a picture of her 18-year-old brother David Ellis who was killed on his second day on the job in 1999, wants employers to take young worker safety seriously.

WORKFORCE DIVERSITY

Guiding Young Workers in Health and Safety

The Canadian Centre for Occupational Health and Safety suggests that to reduce the likelihood of accidents and injuries to young workers, the following basic steps should be observed:

1. *Assign suitable work.* Avoid assigning jobs that require long training times, a high degree of skill, a lot of responsibility, critical or risky tasks, or working alone.

2. *Understand young workers.* Young workers think differently than older and more experienced employees do. Young workers tend to take risks and are unrealistic about their own mortality; they may be reluctant to ask questions for fear of appearing unknowledgeable; and because of a lack of understanding, they may decide to make changes to the job in unexpected and possibly risky ways.

3. *Provide training.* Tell young workers not to perform any task until they have been properly trained; not to leave their work area unless they are told to do so, as other worksites may have special hazards; and to ask someone if they are unsure of anything. Make sure that any young worker who must use hazardous equipment is given detailed training on safety features. If young workers must wear protective equipment, make sure they know when they need to wear it, where to find it, how to use it, and how to care for it. Finally, provide training on what to do in case of emergency.

4. *Supervise.* Effective supervision of young workers requires that supervisors be qualified to organize and direct work; that they know the laws and regulations that apply to the job; and that they know the actual and potential hazards in the workplace.

Source: Canadian Centre for Occupational Health and Safety (CCOHS), "Employers: Guiding Young Workers in Health and Safety," www.ccohs.ca/youngworkers/employers.html. Reproduced with the permission of CCOHS (2009).

In summary, these findings provide a partial list of the human traits that have been found to be related to higher accident rates, and they suggest that, for specific jobs, it seems to be possible to identify accident-prone individuals and to screen them out. Overall, it seems that accidents can have multiple causes. With that in mind, accident prevention will be discussed.

HOW TO PREVENT ACCIDENTS

In practice, accident prevention involves reducing unsafe conditions and reducing unsafe acts.

Reducing Unsafe Conditions

Reducing unsafe conditions is an employer's first line of defence. Safety engineers can design jobs to remove or reduce physical hazards. In addition, supervisors and managers play a role in reducing unsafe conditions by ensuring that employees wear personal protective equipment, an often difficult chore. However, only 4 percent of accidents stem from unsafe working conditions, and therefore more attention will be paid to accident prevention methods that focus on changing employee behaviours.

Reducing Unsafe Acts

Reducing unsafe acts is the second basic approach, and there are four specific actions that can help to reduce unsafe acts.

Selection Testing

Employee Reliability Inventory
www.eri.com

Certain selection tests can help screen out accident-prone individuals before they are hired. For example, measures of muscular coordination can be useful because coordination is a predictor of safety for certain jobs. Tests of visual skills can be important because good vision plays a part in preventing accidents in many occupations, including operating machines and driving. A test called the Employee Reliability Inventory (ERI), which measures reliability dimensions such as emotional maturity, conscientiousness, safe job performance, and courteous job performance, can also be helpful in selecting employees who are less likely to have accidents.

Research INSIGHT

A Canadian study conducted in a major industrial plant compared injury costs for a group of employees that were subjected to post-offer screening to assess their physical capability to perform job duties, and another group that did not receive post-offer screening. Injury costs over five years for the screened group were $6 500 and for the non-screened group were $2 073 000—a highly significant difference.[29]

Many employers would like to inquire about applicants' workers' compensation history before hiring, in part to avoid habitual workers' compensation claimants and accident-prone individuals. However, inquiring about an applicant's workers' compensation injuries and claims can lead to allegations of discrimination based on disability. Similarly, applicants cannot be asked whether they have a disability, nor can they be asked to take tests that tend to screen out those with disabilities.

Employers can ask each applicant whether he or she has the ability to perform the essential duties of the job and ask, "Do you know of any reason why you would not be able to perform the various functions of the job in question?" Candidates can also be asked to demonstrate job-related skills, provided that every applicant is required to do so. Any selection test that duplicates the physical requirements of the job at realistic levels and the type of work expected does not violate human rights law, as long as it is developed and imposed honestly and in good faith to test whether or not the applicant can meet production requirements.[30]

Top-Management Commitment

Studies consistently find that successful health and safety programs require a strong management commitment. An example of the importance of top-management commitment is provided in the Strategic HR box. This commitment manifests itself in senior managers being personally involved in safety activities on a routine basis, giving safety matters high priority in company meetings and production scheduling, giving the company safety officer high rank and status, and including safety training in new workers' training. For example, linking managers' bonuses to safety improvements can reinforce a firm's commitment to safety and encourage managers to emphasize safety. HR managers have an important role to play in communicating the importance of health and safety to senior management by demonstrating how it affects the bottom line.

Training and Education

Safety training is another technique for reducing accidents. The Canadian Centre for Occupational Health and Safety and several safety associations, such as the Industrial Accident Prevention Association (IAPA), are available to partner in training efforts. The Canadian Federation of Independent Business offers online training leading to a Small Business Health and Safety (SBHS) certificate.

All employees should be required to participate in occupational health and safety training programs, and opportunities for employee input into the content and design of such programs is advisable. The training should include a practical evaluation process to ensure that workers are applying the acquired knowledge and following recommended safety procedures. Such training is especially appropriate for new employees.

Industrial Accident Prevention Association
www.iapa.ca

Safety posters can also help reduce unsafe acts. However, posters are no substitute for a comprehensive safety program; instead, they should be combined with other techniques, like screening and training, to reduce unsafe conditions and acts. Posters with pictures may be particularly valuable for immigrant workers if their first language is not the language of the workplace.

An Ethical Dilemma

Is it ethical to provide safety training in English to immigrant workers who speak little English in order to reduce costs?

STRATEGIC HR

Top Management Commitment to Safety at Steelcase Canada Pays Off

"Quite exceptional." That's how Tony Grech, a field consultant for the Industrial Accident Prevention Association (IAPA), describes the lost-time injury rates at Steelcase Canada's facility in Markham, Ontario, where their 460 employees manufacture office furniture. The company's lost-time injury rates were 79 percent to 87 percent lower than its associated rate group from 2001 to 2005.

The high scores were the result of a reinvigorated commitment to health and safety at the company, according to Mike Fenuta, manager of health and safety. "The key was ownership from our leadership," said Fenuta. "They really started integrating that and made it an accountability across the board, not only from senior executives but right down to the shop-floor employee, where safety was discussed on a daily basis."

Steelcase set up a joint health and safety committee, as required by law, but decided to go beyond that in establishing safety teams that met weekly for each area of responsibility. These then developed into safety and quality teams that "have now become part of the business," said Fenuta.

"We've always believed people are our most important asset and we have to invest in them, just like we would in hard assets like equipment. We've been establishing standards that not only meet the requirements but are one step beyond. Most of the time we are ahead of the curve."

Consequently morale has improved because of the safer environment and employees feel more appreciated. New employees are also given an extensive orientation so they "get on board a lot quicker with quality issues and adherence to safety issues," said Steve Taylor, environmental and plant engineer at Steelcase.

And, "if you take care of people, they produce good quality products, which in return are delivered to customers on time, and that takes care of your financials," said Fenuta.

There are definite savings, both tangible and intangible, from improved health and safety, said Taylor. For one, Steelcase has received significant rebates every year through an experience rating system run by Ontario's Workplace Safety and Insurance Board. Taylor said Steelcase has averaged more than $250 000 in annual savings. The better health and safety conditions have also reduced the absentee rate, so additional "floater" labour hired to cover routine absence is no longer needed, meaning two fewer employees and no need for extra staff.

Over the past 10 years, health and safety has become a fundamental part of the company's culture. "It's a major cultural shift and it takes years to develop this," said Grech. "It's not done overnight."

Source: S. Dobson, "Good Health and Safety Brings Enviable Rewards," *Canadian HR Reporter* (February 12, 2007). Reprinted by permission of Canadian HR Reporter. © Copyright Thomson Reuters Canada Ltd., (2012) Toronto, Ontario, 1-800-387-5164. Web: www.hrreporter.com

Positive Reinforcement

Safety programs based on positive reinforcement can improve safety behaviour at work. Employees often receive little or no positive reinforcement for performing safely. One approach is to establish and communicate a reasonable goal (in terms of observed incidents performed safely) so that workers know what is expected of them in terms of good performance. Employees are encouraged to increase their performance to the new safety goal for their own protection and to decrease costs for the company. Various observers (such as safety coordinators and senior managers) walk through the plant regularly, collecting safety data. The results are then posted on a graph charting the percentage of incidents performed safely by the group as a whole, thus providing workers with feedback on their safety performance. Workers can compare their current safety performance with their assigned goal. In addition, supervisors should praise workers when they perform selected activities safely.[31]

For example, UPS Canada honours drivers who have achieved 25 years or more of safe driving with a special badge to add to their uniform. The drivers are part of UPS's prestigious Circle of Honour, the company's highest level of driving recognition.[32]

Controlling Workers' Compensation Costs

Workers' compensation costs are often the most expensive benefit provided by an employer. For example, the average workplace injury in Ontario costs more than $59 000 in workers' compensation benefits. Indirect costs are estimated to be about four times the direct costs.[33] Each firm's workers' compensation premiums are proportional to its workers' compensation experience rate. Thus, the more claims a firm has, the more the firm will pay in premiums. A new online tool is available for small businesses in Ontario to calculate the true costs of a workplace injury, as explained in the Entrepreneurs and HR box.

ENTREPRENEURS and HR

Small Business Safety Calculator

Statistics from Ontario's Workplace Safety and Insurance Board (WSIB) show that the job fatality rates of small businesses are 6.7 times higher than those for larger businesses, and lost-time injury rates are 10 percent higher. When a worker in Ontario is injured on the job, the WSIB pays for costs associated with the injury claim, including health, rehabilitation, and disability costs. However, injuries cost small businesses in many other areas not covered by WSIB insurance. The Industrial Accident Prevention Association (IAPA)'s free small business safety calculator will help businesses identify and quantify these costs, including the following:

- **Incident Costs**—time to provide first aid; time for transportation to hospital/clinic/home; lost productivity of all affected workers; time to make area safe; cost of first aid supplies and equipment used; cost of ambulance or taxi

- **Investigation Costs**—time to investigate the accident; time spent to complete an accident investigation report; time to complete related paperwork for the company; time taken to report the incident to the WSIB and meet with WSIB officers; follow-up meetings to discuss the accident

- **Damage Costs**—time to assess the damage; time to repair or replace equipment; time to coordinate repair work; clean-up time; cost of outside contractors and materials for clean up; cost to dispose of damaged equipment; cost of replacement parts, equipment, or lost product

- **Replacement Costs**—time to hire or relocate replacement worker; relocation or rescheduling of another worker; trainer time for new or relocated worker; trainee time for new or relocated worker; cost to hire a replacement worker

- **Productivity Costs**—lost productivity due to disruption; time spent managing the injury claim; reduced productivity of injured worker after he or she returns to work

The IAPA small business safety calculator is modelled after one created by WorkSafeBC. It was re-engineered for use in Ontario and specifically for those companies that fall within one of IAPA's 12 industry groups: glass, stone, and ceramics; chemical and plastics; food and beverage; agri-business; high-tech; industrial auto sales; leather, rubber, and tanners; metal trades; office and related services; printing trades; textile and allied trades; and woodworking. The calculator is available online at www.iapa.ca/sbc.

Source: "Calculating the Costs of Workplace Injuries," *Canadian HR Reporter* (April 9, 2007).

Tips : FOR THE FRONT LINE

RPC

Ensures compliance with
legislated reporting requirements

Ensures adequate
accommodation, modified work,
and graduated return-to-work
programs are in place

Ensures that modifications to the
work environment are consistent
with worker limitations

Before the Accident

The appropriate time to begin "controlling" workers' compensation claims is before the accident happens, not after. This involves taking all the steps previously summarized. For example, firms should remove unsafe conditions, screen out employees who might be accident-prone for the job in question (without violating human rights legislation), and establish a safety policy and loss control goals.

After the Accident—Facilitating the Employee's Return to Work

Employers should provide first aid, make sure that the worker gets quick medical attention, make it clear that they are interested in the injured worker and his or her fears and questions, document the accident, file any required accident reports, and encourage a speedy return to work. Perhaps the most important and effective thing an employer can do to reduce costs is to develop an aggressive return-to-work program.

The National Institute of Disability Management and Research (NIDMAR) in Victoria, British Columbia, recommends following the three Cs: (1) *commitment* to keeping in touch with the worker and ensuring his or her return to work; (2) *collaboration* among the parties involved, including medical, family, and workers' compensation; and (3) *creativity* in focusing on how to use the worker's remaining abilities on the job.[34]

Specific actions to encourage early return to work can be internal or external to the organization. Internally, an employer can set up rehabilitation committees to identify modified work, including relevant stakeholders, such as the employee and his or her colleagues, HR professionals, union representatives, and managers.

Functional abilities evaluations (FAEs) are an important step in facilitating the return to work. The FAE is conducted by a healthcare professional with an aim to

- improve the chances that the injured worker will be safe on the job
- help the worker's performance by identifying problem areas of work that can be addressed by physical therapy or accommodated through job modification
- determine the level of disability so that the worker can either go back to his or her original job or be accommodated[35]

Externally, the employer can work with the employee's family to ensure that they are supportive, mobilize the resources of the EAP to help the employee, ensure that physical and occupational therapists are available, and make the family physician aware of workplace accommodation possibilities.

OCCUPATIONAL HEALTH AND SAFETY CHALLENGES IN CANADA

A number of health-related issues and challenges can undermine employee performance at work. These include alcoholism and substance abuse, stress and burnout, repetitive strain injuries, workplace toxins, workplace smoking, influenza pandemics, and workplace violence.

Substance Abuse

The effects of substance abuse on the employee and his or her work are severe. Both the quality and quantity of work decline sharply, and safety may be compromised. When dealing with alcohol and substance abuse on the job, employers must balance conflicting legal obligations. On the one hand, under human rights laws, alcoholism and drug addiction are considered to be disabilities. On the other hand, under occupational health and safety legislation, employers are responsible for maintaining due diligence. As a result, employers worry that when they accommodate an employee with an addiction, they may not be ensuring a safe work environment for other employees.[36]

Further, drug and alcohol testing in Canada is only legal in situations where three conditions determined by the Supreme Court are met:

1. The test is rationally connected to the performance of the job.
2. The test is adopted in an honest and good-faith belief that it is necessary for the fulfillment of a legitimate work-related purpose.
3. The test is reasonably necessary to the accomplishment of the work-related purpose.[37]

Random drug tests do not measure actual impairment and are therefore unjustifiable. Arbitrary alcohol testing of one or more employees but not others is not usually justifiable, but for employees in safety-sensitive positions, such as airline pilots, it may be justifiable. "For cause" and "post-incident" testing for either alcohol or drugs may be acceptable in specific circumstances. Positive test results should generally result in accommodation of the employee. Immediate dismissal is not generally justifiable.[38]

Recognizing the substance abuser on the job can pose a problem. The early symptoms can be similar to those of other problems and thus hard to classify. Problems range from tardiness to prolonged, unpredictable absences in later stages of addiction. Supervisors should be the company's first line of defence in combating substance abuse in the workplace, but they should not try to be company detectives or medical diagnosticians. Guidelines for supervisors should include the following:[39]

- If an employee appears to be under the influence of drugs or alcohol, ask how the employee feels and look for signs of impairment, such as slurred speech. An employee judged to be unfit for duty may be sent home but not fired on the spot.

- Make a written record of observed behaviour and follow up each incident. In addition to issuing a written reprimand, managers should inform workers of the number of warnings that the company will tolerate before requiring termination. Regardless of any suspicion of substance abuse, concerns should be focused on work performance, expected changes, and available options for help.

- Troubled employees should be referred to the company's employee assistance program.

The four traditional techniques for dealing with substance abuse are discipline, discharge, in-house counselling, and referral to an outside agency. Discharge is used to deal with alcoholism and drug problems only after repeated attempts at rehabilitation have failed. In-house counselling can be offered by the employer's medical staff or the employee assistance plan. External agencies such as Alcoholics Anonymous can also be used.

Hints | TO ENSURE LEGAL COMPLIANCE

RPC

Ensures that policies for required medical testing fall within the limits of statute and contract

Tips | FOR THE FRONT LINE

Bellwood Health Services Inc.
www.bellwood.ca

Shepell.fgi
www.shepellfgi.com

In Grande Prairie, Alberta, a clinic was established by the Alberta Alcohol and Drug Abuse Commission as a result of requests from the business community for a treatment centre that could deal with workplace-specific issues. It offers quick enrollment in its 30-day alcohol treatment program or the 50-day cocaine treatment program for $175 per day, plus months of follow-up, helping 180 clients a year return to work as soon as possible.[40]

Job-Related Stress

Workplace stress is a pervasive problem that is getting worse. Job stress has serious consequences for both the employee and the organization. The human consequences of job stress include anxiety, depression, anger, and various physical consequences, such as cardiovascular disease, headaches, and accidents. In Canada, the total cost of mental health problems approximates 17 percent of payroll, and the overall economic impact of work-related mental health problems is estimated to be $51 billion annually.[41] Stress also has serious consequences for the organization, including reductions in productivity and increased absenteeism and turnover.[42] Lost productivity at work due to health-related issues can cost the average Canadian organization up to $10 million each year.[43] Mental health issues are the leading cause of both short- and long-term disability claims.[44] Many organizations make physical safety a priority, but too often work environments that clearly have the potential for serious consequences from stress are simply tolerated.[45] Perhaps this reflects the fact that two-thirds of companies underestimate the prevalence of mental illness in the workplace, and only 13 percent of senior executives have a strong awareness of the impact of mental health on their workplaces.[46] As reflected in **Figure 14.6**, there are common indicators that a colleague is reaching their stress threshold.

Organizations begin to suffer when too many employees feel that the relentless pace of work life is neither sustainable nor healthy. Why is this

| FIGURE **14.6** | Warning Signs: How Can You Tell if an Employee Is Reaching Their Stress Threshold? |

How can you tell if a colleague has reached the breaking point? Experts note some possible indicators:

- Skipping group lunches: a signal someone feels demoralized and not part of their work community
- Coming to work late: one of the first hints that stress is eating away at motivation
- Calling in sick frequently: if people feel they aren't getting a break at work, they may start taking them on their own
- Withdrawing: when someone uncharacteristically retreats from water cooler talk and office banter, it may indicate an unhealthy distancing from colleagues
- Obsessing: if colleagues focus on seemingly insignificant matters or isolated incidents, it may mean they are angry or can no longer cope with the big picture

Source: Mitchell Messer, director of the Anger Institute in Chicago; R. Brayton Bowen, president of The Howland Group, a management-consulting firm. Printed in "Stressed Out: Can Workplace Stress Get Worse?" *Wall Street Journal* (January 16, 2001), p. 1.

happening? Employees are being asked to do more with less, creating work overload, increased time pressures, and tighter deadlines (almost one-third of Canadian workers consider themselves workaholics).[47] More people are working in "precarious" employment, such as temporary or part-time work with no benefits.[48] The sheer volume of email imposes terrific amounts of pressure and distraction on employees, taking a toll on their emotional equilibrium. Psychopathic bosses with no consciences, called "snakes in suits," can wreak havoc with other employees. The result is a corporate climate characterized by fatigue, depression, and anxiety.[49]

Job stress has two main sources: environmental factors and personal factors. First, a variety of external, *environmental factors* can lead to job stress. Two factors are particularly stress-inducing. The first is a high-demand job, such as one with constant deadlines coupled with low employee control. The second is high levels of mental and physical effort combined with low rewards in terms of compensation or acknowledgement.[50] Healthcare workers, whose jobs typically include these factors, are more stressed than any other group.[51] However, no two people react to the same job in an identical way, since *personal factors* also influence stress. For example, Type A personalities—people who are workaholics and who feel driven to always be on time and meet deadlines—normally place themselves under greater stress than do others. Similarly, one's patience, tolerance for ambiguity, self-esteem, health and exercise, and work and sleep patterns can also affect how one reacts to stress. Add to job stress the stress caused by non-job-related issues like divorce, postpartum depression, seasonal affective disorder, and work–family conflict, and many workers are problems waiting to happen.

Yet stress is not necessarily dysfunctional. Too little stress creates boredom and apathy. Performance is optimal at a level of stress that energizes but does not wear someone out.[52] Others find that stress may result in a search that leads to a better job or to a career that makes more sense given the person's aptitudes. A modest level of stress may even lead to more creativity if a competitive situation results in new ideas being generated.

Reducing Job Stress

There are things that a person can do to alleviate stress, ranging from commonsense remedies, such as getting more sleep, eating better, and taking vacation time, to more exotic remedies, such as biofeedback and meditation. Finding a more suitable job, getting counselling through an EAP or elsewhere, and planning and organizing each day's activities are other sensible responses.[53]

The organization and its HR specialists and supervisors can also play a role in identifying and reducing job stress. Offering an EAP is a major step toward alleviating the pressure on managers to try to help employees cope with stress. About 40 percent of EAP usage is related to stress at work. For the supervisor, important activities include monitoring each employee's performance to identify symptoms of stress and then informing the person of the organizational remedies that may be available, such as EAPs, job transfers, or other counselling. Also important are fair treatment and permitting the employee to have more control over his or her job.[54]

An Ethical : Dilemma

Is it ethical for an organization to ignore the issue of job stress entirely?

Research :INSIGHT

The importance of control over a job was illustrated by the results of a study in which the psychological strain caused by job stress was reduced by the amount of control that employees had over their job. The less stressful jobs did have high demands in terms of quantitative workload, the amount of attention that the employees had to pay to their work, and work pressure; however, they also ranked high in task clarity, job control, supervisory support, and employee skill utilization. The researchers conclude that "to achieve a balanced system, that is, to reduce psychological strain, [job] demands and [ambiguity regarding the future of the job] need to be lowered, while skill utilization, task clarity, job control, and supervisor support need to be increased."[55]

HR executives need to become advocates for employee mental health within the senior management team. Today's highly valued employees who are driving corporate productivity, innovation, and performance tend to be young knowledge workers, precisely the type of worker most prone to depression and stress.[56]

Burnout

burnout The total depletion of physical and mental resources caused by excessive striving to reach an unrealistic work-related goal.

Many people fall victim to **burnout**—the total depletion of physical and mental resources—because of excessive striving to reach an unrealistic work-related goal. Burnout begins with cynical and pessimistic thoughts and leads to apathy, exhaustion, withdrawal into isolation, and eventually depression.[57] Burnout is often the result of too much job stress, especially when that stress is combined with a preoccupation with attaining unattainable work-related goals. Burnout victims often do not lead well-balanced lives; virtually all of their energies are focused on achieving their work-related goals to the exclusion of other activities, leading to physical and sometimes mental collapse. This need not be limited to upwardly mobile executives; for instance, social workers caught up in their clients' problems are often burnout victims.

What can a candidate for burnout do? Here are some suggestions:

Tips :FOR THE FRONT LINE

- *Break patterns.* First, survey how you spend your time. Are you doing a variety of things, or the same thing over and over? The more well-rounded your life is, the better protected you are against burnout. If you have stopped trying new activities, start them again—for instance, travel or new hobbies.

- *Get away from it all periodically.* Schedule occasional periods of introspection during which you can get away from your usual routine, perhaps alone, to seek a perspective on where you are and where you are going.

- *Reassess goals in terms of their intrinsic worth.* Are the goals that you have set for yourself attainable? Are they really worth the sacrifices that you will have to make?

- *Think about work.* Could you do as good a job without being so intense or while also pursuing outside interests?

- *Reduce stress.* Organize your time more effectively, build a better relationship with your boss, negotiate realistic deadlines, find time during the day for detachment and relaxation, reduce unnecessary noise around your office, and limit interruptions.

Workers' Compensation and Stress-Related Disability Claims

All Canadian jurisdictions provide benefits for post-traumatic stress caused by a specific and sudden workplace incident. However, when it comes to chronic stress, there is very limited or no coverage, depending on the jurisdiction.[58]

The rationale is that stress has multiple causes, including family situations and personal disposition. Research suggests, however, that a significant portion of chronic stress is often work related. In particular, high-demand/low-control jobs (such as an administrative assistant with several demanding bosses) are known to be "psychotoxic." Consequently, employees who are denied workers' compensation benefits for chronic stress that they believe to be work related are suing their employers. The courts are recognizing these claims and holding employers responsible for actions of supervisors who create "poisoned work environments" through harassment and psychological abuse. Courts are finding that a fundamental implied term of any employment relationship is that the employer will treat the employee fairly and with respect and dignity and that the due diligence requirement includes protection of employees from psychological damage as well as physical harm.[59]

Repetitive Strain Injuries

repetitive strain injuries (RSIs)
Activity-related soft-tissue injuries of the neck, shoulders, arms, wrists, hands, back, and legs.

RSI Clinic
www.treatpain.ca/RSI_CLINIC.html

Human Systems Inc.
www.humansys.com

Human Factors and Ergonomics Society
www.hfes.org

Repetitive strain injuries (**RSIs**) are rapidly becoming the most prevalent work-related injury because of the increasing number of "knowledge" workers who use computers. RSI is an umbrella term for a number of "overuse" injuries affecting muscles, tendons, and nerves of the neck, back, chest, shoulders, arms, and hands. Typically arising as aches and pains, these injuries can progress to become crippling disorders that prevent sufferers from working and from leading normal lives. Warning signs of RSI include tightness or stiffness in the hands, elbow, wrists, shoulders, and neck; numbness and tingling in the fingertips; hands falling asleep; and frequent dropping of tools.[60]

A variety of workplace factors can play a role in the development of RSIs, including repetition, work pace, awkward or fixed positions, forceful movements, vibration, cold temperatures, and insufficient recovery time. RSIs are costly for employers in terms of compensation claims, overtime, equipment modification, retraining, and lost productivity. As with any other workplace safety issue, employers are required under occupational health and safety law to put controls in place to prevent RSIs. British Columbia has the most rigorous requirements regarding protection of workers against RSIs, and unions are calling for other provinces to follow suit. Employers must advise and train workers about the risk of RSIs from workplace activity, identify and assess job-related RSI risk factors, encourage workers to report RSI symptoms early, and use ergonomic interventions.[61]

Ergonomics

ergonomics An interdisciplinary approach that seeks to integrate and accommodate the physical needs of workers into the design of jobs. It aims to adapt the entire job system—the work, environment, machines, equipment, and processes—to match human characteristics.

Poorly designed workstations, bad posture, and long periods of time working on computers are common conditions leading to RSIs, and these are easily preventable. **Ergonomics** is the art of fitting the workstation and work tools to the individual, which is necessary because there is no such thing as an average body. **Figure 14.7** illustrates ergonomic factors at a computer workstation. The most important preventive measure is to have employees take short breaks every half-hour or hour to do simple stretches at their workstations.[62]

Ergonomically designed workstations have been found to increase productivity and efficiency, as well as reduce injuries. The Institute for Work and Health studied 200 tax collectors who were in sedentary, computer-intensive jobs. Workers who were given a highly adjustable chair combined with a 90-minute

FIGURE **14.7**   Computer Ergonomics

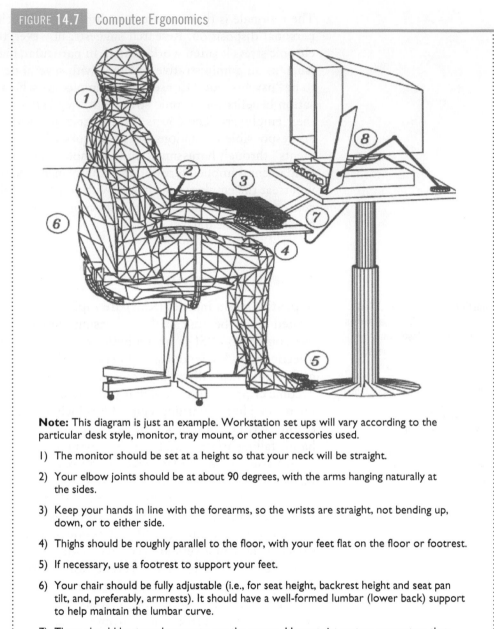

Note: This diagram is just an example. Workstation set ups will vary according to the particular desk style, monitor, tray mount, or other accessories used.

1) The monitor should be set at a height so that your neck will be straight.

2) Your elbow joints should be at about 90 degrees, with the arms hanging naturally at the sides.

3) Keep your hands in line with the forearms, so the wrists are straight, not bending up, down, or to either side.

4) Thighs should be roughly parallel to the floor, with your feet flat on the floor or footrest.

5) If necessary, use a footrest to support your feet.

6) Your chair should be fully adjustable (i.e., for seat height, backrest height and seat pan tilt, and, preferably, armrests). It should have a well-formed lumbar (lower back) support to help maintain the lumbar curve.

7) There should be enough space to use the mouse. Use a wrist rest or armrest so that your wrist is straight and your arm muscles are not overworked.

8) Use an adjustable document holder to hold source documents at the same height, angle, and distance as the monitor.

Source: Computer Ergonomics: Workstation Layout and Lighting (Toronto, ON: Ontario Ministry of Labour Health and Safety Guidelines, 2004). © Queen's Printer for Ontario, 2004. Reproduced with permission.

Research INSIGHT

ergonomics training session reported less musculoskeletal pain over their work-day, compared with workers who received just the training or nothing at all. Productivity increased nearly 18 percent because of the reduction in pain and more effective use of workspaces.[63]

Ergonomics will become more and more important as the workforce ages, and the physical demands of work will need to be adapted to accommodate some of the many physical changes typically associated with aging, including changes in muscular strength, hand function, cardiovascular capacity, vision, and hearing.

Video Display Terminals

The physical demands of new technologies have brought a new set of RSIs. The fact that many workers today must spend hours each day working with video display terminals (VDTs) is creating new health problems at work. Short-term eye problems, like burning, itching, and tearing, as well as eyestrain and eye soreness are common complaints among video display operators. Backaches and neck aches are also widespread among display users. These often occur because employees try to compensate for display problems like glare and immovable keyboards by manoeuvring into awkward body positions.

Researchers also found that employees who used VDTs and had heavy workloads were prone to psychological distress, such as anxiety, irritability, and fatigue. There is also a tendency for computer users to suffer from RSIs, such as *carpal tunnel syndrome* (a tingling or numbness in the fingers caused by the narrowing of a tunnel of bones and ligaments in the wrist) caused by repetitive use of the hands and arms at uncomfortable angles.[64]

Tips FOR THE FRONT LINE

General recommendations regarding the use of VDTs include giving employees rest breaks every hour, designing maximum flexibility into the workstation so that it can be adapted to the individual operator, reducing glare with devices, such as shades over windows and terminal screens, and giving VDT workers a complete pre-placement vision exam to ensure that vision is properly corrected to reduce visual strain.[65]

Workplace Toxins

The leading cause of work-related deaths around the world is cancer. Hundreds of Canadian workers die from occupational cancer each year.[66] There is an erroneous perception that cancer-causing agents in the workplace are disappearing. Employers often face significant costs to eliminate carcinogens in the workplace, and unions are often so preoccupied with wage and benefit increases that they don't bring the issue to the bargaining table (although the Canadian Labour Congress has launched an initiative to reduce work-related cancers by releasing an information kit for workers on cancer-causing materials on the job).[67] In addition to known carcinogens, such as asbestos and benzene, new chemicals and substances are constantly being introduced into the workplace without adequate testing.[68] Workers' compensation laws in several provinces have been amended to provide benefits to firefighters who develop specific job-related cancers.[69]

Workplace Smoking

Smoking is a serious problem for employees and employers. Employers face higher costs for healthcare and disability insurance, as smoking is associated with numerous health problems. Employees who smoke have reduced productivity and a significantly greater risk of occupational accidents than do non-smokers. Employees who smoke also expose non-smoking co-workers to toxic second-hand smoke.

Smokers who are also exposed to other carcinogens in the workplace, such as asbestos, have dramatically higher rates of lung cancer. The effects of on-the-job exposure to radon on lung cancer rates were found to last up to 14 years, and the cancer rates were greatly increased for smokers.[70]

Most Canadian jurisdictions have banned smoking in workplaces. Health Canada is urging employers to implement smoking cessation programs for employees to achieve better health for employees, better business results, legislative compliance, increased employee satisfaction (especially for the 80 percent of Canadians who do not smoke), and avoidance of litigation.[71]

Viral Pandemic

Recent major outbreaks of viral diseases like influenza have alarmed people around the world and reminded everyone that a major viral pandemic is inevitable at some time in the future. A 2006 study by the Conference Board of Canada found that although almost 80 percent of executives are concerned about the impact of a pandemic on their organization, only 4 percent of their organizations had developed a pandemic preparedness plan.[72]

HR will be a key player in responding to a pandemic as most employers are planning to continue their business operations using the existing workforce— in other words, with substantially fewer employees. Immediate decisions will be required regarding telecommuting and working at remote worksites, compensation for absent employees, and maintenance of occupational health for employees who are working on company premises.[73] Even in the plans that do exist, there is little detail on the status of quarantined employees, compensating employees who cover for absent co-workers, responding to employee refusals to work in an unsafe environment, and business shutdown if health and safety officers declare the entire workplace to be unsafe.[74]

The Canadian Pandemic Influenza Plan
www.phac-aspc.gc.ca/cpip-pclcpi

A pandemic preparedness plan should address prevention, containment, response to employee work refusals, creation of a pandemic preparation and response team, viability of continuing company operations, security of company premises, sickness/disability coverage, leaves to care for sick family members or children at home if schools are closed, and visitors to company premises.[75] Communication will be a critical component of pandemic management (likely using email, intranet, and hotlines), particularly if travel bans are imposed.[76] Unionized organizations will also need to consult their collective agreements and may wish to consult with the union when making pandemic preparedness plans.[77]

Recently amended Ontario legislation provides that if an emergency is declared by the government, then 10 unpaid days of leave will be available to employees who need to care for sick family members, in addition to the already existing 10 unpaid days available in these circumstances.[78]

Although the risk of a pandemic occurring in any one year may be small, the potential consequences are so serious that business leaders are well advised to prepare their organizations.[79]

Violence at Work

Workplace violence is defined by the International Labour Organization (ILO) as incidents in which an employee is abused, threatened, or assaulted in circumstances relating to work, and it includes harassment, bullying, intimidation, physical threats, assaults, and robberies. Most workplace violence arises from members of the public—customers or strangers—rather than co-workers.

Health Minister Leona Aglukkaq speaking at a news conference in Ottawa about the swine flu outbreak. Employers that lack pandemic plans should start putting them together now, according to experts.

Canada is the fourth-worst country in the world for workplace violence (the United States is seventh) according to ILO data.[80]

The first-ever Statistics Canada report on criminal victimization in the workplace, released in 2007, indicated that one in every five violent incidents in Canada (such as physical and sexual assault, or armed robbery) occurred in the workplace. Physical assault was the most common violent incident, representing 71 percent of all incidents of workplace violence.[81] Violence against employees at work is particularly prevalent for women in healthcare professions. More than one-third of nurses are physically assaulted and almost half suffer emotional abuse.[82] Reports of abuse of nurses by clinical area of practice are shown in **Figure 14.8.**

Workplace Violence and the Law

Most Canadian jurisdictions now have workplace violence legislation in place covering physical violence, and some include psychological/emotional violence as well. Human rights laws across the country prohibit various forms of harassment and bullying. Employers may be found vicariously liable for the violent acts of their employees on the basis that the employer negligently hired or negligently retained someone whom they should reasonably have known could cause the violent act; employers may also be found liable when they are aware of violent incidents and fail to respond.[83]

Prevention and Control of Workplace Violence

Tips FOR THE FRONT LINE

There are several concrete steps that employers can take to reduce the incidence of workplace violence. These include identifying jobs with high risk of violence,

FIGURE **14.8**   Reports of Abuse by Clinical Area of Practice

Reports of abuse by clinical area of practice

Clinical area	Percent
Geriatrics or long-term care	50%
Palliative care	47%
Psychiatry or mental health	44%
Critical care	44%
Emergency room	42%

Source: Statistics Canada, Factors Related to On-the-Job Abuse of Nurses by Patients, *Health Reports*, 20, no. 2 (2009), pp. 7–19.

Canadian Initiative on Workplace
Violence
www.workplaceviolence.ca

instituting a workplace violence policy, creating a healthy work environment, heightening security measures, training for violence reduction, and improving employee screening.

Identify Jobs with High Risk of Violence Kevin Kelloway, a researcher at Saint Mary's University in Halifax, has identified three job characteristics that are reliable predictors of workplace violence. First, the instigator of the violence specifically enters the work environment with the intent to engage in criminal behaviour (theft, for instance) and generally has no other legitimate reason to be in the workplace; most at risk are jobs like taxi drivers or gas station attendants. Second, the instigator is the recipient of a service or object offered at the targeted workplace (for example, a nurse or social worker). Third, the risk of violence from a potential or former employee is increased (for example, a disgruntled employee). Identifying and redressing these hazards and risk factors, such as installing safety shields for taxi drivers and bus drivers, can help to reduce victimization.[84]

Institute a Workplace Violence Policy Firms should develop, support, and communicate a workplace violence policy that clearly communicates management's commitment to preventing violent incidents. The policy should state that no degree or type of violence is acceptable in the workplace; provide definitions of prohibited conduct; specify consequences of violating the policy; encourage reporting of violent incidents; include prohibitions and sanctions for retaliation or reprisal; and specify that all physical assaults will be reported to police.[85]

Create a Healthy Work Environment According to Julian Barling, a researcher at Queen's University, a healthy work environment with professional supervision is the best way to reduce violence on the part of employees. Leaders, managers, and supervisors should express real concern for employees and treat people fairly, as acts of revenge typically occur in response to perceived injustice.[86]

Heighten Security Measures Security precautions to reduce the risk of workplace violence include improving external lighting, using drop safes to minimize cash on hand and posting signs noting that only a limited amount of cash is on hand, installing silent alarms and surveillance cameras, increasing the number of staff members on duty, and closing establishments during high-risk hours late at night and early in the morning. In workplaces serving members of the public, some important precautions for employee safety include providing staff training in conflict resolution and defusing anger; having security staff to refuse admittance to anyone who appears intoxicated, visibly angry, or threatening; and instituting a recognizable "help" signal to alert other staff members that assistance is required.[87]

Provide Workplace Violence Training Workplace violence training explains what workplace violence is, identifies its causes and signs, and offers tips on how to prevent it and what to do when it occurs. Supervisors can also be trained to identify the typical perpetrator—male, aged 25 to 40, bad at handling stress, a constant complainer, has a tendency to make verbal threats and physical or verbal outbursts, harbours grudges, and brandishes weapons to gain attention.[88]

Improve Employee Screening Screening out potentially violent applicants means instituting a sound pre-employment investigation of all information provided.

Sample interview questions to ask might include "What frustrates you?" and "Who was your worst supervisor and why?"[89] As sensible as it is to try to screen out potentially violent employees, doing so incurs the risk of liability and lawsuits. Human rights legislation limits the use of criminal records in hiring decisions.

EMPLOYEE WELLNESS PROGRAMS

employee wellness program
A program that takes a proactive approach to employee health and well-being.

Strength Tek
www.strengthtek.com

Healthy Workplace Month
www.healthyworkplacemonth.ca

There are three elements in a healthy workplace: the physical environment, the social environment, and health practices. **Employee wellness programs** take a proactive approach to all these areas of employee well-being (as opposed to EAPs, which provide reactive management of employee health problems). Wellness should be viewed as a management strategy to achieve measurable outcomes related to productivity, cost reduction, recruitment/retention, and profit, as shown in **Figure 14.9**. TELUS has a 50-year-old wellness program in which managers are held accountable—if absenteeism increases in their department, their bonus decreases![90] The company believes that a focus on wellness and enhancing corporate competitiveness are one and the same. Its long-term experience has netted a savings of three dollars for every dollar spent on wellness.

Experience has shown that wellness programs are very effective; there is overwhelming evidence that money invested in a wellness program is returned many times over.[91] For example, Seven Oaks General Hospital in Winnipeg, which

---

FIGURE **14.9**   Benefits for Employers from Action on the Determinants of Health

PRODUCTIVITY
- Reduced absenteeism
- Reduced distractions
- Improved performance
- Improved skills

COST REDUCTION
- Reduced workplace accidents and injuries
- Reduced compensation claims
- Reduced benefits costs

RECRUITMENT AND RETENTION
- Improved retention rates
- Improved employee engagement

PROFIT
- Reduced turnover costs
- Improved customer service and retention
- Improved recruitment competitiveness

Source: Daniel Munro, *Healthy People, Healthy Performances, Healthy Profits: The Case for Business Action on the Socio-Economic Determinants of Health* (Ottawa, ON: Conference Board of Canada, 2008). Reprinted by permission of The Conference Board of Canada, Ottawa.

has a 10-year-old Wellness Institute, reports a turnover rate of 4.5 percent, well under half of the industry average in Winnipeg of 11.9 percent.[92] A study of heart health wellness initiatives reported a return on investment of 415 percent.[93] NCR Canada saved $600 000 in direct and indirect costs during the first year of its wellness program; absenteeism was cut by more than half after 12 months and was still one-third lower after 36 months.[94]

One expert predicts that, over the next 25 years, prevention and wellness will be the next great leap forward in healthcare, as employees become more broadly recognized as the most important assets of organizations. A focus on wellness will also be driven by the shrinking workforce, an increase in postponed retirement, increased awareness of mental health, and medical and technological advances.[95]

Wellness initiatives often include stress management, nutrition and weight management, smoking cessation programs, tai chi, heart health (such as screening cholesterol and blood pressure levels), physical fitness programs, and workstation wellness through ergonomics. Even simple things like providing safe bicycle lockup and change rooms or making fresh fruit and water available can make a difference.[96] Wellness and prevention efforts need to be understood and undertaken as a process—a long-term commitment to a holistic focus on the total person.

Chapter SUMMARY

1. Employers and employees are held jointly responsible for maintaining the health and safety of workers, including participation on joint health and safety committees. Employers are responsible for "due diligence"—taking every reasonable precaution to ensure the health and safety of their workers. Supervisors are responsible for ensuring workplace policies are well communicated and adhered to by employees, and that employees concerns are dealt with in a safe and systematic manner. Employees are responsible for protecting their own health and safety and that of their co-workers. Employees have the right to know about workplace safety hazards, the right to participate in the occupational health and safety process, and the right to refuse unsafe work.

2. The Workplace Hazardous Materials Information System (WHMIS) is a Canada-wide, legally mandated system designed to protect workers by providing crucial information about hazardous materials and substances in the workplace. WHMIS requires labelling of hazardous material containers, material safety data sheets, and employee training.

3. There are three basic causes of accidents—chance occurrences, unsafe conditions, and unsafe acts on the part of employees. In addition, three other work-related factors—the job itself, the work schedule, and the psychological climate—also contribute to accidents.

4. One approach to preventing accidents is to reduce unsafe conditions by identifying and removing potential hazards. Another approach to improving safety is to reduce unsafe acts—for example, through selection and placement, education and training, positive reinforcement, top-management commitment, and monitoring work overload and stress.

5. Employee wellness programs aim to improve employees' health and reduce costs for sickness and disability claims, workers' compensation, and absenteeism. Wellness initiatives include physical fitness programs, smoking cessation programs, relaxation classes, and heart health monitoring.

6. Substance abuse is an important and growing health problem among employees. Techniques to deal with this challenge include disciplining, discharge, in-house counselling, and referrals to an outside agency. Stress, depression, and burnout are other potential health problems at work. Job stress can be reduced by ensuring that employees take breaks each day, providing access to counselling, and giving employees more control over their jobs. Repetitive strain injuries occur as a result of repetitive movements, awkward postures, and forceful exertion. Ergonomics is very effective at reducing RSIs.

7. Workplace toxins can be carcinogenic, and some governments are providing workers' compensation benefits to workers with job-related cancer. Employees who smoke have reduced productivity and greater health costs. Governments across Canada have increasingly banned workplace smoking. Violence against employees is a serious problem at work. Steps that can reduce workplace violence include improved security arrangements, better employee screening, and workplace violence training.

MyManagementLab

Visit MyManagementLab to access a personalized Study Plan and additional study tools for this chapter.

Key TERMS

burnout *(p. 402)*
employee wellness program *(p. 409)*
ergonomics *(p. 403)*
Lost-time injury rate *(p. 382)*

occupational health and safety legislation *(p. 383)*
repetitive strain injuries (RSIs) *(p. 403)*
Workplace Hazardous Materials Information System (WHMIS) *(p. 386)*

Review and Discussion QUESTIONS

1. Discuss the purpose of occupational health and safety legislation and who the agents responsible for enforcing it are.

2. Explain the differences and similarities in the employer, supervisor, and employee roles and responsibilities in maintaining safe workplace conditions.

3. Explain factors that contribute to unsafe acts, and identify how these factors can be controlled to reduce unsafe working conditions.

4. Describe how to reduce workers' compensation costs, both before and after an accident.

5. Explain the four traditional techniques for dealing with substance abuse.

6. Analyze the legal and safety issues concerning workplace toxins.

7. Identify factors contributing to violence at work and explain how to reduce these factors.

Critical Thinking QUESTIONS

1. What is your opinion on the following question: "Is there such a thing as an accident-prone person?" What is the impact of your answer to this question on how organizations can manage occupational health and safety in an organization?

2. Young people have a disproportionately high number of workplace accidents. In your opinion, what factors have impacted this statistic? Why do you think that is? What role does the organization play in reducing workplace accidents among younger employees? What role do younger employees play in reducing workplace accidents?

3. Develop guidelines for determining the point at which to terminate an employee who shows tendencies of violence in the workplace. Assess a situation from the position of kitchen staff at a large restaurant. Reminder: Your guidelines must stay within legal limits and should also be realistic.

4. You notice that one of your employees consistently comes in to work on Monday morning nursing a hangover. For most of the morning, she appears distant and reclusive. Do you approach her to discuss the situation, or do you feel that is an invasion of privacy?

5. Given the disappointing progress in reducing workplace injuries and deaths, do you think that the "corporate killing" law should be used more aggressively?

6. Assume that you have an employee working in your company who has been treated several times already for substance abuse through the company counselling program. Today, the manager found him "stoned" again, trying to operate a piece of equipment in an unsafe manner. The manager just came to you and said "Fire him! I've had enough! He's not only endangering himself, but other workers." The company has a no substance use while at work and zero tolerance for arriving at work in an impaired state policy that all employees are aware of and have signed off on as part of the code of conduct. What steps can/should your company take in this circumstance?

Experiential EXERCISES

1. In a group of four to six students, spend about 30 to 45 minutes in and around one of the buildings on your campus identifying health and safety hazards. Research whether or not these unsafe conditions violate the applicable health and safety legislation. Develop recommendations to enhance building safety for each location and debrief your colleagues on these recommendations.

2. Review a workplace-violence consulting website and contact a workplace-violence consultant. Gather information on what advice is provided to clients on preventing workplace violence, and ask for a sample workplace-violence policy. Prepare a brief presentation to the class on your findings.

3. On your own, identify the workplace hazards that might be present in the following workplaces:

   • car repair and auto body shop
   • home renovations supplies and equipment storage area
   • live concert venue
   • health clinic dealing with homeless people
   • office with many employees working on computers and paper files
   • chemical plant finished product storage area

   Think about what these companies can and should do to ensure that their employees are safe at work. Once you have completed your own list of answers, work with a group of four or five other students to compare your lists. Brainstorm other hazards and solutions.

4. Conduct an Internet search on Canadian websites to find a material safety data sheet (MSDS) for chlorine laundry bleach for home use. Compare the information on this sheet to the information shown in the MSDS for propane in Figure 14.3 on pages 388–389. Have all of the same areas been covered and to the same depth? Compare this information to the information found on the label

of a bottle of bleach. What is different? What have you learned that you did not know? Bring the results of your research to class for a discussion on the importance of MSDS information to employees in different types of organizations.

5. Depression has been described as a "clear and present danger" to business, as it manifests itself in alcoholism, absenteeism, injury, physical illness, and lost productivity. Estimates suggest that an employee with depression who goes untreated costs the company twice what treatment costs per year. A Harvard University study projects that, by 2020, depression will become the biggest source of lost workdays in developed countries; the World Health Organization predicts that depression will rank second as a cause of disability on a global basis by the same year. Young workers (aged 15 to 24) are most at risk.

Assuming the role of a career counsellor to newly hired graduates in a large retail company (Sears, Costco, Walmart, and so on), explain the employee and employer outcomes of stress and depression in an informed and actionable way.

Running CASE

Running Case: LearnInMotion.com

The New Health and Safety Program

At first glance, a dot-com is one of the last places you would expect to find potential health and safety hazards—or so Jennifer and Pierre thought. There is no danger of moving machinery, no high-pressure lines, no cutting or heavy lifting, and certainly no forklift trucks. However, there are health and safety problems.

In terms of unsafe conditions, for instance, two things dot-com companies have lots of are cables and wires. There are cables connecting the computers to each other and to the servers, and in many cases separate cables running from some computers to separate printers. There are 10 telephones in the office, all on five-metre phone lines that always seem to be snaking around chairs and tables. There is, in fact, an astonishing amount of cable considering that this is an office with fewer than 10 employees. When the installation specialists wired the office (for electricity, high-speed DSL, phone lines, security system, and computers), they estimated that they used more than five kilometres of cable of one sort or another. Most of the cables are hidden in the walls or ceilings, but many of them snake their way from desk to desk and under and over doorways.

Several employees have tried to reduce the nuisance of having to trip over wires whenever they get up by putting their plastic chair pads over the wires closest to them. However, that still leaves many wires unprotected. In other cases, they brought in their own packing tape and tried to tape down the wires in those spaces where they are particularly troublesome, such as across doorways.

The cables and wires are one of the more obvious potential accident-causing conditions. The firm's programmer, before he left the firm, had tried to repair the main server while the unit was still electrically alive. To this day, they are not exactly sure where he stuck the screwdriver, but the result was that he was "blown across the room," as Pierre puts it. He was all right, but it was still a scare.

And although the company has not received any claims yet, every employee spends hours at his or her computer, so carpal tunnel syndrome is a risk, as are eyestrain and strained backs. One recent incident particularly scared them. The firm uses independent contractors to deliver the firm's book- and CD-ROM–based courses in Toronto and two other cities. A delivery person was riding his bike at the corner of King and Bay Streets in Toronto, where he was struck by a car. Luckily he was not hurt, but the bike's front wheel was wrecked, and the close call got Pierre and Jennifer thinking about their lack of a safety program.

It's not just the physical conditions that concern the company's two owners. They also have some concerns about potential health problems, such as job stress and burnout. Although the business may be (relatively) safe with respect to physical conditions, it is also relatively stressful in terms of the demands it makes in terms of hours and deadlines. It is not at all uncommon for employees to get to work by 7:30 or 8 A.M. and to work through until 11 P.M. or midnight, at least five and sometimes six or seven days per week. Getting the company's new calendar fine-tuned and operational requires 70-hour work-weeks for three weeks from five of LearnInMotion's employees.

The bottom line is that both Jennifer and Pierre feel quite strongly that they need to do something about implementing a health and safety plan. Now they want you, their management consultant, to help them actually do it.

QUESTIONS

1   If LearnInMotion happened to receive a visit from the Ministry of Labour, what specific areas do you feel they would be ordered to change and why?

2   As owners of LearnInMotion, do Jennifer and Pierre have specific responsibilities for ensuring their employees' health and safety is maintained and for having a health and safety policy in place which is subsequently enforced?

3   What unsafe conditions and acts were described in this case?

Case INCIDENT

Ramona's Health and Safety Nightmare

Ramona McKenzie was on her way to work on a cloudy Monday morning when she got the call on her cellphone that no human resources manager wants to receive: An employee had just been injured at her workplace.

While turning into the company driveway, Ramona sees an ambulance, the injured worker, and a number of other employees surrounding the injured worker. Ramona parks her car, rushes over to where the employee is lying, and inquires about what happened.

The injured employee informs Ramona that she fell on the way into the building because no salt had been laid earlier in the morning to melt the ice on the parking lot. At this point, the ambulance takes the injured employee to the hospital and Ramona asks to speak to the plant manager in his office.

Shaken by everything that had occurred, Ramona asks the plant manager to find out why no salt had been put on the parking lot, as this was the norm after a significant snowfall. The plant manager informs Ramona that he would do this but also notes that the injured worker was wearing high-heeled shoes while on her way into the building. He also says that the employee arrived to work unusually early, before

any other workers, since she felt she had a few tasks she wanted to complete for a meeting scheduled at noon and wanted more time to prepare. She claimed that she informed her supervisor very casually at the end of the day yesterday that she may be arriving to work early to finish the project by the deadline.

Now that you know the facts of this scenario, please assist Ramona by answering the following questions.

QUESTIONS

1   Could this accident have been prevented? If yes, how? If no, why not?

2   Who is responsible for this accident?

3   What does Ramona have to do to ensure a smooth return to work for the injured worker after the accident?

MyManagementLab

Visit MyManagementLab to access a personalized Study Plan and additional study tools for this chapter.

   To view the CBC videos, read a summary, and answer discussion questions, go to MyManagementLab

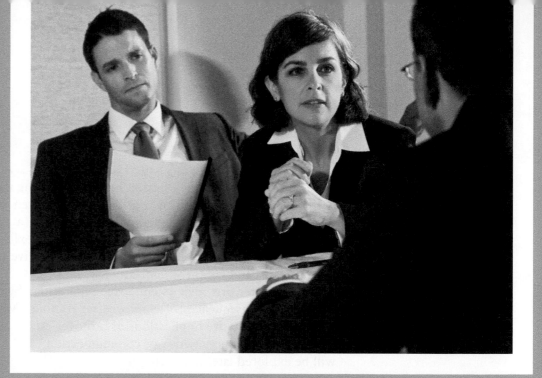

CHAPTER 15

Managing Employee Separations:

Foundations of Employee Engagement, Communication, and Turnover Management

LEARNING OUTCOMES

AFTER STUDYING THIS CHAPTER, YOU SHOULD BE ABLE TO

DEFINE voluntary and involuntary turnover and explain the impact of each.

DISCUSS the drivers and outcomes of each turnover method.

ANALYZE important HR considerations in ensuring fairness in dismissals, layoffs, and terminations.

DISCUSS the three foundations of a fair and just disciplinary process.

DEFINE wrongful dismissal and constructive dismissal.

EXPLAIN the six steps in the termination interview.

EXPLAIN various techniques for ensuring effective employee communication in organizations to help manage turnover.

REQUIRED PROFESSIONAL CAPABILITIES (RPC)

- Uses communication strategies to advance organizational objectives

- Develops and implements programs for employee involvement

- Develops and maintains the trust and support of collaborators, including the immediate supervisor, subordinates, and internal clients

- Gathers and analyzes information on organizational context (climate, culture) to highlight key issues

- Recommends or initiates actions in response to known or suspected incidents of misconduct

- Participates in the termination process by preparing termination notices, conducting exit interviews, and arranging outplacement services

- Monitors and reports on the progress of major change initiatives

- Develops processes to engage and involve employees in achieving the objectives of the organization

- Provides advice on issues relating to labour and employee relations, including hiring, discipline, and termination

- Contributes to development of an environment that fosters effective working relationships

THE IMPORTANCE OF MANAGING EMPLOYEE SEPARATIONS

Issues of recruitment and selection focus on growing the human resource talent within an organization. The role of HRM is often overlooked in managing employee engagement and communication during a time of employee separations. Who leaves, how they are treated during the exit, what the cause or nature of the exit is, and how remaining employees perceive this all impacts the long-term sustainability of the organization.

This chapter first reviews employee separations by categorizing the possible causes and consequences of employee separations. Methods of reducing turnover and the negative implications of turnover on remaining employees (including legal compliance, two-way communication, and fair treatment programs) will be explored later in the chapter.

MANAGING TURNOVER

Employee exits can become a huge challenge for organizations. The time, money, and resources invested in recruiting, training, and maintaining employees is lost when employees exit a firm. Additionally, employee exits disrupt the organization's ability to produce and maintain the right quantity and quality of talent and derail the organization's focus on larger strategic issues. For example, the retail sector often has high turnover levels, with very few long-tenured employees. Similarly, in the hospitality industry, one in every five employees leaves the company in any given year.[1]

turnover The termination of an individual's employment with an organization.

An organization's labour force is in constant fluctuation as employees continuously enter and exit the workforce. **Turnover** refers to the termination of an individual's employment with an organization. Turnover can be either permanent or temporary and can be a result of action taken by either the employee or employer. There are many possible reasons for an employee to separate from a firm. An online study of over 1 000 Canadians asked people why they left their last employer. Results are highlighted in **Figure 15.1** on the next page. The most common reason given by those interviewed was downsizing or restructuring activity, followed by a desire to find new challenges, then ineffective leadership.

voluntary turnover Employee-initiated termination of employment, such as quits, retirement, or resignation.

involuntary turnover Employer-initiated termination of employment, such as dismissal or layoff.

Overall, the reasons for turnover can be classified into two subgroups: voluntary and involuntary. **Voluntary turnover** is employee initiated, usually in the form of quits or retirement. The decision to discontinue employment with the firm is made by the employee, without management enticement. **Involuntary turnover** is employer initiated and is usually in the form of dismissals or layoffs. Regardless, the employee has little or no personal say in this turnover decision. Employee exits from a firm are usually a mix of voluntary and involuntary turnover.

A study of over 34 000 workers in the Canadian labour force examined voluntary and involuntary turnover from 2000–2004. As an employee gains tenure in a company, his or her likelihood of quitting or being dismissed or laid off is significantly reduced. Additionally, individuals who hold occupations in management and administration-related positions are less likely to be laid off than individuals in other occupations. However, on average,

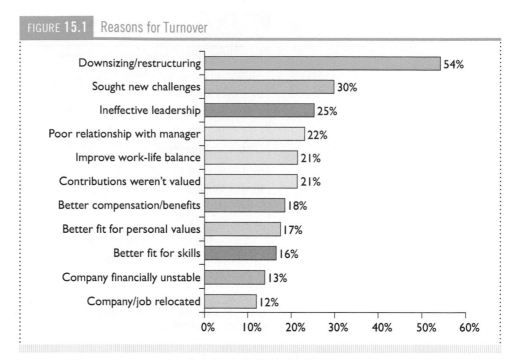

FIGURE **15.1**   Reasons for Turnover

Source: News 4, "Reasons for Turnover," *Canadian HR Reporter,* June 16, 2008. Reprinted by permission of Canadian HR Reporter. © Copyright Thomson Reuters Canada Ltd., (2012) Toronto, Ontario, 1-800-387-5164. Web: www.hrreporter.com.

the personality characteristics of employees who get laid off in relation to those who quit are opposite. For example, higher education reduces the likelihood that an employee will be laid off, but increases the probability that they will quit. Employees in the goods industry are more likely to experience a layoff, whereas employees in the service industry are more likely to voluntarily leave their job via quitting.[2]

The Cost of Turnover

In Canada, from 1978–1995, the temporary employment separation rate per year ranged from 18.9 to 23.8 percent, while the layoff rate ranged from 12.6 to 16.4 percent per year. Combined, these statistics suggest that temporary and permanent rates of employee separation have affected 30 to 40 percent of employees annually. Turnover rates vary by industry (for example, the construction industry and consumer services industries typically have the highest turnover levels in Canada, while public services has the lowest turnover levels), by the size of the company (smaller organizations typically have higher turnover rates), and by age (older workers are less likely to experience turnover than younger workers).[3]

It is not surprising that over 50 percent of Canadian organizations admit that they experience difficulties recruiting and retaining talent.[4] Some companies are in a constant search for talent, like supermarkets, where the industry-wide turnover rate for courtesy clerks or cashiers is 300 percent.[5] Translated, that means that, on average, each cashier will work for four months at a time before the position will be vacated. The challenge is that the cost of turnover ranges from 150 percent of salary to 250 percent of salary.[6] Ultimately, the combination of having a company incur the cost of turnover as well as the cost of day-to-day operations can be economically damaging.

FIGURE **15.2** The Estimated Direct Cost of Turnover

Number of terminated/resigned employees	725 000
Number of active employees	1 300 000
Employee turnover	55.7%
But for every ONE employee who leaves:	
Cost of recruiting/advertising	$25
Cost of interviewing	$60
Cost of orientation	$60
Cost of training	$600
Administrative cost	$20
Hourly wage of a new employee (not including payroll costs, benefits, etc.)	$6
Total direct cost for ONE new employee	$1950
Total direct cost of all employee turnover	$1.4 billion

Source: A. Heller, "The People Factor: Supermarkets Investment in "Return On People" Provides Results in a Changing Labor Environment" *Supermarket News*, 52, no. 18 (May 3, 2004), p. 32.

As highlighted in **Figure 15.2**, the estimated direct cost of turnover per year can reach $1.4 billion, and the impact on customer loyalty can be two to three times the direct cost of loyalty. Reducing turnover even 10 percent could potentially result in direct savings of roughly $140 million per year.

Direct costs associated with turnover are often easier to estimate given that they are more visible (for example, cost of advertising and interviewing, cost of moving expenses offered to the new candidate), while indirect costs associated with turnover are often overlooked, but are still considerable (for example, lost productivity during the employment gap, training curve productivity losses). There are four main components associated with the cost of the turnover:

Tips FOR THE FRONT LINE

- Separation costs—the cost of exit interviews, administrative functions associated with the turnover, and separation or severance pay
- Vacancy costs—the net savings or cost incurred of increased overtime, the use of temporary workers, and the loss of sales associated with the vacancy
- Replacement costs—the cost of recruiting and hiring a replacement to fill the vacant position (including the cost of interviews, testing, administrative expenses, travel/moving expenses, and so on)
- Training costs—formal and informal training (including the performance differential between employees exiting the organization and their replacements)[7]

Voluntary Turnover

Voluntary turnover includes quitting, resignations, and retirements, presenting a specific and immediate challenge to organizational success. In voluntary turnover, the employee initiates the termination of employment. Often, departing employees migrate to competing firms and create situations where their knowledge, skills, and abilities developed within the firm can be used to disadvantage the firm. As a result, voluntary turnover presents unanticipated challenges of replacing and retraining employees.

Research INSIGHT

A review of turnover research identifies predictors of voluntary turnover. Individual-level variables found to have a statistically significant relationship with voluntary job loss are (1) low organizational commitment, (2) low role clarity, (3) low tenure, (4) high role conflict, and (5) low overall job satisfaction. Additionally, age and marital status were negatively correlated with voluntary turnover, while education was positively correlated with voluntary turnover.[8]

The biggest challenge of voluntary turnover is the lack of managerial control. Voluntary turnover can be functional (where bad performers leave and good performers stay), which can help reduce suboptimal organizational performance, or dysfunctional (where good performers leave and bad performers stay), which can be detrimental to a firm's success.[9]

Two researchers, Abbasi and Hollman, argue that eroding employee loyalty has the potential to radically affect a firm's ability to prosper in today's competitive economy, leaving even the most ambitious firms struggling to keep the most productive and talented employees. They highlight five reasons for employee turnover within an organization:[10]

(1) suboptimal hiring practices

(2) difficult managerial style

(3) lack of recognition

(4) lack of competitive compensation systems

(5) toxic workplace environments

In addition to the reasons outlined above, voluntary turnover also includes unexplained reasons, known as the "hobo phenomena."[11]

Tips FOR THE FRONT LINE

While an employer cannot always predict the reasoning behind voluntary turnover, it is important to try to understand which types of employees are likely to leave and why. This helps manage and prevent dysfunctional or excessive turnover. This information can be collected in exit interviews, staff surveys, and annual HR reviews.[12] Collecting this type of information can lead to trends that companies can use to screen certain types of individuals in the selection process. Additionally, these trends may lead organizations to develop methods of reducing turnover amongst current employees. In doing so, organizations obtain the information required to reduce turnover, retain effective employees, and decrease direct costs associated with turnover.

Quits

quitting Voluntary, employee-initiated resignation.

Quitting is legally recognized as a voluntary resignation in which the employee terminates the employment relationship, often in the form of a resignation letter. In Canada, employment-related legislation clearly identifies employer responsibilities at the time of involuntary turnover (such as minimum notice periods and severance pay), but there exist no equivalent employer-oriented protections in the case of employee-initiated turnover.

Employees often elect to leave a company based on work-related factors (for example, the employee dislikes the boss, too much pressure or stress), or non-work-related factors (return to school, moving).[13] Either way, employee quits are most often caused by low job satisfaction.[14]

Competitive factors often play a significant role in a person's desire to resign from a company, including opportunities for employment in other organizations.

Consequently, perceived job alternatives and high labour demands influence an employee's perception of ease of employment in other organizations, and are often carefully considered by the employee prior to resignation. Globalization, technological advancements, and market pressures have created an increasingly turbulent economy, and over the last few decades large-scale labour mobility has become the norm. The result has been a decline in employee job tenure and job stability.

To adapt to a constantly changing environment, individual employees are more willing to look for horizontal and vertical career advancement opportunities outside of the organization. The notion of "cradle-to-grave" jobs that permeated the employment relationship prior to the 1980s no longer exists. A leading researcher best captures this change: "If the traditional, lifetime employment relationship was like a marriage, then the new employment relationship is like a lifetime of divorces and remarriages."[15]

Retirement

The origins of mandatory retirement in Canada are largely routed in the industrial revolution of the late 1800s and early 1900s. At a time when the skilled workforce was being replaced by an unskilled, assembly and task-oriented workforce, employers were forcing employees to take retirement at age 65 so they could replace older and often more expensive workers with younger and less costly labour. Governments responded by introducing a series of acts aimed at providing financial support for people reaching "retirement age" to prevent poverty amongst the oldest generation. In the early 1900s, average male life expectancy was 47 years and female life expectancy was 50 years.[16] As a result, mandatory retirement at the age of 65 was not a reality for a significant portion of the workforce. Medical discoveries, eradication of infectious diseases, and implementation of public health measures (like water chlorination) have resulted in a significant increase in average lifespan on an international scale. According to Statistics Canada, average life expectancy for men in 2011 was 78.3 years, while average life expectancy for women was 83 years.

However, a combination of legal advancements on anti-discriminatory employment policies (such as age-based discrimination), labour scarcity, and peoples' desires to choose their own lifestyle, circumstances, and priorities has resulted in the abolishment of mandatory retirement in Canada.

The result has been a shift from categorizing retirement as voluntary turnover rather than as a form of involuntary turnover. The average age of retirement for public sector employees is 60 years of age and 62 for private sector employees. However, there is a large range of possible retirement ages, with some 40 year olds eligible to retire from their organization while some 87 year olds continue to be employed.[17]

One of the challenges associated with the retirement of employees, from an organizational standpoint, is the difficulty in predicting when employees will retire. Developing succession or replacement plans around potential retires and finding ways to their transfer tacit and social knowledge becomes paramount to how an organization deals with retirement. Some companies are managing the labour shortage created by retiring employees by offering **"retirees on call"** programs, where retirees can come back on a part-time or as-needed basis, or by offering **"phased retirement,"** where employees gradually reduce the number of hours that they work.[18]

retirees on call A program where retirees can continue to work on a part-time or as needed basis post-retirement.

phased retirement potential retirees gradually reduce the number of hours worked per week over time.

pre-retirement counselling
Counselling provided to employees some months (or even years) before retirement, which covers such matters as benefits advice, second careers, and so on.

The Retirement Education Centre
www.iretire.org

The Financial Education Institute of Canada
www.financialknowledgeinc.com

T.E. Financial Consultants
www.tefinancial.com

An employee contemplating different retirement options

Hints : **TO ENSURE LEGAL COMPLIANCE**

Tips : **FOR THE FRONT LINE**

Court decisions have confirmed that employers do have some legal responsibility to help employees prepare for retirement.[19] Most employers provide some type of formal **pre-retirement counselling** aimed at easing the passage of their employees into retirement.[20] Retirement education and planning firms provide services to assist upcoming retirees with such issues as lifestyle goals (including part-time or volunteer work, or moving to another country), financial planning, relationship issues, and health issues. Both individual and group transition counselling are offered in seminars and workshops featuring workbooks, questionnaires, discussions, group exercises, and software products.[21]

Involuntary Turnover

There are many reasons why an organization might engage in involuntary turnover. Job performance may be below acceptable standards and the organization decides to dismiss an employee. Economic or financial pressures may result in a decision to downsize through mass layoffs. The organization may be engaging in a new strategic direction and has choosen to close down or outsource one or more business units. In any of these cases, the decision to terminate employment is made by the organization and its agents, not by the individual employee. Employee dismissal and downsizing are two of the most common situations in which employees perceive that they are treated unfairly. This reaction is not surprising given the negative ramifications to the employee in each case (job loss). Thus, it is important for all managers and HR professionals to be aware of how to conduct involuntary turnover fairly and legally.

Specifically, employer-initiated termination should be fair and occur after all reasonable steps to rehabilitate or salvage the employment relationship through employee discipline have failed. The legal system in Canada has repeatedly articulated the rights of employees to fair treatment, not only during the term of employment but also during the discipline and dismissal process. A fair and just disciplinary process is based on three foundations: rules and regulations, progressive discipline, and an appeals process.

Rules and Regulations

A set of clear expectations informs employees ahead of time as to what is and is not considered acceptable behaviour in the workplace. Employees must be informed, preferably in writing, of what behaviours or actions are not permitted. This is usually done during the employee's orientation (and included in the employee orientation handbook), or when rules or regulations in the workplace change. Examples of such rules include:

- Poor work performance is not acceptable. Each employee is expected to perform his or her work properly and efficiently, and to meet established standards of quality.

- Liquor and drug use is not permitted on work premises. The use of either during working hours or working under the influence of drugs or alcohol is strictly prohibited.
- Safety rules must be followed at all times.

An Ethical | **Dilemma**

Is it ethical to apply disciplinary action in cases of ongoing absenteeism and tardiness because of family responsibilities? What other approach could be used?

Progressive Discipline

A system of progressive penalties is the second foundation of effective discipline. Penalties may range from verbal warnings, to written warnings, to suspension (paid or unpaid) from the job, and finally to dismissal. The severity of the penalty is usually a function of the type of offence and the number of times the offence has occurred. For example, most companies issue warnings for the first instance of unexcused lateness. However, for chronic lateness, dismissal is the more usual disciplinary action.

Finally, there should be an appeals process as part of the disciplinary process; this helps to ensure procedural fairness.

Dismissal for Just Cause

dismissal Involuntary termination of an employee's employment.

dismissal for just cause An employer-initiated termination based on an employee's poor behaviours; in these situations, no severance, reasonable notice periods, or additional payments beyond what the employee has already earned are owed.

Dismissal is the most drastic disciplinary step that can be taken toward an employee and one that must be handled with deliberate care. While dismissals damage the goodwill of a company as well as sever the employment relationship, there are undoubtedly times when dismissal is required, and in these instances it should be carried out forthrightly.[22] In cases where an employee was **dismissed for just cause**, it is considered an employer-initiated termination based on an employee's poor behaviours, therefore no severance, reasonable notice periods, or additional payments beyond what the employee has already earned are owed (for example, earned vacation time that is unused must be paid out). In cases of dismissal for just cause, the onus of proof lies on management to prove that performance in the past was below acceptable levels and that the organization provided feedback and allowed for opportunities to correct behaviours that led to poor performance (as discussed in detail in Chapter 10). In Canada, research finds that the group of employees who lose their jobs due to dismissal are no different in terms of age, gender, education, occupation, and industry than those who remain employed (no turnover).[23]

There is no clear definition of what behaviour constitutes "just cause" for dismissal.[24] Any allegation of just cause must be considered using a contextual approach, looking at not only the alleged behaviour, but the entirety of the employment relationship.[25] If an employer is considering making an allegation of just cause, it is crucial to investigate fully and fairly before any decision is made. The fundamental question is whether or not the employee has irreparably harmed the relationship to the point that it would be unreasonable to expect the employer to continue the employment relationship.[26]

Just cause can often be demonstrated in cases of disobedience, incompetence, dishonesty, insubordination, fighting, and persistent absence or lateness.[27] However, just cause cannot be assessed in isolation and may vary depending on the possible consequences of the misconduct, the status of the employee, and the circumstances of the case. The burden of proof rests with the employer in cases of dismissal or layoff. In Canada, courts often do not accept the

insubordination Wilful disregard or disobedience of the boss' authority or legitimate orders; criticizing the boss in public.

assertion of just cause by the employer, and unions almost never do—one union alleged that a death threat made by an employee to his supervisor was "mild insubordination."[28]

Employee misconduct (including theft, expense account fraud, abuse of sick leave, and so on) is a fundamental violation of the employment relationship and can constitute just cause.[29] Unfortunately, the prevalence of theft behaviour is alarming. For example, an Ernst & Young study estimated that 47 percent of retail "inventory shrinkage" is attributable to employees, and the Retail Council of Canada estimates that employee theft costs Canadian businesses about $1 billion per year.[30] Air Canada estimates that it loses up to 9 percent of its cabin stock each year to employee theft, or about $9 per day per employee.[31]

Insubordination is a form of misconduct that often provides grounds for just cause dismissal, although it may be relatively difficult to describe and to prove. To that end, it is important to communicate to employees that some acts are considered insubordinate whenever and wherever they occur. These generally include the following:[32]

1. Direct disregard of the boss' authority; refusal to obey the boss' reasonable instructions—particularly in front of others.
2. Deliberate defiance of clearly stated company policies, rules, regulations, and procedures.
3. Public criticism of the boss; contradicting or arguing with him or her.
4. Contemptuous display of disrespect—making insolent comments and portraying these feelings in terms of the employee's attitude on the job.
5. Disregard for the chain of command, shown by going around the immediate supervisor or manager with a complaint, suggestion, or political manoeuvre.
6. Participation in (or leadership of) an effort to undermine and remove the boss from power.

A recent example of dismissal for just cause based on insubordination involved a Calgary stockbroker who was fired after he brought a prostitute to his office after hours and left her there alone following a dispute about payment. The woman was left alone in the reception area where she could have accessed confidential client and company data after he left. She showed up at the office the next day demanding payment, which resulted in the dismissal of the stockbroker. The court said the stockbroker's conduct exhibited contempt for his employer, his co-workers, and their reputation in the business community.[33]

Figure 15.3 provides guidelines on insubordination used by the Saskatchewan government to assist managers and supervisors in dealing with insubordination.

Layoff

As organizations adapt to ever-changing demands, markets, technologies, and competitors, layoffs have become an accepted and familiar organizational activity. "Downsizing" refers to an intentional decision made by executives within the organization that involves a reduction of the workforce to improve efficiency

layoff The temporary withdrawal of employment to workers for economic or business reasons.

or effectiveness of the organization by affecting the work process.[34] A **layoff**, in which workers are sent home for a period of time (often undefined), is a situation in which three conditions are present: (1) There is no work available for the employees, (2) management expects the no-work situation to be temporary and probably short term, and (3) management intends to recall the employees when work is again available.[35] Alternative names for layoffs include downsizing, rightsizing, reduction in workforce, and mass terminations, to list just a few. Layoffs that involve unionized employees are almost always based on seniority or conditions outlined in the collective bargaining agreement. However, layoffs that occur in non-unionized environments or affect non-unionized employees

FIGURE 15.3   Saskatchewan Public Service Commission Corrective Discipline Guidelines for Insubordination

Saskatchewan Public Service Commission

Human Resource Manual
www.gov.sk.ca/psc/hrmanual

Section: PS 803-Guidelines

Corrective Discipline Guidelines
Part E: Insubordination

Date issued: 1982 11 17

Revision date: 1990 09 30

The following sets out guidelines to assist managers and supervisors in dealing with the discipline situation.

1. Insubordination - A Special Case

Insubordination is defined as the refusal of an employee to carry out the order of a supervisor. Employees are required, under the Public Service Employment Regulations Section 15.1, to carry out such orders. Employees may disagree with such orders. However, the proper employee response is to obey the order and seek redress via grievance action. The rule of "obey now - grieve later" is well founded in arbitration decisions.

Note however, that the "obey now - grieve later" rule does not apply to all orders given by supervisors. Some exceptions are as follows:

- where the order given is not related to work, e.g., deliver my personal mail as opposed to deliver departmental mail, etc. An employee may be directed and is required to perform work duties not found in his job description. However, the employee may later grieve the assignment of these duties.

- where the employee has reasonable grounds for believing that obeying the order given would endanger health and/or safety.

- where the order given is illegal.

- where the order is given by someone without authority. Note however that all orders need not be given by one's immediate supervisor. Where the employee knows that the order is being given by his supervisor's superior, such orders must be followed.

- where the order interferes with personal appearance or privacy, e.g., a search of one's personal effects where there is suspected theft, that one shave a beard, cut ones hair, wear certain clothes, etc. Note however that appearance or clothing rules may apply where they are a direct job requirement, e.g., uniforms for regulatory staff, cleanliness when preparing food, etc. The refusal of an employee to submit himself to a search of personal effects when management has reasonable grounds for such a request should be recorded. Inform the employee discipline action may be taken; consult with your personnel advisor on how to proceed.

- where the employee has a reasonable personal excuse, e.g., the employee was provoked into refusing the order, where the employee has a legitimate and reasonable personal excuse and gives it at the time of refusal - personal illness, death in the family, etc. Note however that mere personal inconvenience is not acceptable, e.g., I'm on my break, it's my bowling night, etc.

continued

FIGURE 15.3   (Continued)

**Saskatchewan
Public Service
Commission**

Human Resource Manual
www.gov.sk.ca/psc/hrmanual

Section: PS 803-Guidelines

2. Insubordination - How to Handle

Among disciplinary offenses, insubordination is common. To have an employee refuse an order can be unsettling for a supervisor. As a result, the following approach is suggested:

- give the order in the normal manner, e.g., would you be kind enough to help out. The employee refuses.

- determine the employee's reason for refusal.

- determine if the employee's refusal is valid.

- if not, inform the employee you will give a formal order and failure to comply could result in disciplinary action.

- if feasible, inform the employee you will give him three (3) to five (5) minutes to consider his response to the order you will give.

- on return or when you give the order, it is desirable to be accompanied by another supervisory representative or employee if possible. This person will act as a witness.

- clearly repeat the order, e.g., as your supervisor I am ordering you to help out; failure could result in disciplinary action.

- if the employee continues to refuse, inform him that the matter will be investigated further and disciplinary action could result.

- record all of the above in writing immediately after the event; note complete details, i.e., the exact order you gave, the exact words of refusal, the time of the order, etc. Have your witness add his comments.

- initiate the employer's policy of Corrective Discipline.

Source: Human Resources Manual, Saskatchewan Public Service Commission, www.psc.gov.sk.ca/Default.aspx?DN=6acee10d-6c70-4392-a536-9aac55f273e5 (accessed July 17, 2009).

occur regularly and are not significantly standardized or influenced by third-party limitations.

Many employers today recognize the enormous investments that organizations have in recruiting, screening, and training their employees. As a result, they are more hesitant to lay off employees at the first signs of business decline. Instead, they are using new approaches to either limit the effects of a layoff or eliminate the layoffs entirely.

There are several alternatives to layoffs. One such alternative is a voluntary reduction in pay, where all employees agree to reductions in their pay to keep everyone working. Other employers arrange to have all or most of their employees accumulate their vacation time and to concentrate their vacations during slow periods. Other employees agree to take voluntary time off, which again has the effect of reducing the employer's payroll and avoiding the need for a layoff. Another way to avoid layoffs is the use of contingent employees hired with the understanding that their work is temporary and they may be laid off at any time.[36] Finally, the work-sharing program, available through Service Canada, allows employers to reduce the workweek by one to three days, and employees can claim employment insurance for the time not worked.

FAIRNESS IN EMPLOYEE SEPARATIONS

Research INSIGHT

A study of 996 recently fired or laid off workers found that wrongful dismissal claims were strongly correlated with the way workers felt they had been treated at the time of termination. They also found a "vendetta effect," where the instances of wrongful dismissal claims became stronger as negative treatment became more extreme, as shown in **Figure 15.4**. The researchers concluded that many wrongful dismissal lawsuits could be avoided if effective human resource practices, specifically treating employees fairly, were employed. Providing clear, honest explanations of termination decisions, and handling the termination in a way that treats people with dignity and respect can be especially favourable to the company's reputation, as well as reduce the employee's negative feelings toward themselves and the company.[37]

Over 30 years of organizational research clearly indicates that employees are sensitive to the treatment they receive, and that they have strong perceptions regarding the fairness of their experiences at work.[38] In respect to employee relations, experts generally define organizational justice in terms of three components: distributive justice, procedural justice, and interactional justice. **Distributive justice** refers to the fairness and justice of the outcome of a decision (Would a comparable employee have the same outcome related to the employee separation?). **Procedural justice** refers to the fairness of the process (Is the process my company uses to make decisions about terminations or

distributive justice Fairness of a decision outcome.

procedural justice Fairness of the process used to make a decision.

FIGURE 15.4   Fair Treatment and Wrongful Dismissal Claims: The Vendetta Effect

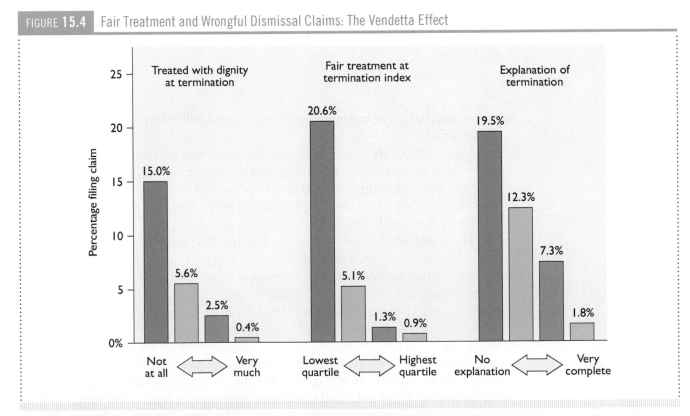

Source: Republished with permission of Sage Publications Inc. Journals, from "The Winding Road from Employee to Complainant: Situational and Psychological Determinants of Wrongful-Termination Claims," by E.A. Lind, J. Greenberg, K.S. Scott, and T.D. Welchans. *Administrative Science Quarterly*, (September 2000) p. 557–590; permission conveyed through Copyright Clearance Center, Inc.

interactional justice Fairness in interpersonal interactions by treating others with dignity and respect.

employee separations fair?). **Interactional justice** refers to the manner in which managers conduct their interpersonal dealings with employees and, in particular, the degree to which they treat employees with dignity and respect as opposed to abuse or disrespect (Does my supervisor treat me with respect when assessing factors related to the separation?).

While a focus on fairness perceptions of employees who exit an organization through employee separations is important from a legal and ethical perspective, perceptions of whether exiting employees were treated fairly and justly also affect employees who remain with the organization. For example, fair treatment of employees whose jobs are lost in layoffs is important for maintaining employee engagement on the part of the "survivors" who continue to come to work in these difficult circumstances. Communicating the news of impending layoffs is a difficult task, but ensuring interactional justice when doing so is critical to maintaining engagement on the part of the employees who will continue working for the organization.

Effectively managing employee separations in Canada includes a focus on both exiting employees (including legal compliance with reasonable notice periods) and remaining employees (employee engagement), as well as effective communication to all employees.

Providing Reasonable Notice

In Canada, the employer–employee relationship is governed by an employment contract—a formal agreement (in writing or based on mutual understanding) made between the two parties. If the contract is for a specific length of time, the contract ends at the expiration date and the employee cannot be prematurely dismissed without just cause.

wrongful dismissal An employee dismissal that does not comply with the law or does not comply with a written or implied contractual arrangement.

More commonly, employees are hired under an implied contract where the understanding is that employment is for an indefinite period of time and may be terminated by either party only when reasonable notice is given.[39] Employers cannot hire and fire employees at will, as is the case in the United States. Canadian employers can only terminate an employee's employment without reasonable notice when just cause exists. If there is no employment contract and just cause is not present, then a termination without reasonable notice is considered unfair and is known as **wrongful dismissal**. Although it is rare for employees to be accused of not providing reasonable notice of their resignation, if they don't they may be forced to pay out a reimbursement fee to the organization in compensation for the profits lost during the employee's absence. As an example, a manager in British Columbia was ordered to compensate his former employer for lost profits when he left without providing any notice and went to work for a competitor.[40]

group termination laws Laws that require an employer to notify employees in the event that they decide to terminate a group of employees.

Group termination laws require employers who are terminating a large group of employees to give employees more notice than that required on termination of an individual employee. The laws are intended to assist employees in situations of plant closings and large downsizings. Most jurisdictions in Canada require employers who are terminating a group of employees (some specify 10 or more, others 25 or more) within a short time to give advance notice to employees and sometimes to their union. The amount of notice varies by jurisdiction and with the number of employees being terminated, but it generally ranges from 6 to 18 weeks. The laws do not prevent the employer from closing down, nor do they require saving jobs; they simply give employees time to seek other work or retraining by giving them advance notice of their termination.

Often, the amount of notice considered reasonable when an employer decides to terminate the employment relationship is beyond the minimum notice requirements of employment/labour standards legislation. A rule of thumb for reasonable notice is about three to four weeks per year of service. The employee sometimes continues to work during the period of notice but usually ceases work at the time that the notice of termination is given. In the latter case, the employee receives a lump-sum of money equal to his or her pay for the period of notice. Payments are often conditional on the employee signing a general release of all legal claims against the employer.

The employee can accept the notice given (and sign any required release form) or can sue for wrongful dismissal if the notice is considered unacceptable. The court will review the circumstances of the dismissal and make a final decision on the amount of notice to be provided. The courts generally award a period of notice based on their assessment of how long it will take the employee to find alternative employment, taking into account the employee's age, salary, length of service, the level of the job, and other factors. Rarely have notice periods exceeded 24 months.[41]

Another important factor in determining notice periods is whether the dismissed employee was induced or lured away from stable employment elsewhere and then terminated because of a business downturn. For example, a senior marketing manager who had worked for Bell Canada for 20 years was urged by two former co-workers to join them at Alcatel. She joined Alcatel with a 50 percent salary increase to offset her pension loss at Bell. She was terminated after 21 months, sued for wrongful dismissal, and was awarded nine months' notice due to the inducement.[42]

Bad-Faith Damages

In 1997, "bad-faith conduct" on the part of the employer in dismissing an employee was added as another factor considered by the courts in determining the period of reasonable notice.[43] At a minimum, employers are required to be candid, reasonable, honest, and forthright with their employees in the course of dismissal and should refrain from engaging in conduct that is unfair or in bad faith, such as being untruthful, misleading, or unduly insensitive. The resulting additional periods of notice are unpredictable, often around three to four months, but sometimes considerably higher.[44] A significant change to the assessment of bad-faith damages was established by a 2008 decision by the Supreme Court of Canada, which ruled that bad-faith damages apply to only the most extreme conduct and that damages should not be provided by extending the notice period but by compensation for actual damages suffered by the employee.[45] Nevertheless, it is still clear that employers must treat employees with dignity and respect at all times, especially at the time of dismissal.[46]

Punitive Damages

In extreme cases, employers may also be ordered to pay punitive damages for harsh and vindictive treatment of an employee, or damages for aggravated or mental distress if the employee suffered undue distress from not being given adequate notice of termination.[47] In 2005, the largest punitive damage award in Canadian history was handed down when Honda Canada was ordered to pay $500 000 to

RPC

Participates in the termination process by preparing termination notices, conducting exit interviews, and arranging outplacement services a terminated employee for its mistreatment of the employee, who was disabled due to chronic fatigue syndrome.[48] The amount was later reduced to $100 000 by an appeal court and eliminated entirely by the Supreme Court of Canada, who ruled in 2008 that punitive damages should only apply in exceptional cases with wrongful acts by the employer that are truly malicious and outrageous.[49]

Constructive Dismissal

constructive dismissal When the employer makes unilateral changes in the employment contract that are unacceptable to the employee, even though the employee has not been formally terminated.

Constructive dismissal is considered to occur when the employer makes unilateral changes in the employment contract that are recognized as unacceptable according to the employee, even though the employee has not been formally terminated.[50] The most common changes in employment status that are considered to constitute constructive dismissal are demotion, reduction in pay and benefits, forced resignation, forced early retirement, forced transfer, and changes in job duties and responsibilities. An employee who believes that he or she has been constructively dismissed can sue the employer for wrongful dismissal. If the judge agrees that constructive dismissal occurred, then a period of notice to be provided to the employee can be determined.

For example, a long-term employee of Ontario Power Generation was affected by a shift in the company's focus that largely eliminated his responsibilities for business development. He was told that he would be "underutilized for the foreseeable future" and that if he didn't like the changes, he could resign or retire. He resigned shortly thereafter and sued for constructive dismissal. The court found that the essential terms of his employment had been substantially changed. The court also discovered that the company had no plan to provide him with work and that he had been constructively dismissed. He was awarded 24 months' pay.[51]

The definition of constructive dismissal was expanded in a recent case where an employee was given two years' notice of a change to his written employment agreement that would reduce the amount in the termination pay clause. The employee disagreed with the change and was told two years later that he had to accept the new terms or "we do not have a job for you." The employee left the company and successfully sued for constructive dismissal.[52]

Avoiding Wrongful Dismissal Suits

Dismissals for cause may result in the employee filing a wrongful dismissal lawsuit. A wrongful dismissal accusation is one in which the terminated employee contends that the employer terminated the employment relationship in violation of relevant law (based on age, gender, or other protected grounds), the contract of employment (implied or explicit), or the employer's own dismissal procedures. More recent accusations have stemmed from how the dismissal was carried out (perceptions of fairness) or employee perception that the reason for the termination did not qualify as "just cause."

There are several steps that can be taken to avoid wrongful dismissal suits:[53]

Hints TO ENSURE LEGAL COMPLIANCE

1. Use employment contracts with a termination clause and with wording clearly permitting the company to dismiss without cause during the probationary period.
2. Document all disciplinary action.
3. Do not allege just cause for dismissal unless it can be proven.

4. Time the termination so that it does not conflict with special occasions, such as birthdays or holidays.

5. Use termination letters in all cases, clearly stating the settlement offer.

6. Schedule the termination interview in a private location at a time of day that will allow the employee to clear out belongings with a minimal amount of contact with other employees.

7. Include two members of management in the termination meeting.

If a wrongful dismissal suit is made against the company, the firm should:[54]

Tips FOR THE FRONT LINE

- Review the claim carefully before retaining an employment lawyer, and investigate for other improper conduct; ask for a legal opinion on the merits of the case; work with the lawyer and provide all relevant facts and documentation; and discuss any possible letter of reference with the lawyer.

- Never allege cause if none exists, and avoid defamatory statements.

- Consider mediation as an option, or offer to settle to save time and money.

Outplacement Counselling

outplacement counselling
A systematic process by which a terminated person is trained and counselled in the techniques of self-appraisal and securing a new position.

Outplacement counselling provides career counselling and job search skills training for terminated employees. The counselling itself is done either by the employer's in-house specialist or by outside consultants. Outplacement counselling is considered part of the terminated employee's severance package.[55]

Outplacement counselling is usually conducted by outplacement firms, such as Drake Beam Morin and Right Management. Middle- and upper-level managers who are dismissed will typically have office space and secretarial services that they can use at local offices of such firms, in addition to the counselling services.

The Termination Interview

termination interview The interview in which an employee is informed of the fact that he or she has been dismissed.

Dismissing an employee is one of the most difficult tasks that a manager will face at work.[56] The dismissed employee, even if warned many times in the past, will often still react with total disbelief or even violence. Guidelines for the **termination interview** itself follow.

1. *Plan the interview.* Carefully schedule the meeting on a day early in the week, and try to avoid Fridays, pre-holidays, and vacation times. Have the employee agreement, human resources file, and release announcement (internal and external) prepared in advance. Be available at a time after the interview in case questions or problems arise, and have phone numbers ready for medical or security emergencies.

2. *Get to the point.* As soon as the employee arrives, give the person a moment to get comfortable and then inform him or her of the decision.

3. *Describe the situation briefly.* In three or four sentences, explain why the person is being let go. For instance, "Production in your area is down 4 percent, and we are continuing to have quality problems. We have talked about these problems several times in the past three months, and the solutions are

Termination interviews are among the most difficult tasks that managers face, but there are guidelines for making them less painful for both parties.

not being followed through. We have to make a change."[57] Remember to describe the situation rather than attacking the employee personally.

4. *Listen.* It is important to continue the interview until the person appears to be talking freely and seems reasonably calm about the reasons for his or her termination and the severance package that he or she is to receive. Behavioural indications can be used to help gauge the person's reaction and to decide how best to proceed. Five major reactions often occur:

- First, some employees will be *hostile and angry,* expressing hurt and disappointment. In such cases, remain objective while providing information on any outplacement or career counselling to be provided, being careful to avoid being defensive or confronting the person's anger.

- Second, some employees may react in a *defensive, bargaining* manner, based on their feelings of fear and disbelief. In this case, it is important to acknowledge that this is a difficult time for the employee and then provide information regarding outplacement counselling without getting involved in any bargaining discussions.

- Third, the employee may proceed in a *formal, controlled* manner, indicative of a suppressed, vengeful reaction and the potential for legal action. In this case, allow the employee to ask any questions pertaining to his or her case (avoiding side issues) in a formal tone while leading into information about the outplacement counselling to be provided.

- Fourth, some employees will maintain a *stoic* façade, masking their shock, disbelief, and numbness. In this case, communicate to the employee that his or her shock is recognized and that the details can be handled later if the employee prefers. Answer any questions arising at that point and provide information on outplacement counselling.

- A fifth reaction is an *emotional* one involving tears and sadness, indicating grief and worry on the part of the employee. Allow the person to cry and provide tissues. When the person regains his or her composure, explain the outplacement counselling process.

An Ethical : Dilemma

Is it ethical to "buy out" an undesirable employee with severance pay and a good letter of reference in order to avoid prolonged wrongful dismissal litigation, even if you know the letter is misleading to potential future employers?

5. *Review all elements of the severance package.* Describe severance payments, benefits, and the way in which references will be handled. However, under no conditions should any promises or benefits beyond those already in the severance package be implied. The termination should be complete when the person leaves.

6. *Identify the next step.* The terminated employee may be disoriented, so explain where he or she should go on leaving the interview. Remind the person whom to contact at the company regarding questions about the severance package or references.

EFFECTIVE EMPLOYEE COMMUNICATION

Employee Engagement

employee engagement The emotional and intellectual involvement of employees in their work, such as intensity, focus, and involvement in his or her job and organization.

Employee engagement is a positive, fulfilling, work-related state of mind characterized by vigour, dedication, and absorption.[58] It is a heightened emotional and intellectual connection that an employee has for his or her job, organization, manager, or co-workers, that in turn influences the employee to apply additional discretionary effort.[59] Engaged employees feel a vested interest in the company's success and are both willing and motivated to perform to levels that exceed the stated job requirements (see **Figure 15.5**).[60]

RPC

Develops processes to engage and involve employees in achieving the objectives of the organization

A closer look at the drivers of employee engagement reveals the importance of fair treatment. Senior management that are concerned about the well-being of their employees, tell the truth, and communicate difficult messages well are treating employees with dignity and respect, which is the cornerstones of interactional justice. Opportunities for growth and development, including increased autonomy and participation in day-to-day decision making, are manifestations of procedural justice. Organizations that strive for excellence and maintain high levels of distributive fairness ensure that their employees' career objectives are clear and their performances are compensated.

One of the most important drivers of employee engagement is effective communication, because an engaged employee is an informed employee who feels valued and critical to their organization's success.[61] It is important for managers to deliver information (facts) about individual performance and organizational success to their employees in combination with effective communication and feedback to maximize employee engagement. It is also important to maximize face-to-face opportunities when delivering information from members of the senior management team.[62]

RPC

Develops and implements programs for employee involvement Uses communication strategies to advance organizational objectives

To increase employee engagement, many firms give employees extensive data on the performance of and prospects for their operations.[63] It must be remembered that employee communication requires careful consideration, as Chrysler

---

FIGURE 15.5   Top Drivers of Attraction, Retention, and Engagement in Canada

TOP FIVE DRIVERS		
Top Attraction Drivers	**Top Retention Drivers**	**Top Engagement Drivers**
Competitive base pay	Have excellent career advancement opportunities	Senior management sincerely interested in employee well-being
Vacation/paid time off	Satisfaction with the organization's people decisions	Organization's reputation for social responsibility
Competitive health care benefits	Ability to balance my work/personal life	Input into decision making in my department
Challenging work	Fairly compensated compared to others doing similar work in my organization	Improved my skills and capabilities over the last year
Career advancement opportunities	Understand potential career track within organization	Understand potential career track within organization

Source: Closing the Engagement Gap: A Road Map for Driving Superior Business Performance. Towers Perrin Workforce Study 2007–2008, p. 21. Copyright 2009 Towers Perrin. Used with permission.

found out in early 2009 when it sent a letter to unionized employees outlining the serious challenges the company was facing and the need to reduce labour costs. Within hours, workers in Windsor, Ontario, spilled out of the plant to burn the letter in protest. The union called the letter a "clear attempt to sidestep and undermine" them.[64]

Suggestion Programs

Employees can often offer well-informed, thoughtful, and creative suggestions regarding issues ranging from malfunctioning vending machines to unlit parking lots to a manager spending too much of the department's money on travel. Dofasco Inc.'s suggestion program has been a success story for decades. Employees can receive cash awards of up to $50 000, depending on the savings realized by implementing the suggestion. Suggestion programs like these have several benefits. They let management continually monitor employees' feelings and concerns while making it clear that employees have several channels through which to communicate concerns and get responses. The net effect is less likelihood that minor employee issues will manifest themselves into organizational concerns.

Employee Opinion Surveys

employee opinion surveys
Communication devices that use questionnaires to ask for employees' opinions about the company, management, and work life.

Many firms also administer periodic anonymous **employee opinion surveys.** For maximum benefit, surveys should be conducted regularly and the results must be provided to participants.[65] An employee satisfaction survey, called the Employee Feedback System (EFS), has been developed by the National Quality Institute and the Workplace Health Research Unit at Brock University.[66] The EFS examines 16 areas ranging from job satisfaction and co-worker cohesion to quality focus and employee commitment.

Employee Feedback System
www.thcu.ca/workplace/sat/pubs/ sat_0065_v102.pdf

Recently, employees began to use blogs to express opinions about their employers, and employer concerns arose about damage to their reputation and possible disclosure of confidential company information. Some corporations, such as IBM, Cisco, and Sun Microsystems, have chosen to trust their employees and have suggested guidelines and specific tactics so that employees can blog without causing themselves or their employers any grief.[67] However, there are also cases where employees have been terminated for posting negative opinions about their employer, and arbitration boards have upheld the terminations, finding that postings about managers, co-workers, and the work environment are sufficient grounds for discharge.[68] A blogging policy is recommended by legal experts and should include directions to refrain from disclosing any confidential company information or embarrassing or demeaning information about the company and its employees.[69]

RPC

Develops and maintains the trust and support of collaborators, including the immediate supervisor, subordinates, and internal clients Gathers and analyzes information on organizational context (climate, culture) to highlight key issues

Communication from Management

To increase employee engagement, many firms give employees extensive data on the performance of and prospects for their operations. Traditionally, newsletters and verbal presentations were the most effective methods used to disseminate information from the company to employees. More recently, organizations have used videos, email, and intranets.[70] Blogs can also be used by senior managers to connect with employees. When Jim Estill sold his company and became CEO of the larger combined operation, he found employees of the acquiring company "treated me like I was some sort of Martian." He started a blog (80 percent company-related content and 20 percent personal) and soon overcame the problem—staff even sent him pictures from their kids' birthday parties! In addition, staff sent the blog to vendors and customers, which elevated him in their eyes as well.[71] One Canadian company used improved management communication to drive huge increases in employee engagement as well as a turnaround in financial results, as described in the Strategic HR box.

STRATEGIC HR

Forensic Technology: Improved Engagement Fuels Company Turnaround

When characters on the hit shows *CSI* and *CSI: New York* study a digital image of a gun's spent cartridge case looking for clues to this week's puzzling murder, they are using a real-life analysis system built by Montreal-based Forensic Technology (FT). The firm is a leader in ballistics and firearms identification technologies.

However, the company was barely making a profit in 2004 and had to downsize by 25 percent. In 2005, salaries were frozen and the generous employee profit-sharing plan was discontinued. In 2006 the company was for sale. Turnover hit 20 percent and stayed there.

"High turnover is a particularly painful experience in most companies, but it is excruciating and very costly in high-tech companies," said Elisabeth Lecavalier, FT vice-president of human resources. "Not only were we losing valued employees with high levels of education and technical skills and knowledge that are tough to find in a very competitive market in Montreal, but replacement costs, time spent in retraining and reintegrating added to the burden. Add to that the demoralizing impact of losing friends and facing additional workload on the employees who stayed. We were faced with a situation that just had to turn around, and turn around fast."

The turnaround began in the fall of 2006 with an internal effort to improve employee engagement and increase retention. FT began with the recognition of a need for strategic alignment of people, processes, and technology. With the support of top management,

the role of human resources became one of a catalyst: conducting research, suggesting new strategies and programs, training, and coordinating and supporting business initiatives. Using focus groups, they developed a new company tag line: "Work that matters." Surveys and focus group discussions identified the key drivers of engagement as career development, recognition, internal communications, and work environment issues (flexibility and social responsibility). Each of these areas was addressed.

A new management development program emphasizing employee engagement encouraged managers to listen to their employees, understand their career aspirations, and provide training and development that would move them toward achieving those aspirations. The President's Award for Excellence recognition program was established, along with a new intranet site with the latest in corporate news. A new community involvement event was instituted where FT employees organize and conduct a learning event for high school students in high-risk areas of the city to show them the value of pursuing their education.

By 2008, FT's turnover fell to less than 4 percent and employee engagement levels rose from 30 percent to close to 65 percent. Employees now have great pride in the company, with one field technician commenting "there is a moral value to what we do."

Chapter SUMMARY

1. Turnover can be voluntary (employee initiated) or involuntary (employer initiated). HR considerations in managing turnover include making sure that there is enough talent to complete production demands as well as minimizing turnover costs to the organization.

2. A fair and just disciplinary process is based on three prerequisites: rules and regulations, a system of progressive penalties, and an appeals process.

3. Employees who are dismissed without just cause must be provided with reasonable notice. This means paying them for several weeks or months in addition to the legally required notice period on termination. If the employee does not believe that the period of notice is reasonable, he or she may file a wrongful dismissal lawsuit. Constructive dismissal occurs when the employer makes unilateral changes in the employment contract that are unacceptable to the employee, even though the employee has not been formally terminated.

4. The six steps in the termination interview are to plan the interview carefully, get to the point, describe the situation, listen until the person has expressed his or her feelings, discuss the severance package, and identify the next step.

5. Employee engagement is a positive, fulfilling, work-related state of mind characterized by vigour, dedication, and absorption. Organizational factors such as senior leadership, opportunities for learning and development, and company image and reputation are the primary influencers of engagement. Outcomes of employee engagement include improvements in recruiting, retention, turnover, individual productivity, customer service, and customer loyalty, as well as growth in operating margins and increased profit margins and revenue growth rates.

6. Techniques for ensuring effective employee communication include suggestion programs, employee opinion surveys, and communication from management.

MyManagementLab

Visit MyManagementLab to access a personalized Study Plan and additional study tools for this chapter.

Key TERMS

constructive dismissal *(p. 429)*
dismissal *(p. 422)*
dismissal for just cause *(p. 422)*
distributive justice *(p. 426)*
employee engagement *(p. 432)*
employee opinion surveys *(p. 433)*
group termination laws *(p. 427)*
insubordination *(p. 423)*
interactional justice *(p. 427)*
involuntary turnover *(p. 416)*
layoff *(p. 424)*

outplacement counselling *(p. 430)*
phased retirement *(p. 420)*
pre-retirement counselling *(p. 421)*
procedural justice *(p. 426)*
quitting *(p. 419)*
retirees on call *(p. 420)*
termination interview *(p. 430)*
turnover *(p. 416)*
voluntary turnover *(p. 416)*
wrongful dismissal *(p. 427)*

Review and Discussion QUESTIONS

1. Explain why organizations today are concerned with voluntary turnover.

2. Describe the issues of reasonable notice in layoffs and how it relates to employee perspectives of fairness or intent to file wrongful dismissal lawsuits.

3. Explain how fairness in employee termination can be ensured, particularly the prerequisites to progressive discipline guidelines.

4. What are the various steps in the termination interview?

5. Discuss some of the issues that should be covered when communicating effectively with employees in the organization.

Critical Thinking QUESTIONS

1. Should a company consider providing termination packages to employees who have ongoing disciplinary problems rather than taking the time and effort to go through the progressive discipline process?

2. Assume that in one department of your organization the voluntary turnover rate is double the rate that other departments have. What factors might contribute to this? What issues would you investigate? Is voluntary turnover necessarily bad and in need of correction?

3. Discuss the options presented as alternatives to layoffs. Which of these would appeal to you, your family members, and friends? Why? What challenges do these alternatives pose to organizations?

Experiential EXERCISES

1. Working individually or in groups, obtain copies of the student handbook for your college or university and determine to what extent there is a formal process through which students can air grievances. Would you expect the process to be effective? Why or why not? Based on contact with students who have used the grievance process, has it been effective?

2. Working individually or in groups, determine the nature of the academic discipline process in your college or university. Does it appear to be an effective one? Based on this chapter, should any modification be made to the student discipline process?

3. A computer department employee made an entry error that ruined an entire run of computer reports. Efforts to rectify the situation produced a second batch of improperly run reports. As a result of the series of errors, the employer incurred extra costs of $2400, plus a weekend of overtime work by other computer department staffers. Management suspended the employee for three days for negligence and also revoked a promotion for which the employee had previously been approved.

Protesting the discipline, the employee stressed that she had attempted to correct her error in the early stages of the run by notifying the manager of computer operations of her mistake. Maintaining that the resulting string of errors could have been avoided if the manager had followed up on her report and stopped the initial run, the employee argued that she had been treated unfairly; she was being severely punished but the manager had not been disciplined at all, even though he had compounded the problem. Moreover, citing her "impeccable" work record and management's acknowledgement that she had always been a "model employee," the employee insisted that the denial of her previously approved promotion was "unconscionable."

(a) In groups, determine what your decision would be if you were the arbitrator. Why? (Your instructor will inform you of the actual arbitrator's decision when you discuss this exercise in class.)

(b) Do you think that the employer handled the disciplinary situation correctly? Why? What would you have done differently?

4. Working with a partner, review the following scenario and discuss your responses.
Maggie sat there stunned. Her boss had just told her that, as a result of the merger with the ABC Company, she would be reporting to the vice-president of customer service and that her title would be associate vice-president of customer service. "This can't be. My job is the VP of customer service. How can I report to another VP?"

Has Maggie been demoted? Constructively dismissed? Discuss the rationale for your answer.

5. You are the HR manager in a small company that has just bought another company in your field. You only learned of the purchase when you were asked to attend a meeting this morning. Somehow, between now and tomorrow at noon, you must come up with a plan to communicate the purchase to your and the other organization's employees. What do you think will be the main concerns of employees in each company? Describe your first steps and the plan for the transition period between now and the closing date of the purchase.

Running CASE

Running Case: LearnInMotion.com

Fair Treatment in Disciplinary Action
Because the employees at LearnInMotion.com use high-cost computer equipment to do their jobs, Jennifer and Pierre have always felt strongly about not allowing employees to eat or drink at their desks. Jennifer was therefore surprised to walk into the office one day to find two employees eating lunch at their desks. There was a large pizza in a box, and the two of them were sipping soft drinks and eating slices of pizza and submarine sandwiches from paper plates. She could see that there were grease and soft drink spills on their desks, and the office smelled of onions and pepperoni. In addition to looking unprofessional, the mess on the desks increased the possibility that the computers could be damaged. One of the employees continued to use his computer with greasy fingers between bites.

Although this was a serious matter, neither Jennifer nor Pierre believes that what the employees were doing is grounds for immediate dismissal, partly because there is no written policy on eating at the workstations. They just assumed that people would use their common sense. The problem is that they do not know what to do. It seems to them that the matter calls for more than just a warning but less than dismissal. As their management consultant, how would you answer the following questions?

QUESTIONS

1 What is a progressive discipline policy, and should LearnInMotion put one in place, formally and in writing within their human resources policy manual?

2 If LearnInMotion puts a progressive disciplinary policy in place and these two employees choose to eat at their desks again, would this constitute "just cause" termination?

3 If LearnInMotion chooses to terminate these two employees right now, would they face any legal ramifications?

Case INCIDENT

An Inappropriate Email

Roger Miller, the director of human resources for Virtual Reality Media, was returning to his office after a half-day training session on how to retain and engage today's top talent when he received a disturbing phone call. Randy, the manager of the multimedia lab, called to let Roger know about an email he had just been copied on.

One of Randy's salespeople, John, had sent all of his fellow staff within the multimedia lab department a very derogatory email describing about Randy; the email said that Randy was a useless supervisor who should not be in a management position as he does not know what he is doing and should be fired.

Randy is very upset and wants Roger to terminate John. This is where you come in to help Roger.

QUESTIONS

1 Assume you are Roger. Specifically, what should you do now?
2 How should you do it?
3 Is this a just cause termination?

MyManagementLab

Visit MyManagementLab to access a personalized Study Plan and additional study tools for this chapter.

 To view the CBC videos, read a summary, and answer discussion questions, go to MyManagementLab

CHAPTER

16 Labour Relations

||||||||||||||||||||||||||||||||||||||||||||||||||||

LEARNING OUTCOMES

AFTER STUDYING THIS CHAPTER, YOU SHOULD BE ABLE TO

DISCUSS the key elements of Canada's labour laws.

OUTLINE the five steps in the labour relations process.

DESCRIBE the five steps in a union organizing campaign.

OUTLINE the three ways to obtain union recognition.

DESCRIBE the three steps in the collective bargaining process.

EXPLAIN the typical steps in a grievance procedure.

||||||||||||||||||||||||||||||||||||||||||||||||||||

REQUIRED PROFESSIONAL CAPABILITIES (RPC)

- Provides advice on the interpretation of the collective agreement

- Collects and presents information required for decision making in the bargaining process

- Effectively handles disagreements and conflicts

- Analyzes and provides advice on employment rights and responsibilities

- Provides advice on interest arbitration.

INTRODUCTION TO LABOUR RELATIONS

labour union (union) An officially recognized association of employees practising a similar trade or employed in the same company or industry who have joined together to present a united front and collective voice in dealing with management.

labour–management relations The ongoing interactions between labour unions and management in organizations.

collective bargaining agreement (union contract) A formal agreement between an employer and the union representing a group of employees regarding terms and conditions of employment.

collective bargaining Negotiations between a union and an employer to arrive at a mutually acceptable collective agreement.

bargaining units The group of employees in a firm, a plant, or an industry that has been recognized by an employer or certified by a labour relations board (LRB) as appropriate for collective bargaining purposes.

Canadian Labour and Business Centre
www.clbc.ca

Ontario Ministry of Labour
www.labour.gov.on.ca

Canadian LabourWatch Association
www.labourwatch.com

A **labour union** (or **union**) is an officially recognized body representing a group of employees who have joined together to present a collective voice in dealing with management. The purposes of unionization are to influence HR policies and practices that affect bargaining unit members, such as pay and benefits; to achieve greater control over the jobs being performed, greater job security, and improved working conditions; and to increase job satisfaction and meet employees' affiliation needs. The term **labour–management relations** refers to the ongoing interactions between labour unions and management in organizations.

The presence of a labour union alters the relationship between employees and the firm and has implications for planning and implementing a business strategy. Managerial discretion and flexibility in dealing with employees and in implementing and administering HR policies and procedures are reduced. For example, union seniority provisions in the **collective bargaining agreement** (**union contract**), negotiated through **collective bargaining**, govern the selection of employees for transfers, promotions, and training programs and specify the order in which employees can be laid off and recalled. Many other terms and conditions of employment for **bargaining unit** members are determined and standardized through collective bargaining, rather than being left to management's discretion.

An organization's *labour relations (LR) strategy,* one component of its HR strategy, is its overall plan for dealing with unions, which sets the tone for its union–management relationship. The decision to accept or avoid unions is the basis of an organization's LR strategy.[1]

Managers in firms choosing a *union acceptance strategy* view the union as the legitimate representative of the firm's employees. Such a relationship can lead to innovative initiatives and win–win outcomes. Managers select a *union avoidance strategy* when they believe that it is preferable to operate in a non-unionized environment. Walmart is well known for its preference to remain non-union (and has even closed stores that have attempted to unionize).[2] To avoid unions, companies can either adopt a *union substitution approach,* in which they become so responsive to employee needs that there is no incentive for them to unionize (as is the case at Dofasco), or adopt a *union suppression approach* when there is a desire to avoid a union at all costs (Walmart challenged the constitutionality of Saskatchewan's labour laws all the way to the Supreme Court of Canada, but lost).[3]

Canada's Labour Laws

Canadian labour laws have two general purposes:

1. To provide a common set of rules for fair negotiations
2. To protect the public interest by preventing the impact of labour disputes from inconveniencing the public.

As with other employment-related legislation, there are 13 provincial/territorial jurisdictions, as well as federal labour relations legislation for employees subject to federal jurisdiction. There are a number of common characteristics in the LR legislation across Canada, which can be summarized as follows:

- Procedures for the certification of a union
- The requirement that a collective agreement be in force for a minimum of one year

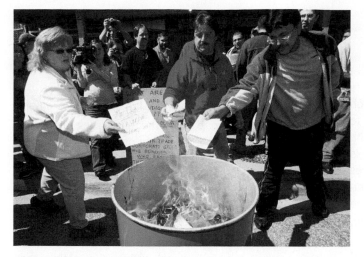

Chrysler workers at the company's assembly plant in Windsor, Ontario, burn letters they received from management. The letters outlined a number of concessions the company is requesting of employees.

- Procedures that must be followed by one or both parties before a strike or lockout is legal
- The prohibition of strikes or lockouts during the life of a collective agreement
- The requirement that disputes over matters arising from interpretation of the collective agreement be settled by final and binding arbitration
- Prohibition of certain specified "unfair practices" on the part of labour and management
- Establishment of a labour relations board or the equivalent; labour relations boards are tripartite—made up of representatives of union and management, as well as a neutral chair or a vice-chair, typically a government representative.

RPC

Analyzes and provides advice on employment rights and responsibilities

Labour relations legislation attempts to balance employees' rights to engage in union activities with employers' rights to manage. For example, managers are prohibited from interfering with and discriminating against employees who are exercising their rights under the LR legislation. One restriction on unions is that they are prohibited from calling or authorizing an unlawful strike.

The Labour Movement in Canada Today

The primary goal of labour unions active in Canada today is to obtain economic benefits and improved treatment for their members. It may involve lobbying for legislative changes pertaining to these issues. This union philosophy, with its emphasis on economic and welfare goals, has become known as **business unionism**. Unions strive to ensure *job security* for their members and to attain *improved economic conditions* and *better working conditions* for their members. Most unions today also become involved in broader political and social issues affecting their members. Activities aimed at influencing government economic and social policies are known as **social (reform) unionism**. For example, unions have recognized the special circumstances of Aboriginal workers, as outlined in the Workforce Diversity box.

Types of Unions

The labour unions in Canada can be classified according to the following characteristics:

1. *Type of worker eligible for membership.* All the early trade unions in Canada were **craft unions**—associations of persons performing a certain type of skill or trade (for example, carpenters or bricklayers). Examples in today's workforce include the British Columbia Teachers' Federation and the Ontario Nurses' Association. An **industrial union** is a labour organization comprising all the workers eligible for union membership in a particular company or industry, irrespective of the type of work performed.
2. *Geographical scope.* Labour unions with head offices in other countries (most often the United States) that charter branches in both Canada and one

business unionism The activities of labour unions focusing on economic and welfare issues, including pay and benefits, job security, and working conditions.

social (reform) unionism Activities of unions directed at furthering the interests of their members by influencing the social and economic policies of governments at all levels, such as speaking out on proposed legislative reforms.

craft union Traditionally, a labour organization representing workers practising the same craft or trade, such as carpentry or plumbing.

industrial union A labour organization representing all workers eligible for union membership in a particular company or industry, including skilled trades people.

Construction Labour Relations
www.clra.org

International Labour News
www.labourstart.org

WORKFORCE DIVERSITY

Collective Agreement Puts Aboriginals First

It's not every day a union agrees to a contract that puts some members behind outside applicants for a job opening, or to a collective agreement that has little to offer when it comes to the privileges of seniority. But the collective agreement at Voisey's Bay Nickel Company is one such rarity. At this mine, located 350 kilometres north of Happy Valley-Goose Bay in Labrador, the Innu and Inuit people, regardless of whether or not they're employees, are always first in line whenever a position, a training opportunity, or a promotion comes up.

That's one of the implications of the two impacts and benefits agreements (IBAs) the nickel company, a subsidiary of Inco, signed with the Innu Nation and the Labrador Inuit Association. Innu and Inuit people are on top of this order of preference, starting with those in the bargaining unit, followed by those already employed by Voisey's Bay and by Innu and Inuit outside candidates. Among non-Aboriginals, priority goes to Labrador residents. Those with union membership rank first, followed by Voisey's Bay employees, and then those in the community.

Inco's IBAs with the Innu and Inuit of Labrador aren't unique. Agreements have been signed in many other resource projects, including Xstrata Nickel's Raglan mine in Quebec, BHP Billiton's Ekati diamond mine in the Northwest Territories, and De Beers Canada's Victor mine in Ontario.

The union also negotiated other benefits not stipulated in the IBAs to reflect the fact that Aboriginals make up more than half of the bargaining unit. For example, National Aboriginal Day on June 21 is now a paid holiday under the collective agreement.

The IBAs also impose obligations on the employer to provide training opportunities for Aboriginals. The training initiatives go back 10 years, when the company first sought out candidates by providing information about the work conditions and kinds of careers available in mining. When the project was under construction, the company drew up its workforce plans and identified areas where the skilled workers were already available and where there were gaps. Then, with funding support from the federal government, the company offered skilled trades training for occupations such as heavy equipment operator and millwright.

"Once they graduated, we then looked for opportunities where we could employ them during the construction phase to give them actual experience," said Wayne Scott, manager of HR at Voisey's Bay.

Source: U. Vu, "Collective Agreement Puts Aboriginals First," *Canadian HR Reporter* (November 6, 2006).

---

or more countriesare known as *international unions*. Labour unions that charter branches in Canada only and have their head office in this country are known as *national unions*. A small number of employees belong to labour unions that are purely *local* in geographical scope.

3. *Labour congress affiliation.* A third way of distinguishing among labour unions is according to affiliation with one or another central labour organization. These central organizations include the following:

- *Canadian Labour Congress (CLC).* The CLC is the major central labour organization in Canada and has over 3 million affiliated union members. Most international and national unions belong to the CLC, as well as all directly chartered local unions, local/district labour councils, and provincial/territorial federations of labour.

- *Confédération des syndicats nationaux (CSN)*—in English, Confederation of National Trade Unions (CNTU). This organization is the Quebec counterpart of the CLC and has more than 300 000 members.

- *American Federation of Labor and Congress of Industrial Organizations (AFL–CIO).* The American counterpart of the CLC is the AFL–CIO. The two organizations operate independently, but since most international unions in the CLC are also members of the AFL–CIO, a certain degree of common interest exists.

American Federation of Labor and Congress of Industrial Organizations (AFL–CIO)
www.aflcio.org

local A group of unionized employees in a particular location.

union steward A union member elected by workers in a particular department or area of a firm to act as their union representative.

The basic unit of the labour union movement in Canada is the **local**, formed in a particular location. For HR managers and front-line supervisors, the union locals are generally the most important part of the union structure. Key players within the local are the elected officials known as **union stewards**, who are responsible for representing the interests and protecting the rights of bargaining unit employees in their department or area. The Strategic HR box discusses a recent trend of expanded memberships at the local union level in Canada.

STRATEGIC HR

UFCW Forms a "Super Local"

Two United Food and Commercial Workers (UFCW) unions merged in late 2011 to form what many are calling North America's largest local union. Collectively, this union represents over 60 000 workers, the majority of which are employed by Loblaw.

UFCW Canada national director Wayne Hanley suggests that the super local is the union's response to challenges such as declining memberships, aggressive employers, and economic volatility. "If we pool our resources, we can give better service" explained Hanley. "You're in a better position because you are not playing one against the other."

In addition to these benefits, a larger union often means less administration (resulting in lower union dues) and the ability to maintain in-house legal expertise and secure more professional training.

CAW president Ken Lewenza suggests that the newly formed UFCW union falls outside of the framework of a local union. "Sixty thousand members would, in many ways, do the work done at the national level," argues Lewenza. "Local to use means local, as in operates in the local community." Regardless, he agrees that larger locals will be a reality for Canadian unions in the future.

Source: D. Harder, "UFCW Creates 'Super Local' of 60,000," *Canadian HR Reporter*, 24, no. 14 (August 15, 2011), p. 8. Reprinted by permission of Canadian HR Reporter. © Copyright Thomson Reuters Canada Ltd., (2012) Toronto, Ontario, 1-800-387-5164. Web: www.hrreporter.com.

Membership Trends

As of 2010, 31.5 percent of Canadian employees were unionized. The membership in unions as a percentage of the labour force has been steadily decreasing, as shown in **Figure 16.1**. Various factors are responsible for membership decline, including a dramatic increase in service sector and white-collar jobs, combined with a decrease in employment opportunities in industries that have traditionally been highly unionized, such as manufacturing. More effective HR practices in non-unionized firms are another contributing factor.[4]

Traditionally, unions have targeted full-time, manufacturing workers (which used to be almost exclusively older males) for membership. Canadian unions are unique in that they have managed to refocus their target on membership to better align with workforce realities. As a result, the rate of decline in union membership is not nearly as significant in Canada as it is elsewhere (for example, the United States). This can be attributed to three significant issues: global competition, demographics, and unionization of white-collar workers in Canada.

Global Competition

Globalization is transforming the dynamics of labour relations in Canada such that employers are being forced to become more militant, and unions are struggling to maintain their influence at the bargaining table.[5] Some unions face the difficult choice of negotiating concessions or watching jobs go to lower-cost countries.

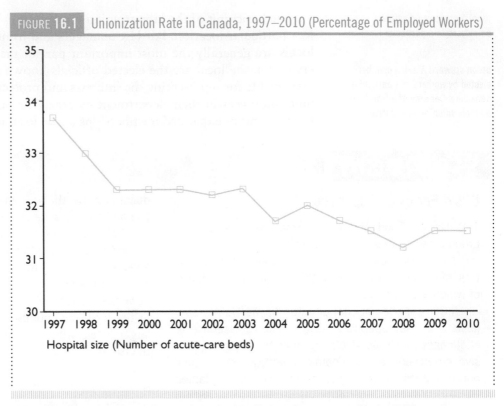

FIGURE 16.1 Unionization Rate in Canada, 1997–2010 (Percentage of Employed Workers)

Note: HRSDC calculations based on Statistics Canada, "Labour force survey estimates (LFS), employees by union coverage, North American Industry Classification System (NAICS), sex and age group, annual" (CANSIM Table 282-0078). Ottawa, ON: Statistics Canada, 2011.

Source: Work-Unionization Rates, http://www4.hrsdc.gc.ca/.3ndic.1t.4r@-eng.jsp?iid=17, Human Resources and Skills Development Canada, 2012. Reproduced with the permission of the Minister of Public Works and Government Services Canada, 2012.

Demographics

The focus of union collective bargaining efforts must align with the workplace demographics. The aging of the workforce and pending labour shortage affects unions as well as HR managers.[6] It has been suggested that unions and management may need to work together to attract and retain workers. Retention concerns may make employers more willing to offer job security in exchange for promises of productivity and flexibility from unions. Pensions and benefits for older workers and retirees has also become more of a union priority.

Unionization of White-Collar Employees

Difficulties in attempting to resolve grievances and lack of job security have led to increased interest in unionization among white-collar workers. Service sector workers, such as those in retail stores, fast-food chains, and government agencies, as well as managers and professionals (including university/college faculty), have been targeted for organizing campaigns. Since these jobs tend to have more women and young people than manufacturing jobs, unions are now focusing more on work–family issues as well as the health and safety risks associated with white-collar jobs, such as the potential for repetitive strain injuries from working at video display terminals (computers or laptops).[7]

THE LABOUR RELATIONS PROCESS

As illustrated in **Figure 16.2,** the labour relations process consists of five steps:

1. Employees decide to seek collective representation.
2. The union organizing campaign begins.
3. The union receives official recognition.
4. Union and management negotiate a collective agreement.
5. Day-to-day contract administration begins.

Each of these five steps will now be reviewed in detail.

Step 1: Desire for Collective Representation

 Research ┊ **INSIGHT**

Based on a review of 36 research studies internationally, three classifications were developed to explain why individuals join unions:[8]

- *Dissonance-based reasons.* When expectations of work (work should be enjoyable and rewarding, for example) and the experience of work (the work environment is unpleasant and pay is low) are in conflict, the desire to join

| FIGURE **16.2** | An Overview of the Labour Relations Process

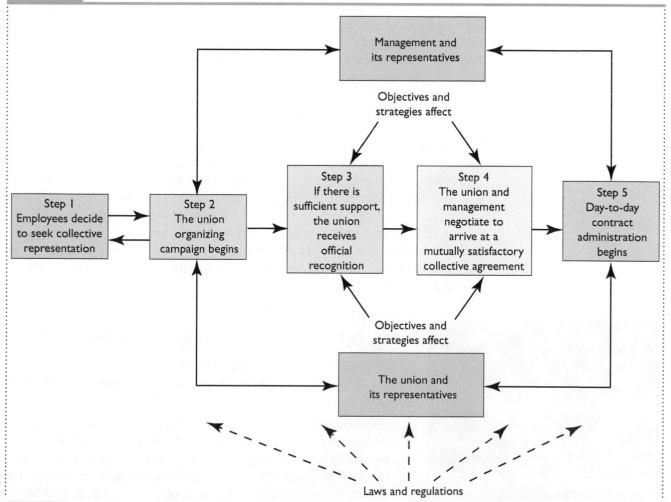

a union is triggered. However if dissonance is the reason why employees want to unionize, then they will only do so if they think the union will be effective in remedying the associated discontent or frustration with the work expectations versus experiences dissonance.

- *Utility-based reasons.* An individual's decision to join a union can also be attributed to a rational calculation of the costs and benefits of unionization, where individuals compare the costs and benefits of remaining non-unionized versus becoming unionized. The selection of which decision to make is largely based on the calculation of the cost/benefit analysis.[9]
- *Political/ideological reasons.* An individual's political or ideological beliefs may influence their understanding of and desire for collective versus individual negotiation of employment terms.[10]

Numerous studies suggest that age, gender, education levels, and other demographic factors are highly correlated with the desire to join a union. However, there is little consistency with the findings of the studies, with the exception of two groups: People over the age of 60 and black workers are consistently likely to have a desire to join a union.[11] It has been theorized that this is largely due to perceptions of employment related discrimination. It has also been suggested that each workplace is unique, so the demographic characteristics of one workforce may impact the desire to join a union in a way that isn't highly generalizable or applicable to a larger population.

Given the fact that, in 2007, the average wage rate for unionized employees was significantly higher than non-unionized employees (average hourly rate full time: unionized = \$24.15, non-unionized = \$20.55: average hourly rate part time: unionized = \$19.99, non-unionized = \$12.56) and average hours worked per week was significantly higher for unionized employees in Canada (unionized = 19.3 hours, non-unionized = 16.9), these expectations seem quite justifiable. Being a union member also has an impact on female workers' ability to achieve pay equity. On average, full-time female unionized workers earned 94 percent of the hourly wages of their male counterparts, and part-time female unionized workers earned 14 percent more than their male counterparts.[12]

However, research studies have made it clear that dissatisfaction alone will not lead to unionization. More important seems to be the employees' belief that it is only through unity that they can protect themselves from the arbitrary whims of management. In other words, it is only when workers are dissatisfied and believe that they are without the ability to change the factors causing dissatisfaction, except through collective action, that they become interested in unionizing.[13]

Step 2: Union Organizing Campaign

Once interest in joining a union has been aroused, the union organizing process begins. There are five steps typically involved in this process:

1. *Employee/union contact.* A formal organizing campaign may be initiated by a union organizer or by employees acting on their own behalf. Most organizing campaigns are begun by employees who get in touch with an existing union.[14] However, large unions have a number of *union organizers* on staff who are

Promoting the benefits of unionization.

responsible for identifying organizing opportunities and launching organizing campaigns. During these initial discussions, employees investigate the advantages of union representation, and the union officials start to gather information about the employees' sources of dissatisfaction.

2. *Initial organizational meeting.* The union organizer then schedules an initial meeting with the individuals who first expressed an interest in unionization and co-workers who subsequently express their support. The aim is to identify employees who would be willing to help the organizer direct the campaign.

3. *Formation of an in-house organizing committee.* This committee comprises a group of employees who are dedicated to the goal of unionization and who are willing to assist the union organizer.

4. *The organizing campaign.* Members of the in-house committee then contact employees, present the case for unionization, and encourage as many employees as possible to sign an **authorization card**, indicating their willingness to be represented by the union in collective bargaining with the employer.

5. *The outcome.* There are a number of possible outcomes to a unionization campaign, including rejection by the majority of eligible employees. For a union to become the bargaining unit for a group of employees, it must be certified by a labour relations board (LRB) or receive official recognition from the employer.

Signs of Organizing Activity

Managers who suspect that a unionization attempt may be underway should watch for a number of the following signs:[15]

- Disappearance of employee lists or directories
- More inquiries than usual about benefits, wages, promotions, and other HR policies and procedures
- Questions about their opinions of unions
- An increase in the number or nature of employee complaints or grievances
- A change in the number, composition, and size of informal groups at lunch and coffee breaks
- The sudden popularity of certain employees (especially if they are the informal leaders)
- The sudden cessation of employee conversation when a member of management approaches, or an obvious change in employees' behaviour toward members of management, expressed either formally or informally
- The appearance of strangers in the parking lot
- The distribution of cards, flyers, or pro-union buttons

Employer Response to an Organizing Campaign

If the employer prefers that the group seeking unionization retain its non-union status, a careful campaign is usually mounted to counteract the union drive. Normally, HR department staff members head up the campaign, although they may be assisted by a consultant or labour lawyer. Absolutely critical to the success of a company's counter-campaign is supervisory training. Supervisors need to be informed about what they can and cannot do or say during the organizing campaign to ensure that they avoid actions that

authorization card A card signed by an employee that indicates his or her willingness to have the union act as his or her representative for purposes of collective bargaining.

Tips : FOR THE FRONT LINE

Labour Relations (Ontario)
www.labour.gov.on.ca/english/lr

might directly or inadvertently provide fuel for the union's campaign and refrain from violating LR legislation.

An Ethical **Dilemma**

Knowing that head office plans to close your facility if a unionization bid is successful, how should you, as a manager, respond to inquiries from employees about the impact of a union?

As much information about the union as possible should be obtained pertaining to dues, strike record, salaries of officers, and any other relevant facts that might cause employees to question the benefits of unionization. Communication strategies can be planned, with the aim of reminding employees about the company's good points, pointing out disadvantages of unionization, and refuting any misleading union claims. The employer's case for remaining non-union should be presented in a factual, honest, and straightforward manner.

Under the law, employers are granted the right to do the following:

Hints TO ENSURE LEGAL COMPLIANCE

- Express their views and opinions regarding unions
- State their position regarding the desirability of remaining non-union
- Prohibit distribution of union literature on company property on company time
- Increase wages, make promotions, and take other HR actions, as long as they would do so *in the normal course of business*. In most jurisdictions, however, once an application for certification is received by the LRB, wages, benefits, and working conditions are frozen until the application is dealt with.
- Assemble employees during working hours to state the company's position, as long as employees are advised of the purpose of the meeting in advance, attendance is optional, and threats and promises are avoided (employers have no obligation to give the union the same opportunity).

Step 3: Union Recognition

A union can obtain recognition as a bargaining unit for a group of workers in three basic ways: (1) voluntary recognition, (2) the regular certification process, and (3) a pre-hearing vote. Bargaining rights can also be terminated in various ways.

Voluntary Recognition

An employer in every Canadian jurisdiction, except Quebec, can voluntarily recognize a union as the bargaining agent for a group of its employees. Although fairly rare, this may occur if an employer has adopted a union acceptance strategy and believes that employees want to be represented by that union.

Regular Certification

certification The procedure whereby a labour union obtains a certificate from the relevant LRB declaring that the union is the exclusive bargaining agent for a defined group of employees in a bargaining unit that the LRB considers appropriate for collective bargaining purposes.

The normal union certification procedure is for the union to present evidence of at least a minimum level of membership support for a bargaining unit that they have defined, in the form of signed authorization cards, to the appropriate LRB, along with an application for **certification**. The minimum level of support required to apply for certification varies by jurisdiction, from 25 percent of the bargaining unit in Saskatchewan to 65 percent in Manitoba.[16] The LRB then determines whether the bargaining unit defined by the union is appropriate for collective bargaining purposes.

In most jurisdictions LRBs can grant *automatic certification* without a vote if the applicant union can demonstrate a high enough level of support for the proposed bargaining unit (generally 50 or 55 percent). Automatic certification may also be granted in some jurisdictions if the employer has engaged in unfair practices. If the level of support is not sufficient for automatic certification, but is above a specified minimum level (between 25 and 45 percent, depending on jurisdiction), the LRB will order and supervise a **representation vote**.[17] Eligible employees have the opportunity to cast a secret ballot, indicating whether or not they want the union to be certified. In some jurisdictions, to gain certification the voting results must indicate that *more than 50 percent of the potential bargaining unit members* are in support of the union. In other jurisdictions, the standard is the support of *more than 50 percent of those voting*.[18] If the union loses, another election cannot be held among the same employees for at least one year. Only about 20 percent of certifications are the result of a vote—roughly four out of five certifications are the result of authorization cards alone.[19]

representation vote A vote conducted by the LRB in which employees in the bargaining unit indicate, by secret ballot, whether or not they want to be represented, or continue to be represented, by a labour union.

Pre-Hearing Votes

In most jurisdictions, a **pre-hearing vote** may be conducted where there is evidence of violations of fair labour practices early in an organizing campaign. In such a case, the LRB may order a vote before holding a hearing to determine the composition of the bargaining unit. The intent is to determine the level of support for the union as quickly as possible, before the effect of any irregularities can taint the outcome. The ballot box is then sealed until the LRB determines whether the bargaining unit is appropriate and, if so, which employees are eligible for membership. If the bargaining unit is deemed appropriate by the LRB, only the votes of potential bargaining unit members are counted, and if the majority of the ballots cast support the union, it is certified.

pre-hearing vote An alternative mechanism for certification, used in situations in which there is evidence of violations of fair labour practices early in the organizing campaign.

Termination of Bargaining Rights

All labour relations acts provide procedures for workers to apply for the **decertification** of their unions. Generally, members may apply for decertification if the union has failed to negotiate a collective agreement within one year of certification, or if they are dissatisfied with the performance of the union. The LRB holds a secret-ballot vote, and if more than 50 percent of the ballots cast (or bargaining unit members, depending on jurisdiction) are in opposition to the union, the union will be decertified. A labour union also has the right to notify the LRB that it no longer wants to continue to represent the employees in a particular bargaining unit. This is known as "termination on abandonment." Once the LRB has declared that the union no longer represents the bargaining unit employees, any collective agreement negotiated between the parties is void.

decertification The process whereby a union is legally deprived of its official recognition as the exclusive bargaining agent for a group of employees.

Step 4: Collective Bargaining

Collective bargaining is the process by which a formal collective agreement is established between labour and management. The collective agreement is the cornerstone of the Canadian LR system. Both union and management representatives are required to bargain in good faith. This means that they must communicate and negotiate, that proposals must be matched with counterproposals, and that both parties must make every reasonable effort to arrive at an agreement.

Steps typically involved in the collective bargaining process include (1) preparation for bargaining, (2) face-to-face negotiations, and (3) obtaining approval for the proposed contract. There are two possible additional steps. First, when talks break down, third-party assistance is required by law in every jurisdiction except Saskatchewan.[20] The second additional step is a strike/lockout or interest arbitration if the parties arrive at a bargaining impasse. Each of these steps will be described next.

Preparation for Negotiations

Good preparation leads to a greater likelihood that desired goals will be achieved. Preparation for negotiations involves planning the bargaining strategy and process and assembling data to support bargaining proposals. Both union and management will gather data on general economic trends, analyze other collective agreements and trends in collective bargaining, conduct an analysis of grievances, review the existing contract or the union's organizing campaign promises, conduct wage and salary surveys at competitor organizations, prepare cost estimates of monetary proposals, and make plans for a possible strike or lockout. In addition, management negotiators will obtain input from supervisors. Union negotiators will obtain input from union stewards, obtain the company's financial information (if it is a public company), gather demographic information on their membership, and obtain input from members.

International Labour Organization
www.ilo.org

Once these steps are completed, each side forms a negotiating team and an initial bargaining plan/strategy is prepared. Initial proposals are then finalized and presented for approval by either senior management or the union membership.

Face-to-Face Negotiations

Under LR legislation, representatives of either union or management can give written notice to the other party of their desire to negotiate a first collective agreement or renew an existing one. Early in the negotiating process, demands are exchanged—often before the first bargaining session. Then both negotiating teams can make a private assessment of the other team's demands. Usually, each team finds some items with which they can agree quite readily and others on which compromise seems likely. Tentative conclusions are also made regarding which items, if any, are potential strike or lockout issues.

caucus session A session in which only the members of one's own bargaining team are present.

Location, Frequency, and Duration of Meetings Negotiations are generally held at a neutral, offsite location, such as a hotel meeting room, so that there is no psychological advantage for either team and so that interruptions and work distractions can be kept to a minimum. Each side generally has another room in which intra-team meetings, known as **caucus sessions**, are held.

Generally, meetings are held as often as either or both parties consider desirable, and they last as long as progress is being made. Marathon bargaining sessions, such as those lasting all night, are not typical until conciliation has been exhausted and the clock is ticking rapidly toward the strike/lockout deadline.

Initial Bargaining Session The initial meeting of the bargaining teams is extremely important in establishing the climate that will prevail during the negotiating sessions that follow. A cordial attitude can help to relax tension and ensure that negotiations

Negotiating a collective agreement.

proceed smoothly. Generally, the first meeting is devoted to an exchange of demands (if this has not taken place previously) and the establishment of rules and procedures that will be used during negotiations.

Subsequent Bargaining Sessions In traditional approaches to bargaining, each party argues for its demands and resists those of the other at each negotiating session. At the same time, both are looking for compromise alternatives that will enable an agreement to be reached. Every proposal submitted must be either withdrawn temporarily or permanently, accepted by the other side in its entirety, or accepted in a modified form. Ideally, both sides should come away from negotiations feeling that they have attained many of their basic bargaining goals and confident that the tentative agreement reached will be acceptable to senior management and the members of the bargaining unit.

For each issue on the table to be resolved satisfactorily, the point at which agreement is reached must be within limits that the union and employer are willing to accept, often referred to as the **bargaining zone**. As illustrated in **Figure 16.3**, if the solution desired by one party exceeds the limits of the other party, then it is outside of the bargaining zone. Unless that party modifies its demands sufficiently to bring them within the bargaining zone, or the other party extends its limits to accommodate such demands, a bargaining deadlock is the inevitable result.

Distributive bargaining is an approach often typified as "win–lose" bargaining because the gains of one party are normally achieved at the expense of the other.[21] It is appropriately involved when the issues being discussed pertain to the distribution of things that are available in fixed amounts, such as wage increases and benefits improvements. However, it may also be used when there is a history of distrust and adversarial relations, even when dealing with issues on which a more constructive approach is possible.

As indicated in Figure 16.3, distributive bargaining is characterized by three distinct components: the initial point, the target point, and the resistance point. The initial point for the union is usually higher than what the union expects to receive from management. The union target point is next, and represents the

RPC

Collects and presents information required for decision making in the bargaining process

bargaining zone The area defined by the bargaining limits (resistance points) of each side, in which compromise is possible, as is the attainment of a settlement satisfactory to both parties.

distributive bargaining A win–lose negotiating strategy where one party gains at the expense of the other.

FIGURE **16.3**   The Bargaining Zone and Characteristics of Distributive Bargaining negotiating team's assessment of what is realistically achievable from management. The union's bargaining zone limit is its resistance point, which represents its minimally acceptable level.

These points are essentially reversed for management. The management team's initial point is its lowest level, which is used at the beginning of negotiations. Next is its target point, the desired agreement level. Management's resistance point forms the other boundary of the bargaining zone.

Integrative bargaining is an approach that assumes that a win–win solution can be found but also acknowledges that one or both sides can be losers if the bargaining is not handled effectively.[22] Integrative bargaining strategies require that both management and union negotiators adopt a genuine interest in the joint exploration of creative solutions to common problems.

Issues pertaining to work rules, job descriptions, and contract language can often be handled effectively by using an integrative approach; these are situations in which management negotiators are not intent on retaining management rights and both sides are committed to seeking a win–win solution. Wage rates and vacation entitlements are more likely to be fixed-sum issues that are handled by a distributive approach.

The objective of integrative bargaining is to establish a creative negotiating relationship that benefits labour and management. Becoming increasingly popular these days is a relatively new integrative approach known as **mutual gains (interest-based) bargaining**, which is another win–win approach to LR issues. All key union and management negotiators are trained in the fundamentals of effective problem solving and conflict resolution. Such training is often extended to other employees to ensure that the principles of mutual gains (interest-based) bargaining are incorporated into the organization's value system and that cooperation becomes a year-round corporate objective.[23]

Solutions must take the interests of each party into account. A joint sense of accountability is fostered and ongoing joint union–management initiatives can result from the negotiating process. In addition, the tools that are used at the bargaining table can be applied to the resolution of all workplace issues. Although mutual gains (interest-based) bargaining has been put into practice in about 40 percent of Canadian negotiations, experts warn that implementation is difficult, as it requires a grassroots culture change.[24]

Thus, the negotiating process is far more complex than it may appear to a casual observer. There are different types of bargaining strategies involved, and each side arrives at the bargaining table with political and organizational interests at stake.

The Contract Approval Process

As mentioned previously, collective agreements must be written documents. However, the parties do not normally execute a formal written document until after the bargaining process has been completed. Instead, the terms and conditions agreed to by the parties are usually reduced to a **memorandum of settlement** and submitted to the constituent groups for final approval.

Generally, final approval for the employer rests with the senior management team. In most cases, the union bargaining team submits the memorandum of settlement to the bargaining unit members for **ratification**. In some jurisdictions, ratification is required by law, and all members of the bargaining unit must be

---

integrative bargaining A negotiating strategy in which the possibility of win–win, lose–win, win–lose, and lose–lose outcomes is recognized, and there is acknowledgement that achieving a win–win outcome will depend on mutual trust and problem solving.

mutual gains (interest-based) bargaining A win–win negotiating approach based on training in the fundamentals of effective problem solving and conflict resolution, in which the interests of all stakeholders are taken into account.

memorandum of settlement A summary of the terms and conditions agreed to by the parties that is submitted to the constituent groups for final approval.

ratification Formal approval by secret-ballot vote of the bargaining unit members of the agreement negotiated between union and management.

given ample opportunity to cast a secret-ballot vote indicating approval or rejection of the proposed contract. If the majority of bargaining unit members vote in favour of the proposal, it goes into effect. If the proposed collective agreement is rejected, union and management negotiators must return to the bargaining table and seek a more acceptable compromise. In such instances, third-party assistance is often sought.

Once approval has been received from the constituent groups, the bargaining team members sign the memorandum of settlement. Once signed, this memorandum serves as the collective agreement until the formal document is prepared and contract administration begins.

Third-Party Assistance and Bargaining Impasses

Legislation in all Canadian jurisdictions provides for conciliation and mediation services. Although the terms *conciliation* and *mediation* are often used interchangeably, they have quite distinct and different meanings.

Conciliation is the intervention of a neutral third party whose primary purpose is to bring the parties together and keep them talking so they can reach a mutually satisfactory collective agreement. The only means available to a conciliator to bring the parties to agreement is persuasion—he or she is not permitted to have any direct input into the negotiation process or to impose a settlement. Conciliation is typically requested after the parties have been negotiating for some time and are starting to reach a deadlock, or after talks have broken down. The aim of conciliation is to try to help the parties avoid the hardship of a strike or lockout.

In all jurisdictions except Saskatchewan, strikes and lockouts are prohibited until third-party assistance has been undertaken (Conciliation is required in all but two jurisdictions.) In most jurisdictions in which third-party assistance is mandatory, strikes/lockouts are prohibited until conciliation efforts have failed and a specified time period has elapsed.[25]

Mediation is the intervention of a neutral third party whose primary purpose is to help the parties fashion a mutually satisfactory agreement. Mediation is usually a voluntary process, typically occurring during the countdown period prior to a strike or lockout or during the strike or lockout itself. The mediator's role is an active one. It often involves meeting with each side separately and then bringing them together in an attempt to assist them in bridging the existing gaps. He or she is allowed to have direct input into the negotiation process but cannot impose a settlement.

When the union and management negotiating teams are unable to reach an agreement, and once the conciliation process has been undertaken (where required), the union may exercise its right to strike or request interest arbitration, and the employer may exercise its right to lock out the bargaining unit members. Alternatively, bargaining unit members may continue to work without a collective agreement once the old one has expired until talks resume and an agreement is reached.

Strikes A **strike** can be defined as a temporary refusal by bargaining unit members to continue working for the employer. When talks are reaching an impasse, unions will often hold a **strike vote**. Legally required in some jurisdictions, such a vote seeks authorization from bargaining unit members to strike if necessary. A favourable vote does not mean that a strike is inevitable.

---

conciliation The often mandatory use of a neutral third party who has no direct input on the negotiation process to help an organization and the union representing a group of its employees communicate more effectively with the aim of coming to a mutually satisfactory collective agreement.

Ontario Ministry of labour—Conciliation
www.labour.gov.on.ca/english/lr/faqs/lr_faq2.php

mediation The often voluntary use of a neutral third party who has direct input on the negotiation process to help an organization and the union representing its employees to reach a mutually satisfactory collective agreement.

strike The temporary refusal by bargaining unit members to continue working for the employer.

strike vote Legally required in some jurisdictions, it is a vote seeking authorization from bargaining unit members to strike if necessary. A favourable vote does not mean that a strike is inevitable.

In fact, a highly favourable strike vote is often used as a bargaining ploy to gain concessions that will make a strike unnecessary. The results of a strike vote also help the union negotiating team members determine their relative bargaining strength. Unless strike action is supported by a substantial majority of bargaining unit members, union leaders are rarely prepared to risk a strike and must therefore be more willing to compromise, if necessary, to avoid a work stoppage.

Since a strike can have serious economic consequences for bargaining unit members, the union negotiating team must carefully analyze the prospects for its success. Striking union members receive no wages and often have no benefits coverage until they return to work, although they may draw some money from the union's strike fund. Work stoppages are also costly for employers, customers, and suppliers.

picket Stationing groups of striking employees, usually carrying signs, at the entrances and exits of the struck operation to publicize the issues in dispute and discourage people from entering or leaving the premises.

When a union goes on strike, bargaining unit members often **picket** the employer. To ensure as many picketers as possible, the union may make strike pay contingent on picket duty. Picketers stand at business entrances, carrying signs advertising the issues in dispute, and attempt to discourage people from entering or leaving the premises.

boycott An organized refusal of bargaining unit members and supporters to buy the products or use the services of the organization whose employees are on strike in an effort to exert economic pressure on the employer.

Another economic weapon available to unions is a **boycott**, which is a refusal to patronize the employer. A boycott occurs when a union asks its members, other union members, the employer's customers/clients, and supporters in the general public not to patronize the business involved in the labour dispute. Such action can harm the employer if the union is successful in gaining a large number of supporters. As with a strike, a boycott can have long-term consequences if former customers/clients develop a bias against the employer's products or services or make a change in buying habits or service provider that is not easily reversed.

lockout The temporary refusal of a company to continue providing work for bargaining unit employees involved in a labour dispute, which may result in closure of the establishment for a time.

The duration and ultimate success of a strike depends on the relative strength of the parties. Once a strike is settled, striking workers return to their jobs. During a labour dispute many people are put under remarkable pressure, and relationships essential to effective post-settlement work dynamics can be tarnished—especially in firms that rely heavily on teamwork. Post-settlement work environments are often riddled with tension, derogatory remarks, and hostility.

Striking members of the Canadian Union of Public Employees, local 3903, picket at York University in Toronto.

Lockout Although not a widely used strategy in Canada, a lockout is legally permissible. This involves the employer prohibiting the bargaining unit employees from entering the company premises as a means of putting pressure on the union to agree to the terms and conditions being offered by management. Sometimes the employer chooses to close operations entirely, which means that non-striking employees are also affected. Most employers try to avoid this option, since doing so means that the well-being of innocent parties is threatened, and a lockout may damage the

An Ethical : Dilemma

Is it ethical for a firm to close the establishment during a labour dispute if that results in non-striking employees being laid off?

firm's public image. Employees at forest products company Stora Enso in Port Hawkesbury, Nova Scotia, were locked out in 2006 after 20 months of bargaining when the union refused to accept a wage rollback of 10 percent, contracting out, and loss of seniority rights. An agreement was ratified five months later, just before the mill closure deadline set by the company.[26]

Unlawful Strikes and Lockouts An unlawful strike is one that contravenes the relevant LR legislation and lays the union and its members open to charges and possible fines or periods of imprisonment if found guilty. For example, it is illegal for a union to call a strike involving employees who do not have the right to strike because of the essential nature of their services, such as nurses or police officers. In all jurisdictions, it is illegal to call a strike during the term of an existing collective agreement.

wildcat strike A spontaneous walkout, not officially sanctioned by the union leadership, which may be legal or illegal, depending on its timing.

A **wildcat strike** is a spontaneous walkout, not officially sanctioned by the union leaders, that is illegal if it occurs during the term of a collective agreement. For example, hotel workers at a Holiday Inn in Toronto, many of them new Canadians in low-end jobs, staged a wildcat walkout for about 45 minutes in November 2007 to protest lagging contract talks.[27]

arbitration The use of an outside third party to investigate a dispute between an employer and union and impose a settlement.

Interest Arbitration Arbitration involves the use of an outside third party to investigate a dispute between an employer and union and impose a settlement. A sole arbitrator or three-person arbitration board may be involved. Arbitrators listen to evidence, weigh it impartially and objectively, and make a decision based on the law or the contract language. An arbitrator is not a judge, however. First, arbitration hearings tend to be much more informal than courtroom proceedings. Second, the arbitrator is not bound by precedents to the extent that a judge is usually held.[28] Third, both the law and court decisions have given the arbitration function considerable power and freedom. Arbitration decisions are final and binding and cannot be changed or revised.

Public Service Grievance Board— Arbitration
www.psab.gov.on.ca/english/psgb/ Arbitration.htm

interest arbitration The imposition of the final terms of a collective agreement.

Interest arbitration may be used to settle an **interest dispute** regarding the terms of a collective agreement by imposing the terms of the collective agreement. The right to interest arbitration is legally mandated for workers who are not permitted to strike, such as hospital and nursing home employees, police officers and firefighters in most jurisdictions, and some public servants.[29] Interest arbitration is also involved when special legislation is passed ordering striking or locked-out parties back to work because of public hardship.

interest dispute A dispute between an organization and the union representing its employees over the terms of a collective agreement.

The Collective Agreement: Typical Provisions

RPC

Provides advice on interest arbitration

The eventual outcome of collective bargaining, whether negotiated by the parties or imposed by an arbitrator, is a formal, written collective agreement.

Union Recognition Clause A *union recognition clause* clarifies the scope of the bargaining unit by specifying the employee classifications included therein or listing those excluded.

union security clause The contract provisions protecting the interests of the labour union, dealing with the issue of membership requirements and, often, the payment of union dues.

Union Security/Checkoff Clause All Canadian jurisdictions permit the inclusion of a **union security clause** in the collective agreement to protect the interests of the labour union. This clause deals with the issue of membership requirements and, often, the payment of union dues. There are various forms of union security clauses:[30]

- A *closed shop* is the most restrictive form of union security. Only union members in good standing may be hired by the employer to perform bargaining unit work. This type of security clause is common in the construction industry.

- In a *union shop,* membership and dues payment are mandatory conditions of employment. Although individuals do not have to be union members at the time that they are hired, they are required to join the union on the day on which they commence work or on completion of probation.

- In a *modified union shop,* the individuals who were bargaining unit members at the time of certification or when the collective agreement was signed are not obliged to join the union, although they must pay dues, but all subsequently hired employees must do both.

An Ethical Dilemma

Given the fact that some workers have religious or other objections to unions, is the Rand formula ethical?

- Under a *maintenance-of-membership arrangement,* individuals voluntarily joining the union must remain members during the term of the contract. Membership withdrawal is typically permitted during a designated period around the time of contract expiration. Dues payment is generally mandatory for all bargaining unit members.

- The *Rand formula* is the most popular union security arrangement. It does not require union membership, but it does require that all members of the bargaining unit pay union dues. It is a compromise arrangement that recognizes the fact that the union must represent all employees in the bargaining unit and should therefore be entitled to their financial support, but also provides the choice to join or not join the union.

- An *open shop* is a type of security arrangement whereby union membership is voluntary and non-members are not required to pay dues.

No-Strike-or-Lockout Provision There must be a clause in every contract in Canada forbidding strikes or lockouts while the collective agreement is in effect. The intent is to guarantee some degree of stability in the employment relationship during the life of the collective agreement, which must be at least one year. Saskatchewan and Quebec are the only jurisdictions that impose a maximum duration of three years.[31] In general, the duration of collective agreements in Canada is increasing.[32] Halifax police accepted a 12-year agreement in 2003.[33]

Management Rights Clause The management rights clause clarifies the areas in which management may exercise its exclusive rights without agreement from the union, and the issues that are not subject to collective bargaining. It typically refers to the rights of management to operate the organization, subject to the terms of the collective agreement. Any rights not limited by the clause are reserved to management.

Arbitration Clause All Canadian jurisdictions require that collective agreements contain a clause providing for the final and binding settlement, by arbitration, of all disputes arising during the term of a collective agreement. Such disputes may relate to the application, interpretation, or administration of the agreement, as well as alleged contraventions by either party.

Step 5: Contract Administration

After a collective agreement has been negotiated and signed, the contract administration process begins. Both union and management are required to abide by the contract provisions. It is also in day-to-day contract administration that the bulk of labour–management relations occurs. Regardless of the amount of time and effort put into the wording of the contract, it is almost inevitable that differences of opinion will arise regarding the application and interpretation of the agreement. Seniority and discipline issues tend to be the major sources of disagreement between union and management.

Seniority

seniority Length of service in the bargaining unit.

Unions typically prefer to have employee-related decisions determined by **seniority**, which refers to length of service in the bargaining unit. In many collective agreements, seniority is the governing factor in layoffs and recalls (the most senior employees are the last to be laid off and the first to be recalled) and a determining factor in transfers and promotions. In some collective agreements, seniority is also the determining factor in decisions pertaining to work assignments, shift preferences, allocation of days off, and vacation time.

Unions prefer the principle of seniority as an equitable and objective decision-making criterion, ensuring that there is no favouritism. Managers often prefer to place greater weight on ability or merit.

Discipline

Almost all collective agreements give the employer the right to make reasonable rules and regulations governing employees' behaviour and to take disciplinary action if the rules are broken. In every collective agreement, bargaining unit members are given the right to file a grievance if they feel that any disciplinary action taken was too harsh or without just cause.

Most collective agreements restrict an employer's right to discipline employees by requiring proof of just cause for the disciplinary action imposed. Since just cause is open to different interpretations, disciplinary action is a major source of grievances. Thus, disciplinary issues must be handled in accordance with the terms of the collective agreement and backed by carefully documented evidence. Even when disciplinary action is handled carefully, the union may argue that there were extenuating circumstances that should be taken into consideration. Supervisors have to strike a delicate balance between fairness and consistency.

When discipline cases end up at arbitration, two independent decisions are made. The first is whether the employee actually engaged in some form of misconduct. Then, if that question is answered in the affirmative, an assessment must be made of whether such misconduct warrants the particular discipline imposed, as well as whether such disciplinary action violated the collective agreement.

Grievance Resolution and Rights Arbitration

grievance A written allegation of a contract violation, filed by an individual bargaining unit member, the union, or management.

A **grievance** is a written allegation of a contract violation relating to a disagreement about its application or interpretation. When such alleged violations or disagreements arise, they are settled through the grievance procedure. A multistep grievance procedure, the last step of which is final and binding arbitration, is found in virtually all collective agreements. Such procedures have been very effective in resolving day-to-day problems arising during the life of the collective agreement.

The primary purpose of the grievance procedure is to ensure the application of the contract with a degree of justice for both parties. Secondary purposes include providing the opportunity for the interpretation of contract language, such as the meaning of "sufficient ability"; serving as a communications device through which managers can become aware of employee concerns and areas of dissatisfaction; and bringing to the attention of both union and management those areas of the contract requiring clarification or modification in subsequent negotiations.

RPC

Effectively handles disagreements and conflicts

Steps in the Grievance Procedure The grievance procedure involves systematic deliberation of a complaint at progressively higher levels of authority in the company and union, and most provide for arbitration as a final step. Grievances are usually filed by individual bargaining unit members. If the issue in contention is one that may affect a number of union members, either at that time or in the future, the union may file a *policy grievance*. Management also has the right to use the grievance procedure to process a complaint about the union, although such use is rare. Although the number of steps and people involved at each grievance procedure vary, **Figure 16.4** illustrates a typical sequence.

As illustrated in Figure 16.4, the typical first step of the grievance procedure is the filing of a written complaint with the employee's immediate supervisor. If the problem is not resolved to the satisfaction of the employee at the first step, he or she may then take the problem to the next higher managerial level designated in the contract, and so on through all the steps available. Time limits are typically provided for resolution at each step. Failure to respond within the specified time limit may result in the grievance being automatically processed at the next step or being deemed to have been withdrawn or resolved. Ninety percent or more of all grievances are settled, abandoned, or withdrawn before arbitration.

rights dispute A disagreement between an organization and the union representing its employees regarding the interpretation or application of one or more clauses in the current collective agreement.

Rights Arbitration Grievances relating to the interpretation or administration of the collective agreement are known as **rights disputes**. If these cannot be resolved internally, they must be referred to arbitration for a final and binding decision. The process involved in resolving such issues is known as **rights arbitration**.

rights arbitration The process involved in the settlement of a rights dispute.

A written arbitration award is issued at the conclusion of most rights arbitration cases, indicating that the grievance has been upheld or overturned. In disciplinary cases, it is also possible for an arbitration award to substitute a penalty that is more or less severe than the one proposed by union or management.

FIGURE **16.4**   A Typical Grievance Procedure

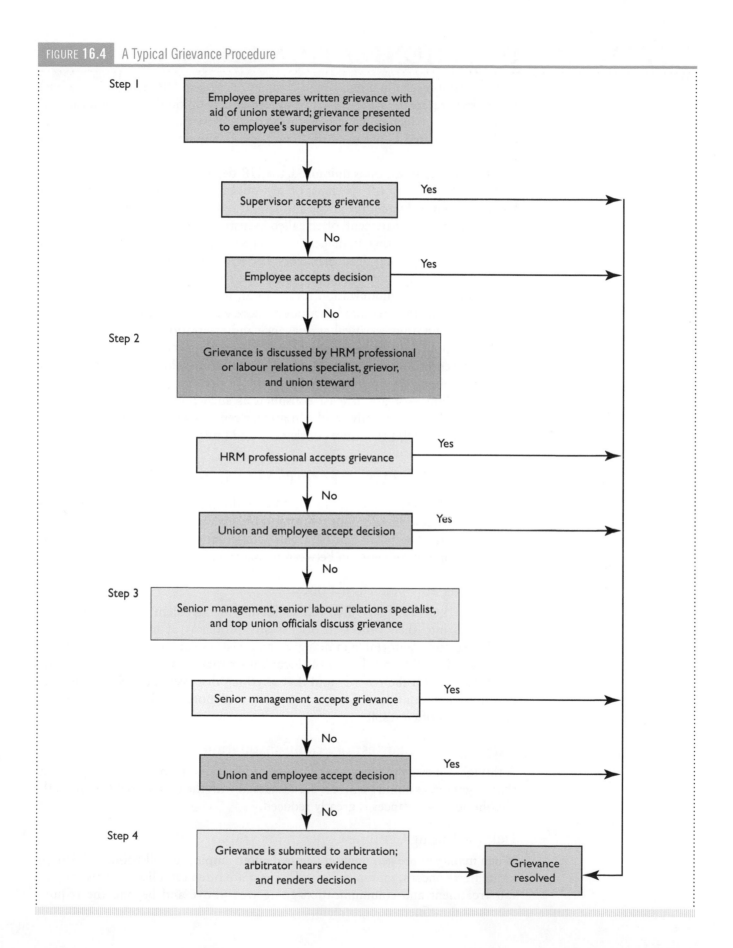

THE IMPACT OF UNIONIZATION ON HRM

Unionization results in a number of changes relating to HRM, all relating back to the requirements of the collective agreement. A union does have an impact on the way in which managers perform their HR responsibilities; when union leaders are treated as partners, they can provide a great deal of assistance with HR functions.

Once an organization is unionized, the HR department is typically expanded by the addition of an LR specialist or section. In a large firm with a number of bargaining units, human resources and labour relations may form two divisions within a broader department, often called industrial relations or labour relations.

In a unionized setting, management has less freedom to make unilateral decisions. This change may lead managers and supervisors to feel that they have lost some of their authority, which can cause resentment, especially since they inevitably find that unionization results in an increase in their responsibilities. Supervisors are often required to produce more written records than ever before, since documentation is critical at grievance and arbitration hearings.

All HR policies must be consistent with the terms of the collective agreement. Union representatives are often involved in the formulation of any policies that affect bargaining unit members—such as those pertaining to disciplinary rules and regulations—or are at least consulted as such policies are being drafted. Unionization also generally results in greater centralization of employee record keeping, which helps to ensure consistency and uniformity.

Tips FOR THE FRONT LINE

Building Effective Labour–Management Relations

One of the biggest challenges to HRM in unionized organizations is to build a cooperative and harmonious working relationship between management and union leaders. The result can be a win–win situation. There are a number of ways to promote cooperation between management and labour.

Instituting an Open-Door Policy

When the key managers involved in labour–management relations welcome employees into their offices to discuss any problems or concerns, and when employees feel comfortable in doing so, many issues can be resolved informally. For example, if the president of the local knows that he or she can approach the LR manager "off the record" and that anything discussed in such sessions will be kept strictly confidential, fewer grievances and more trusting and harmonious relationships often result.

Extending the Courtesy of Prior Consultation

Although not every management decision requires union approval, if any actions that might affect union members are discussed with the union executive first, the likelihood of grievances is greatly reduced.

Demonstrating Genuine Concern for Employee Well-Being

When managers are genuinely concerned about employee well-being and demonstrate that concern, mutual trust and respect are often established. This involves fair treatment and communication going well above and beyond the requirements of the collective agreement.

Forming Joint Committees and Holding Joint Training Programs

Forming labour–management committees to investigate and resolve complex issues can lead to innovative and creative solutions, as well as to a better relationship. When a contract is first signed, it can be beneficial to hold a joint training program to ensure that supervisors and union stewards are familiar with the terms and conditions specified therein and that they understand the intent of the negotiating teams. Such training can reduce misunderstandings and the likelihood of disagreement regarding interpretation of contract language.

Meeting Regularly

Whether required by the collective agreement or voluntarily instituted, regularly scheduled union–management meetings can result in more effective communication and the resolution of problems/concerns before they become formal grievance issues.

Using Third-Party Assistance

To build a better relationship, it is often beneficial to bring in a consultant or a government agency representative to help identify common goals and objectives and ways in which trust and communication can be strengthened.

Chapter SUMMARY

1. Canada's labour laws provide a common set of rules for fair negotiations and ensure the protection of public interest by preventing the impact of labour disputes from inconveniencing the public. Tripartite labour relations boards across the country administer labour relations laws. These laws try to balance employees' rights to engage in union activity with employers' management rights.

2. There are five steps in the LR process: (i) employees' decision to seek collective representation, (ii) the union organizing campaign, (iii) official recognition of the union, (iv) negotiation of a collective agreement, and (v) day-to-day contract administration.

3. The union organizing process involves five steps, which typically include (i) employee/union contact, (ii) an initial organizational meeting, (iii) the formation of an in-house organizing committee, (iv) an organizing campaign, and (v) the outcome—certification, recognition, or rejection.

4. There are three basic ways in which a union can obtain recognition as a bargaining unit for a group of workers: voluntary recognition, the regular certification process, and a pre-hearing vote.

5. The three steps in the collective bargaining process are preparation for negotiations, face-to-face negotiations, and obtaining approval for the proposed contract. Two possible additional steps are third-party assistance if talks break down and a strike/lockout or interest arbitration if the parties arrive at a bargaining impasse.

6. Typical steps in a grievance procedure involve presenting a written grievance to the worker's immediate supervisor, then to an HR/LR specialist, then to senior management, and finally to an arbitrator for final and binding rights arbitration.

MyManagementLab

Visit MyManagementLab to access a personalized Study Plan and additional study tools for this chapter.

Key TERMS

arbitration *(p. 455)*
authorization card *(p. 447)*
bargaining unit *(p. 440)*
bargaining zone *(p. 451)*
boycott *(p. 454)*
business unionism *(p. 441)*
caucus session *(p. 450)*
certification *(p. 448)*
collective bargaining *(p. 440)*
collective bargaining agreement
    (union contract) *(p. 440)*
conciliation *(p. 453)*
craft union *(p. 441)*
decertification *(p. 449)*
distributive bargaining *(p. 451)*
grievance *(p. 458)*
industrial union *(p. 441)*
integrative bargaining *(p. 452)*
interest arbitration *(p. 455)*
interest dispute *(p. 455)*

labour–management relations *(p. 440)*
labour union (union) *(p. 440)*
local *(p. 443)*
lockout *(p. 454)*
mediation *(p. 453)*
memorandum of settlement *(p. 452)*
mutual gains (interest-based) bargaining *(p. 452)*
picket *(p. 454)*
pre-hearing vote *(p. 449)*
ratification *(p. 452)*
representation vote *(p. 449)*
rights arbitration *(p. 458)*
rights dispute *(p. 458)*
seniority *(p. 457)*
social (reform) unionism *(p. 441)*
strike *(p. 453)*
strike vote *(p. 453)*
union security clause *(p. 455)*
union steward *(p. 443)*
wildcat strike *(p. 455)*

Review and Discussion QUESTIONS

1. Cite three examples of unfair labour practices on the part of management and three on the part of unions.

2. Explain three of the challenges facing the union movement in Canada today.

3. Describe five signs to which managers should be alert to detect an organizing campaign.

4. Explain the bargaining zone and draw a diagram to illustrate this concept.

5. Explain the six common forms of union security clause.

6. Explain how arbitration differs from conciliation and mediation and differentiate between interest arbitration and rights arbitration.

Critical Thinking QUESTIONS

1. Discuss why Dofasco, a company that has remained union-free for many years, allowed the United Steelworkers access to its workers in Hamilton to try to sign them up as union members. In your opinion, why was this attempt by the union unsuccessful?

2. "If supervisors communicate effectively with employees, deal with their concerns, and treat them fairly, employees are far less likely to be interested in forming or joining a union." Do you agree or disagree with this statement? Why?

3. Two possible approaches to labour relations are union acceptance and union avoidance. Determine which of these strategies seems to have been adopted in a firm in which you have been employed or with which you are familiar. Provide evidence to back up your answer.

4. As the LR specialist, what steps would you take to prepare the firm and management team if you believed that a strike was a possible outcome of the upcoming negotiations?

5. As the HR manager, how would you handle a situation in which a supervisor has knowingly violated the collective agreement when scheduling overtime?

Experiential EXERCISES

1. Assume that you are the vice-president of HR at a relatively new non-union firm that has been experiencing rapid growth. In view of the management team's desire to remain non-union, you have been asked to prepare a report to the other senior management team members making specific recommendations regarding strategies that the firm should adopt to help ensure that the employees will have no desire to unionize.

2. Working with two or three classmates, devise a management counter-campaign to a unionization attempt, ensuring that all recommended courses of action are legal.

3. Obtain a copy of two collective agreements. Compare and contrast the following provisions: union recognition, management rights, union security, grievance procedures, and arbitration clauses. What do you think led to the differences? Which contract do you think in its entirety is better for employees? Why?

4. Read the following scenario and then, based on the role your team has been assigned by your instructor and the preparation time allowed, develop a negotiating strategy, including your bargaining zone that you think will enable you to reach a fair and reasonable outcome for all parties. Before coming to the bargaining table, pick a chief negotiator for your team. Negotiate a settlement.

Scenario

ABC manufacturing is a large multinational machinery and heavy equipment manufacturer. The last two years have been very difficult, with more competition coming from offshore companies whose labour costs are much lower than those in Canada. The company is losing money and is considering whether to lay off workers in one or more of its Canadian plants, perhaps opening a new plant in Mexico or somewhere else in Central America. The union contract is up and negotiations will begin soon.

5. Research past issues of Canadian HR publications and find at least two labour arbitration awards, one that finds in favour of the organization and the other that finds in favour of the union. Prepare a brief presentation on what you find fair/unfair in these settlements. Be prepared to discuss why you think this.

Running CASE

The Grievance

When coming in to work one day, Pierre was surprised to be taken aside by Jason, one of their original employees, who met him as he was parking his car. "Jennifer told me I was suspended for two days without pay because I came in late last Thursday," said Jason. "I'm really upset, but around here Jennifer's word seems to be law, and it sometimes seems like the only way anyone can file a grievance is by meeting you like this in the parking lot."

Pierre was very disturbed by this revelation and promised the employee that he would discuss the situation with Jennifer. He began mulling over possible alternatives.

QUESTIONS

1   Does LearnInMotion run the potential risk of becoming unionized through its reactive managerial policy by one instead of both owners?

2   What are the primary reasons why people unionize?

3   Should a union wish to organize LearnInMotion employees, what are the five steps in the labour relations process a union must go through?

Case INCIDENT

Strategy

"They want what?" the mayor exclaimed.

"Like I said," the town clerk replied, "17 percent over two years."

"There is no way that the taxpayers will accept a settlement anywhere near that," reiterated the mayor. "I don't care if the garbage doesn't get collected for a century. We can't do more than 8 percent over the next two years."

The town clerk looked worried. "How much loss of service do you think the public will accept? Suppose they do go on strike? I'm the one who always gets the complaints. Then there's the health problem with rats running all over the place! Remember over in Neibringtown, when that little kid was bitten? There was a hell of an outcry."

The mayor agreed. "Garbage collectors always have strong bargaining power, but, if I don't fight this, I'll be voted out in the next election. I say we offer 6 percent over 18 months. Then we can go either way—6 percent over 12 months or 8 percent over two years."

"I wonder if we have any other options?" worried the town clerk.

"Well, we could threaten not to hire any more union personnel and to job out the collection service to private contractors if the union isn't cooperative," mused the mayor.

"That's a good idea!" The town clerk sounded enthusiastic. "Also, we can mount a newspaper advertising campaign to get the public behind us. If we play on the fear of massive tax increases, the garbage collectors won't have much public sympathy."

"What about asking the union to guarantee garbage collection for older citizens during a strike? If they refuse, they'll look bad in the public eye; if they accept, we are rid of a major problem. Most people can bring their trash to a central collection point. Not all older citizens can," chuckled the mayor. "We can't lose on that issue!"

"Okay then," said the town clerk. "It looks like we have the beginning of a bargaining strategy here. Actually, I feel better now. I think we're in a rather strong position."

QUESTIONS

1 Discuss the plight of public sector unions faced with the reality of a limited tax base and public pressure to lower taxes.

2 Is the town clerk right? Is the town in a good bargaining position? Explain your answer.

3 What strengths does the union have in its position?

4 If you were a labour relations consultant, would you agree with the present strategy? What alternatives, if any, would you propose?

Source: R.W. Mondy, R.M. Noe, S.R. Premeaux, and R.A. Knowles, *Human Resource Management*, Second Canadian Edition (Toronto, ON: Pearson Education Canada, 2001), p. 386.

MyManagementLab

Visit MyManagementLab to access a personalized Study Plan and additional study tools for this chapter.

 To view the CBC videos, read a summary, and answer discussion questions, go to MyManagementLab

CHAPTER

17

Managing Human Resources in a Global Business

LEARNING OUTCOMES

AFTER STUDYING THIS CHAPTER, YOU SHOULD BE ABLE TO

EXPLAIN how global movement of labour has an impact on HRM in Canada.

DESCRIBE the influence of intercountry differences on the workplace.

EXPLAIN how to improve global assignments through employee selection.

DISCUSS the major considerations in formulating a compensation plan for international employees.

DESCRIBE the main considerations in repatriating employees from abroad.

EXPLAIN the role and influence of international talent on Canadian organizations.

DISCUSS challenges immigrants to Canada face and **IDENTIFY** the role of multiple stakeholders in ensuring successful integration of talent in Canada.

REQUIRED PROFESSIONAL CAPABILITIES (RPC)

- Contributes to an environment that fosters effective working relationships

- Researches, analyzes, and reports on potential people issues affecting the organization

- Provides support and expertise to managers and supervisors with respect to managing people

- Keeps current with emerging HR trends

THE GLOBALIZATION OF BUSINESS AND STRATEGIC HR

workforce mobility The focus on managing the recruitment, relocation, and retention of employees who complete work-related tasks and activities outside of the core or primary head office or region of the company.

In the 21st century, **workforce mobility** programs focus on managing the recruitment, relocation, and retention of employees who complete work-related tasks and activities outside of the core or primary head office or region of the company. These programs are enabled by technological advancements, globalization, tight labour markets, and customer demands and have a direct impact on company profits. Research by Runzheimer International shows that organizations can improve profitability by 1 to 4 percent simply by making workforce mobility management a strategic priority and by managing mobility programs in a more integrated way. This is because disjointed management of mobility programs often results in employee confusion, aggravation, frustration, and disengagement.[1]

The globalization of business is now the norm. European market unification is ongoing and the economies of Brazil, Russia, India, and China are burgeoning. Huge Canadian companies like Noranda, Alcan, and Molson have long had extensive overseas operations, but today the vast majority of companies are finding that their success depends on their ability to market and manage overseas operations. Thousands of Canadian corporations with international operations are now relocating employees overseas on a regular basis. These employees, called **expatriates**, are citizens of the country where the parent company is based who are sent to work in another country.

expatriate Employees who are citizens of the country where the parent company is based who are sent to work in another country.

immigrant A person residing in Canada who was born outside of Canada (excluding temporary foreign workers, Canadian citizens born outside of Canada and those with student or work visas).

Canada is also increasingly influenced by globalization within our borders. According to Statistics Canada, an **immigrant** is a person residing in Canada who was born outside of Canada (excluding temporary foreign workers, Canadian citizens born outside of Canada, and those with student or working visas).[2] Roughly one in every five persons residing in Canada is foreign born. In addition, most of the labour force growth over the last decade has been attributable to immigration, and immigrants continue to be a critical component of Canada's workforce.

Thus, the impact of globalization on the human resource management landscape of Canada includes both Canadians working internationally and international members (mainly immigrants) working in Canada. This chapter reviews both elements of global HRM.

HOW INTERCOUNTRY DIFFERENCES AFFECT HRM

To a large extent, companies operating only within Canada's borders have the luxury of dealing with a relatively limited set of economic, cultural, and legal variables. However, a company that is operating multiple units abroad does not operate in an environment of such relative homogeneity with respect to HRM. For example, minimum legally mandated holidays may range from none in the United States to five weeks per year in Luxembourg. In addition, there are country-specific regulations that affect employees; as an example, there are no formal requirements for employee participation in Italy, but in Denmark, employee representatives on boards of directors are required in companies with more than 30 employees.

Another troubling issue is the need for tight security and terrorism awareness training for employees sent to countries with an increased risk of kidnapping of foreign executives.[3] The point is that managing the HR functions in multinational companies is complicated enormously by the need to adapt HR policies and procedures to the differences among countries in which each subsidiary is based. The following are some intercountry differences that demand such adaptation.[4]

Cultural Factors

RPC

Contributes to an environment that fosters effective working relationships

Wide-ranging cultural differences from country to country demand corresponding differences in HR practices among a company's foreign subsidiaries. The first step is understanding the differences in underlying cultural values in different societies. Major studies have clarified some basic dimensions of international cultural differences. For example, societies differ in power distance—the extent to which the less powerful members of institutions accept and expect that power will be distributed unequally.[5] The institutionalization of such an inequality is higher in some countries (such as Mexico and Japan) than in others (such as Sweden and the Netherlands).

Societies also differ when it comes to individualism versus collectivism—the degree to which ties between individuals are normally loose rather than close. In more individualistic countries, such as Canada and the United States, individuals look out for themselves and their immediate families. However, in more collectivist countries, such as China and Pakistan, an individual's identity is strongly linked to their extended family group, and sometimes even to their work group. Interestingly, the one-child policy in China has resulted in a younger generation that is much more individualistic, known for job-hopping and lack of company loyalty.[6]

A recent major worldwide study of cultural dimensions found that societies differ in their attitudes to gender egalitarianism. Global competition has produced an interesting change in male-dominated mining operations in Australia, as described in the Workforce Diversity box.

WORKFORCE DIVERSITY

Mummy Crew in Monster Trucks

Mining companies in Australia are finding that women often make better drivers than men. They take fewer risks, and are more careful behind the wheel of the massive dump trucks that they operate. Coupled with the skills they acquire over time, what this means is that they reduce the wear and tear on the huge truck tires that are costly to replace in the industry. As Billy Adams writes, in a 2007 article for the *Sunday Morning Post* titled "Women rule in monster trucks," such expensive equipment requires "a skilled pair of hands at the controls."

There are only a handful of companies in the world that make mine tires, so they have a captive market and are in a position to sell their products at a premium. A single tire costs at least AUD$50 000 (approximately CAD$50 900), with an average lifespan of just 5500 hours. Mining companies already spend a lot of money on road maintenance to get the most out of their truck tires, so the gentler way in which their female employees handle their heavy equipment makes it last longer, resulting in significant cost savings.

The industry would not have known this if it weren't for the chronic shortage of skilled workers in recent decades. According to Adams' article, the Minerals Council of Australia estimated that by 2015, the mining industry would need to find 70 000 employees on top of the 120 000 that are already in jobs. This is easier said than done. So some years ago, a forward-thinking company in northern Queensland introduced six-hour day shifts that last between nine and three o'clock, recruiting a new wave of female workers who came to be known as the "Mummy Crew." Every morning a bus would drop their children off at school then take the moms to work at the mine. It was a success story where management believed the new employees had changed the workplace dynamics, and where existing employees began to find fewer discrimination issues, finding the company to be a more pleasant place for everyone.

Source: Based on B. Adams, "Women Rule in Monster Trucks," *Sunday Morning Post* (December 23, 2007), p. 10.

Such intercountry cultural differences have several HR implications. First, they suggest the need for adapting HR practices, such as training and pay plans, to local cultural norms. They also suggest that HR staff members in a foreign subsidiary should include host-country citizens. A high degree of sensitivity and empathy for the cultural and attitudinal demands of co-workers is always important when selecting expatriate employees to staff overseas operations. Such sensitivity is especially important when the job is HRM and the work involves "human" jobs like interviewing, testing, orienting, training, counselling, and (if need be) terminating.

Economic Systems

Differences in economic systems among countries also translate into intercountry differences in HR practices. In free enterprise systems, for instance, the need for efficiency tends to favour HR policies that value productivity, efficient workers, and staff cutting where market forces dictate. Moving along the scale toward more socialist systems, HR practices tend to shift toward preventing unemployment, even at the expense of sacrificing efficiency. For example, in communist Vietnam, workplace culture involves a siesta after lunch for workers, and managers spend a lot time out of the office enhancing personal and social relationships.[7]

A worker walks past a broken electricity transformer in Lagos, Nigeria. Despite having one of the world's great energy reserves, corruption and mismanagement have left Africa's oil giant chronically short of electricity.

Legal Systems

Labour laws vary considerably around the world. China, for instance, continues to update its labour laws, which now include many similarities to those in the west. Discrimination is prohibited on most of the grounds commonly found in western countries, with the exception of age. However, enforcement of labour laws is haphazard.[8]

When it comes to employee termination, the amount of notice with pay to be provided, continuation of benefits, notification of unions, and minimum length of service to qualify for severance payments vary significantly and can in some cases have a major impact on labour costs.[9]

Health and safety laws vary from non-existent in many African states to Britain's new Corporate Manslaughter and Corporate Homicide Act, which tightens liability of senior management for health and safety offences.[10] In other countries like China, worker health and safety laws exist but are largely unenforced.[11]

Labour Cost Factors

Differences in labour costs may also produce differences in HR practices. To maintain the competitive advantage of lower labour costs in China, the concept of investing in employees through training and development is seen as an unnecessary cost.[12] High labour costs can require a focus on efficiency and on HR practices (like pay for performance) aimed at improving employee performance.

International Labour Organization
www.ilo.org

Industrial Relations Factors

Industrial relations, and specifically the relationship among the workers, the union, and the employer, vary dramatically from country to country and have an enormous impact on HRM practices. In Germany, for instance, co-determination is the rule: that is, employees have the legal right to a voice in setting company policies. In this and several other countries, workers elect their own representatives to the supervisory board of the employer, and there is also a vice-president for labour at the top management level.[13] Conversely, in many other countries, the state interferes little in the relations between employers and unions. In China, for instance, company unions fall under the administration of the local Communist Party committee, which often shares long-term goals with the company. Thus, unions seldom play an effective role in labour disputes.[14]

RPC

Researches, analyzes, and reports on potential people issues affecting the organization

Summary

In summary, intercountry variations in culture, economic systems, labour costs, and legal and industrial relations systems complicate the task of selecting, training, and managing employees abroad. These variations result in corresponding differences that make the job of expatriate managers much more complex and difficult than when at home. International assignments thus run a relatively high risk of failing unless these differences are taken into account when selecting, training, and compensating international assignees.

GLOBAL RELOCATION

The number of expatriates working abroad is continuing to increase. One survey showed that the number of expatriates doubled between 2005 and 2008. The number of "global nomads" (employees who continuously move from country to country on multiple assignments) has also increased.[15] In addition, there has been a gradual increase in the number of female expatriates, who have long been underrepresented in the expatriate ranks.[16] Expatriates may be not only invaluable but also irreplaceable in the near future as the global labour pool contracts in most western countries as well as Japan and China.[17] Overall, relocation policies are becoming more flexible, as the majority of all services are provided on a case-by-case basis.[18]

Family issues rank as the number one concern when it comes to employee relocations, and many employees are reluctant to accept expatriate assignments for this reason.[19] Employees who are considering an international assignment will also want to know how working and living in another country will affect their compensation, benefits, and taxes, and what kind of relocation assistance they will receive. From a practical perspective, some of the most pressing challenges are techniques used to recruit, select, train, compensate, and provide family support for employees who are based abroad, such as the following:

Tips : **FOR THE FRONT LINE**

1. *Candidate identification, assessment, and selection.* In addition to the required technical and business skills, key traits to consider for global assignments include cultural sensitivity, interpersonal skills, and flexibility.

2. *Cost projections.* The average cost of sending an employee and his or her family on an overseas assignment is reportedly between three and five times the employee's pre-departure salary; as a result, quantifying total costs for a global assignment and deciding whether to use an expatriate or a local employee are essential in the budgeting process.

3. *Assignment letters.* The assignee's specific job requirements and remuneration, vacation, home leave, and repatriation arrangements will have to be documented and formally communicated in an assignment letter.[20]

4. *Compensation, benefits, and tax programs.* There are many ways in which to compensate employees who are transferred abroad, given the vast differences in living expenses around the world. Some common approaches to international pay include home-based pay plus a supplement and destination-based pay.

5. *Relocation assistance.* The assignee will probably have to be assisted with such matters as maintenance of a home and automobiles, shipment and storage of household goods, and so forth. The average cost of a permanent international relocation for a Canadian employee is between $50 000 and $100 000.[21]

6. *Family support.* Cultural orientation, educational assistance, and emergency provisions are just some of the matters to be addressed before the family is moved abroad.

The last two issues relate to the heightened focus on the spouse and family, who are vitally important in today's climate of relocation refusals because of concerns about a mother-in-law's homecare, the children's education, a spouse's career, and the difficulty of adjusting to new surroundings while juggling family responsibilities at the same time as focusing on the new job. Although the typical expatriate has traditionally been a male with a non-working spouse, dual career families are now the norm. Major work–life balance relocation challenges thus include career assistance for the spouse and education and school selection assistance for the children.[22] Cross-cultural and language training programs will also probably be required. Policies for repatriating the expatriate when he or she returns home are another matter that must be addressed.

Sending employees abroad and managing HR globally is complicated by the nature of the countries into which many firms are expanding. Today's expatriates are heading to China (now the most likely destination for a foreign assignment) and other emerging economies.[23] Strategic HR involvement in the design and implementation of a global expansion strategy is required right from the start. Extensive research may be required with regard to local hiring practices, the availability of skilled labour, and employment regulations. Drivers of employee engagement vary across countries, but one company (DHL) found that an engagement strategy based on communication drove spectacular growth in their emerging markets division, as described in the Strategic HR box.

STRATEGIC HR

Employee Engagement Program Drives Business Results at DHL

Employees form the backbone of any successful organization. Valued members of staff can make, or break, a company's success, so it is essential that employers do their best to keep them happy. However, one of the most effective ways to create and maintain staff satisfaction is arguably one of the least practiced: Communication is the key to employee engagement. On a practical level, internal communications help employees understand a company's vision, values, and culture, while on a more subliminal level, good internal communication is one of the most effective ways to build strong relationships and forge a sense of fulfillment.

DHL's emerging markets division was one of the first to realize this. Started as a separate region in 2000, the division serves 93 countries across a 14-hour time zone. The countries are grouped by area: Russia and the Commonwealth of Independent States; southeast Europe and north Africa; the Middle East, sub-Saharan Africa, and Turkey. "By aligning these countries according to similar needs, issues, potential and expectations, we made our venture into new territory more manageable," said David Wild, general manager at DHL United Arab Emirates. "However, we were determined to be aware and to acknowledge that all the countries are diverse in culture, language, and standards. This was the key to our success in these emerging markets." The emerging markets division now contributes some 200 000 customers to the company's 4.2 million across the globe.

In 2006, Maverick Events Worldwide developed a method under which all messages within the emerging markets division of DHL could be delivered across the entire workforce. It created the "Mission Possible" brand, which was based on the *Mission Impossible* movie, as it considered film to be one to the few media capable of translation across a culturally diverse region.

A movie, filmed in 14 countries, was produced featuring DHL senior managers delivering their messages. All staff were "agents" taking part in a mission to make the emerging markets division the fastest growing and most profitable in DHL. They were issued with "agent packs" containing the tools they needed to complete their mission.

"Mission Possible" was directly responsible for additional revenue of €316 million in 12 months. The emerging markets division saw 18 percent annual growth using "Mission Possible" as its internal focus. The campaign was subsequently taken forward into other regions of the DHL group.

Source: Adapted from C. Edmonds, "Delivering an International HR Strategy at DHL," *Human Resources Management International Digest*, 17, no. 1 (2009), pp. 32–34. © Emerald Group Publishing Limited all rights reserved.

Why Expatriate Assignments Fail

expatriate assignment failure
Early return of an expatriate from a global assignment.

Research INSIGHT

Global mobility management is important because the cost of **expatriate assignment failure**—early return from an expatriate assignment—can reach a million dollars.[24] There is some evidence that the rate of early departures, at least, is declining. This appears to be because more employers are taking steps to reduce expatriates' problems abroad. For example, they are selecting expatriates more carefully, helping spouses to get jobs abroad, and providing more ongoing support to the expatriate and his or her family.[25] As another example, some companies have formal "global buddy" programs. Here, local managers assist new expatriates with advice on things such as office politics, norms of behaviour, and where to receive emergency medical assistance.[26]

Discovering why expatriate assignments fail is an important research task, and experts have made considerable progress. Personality is one factor. For example, in a study of 143 expatriate employees, extroverted, agreeable, and emotionally stable individuals were less likely to want to leave early.[27] Furthermore, the person's intentions are important. For example, people who want expatriate careers try harder to adjust to such a life.[28]

Non-work factors like family pressures usually loom large in expatriate failures. In one study, managers listed, in descending order of importance for leaving early, inability of spouse to adjust, manager's inability to adjust, other family problems, manager's personal or emotional immaturity, and inability to cope with larger overseas responsibility.[29] Managers of European firms emphasized only the inability of the manager's spouse to adjust as an explanation for the expatriate's failed assignment. Other studies similarly emphasize the effects of a dissatisfied spouse on the international assignment.[30]

Canadian companies have reported low failure rates for expatriates relative to other countries, particularly the United States, which has a failure rate of 40 to 50 percent.[31] Canadians may be more culturally adaptable than their American counterparts because they are already familiar with bilingualism and multiculturalism. In fact, Canadian executives are in demand across the globe. The country's diverse ethnic makeup has produced a generation of business leaders who mix easily with different cultures.[32]

Many employers have tried to eliminate issues that lead to expatriate assignment failures by shortening the assignment length and having the family remain at home. Expatriate assignments have traditionally been for terms of three to five years, but recently there has been a trend toward short-term global assignments instead of permanent relocations.[33] A recent survey, by global consulting firm KPMG, found that short-term assignments of less than 12 months are almost as prevalent as long-term assignments (more than five years),[34] as shown in **Figure 17.1**.

Short-term assignment alternatives include frequent extended business trips with corresponding time spent back at home, short-term assignments of between three months and a year with frequent home leave (once every 12 weeks on

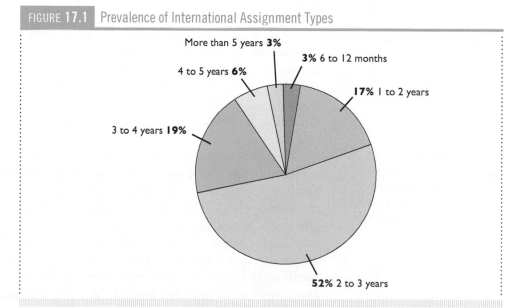

FIGURE 17.1 Prevalence of International Assignment Types

- More than 5 years **3%**
- 4 to 5 years **6%**
- **3%** 6 to 12 months
- **17%** 1 to 2 years
- 3 to 4 years **19%**
- **52%** 2 to 3 years

Source: Based on *Survey 2011 Global Assignment Policies and Practices*, KPMG, p. 9, www.kpmginstitutes. com/taxwatch/insights/2011/pdf/gapp-survey-2011.pdf.

average), and the dual household arrangement, where the employee's family remains at home and the employee sets up a small household for himself or herself in the foreign country. Often, firms neglect to prepare employees for short-term assignments in the same way they do for the long-term variety, which leads to problems such as lack of cross-cultural awareness, extreme loneliness, and feeling undervalued on returning to the home office.[35] Companies that provide strong support to expatriate employees stand a higher chance of success.[36]

CONSIDERATIONS IN GLOBAL HRM

Careful screening is just the first step in ensuring that a foreign assignee is successful. The employee may then require special training and, additionally, international HR policies must be formulated for compensating the firm's overseas managers and maintaining healthy labour relations.

Canadian Employee Relocation Council
www.cerc.ca

Transition Dynamics
www.transition-dynamics.com

The Expatriate Group
www.expat.ca

ethnocentric staffing policy
Policies that align wit the attitude that home-country managers are superior to those in the host country".

polycentric staffing policy
Policies that align with the belief that only host-country managers can understand the culture and behaviour of the host-country market.

geocentric staffing policy Policies that aligned with the belief that the best manager for any specific position anywhere on the globe may be found in any of the countries in which the firm operates.

Global Staffing Policy

There are three international staffing policies. An **ethnocentric staffing policy** is based on the attitude that home-country managers are superior to those in the host country, and all key management positions are filled by parent-country nationals. At Royal Dutch Shell, for instance, virtually all financial controllers around the world are Dutch nationals. Reasons given for ethnocentric staffing policies include lack of qualified host-country senior management talent, a desire to maintain a unified corporate culture and tighter control, and the desire to transfer the parent firm's core competencies (for example, a specialized manufacturing skill) to a foreign subsidiary more expeditiously.

A **polycentric staffing policy** is based on the belief that only host-country managers can understand the culture and behaviour of the host-country market, and therefore foreign subsidiaries should be staffed with host-country nationals and its home office headquarters with parent-country nationals. This may reduce the local cultural misunderstandings that expatriate managers may exhibit. It will also almost undoubtedly be less expensive. One expert estimates that an expatriate executive can cost a firm up to three times as much as a domestic executive because of transfer expenses and other expenses such as schooling for children, annual home leave, and the need to pay income taxes in two countries.

A **geocentric staffing policy** assumes that management candidates must be searched for globally, on the assumption that the best manager for any specific position anywhere on the globe may be found in any of the countries in which the firm operates. This allows the global firm to use its human resources more efficiently by transferring the best person to the open job, wherever he or she may be. It can also help to build a stronger and more consistent culture and set of values among the entire global management team. Team members here are continually interacting and networking with one another as they move from assignment to assignment around the globe and participate in global development activities.

Selection for Global Assignments

International managers can be expatriates, locals (citizens of the countries where they are working), or third-country nationals (citizens of a country other than the parent or the host country), such as a British executive working in a Tokyo subsidiary of a Canadian multinational bank.[37] Expatriates represent a minority of managers; most managerial positions are filled by locals rather than expatriates in both headquarters and foreign subsidiary operations.

An Ethical ⫶ Dilemma

How ethical is it for a multinational organization to recruit expatriate staff for managerial positions when similarly qualified staff can be identified in the host country?

There are several reasons to rely on local, host-country management talent for filling the foreign subsidiary's management ranks. Many people simply prefer not to work in a foreign country, and in general the cost of using expatriates is far greater than the cost of using local management talent. The multinational corporation may be viewed locally as a "better citizen" if it uses local management talent, and indeed some governments actually press for the localization of management. There may also be a fear that expatriates, knowing that they are posted to the foreign subsidiary for only a few years, may overemphasize short-term projects rather than focus on perhaps more necessary long-term tasks.

There are also several reasons for using expatriates—either parent-country or third-country nationals—for staffing subsidiaries. The major reason is technical competence. In other words, employers may be unable to find local candidates with the required technical qualifications. Multinationals also increasingly view a successful stint abroad as a required step in leadership development. Control is another important reason. Multinationals sometimes assign expatriates from their headquarters staff abroad on the assumption that these managers are more steeped in the firm's policies and culture and more likely to unquestioningly implement headquarters' instructions.

Orienting and Training Employees for Global Assignments

Cross-cultural training is very important for creating realistic expectations, which in turn are strongly related to cross-cultural adjustment.[38] A four-step approach to cross-cultural training is often used. Level 1 training focuses on the impact of cultural differences and on raising trainee awareness of such differences in terms of their impact on business outcomes. Even transfers to the United States from Canada can involve culture shock. Level 2 training focuses on attitudes and aims at getting participants to understand how attitudes (both negative and positive) are formed and how they influence behaviour (for example, unfavourable stereotypes may subconsciously influence how a new manager responds to and treats his or her new foreign employees). Level 3 training provides factual knowledge about the target country, while Level 4 training provides skill building in areas like language and adjustment and adaptation skills. The depth of training is of the utmost importance. If firms are going to provide cross-cultural training, it needs to be in-depth and done with care. For example, language training must include nonverbal communication awareness, as it varies so widely across the world.[39]

Orientation and training for international assignments can help employees (and their families) to avoid "culture shock" and better adjust to their new surroundings.

In addition to cross-cultural training, leadership development opportunities are often an important learning component of expatriate assignment.[40] At IBM, for instance, such development includes the use of a series of rotating assignments that permits overseas managers to grow professionally. At the same time, IBM and other major firms have established management development centres around the world where executives can go to hone their skills. Beyond that, classroom programs (such as those at the London Business School, or at INSEAD in France) provide overseas executives with the opportunities that they need to hone their functional and leadership skills.

International Compensation

The concept of international compensation management can present some unexpected and complicated problems. Compensation programs throughout a global firm must be both integrated (to maximize overall effectiveness) and differentiated (to effectively motivate and meet the specific needs of the various categories and locations of employees). On the one hand, there is logic in maintaining company-wide pay scales and policies so that, for instance, divisional marketing directors throughout the world are all paid within the same narrow range. This reduces the risk of perceived inequities and dramatically simplifies the job of keeping track of disparate country-by-country wage rates. However, most multinational companies have recognized the need to make executive pay decisions on a global level, and executive pay plans are gradually becoming more uniform.[41] As shown in **Figure 17.2**, the majority of global assignment compensation (60 percent) is aligned to pay expatriates according to compensation levels in their own country.

| FIGURE **17.2** | Approaches to Compensation for Global Assignments, 2011 |

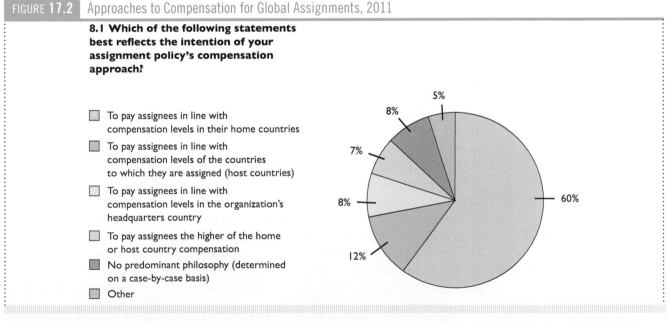

8.1 Which of the following statements best reflects the intention of your assignment policy's compensation approach?

- ☐ To pay assignees in line with compensation levels in their home countries
- ☐ To pay assignees in line with compensation levels of the countries to which they are assigned (host countries)
- ☐ To pay assignees in line with compensation levels in the organization's headquarters country
- ☐ To pay assignees the higher of the home or host country compensation
- ☐ No predominant philosophy (determined on a case-by-case basis)
- ☐ Other

5%
8%
7%
8%
12%
60%

Source: Based on *Survey 2011 Global Assignment Policies and Practices*, KPMG, p. 37, www.kpmginstitutes.com/taxwatch/insights/2011/pdf/gapp-survey-2011.pdf.

On the other hand, the practice of not adapting pay scales to local markets can present an HR manager with more problems than it solves. The fact is that living in Tokyo is many times more expensive than living in Calgary, while the cost of living in Bangalore, India, is considerably lower than living in Toronto.[42] If these cost-of-living differences are not considered, it may be almost impossible to get managers to accept assignments in high-cost locations. One way to handle the problem is to pay a similar base salary companywide and then add on various allowances according to individual market conditions.[43]

Compensation professionals also face the challenge of designing programs that motivate local employees in each country as well as internationally mobile employees of all nationalities. Some multinational companies deal with this problem by conducting their own annual compensation surveys. Others use a global career progression framework that includes the flexibility to accommodate local practices and still maintain organization-wide consistency.[44]

The Balance Sheet Approach

balance sheet approach A method of formulating expatriate pay based on equalizing purchasing power across countries.

The most common approach to formulating expatriate pay is to equalize purchasing power across countries, a technique known as the **balance sheet approach**. The basic idea is that each expatriate should enjoy the same standard of living that he or she would have had at home. The employer estimates what the cost of major expenses like housing would be in the expatriate's home country and the equivalent cost of each in the host country. Any differences—such as higher housing expenses—are then paid by the employer.

An Ethical ⋮ Dilemma

Is it ethical to pay expatriates using the balance sheet approach when local staff at the same level receive far less compensation?

In practice, this involves building the expatriate's total compensation around five or six separate components, as shown in **Figure 17.3**. For example, base salary will normally be in the same range as the manager's home-country salary. In addition, however, there might be a mobility premium. This is paid as a percentage of the executive's base salary, in part to compensate the manager for the cultural and physical adjustments that he or she will have to make.[45] There may also be several allowances, including a housing allowance and an education allowance for the expatriate's children.

Variable Pay

As organizations around the world have shifted their focus to individual performance differentiation, there has been a rise in the prevalence of individual performance rewards, although the widespread use of team awards remains in a few Asian countries.[46] Across the globe, over 85 percent of companies offer at least one type of broad-based variable pay program, as shown in **Figure 17.4**. Target bonuses for management and professional employees, as a percentage of base salary, have become quite similar globally. Although broad-based variable pay was a lot less common in the past, it has now gone global and is an integral part of the compensation landscape for management and professional employees in every region.

International EAPs

Employee assistance programs (EAPs) are also going global, helping expatriates take care of their mental health, which is often affected by the stressful relocation process. A worldwide survey found that more than half of expatriates

FIGURE **17.3** | Balance Sheet Approach

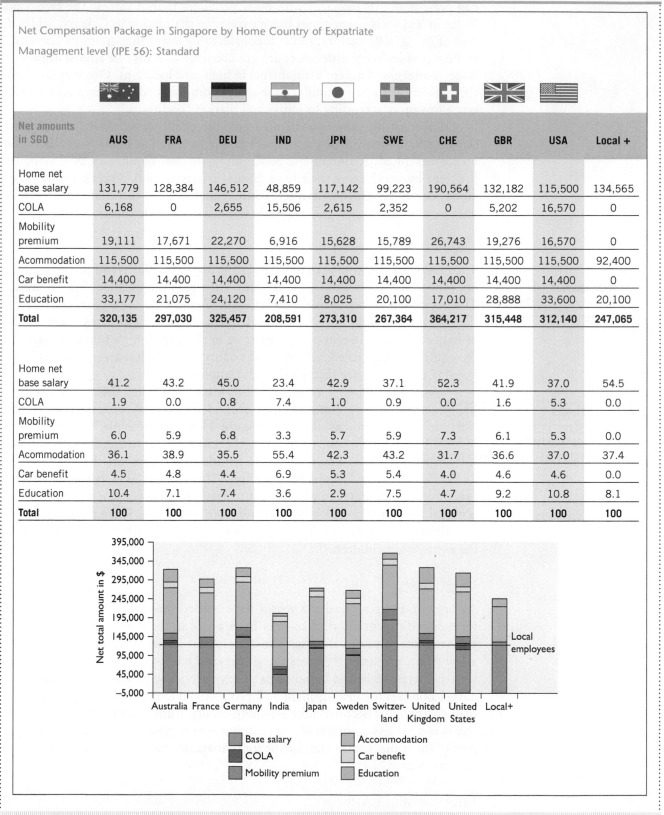

Net Compensation Package in Singapore by Home Country of Expatriate

Management level (IPE 56): Standard

Net amounts in SGD	AUS	FRA	DEU	IND	JPN	SWE	CHE	GBR	USA	Local +
Home net base salary	131,779	128,384	146,512	48,859	117,142	99,223	190,564	132,182	115,500	134,565
COLA	6,168	0	2,655	15,506	2,615	2,352	0	5,202	16,570	0
Mobility premium	19,111	17,671	22,270	6,916	15,628	15,789	26,743	19,276	16,570	0
Acommodation	115,500	115,500	115,500	115,500	115,500	115,500	115,500	115,500	115,500	92,400
Car benefit	14,400	14,400	14,400	14,400	14,400	14,400	14,400	14,400	14,400	0
Education	33,177	21,075	24,120	7,410	8,025	20,100	17,010	28,888	33,600	20,100
Total	**320,135**	**297,030**	**325,457**	**208,591**	**273,310**	**267,364**	**364,217**	**315,448**	**312,140**	**247,065**
Home net base salary	41.2	43.2	45.0	23.4	42.9	37.1	52.3	41.9	37.0	54.5
COLA	1.9	0.0	0.8	7.4	1.0	0.9	0.0	1.6	5.3	0.0
Mobility premium	6.0	5.9	6.8	3.3	5.7	5.9	7.3	6.1	5.3	0.0
Acommodation	36.1	38.9	35.5	55.4	42.3	43.2	31.7	36.6	37.0	37.4
Car benefit	4.5	4.8	4.4	6.9	5.3	5.4	4.0	4.6	4.6	0.0
Education	10.4	7.1	7.4	3.6	2.9	7.5	4.7	9.2	10.8	8.1
Total	**100**	**100**	**100**	**100**	**100**	**100**	**100**	**100**	**100**	**100**

Source: From C. Mestre, A. Rossier-Renaud, and M. Berger, "Better Benchmarks for Global Mobility," *Workspan* (April 2009), p. 75. Contents © 2009 Workspan. Reprinted with permission from WorldatWork. No part of this may be reproduced, excerpted or redistributed in any form without express written permission from WorldatWork.

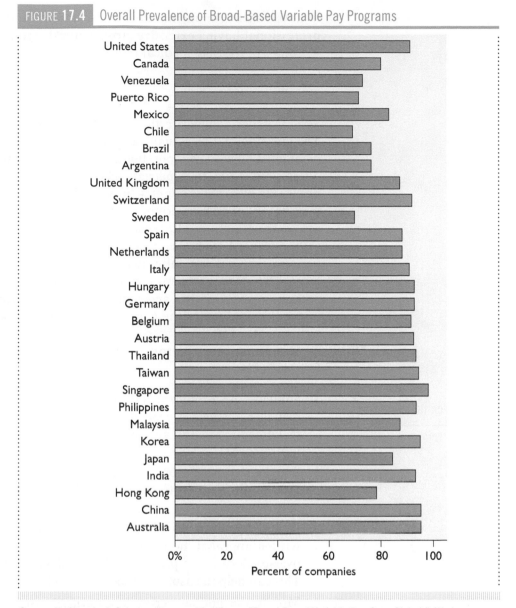

FIGURE **17.4** Overall Prevalence of Broad-Based Variable Pay Programs

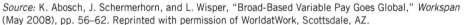

Source: K. Abosch, J. Schermerhorn, and L. Wisper, "Broad-Based Variable Pay Goes Global," *Workspan* (May 2008), pp. 56–62. Reprinted with permission of WorldatWork, Scottsdale, AZ.

are weighed down by added stress caused by longer hours, extended workdays/workweeks, and cultural differences, among other factors. Two-thirds feel the strain of managing the demands of work and the well-being of family.[47] The proactive approach is to contact employees before departure to explain the program's services; then, about three months after arrival, families are contacted again. By this time, they have usually run into some challenges from culture shock and will welcome some assistance. The expatriates and their families have then established a connection with the EAP to use for ongoing support.[48]

Problems such as homesickness, boredom, withdrawal, depression, compulsive eating and drinking, irritability, marital stress, family tension, and conflict are all common reactions to culture shock. Employees on short-term assignment without their families can experience extreme loneliness. Treatment for psychiatric illnesses varies widely around the world, as do the conditions in government-run mental health institutions, and consultation with an EAP professional having extensive cross-cultural training may be critical in ensuring that appropriate medical treatment is obtained.[49]

Performance Appraisal of Global Managers

Several issues complicate the task of appraising an expatriate's performance. The question of who actually appraises the expatriate is crucial. Local management must have some input, but the appraisal may then be distorted by cultural differences. Thus, an expatriate manager in India may be evaluated somewhat negatively by his host-country bosses, who find the use of participative decision making or other behaviours on the part of the expatriate to be inappropriate in their culture. However, home-office managers may be so geographically distanced from the expatriate that they cannot provide valid appraisals because they are not fully aware of the situation that the manager actually faces. Therefore, problems can arise if the expatriate is measured by objective criteria, such as profits and market share, but local events, such as political instability, undermine the manager's performance while remaining "invisible" to home-office staff.

Suggestions for improving the expatriate appraisal process include the following:[50]

Tips : FOR THE FRONT LINE

1. Stipulate the assignment's difficulty level. For example, being an expatriate manager in China is generally considered to be more difficult than working in England, and the appraisal should take such difficulty-level differences into account.

2. Weight the evaluation more toward the onsite manager's appraisal than toward the home-site manager's distant perceptions of the employee's performance.

3. If, however (as is usually the case), the home-site manager does the actual written appraisal, he or she should use a former expatriate from the same overseas location to provide background advice during the appraisal process. This can help to ensure that unique local issues are considered.

4. Modify the normal performance criteria used for that particular position to fit the overseas position and characteristics of that particular locale. For example, "maintaining positive labour relations" might be more important in Chile, where labour instability is more common, than it would be in Canada.

5. Attempt to give the expatriate manager credit for relevant insights into the functioning of the operation and specifically the interdependencies of the domestic and foreign operations. In other words, do not just appraise the expatriate manager in terms of quantifiable criteria, like profits or market share. His or her recommendations regarding how home-office/foreign-subsidiary communication might be enhanced and other useful insights should also affect the appraisal.

International Labour Relations

Firms opening subsidiaries abroad will find substantial differences in labour relations practices among the world's countries and regions. For example, Walmart, which has successfully resisted unionization in most of the world, had to accept unions in many of its stores in China.[51] In Eastern Europe, unionization rates have plummeted since the fall of the Iron Curtain resulting in a competitive advantage, with wages averaging only one-third of those in Western Europe.[52]

Some important differences between labour relations practices in Europe and North America include the following:[53]

- *Centralization.* In general, collective bargaining in Europe is likely to be industry-wide or regionally oriented, whereas North American collective bargaining generally occurs at the enterprise or plant level.

- *Employer organization.* Because of the prevalence of industry-wide bargaining, the employer's collective bargaining role tends to be performed primarily by employer associations in Europe; individual employers in North America generally (but not always) represent their own interests when bargaining collectively with unions.

- *Union recognition.* Union recognition for collective bargaining in Europe is much less formal than in North America. For example, in Europe there is no legal mechanism requiring an employer to recognize a particular union; even if a union claims to represent 80 percent of an employer's workers, another union can try to organize and bargain for the other 20 percent.

- *Content and scope of bargaining.* North American labour–management agreements tend to focus on wages, hours, and working conditions. European agreements tend to be brief and simple and to specify minimum wages and employment conditions.

- *Worker participation.* Worker participation has a long and relatively extensive history in Europe. In many countries, works councils are required. A works council is a committee in which plant workers consult with management about certain issues or share in the governance of the workplace.[54]

REPATRIATION

repatriation The process of moving the expatriate and his or her family back home from the foreign assignment.

Repatriation is the process of moving the expatriate and his or her family back home from the foreign assignment. Sometimes, repatriation can be more difficult than going abroad.[55] Up to half of expatriates leave their organization following a repatriation, usually because they are not able to use their newly developed skills and capabilities in their roles on their return.[56] Their expert knowledge and international expertise often ends up with the competition.

Several repatriation problems are very common. One is the expatriate's fear that he or she has been "out of sight, out of mind" during an extended foreign stay and has thus lost touch with the parent firm's culture, top executives, and those responsible for the firm's management selection processes. Indeed, such fears can be well founded: Many repatriates are temporarily placed in mediocre or makeshift jobs. Ironically, the company often undervalues the cross-cultural skills acquired abroad, and the international posting becomes a career-limiting, rather than career-enhancing, move. Many are shocked to find that the executive trappings of the overseas job (private schools for the children and a company car and driver, for instance) are lost on return, and that the executive is again just a small fish in a big pond. Perhaps more exasperating is the discovery that some of the expatriate's former colleagues have been more rapidly promoted while he or she was overseas. Even the expatriate's family may undergo a sort of reverse culture shock, as the spouse and children face the often daunting task of picking up old friendships and habits or starting schools anew on their return.[57]

Progressive multinationals anticipate and avoid these problems by taking a number of sensible steps:[58]

Tips : **FOR THE FRONT LINE**

1. *Writing repatriation agreements.* Many firms use repatriation agreements, which guarantee in writing that the international assignee will not be kept abroad longer than some period (such as five years) and that on return he or she will be given a mutually acceptable job.

2. *Assigning a sponsor.* The employee should be assigned a sponsor/mentor (such as a senior manager at the parent firm's home office). This person's role is to look after the expatriate while he or she is away. This includes keeping the person apprised of significant company events and changes back home, monitoring his or her career interests, and nominating the person to be considered for key openings when the expatriate is ready to come home.

3. *Providing career counselling.* Provide formal career counselling sessions to ensure that the repatriate's job assignments on return will meet his or her needs.

4. *Keeping communication open.* Keep the expatriate "plugged in" to home-office business affairs through management meetings around the world and frequent home leave combined with meetings at headquarters. Only 18 percent of companies in a 2006 Watson Wyatt global survey had a global communication plan in place to keep employees around the world informed about what the company was doing.

5. *Offering financial support.* Many firms pay real estate and legal fees and help the expatriate to rent or in some other way to maintain his or her residence so that the repatriate and his or her family can actually return "home."

6. *Developing reorientation programs.* Provide the repatriate and his or her family with a reorientation program to facilitate the adjustment back into the home culture.

7. *Building in return trips.* Expatriates can benefit from more frequent trips to the home country to ensure that they keep in touch with home-country norms and changes during their international assignment.

MANAGING GLOBAL WORKERS WITHIN CANADA

RPC

Keeps current with emerging HR trends

The successful integration of immigrants and foreign workers into the Canadian labour market is increasingly becoming of interest to organizations, Canadian public policy makers, and HR professionals alike. The issues of underemployment of immigrants and foreign workers is especially critical today, given the aging workforce, the rate of immigration to Canada (almost one in every five persons residing in Canada is foreign born), and our dependence on immigrants to maintain our labour force size. Additionally, the labour and talent scarcity further fuels the need for successful integration and utilization of immigrants in the Canadian labour force. In 2010, the top six source countries of immigrants to Canada were China, the Philippines, India, the United States, the United Kingdom, and France.[59]

Canadian employers note that hiring immigrants increases the employer's language skills, generation of new ideas, and enhances the company's reputation.[60] Research has found that diverse groups make higher-quality decisions, generate more creative ideas, use more creative problem-solving techniques, and have the potential for higher rates of productivity.[61] A survey of human resources professionals found that 91 percent of respondents felt that diversity initiatives help the organization maintain a competitive advantage, largely through enhanced corporate culture, employee morale, retention, and recruitment.[62]

Immigrant workers in Canada can face unique challenges that hinder full employment or integration into the workforce. In 1980, recent male immigrants to Canada who were employed earned, on average, 85 cents for every dollar that Canadian-born males earned; by 2005, the ratio dropped to 63 cents for every dollar.[63] In addition, unemployment rates among new immigrants (those who have been in Canada for less than five years) are significantly higher than rates of those born in Canada or immigrants who are have been in Canada for longer periods of time (see **Figure 17.5**).

A survey by Statistics Canada found that 70 percent of newcomers said they had encountered problems or barriers in the job-finding process. The results can be broadly categorized into a lack of Canadian work experience, poor transferability of foreign credentials, and a lack of literacy skills in either of the official languages (English or French; see **Figure 17.6**).

The unemployment level and challenges of employment represent only part of the obstacles of immigrant and foreign workforce integration in Canada. Another significant challenge is the underutilization of immigrant skills because they are being hired for positions that they are overqualified to perform. Statistics Canada has reported that the percentage of long-term immigrants who had successfully completed a university degree and who only found jobs with low educational requirements (such as clerks, truck drivers, salespeople, cashiers, and taxi drivers) rose steadily between 1991 and 2006. The resulting skills mismatch puts pressure on HR departments to find the right talent needed for a position, on the organization to provide more extensive training and development programs, and on society as a whole because of the lost value of experience and knowledge acquired by its members.[64]

FIGURE **17.5**   Unemployment Rates of Population Ages 25 to 54 and by Educational Attainment, 2010

	All education levels	No degree, certificate or diploma	High school graduate	Post-secondary certificate or diploma	University degree
Born in Canada	6.1	12.9	7.1	5.6	3.5
Landed immigrants	9.5	14.9	10.1	8.9	8.6
Immigrants, landed 5 or less years earlier	14.7	18	16.2	14.3	14.4
Immigrants, landed 5 to 10 years earlier	9.5	16.1	11.9	9.1	8.2
Immigrants, landed more than 10 years earlier	8.1	14	8.9	7.7	6

Source: Statistics Canada 2011.

Source: CanadaImmigrants.com, "Canada Immigrants' Earning Statistics," www.canadaimmigrants.com/immigrants_earnings.asp.

FIGURE **17.6**   Immigrant Job Search Difficulties in Canada, 2005

Immigrants and Employers Agree on the Main Obstacles to Employment

	Immigrant Job Seekers	Managers Expecting to Hire
Percent of Immigrants reporting problems in finding employment / Percent of Managers expecting problems hiring foreign-trained workers	70%	72%
Most Commonly Cited Problems		
Lack of Canadian Work Experience	26%	46%
Transferability of Foreign Credentials	24%	52%
Lack of Official Language Skills	22%	66%

Sources: Immigrant job seek data from Statistics Canada Longitudinal Survey of Immigrants to Canada, Catalogue no. 89-611-XIE; Managers data from Canadian Labour and Business Centre's Viewpoints 2002 Survey.

Source: Immigrant job seeker data from Statistics Canada Longitudinal Survey of Immigrants to Canada, Catalogue no. 89-611-XIE; Managers data from Canadian Labour and Business Centre's Viewpoints 2002 Survey.

Barrier 1: Lack of Canadian Experience

Work experience helps individuals develop skills in communication, work patterns, and team work that are recognized and valued by organizations. It can help people identify career paths and requirements of desired positions. It can shape perceptions of the world of work and set expectations of the employer. It can also provide an opportunity for individuals to network with others, which can assist their future job search efforts.

A barrier to the successful employment of immigrants is identified as the lack of Canadian experience. Understandably, most employers look for familiar references when assessing candidates, such as experiences and companies that they recognize on résumés or during interviews. Often immigrants feel like they are in a Catch-22 situation where they cannot secure a job without the proven Canadian experience, and they cannot acquire the Canadian experience without securing a job.

This situation is deepened because of a lack of recognition for foreign work, which is consistently discounted in the Canadian labour market.[65] As immigrants enter the Canadian workforce, research on earnings shows low, or even zero, returns (monetary recognition) for their foreign work experience.[66] When only their Canadian work experience is taken into account, immigrants' earnings are similar to those of the Canadian-born with the same years of Canadian experience, regardless of how many years of international experience the immigrant had prior to joining the Canadian workforce. These results suggest a significant inability to transfer and recognize skills and experiences immigrants acquired in their country of origin to the Canadian labour market, representing a lost value to the immigrant.

Almost two in every three new immigrants fail to find employment in the same field in which they were employed in their native country. For example, before arriving in Canada, only 10.2 percent of men and 12.1 percent of women were employed in sales and service-related occupations. Six months after arrival in Canada, 24.9 percent of men and 37.3 percent of women were employed in these occupations.[67]

Tips FOR THE FRONT LINE

Options to help overcome challenges associated with lack of Canadian experience and devaluation of foreign experience include the following:[68]

1. Educate employers, recruiters, and hiring managers to develop skills needed to recognize and effectively interpret skills from different countries.

2. Provide clear statements in job descriptions as to the extent and nature of work experience required to complete job requirements. Offer candidates an opportunity to demonstrate the skills in a simulated or field setting.

3. Use apprenticeships effectively. Some trades mandate apprenticeships (for example, in Ontario there are 20 trades with a mandatory apprenticeship component), whereas others are voluntary. This creates an option where apprenticeships can be used to develop and evaluate the skills of foreign-trained workers. Alternatively, some provinces (like Alberta) allow immigrants with significant foreign experience in a trade the opportunity to write an exam to receive certification.

4. Partner with industry-based assessment centres (for example, Workplace Integration of Skilled Newcomers in the Trades, Internationally Educated Engineer Qualification Bridging Program) to develop bridging programs to integrate foreign experience of immigrants.

At the same time, immigrants to Canada have a responsibility toward learning about Canadian workplace norms and customs and presenting their experiences or qualifications to Canadian recruiters in a clear and effective way. There must also be an awareness of Canadian laws and regulations. There are many ways organizations can help with this, as discussed in the Global HRM box.

GLOBAL HRM

Successful Integration of Immigrants in Canada

There are many examples of innovative, forward-thinking companies that have developed initiatives to aid in the successful integration of immigrants into their workforce. The result is a competitive advantage and ability to recognize and recruit strong talent.

- RBC requires recruiters and managers to be trained in cross-cultural awareness to help interpret and understand past experiences related to the job. This represents a two-way mutual understanding approach to recruitment.

- Assiniboine Credit Union assumes an organic approach by training managers and employees on diversity and cultural awareness, offering a mentorship or buddy program, and regularly soliciting and communicating feedback from the programs, which then aids in modifying the programs.

- Manulife offers paid internships (of 4 to 12 months) and formalizes the process by having clear indications of who is eligible for the programs offered (must be in Canada less than three years, have at least three years of foreign experience, and so on).

Source: Based on G. Larose and G. Tillman, "Valorizing Immigrants' Non-Canadian Work Experience," (Ottawa, ON: Work and Learning Knowledge Centre, 2009).

Barrier 2: Poor Transferability of Foreign Education or Training

While finding a job can be difficult for many, the employment prospects for new immigrants are often diminished due to poor recognition of foreign qualifications. Licensing bodies of certain trades and professions may not accept foreign-obtained certification, and employers have difficulty assessing foreign education in a meaningful way.[69] In 2008, over 42 percent of new immigrants were working in occupations that required lower levels of education than what they had attained. Of Canadian-born workers, the rate was 28 percent.[70]

The result is the underutilization of foreign workers in Canada. A study of over 7 700 new immigrants found that within four years after landing in Canada, only 28 percent with foreign credentials had received recognition for these credentials (meaning that the employer/institution recognizes the credential as being legitimate within determined standards).[71] Women and older immigrants are less likely to have foreign education recognized in Canada. Also, immigrants from South Korea, the Philippines, and France have the lowest rates of full foreign credentials recognition, while immigrants from the United States and United Kingdom have the highest rates.[72]

Canadian literature on the assessment of foreign training, using prior learning assessment and recognition (PLAR) methods, is extensive. PLAR is a system meant to aide in the recognition of the learning adults acquire outside of formal Canadian education; it attempts to standardize recognition of skills and abilities in a meaningful way. Many colleges and universities in Canada rely on PLAR to evaluate foreign credentials.

Barrier 3: Lack of Literacy Skills

Literacy is the ability to identify, understand, interpret, create, communicate, compute, and use printed and written materials associated with varying contexts. In a global economy, it is critical that employees have the ability to express themselves in the official language(s) of the country they are employed in. The education levels of new immigrants have been steadily rising over recent years due to changes in immigration criteria.

Literacy and adult education falls mainly under the jurisdiction of provincial and territorial governments. The federal government plays a role in developing policy and delivering some funding for literacy initiatives. In May 2007, Citizenship and Immigration Canada established the Foreign Credential Referral Office (FCRO) to guide, monitor, and facilitate the assessment of foreign credentials. In October 2010, the FCRO took over responsibility from HRSDC for the Canadian Immigrant Integration Program. That year, the FCRO aided in online and over the phone inquiries from over 25 000 immigrants.[73]

Six months after arrival in Canada, only three in every five immigrants report that they are able to speak English well or very well, and only one in every ten immigrants report the same about French.[74] Language training increases an immigrant's likelihood of gaining employment or advancing within an organization. Roughly 45 percent of new immigrants partake in language training in English once employed in Canada, and 10 percent are trained in French.[75]

Language ability has also been shown to improve labour-market outcomes among educated immigrants.[76] The earnings differential between immigrants and Canadian-born individuals would narrow by about 20 percent if immigrants had the same average literacy scores as the native born. Consequently, this would eliminate more than half of the immigrant earnings disadvantage among university educated workers alone. The variance and in some cases lack of literacy skills in Canada's official languages is viewed as a significant barrier to the successful integration of immigrants in the labour market.

Thus, while literacy deficiencies among immigrants have an important impact on earnings differentials, the impact is decidedly smaller than the effect of low returns associated with foreign experience among the highly educated. Controlling for literacy does not affect the relative patterns of returns to foreign- and Canadian-acquired experience. Immigration is vital to Canada's population growth and economic prosperity. Yet, while demand for their skills grows, many highly competent newcomers to Canada remain underemployed.

Chapter SUMMARY

1. Globalization affects HRM in two significant ways. First, workforce mobility forces companies to focus on international recruitment, retention, and relations strategies to take advantage of the skills workers who are not born in Canada offer. Second, immigrants into Canada present a significant source of labour force growth, and successful integration of these immigrants can yield significant benefits for the organization

2. Intercountry differences include cultural factors (such as power distance, individualism versus collectivism, and gender egalitarianism), economic systems, labour cost factors, and industrial relations factors. These affect HRM in a variety of ways.

3. Global relocation strategies must consider effective selection, training, compensation, labour relations, and performance appraisals for expatriates and global managers. For example, in reference to compensation, the balance sheet approach allows the employer to estimate expenses for income taxes, housing, and goods and services and pay supplements to the expatriate in such a way as to maintain the same standard of living that he or she would have had at home.

4. Repatriation problems are common but can be minimized. They include the often well-founded fear that the expatriate is "out of sight, out of mind" and difficulties in re-assimilating the expatriate's family back into home-country culture. Suggestions for avoiding these problems include using repatriation agreements, assigning a home-country sponsor/mentor, offering career counselling, keeping the expatriate plugged in to home-office business, building in return trips, providing financial support to maintain the expatriate's home-country residence, and offering reorientation programs to the expatriate and his or her family.

5. Newcomers to Canada face a variety of challenges associated with securing full employment. Specifically, a lack of Canadian work experience, poor transferability of foreign credentials, and a lack of language skills in English or French are seen as the greatest barriers to employment for newcomers, according to both immigrants and employers.

6. These barriers result in significant underemployment of immigrants, or a skills mismatch, which further exasperates the skills shortage that employers experience.

7. Newcomers to Canada and employers can benefit from modifying recruitment and selection procedures to offer opportunities to assess the skills of immigrants as part of the selection process, using apprenticeships effectively, partnering with assessment centres to recognize skills, and educating employers, recruiters, and managers about how to recognize and interpret skills from another country.

MyManagementLab

Visit MyManagementLab to access a personalized Study Plan and additional study tools for this chapter.

Key TERMS

balance sheet approach *(p. 477)*
ethnocentric staffing policy *(p. 474)*
expatriate *(p. 467)*
expatriate assignment failure *(p. 472)*
geocentric staffing policy *(p. 474)*

immigrant *(p. 467)*
polycentric staffing policy *(p. 474)*
repatriation *(p. 481)*
workforce mobility *(p. 467)*

Review and Discussion QUESTIONS

1. Specifically, what are some of the uniquely international activities that an international HR manager typically engages in?

2. Explain three broad global HR challenges.

3. Discuss the reasons why expatriate assignments fail and what is being done to reduce the failure rate.

4. How does compensation of an expatriate differ from that of a home-office manager? How can some of the unique problems of compensating the expatriate be avoided?

5. Describe five actions that can be taken by expatriate managers in other countries to increase their personal safety.

6. What are the three biggest obstacles to securing full employment of immigrants and foreign workers in Canada? How can these be managed?

7. Why is the issue of underemployment of foreign-trained persons important to Canadian employers?

Critical Thinking QUESTIONS

1. You are president of a small business. In what ways do you expect that being involved in international business activity will affect HRM in your business?

2. A firm is about to send its first employees overseas to staff a new subsidiary. The president asks why such assignments fail and what can be done to avoid such failures. Write a memo in response to these questions.

3. What can an organization do to ensure that the skills acquired on an international assignment

are used when the employee returns to his or her home country?

4. How would you assess the credentials of foreign-trained persons? What agencies are available for you to contact?

5. What obstacles to successful integration of global talent do you think exist in your company? What solutions can you recommend to overcome these obstacles?

Experiential EXERCISES

1. Choose three traits that are useful for selecting international assignees, and create a straightforward test (not one that uses pencil and paper) to screen candidates for these traits.

2. Describe the most common approach to formulating expatriate pay. Use a library source to determine the relative cost of living in five countries this year, and explain the implications of such differences for drafting a pay plan for managers being sent to each country.

3. Either in pairs or groups of four or five, develop an outline for an initial four-hour cross-cultural training program. What training resources, tools, and processes might you use? Be prepared to give a rationale for your program.

4. Check online and find at least two websites that deal with or otherwise discuss the expatriate experience, and note the concerns and suggestions expressed. Compare these to the text discussion. How do the actual expatriate experiences you found influence your current attitude toward working overseas? What are your major concerns? What excites you?

Running CASE

Running Case: LearnInMotion.com

Going Abroad

According to its business plan and in practice, LearnInMotion.com "acquires content globally but delivers it locally." In other words, all the content and courses and other material that it lists on its site come from content providers all over the world. However, the "hard copy" (book and CD-ROM) courses are delivered, with the help of independent contracting delivery firms, locally in Ontario and Quebec.

Now the company is considering an expansion. Although the most logical strategic expansion would probably entail adding cities in Canada, one of LearnInMotion's major content providers—a big training company in England—believes there is a significant market for LearnInMotion services in England, particularly in London, Oxford, and Manchester (all of which are bustling business centres, and all of which have well-known universities). The training company has offered to finance and co-own a branch of LearnInMotion in London. They want it housed in the training firm's new offices in Mayfair, near Shepherd Market, in London. This is an easily accessible (if somewhat expensive) area, within easy walking distance of Hyde Park and not far from the London Underground Piccadilly line, which runs directly through the city to Heathrow airport.

Everyone concerned wants to make sure the new operation can "hit the ground running." This means either Jennifer or Pierre will have to move to London almost at once and take one salesperson and one of the content management people along. Once there, this small team could hire additional employees locally, and then, once the new operation is running successfully, return to Ottawa, probably within three or four months.

Jennifer and Pierre have decided to go ahead and open the London office, but this is not a decision they've taken lightly, since there are many drawbacks to doing so. The original, Ottawa-based site is not generating anywhere near the sales revenue it was supposed to at this point, and being short three key employees is not going to help. Neither the board of directors nor the representatives of the venture capital fund were enthusiastic about the idea of expanding abroad. However, they went along with it, and the deciding factor was probably the cash infusion that the London-based training firm was willing to make. It basically provided enough cash to run not just the London operation but the one in Ottawa as well for an additional six months.

Having made the decision to set up operations abroad, Jennifer and Pierre now need to turn to the multitude of matters involved in the expansion—for instance, obtaining the necessary licenses to open the business in England and arranging for phone lines (all carried out with the assistance of the London-based training firm). However, it's also obvious to Jennifer and Pierre that there are considerable human resources management implications involved in moving LearnInMotion employees abroad and in staffing the operation once they're there. Now they want you, their management consultant, to help them actually do it.

QUESTIONS

1   What intercountry differences will affect the human resources management practices of LearnInMotion?

2   Should LearnInMotion use a global selection policy to source talent for their London operation?

3   How should LearnInMotion implement a global HR system?

Case INCIDENT

"Boss, I Think We Have a Problem"

Central Steel Door Corporation has been in business for about 20 years, successfully selling a line of steel industrial-grade doors as well as the hardware and fittings required for them. Focusing mostly on the United States and Canada, the company had gradually increased its presence from the New York City area, first into New England and then down the Atlantic coast, then through the Midwest and west, and finally into Canada. The company's basic expansion strategy was always the same: Choose an area, open a distribution centre, hire a regional sales manager, then let that regional sales manager help staff the distribution centre and hire local sales reps.

Unfortunately, the company's traditional success in finding sales help for its North American locations has not extended to its overseas operations. With the introduction of the new European currency in 2002, Mel Fisher, president of Central Steel Door, decided to expand his company abroad into Europe. However, the expansion has not gone smoothly at all. He tried for three weeks to find a sales manager by advertising in the *International Herald Tribune*, which is read by businesspeople in Europe and by American expatriates living and working in Europe.

Although the ads placed in the *Tribune* also run for about a month on the *Tribune's* website, Fisher has so far received only five applications. One came from a possibly viable candidate, whereas four came from candidates whom Fisher refers to as "lost souls"—people who seem to have spent most of their time travelling aimlessly from country to country sipping espresso in sidewalk cafés. When asked what he had done for the last three years, one told Fisher he'd been on a "walkabout."

Other aspects of his international HR activities have been equally problematic. Fisher alienated two of his US sales managers by sending them to Europe to temporarily run the European operations, but neglecting to work out a compensation package that would cover their relatively high living expenses in Germany and Belgium. One ended up staying the better part of the year, and Fisher was rudely surprised to be informed by the Belgian government that his sales manager owed thousands of dollars in local taxes. The managers had hired about 10 local people to staff each of the two distribution centres. However, without full-time local European sales managers, the level of sales was disappointing, so Fisher decided to fire about half of the distribution centre employees. That's when he got an emergency phone call from his temporary sales manager in Germany: "I've just been told that all these employees should have had written employment agreements and that we can't fire any-one without at least one year's notice, and the local authorities here are really up in arms. Boss, I think we have a problem."

QUESTIONS

1 Based on this chapter and the case incident, com-pile a list of 10 international HR mistakes Fisher has made so far.

2 How would you have gone about hiring a European sales manager? Why?

3 What would you do now if you were Fisher?

MyManagementLab

Visit MyManagementLab to access a personalized Study Plan and additional study tools for this chapter.

 To view the CBC videos, read a summary, and answer discussion questions, go to MyManagementLab.

Notes

Chapter 1

1. O. Parker, *The Strategic Value of People: Human Resource Trends and Metrics* (Ottawa, ON: The Conference Board of Canada, July 2006); E. Andrew, "Most Canadian Companies Are Still Not Treating Human Resources as a Serious Strategic Issue," *Workspan Focus Canada* (February 2006), pp. 14–16; S. Prashad, "All Aligned: How to Get HR on Board with Business," *HR Professional* (February/March 2005), pp. 19–29.

2. O. Parker, *It's the Journey That Matters: 2005 Strategic HR Transformation Study Tour*. (Ottawa, ON: The Conference Board of Canada, March 2006).

3. N. Bontis, "Made to Measure: Linking Human Capital Metrics with Organizational Performance," *HR Professional* (August/September 2007), pp. 16–20; B. Becker, M. Huselid, P.S. Pickus, and M.F. Spratt, "HR as a Source of Shareholder Value: Research and Recommendations," *Human Resource Management* 36, no. 1 (Spring 1997), pp. 39–47; B. Becker and B. Gerhart, "The Impact of Human Resource Management on Organizational Performance: Progress and Prospects," *Academy of Management Journal*, 39, no. 4 (August 1996), pp. 779–801; M. Huselid, "The Impact of Human Resources Management Practices on Turnover, Productivity, and Corporate Performance," *Academy of Management Journal*, 38 (1995), pp. 635–672; P. Wright, G. McMahan, B. McCormick, and S. Sherman, "Strategy, Core Competence, and HR Involvement as Determinants of HR Effectiveness and Refinery," *Human Resource Management*, 37, no. 37 (1998), pp. 17–31.

4. C. Clegg, M. Patterson, A. Robinson, C. Stride, T.D. Wall, and S.J. Wood, "The Impact of Human Resource and Operational Management Practices on Company Productivity: A Longitudinal Study," *Personnel Psychology*, 61 (Autumn 2008), pp. 467–501.

5. A. Lado and M.C. Wilson, "Human Resource Systems and Sustained Competitive Advantage: A Competency-Based Perspective," *Academy of Management Review*, 19 (1994), pp. 699–727.

6. J.E. Delery and D.H. Doty, "Modes of Theorizing in Strategic Human Resource Management: Tests of Universalistic, Contingency, and Configurational Performance Predictions," *Academy of Management Journal*, 39, no. 4 (1996), pp. 802–835.

7. M. Huselid, "The Impact of Human Resources Management Practices on Turnover, Productivity, and Corporate Performance," *Academy of Management Journal*, 38 (1995), pp. 635–672.

8. F.W. Taylor, "The Principles of Scientific Management," in J.M. Sharfritz and J.S. Ott (eds.), *Classics of Organization Theory*, 2nd ed. (Chicago, IL: The Dorsey Press, 1987), pp. 66–81.

9. D.G. Nickels, J.M. McHugh, S.M. McHugh, and P.D Berman, *Understanding Canadian Business*, 2nd ed. (Toronto, ON: Irwin, 1997), p. 220.

10. This discussion is based on E.E. Lawler III, "Human Resources Management," *Personnel* (January 1988), pp. 24–25.

11. J. Miller, "HR Outsourcing and the Bottom Line," *Workspan* (October 2008), pp. 76–81; J. Berkow, "People Skills Required," *National Post* (October 19, 2005).

12. R.J. Cattaneo and A.J. Templer, "Determining the Effectiveness of Human Resources Management," in T.H. Stone (ed.), *ASAC: Personnel and Human Resources Division Proceedings* (Halifax, NS: St. Mary's University, June 1988), p. 73.

13. T. Belford, "HR Focusing on How It Can Add Value," *Globe and Mail* (March 25, 2002), p. B11.

14. S. Dobson, "Business Acumen Critical for HR: Survey," *Canadian HR Reporter* (May 9, 2011).

15. S. Modi, "Is the CEO the New Chief Talent Officer in Global Recruitment and HR?" Monster Thinking, (July 6, 2011), www.monsterthinking.com/ 2011/07/06/is-the-ceo-the-new-chief-talent-officer-in-global-recruitment-and-hr/ (accessed September 26, 2011).

16. R. Wright, *Measuring Human Resources Effectiveness Toolkit* (Ottawa, ON: The Conference Board of Canada, 2004); U. Vu, "The HR Leader's Contribution in an Engaged Organization," *Canadian HR Reporter* (May 22, 2006); D. Brown, "Measuring Human Capital Crucial, ROI Isn't, Says New Think-Tank Paper," *Canadian HR Reporter* (October 25, 2004), pp. 1, 4; J. Douglas and T. Emond, "Time to Pop the Question: Are Your Employees Engaged?" *WorldatWork Canadian News* (Third Quarter, 2003), pp. 12–14.

17. R. Baumruk, "The Missing Link: The Role of Employee Engagement in Business Success," *Workspan* (November 2004), pp. 48–52; N. Winter, "Tuned In and Turned On," *Workspan* (April 2003), pp. 48–52.

18. D.S. Cohen, "Behaviour-Based Interviewing," *Human Resources Professional* (April/May 1997), p. 29.

19. *CCHRA Awareness Study* (Toronto, ON: CCHRA and Ekos Research Associates, 2008).

20. B.E. Becker, M.A. Huselid, and D. Ulrich, *The HR Scorecard: Linking People, Strategy and Performance* (Boston, MA: Harvard Business School Press, 2001); D. Brown, "Measuring the Value of HR," *Canadian HR Reporter* (September 24, 2001), pp. 1, 5. See also E. Beaudan, "The Failure of Strategy: It's All in the Execution, *Ivey Business Journal* (January/February 2001).

21. A. Aijala, B. Walsh, and J. Schwartz, *Aligned at the Top: How Business and HR Executives View Today's Most Significant People Challenges—And What They're Doing About It.* Deloitte Development LLC, 2007.

22. *Canada's Demographic Revolution: Adjusting to an Aging Population* (Ottawa, ON: The Conference Board of Canada, March 2006).

23. O. Parker, *The Strategic Value of People: Human Resource Trends and Metrics* (Ottawa, ON: The Conference Board of Canada, July 2006).

24. R. Kaplan and D. Norton, *The Strategy-Focused Organization: How Balanced Scorecard Companies Thrive in the New Business Environment* (Boston, MA: Harvard Business School Press, 1996); S. Mooraj, D. Oyon, and D. Hostettler, "The Balanced Scorecard: A Necessary Good or an Unnecessary Evil?" *European Management Journal* 17, no. 5 (October 1999), pp. 481–491; B. Becker, M. Huselid, and D. Ulrich, *The HR Scorecard: Linking People, Strategy and Performance* (Boston, MA: Harvard Business School Press, 2001); M. Huselid, B. Becker, and R. Beatty, *The Workforce Scorecard: Managing Human Capital to Execute Strategy* (Boston, MA: Harvard Business School Press, 2006).

25. G. Ferris, D. Frink, and M.C. Galang, "Diversity in the Workplace: The Human Resources Management Challenge," *Human Resource Planning* 16, no. 1 (1993), p. 42.

26. "Study: Canada's Visible Minority Population in 2017," *The Daily*, Statistics Canada (March 2005); *Canada's Ethnocultural Portrait: The Changing Mosaic*, Statistics Canada, Catalogue No. 96 F0030 XIE 2001 0082004.

27. Statistics Canada, "Wives as Primary Breadwinners," *Perspectives* (August 2006), p. 3, Catalogue # 75-001-XIE; Statistics Canada, "Labour Force Characteristics by Age and Sex," CANSIM Table 282-0087, www.statcan,gc,ca/subjects-sujets/labour-travail/lfs-epa/t090710al-eng.htm (accessed July 31, 2009).

28. M. Hutchinson, "Aboriginal Workforce Poised to Replace Retiring Baby Boomers," http://www.aboriginalhr.ca/en/programs/MAI/Business_case (August 17, 2006).

29. C. Williams, "Disability in the Workplace," *Perspectives on Labour and Income* 18, no. 1 (February 2006), pp. 16–24.

30. S.P. Eisner, "Managing Generation Y," *S.A.M. Advanced Management Journal,* 70, no. 4 (2005), pp. 4–15; "Canadians Plan to Work Past Traditional Retirement Age, Survey Finds," www.worldatwork.org/waw/

adimComment?id=3085&printable (March 11, 2009); "More Than Half of Canadians Plan to Work in Retirement," *Canadian HR Reporter* (January 8, 2007).

31. S. Dobson, "Age-Free Culture Goal of Top Employers," *Canadian HR Reporter* (January 12, 2009).

32. A. Belanger, L. Martel, and E. Caron-Malenfant, *Population Projections for Canada, Provinces and Territories: 2005–2031*, Statistics Canada, Catalogue No. 91-520-XIE (December 2005), pp. 16–17; *Canada's Demographic Revolution: Adjusting to an Aging Population* (Ottawa, ON: The Conference Board of Canada, March 2006).

33. Based on material cited in "News and Views: Flex Appeal," compiled by M. Griffin, *HR Professional* (February/March 1999), p. 10; research reported by P.L. Nyhof in "Managing Generation X: The Millennial Challenge," *Canadian HR Reporter* (May 22, 2000), pp. 7–8; R. Berry, "Observations on Generational Diversity," *Profiles in Diversity Journal* 4, no. 3 (2002).

34. A. Glass, "Understanding Generational Differences for Competitive Success," *Industrial and Commercial Training,* 39, no. 2 (2007), pp. 98–103.

35. Jean-Philippe Naud, "Generation Y at Work," *WorldatWork Canadian News* (Second Quarter, 2005), pp. 6–8; D. Piktialis, "The Generational Divide in Talent Management," *Workspan* (March 2006), pp. 10–12; G. Kovary and A. Buahene, "Recruiting the Four Generations," *Canadian HR Reporter* (May 23, 2005), p. R6.

36. *Managing Tomorrow's People: The Future of Work to 2020.* (London UK: PricewaterhouseCoopers, 2007).

37. Statistics Canada, *Labour Force Historical Review*, Catalogue No.71F0004XCB, 2007.

38. A. Campbell and N. Gagnon, *Literacy, Life and Employment: An Analysis of Canadian International Adult Literacy Survey (IALS) Microdata* (Ottawa, ON: Conference Board of Canada, January 2006).

39. P. Bleyer, "Let's Make Productivity Work for Canadians," Canadian Council on Social Development, 2005, www.ccsd.ca/pr/2005/ccsd_prebudget.htm (accessed January 6, 2007).

40. J. Bernier, *The Scope of Federal Labour Standards and Nontraditional Work Situations* (Submission to the Federal Labour Standards Review, October 2005), pp. 5–13.

41. M. Townson, *Women in Non-Standard Jobs: The Public Policy Challenge* (Ottawa, ON: Status of Women Canada, 2003); M. Townson, "The Impact of Precarious Employment," in L.O. Stone (ed.), *New Frontiers of Research on Retirement,* Statistics Canada, Catalogue No. 75-511-XIE, 2006, pp. 355–382; R.P. Chaykowski, *Non-standard Work and Economic Vulnerability*, Canadian Policy Research Network, Vulnerable Workers Series, No. 3 (March 2005); G. Valeé, *Towards Enhancing the Employment Conditions of Vulnerable Workers: A Public Policy Perspective,* Canadian Policy Research Network, Vulnerable Workers Series, No. 2 (March 2005).

42. M. Vartiainen, M. Hakonen, S. Koivisto, P. Mannonen, M. P. Nieminen, V. Ruohomaki, and A. Vartola, *Distributed and Mobile: Places, People and Technology* (Helsinki Finland: Oy Yliopistokustannus University Press, 2007), p. 75.

43. C. Clark, "The World Is Flat: Work-Life Trends to Watch," *Workspan* (January 2009), pp. 17–19.

44. K. Williams, "Privacy in a Climate of Electronic Surveillance," *Workplace News* (April 2005), p. 10.

45. P. Benimadhu, "Startling Business Shifts Causing a Rethink of Work," *InsideEdge* (Summer 2008), p. 10.

46. "Multinational Corporation," http://en.wikipedia.org/wiki/Multinational_corporation (accessed August 17, 2006).

47. S. Nolen, "Step 1: Keep Workers Alive," *Globe and Mail* (August 5, 2006), pp. B4–B5.

48. U. Vu, "Climate Change Sparks Attitude Shift," *Canadian HR Reporter* (March 26, 2007), p. 11.

49. S. Dobson, "Fairmont Finds It's Easy Being Green," *Canadian HR Reporter* (March 26, 2007).

50. R. Stringer, *Leadership and Organizational Climate* (Upper Saddle River, NJ: Prentice-Hall, 2002).

51. This section is based on www.cchra.ca.

52. C. Balthazard, "The Difference between a Professional Association and a Regulatory Body," *Canadian HR Reporter* (August 11, 2008); C. Balthazard, "Regulatory Agenda at HRPA," *Canadian HR Reporter* (November 3, 2008).

53. This section is based on www.cchra.ca.

54. S. Klie, "Senior HR Designation Unveiled," *Canadian HR Reporter* (July 7, 2009).

Chapter 2

1. S. Dobson, "Business Acumen Critical for HR: Survey," *Canadian HR Reporter* (May 9, 2011).

2. P. Verge and G. Vallee, "Un droit du travail? Essai sur la spicifite du droit du travail," Editions Yvon Blais, Cowansville, (1997).

3. J. Sack, "U.S. and Canadian Labour Law: Significant Distinctions", *ABA Journal of Labor & Employment Law*, 25, no. 2 (2010), pp. 241–259.

4. Canadian Charter of Rights and Freedoms, as part of the Constitution Act of 1982.

5. Canadian Charter of Rights and Freedoms, Section 15(1).

6. *Annual Report of the Canadian Human Rights Commission* (Ottawa, ON: Government of Canada, 1991), p. 65.

7. A.P. Aggarwal, *Sex Discrimination: Employment Law and Practices* (Toronto, ON: Butterworths Canada, 1994).

8. H.J. Jain, "Human Rights: Issues in Employment," *Human Resources Management in Canada* (Toronto, ON: Prentice-Hall Canada, 1995), p. 50.

9. Ontario Human Rights Commission, *Human Rights at Work* (Toronto, ON: Government of Ontario, 1999), pp. 63–64.

10. S. Rudner, "Just Cause—Back from the Dead?" *Canadian HR Reporter* (September 22, 2008); M. Bélanger and R. Ravary, "Supreme Court of Canada Sets Limits on Employer's Duty to Accommodate," *McCarthy Tétrault e-Alert* (July 24, 2008); D. Elenbaas, "Undue Hardship: Supreme Court of Canada Clarifies the Standard—or Does it?" *Ultimate HR Manual*, 39 (August 2008), pp. 1–3.

11. According to Raj Anand, partner with WeirFoulds LLP and former chief commissioner of the Ontario Human Rights Commission. Presentation on "Equity, Diversity and Accommodation" at Osgoode Hall Law School, April 7, 2011.

12. "Policy and Guidelines on Disability and the Duty to Accommodate," Ontario Human Rights Commission (December, 2009), www.ohrc.on.ca/en/resources/Policies/PolicyDisAccom2/pdf (accessed September 26, 2011).

13. British Columbia (Public Service Employee Relations Commission) v. BCGSEU, [1999] 3 S.C.R. 3 at para. 68.

14. According to the US National Library of Medicine, www.ncbi.nlm.nih.gov/pubmedhealth/PMH0001295.

15. "Disability and the Duty to Accommodate: Your Rights and Responsibilities," Ontario Human Rights Commission, www.ohrc.on.ca/en/issues/disability (accessed November 23, 2011).

16. J.R. Smith, "Bipolar Employee Awarded $80,000" *Canadian HR Reporter* (April 7, 2008); C. Hall, "Just Because You Can't See Them Doesn't Mean They're Not There: 'Invisible Disabilities,'" *Ultimate HR Manual*, 34 (March 2008), pp. 1–3; "Duty to Accommodate Mental Health Disability Upheld in Landmark Ontario Human Rights Decision," *Ultimate HR Manual*, 33 (February 2008), p. 6.

17. According to the Supreme Court Ruling by Brian Dickson Chief Justice of Canadia, Janzen v. Platy Enterprises Ltd., 1989.

18. S. Klie, "Harassment Twice as Bad for Minority Women," *Canadian HR Reporter* (April 10, 2006).

19. S. Dobson, "Tackling the Bullies," *Canadian HR Reporter* (March 9, 2009).

20. B. Kuretzky, "When Push Comes to Shove," *Workplace News* (November/December 2005), p. 22; U. Vu, "Employers Waiting for Courts to Define Bullying," *Canadian HR Reporter* (September 12, 2005), pp. 1, 13.

21. "Saskatchewan's Anti-Bullying Law Now in Effect," *Canadian HR Reporter* (October 4, 2007); S. Rudner, "Psychological Harassment Hurts Employees, Productivity," *Canadian HR Reporter* (October 21, 2007).

22. J.R. Smith, "Employers: Don't Let Workplace Harassment Catch You Off Guard," *Canadian HR Reporter* (October 22, 2007); *Anti-Harassment Policies for the Workplace: An Employer's Guide* (Canadian Human Rights Commission, March 2006), p. 3.

23. J.R. Smith, "Employer's Damage Control Leads to Big-Time Damages," *Canadian HR Reporter* (June 1, 2009); "Employer Vicariously Liable for Supervisor's Abusive Conduct," *Ultimate HR Manual*, 49 (June 2009), p. 7.

24. A.P. Aggarwal, *Sexual Harassment in the Workplace*, 2nd ed. (Toronto, ON: Butterworths Canada, 1992), pp. 10–11.

25. N.C. MacDonald, "Keeping the Bedroom out of the Boardroom," *Canadian HR Reporter* (October 22, 2007).

26. *Anti-Harassment Policies for the Workplace: An Employer's Guide* (Canadian Human Rights Commission, March 2006), pp. 16–25.

27. "Construction Firms Fight B.C. Human Rights Ruling," *HR Professional* (April/May 2009), p. 13.

28. S. Klie, "Muslims Face Discrimination in Workplace," *Canadian HR Reporter* (February 27, 2006).

29. "Key Provisions of Ottawa's Same-Sex Legislation," *Canadian HR Reporter* (March 27, 2000), p. 11.

30. Canadian Human Rights Commission, www.chrc-ccdp.ca/adr/settlements/archives2/page5-en.asp (accessed August 13, 2006).

31. Canadian Human Rights Commission, www.chrc-ccdp.ca/discrimination/age-en.asp (accessed August 13, 2006).

32. Ontario Human Rights Commission, www.ohrc.on.ca/english/publicatoins/age-policy_5.shtml (accessed June 2, 2006).

33. H. Levitt and L-K Hum, "Accommodating Family Status," *Canadian HR Reporter* (January 12, 2009).

34. L. Corrente, "Accommodating Family Status," Torkin Maines Presentation (June 8, 2005).

35. R.S. Abella, *Equality in Employment: A Royal Commission Report* (Ottawa, ON: Supply and Services Canada, 1984).

36. A.B. Bakan and A. Kobyashi, *Employment Equity Policy in Canada: An Interprovincial Comparison* (Ottawa, ON: Status of Women Canada, March 2000), pp. 9–10.

37. *Women in Canada: Work Chapter Updates*, Statistics Canada, Catalogue No. 89F0133XIE, 2006.

38. S. Klie, "Feds Discriminated Against Nurses," *Canadian HR Reporter* (February 25, 2008).

39. K.A. Zavitz, "Intolerance Costly Problem for Employers," *Canadian HR Reporter* (December 15, 2008).

40. C. Williams, "Disability in the Workplace," *Perspectives on Labour and Income* 7, no. 2 (February 2006), pp. 16–23.

41. "2006 Census: Ethnic Origin, Visible Minorities, Place of Work and Mode of Transportation," Statistics Canada (April 2, 2008), www.statcan.gc.ca/daily-quotidien/080402/dq080402a-eng.htm (accessed September 26, 2011).

42. W. Cukier and M. Yap, *DiverseCity Counts: A Snapshot of Diversity in the Greater Toronto Area.* (Toronto, ON: The Diversity Institute, Ryerson University, May 2009).

43. P. Israel, "Employee Misconduct . . . Employer Responsibility?" *Canadian HR Reporter* (May 20, 2002), p. 5.

44. P. Israel, "Spying on Employees . . . and It's Perfectly Legal," *Canadian HR Reporter* (April 21, 2003), p. 5.

45. M. Draaisma, "Computer Use Policy in Workplace Is a Must, Says Toronto Lawyer," *Ultimate HR Manual* (May 2009), pp. 1–4.

46. A.P. Cleek, "Six Steps to an Effective Workplace Blogging Policy," *Ultimate HR Manual* (August 2007), pp. 6–7.

47. E. Kuzz, "More Rules for Employee Information Protection," *Canadian HR Reporter* (September 9, 2002), p. 16; D. Brown, "10 Months to Get Ready," *Canadian HR Reporter* (February 24, 2003), pp. 1, 11.

48. D. Fallows, "Technology Paves the Way for Big Brother," *Canadian HR Reporter* (April 9, 2007).

49. M. Draaisma, "Computer Use Policy in Workplace Is a Must, Says Toronto Lawyer," *Ultimate HR Manual* (May 2009), pp. 1–4; S. Rudner, "The High Cost of Internet, E-mail Abuse," *Canadian HR Reporter* (January 31, 2005), pp. R5–R6; N. MacDonald, "You've Got E-mail Problems," *Canadian HR Reporter* (March 10, 2003), pp. G5, G10.

50. K. Williams, "Privacy in a Climate of Electronic Surveillance," *Workplace News* (April 2005), p. 10; S. Hood, "What's Private, What's Not?" *HR Professional* (February/March 2006), pp. 20–28; P. Strazynski, "Falsely Accused Employee Gets $2.1 Million," *Canadian HR Reporter* (July 14, 2008).

Chapter 3

1. "Companies Continue to Invest in HR Technology to Manage Workforce, Towers Perrin Reports." www.hrtools.com/training_performance/companies_continue_to_invest_in_hr_technology_to_manage_workforce_towers_perrin_reports.aspx (accessed August 26, 2008); Towers Perrin, www.towersperrin.com (accessed August 20, 2008).

2. S. Shrivastava and J.B. Shaw, "Liberating HR through Technology," *Human Resource Management* (Fall 2003), p. 201.

3. W.J. Jones and R.C. Hoell, "Human Resource Information System Courses: An Examination of Instructional Methods," *Journal of Information Systems Education* (Fall 2005), p. 321.

4. A.S. Targowski and S.P. Deshpande, "The Utility and Selection of an HRIS," *Advances in Competitiveness Research* (Autumn 2001), p. 42.

5. S. Shrivastava and J.B. Shaw, "Liberating HR through Technology," *Human Resource Management* (Fall 2003), p. 201.

6. R. Zampetti and L. Adamson, "Web-Based Employee Self-Service: A Win–Win Proposition for Organizations and Employees," in A.J. Walker (ed.), *Web-Based Human Resources* (New York, NY: McGraw-Hill, 2001), p. 15.

7. P. Vernon, "Delivering on the Promise of HR Transformation" (November 29, 2004), www.humanresourcesmagazine.com.au/articles/CB/0C0293CB.asp?Type=61&Category=872 (accessed August 20, 2009).

8. Ibid.

9. J. Schramm, "HR Technology Competencies: New Roles for HR Professionals," *2006 SHRM Research Quarterly*, p. 2.

10. P. Vernon, "Delivering on the Promise of HR Transformation" (November 29, 2004), www.humanresourcesmagazine.com.au/articles/CB/0C0293CB.asp?Type=61&Category=872 (accessed August 20, 2009).

11. J. Collison, "2005 HR Technology Survey Report," SHRM Research, p. vii.

12. "HRIS for the HRIS Professional: What You Need to Know," *HR Focus* (June 2005), pp. 10–11.

13. E.E. Lawler III, "From Human Resource Management to Operational Effectiveness," *Human Resource Management* (Summer 2005), pp. 165–169.

14. W. Brockbank, "If HR Were Really Strategically Proactive: Present and Future Directions in HR's Contribution to Competitive Advantage," *Human Resource Management* (Winter 1999), pp. 337–352.

15. "2008 HR Service Delivery Report." www.towersperrin.com/tp/getwebcachedoc?web=USA/2008/200810/HRSDExecutiveReport2008.pdf (accessed September 2008).

16. S. Shrivastava and J.B. Shaw, "Liberating HR through Technology," *Human Resource Management* (Fall 2003), p. 201.

17. J. Johnston, "What Does It Take to Put in an HRMS?" *Canadian HR Reporter* (October 22, 2001), p. G3.

18. A. Doran, "HRMS in the New Millennium: What Will the Next 10 years Bring Us and What Is the International Perspective?" in *21 Tomorrows New Formula: Concept-Driven Innovation through Strategic HR* (2000), pp. 29–35.

19. W.J. Jones and R.C. Hoell, "Human Resource Information System Courses: An Examination of Instructional Methods," *Journal of Information Systems Education* (Fall 2005), pp. 321–329

20. A.R. Hendrickson, "Human Resource Information Systems: Backbone Technology of Contemporary Human Resources," *Journal of Labor Research* (Summer 2003), p. 381.

21. M.J. Kavanaugh and M. Thite, *Human Resource Information Systems* (Thousand Oaks, CA: Sage Publications, 2009).

22. Ibid.

23. E.W.T. Ngai and F.K.T. Wat, "Human Resource Information Systems: A Review and Empirical Analysis," Department of Management and Marketing, The Hong Kong Polytechnic University (July 7, 2004), p. 297.

24. R. Zampetti and L. Adamson, "Web-Based Employee Self-Service: A Win–Win Proposition for Organizations and Employees," in A.J. Walker (ed.), *Web-Based Human Resources* (New York, NY: McGraw-Hill, 2001), p. 15.

25. M. Mayfield, "Human Resource Information Systems: A Review and Model Development," *Advances in Competitiveness Research* (January 1, 2003), pp. 139–152.

26. A.R. Hendrickson, "Human Resource Information Systems: Backbone Technology of Contemporary Human Resources," *Journal of Labor Research* (Summer 2003), p. 381.

27. A.S. Targowski and S.P. Deshpande, "The Utility and Selection of an HRIS," *Advances in Competitiveness Research* (Autumn 2001), p. 42.

28. M.J. Kavanaugh and M. Thite, *Human Resource Information Systems* (California: Sage Publications, 2009).

29. M. Mayfield, "Human Resource Information Systems: A Review and Model Development," *Advances in Competitiveness Research* (January 1, 2003), pp. 139–152.

30. Human Resources and Social Development Canada, "Employment Equity Computerized Reporting System (EECRS) Software," www.hrsdc.gc.ca/asp/gateway.asp?hr=en/lp/lo/lswe/we/ee_tools/software/eecrs/index-we.shtml&hs—wzp (accessed August 17, 2006).

31. J. Sullivan, "The Six Levels of HRIS Technology," in R.H. Stambaugh (ed.), *21 Tomorrows: HR Systems in the Emerging Workplace of the 21st Century* (Dallas, TX: Rector Duncan & Associates, 2000), pp. 79–86.

32. W.J. Jones and R.C. Hoell, "Human Resource Information System Courses: An Examination of Instructional Methods," *Journal of Information Systems Education* (Fall 2005), p. 326.

33. J.W. Boudreau, "Talentship and HR Measurement and Analysis: From ROI to Strategic Organizational Change," *Human Resource Planning* (2006), p. 30.

34. G. Safran, "Getting the I out of your HRIS," *Canadian HR Reporter* (February 26, 2001), p. 21.

35. J. Schramm, "HR Technology Competencies: New Roles for HR Professionals," *2006 SHRM Research Quarterly*, (2006) p. 2.

36. J. Johnston, "What Does It Take to Put in an HRMS?" *Canadian HR Reporter* (October 22, 2001), p. G3.

37. S. Shrivastava and J.B. Shaw, "Liberating HR through Technology," *Human Resource Management* (Fall 2003), pp. 201–215.

38. A.R. Hendrickson, "Human Resource Information Systems: Backbone Technology of Contemporary Human Resources," *Journal of Labor Research* (Summer 2003), p. 381.

39. J.G. Meade, *The Human Resources Software Handbook* (San Francisco, CA: Jossey-Bass/Pfeiffer, 2003). p. 85.

40. "Bridgefield Group ERP/Supply Chain Glossary," http://bridgefieldgroup.com/bridgefieldgroup/glos2.htm (accessed June 29, 2006).

41. A.R. Hendrickson, "Human Resource Information Systems: Backbone Technology of Contemporary Human Resources," *Journal of Labor Research* (Summer 2003), p. 381–394; J.G. Meade, *The Human Resources Software Handbook* (San Francisco, CA: Jossey-Bass/Pfeiffer, 2003). p. 85.

42. SAP AG, www.en.wikipedia.org/wiki/SAP_(company) (accessed June 17, 2006); SAP Canada, www.sap.com (accessed January 8, 2007).

43. PeopleSoft, http://en.wikipedia.org/ciki/PeopleSoft (accessed June 17, 2006); Oracle, www.oracle.com (accessed June 17, 2006).

44. V. Gerson, "CIBC Taps PeopleSoft HR System," *Bank Systems + Technology* (February 2002), p. 16.

45. Halogen Software, www.halogensoftware.com (accessed June 29, 2006).

46. S. Shrivastava and J.B. Shaw, "Liberating HR through Technology," *Human Resource Management* (Fall 2003), pp. 201–215; J.G. Meade, *The Human Resources Software Handbook* (San Francisco, CA: Jossey-Bass/Pfeiffer, 2003), p. 85.

47. J.G. Meade, *The Human Resources Software Handbook* (San Francisco, CA: Jossey-Bass/Pfeiffer, 2003), p. 85.

48. J.C. Hubbard, K.A. Forcht, and D.S. Thomas, "Human Resource Information Systems: An Overview of Current Ethical and Legal Issues," *Journal of Business Ethics* (September 1998), pp. 1320–1321.

49. K.A. Kovach, A.A. Hughes, P. Fagan, and P.G. Maggitti, "Administrative and Strategic Advantages of HRIS," *Employment Relations Today* (Summer 2002), p. 46.

50. J. Caplan, "eHR in Greater China: The Future of HR Takes Flight," *China Staff* (March 2004), p. 3.

51. B. Jorgensen, "eHR Is Playing a Larger Role in Corporate Communications, but Companies Must Make a Business for Additional Spending," *Electronic Business* (August 2002), p. 36.

52. "Which HRIS Technologies Best Support the Vital Workplace?" *HR Focus* (February 2000), p. 6.

53. "Glossary of Distance Education Terms," www.tamu.edu/ode/glossary.html (accessed January 8, 2007).

54. G. Downey, "Use of Self-Service HR Skyrockets," *Computing Canada* (February 1, 2002), pp. 1–2.

55. R. Zampetti and L. Adamson, "Web-Based Employee Self-Service: A Win–Win Proposition for Organizations and Employees," in A.J. Walker (ed.), *Web-Based Human Resources.* (New York, NY: McGraw-Hill, 2001), p. 15; H.C. Gueutal and D.L. Stone, *The Brave New World of eHR* (San Francisco, CA: Jossey-Bass, 2005), p. 192.

56. R. Zampetti and L. Adamson, "Web-Based Employee Self-Service: A Win–Win Proposition for Organizations and Employees," in A.J. Walker (ed.), *Web-Based Human Resources* (New York, NY: McGraw-Hill, 2001), p. 15.

57. "Do More to Get More from HR Systems," *HR Focus* (June 2006), p. 3.

58. P. MacInnis, "Toronto Police Services Ramps Up for Self-Serve HR," *Computing Canada* (October 11, 2002), p. 10.

59. D. Robb, "Unifying Your Enterprise with a Global HR Portal," *HRMagazine* (March 2006), p. 110.

60. "Do More to Get More from HR Systems," *HR Focus* (June 2006), p. 3.

61. Ibid.

62. Industry Canada, "Strategis: Canada's Business and Consumer Site," http://strategis.ic.gc.ca (accessed January 8, 2007).

63. 2008 HR Service Delivery Report, www.towersperrin.com/tp/getwebcachedoc?web=USA/2008/200810/HRSDExecutiveReport2008.pdf (accessed September 2008).

64. J.G. Meade, *The Human Resources Software Handbook* (San Francisco, CA: Jossey-Bass/Pfeiffer, 2003), p. 85.

65. "What's New," *HRMagazine* (January 2005), p. 107.

66. ExecuTRACK Solutions, www.executrack.com (accessed June 29, 2006).

67. Organizational Charts by Human Concepts, www.orgplus.com (accessed June 29, 2006).

68. "Companies Aim to Transform HR Delivery Strategy to Meet New Employee Needs, Watson Wyatt Study Finds," www.watsonwyatt.com/news/press.asp?ID=17525 (accessed August 20, 2009).

69. T.J. Keebler and D.W. Rhodes, "E-HR Becoming the 'Path of Least Resistance,'" *Employment Relations Today* (Summer 2002), pp. 57–58.

70. D. Brown, "eHR—Victim of Unrealistic Expectations," *Canadian HR Reporter* (March 11, 2002), p. 2.

71. J. Collison, "2005 HR Technology Survey Report," *SHRM Research*, pp. 3–4.

72. S. Shrivastava and J.B. Shaw, "Liberating HR through Technology," *Human Resource Management* (Fall 2003), p. 205

73. J. Sullivan, "The Six Levels of HRIS Technology," in R.H. Stambaugh (ed.), *21 Tomorrows: HR Systems in the Emerging Workplace of the 21st Century* (Dallas, TX: Rector Duncan & Associates, 2000), pp. 79–86.

74. National Center for Education Statistics, US Department of Education, Institute of Education Sciences, Technology @ Your Fingertips Glossary. http://nces.ed.gov/pubs98/tech/glossary.asp (accessed June 29, 2006).

75. J. Sullivan, "The Six Levels of HRIS Technology," in R.H. Stambaugh (ed.), *21 Tomorrows: HR Systems in the Emerging Workplace of the 21st Century* (Dallas, TX: Rector Duncan & Associates, 2000), pp. 79–86.

76. R. Henson, "HR 20/20: Clarifying the View of HR in Year 2020," in R.H. Stambaugh (ed.), *21 Tomorrows: HR Systems in the Emerging Workplace of the 21st Century* (Dallas, TX: Rector Duncan & Associates, 2000), pp. 11–16.

77. Hackett Group, *World-Class HR Metrics: World-Class Spend Less Yet Achieve Higher effectiveness* (accessed July 25, 2006).

78. R. Zampetti and L. Adamson, "Web-Based Employee Self-Service: A Win–Win Proposition for Organizations and Employees," in A. J. Walker (ed.), *Web-Based Human Resources* (New York, NY: McGraw-Hill, 2001), p. 15.

79. "HRIS in 2010 (or Sooner!): Experts Predict Use of Wrist Mounted Devices, Virtual HR Access, and HR Voice Recognition," *Managing HR Information Systems* (February 2002), pp. 1–4.

80. "Companies Aim to Transform HR Delivery Strategy to Meet New Employee Needs, Watson Wyatt Study Finds," www.watsonwyatt.com/news/press.asp?ID=17525 (accessed August 20, 2009).

81. J. Sullivan, Ph.D., "The Six Levels of HRIS Technology," in R.H. Stambaugh (ed.), *21 Tomorrows: HR Systems in the Emerging Workplace of the 21st Century* (Dallas, TX: Rector Duncan & Associates, 2000), pp. 79–86.

82. L.A. Weatherly, "HR Technology: Leveraging the Shift to Self-Service—It's Time to Go Strategic," *HRMagazine* (March 2005), p. A1.

83. "Human Resource Outsourcing Gains Traction, Says Aberdeen Group: Report Cites Growing Use of Outsourcing," *Business Wire* (January 23, 2006), p. 1.

Chapter 4

1. R. I. Henderson (ed.), *Compensation Management in a Knowledge-Based World* (Upper Saddle River, NJ: Prentice-Hall, 2003), pp. 135–138.; See also P.W. Wright and K. Wesley, "How to Choose the Kind of Job Analysis You Really Need," *Personnel*, 62 (May 1985), pp. 51–55; C.J. Cranny and M.E. Doherty, "Importance Ratings in Job Analysis: Note on the Misinterpretation of Factor Analyses," *Journal of Applied Psychology* (May 1988), pp. 320–322.

2. J. Heerwagen, K. Kelly, and K. Kampschroer, "The Changing Nature of Organizations, Work, and Workplace," *Whole Building Design Group (WBDG), National Institute of Building Sciences* (February 2006).

3. C. Babbage, *On the Economy of Machinery and Manufacturers* (London: Charles Knight, 1832), pp. 169–176; reprinted In Joseph Litterer, *Organizations* (New York: John Wiley and Sons, 1969), pp. 73–75.

4. F. Herzberg, "One More Time, How Do You Motivate Employees?" *Harvard Business Review*, 46 (January–February 1968), pp. 53–62.

5. Next two sections based on Jeffrey Shippmann et al., "The Practice of Competency Modeling," *Personnel Psychology,* 53, no. 3 (2000), p. 703;

P. Singh, "Job Analysis for a Changing Workplace," *Human Resource Management Review*, 18 (2008), pp. 87–99.

6. Adapted from Richard Mirabile, "Everything You Wanted to Know About Competency Modeling," *Training and Development,* 51, no. 8 (August 1997), pp. 73–78.

7. Dennis Kravetz, "Building a Job Competency Database: What the Leaders Do," Kravetz Associates (Bartlett, Illinois, 1997).

8. G.M. Parker, *Cross-Functional Teams: Working with Allies, Enemies and Other Strangers* (San Francisco: Jossey-Bass, 2003), p. 68.

9. "Collaboration for Virtual Teams," *HR Professional* (December 2002/January 2003), p. 44.

10. Note that the PAQ (and other quantitative techniques) can also be used for job evaluation.

11. E. Cornelius III, F. Schmidt, and T. Carron, "Job Classification Approaches and the Implementation of Validity Generalization Results," *Personnel Psychology,* 37 (Summer 1984), pp. 247–260; E. Cornelius III, A. DeNisi, and A. Blencoe, "Expert and Naïve Raters Using the PAQ: Does It Matter?" *Personnel Psychology,* 37 (Autumn 1984), pp. 453–464; L. Friedman and R. Harvey, "Can Raters with Reduced Job Description Information Provide Accurate Position Analysis Questionnaire (PAQ) Ratings?" *Personnel Psychology,* 34 (Winter 1986), pp. 779–789; R. J. Harvey et al., "Dimensionality of the Job Element Inventory: A Simplified Worker-Oriented Job Analysis Questionnaire," *Journal of Applied Psychology* (November 1988), pp. 639–646; S. Butler and R. Harvey, "A Comparison of Holistic versus Decomposed Rating of Position Analysis Questionnaire Work Dimensions," *Personnel Psychology* (Winter 1988), pp. 761–772.

12. This discussion is based on H. Olson et al., "The Use of Functional Job Analysis in Establishing Performance Standards for Heavy Equipment Operators," *Personnel Psychology,* 34 (Summer 1981), pp. 351–364.

13. Human Resources Development Canada, *National Occupation Classification Career Handbook*, (2006).

14. R. J. Plachy, "Writing Job Descriptions That Get Results," *Personnel* (October 1987), pp. 56–58. See also M. Mariani, "Replace with a Database," *Occupational Outlook Quarterly,* 43 (Spring 1999), pp. 2–9.

15. J. Evered, "How to Write a Good Job Description," *Supervisory Management* (April 1981), p. 16.

16. Ibid, p. 18.

17. P.H. Raymark, M.J. Schmidt, and R.M. Guion, "Identifying Potentially Useful Personality Constructs for Employee Selection," *Personnel Psychology* 50 (1997), pp. 723–726.

Chapter 5

1. *Performance and Potential 2000–2001: Seeking Made in Canada Solutions* (Ottawa, ON: Conference Board of Canada, 2000), p. 51.

2. HRSDC, Looking Ahead: A 10-Year Outlook for the Canadian Labour Market (2006–2015), Statistics Canada, January 29, 2007, www.hrsdc.gc.ca/eng/publications_resources/research/categories/labour_market_e/sp_615_10_06/supply.shtml (accessed September 26, 2011).

3. S. Klie, "Guesses Just Don't Cut It Anymore," *Canadian HR Reporter* (March 24, 2008).

4. This is a modification of a definition found in P. Wallum, "A Broader View of Succession Planning," *Personnel Management* (September 1993), pp. 43–44.

5. "Succession Planning for Family Business," BDO Canada (September 12, 2010), www.bdo.ca/library/publications/familybusiness/succession/planning1.cfm (accessed September 26, 2011).

6. HRSDC, Looking Ahead: A 10-Year Outlook for the Canadian Labour Market (2006–2015), Statistics Canada, (January 29, 2007), www.hrsdc.gc.ca/eng/publications_resources/research/categories/labour_market_e/sp_615_10_06/supply.shtml (accessed September 26, 2011).

7. A. Coughlin, *Alberta's Labour Shortage Just the Tip of the Iceberg* (Conference Board of Canada Executive Action, 2006); G. Hodgson and

G. McGowan, "Taking Sides: Is Alberta's Labour Shortage a Doomsday Scenario?" *Canadian HR Reporter* (July 17, 2006); P. Brethour, "Oil Patch Labour Crisis Seen Spreading to Rest of Country; "Husky Head Raises Alarm Over Rising Costs, Saying Projects at Risk," *Globe and Mail* (April 20, 2006), http://www.theglobeandmail.com/report-on-business/oil-patch-labour-crisis-seen-spreading-to-rest-of-country/article707140/ (accessed September 9, 2012).

8. "Mining Industry Needs 80,000 Workers," *Canadian HR Reporter* (March 26, 2007), p. 2; S. Klie, "Construction Demand Outpaces Labour Growth," *Canadian HR Reporter* (September 10, 2007); "Non-profits Facing Labour Shortage," *Canadian HR Reporter* (July 9, 2007); U. Vu, "Mounties Prepare For Recruiting Spree," *Canadian HR Reporter* (October 23, 2006); "Manufacturing Sector Labours to Address Human Resources Issues," Conference Board of Canada, *InsideEdge* (Spring 2008), p. 18; S. Klie, "Short Circuiting Labour Supply," *Canadian HR Reporter* (December 15, 2008).

9. *Canadian Perspectives on ICT Outsourcing and Offshoring* (Toronto ON: IDC, 2007); S. Klie, "IT Offshoring Growing," *Canadian HR Reporter* (October 22, 2007); L. Young, "IT University Enrolment Plunges," *Canadian HR Reporter* (December 3, 2007); S; Klie, "Price Tag of IT Shortage: $10 Billion Per Year," *Canadian HR Reporter* (February 11, 2008); S. Klie, "Women Could Solve IT Worker Shortage," *Canadian HR Reporter* (October 20, 2008).

10. H. Sokoloff, "Legal Exodus," *National Post* (March 17, 2005), p. FP3; "Baby Boomers an HR Problem for Funeral Services," *Canadian HR Reporter* (January 16, 2006), p. 2; "Today's Forecast: Meteorologist Shortage," *Canadian HR Reporter* (December 5, 2005), p. 2; "Engineers in Short Supply," *Canadian HR Reporter* (November 21, 2005), p. 2; S. Klie, "Fewer Accountants Is a Bad Thing—Really," *Canadian HR Reporter* (February 13, 2006), p. 3; "Alberta Labour Shortage Draining Civil Service," *Canadian HR Reporter* (January 30, 2006), p. 2.

11. A.L. Delbecq, A.H. Van DelVen, and D.H. Gustafson, *Group Techniques for Program Planning: A Guide to Nominal and Delphi Processes* (Glenview, IL: Scott Foresman, 1975).

12. G. Milkovich, A.J. Annoni, and T.A. Mahoney, "The Use of Delphi Procedures in Manpower Forecasting," *Management Science* (1972), pp. 381–388.

13. "Feds Help Employers Avoid Layoffs," *HR Professional* (June/July 2009), p. 12.

14. W.F. Cascio and C.E. Young, "Financial Consequences of Employment Change Decisions in Major U.S. Corporations: 1982–2000," in K.P. DeMeuse and M.L. Marks (eds.), *Resizing the Organization*, pp. 131–156 (San Francisco, CA: Jossey-Bass, 2003).

15. M. MacKillop, "Ballpark Justice," *Human Resources Professional* (September 1994), pp. 10–11.

Chapter 6

1. G. Bouchard, "Strong Employer Brand Can Tap Scarce Resource: Talent," *Canadian HR Reporter* (November 19, 2007), p. 10.

2. "Effective Recruiting Tied to Stronger Financial Performance," *WorldatWork Canadian News* (Fourth Quarter, 2005), pp. 18–19.

3. K. Peters, "Public Image Ltd.," *HR Professional* (December 2007/January 2008), pp. 24–30; S. Klie, "Getting Employees to Come to You," *Canadian HR Reporter* (November 19, 2007), pp. 9–10; S. Klie, "Tuning into TV's Recruitment Reach," *Canadian HR Reporter* (September 25, 2006).

4. G. Bouchard, "Strong Employer Brand Can Tap Scarce Resource: Talent," *Canadian HR Reporter* (November 19, 2007), p. 10.

5. K. Peters, "Public Image Ltd.," *HR Professional* (December 2007/January 2008), pp. 24–30; G. Bouchard, "Strong Employer Brand Can Tap Scarce Resource: Talent," *Canadian HR Reporter* (November 19, 2007), p. 10; M. Morra, "Best in Show," *Workplace News* (September/October 2006), pp. 17–21; M. Shuster, "Employment Branding: The Law of Attraction!" *Workplace* (January/February 2008), pp. 14–15.

6. M. Morra, "Best in Show," *Workplace News* (September/October 2006), pp. 17–21.

7. G. Bouchard, "Strong Employer Brand Can Tap Scarce Resource: Talent," *Canadian HR Reporter* (November 19, 2007), p. 10.

8. S. Klie, "Getting Employees to Come to You," *Canadian HR Reporter* (November 19, 2007), pp. 9–10; M. Shuster, "Employment Branding: The Law of Attraction!" *Workplace* (January/February 2008), pp. 14–15.

9. K. Peters, "Public Image Ltd.," *HR Professional* (December 2007/January 2008), pp. 24–30; S. Dobson, "The Little School Bus Company That Could," *Canadian HR Reporter* (April 23, 2007).

10. M. Shuster, "Employment Branding: The Law of Attraction!" *Workplace* (January/February 2008), pp. 14–15.

11. A. Watanabe, "From Brown to Green, What Colour Is Your Employment Brand?" *HR Professional* (February/March 2008), pp. 47–49.

12. M. Morra, "Best in Show," *Workplace News* (September/October 2006), pp. 17–21.

13. R. Milgram, "Getting the Most Out of Online Job Ads," *Canadian HR Reporter* (January 28, 2008).

14. K. Peters, "Public Image Ltd.," *HR Professional* (December 2007/January 2008), pp. 24–30; S. Klie, "Getting Employees to Come to You," *Canadian HR Reporter* (November 19, 2007), pp. 9–10.

15. S. Klie, "Getting Employees to Come to You," *Canadian HR Reporter* (November 19, 2007), pp. 9–10; M. Shuster, "Employment Branding: The Law of Attraction!" *Workplace* (January/February 2008), pp. 14–15.

16. "Recruitment Tops HR Areas Expecting 'Enormous Change,'" *Canadian HR Reporter* (December 6, 2004), p. G3; *Hewitt Associates Timely Topic Survey* (February 2004).

17. H.N. Chait, S.M. Carraher, and M.R. Buckley, "Measuring Service Orientation with Biodata," *Journal of Management Issues* (Spring 2000), pp. 109–120; V.M. Catano, S.F. Cronshaw, R.D. Hackett, L.L. Methot, and W.H. Weisner, *Recruitment and Selection in Canada*, 2nd ed. (Scarborough, ON: Nelson Thomson Learning, 2001), p. 307; J.E. Harvey-Cook and R.J. Taffler, "Biodata in Professional Entry-Level Selection: Statistical Scoring of Common-Format Applications," *Journal of Occupational and Organizational Psychology* (March 1, 2000), pp. 103–118; Y.Y. Chung, "The Validity of Biographical Inventories for the Selection of Salespeople," *International Journal of Management* (September 2001).

18. L. Petrecca, "With 3000 Job Applications a Day, Google Can Be Picky," *USA Today* (May 18, 2010), (accessed September 9, 2012). http://www.usatoday.com/money/workplace/2010-05-19-jobs19_VA_N.htm

19. D. Dahl and P. Pinto, "Job Posting, an Industry Survey," *Personnel Journal* (January 1977), pp. 40–41.

20. J. Daum, "Internal Promotion—Psychological Asset or Debit? A Study of the Effects of Leader Origin," *Organizational Behavior and Human Performance*, 13 (1975), pp. 404–413.

21. See, for example, A. Harris, "Hiring Middle Management: External Recruitment or Internal Promotion?" *Canadian HR Reporter* (April 10, 2000), pp. 8–10.

22. M. Sharma, "Welcome Back!" *HR Professional* (February/March 2006), pp. 38–40; E. Simon, "You're Leaving the Company? Well, Don't Be a Stranger," *Globe and Mail* (December 22, 2006), p. B16.

23. U. Vu, "Encana Builds Talent Pipeline into High School Classrooms," *Canadian HR Reporter* (April 11, 2005), p. 3.

24. Halifax Career Fair, www.halifaxcareerfairs.com (accessed May 31, 2009).

25. Career Edge, www.careeredge.ca (accessed May 31, 2009).

26. N. Laurie and M. Laurie, "No Holds Barred in Fight for Students to Fill Internship Programs," *Canadian HR Reporter* (January 17, 2000), pp. 15–16.

27. Human Resources Professionals Association of Ontario, www.hrpao.org (accessed June 25, 2003).

28. D. Hurl, "Letting the Armed Forces Train Your Managers," *Canadian HR Reporter* (December 3, 2001), pp. 8–9.

29. L. MacGillivray, "Cashing in on the Canadian Forces," *Workplace Today* (October 2001), pp. 40–41.

30. L. Blake, "Ready-Trained, Untapped Source of Skilled Talent—Courtesy Canadian Forces," *Workplace*, www.workplace-mag.com (accessed December 2, 2008).

31. U. Vu, "Security Failures Expose Résumés," *Canadian HR Reporter* (May 24, 2003); P. Lima, "Talent Shortage? That Was Yesterday. Online Recruiters Can Deliver More Candidates for Your Job Openings and Help You Find Keepers," *Profit: The Magazine for Canadian Entrepreneurs* (February/March 2002), pp. 65–66; "Online Job Boards," *Canadian HR Reporter* (February 11, 2002), pp. G11–G15.

32. U. Vu, "Security Failures Expose Résumés," *Canadian HR Reporter* (May 24, 2003).

33. S. Bury, "Face-Based Recruiting," *Workplace* (September/October 2008), pp. 19–21.

34. G. Stanton, "Recruiting Portals Take Centre Stage in Play for Talent," *Canadian HR Reporter* (September 25, 2000), pp. G1–G2.

35. A. da Luz, "Video Enhances Online Job Ads," *Canadian HR Reporter* (February 11, 2008).

36. D. Brown, "Canadian Government Job Boards Lag on Best Practices," *Canadian HR Reporter* (January 13, 2003), p. 2.

37. T. Martell, "Résumé Volumes Push Firms to Web," *ComputerWorld Canada* (April 7, 2000), p. 45.

38. A. Altass, "E-Cruiting: A Gen X Trend or Wave of the Future?" *HR Professional* (June–July 2000), p. 33.

39. "Corporate Spending Millions on Ineffective Web Recruiting Strategies," *Canadian HR Reporter* (September 25, 2000), p. G5.

40. A. Snell, "Best Practices for Web Site Recruiting," *Canadian HR Reporter* (February 26, 2001), pp. G7, G10.

41. D. Brown, "Who's Looking Online? Most Firms Don't Know," *Canadian HR Reporter* (August 13, 2001), pp. 2, 12; "Corporate Spending Millions on Ineffective Web Recruiting Strategies," *Canadian HR Reporter* (September 25, 2000), p. G5; A. Snell, "Best Practices for Web Site Recruiting," *Canadian HR Reporter* (February 26, 2001), pp. G7, G10.

42. Service Canada, Job Bank, http://jb-ge.hrdc-drhc.gc.ca (accessed May 31, 2009).

43. J.A. Parr, "7 Reasons Why Executive Searches Fail," *Canadian HR Reporter* (March 12, 2001), pp. 20, 23.

44. Association of Canadian Search, Employment and Staffing Services (ACSESS), www.acsess.org (accessed August 8, 2006).

45. Statistics Canada, *The Daily* (April 8, 2005); Association of Canadian Search, Employment and Staffing Services (ACSESS), "Media Kit: Media Fact Sheet," www.acsess.org/NEWS/factsheet.asp (accessed May 31, 2009).

46. A. Doran, "Technology Brings HR to Those Who Need It," *Canadian HR Reporter* (October 6, 1997), p. 8.

47. S. Bury, "Face-Based Recruiting," *Workplace* (September/October 2008), pp. 19–21.

48. D. Harder, "Recruiting in Age of Social Networking," *Canadian HR Reporter* (April 21, 2008).

49. L. Barrington and J. Shelp, "Looking for Employees in All the Right Places," *The Conference Board Executive Action Series* (December 2005).

50. A. Pell, *Recruiting and Selecting Personnel* (New York, NY: Regents, 1969), pp. 16–34.

51. T. Lende, "Workplaces Looking to Hire Part-Timers," *Canadian HR Reporter* (April 22, 2002), pp. 9, 11.

52. K. LeMessurier, "Temp Staffing Leaves a Permanent Mark," *Canadian HR Reporter* (February 10, 2003), pp. 3, 8.

53. A. Ryckman, "The 5 Keys to Getting Top Value from Contractors," *Canadian HR Reporter* (December 2, 2002), p. 25; S. Purba, "Contracting Works for Job Hunters," *Globe and Mail* (April 24, 2002).

54. "Flexible Staffing in the Aerospace Industry," *Airfinance Journal I Aircraft Economic Yearbook* (2001), pp. 14–17.

55. M. Potter, "A Golden Opportunity for Older Workers to Energize Firms," *Canadian HR Reporter* (April 25, 2005), p. 13.

56. L. Cassiani, "Looming Retirement Surge Takes on New Urgency," *Canadian HR Reporter* (May 21, 2001), pp. 1, 10.

57. O. Parker, *Too Few People, Too Little Time: The Employer Challenge of an Aging Workforce* (Ottawa, ON: The Conference Board of Canada Executive Action, July 2006).

58. K. Thorpe, *Harnessing the Power: Recruiting, Engaging, and Retaining Mature Workers.* (Ottawa, ON: Conference Board of Canada, 2008).

59. S.B. Hood, "Generational Diversity in the Workplace," *HR Professional* (June/July 2000), p. 20.

60. G. Kovary and A. Buahene, "Recruiting the Four Generations," *Canadian HR Reporter* (May 23, 2005), p. R6.

61. S. Klie, "Firm Asks Students: What Do You Want?" *Canadian HR Reporter* (May 5, 2008).

62. Inclusion Network, www.inclusionnetwork.ca (accessed May 31, 2009); Aboriginal Human Resource Council, http://aboriginalhr.ca (accessed May 31, 2009).

63. Society for Canadian Women in Science and Technology, www.harbour.sfu.ca/scwist/index_files/Page1897.htm (accessed May 31, 2009); C. Emerson, H. Matsui, and L. Michael, "Progress Slow for Women in Trades, Tech, Science," *Canadian HR Reporter* (February 14, 2005), p. 11.

64. WORKInk, www.workink.com (accessed May 31, 2009).

Chapter 7

1. D. Brown, "Waterloo Forced to Fire Top Bureaucrat Weeks After Hiring," *Canadian HR Reporter* (October 11, 2004), p. 3.

2. British Columbia Criminal Records Review Act, www.pssg.gov.bc.ca/criminal-records-review/index.htm (accessed May 31, 2009).

3. C. Kapel, "Giant Steps," *Human Resources Professional* (April 1993), pp. 13–16.

4. P. Lowry, "The Structured Interview: An Alternative to the Assessment Center?" *Public Personnel Management,* 23, no. 2 (Summer 1994), pp. 201–215.

5. Steps two and three are based on the Kepner-Tregoe Decision-Making Model.

6. S.A. Way and J.W. Thacker, "Selection Practices: Where Are Canadian Organizations?" *HR Professional* (October/November 1999), p. 34.

7. L.J. Katunich, "How to Avoid the Pitfalls of Psych Tests," *Workplace News Online* (July 2005), p. 5; *Testing and Assessment—FAQ/Finding Information About Psychological Tests,* APA Online, www.apa.org/science/faq-findtests.html (accessed August 1, 2006).

8. M. McDaniel et al., "The Validity of Employment Interviews: A Comprehensive Review and Meta-analysis," *Journal of Applied Psychology,* 79, no. 4 (1994).

9. "Hiring: Psychology and Employee Potential," *HR Professional* (August/September 2008), p. 16.

10. Ibid.

11. S. Bakker, "Psychometric Selection Assessments," *HR Professional* (April/May 2009), p. 21.

12. Canadian Psychological Association, *Guidelines for Educational and Psychological Testing,* www.cpa.ca/documents/PsyTest.html (accessed May 31, 2009).

13. R.M. Yerkes, "Psychological Examining in the U.S. Army: Memoirs of the National Academy of Sciences," Washington DC: U.S. Government Printing Office, Vol. 15 (1921).

14. F.L. Schmidt and J. Hunter, "General Mental Ability in the World of Work: Occupational Attainment and Job Performance," *Journal of Personality and Social Psychology,* 86, no. 1 (2004), 162–173.

15. M. Zeidner, I. G. Matthews, and R.D. Roberts, "Emotional Intelligence in the Workplace: A Critical Review" *Applied Psychology: An International Review*, 53, no.3 (2004), pp. 371–399

16. "Emotional Intelligence Testing," *HR Focus* (October 2001), pp. 8–9.

17. Results of meta-analyses in one recent study indicated that isometric strength tests were valid predictors of both supervisory ratings of physical performance and performance on work simulations. See B.R. Blakley, M. Quinones, M.S. Crawford, and I.A. Jago, "The Validity of Isometric Strength Tests," *Personnel Psychology*, 47 (1994), pp. 247–274.

18. C. Colacci, "Testing Helps You Decrease Disability Costs," *Canadian HR Reporter* (June 14, 1999), p. G4.

19. K. Gillin, "Reduce Employee Exposure to Injury with Pre-Employment Screening Tests," *Canadian HR Reporter* (February 28, 2000), p. 10.

20. This approach calls for construct validation, which, as was pointed out, is extremely difficult to demonstrate.

21. Myers-Briggs Type Indicator (MBTI) Assessment, www.cpp.com/products/mbti/index.asp (accessed May 31, 2009).

22. See, for example, D. Cellar et al., "Comparison of Factor Structures and Criterion Related Validity Coefficients for Two Measures of Personality Based on the Five-Factor Model," *Journal of Applied Psychology*, 81, no. 6 (1996), pp. 694–704; J. Salgado, "The Five Factor Model of Personality and Job Performance in the European Community," *Journal of Applied Psychology*, 82, no. 1 (1997), pp. 30–43.

23. M.R. Barrick and M.K. Mount, "The Big Five Personality Dimensions and Job Performance: A Meta-Analysis," *Personnel Psychology*, 44 (Spring 1991), pp. 1–26.

24. C. Robie, K. Tuzinski, and P. Bly, "A Survey of Assessor Beliefs and Practices Related to Faking," *Journal of Managerial Psychology* (October 2006), pp. 669–681.

25. C. Robie, "Effects of Perceived Selection Ratio on Personality Test Faking," *Social Behavior and Personality*, 34, no. 10 (2006), 1233–1244.

26. E. Silver and C. Bennett, "Modification of the Minnesota Clerical Test to Predict Performance on Video Display Terminals," *Journal of Applied Psychology*, 72, no. 1 (February 1987), pp. 153–155.

27. L. Siegel and I. Lane, *Personnel and Organizational Psychology* (Homewood, IL: Irwin, 1982), pp. 182–183.

28. J. Weekley and C. Jones, "Video-Based Situational Testing," *Personnel Psychology*, 50 (1997), p. 25.

29. Ibid, pp. 26–30.

30. D. Chan and N. Schmitt, "Situational Judgment and Job Performance," *Human Performance*, 15, no. 3 (2002), pp. 233–254.

31. S. Klie, "Screening Gets More Secure," *Canadian HR Reporter* (June 19, 2006).

32. Canadian Human Rights Commission, *Canadian Human Rights Commission Policy on Alcohol and Drug Testing* (June 2002).

33. M. McDaniel et al., "The Validity of Employment Interviews: A Comprehensive Review and Meta-Analysis," *Journal of Applied Psychology*, 79, no. 4 (1994), p. 599.

34. J.G. Goodale, *The Fine Art of Interviewing* (Englewood Cliffs, NJ: Prentice Hall Inc., 1982), p. 22; see also R.L. Decker, "The Employment Interview," *Personnel Administrator*, 26 (November 1981), pp. 71–73.

35. M. Campion, E. Pursell, and B. Brown, "Structured Interviewing: Raising the Psychometric Properties of the Employment Interview," *Personnel Psychology*, 41 (1988), pp. 25–42.

36. M. McDaniel et al., "The Validity of Employment Interviews: A Comprehensive Review and Meta-Analysis," *Journal of Applied Psychology*, 79, no. 4 (1994).

37. D.S. Chapman and P.M. Rowe, "The Impact of Video Conferencing Technology, Interview Structure, and Interviewer Gender on Interviewer Evaluations in the Employment Interview: A Field Experiment," *Journal of Occupational and Organizational Psychology*, 74 (September 2001), pp. 279–298.

38. M. McDaniel et al., "The Validity of Employment Interviews: A Comprehensive Review and Meta-Analysis," *Journal of Applied Psychology*, 79, no. 4 (1994), p. 601.

39. Ibid.

40. "Lights, Camera...Can I Have a Job?" *Globe and Mail* (March 2, 2007), p. C1; A. Pell, *Recruiting and Selecting Personnel* (New York, NY: Regents, 1969), p. 119.

41. J.G. Goodale, *The Fine Art of Interviewing* (Englewood Cliffs, NJ: Prentice Hall Inc., 1982), p. 26.

42. See R.D. Arvey and J.E. Campion, "The Employment Interview: A Summary and Review of Recent Research," *Personnel Psychology*, 35 (1982), pp. 281–322; M. Heilmann and L. Saruwatari, "When Beauty Is Beastly: The Effects of Appearance and Sex on Evaluation of Job Applicants for Managerial and Nonmanagerial Jobs," *Organizational Behavior and Human Performance*, 23 (June 1979), pp. 360–722; C. Marlowe, S. Schneider, and C. Nelson, "Gender and Attractiveness Biases in Hiring Decisions: Are More Experienced Managers Less Biased?" *Journal of Applied Psychology*, 81, no. 1 (1996), pp. 11–21; V. Galt, "Beauty Found Not Beastly in the Job Interview," *Globe and Mail* (April 15, 2002).

43. A. Pell, "Nine Interviewing Pitfalls," *Managers* (January 1994), p. 29; T. Dougherty, D. Turban, and J. Callender, "Confirming First Impressions in the Employment Interview: A Field Study of Interviewer Behavior," *Journal of Applied Psychology*, 79, no. 5 (1994), p. 663.

44. See A. Pell, "Nine Interviewing Pitfalls," *Managers* (January 1994), p. 29; P. Sarathi, "Making Selection Interviews Effective," *Management and Labor Studies*, 18, no. 1 (1993), pp. 5–7; J. Shetcliffe, "Who, and How, to Employ," *Insurance Brokers' Monthly* (December 2002), pp. 14–16.

45. G.J. Sears and P.M. Rowe, "A Personality-Based Similar-to-Me Effect in the Employment Interview: Conscientious, Affect-versus-Competence Mediated Interpretations, and the Role of Job Relevance," *Canadian Journal of Behavioural Sciences*, 35 (January 2003), p. 13.

46. This section is based on E.D. Pursell, M.A. Campion, and S.R. Gaylord, "Structured Interviewing: Avoiding Selection Problems," *Personnel Journal*, 59 (1980), pp. 907–912; G.P. Latham, L.M. Saari, E.D. Pursell, and M.A. Campion, "The Situational Interview," *Journal of Applied Psychology*, 65 (1980), pp. 422–427; see also M. Campion, E. Pursell, and B. Brown, "Structured Interviewing: Raising the Psychometric Properties of the Employment Interview," *Personnel Psychology*, 41 (1988), pp. 25–42; J.A. Weekley and J.A. Gier, "Reliability and Validity of the Situational Interview for a Sales Position," *Journal of Applied Psychology*, 72 (1987), pp. 484–487.

47. A. Pell, *Recruiting and Selecting Personnel* (New York, NY: Regents, 1969), pp. 103–115.

48. W.H. Wiesner and R.J. Oppenheimer, "Note-Taking in the Selection Interview: Its Effect upon Predictive Validity and Information Recall," *Proceedings of the Annual Conference Meeting. Administrative Sciences Association of Canada* (Personnel and Human Resources Division, 1991), pp. 97–106.

49. V. Tsang, "No More Excuses," *Canadian HR Reporter* (May 23, 2005); L.T. Cullen, "Getting Wise to Lies," *TIME* (May 1, 2006), p. 27.

50. Ibid.

51. L. Fischer, "Gatekeeper," *Workplace News* (August 2005), pp. 10–11.

52. "Background Checks," *HR Professional* (June/July 2008), p. 16.

53. T. Humber, "Recruitment Isn't Getting Any Easier," *Canadian HR Reporter* (May 23, 2005).

54. C. Hall and A. Miedema, "But I Thought You Checked?" *Canadian HR Reporter* (May 21, 2007).

55. R. Zupek, "Is Your Future Boss Researching You Online?" CareerBuilder.ca, www.careerbuilder.ca/blog/2008/10/09/cb-is-your-future-boss-researching-you-online (accessed May 24, 2009).

56. J.R. Smith, "Damaging Reference Survives Alberta Privacy Challenge," *Canadian HR Reporter* (January 28, 2008).

57. A.C. Elmslie, "Writing a Reference Letter—Right or Wrong?" *Ultimate HR Manual*, 44 (January 2009), pp. 1–3.

58. A. Moffat, "The Danger of Digging too Deep," *Canadian HR Reporter* (August 11, 2008); see also P. Israel, "Providing References to Employees: Should You or Shouldn't You?" *Canadian HR Reporter* (March 24, 2003), pp. 5–6; T. Humber, "Name, Rank and Serial Number," *Canadian HR Reporter* (May 19, 2003), pp. G1, G7.

59. J.A. Breaugh, "Realistic Job Previews: A Critical Appraisal and Future Research Directions," *Academy of Management Review*, 8, no. 4 (1983), pp. 612–619.

60. P. Buhler, "Managing in the '90s: Hiring the Right Person for the Job," *Supervision* (July 1992), pp. 21–23; S. Jackson, "Realistic Job Previews Help Screen Applicants and Reduce Turnover," *Canadian HR Reporter* (August 9, 1999), p. 10.

61. S. Jackson, "Realistic Job Previews Help Screen Applicants and Reduce Turnover," *Canadian HR Reporter* (August 9, 1999), p. 10.

62. B. Kleinmutz, "Why We Still Use Our Heads Instead of Formulas: Toward an Integrative Approach," *Psychological Bulletin*, 107 (1990), pp. 296–310.

Chapter 8

1. M. Akdere and S. Schmidt, "Measuring the Effects of Employee Orientation Training on Employee Perception," *The Business Review* (Summer 2007), pp. 322–327.

2. B.W. Pascal, "The Orientation Wars," *Workplace Today* (October 2001), p. 4.

3. B. Pomfret, "Sound Employee Orientation Program Boosts Productivity and Safety," *Canadian HR Reporter* (January 25, 1999), pp. 17–19.

4. L. Shelat, "First Impressions Matter—A Lot," *Canadian HR Reporter* (May 3, 2004), pp. 11, 13.

5. For a recent discussion of socialization, see, for example, G. Chao et al., "Organizational Socialization: Its Content and Consequences," *Journal of Applied Psychology*, 79, no. 5 (1994), pp. 730–743.

6. S. Jackson, "After All That Work in Hiring, Don't Let New Employees Dangle," *Canadian HR Reporter* (May 19, 1997), p. 13.

7. A. Macaulay, "The Long and Winding Road," *Canadian HR Reporter* (November 16, 1998), pp. G1–G10.

8. R. Biswas, "Employee Orientation: Your Best Weapon in the Fight for Skilled Talent," *Human Resources Professional* (August/September 1998), pp. 41–42.

9. "Employee Onboarding Guides New Hires," *Workspan* (January 2009), p. 119.

10. D. Chhabra, "What Web-Based Onboarding Can Do for Your Company," *Workspan* (May 2008), pp. 111–114.

11. R. Harrison, "Onboarding: The First Step in Motivation and Retention," *Workspan* (September 2007), pp. 43–45.

12. D. Barnes, "Learning Is Key to Post-Merger Success," *Canadian HR Reporter* (July 12, 1999), pp. 16–17.

13. C. Gibson, "Online Orientation: Extending a Welcoming Hand to New Employees," *Canadian HR Reporter* (November 30, 1998), pp. 22–23.

14. "Onboarding: Virtual Orientation at IBM," *HR Professional* (August/September 2008), p. 12.

15. D. Brown, "Execs Need Help Learning the Ropes Too," *Canadian HR Reporter* (April 22, 2002), p. 2.

16. Ibid.

17. "The Critical Importance of Executive Integration," *Drake Business Review* (December 2002), pp. 6–8.

18. S. Mingail, "Employers Need a Lesson in Training," *Canadian HR Reporter* (February 11, 2002), pp. 22–23.

19. U. Vu, "Trainers Mature into Business Partners," *Canadian HR Reporter* (July 12, 2004), pp. 1–2.

20. S. Klie, "Training Isn't Always the Answer," *Canadian HR Reporter* (December 5, 2005), pp. 13–14.

21. V. Galt, "Training Falls Short: Study," *Globe and Mail* (July 9, 2001), p. M1.

22. D. Harder, "Sierra Systems Earns Top Marks for Training," *Canadian HR Reporter* (February 2, 2009).

23. *Knowledge Matters: Skills and Learning for Canadians* (Government of Canada, 2002), p. 3, www11.sdc.gc.ca/sl-ca/doc/summary.shtml (accessed June 7, 2006).

24. A. Tomlinson, "More Training Critical in Manufacturing," *Canadian HR Reporter* (November 4, 2002), p. 2.

25. D. Brown, "PM Calls for Business to Spend More on Training," *Canadian HR Reporter* (December 16, 2002), pp. 1, 11; D. Brown, "Budget Should Include More for Training: Critics," *Canadian HR Reporter* (March 10, 2003), pp. 1–2; D. Brown, "Legislated Training, Questionable Results," *Canadian HR Reporter* (May 6, 2002), pp. 1, 12.

26. N.L. Trainor, "Employee Development the Key to Talent Attraction and Retention," *Canadian HR Reporter* (November 1, 1999), p. 8.

27. Bank of Montreal, www.bmo.com (accessed May 31, 2009).

28. L. Johnston, "Employees Put High Price on Learning, Development," *Canadian HR Reporter* (November 3, 2008); S. Klie, "Higher Education Leads to Higher Productivity," *Canadian HR Reporter* (December 3, 2007).

29. D. LaMarche-Bisson, "There's More than One Way to Learn," *Canadian HR Reporter* (November 18, 2003), p. 7.

30. M. Belcourt, P.C. Wright, and A.M. Saks, *Managing Performance through Training and Development*, 2nd ed. (Toronto, ON: Nelson Thomson Learning, 2000); see also A.M. Saks and R.R. Haccoun, "Easing the Transfer of Training," *Human Resources Professional* (July–August 1996), pp. 8–11.

31. J.A. Colquitt, J.A. LePine, and R.A. Noe, "Toward an Integrative Theory of Training Motivation: A Meta-Analytic Path Analysis of 20 Years of Research," *Journal of Applied Psychology*, 85 (2000), pp. 678–707.

32. M. Georghiou, "Games, Simulations Open World of Learning," *Canadian HR Reporter* (May 5, 2008).

33. K.A. Smith-Jentsch et al., "Can Pre-Training Experiences Explain Individual Differences in Learning?" *Journal of Applied Psychology*, 81, no. 1 (1986), pp. 100–116.

34. J.A. Cannon-Bowers et al., "A Framework for Understanding Pre-Practice Conditions and Their Impact on Learning," *Personnel Psychology*, 51 (1988), pp. 291–320.

35. Based on K. Wexley and G. Latham, *Developing and Training Human Resources in Organizations* (Glenview, IL: Scott, Foresman, 1981), pp. 22–27.

36. G. Na, "An Employer's Right to Train," *Canadian HR Reporter* (October 6, 2008).

37. B.M. Bass and J.A. Vaughan, "Assessing Training Needs," in C. Schneier and R. Beatty, *Personnel Administration Today* (Reading, MA: Addison-Wesley, 1978), p. 311; see also R. Ash and E. Leving, "Job Applicant Training and Work Experience Evaluation: An Empirical Comparison of Four Methods," *Journal of Applied Psychology*, 70, no. 3 (1985), pp. 572–576; J. Lawrie, "Break the Training Ritual," *Personnel Journal*, 67, no. 4 (April 1988), pp. 95–77; T. Lewis and D. Bjorkquist, "Needs Assessment—A Critical Reappraisal," *Performance Improvement Quarterly*, 5, no. 4 (1992), pp. 33–54.

38. See, for example, G. Freeman, "Human Resources Planning—Training Needs Analysis," *Human Resources Planning*, 39, no. 3 (Fall 1993), pp. 32–34.

39. J.C. Georges, "The Hard Realities of Soft Skills Training," *Personnel Journal*, 68, no. 4 (April 1989), pp. 40–45; R.H. Buckham, "Applying Role Analysis in the Workplace," *Personnel*, 64, no. 2 (February 1987), pp. 63–65; J.K. Ford and R. Noe, "Self-Assessed Training Needs: The Effects of Attitudes towards Training, Management Level, and Function," *Personnel Psychology*, 40, no. 1 (Spring 1987), pp. 39–54.

40. K. Wexley and G. Latham, *Developing and Training Human Resources in Organizations* (Glenview, IL: Scott, Foresman, 1981), p. 107.

41. "German Training Model Imported," *BNA Bulletin to Management* (December 19, 1996), p. 408; L. Burton, "Apprenticeship: The Learn While You Earn Option," *Human Resources Professional* (February/March 1998), p. 25; H. Frazis, D.E. Herz, and M.W. Harrigan, "Employer-Provided Training: Results from a New Survey," *Monthly Labor Review*, 118 (1995), pp. 3–17.

42. "Apprenticeship Grant Gets Going," *Canadian HR Reporter* (January 25, 2007); "New Funding for Apprenticeships," *Canadian HR Reporter* (May 3, 2004), p. 2; "Ontario Boosts Apprenticeship Program with $37 Million Investment," *Canadian HR Reporter* (April 7, 2000); ThinkTrades (Alberta Aboriginal Apprenticeship Project), www.thinktrades.com/candidates.htm (accessed June 13, 2006).

43. N. Day, "Informal Learning Gets Results," *Workforce* (June 1998), p. 31.

44. S. Williams, "'Classroom' Training Alive and Changing," *Canadian HR Reporter* (October 6, 2008).

45. M. Emery and M. Schubert, "A Trainer's Guide to Videoconferencing," *Training* (June 1993), p. 60.

46. G.N. Nash, J.P. Muczyk, and F.L. Vettori, "The Role and Practical Effectiveness of Programmed Instruction," *Personnel Psychology*, 24 (1971), pp. 397–418.

47. K. Wexley and G. Latham, *Developing and Training Human Resources in Organizations* (Glenview, IL: Scott, Foresman, 1981), p. 141; see also R. Wlozkowski, "Simulation," *Training and Development Journal*, 39, no. 6 (June 1985), pp. 38–43.

48. "Pros and Cons of E-learning," *Canadian HR Reporter* (July 16, 2001), pp. 11, 15; D. Murray, *E-learning for the Workplace* (Ottawa, ON: Conference Board of Canada, 2001); see also M. Rueda, "How to Make E-Learning Work for Your Company," *Workspan* (December 2002), pp. 50–53; U. Vu, "Technology-Based Learning Comes of Age," *Canadian HR Reporter* (April 21, 2003), pp. 3, 17.

49. S. Mingail, "Good E-Learning Built on Good Instructional Design," *Canadian HR Reporter* (March 22, 2004), p. 12.

50. S. Carliner, M. Ally, N. Zhao, L. Bairstow, S. Khoury, and L. Johnston, *A Review of the State of the Field of Workplace Learning: What We Need to Know About Competencies, Diversity, E-Learning, and Human Performance Impact* (Canadian Society for Training and Development, 2006).

51. G. Siemens, "5 Things to Watch in E-learning," *Canadian HR Reporter* (October 6, 2008).

52. See, for example, T. Falconer, "No More Pencils, No More Books!" *Canadian Banker* (March/April 1994), pp. 21–25.

53. M. Georghiou, "Games, Simulations Open World of Learning," *Canadian HR Reporter* (May 5, 2008).

54. W. Powell, "Like Life?" *Training & Development* (February 2002), pp. 32–38; see also A. Macaulay, "Reality-Based Computer Simulations Allow Staff to Grow through Failure," *Canadian HR Reporter* (October 23, 2000), pp. 11–12.

55. S. Klie, "L'Oreal Plays Games with Training," *Canadian HR Reporter* (October 6, 2008).

56. A. Czarnecki, "Interactive Learning Makes Big Dent in Time, Money Requirements for T&D," *Canadian HR Reporter* (November 18, 1996), pp. L30–L31.

57. L. Young, "Self-Directed Computer-Based Training That Works," *Canadian HR Reporter* (April 24, 2000), pp. 7–8.

58. F. Manning, "The Misuse of Technology in Workplace Learning," *Canadian HR Reporter* (April 24, 2000), pp. 7, 10; T. Purcell, "Training Anytime, Anywhere," *Canadian HR Reporter* (July 16, 2001), pp. 11, 15; L. Cassini, "Student Participation Thrives in Online Learning Environments," *Canadian HR Reporter* (May 2, 2001), p. 2.

59. O. Diss, "Deploying a New E-Learning Program?" *HR Professional* (October–November 2005), p. 16.

60. P. Weaver, "Preventing E-Learning Failure," *Training & Development* (August 2002), pp. 45–50; K. Oakes, "E-Learning," *Training & Development* (March 2002), pp. 73–75; see also P. Harris, "E-Learning: A Consolidation Update," *Training & Development* (April 2002), pp. 27–33; C.R. Taylor, "The Second Wave," *Training & Development* (October 2002), pp. 24–31; E. Wareham, "The Educated Buyer," *Computing Canada* (February 18, 2000), p. 33; A. Tomlinson, "E-Learning Won't Solve All Problems," *Canadian HR Reporter* (April 8, 2002), pp. 1, 6.

61. P. Weaver, "Preventing E-Learning Failure," *Training & Development* (August 2002), pp. 45–50.

62. M. Belcourt, P.C. Wright, and A.M. Saks, *Managing Performance through Training and Development*, 2nd ed. (Toronto, ON: Nelson Thomson Learning, 2002), pp. 188–202.

63. Ibid, p. 9.

64. D. Kirkpatrick, "Effective Supervisory Training and Development," Part 3, "Outside Programs," *Personnel*, 62, no. 2 (February 1985), pp. 39–42. Among the reasons training might not pay off on the job are a mismatching of courses and trainees' needs, supervisory slip-ups (with supervisors signing up trainees and then forgetting to have them attend the sessions when the training session is actually given), and lack of help in applying skills on the job.

65. N.L. Trainor, "Evaluating Training's Four Levels," *Canadian HR Reporter* (January 13, 1997), p. 10.

66. C. Knight, "Awards for Literacy Announced," *Canadian HR Reporter* (December 29, 1997), p. 10.

67. *Reading the Future: Planning to Meet Canada's Future Literacy Needs* (Ottawa, ON: Canadian Council on Learning, 2008).

68. "New Report Reveals the Future of Literacy in Canada's Largest Cities," Canadian Council on Learning, www.ccl-cca.ca/CCL/Newsroom/Releases/20100908literacy2031.html (accessed July 7, 2011).

69. S. Coulombe, J-F. Tremblay, and S. Marchand, *International Adult Literacy Study: Literacy Scores, Human Capital and Growth Across 14 OECD Countries*, Statistics Canada, Catalogue No. 89-552-MIE, 2004; S. Mingal, "Tackling Workplace Literacy a No-Brainer," *Canadian HR Reporter* (November 22, 2004), pp. G3, G10; D. Brown, "Poor Reading, Math Skills a Drag on Productivity, Performance," *Canadian HR Reporter* (February 28, 2005), pp. 1, 10.

70. U. Vu, "Workplace Language Training Gets Cash Boost," *Canadian HR Reporter* (May 19, 2008); K. Wolfe, "Language Training for the Workplace," *Canadian HR Reporter* (June 6, 2005), pp. 1, 13.

71. R. Rosen and P. Digh, "Developing Globally Literate Leaders," *Training & Development* (May 2001), pp. 70–81.

72. B. Siu, "Cross-Cultural Training and Customer Relations: What Every Manager Should Know," *Canadian HR Reporter* (November 15, 1999), pp. G3, G15.

73. D. Roberts and B. Tsang, "Diversity Management Training Helps Firms Hone Competitive Edge," *Canadian HR Reporter* (June 19, 1995), pp. 17–18.

74. L. Young, "Retail Sector Seeks to Upgrade Education, Training to Solve Human Resource Woes," *Canadian HR Reporter* (February 8, 1999), p. 11; see also B. Nagle, "Superior Retail Training Blends Customer Service, Product Knowledge," *Canadian HR Reporter* (July 15, 2002), pp. 7–8; D. Brown, "Is Retail Ready to Buy Training?" *Canadian HR Reporter* (July 15, 2002), pp. 7–8.

75. Canadian Retail Institute, www.retaileducation.ca/cms/sitem.cfm/certification_&_training (accessed May 31, 2009).

76. Based on J. Laabs, "Team Training Goes Outdoors," *Personnel Journal* (June 1991), pp. 56–63; see also S. Caudron, "Teamwork Takes Work," *Personnel Journal*, 73, no. 2 (February 1994), pp. 41–49.

77. B. Donais, "Training Managers in Handling Conflict," *Canadian HR Reporter* (March 12, 2007); A. Tomlinson, "A Dose of Training for Ailing First-Time Managers," *Canadian HR Reporter* (December 3, 2001), pp. 7, 10.

78. L.C. McDermott, "Developing the New Young Managers," *Training & Development* (October 2001), pp. 42–48; A. Tomlinson, "A Dose of Training for Ailing First-Time Managers," *Canadian HR Reporter* (December 3, 2001), pp. 7, 10.

Chapter 9

1. Towers Perrin, *Talent Management: The State of the Art* (Toronto, ON: Towers Perrin, 2005); E. Chadnick, "Is HR Prepared to Keep the Keepers?" *Canadian HR Reporter* (January 29, 2007).

2. S. O'Neal and J. Gebauer, "Talent Management in the 21st Century: Attracting, Retaining and Engaging Employees of Choice," *WorldatWork Journal* (First Quarter, 2006), pp. 6–17.

3. Quoted from F. Otte and P. Hutcheson, *Helping Employees Manage Careers* (Englewood Cliffs, NJ: Prentice Hall, 1992), pp. 5–6.

4. M. Duarte, "O indivíduo e a organização: Perspectivas de desenvolvimento" (The Individual and the Organization: Perspectives of Development)," *Psychologica (Extra-Série)* (2004), pp. 549–557.

5. M. Savickas, L. Nota, J. Rossier, J. Dauwalder, M. Duarte, J. Guichard, S. Soresi, R. Van Esbroeck, and A. Van Vianen, "Life Designing: A Paradigm for Career Construction in the 21st Century," *Journal of Vocational Behavior* (May 2009), pp. 239–250.

6. M. Duarte, "O indivíduo e a organização: Perspectivas de desenvolvimento" (The Individual and the Organization: Perspectives of Development)," *Psychologica (Extra-Série)* (2004), pp. 549–557.

7. W. Enelow, *100 Ways to Recession-Proof Your Career* (Toronto, ON: McGraw-Hill, 2002), p. 1.

8. P. Linkow, "Winning the Competition for Talent: The Role of the New Career Paradigm in Total Rewards," *Workspan* (October 2006), pp. 28–32.

9. M. Watters and L. O'Connor, *It's Your Move: A Personal and Practical Guide to Career Transition and Job Search for Canadian Managers, Professionals and Executives* (Toronto, ON: HarperCollins, 2001).

10. For example, one survey of Baby Boomers concluded that "allowed to excel" was the most frequently mentioned factor in overall job satisfaction in an extensive attitude survey of Canadian supervisors and middle managers between 30 and 45 years of age; J. Rogers, "Baby Boomers and Their Career Expectations," *Canadian Business Review* (Spring 1993), pp. 13–18.

11. See, for example, R. Chanick, "Career Growth for Baby Boomers," *Personnel Journal,* 71, no. 1 (January 1992), pp. 40–46.

12. R. Sheppard, "Spousal Programs and Communication Curb Relocation Rejections," *Canadian HR Reporter* (November 1, 1999), p. 17.

13. D. Quinn Mills, *Labor–Management Relations* (New York, NY: McGraw-Hill, 1986), pp. 387–396.

14. G. Dessler, *Winning Commitment* (New York, NY: McGraw-Hill, 1993), pp. 144–149.

15. See J. Famularo, *Handbook of Modern Personnel Administration* (New York, NY: McGraw-Hill, 1972), p. 17.

16. J. Swain, "Dispelling Myths about Leadership Development," *Canadian HR Reporter* (June 3, 2002), p. 27.

17. J. Cooper, "Succession Planning: It's Not Just for Executives Anymore," *Workspan* (February 2006), pp. 44–47.

18. Ibid.

19. P. Cantor, "Succession Planning: Often Requested, Rarely Delivered," *Ivey Business Journal* (January/February 2005), pp.1–11.

20. R. Cheloha and J. Swain, "Talent Management System Key to Effective Succession Planning," *Canadian HR Reporter* (October 10, 2005), pp. 5, 8.

21. U. Vu, "Beware the Plan That's Led Too Much by HR," *Canadian HR Reporter* (October 10, 2005), pp. 6–7.

22. For discussions of the steps in succession planning, see, for example, K. Nowack, "The Secrets of Succession," *Training and Development* (November 1994), pp. 49–55; D. Brookes, "In Management Succession, Who Moves Up?" *Human Resources* (January/February 1995), pp. 11–13.

23. "Half of Companies Fail to Update Succession Plans," *Workplace e-Newsletter,* www.workplace-mag.com/Half-of-companies-fail-to-update-succession-plans.html (accessed May 31, 2009).

24. K. Spence, "The Employee's Role in Succession Planning," *Canadian HR Reporter* (February 14, 2000), p. 13.

25. J. Orr, "Job Rotations Give Future Leaders the Depth They Need," *Canadian HR Reporter* (January 30, 2006), pp. 17, 20.

26. D. Yoder, H.G. Heneman, J. Turnbull, and C.H. Stone, *Handbook of Personnel Management and Labor Relations* (New York, NY: McGraw Hill, 1958); see also J. Phillips, "Training Supervisors Outside the Classroom," *Training and Development Journal,* 40, no. 2 (February 1986), pp. 46–49.

27. K. Wexley and G. Latham, *Developing and Training Human Resources in Organizations* (Glenview, IL: Scott, Foresman, 1981), p. 207.

28. D. Brown, "Action Learning Popular in Europe, Not Yet Caught on in Canada," *Canadian HR Reporter* (April 25, 2005), pp. 1–17.

29. IPM Management Training and Development, "Workplace.ca," www.workplace.ca (accessed March 31, 2003).

30. L. Cassiani, "Taking Team Building to New Heights," *Canadian HR Reporter* (February 26, 2001), pp. 8, 17.

31. J. Famularo, *Handbook of Modern Personnel Administration* (New York, NY: McGraw-Hill, 1972), pp. 21.7–21.8.

32. L. Morin and S. Renaud, "Corporate University Basics," *Workplace Gazette,* 7, no. 4, pp. 61–71.

33. E. Lazarus, "Corporate University," *HR Professional* (June/July 2006), pp. 28–29; "City of Richmond Wins International Award," www.richmond.ca/__shared/printpages/page4754.htm (accessed May 8, 2009).

34. Based on A. Kraut, "Developing Managerial Skill via Modeling Techniques: Some Positive Research Findings—A Symposium," *Personnel Psychology,* 29, no. 3 (Autumn 1976), pp. 325–361.

35. K. Wexley and G. Latham, *Developing and Training Human Resources in Organizations* (Glenview, IL: Scott, Foresman, 1981), p. 193.

36. J. Hinrichs, "Personnel Testing," in M. Dunnette (ed.), *Handbook of Industrial and Organizational Psychology* (Chicago, IL: Rand McNally, 1976), p. 855.

37. J. Kay, "At Harvard on the Case," *National Post Business* (March 2003), pp. 68–78.

38. A.M. Young and P.L. Perrewé, "What Did You Expect? An Examination of Career-Related Support and Social Support Among Mentors and Protégés," *Journal of Management,* 20 (2000), pp. 611–632; "Mentoring Makes Better Employees," *Workplace Today* (June 2001), p. 12; S. Butyn, "Mentoring Your Way to Improved Retention," *Canadian HR Reporter* (January 27, 2003), pp. 13, 15.

39. S. Klie, "Mentoring Accelerates Leadership Development," *Canadian HR Reporter* (March 23, 2009).

40. A.K. Buahene and G. Kovary, "Reversing the Roles: Why Gen Ys Can Make Great Mentors," *Canadian HR Reporter* (May 4, 2009).

41. D. Crisp, "Leadership Values Evolving," *Canadian HR Reporter* (September 8, 2008); S. Klie, "Holistic Approach to Developing Leaders Best," *Canadian HR Reporter* (October 27, 2008).

42. D. Brown, "Banking on Leadership Development," *Canadian HR Reporter* (January 17, 2005), pp. 7, 9.

43. Maple Leaf Foods, "Developing Leaders," www.mapleleaf.com/Working/YourDevelopment.aspx (accessed June 13, 2006).

44. R.J. Kramer, "Growing the New Business Leader," *The Conference Board Executive Action Series,* no. 208 (September 2006).

45. E. Chadnick, "Is HR Prepared to Keep the Keepers?" *Canadian HR Reporter* (January 29, 2007).

46. L. Finkelstein, "Coaching SaskEnergy to Higher Performance," *Canadian HR Reporter* (December 1, 2008).

47. Banff Centre, www.banffcentre.ca/departments/leadership/programs/framework.asp#model (accessed May 31, 2009).

Chapter 10

1. J.T. Rich, "The Solutions for Employee Performance Management," *Workspan* (February 2002), pp. 32–37.

2. J.A. Rubino, "Aligning Performance Management and Compensation Rewards Successfully," *WorldatWork Canadian News* (Fourth Quarter, 2004), pp. 12–16.

3. P. Nel, O. Van Dyk, G. Haasbroek, H. Schultz, T. Sono, and A. Werner, *Human Resource Management,* (Cape Town, South Africa: Oxford University Press, 2004).

4. D. Brown, "HR Improving at Performance Management," *Canadian HR Reporter* (December 2, 2002), pp. 1, 14.

5. "The Performance-Management Process," *Workspan* (October 2006), p. 96.

6. R. Thorndike, "Concepts of Culture-Fairness," *Journal of Educational Measurement* (Summer, 1971), pp. 63–70.

7. S. Motowidlo and J. Van Scotter, "Evidence That Task Performance Should Be Distinguished from Contextual Performance," *Journal of Applied Psychology* (November 1993), pp. 475–480.

8. R. Tett, K. Fox, and P. Palmer, "Task and Contextual Performance as Formal and Expected Work Behaviors," Paper presented at the 18th annual Society of Industrial Organizational Psychologists conference (Orlando, FL, April, 2002).

9. A. Sung and E. Todd, "Line of Sight: Moving Beyond the Catchphrase," *Workspan* (October 2004), pp. 65–69.

10. For further discussion, see G. English, "Tuning Up for Performance Management," *Training and Development Journal* (April 1991), pp. 56–60.

11. C.L. Hughes, "The Bell-Shaped Curve That Inspires Guerrilla Warfare," *Personnel Administrator* (May 1987), pp. 40–41.

12. R. Girard, "Are Performance Appraisals Passé?" *Personnel Journal,* 67, no. 8 (August 1988), pp. 89–90.

13. D. Bernardin and P. Smith, "A Clarification of Some Issues Regarding the Development and Use of Behaviorally Anchored Ratings Scales (BARS)," *Journal of Applied Psychology* (August 1981), pp. 458–463.

14. D. Bownas and H. Bernardin, "Critical Incident Technique," in S. Gael (Ed.), *The Job Analysis Handbook for Business, Industry, and Government* (New York, NY: Wiley, 1988), pp. 1120–1137.

15. N. Hauenstein, R. Brown, and A. Sinclair, "BARS and Those Mysterious, Missing Middle Anchors," *Journal of Business and Psychology* (May 2010), pp. 663–672.

16. J. Goodale and R. Burke, "Behaviorally Based Rating Scales Need Not Be Job Specific," *Journal of Applied Psychology,* 60 (June 1975).

17. K.R. Murphy and J. Constans, "Behavioral Anchors as a Source of Bias in Rating," *Journal of Applied Psychology,* 72, no. 4 (November 1987), pp. 573–577.

18. E. Mone and M. London, *Employee Engagement through Effective Performance Management: A Manager's Guide* (New York, NY: Routledge, 2009).

19. S. Kerr and S. Landouer, "Using Stretch Goals to Promote Organizational Effectiveness and Personal Growth: General Electric and Goldman Sachs," *Academy of Management Executive* (November 2004), pp. 134–138.

20. C. Maslach and M. Leiter, "Early Predictors of Job Burnout and Engagement," *Journal of Applied Psychology* (May 2008), pp. 498–512.

21. M. Levy, "Almost-Perfect Performance Appraisals," *Personnel Journal,* 68, no. 4 (April 1989), pp. 76–83.

22. P. Loucks, "Plugging into Performance Management," *Canadian HR Reporter* (February 26, 2007).

23. C. Howard, "Appraise This!" *Canadian Business* (May 23, 1998), p. 96.

24. E. Farndale, V. Hope-Hailey, and C. Kelliher, "High Commitment Performance Management: The Roles of Justice and Trust," *Personnel Review* (2011), pp. 5–23.

25. E. Mone, C. Eisinger, K. Guggenheim, B. Price, and C. Stine, "Performance Management at the Wheel: Driving Employee Engagement in Organizations," *Journal of Business and Psychology* (May 2011), pp. 205–212.

26. K.S. Teel, "Performance Appraisal: Current Trends, Persistent Progress," *Personnel Journal,* 59, no. 4 (April 1980), pp. 296–316.

27. D. Brown, "Performance Management Systems Need Fixing: Survey," *Canadian HR Reporter* (April 11, 2005), pp. 1, 10; M. Waung and S. Highhouse, "Fear of Conflict and Empathic Buffering: Two Explanations for the Inflation of Performance Feedback," *Organizational Behavior and Human Decision Processes,* 71 (1997), pp. 37–54.

28. Y. Ganzach, "Negativity (and Positivity) in Performance Evaluation: Three Field Studies," *Journal of Applied Psychology,* 80 (1995), pp. 491–499.

29. T.J. Maurer and M.A. Taylor, "Is Sex by Itself Enough? An Exploration of Gender Bias Issues in Performance Appraisal," *Organizational Behavior and Human Decision Processes,* 60 (1994), pp. 231–251; see also C.E. Lance, "Test for Latent Structure of Performance Ratings Derived from Wherry's (1952) *Theory of Ratings,*" *Journal of Management,* 20 (1994), pp. 757–771.

30. S.E. Scullen, M.K. Mount, and M. Goff, "Understanding the Latent Structure of Job Performance Ratings," *Journal of Applied Psychology,* 85 (2001), pp. 956–970.

31. A.M. Saks and D.A. Waldman, "The Relationship between Age and Job Performance Evaluations for Entry-Level Professionals," *Journal of Organizational Behavior,* 19 (1998), pp. 409–419.

32. W.C. Borman, L.A. White, and D.W. Dorsey, "Effects of Ratee Task Performance and Interpersonal Factors in Supervisor and Peer Performance Ratings," *Journal of Applied Psychology,* 80 (1995), pp. 168–177.

33. K. Murphy, W. Balzer, M. Lockhart, and E. Eisenman, "Effects of Previous Performance on Evaluations of Present Performance," *Journal of Applied Psychology,* 70, no. 1 (1985), pp. 72–84; see also K. Williams, A. DeNisi, B. Meglino, and T. Cafferty, "Initial Decisions and Subsequent Performance Ratings," *Journal of Applied Psychology,* 71, no. 2 (May 1986), pp. 189–195.

34. S. Appelbaum, M. Roy, and T. Gillilan, "Globalization of Performance Appraisals: Theory and Applications," *Management Decision* (2011), pp. 570–585.

35. J. Hedge and M. Cavanagh, "Improving the Accuracy of Performance Evaluations: Comparison of Three Methods of Performance Appraiser Training," *Journal of Applied Psychology,* 73, no. 1 (February 1988), pp. 68–73.

36. B. Davis and M. Mount, "Effectiveness of Performance Appraisal Training Using Computer Assistance Instruction and Behavior Modeling," *Personnel Psychology,* 37 (Fall 1984), pp. 439–452.

37. T. Athey and R. McIntyre, "Effect of Rater Training on Rater Accuracy: Levels of Processing Theory and Social Facilitation Theory Perspectives," *Journal of Applied Psychology,* 72, no. 4 (November 1987), pp. 567–572.

38. M.M. Greller, "Participation in the Performance Appraisal Review: Inflexible Manager Behavior and Variable Worker Needs," *Human Relations,* 51 (1998), pp. 1061–1083.

39. R. Arvey, and J. Campion, (1982). "The Employment Interview: A Summary and Review of Recent Research," *Personnel Psychology* (June 1982), pp. 281–322; W. Wiesner and S. Cronshaw, "A Meta-Analytic Investigation of the Impact of Interview Format and Degree of Structure on the Validity of the Employment Interview," *Journal of Occupational Psychology* (1988), pp. 275–290; K. Murphy, and J. Cleveland, *Understanding Performance Appraisal: Social, Organizational, and Goal-Based Perspectives* (Thousand Oaks, CA: Sage, 1995).

40. B.D. Cawley, L.M. Keeping, and P.E Levy, "Participation in the Performance Appraisal Process and Employee Reactions: A Meta-Analytic Review of Field Investigations," *Journal of Applied Psychology,* 83 (1998), pp. 615–633.

41. J.W. Lawrie, "Your Performance: Appraise It Yourself!" *Personnel,* 66, no. 1 (January 1989), pp. 21–33; includes a good explanation of how self-appraisals can be used at work; see also A. Furnham and P. Stringfield, "Congruence in Job-Performance Ratings: A Study of 360° Feedback Examining Self, Manager, Peers, and Consultant Ratings," *Human Relations,* 51 (1998), pp. 517–530.

42. P.A. Mabe III and S.G. West, "Validity of Self-Evaluation of Ability: A Review and Meta-Analysis," *Journal of Applied Psychology,* 67, no. 3 (1982), pp. 280–296.

43. J. Russell and D. Goode, "An Analysis of Managers' Reactions to Their Own Performance Appraisal Feedback," *Journal of Applied Psychology*, 73, no. 1 (February 1988), pp. 63–67; M.M. Harris and J. Schaubroeck, "A Meta-Analysis of Self–Supervisor, Self–Peer, and Peer–Supervisor Ratings," *Personnel Psychology*, 41 (1988), pp. 43–62.

44. V.V. Druskat and S.B. Wolff, "Effects and Timing of Developmental Peer Appraisals in Self-Managing Work Groups," *Journal of Applied Psychology*, 84 (1999), pp. 58–74.

45. M.M. Harris and J. Schaubroeck, "A Meta-Analysis of Self–Supervisor, Self–Peer, and Peer–Supervisor Ratings," *Personnel Psychology*, 41 (1988), pp. 43–62.

46. W.C. Borman, "The Rating of Individuals in Organizations: An Alternate Approach," *Organizational Behavior and Human Performance*, 12 (1974), pp. 105–124.

47. H.J. Bernardin and R.W. Beatty, "Can Subordinate Appraisals Enhance Managerial Productivity?" *Sloan Management Review* (Summer 1987), pp. 63–73.

48. M. London and A. Wohlers, "Agreement between Subordinate and Self-Ratings in Upward Feedback," *Personnel Psychology*, 44 (1991), pp. 375–390.

49. Ibid, p. 376.

50. D. Antonioni, "The Effects of Feedback Accountability on Upward Appraisal Ratings," *Personnel Psychology*, 47 (1994), pp. 349–355.

51. T.J. Maurer, N.S. Raju, and W.C. Collins, "Peer and Subordinate Performance Appraisal Measurement Equivalence," *Journal of Applied Psychology*, 83 (1998), pp. 693–702.

52. R. Reilly, J. Smither, and N. Vasilopoulos, "A Longitudinal Study of Upward Feedback," *Personnel Psychology*, 49 (1996), pp. 599–612.

53. K. Nowack, "360-Degree Feedback: The Whole Story," *Training and Development* (January 1993), p. 69; for a description of some of the problems involved in implementing 360-degree feedback, see M. Budman, "The Rating Game," *Across the Board*, 31, no. 2 (February 1994), pp. 35–38.

54. C. Romano, "Fear of Feedback," *Management Review* (December 1993), p. 39; see also M.R. Edwards and A.J. Ewen, "How to Manage Performance and Pay with 360-Degree Feedback," *Compensation and Benefits Review*, 28, no. 3 (May/June 1996), pp. 41–46.

55. G.P. Latham, J. Almost, S. Mann, and C. Moore, "New Developments in Performance Management," *Organizational Dynamics*, 34, no. 1 (2005), pp. 77–87; R. Brillinger, "The Many Faces of 360-Degree Feedback," *Canadian HR Reporter* (December 16, 1996), p. 21.

56. J.F. Milliman, R.A. Zawacki, C. Norman, L. Powell, and J. Kirksey, "Companies Evaluate Employees from All Perspectives," *Personnel Journal*, 73, no. 11 (November 1994), pp. 99–103.

57. R. Brillinger, "The Many Faces of 360-Degree Feedback," *Canadian HR Reporter* (December 16, 1996), p. 20.

58. Ibid.

59. D.A. Waldman, L.A. Atwater, and D. Antonioni, "Has 360-Degree Feedback Gone Amok?" *Academy of Management Executive*, 12 (1998), pp. 86–94.

60. P.E. Levy, B.D. Cawley, and R.J. Foti, "Reactions to Appraisal Discrepancies: Performance Ratings and Attributions," *Journal of Business and Psychology*, 12 (1998), pp. 437–455.

61. M. Derayeh and S. Brutus, "Learning from Others' 360-Degree Experiences," *Canadian HR Reporter* (February 10, 2003), pp. 18, 23.

62. A.S. DeNisi and A.N. Kluger, "Feedback Effectiveness: Can 360-Degree Appraisal Be Improved?" *Academy of Management Executive*, 14 (2000), pp. 129–139.

63. T. Bentley, "Internet Addresses 360-Degree Feedback Concerns," *Canadian HR Reporter* (May 8, 2000), pp. G3, G15.

64. D. Brown, "Performance Management Systems Need Fixing: Survey," *Canadian HR Reporter* (April 1, 2005), pp. 1, 10.

65. See also J. Greenberg, "Using Explanations to Manage Impressions of Performance Appraisal Fairness," *Employee Responsibilities and Rights Journal*, 4, no. 1 (March 1991), pp. 51–60.

66. R.G. Johnson, *The Appraisal Interview Guide*, Chapter 9 (New York, NY: AMACOM, 1979).

67. J. Block, *Performance Appraisal on the Job: Making It Work* (New York, NY: Executive Enterprises Publications, 1981), pp. 58–62; see also T. Lowe, "Eight Ways to Ruin a Performance Review," *Personnel Journal*, 65, no. 1 (January 1986).

68. J.W. Smither and M. London, "Best Practices in Performance Management," in J.W. Smither & M. London (Eds.), *Performance Management: Putting Research into Action* (San Francisco, CA: Jossey-Bass, 2009).

69. J. Block, *Performance Appraisal on the Job: Making It Work* (New York, NY: Executive Enterprises Publications, 1981), pp. 58–62.

70. M. Feinberg, *Effective Psychology for Managers* (New York, NY: Simon & Schuster, 1976).

71. J. Pearce and L. Porter, "Employee Response to Formal Performance Appraisal Feedback," *Journal of Applied Psychology*, 71, no. 2 (May 1986), pp. 211–218.

72. D.B. Jarvis and R.E. McGilvery, "Poor Performers," *HR Professional* (June/July 2005), p. 32.

73. L. Axline, "Ethical Considerations of Performance Appraisals," *Management Review* (March 1994), p. 62.

74. M. McDougall and L. Cassiani, "HR Cited in Unfair Performance Review," *Canadian HR Reporter* (September 10, 2001), pp. 1, 6.

75. "Health Worker's Performance Review Unfair," *Workplace Today* (June 2001), p. 23.

76. G. Barrett and M. Kernan, "Performance Appraisal and Terminations: A Review of Court Decisions Since Brito v. Zia with Implications for Personnel Practices," *Personnel Psychology*, 40, no. 3 (Autumn 1987), pp. 489–504.

77. J. Kochnarski and A. Sorenson, "Managing Performance Management," *Workspan* (September 2005), pp. 20–37.

78. E.E. Lawler and M. McDermott, "Current Performance Management Practices," *WorldatWork Journal*, 12, no. 2, pp. 49–60.

79. D. Bell, J. Blanchet, and N. Gore, "Performance Management: Making It Work Is Worth the Effort," *WorldatWork Canadian News*, 12, no. 11 (Fourth Quarter, 2004), pp. 1, 27–28.

Chapter 11

1. S. O'Neal, "Total Rewards and the Future of Work," *Workspan* (January 2005), pp. 18–26; S. Watson, "Total Rewards: Building a Better Employment Deal," *Workspan* (December 2003), pp. 48–51.

2. S. O'Neal, "Total Rewards and the Future of Work," *Workspan* (January 2005), pp. 18–26; L. Wright, "Total Rewards Can Mean More HR Work than You Think," *Canadian HR Reporter* (October 6, 2003), pp. 9, 12; K.D. Scott, D. Morajda, and J.W. Bishop, "Increase Company Competitiveness: 'Tune Up' Your Pay System," *WorldatWork Journal* (First Quarter, 2002), pp. 35–42.

3. *Towers Perrin 2007–2008 Global Workforce Study* (Stamford CT: Towers Perrin, 2008), www.towersperrin.com/tp/getwebcachedoc?webc=HRS/USA/2008/200802/GWS_handout_web.pdf (accessed September 26, 2011).

4. "Employee Attraction and Retention," Western Compensation and Benefits Consultants, www.wcbc.ca/news/attractionretention (accessed September 26, 2011).

5. J. Dawe, "Compassionate Care Benefit: A New Alternative for Family Caregivers," *Workplace Gazette* (Summer 2004); S. Klie, "Feds Expand Eligibility for Compassionate Care," *Canadian HR Reporter* (July 17, 2006).

6. "GM, Daimler-Chrysler Workers Ratify Agreements," *Workplace Today* (December 1999), p. 11.

7. Harold Jones, "Union Views on Job Evaluations: 1971 vs. 1978," *Personnel Journal*, 58 (February 1979), pp. 80–85.

8. R. Sahl, "Job Content Salary Surveys: Survey Design and Selection Features," *Compensation and Benefits Review* (May–June 1991), pp. 14–21.

9. M.A. Thompson, "Rewards, Performance Two Biggest Words in HR Future," *WorldatWork Canadian News*, 10 (2002), pp. 1, 2, 11.

10. E. Sibray and J.B. Cavallaro, "Case Study: Market Data and Job Evaluation Equals the Best of Both Worlds," *Workspan*, (July 2007), pp. 27–30.

11. Job analysis can be a useful source of information on compensable factors, as well as on job descriptions and job specifications. For example, a quantitative job analysis technique like the position analysis questionnaire generates quantitative information on the degree to which the following five basic factors are present in each job: having decision making/communication/social responsibilities, performing skilled activities, being physically active, operating vehicles or equipment, and processing information. As a result, a job analysis technique like the PAQ is actually also appropriate as a job evaluation technique (or, some say, more appropriate), in that jobs can be quantitatively compared with one another on those five dimensions, and their relative worth thus ascertained.

12. H. Risher, "Job Evaluation: Validity and Reliability," *Compensation and Benefits Review*, 21 (January–February 1989), pp. 22–36.

13. S. Werner, R. Konopaske, and C. Touhey, "Ten Questions to Ask Yourself about Compensation Surveys," *Compensation and Benefits Review*, 31 (May/June 1999), pp. 54–59.

14. P. Cappelli, *The New Deal at Work: Managing the Market-Driven Workforce* (Boston, MA: Harvard Business School Press, 1999).

15. S. Werner, R. Konopaske, and C. Touhey, "Ten Questions to Ask Yourself about Compensation Surveys," *Compensation and Benefits Review*, 31 (May/June 1999), pp. 54–59.

16. "Compensation Surveys on the Internet," *Canadian HR Reporter* (February 10, 1997), p. 6.

17. F.W. Cook, "Compensation Surveys Are Biased," *Compensation and Benefits Review* (September–October 1994), pp. 19–22.

18. K.R. Cardinal, "The Art and Science of the Match, or Why Job Matching Keeps Me Up at Night," *Workspan* (February 2004), pp. 53–56; S. Werner, R. Konopaske, and C. Touhey, "Ten Questions to Ask Yourself about Compensation Surveys," *Compensation and Benefits Review*, 31 (May/June 1999), pp. 1–6; see also U. Vu, "Know How Pays in Comp Surveys," *Canadian HR Reporter* (April 7, 2003), p. 13.

19. D. Hofrichter, "Broadbanding: A 'Second Generation' Approach," *Compensation and Benefits Review* (September–October 1993), pp. 53–58; see also G. Bergel, "Choosing the Right Pay Delivery System to Fit Banding," *Compensation and Benefits Review*, 26 (July–August 1994), pp. 34–38.

20. C. Bacca and G. Starzmann, "Clarifying Competencies: Powerful Tools for Driving Business Success," *Workspan* (March 2006), pp. 44–46.

21. Ibid.

22. P.K. Zingheim and J.R. Schuster, "Reassessing the Value of Skill-Based Pay," *WorldatWork Journal* (Third Quarter, 2002).

23. R. Long, "Paying for Knowledge: Does It Pay?" *Canadian HR Reporter* (March 28, 2005), pp. 12–13.

24. S. St.-Onge, "Competency-Based Pay Plans Revisited," *Human Resources Professional* (August/September 1998), pp. 29–34; J. Kochanski and P. Leblanc, "Should Firms Pay for Competencies: Competencies Have to Help the Bottom Line," *Canadian HR Reporter* (February 22, 1999), p. 10.

25. F. Giancola, "Skill-Based Pay—Issues for Consideration," *Benefits & Compensation Digest*, 44, no. 5 (May 2007), pp. 10–15.

26. D. Tyson, *Canadian Compensation Handbook* (Toronto, ON: Aurora Professional Press, 2002).

27. P.K. Zingheim, J.R. Schuster, and M.G. Dertien, "Measuring the Value of Work: The 'People-Based' Pay Solution," *WorldatWork Journal* (Third Quarter, 2005), pp. 42–49.

28. D. Yoder, *Personnel Management and Industrial Relations* (Englewood Cliffs, NJ: Prentice Hall, 1970), pp. 643–645.

29. B.R. Ellig, "Executive Pay: A Primer," *Compensation & Benefits Review* (January–February 2003), pp. 44–50.

30. "The Top 1000: Top 50 Highest Paid Executives, 2007," www.reportonbusiness.com/v5/content/tp1000-2007/index.php?view-top_50_execs (accessed November 26, 2008).

31. H.L. Tosi, S. Werner, J.P. Katz, and L.R. Gomez-Mejia, "How Much Does Performance Matter? A Meta-Analysis of CEO Pay Studies," *Journal of Management*, 26 (2000), pp. 301–339.

32. M.A. Thompson, "Investors Call for Better Disclosure of Executive Compensation in Canada," *Workspan Focus Canada* (2006), pp. 5–6.

33. P. Moran, "Equitable Salary Administration in High-Tech Companies," *Compensation and Benefits Review*, 18 (September–October 1986), pp. 31–40.

34. R. Sibson, *Compensation* (New York, NY: AMACOM, 1981), p. 194.

35. B. Bridges, "The Role of Rewards in Motivating Scientific and Technical Personnel: Experience at Elgin AFB," *National Productivity Review* (Summer 1993), pp. 337–348.

36. M. Drolet, "The Male–Female Wage Gap," *Perspectives*, Statistics Canada (Spring 2002), pp. 29–37; E. Carey, "Gender Gap in Earnings Staying Stubbornly High," *Toronto Star* (March 12, 2003), p. A9.

37. "Female Grads Make Less than Males," *Canadian HR Reporter* (April 19, 2004), p. 2.

38. D. Brown, "StatsCan Unable to Explain Gender Wage Gap," *Canadian HR Reporter* (January 31, 2000), p. 3.

39. "PSAC Prepares for Federal Court of Appeal Hearing on Pay Equity Complaint at Canada Post," (July 10, 2008), www.psac.com/news/2008/what/2080710-e.shtml (accessed March 23, 2009).

40. "Air Canada Loses Pay Equity Decision, For Now," *Canadian HR Reporter* (February 13, 2006), p. 2.

41. D. Brown, "StatsCan Unable to Explain Gender Wage Gap," *Canadian HR Reporter* (January 31, 2000), p. 3.

Chapter 12

1. A. Cowan, *Compensation Planning Outlook 2011* (Ottawa, ON: Conference Board of Canada, 2011).

2. P.K. Zingheim and J.R. Schuster, *Pay People Right! Breakthrough Reward Strategies to Create Great Companies* (San Francisco, CA: Jossey-Bass, 2000); D. Brown, "Top Performers Must Get Top Pay," *Canadian HR Reporter* (May 8, 2000), pp. 7, 10; V. Dell'Agnese, "Performance-Based Rewards, Line-of-Sight Foster Ownership Behaviour in Staff," *Canadian HR Reporter* (October 8, 2001), p. 10.

3. S. Klie, "'Employees First' at CPX," *Canadian HR Reporter* (September 26, 2005), pp. 1, 3.

4. R. Henderson, *Compensation Management* (Reston, VA: Reston, 1979), p. 363. For a discussion of the increasing use of incentives for blue-collar employees, see, for example, R. Henderson, "Contract Concessions: Is the Past Prologue?" *Compensation and Benefits Review*, 18, no. 5 (September–October 1986), pp. 17–30; see also A.J. Vogl, "Carrots, Sticks and Self-Deception," *Across-the-Board*, 3, no. 1 (January 1994), pp. 39–44.

5. D. Belcher, *Compensation Administration* (Englewood Cliffs, NJ: Prentice Hall, 1973), p. 314.

6. For a discussion of these, see T. Wilson, "Is It Time to Eliminate the Piece Rate Incentive System?" *Compensation and Benefits Review* (March–April 1992), pp. 43–49.

7. Measured day work is a third type of individual incentive plan for production workers. See, for example, M. Fein, "Let's Return to MDW for Incentives," *Industrial Engineering* (January 1979), pp. 34–37.

8. A. Saunier and E. Hawk, "Realizing the Potential of Teams through Team-Based Rewards," *Compensation and Benefits Review* (July–August 1994), pp. 24–33; S. Caudron, "Tie Individual Pay to Team Success," *Personnel Journal,* 73, no. 10 (October 1994), pp. 40–46.

9. Some other suggestions are equal payments to all members on the team; differential payments to team members based on their contributions to the team's performance; differential payments determined by a ratio of each group member's base pay to the total base pay of the group. See K. Bartol and L. Hagmann, "Team-Based Pay Plans: A Key to Effective Teamwork," *Compensation and Benefits Review* (November–December 1992), pp. 24–29.

10. J. Nickel and S. O'Neal, "Small Group Incentives: Gainsharing in the Microcosm," *Compensation and Benefits Review* (March–April 1990), p. 24; see also J. Pickard, "How Incentives Can Drive Teamworking," *Personnel Management* (September 1993), pp. 26–32; S. Caudron, "Tie Individual Pay to Team Success," *Personnel Journal* (October 1994), pp. 40–46; For an explanation of how to develop a successful group incentive program, see K.D. Scott and T. Cotter, "The Team That Works Together Earns Together," *Personnel Journal,* 63 (March 1984), pp. 59–67.

11. L.N. McClurg, "Team Rewards: How Far Have We Come?" *Human Resource Management,* 40 (Spring 2001), pp. 73–86; see also A. Gostick, "Team Recognition," *Canadian HR Reporter* (May 21, 2001), p. 15.

12. W.E. Reum and S. Reum, "Employee Stock Ownership Plans: Pluses and Minuses," *Harvard Business Review,* 55 (July–August 1976), pp. 133–143; R. Bavier, "Managerial Bonuses," *Industrial Management* (March–April 1978), pp. 1–5; see also J. Thompson, L. Murphy Smith, and A. Murray, "Management Performance Incentives: Three Critical Issues," *Compensation and Benefits Review,* 18, no. 5 (September–October 1986), pp. 41–47.

13. A. Cowan, *Compensation Planning Outlook 2009* (Ottawa, ON: Conference Board of Canada, 2009).

14. B.R. Ellig, "Incentive Plans: Short-Term Design Issues," *Compensation Review,* 16, no. 3 (Third Quarter, 1984), pp. 26–36; B. Ellig, *Executive Compensation—A Total Pay Perspective* (New York, NY: McGraw-Hill, 1982), p. 187.

15. F.D. Hildebrand Jr., "Individual Performance Incentives," *Compensation Review,* 10 (Third Quarter, 1978), p. 32.

16. Ibid., pp. 28–33.

17. P. Brieger, "Shareholders Target CEO Compensation," *Financial Post* (April 7, 2003), p. FP5; see also S.M. Van Putten and E.D. Graskamp, "End of an Era? The Future of Stock Options," *Compensation and Benefits Review* (September–October 2002), pp. 29–35; N. Winter, "The Current Crisis in Executive Compensation," *WorldatWork Canadian News* (Fourth Quarter, 2002), pp. 1–3; R.M. Kanungo and M. Mendonca, *Compensation: Effective Reward Management* (1997), p. 237.

18. A. Cowan, *Compensation Planning Outlook 2011* (Ottawa, ON: Conference Board of Canada, 2011).

19. R. Levasseur and D. D'Alessandro, "Preparing for Changes in Executive Compensation," *Workspan Canada: Workspan Focus* (January 2009), pp. 101–104.

20. A. Cowan, *Compensation Planning Outlook 2011* (Ottawa, ON: Conference Board of Canada, 2011).

21. R. Murrill, "Executive Share Ownership," *Watson Wyatt Memorandum,* 11, no. 1 (March 1997), p. 11.

22. R.J. Long, "Ensuring Your Executive Compensation Plan Is an Asset Rather Than a Liability," *Canadian HR Reporter* (October 19, 1998), pp. 15–16; see also D. Brown, "Bringing Stock Options Back to the Surface," *Canadian HR Reporter* (May 7, 2001), p. 2.

23. I. Huss and M. Maclure, "Broad-Based Stock Option Plans Take Hold," *Canadian HR Reporter* (July 17, 2000), p. 18; J. Staiman and C. Thompson, "Designing and Implementing a Broad-Based Stock Option Plan," *Compensation and Benefits Review* (July–August 1998), p. 23.

24. *CPP Investment Board Proxy Voting Principles and Guidelines* (February 7, 2006).

25. R. Levasseur and D. D'Alessandro, "Preparing for Changes in Executive Compensation," *Workspan Canada: Workspan Focus* (January 2009), pp. 101–104.

26. P. Singh and N.C. Agarwal, "Executive Compensation: Examining an Old Issue from New Perspectives," *Compensation and Benefits Review* (March/April 2003), pp. 48–54.

27. R. Levasseur and D. D'Alessandro, "Preparing for Changes in Executive Compensation," *Workspan Canada: Workspan Focus* (January 2009), pp. 101–104.

28. J. Tallitsch and J. Moynahan, "Fine-Tuning Sales Compensation Programs," *Compensation and Benefits Review,* 26, no. 2 (March–April 1994), pp. 34–37.

29. Straight salary by itself is not, of course, an incentive compensation plan as we use the term in this chapter; J. Steinbrink, "How to Pay Your Sales Force," *Harvard Business Review,* 57 (July–August 1978), pp. 111–122.

30. T.H. Patten, "Trends in Pay Practices for Salesmen," *Personnel,* 43 (January–February 1968), pp. 54–63; see also C. Romano, "Death of a Salesman," *Management Review,* 83, no. 9 (September 1994), pp. 10–16.

31. D. Harrison, M. Virick, and S. William, "Working Without a Net: Time, Performance, and Turnover Under Maximally Contingent Rewards," *Journal of Applied Psychology,* 81 (1996), pp. 331–345.

32. G. Stewart, "Reward Structure as Moderator of the Relationship between Extroversion and Sales Performance," *Journal of Applied Psychology,* 81 (1996), pp. 619–627.

33. In the salary plus bonus plan, salespeople are paid a basic salary and are then paid a bonus for carrying out specified activities. For a discussion of how to develop a customer-focused sales compensation plan, see, for example, M. Blessington, "Designing a Sales Strategy with the Customer in Mind," *Compensation and Benefits Review* (March–April 1992), pp. 30–41; S.S. Sands, "Ineffective Quotas: The Hidden Threat to Sales Compensation Plans," *Compensation and Benefits Review* (March/April 2000), pp. 35–42.

34. E. Maggio, "Compensation Strategies Pulling You in Different Directions?" *Canadian HR Reporter* (October 4, 1999), pp. 11, 19; see also B. Serino, "Non-Cash Awards Boost Sales Compensation Plans," *Workspan* (August 2002), pp. 24–27.

35. B. Weeks, "Setting Sales Force Compensation in the Internet Age," *Compensation and Benefits Review* (March/April 2000), pp. 25–34.

36. See, for example, W. Kearney, "Pay for Performance? Not Always," *MSU Business Topics* (Spring 1979), pp. 5–16; see also H. Doyel and J. Johnson, "Pay Increase Guidelines with Merit," *Personnel Journal,* 64 (June 1985), pp. 46–50.

37. J. Pfeffer and R.I. Sutton, *Hard Facts, Dangerous Half-Truths, and Total Nonsense* (Boston MA: Harvard Business School Press, 2006).

38. W. Seithel and J. Emans, "Calculating Merit Increases: A Structured Approach," *Personnel,* 60, no. 5 (June 1985), pp. 56–68; D. Gilbert and G. Bassett, "Merit Pay Increases Are a Mistake," *Compensation and Benefits Review,* 26, no. 2 (March–April 1994), pp. 20–25.

39. S. Minken, "Does Lump Sum Pay Merit Attention?" *Personnel Journal* (June 1988), pp. 77–83; J. Newman and D. Fisher, "Strategic Impact Merit Pay," *Compensation and Benefits Review* (July–August 1992), pp. 38–45.

40. Based primarily on R. Sibson, *Compensation* (New York, NY: AMACOM, 1981), pp. 189–207; C. Shelton and L. Shelton, "What HR Can Do about the 'Opt-Out' Revolution (Guest Commentary)," *Canadian HR Reporter* (May 8, 2006).

41. A. Cowan, *Compensation Planning Outlook 2009* (Ottawa, ON: Conference Board of Canada, 2009).

42. B. Duke, "Are Profit-Sharing Plans Making the Grade?" *Canadian HR Reporter* (January 11, 1999), pp. 8–9.

43. D.E. Tyson, *Profit-Sharing in Canada: The Complete Guide to Designing and Implementing Plans That Really Work* (Toronto, ON: Wiley, 1996), pp. 200–207.

44. C. Baarda, *Compensation Planning Outlook 2006* (Ottawa, ON: Conference Board of Canada, 2006).

45. R. Murrill, "Executive Share Ownership," *Watson Wyatt Memorandum,* 11, no. 1 (March 1997), p. 11.

46. P. Robertson, "Increasing Productivity through an Employee Share Purchase Plan," *Canadian HR Reporter* (September 20, 1999), pp. 7, 9.

47. C. Beatty, "Our Company: Employee Ownership May Sound Drastic, but It Can Work," *HR Professional* (June/July 2004), p. 20.

48. B.W. Thomas and M.H. Olson, "Gainsharing: The Design Guarantees Success," *Personnel Journal* (May 1988), pp. 73–79; see also "Aligning Compensation with Quality," *Bulletin to Management, BNA Policy and Practice Series* (April 1, 1993), p. 97.

49. See T.A. Welbourne and L. Gomez Mejia, "Gainsharing Revisited," *Compensation and Benefits Review* (July–August 1988), pp. 19–28.

50. Paraphrased from W. Imberman, "Boosting Plant Performance with Gainsharing," *Business Horizons* (November–December 1992), p. 77; for other examples, see T. Ross and L. Hatcher, "Gainsharing Drives Quality Improvement," *Personnel Journal* (November 1992), pp. 81–89; see also J. McAdams, "Employee Involvement and Performance Reward Plans: Design, Implementation, and Results," *Compensation and Benefits Review,* 27, no. 2 (March 1995), pp. 45–55.

51. P.K. Zingheim and J.R. Schuster, "Value Is the Goal," *Workforce* (February 2000), pp. 56–61.

52. "US Airways Employees to Get Profit Sharing Checks," *Entertainment Close-Up* (March 19, 2011).

53. R.J. Long, "Ensuring Your Executive Compensation Plan Is an Asset Rather Than a Liability," *Canadian HR Reporter* (October 19, 1998), pp. 15–16; see also D. Brown, "Bringing Stock Options Back to the Surface," *Canadian HR Reporter* (May 7, 2001), p. 2.

54. J. Cameron and W.D. Pierce, *Rewards and Intrinsic Motivation: Resolving the Controversy* (Westport, CT: Bergin & Garvey, 2002); see also G. Bouchard, "When Rewards Don't Work," *Globe and Mail* (September 25, 2002), p. C3.

55. P.K. Zingheim and J.R. Schuster, *Pay People Right! Breakthrough Reward Strategies to Create Great Companies* (San Francisco, CA: Jossey-Bass, 2000).

56. S. Gross and J. Bacher, "The New Variable Pay Programs: How Some Succeed, Why Some Don't," *Compensation and Benefits Review* (January February 1993), pp. 55–56; see also G. Milkovich and C. Milkovich, "Strengthening the Pay–Performance Relationship: The Research," *Compensation and Benefits Review* (November–December 1992), pp. 53–62; J. Schuster and P. Zingheim, "The New Variable Pay: Key Design Issues," *Compensation and Benefits Review* (March–April 1993), pp. 27–34.

57. D. Belcher, *Compensation Administration* (Englewood Cliffs, NJ: Prentice Hall, 1973), pp. 309–310.

58. C. Kapel and T. Kinsman-Berry, "Seven Key Factors for Effective Incentive Plans," *Canadian HR Reporter* (October 4, 1999), pp. 12–13.

59. A. Avalos, "Recognition: A Critical Component of the Total Rewards Mix," *Workspan* (July 2007), pp. 32–35.

60. K. Izuma, D.N. Saito, and N. Sadato, "Processing of Social and Monetary Rewards in the Human Striatum," *Neuron,* 58, no. 2 (April 24, 2008), pp. 284–294.

61. J. Mills, "Gratitude à la carte," *Workplace News* (January 2005), p. 12; L. McKibbon-Brown, "Beyond the Gold Watch: Employee Recognition Today," *Workspan* (April 2003), pp. 44–46.

62. A. Welsh, "The Give and Take of Recognition Programs," *Canadian HR Reporter* (September 22, 1997), pp. 16–17, 22; J.M. Kouzas and B.Z. Posner, *Encouraging the Heart: A Leader's Guide to Rewarding and Recognizing Others* (San Francisco, CA: Wiley, 2003); D. Brown, "Canada Wants Nurses Again, but Will Anyone Answer the Call?" *Canadian HR Reporter* (January 15, 2001), pp. 1, 14, 15.

63. J.M. Kouzas and B.Z. Posner, *Encouraging the Heart: A Leader's Guide to Rewarding and Recognizing Others* (San Francisco, CA: Wiley, 2003); see also B. Nelson, "Why Managers Don't Recognize Employees," *Canadian HR Reporter* (March 11, 2002), p. 9; L. Cassiani, "Lasting Impressions through Recognition," *Canadian HR Reporter* (March 12, 2001), p. 7; J. Mills, "A Matter of Pride: Rewarding Team Success," *Canadian HR Reporter* (March 8, 1999), p. 16; L. Young, "How Can I Ever Thank You?" *Canadian HR Reporter* (January 31, 2000), pp. 7, 9.

64. E. Wright and K. Ryan, "Thanks a Million (More or Less)," *Canadian HR Reporter* (March 9, 1998), pp. 19, 21, 23; see also "How to Sell Recognition to Top Management," *Canadian HR Reporter* (June 1, 1998), p. 21; B. Nelson, "Cheap and Meaningful Better than Expensive and Forgettable," *Canadian HR Reporter* (August 13, 2001), p. 22.

65. L. Davidson, "The Power of Personal Recognition," *Workforce* (July 1999), pp. 44–49; see also A. Gostick and C. Elton, "Show Me the Rewards," *Canadian HR Reporter* (March 12, 2001), pp. 7, 10; V. Scott and B. Phillips, "Recognition Program Links Achievement to Corporate Goals," *Canadian HR Reporter* (December 14, 1998), pp. 22–23; R. Clarke, "Building a Recognition Program: Alternatives and Considerations," *Canadian HR Reporter* (November 2, 1998), pp. 17, 19; E. Wright and K. Ryan, "Thanks a Million (More or Less)," *Canadian HR Reporter* (March 9, 1998), pp. 19, 21, 23; L. Davidson, "The Power of Personal Recognition," *Workforce* (July 1999), pp. 44–49; D. Brown, "Recognition an Integral Part of Total Rewards," *Canadian HR Reporter* (August 12, 2002), pp. 25, 27.

66. U. Vu, "Green Recognition a Mere Whisper," *Canadian HR Reporter* (August 11, 2008); U. Vu, "What Green Recognition Looks Like," *Canadian HR Reporter* (August 11, 2008).

67. J. Jackson, "The Art of Recognition," *Canadian HR Reporter* (January 15, 2001), p. 22; see also B.P. Keegan, "Incentive Programs Boost Employee Morale," *Workspan* (March 2002), pp. 30–33; S. Nador, "Beyond Trinkets and Trash," *Canadian HR Reporter* (May 20, 2002), pp. 15, 19.

68. H. Hilliard, "How to Reward Top Performers When Money Is No Object," *Canadian HR Reporter* (August 13, 2001), pp. 21, 23.

69. A. Welsh, "The Give and Take of Recognition Programs," *Canadian HR Reporter* (September 22, 1997), pp. 16–17, 22; E. Wright and K. Ryan, "Thanks a Million (More or Less)," *Canadian HR Reporter* (March 9, 1998).

70. L.J. Blake, "Montana's Cookhouse Serves Up Recognition," *Workplace* (September–October 2008), pp. 14–16; D. Irvine, "Bring Back that Lovin' Feeling," *Canadian HR Reporter* (November 3, 2008); T. Humber, "Beyond the Gold Watch," *Canadian HR Reporter* (January 30, 2006), pp. 23, 29; S. Singh, "'Tis the Season for Recognition," *Canadian HR Reporter* (December 5, 2005), pp. 19–20.

Chapter 13

1. Based on F. Hills, T. Bergmann, and V. Scarpello, *Compensation Decision Making* (Fort Worth, TX: The Dryden Press, 1994), p. 424; see also L.K. Beatty, "Pay and Benefits Break Away from Tradition," *HR Magazine,* 39 (November 1994), pp. 63–68.

2. R.K. Platt, "A Strategic Approach to Benefits," *Workspan* (July 2002), pp. 23–24.

3. S. Beech and J. Tompkins, "Do Benefits Plans Attract and Retain Talent?" *Benefits Canada* (October 2002), pp. 49–53.

4. F. Holmes, "Talking about an Evolution," *Benefits Canada* (September 2001), pp. 30–32; J. Thomas and M. Chilco, "Coming of Age," *Benefits Canada* (March 2001), pp. 36–38.

5. "EI Top-Ups Common—Survey," *Canadian HR Reporter* (February 23, 1998), p. 15.

6. S. Klie, "Feds Expand Eligibility for Compassionate Care," *Canadian HR Reporter* (July 17, 2006).

7. "Tragedy Leaves of Absence," *HR Professional* (October/November 2008), p. 16.

8. D. Gunch, "The Family Leave Act: A Financial Burden?" *Personnel Journal* (September 1993), p. 49.

9. H. Amolins, "Workers Must Cooperate in Return to Work," *Canadian HR Reporter* (November 3, 1997), p. 8; C. Knight, "Ontario Businesses Ready for New WCB," *Canadian HR Reporter* (November 17, 1997), p. 9.

10. U. Vu, "How Purolator Dealt with Skyrocketing Costs," *Canadian HR Reporter* (March 13, 2006).

11. S. Pellegrini, "Considering Critical," *Benefits Canada* (April 2002), pp. 71–73.

12. "Employee Benefits in Small Firms," *BNA Bulletin to Management* (June 27, 1991), pp. 196–197.

13. "Employee Benefits," *Commerce Clearing House Ideas and Trends in Personnel* (January 23, 1991), pp. 9–11.

14. S. Dobson, "Health-Care Costs Maintain Dramatic Rise," *Canadian HR Reporter* (July 13, 2009).

15. *Canadian Health Care Trend Survey Results 2009* (Toronto, ON: Buck Consultants).

16. C. Kapel, "Unitel Asks Employees to Share Costs," *Canadian HR Reporter* (June 17, 1996), p. 17; see also J. Sloane and J. Taggart, "Runaway Drug Costs," *Canadian HR Reporter* (September 10, 2001), pp. 17–18; "Deductibles Could Be Making a Comeback," *Canadian HR Reporter* (February 26, 2001), pp. 2, 16.

17. J. Norton, "The New Drug Invasion," *Benefits Canada* (June 1999), pp. 29–32.

18. S. Felix, "Healthy Alternative," *Benefits Canada* (February 1997), p. 47; A. Dimon, "Money Well Spent," *Benefits Canada* (April 1997), p. 15.

19. A. Dimon, "Money Well Spent," *Benefits Canada* (April 1997), p. 15.

20. D. Jones, "Accounting for Health: The Present and Future of HCSAs and Other Consumer-Driven Health Care Products in Canada," *Benefits Canada* (January 2009), pp. 21–23.

21. J. Taggart, "Health Spending Accounts: A Prescription for Cost Control," *Canadian HR Reporter* (October 22, 2001), pp. 16, 18; see also "How Spending Accounts Work," *Canadian HR Reporter* (February 24, 2003), p. 16.

22. K. Gay, "Post-Retirement Benefits Costing Firms a Fortune," *Financial Post* (June 2, 1995), p. 18; S. Lebrun, "Turning a Blind Eye to Benefits," *Canadian HR Reporter* (February 24, 1997), p. 2; S. Pellegrini, "Keep Benefits Costs Low by Assessing Retiree Health," *Canadian HR Reporter* (June 14, 1999), pp. 9–10; M. Warren, "Uncovering the Costs," *Benefits Canada* (November 1996), p. 41; G. Dufresne, "Financing Benefits for Tomorrow's Retirees," *Canadian HR Reporter* (April 6, 1998), p. 11.

23. A. Khemani, "Post-Retirement Benefits Liability Grows," *Canadian HR Reporter* (November 4, 1996), p. 17; see also M. Warren, "Retiree Benefits Come of Age," *Benefits Canada* (May 2000), pp. 73–77.

24. *2008 Post-Retirement Trends* (Toronto, ON: Mercer Human Resources Consulting).

25. W. Pyper, "Aging, Health and Work," *Perspectives on Labour and Income* (Spring 2006), p. 48; S. Klie, "Private Health Coverage Enters Benefits Realm," *Canadian HR Reporter* (September 12, 2005), pp. 1, 22.

26. "Managing Episodic Disabilities Course," *HR Professional* (February–March 2009), p. 18.

27. A. Blake, "A New Approach to Disability Management," *Benefits Canada* (March 2000), pp. 58–64; P. Kulig, "Returning the Whole Employee to Work," *Canadian HR Reporter* (March 9, 1998), p. 20; see also A. Gibbs, "Gearing Disability Management to the Realities of Working Life," *Canadian HR Reporter* (December 2, 2002), p. G7.

28. J. Curtis and L. Scott, "Making the Connection," *Benefits Canada* (April 2003), pp. 75–79.

29. N. Rankin, "A Guide to Disability Management," *Canadian HR Reporter* (March 22, 1999), pp. 14–15.

30. *Staying@Work: Effective Presence at Work,* 2007 Survey Report—Canada (Toronto, ON: Watson Wyatt); "Mental Health Claims on the Rise in Canada," *WorldatWork Canadian News* (Third Quarter, 2005), pp. 15–16; D. Brown, "Mental Illness a Top Concern but Only Gets Band-Aid Treatment," *Canadian HR Reporter* (May 9, 2005), pp. 1, 3; "Mental Health Biggest Workplace Barrier, Women Say," *Canadian HR Reporter* (January 17, 2005), p. 2.

31. P. Weiner, "A Mental Health Priority for Canada's Employers," *Workspan* (January 2009), pp. 91–95.

32. J. Melnitzer, "Down and Out," *Workplace News* (September/October 2005), pp. 20–23; M. Burych, "Baby Blues," *Benefits Canada* (October 2000), pp 33–35.

33. B. Hayhoe, "The Case for Employee Retirement Planning," *Canadian HR Reporter* (May 20, 2002), p. 18.

34. J. Nunes, "Defined Benefit or Defined Contribution, It's Always Costly," *Canadian HR Reporter* (November 5, 2001), pp. 7, 9.

35. Ibid.

36. S. Klie, "Little guarantee for Ontario pensions," *Canadian HR Reporter* (May 4, 2009); S. Dobson, "Costs top list of concerns for DB plan sponsors: Survey," *Canadian HR Reporter* (March 24, 2008).

37. A. Scappatura, "DB Plans Endangered," *Canadian HR Reporter* (June 15, 2009); T. Humber, "The Death of the DB Pension," *Canadian HR Reporter* (March 23, 2009); S. Dobson, "Ottawa Provides Pension Relief," *Canadian HR Reporter* (December 15, 2008); D. Birschel, "Alberta and British Columbia Provide Pension Solvency Relief," *Benefits Quarterly*, 25, no. 2 (2009), p. 66.

38. S. Dobson, "Workers Postpone Retirement to Save Money," *Canadian HR Reporter* (May 18, 2009); "Canadians Delaying Retirement Due to Economic Slowdown," *Workspan* (January 2009), pp. 106–107; S. Klie, "Workers Delay Retirement as Economy Tanks," *Canadian HR Reporter* (January 26, 2009).

39. T. Piskorski, "Minimizing Employee Benefits Litigation through Effective Claims Administration Procedures," *Employee Relations Law Journal*, 20, no. 3 (Winter 1994–95), pp. 421–431.

40. A. Rappaport, "Phased Retirement: An Important Part of the Evolving Retirement Scene," *Benefits Quarterly*, 25, no. 2 (2009), pp. 38–50; R. Castelli, "Phased Retirement Plans, *HR Professional* (December 2008/ January 2009), p. 23.

41. D. Brown, "New Brunswick Nurses Find Phased Retirement Solution," *Canadian HR Reporter* (September 22, 2003), pp. 1, 12; Y. Saint-Cyr, "Phased Retirement Agreements," *Canadian Payroll and Employment Law News*, www. hrpao.org/HRPAO/HRResourceCentre/LegalCentre/ (accessed July 11, 2005).

42. *Towers Perrin 2004 SERP Report: Supplementary Pensions Under Pressure* (Toronto, ON: Towers Perrin).

43. L. Burger, "Group Legal Service Plans: A Benefit Whose Time Has Come," *Compensation and Benefits Review*, 18 (July–August 1986), pp. 28–34.

44. "Financial Distress Impacts Health and Productivity: Employees Turning to EAP for Help," Shepell-fgi Research Group, 2009 Series, 5, no. 1; A. Scappatura, "EAP Use Soars as Economy Tanks: Study," *Canadian HR Reporter* (March 23, 2009); "Requests for Help through EAP Up Significantly," *Workspan* (February 2009), p. 13.

45. J. Hobel, "EAPs Flounder without Manager Support," *Canadian HR Reporter* (June 2, 2003), p. 7; P. Davies, "Problem Gamblers in the Workplace," *Canadian HR Reporter* (November 4, 2002), p. 17; A. Sharratt, "When a Tragedy Strikes," *Benefits Canada* (November 2002), pp. 101–105.

46. R. Csiernik, "The Great EAP Question: Internal or External?" *Canadian HR Reporter* (August 20, 2007).

47. R. Csiernik, "What to Look for in an External EAP Service," *Canadian HR Reporter* (May 31, 2004), p. 7; D. Sharar, "With HR Chasing Lowest Price, EAPs Can't Improve Quality," *Canadian HR Reporter* (May 31, 2004), pp. 6, 8; A. Davis, "Helping Hands," *Benefits Canada* (November 2000), pp. 117–121.

48. "100 Best Companies to Work For," *Fortune* (January 2000), http://money.cnn.com/magazines/fortune/fortune_archive/2000/01/10/271718/index.htm (accessed September 4, 2012).

49. C. Foster, "Workers Don't Leave Problems at Home," *Canadian HR Reporter* (May 7, 2007).

50. S. Dobson, "Is Backup Care Worth the Investment?" *Canadian HR Reporter* (November 3, 2008); D. Brown, "Bringing the Family to Work," *Canadian HR Reporter* (November 6, 2000), pp. 19–20.

51. "Employer-Sponsored Child Care Can Be Instrumental in Attraction and Retention," *Workspan* (January 2009), p. 10.

52. D. McCloskey, "Caregiving and Canadian Families," *Transition Magazine* (Summer 2005), p. 1; B. Parus, "Who's Watching Grandma? Addressing the Eldercare Dilemma," *Workspan* (January 2004), pp. 40–43.

53. "Elder Care to Eclipse Child Care, Report Says," *Canadian HR Reporter* (August 14, 1995), p. 11; A. Vincola, "Eldercare—What Firms Can Do to Help," *Canadian HR Reporter* (June 5, 2000), p. G3.

54. S. Klie, "Employers Can Help with 'Long Goodbye'," *Canadian HR Reporter* (August 13, 2007).

55. D. Dyck, "Make Your Workplace Family-Friendly," *Canadian HR Reporter* (December 13, 1999), pp. G5, G10.

56. E.E. Kossek and C. Ozeki, "Work-Family Conflict, Policies, and the Job-Life Satisfaction Relationship: A Review and Direction for Organizational Behavior–Human Resources Research," *Journal of Applied Psychology,* 83, (1998), pp. 139–149.

57. B. Ellig, *Executive Compensation—A Total Pay Perspective* (New York, NY: McGraw-Hill, 1982), p. 141.

58. B. Jaworski, "'I'll Have My People Call Your People '" *Canadian HR Reporter* (March 27, 2006).

59. W. White and J. Becker, "Increasing the Motivational Impact of Employee Benefits," *Personnel* (January–February 1980), pp. 32–37; B. Olmsted and S. Smith, "Flex for Success!" *Personnel,* 66, no. 6 (June 1989), pp. 50–55.

60. B. McKay, "The Flexible Evolution," *Workplace News* (January/February 2006), pp. 14–15.

61. Ibid.

62. D. Brown, "Everybody Loves Flex," *Canadian HR Reporter* (November 18, 2002), pp. 1, 11; R. Dawson and B. McKay, "The Flexibility of Flex," *WorldatWork Canadian News* (Fourth Quarter, 2005), pp. 1, 6–13.

63. J. Tompkins, "Moving Out: A Look at Comprehensive Benefits Outsourcing," *Canadian HR Reporter* (May 5, 1997), p. 9.

64. N. Chaplick, "Enter at Your Own Risk," *Benefits Canada* (May 2000), pp. 37–39; see also M. Reid, "Legal Aid," *Benefits Canada* (June 2000), pp. 46–48; S. Deller, "Five Hot Survival Tips for Communicating Benefits," *Canadian HR Reporter* (July 13, 1998), pp. 9, 19.

65. C. Davenport, "Employers Twig to Value of Ongoing Pension Communication," *Canadian HR Reporter* (December 16, 1996), p. 33.

Chapter 14

1. D. Brown, "Wellness Programs Bring Healthy Bottom Line," *Canadian HR Reporter* (December 17, 2001), pp. 1, 14.

2. Association of Workers' Compensation Boards of Canada, www.awcbc.ca (accessed July 15, 2009); "Working to Death—Millions Die Each Year Due to Work-Related Accidents and Diseases," *IAPA Press Release* (April 19, 2006), www.iapa.ca/about_iapa/2006_apr19_press.asp (accessed June 20, 2006).

3. H. Bryan, "Attitude Is Everything," *WorkSafe Magazine* (October 2005), p. 18.

4. S. De Léséleuc, "Criminal Victimization in the Workplace," Canadian Centre for Justice Statistics Profile Series (2004), http://downloads.workplaceviolencenews.com/criminal_victimization_in_the_workplace.pdf (accessed September 26, 2011).

5. Based on T.A. Opie and L. Bates, *1997 Canadian Master Labour Guide* (CCH Canada Inc.), pp. 1015–1034.

6. C.A. Edwards and C.E. Humphrey, *Due Diligence Under the Occupational Health and Safety Act: A Practical Guide* (Toronto, ON: Carswell/Thomson Canada, 2000).

7. N. Keith, "The Omniscient Employer: The Need to See the Unforeseeable," *Workplace* (March/April 2008), pp. 16–19.

8. M. Pilger, "Conducting a Hygiene Assessment," *Canadian HR Reporter* (April 10, 2000), pp. G3, G4; J. Montgomery, *Occupational Health and Safety* (Toronto, ON: Nelson Canada, 1996), p. 97; D. Brown, "Joint H&S Committees: An Opportunity, Not a Nuisance," *Canadian HR Reporter* (October 20, 2002), pp. 7, 10.

9. P. Strahlendorf, "What Supervisors Need to Know," *OH&S Canada* (January/February 1996), pp. 38–40; N. Tompkins, "Getting the Best Help from Your Safety Committee," *HR Magazine,* 40, no. 4 (April 1995), p. 76.

10. J. Grant and D. Brown, "The Inspector Cometh," *Canadian HR Reporter* (January 31, 2005), pp. 13, 17; "It's Time to Wake Up to Health and Safety: Ministry of Labour Increases Number of Inspectors," *Safety Mosaic,* 8 (Spring 2005), pp. 5–6.

11. "Alberta Imposes Record Penalties for OH&S Violations," *Workplace,* www.workplace-mag.com/Alberta-imposes-record-penalties-for-ohs-violations.html (accessed July 16, 2009).

12. S. Klie, "Individuals Targeted under OHS," *Canadian HR Reporter* (March 12, 2007); R. Stewart, "Legal Duties of the Front Line," *Canadian HR Reporter* (March 12, 2007).

13. "Employer Jailed for H&S Violation," *Canadian HR Reporter* (April 8, 2002), p. 2; see also T. Humber, "Putting the Boss Behind Bars?" *Canadian HR Reporter* (April 7, 2003).

14. "Quebec Employer First to Be Criminally Convicted in Death of Worker," *Canadian HR Reporter* (February 7, 2008); "C-45 Conviction Nets $110K Fine," *Canadian HR Reporter* (April 7, 2008).

15. J. Montgomery, *Occupational Health and Safety* (Toronto, ON: Nelson Canada, 1996), p. 34.

16. K. Prisciak, "Health, Safety & Harassment?" *OH&S Canada* (April/May 1997), pp. 20–21.

17. Dupont Canada, www2.dupont.com/DuPont_Home/en_CA/index.html (accessed June 20, 2006).

18. *A Safety Committee Man's Guide,* Aetna Life and Casualty Insurance Company, Catalog 872684.

19. J. Roughton, "Job Hazard Analysis," *OH&S Canada* (January/February 1996), pp. 41–44.

20. A. Fowler, "How to Make the Workplace Safer," *People Management,* 1, no. 2 (January, 1995), pp. 38–39.

21. List of unsafe acts from *A Safety Committee Man's Guide,* Aetna Life and Casualty Insurance Company; E. McCormick and J. Tiffin, *Industrial Psychology* (Englewood Cliffs, NJ: Prentice Hall, 1974).

22. E. McCormick and J. Tiffin, *Industrial Psychology* (Englewood Cliffs, NJ: Prentice Hall, 1974), pp. 522–523; David DeJoy, "Attributional Processes and Hazard Control Management in Industry," *Journal of Safety Research,* 16 (Summer 1985), pp. 61–71.

23. E. McCormick and J. Tiffin, *Industrial Psychology* (Englewood Cliffs, NJ: Prentice Hall, 1974), p. 523.

24. A. Campbell, *All Signs Point to Yes: Literacy's Impact on Workplace Health and Safety* (Ottawa, ON: The Conference Board of Canada, 2008).

25. S. Dobson, "Evidence of Link between Literacy, Safety," *Canadian HR Reporter* (December 1, 2008).

26. A. Campbell, *All Signs Point to Yes: Literacy's Impact on Workplace Health and Safety* (Ottawa, ON: The Conference Board of Canada, 2008).

27. "IAPA Wins First Place at International Film and Multimedia Festival," *Workplace* e-newsletter (July 18, 2008).

28. M. Blum and J. Nayler, *Industrial Psychology* (New York, NY: Harper & Row, 1968), p. 522.

29. L. Scott, "Measuring Employee Abilities," *Benefits Canada* (September 2002), pp. 41–49.

30. K. Gillin, "Reduce Employee Exposure to Injury with Pre-Employment Screening Tests," *Canadian HR Reporter* (February 28, 2000), p. 10.

31. M. Shaw, "Rewarding Health and Safety," *Canadian HR Reporter* (December 2, 2002), pp. 19–20.

32. "Rewarding Safety: 70 Million Kilometres and Counting," *Workplace* (November/December 2008).

33. M. Morra, "Fun, with Caution," *Workplace* (March/April 2008), pp. 1; L. Scott, "Measuring Employee Abilities," *Benefits Canada* (September 2002), pp. 41–49.

34. A. Dunn, "Back in Business," *Workplace News* (April 2005), pp. 16–17.

35. Ergomed Solutions, http://ergomedsolutions.com/functionalabilitieseval uationsp17.php (accessed July 15, 2009); C. Colacci, "Meet Your Return to Work Obligations with a Functional Abilities Evaluation," *Canadian HR Reporter* (April 10, 2000), p. G5.

36. C. Hall, "Sobering Advice," *Workplace News,* 11, no. 10 (November/December 2005), pp. 11–12.

37. *British Columbia (Public Service Employee Relations Commission) v. B.C.G.S.E.U.,* (1999) 176 D.L.R. (4th) 1 (S.C.C.) [*Meiorin*].

38. Policy on Drug and Alcohol Testing, Ontario Human Rights Commission, www.ohrc.on.ca/en/resources/Policies/PolicyDrugAlch (accessed July 16, 2009).

39. D. McCutcheon, "Confronting Addiction," *HR Professional* (June/July 2009), p. 39.

40. D. O'Meara, "Sober Second Chance," *Alberta Venture,* 9, no. 2 (March 2005), http://albertaventure.com/2005/03/sober-second-chance/?year=2005 (accessed September 4, 2012).

41. A. Nicoll, *Time for Action: Managing Mental Health in the Workplace* (Toronto, ON: Mercer Human Resources Consulting), (2008); L. Duxbury and C. Higgins, *Exploring the Link between Work–Life Conflict and Demands on Canada's Health Care System: Report Three* (Public Health Agency of Canada: March 2004).

42. *Mental Health at Work: Booklet 1.* IRSST (Laval University, 2005).

43. *Staying@Work: Effective Presence at Work: 2007 Survey Report:Canada* (Toronto, ON: Watson Wyatt).

44. Ibid.

45. D. Crisp, "Leaders Make the Difference," in A. Shaw, "Toxic Workplaces as Bad as Unsafe Ones," *Canadian HR Reporter* (April 21, 2008).

46. A. Nicoll, *Time for Action: Managing Mental Health in the Workplace* (Toronto, ON: Mercer Human Resources Consulting), (2008).

47. Statistics Canada, "Study: Workaholics and Time Perception," *The Daily* (May 15, 2007).

48. "Is Your Job Making You Sick?" *Canadian HR Reporter* (September 17, 2008).

49. J.W. Simpson, "Psychopaths Wear Suits, Too," *National Post* (May 10, 2006), p. WK6; A. Gill, "The Psychopath in the Corner Office," *Globe and Mail* (May 27, 2006), p. F1; "Push for Productivity Taking its Toll," *Canadian HR Reporter* (November 6, 2001), p. 15; D. Brown, "Doing More with Less Hurts Employees and Productivity," *Canadian HR Reporter* (October 7, 2002), pp. 3, 13; A. Sharratt, "Silver Linings," *Benefits Canada* (March 2003), pp. 51–53.

50. J. Santa-Barbara, "Preventing the Stress Epidemic," *Canadian HR Reporter* (March 8, 1999), p. 19; see also A. Chiu, "Beyond Physical Wellness: Mental Health Issues in the Workplace," *Canadian HR Reporter* (February 26, 2001), p. 4; L. Hyatt, "Job Stress: Have We Reached the Breaking Point?" *Workplace Today* (January 2002), pp. 14, 15, 37.

51. "Health Care Workers Most Stressed," *Canadian HR Reporter* (November 15, 2007)

52. P. Crawford-Smith, "Stressed Out," *Benefits Canada* (November 1999), pp. 115–117.

53. *Stress at Work: Taking Control* (Industrial Accident Prevention Association, 2002); J. Newman and T. Beehr, "Personal and Organizational Strategies for Handling Job Stress: A Review of Research and Opinion," *Personnel Psychology* (Spring 1979), pp. 1–43; see also Bureau of National Affairs, "Work Place Stress: How to Curb Claims," *Bulletin to Management* (April 14, 1988), p. 120.

54. T. Humber, "Stress Attack," *Canadian HR Reporter* (February 10, 2002), pp. G1, G10; M. Shain, "Stress and Satisfaction," *OH&S Canada* (April/May 1999), pp. 38–47.

55. P. Carayon, "Stressful Jobs and Non-Stressful Jobs: A Cluster Analysis of Office Jobs," *Ergonomics,* 37, no. 2 (1994), pp. 311–323.

56. *Workplace Mental Health Indicators: An EAP's Perspective,* Shepell-fgi Research Group, 2005, Series 1, Vol. 1, Issue 1.

57. A. Pihulyk, "When the Job Overwhelms," *Canadian HR Reporter* (January 14, 2002), p. 11.

58. P. Kishchuk, *Yukon Workers' Compensation Act Subsection 105.1 Research Series: Expansion of the Meaning of Disability* (March 2003).

59. M. Gibb-Clark, "The Case for Compensating Stress Claims," *Globe and Mail* (June 14, 1999), p. M1; L. Young, "Stressed Workers Are Suing Employers," *Canadian HR Reporter* (May 3, 1999), pp. 1, 6; D. Brown, "Liability Could Extend to Mental Damage," *Canadian HR Reporter* (October 9, 2000), pp. 1, 8.

60. OPSEU Online, "International RSI Awareness Day—February 28, 2006," www.opseu.org/hands/rsi2006.htm (accessed May 18, 2006); J. Hampton, "RSIs: The Biggest Strain Is on the Bottom Line," *Canadian HR Reporter* (February 10, 1997), pp. 15, 19; see also G. Harrington, "Pushing Ergonomics into Place," *Canadian HR Reporter* (April 24, 1995), pp. 11–12.

61. "Prevent Workplace Pains and Strains! It's Time to Take Action!" Ontario Ministry of Labour, www.labour.gov.on.ca/english/hs/ergonomics/is_ergonomics.html (accessed May 25, 2006).

62. S.B. Hood, "Repetitive Strain Injury," *Human Resources Professional* (June/July 1997), pp. 29–34.

63. "Ergonomic Intervention Improves Worker Health and Productivity," *Institute for Work and Health* (December 15, 2003), www.iwh.on.ca/media/ergonomic.php (accessed July 8, 2006); "Ergonomic Intervention Improves Worker Health and Productivity," *Workplace News* (February 2004), p. 16.

64. J.A. Savage, "Are Computer Terminals Zapping Workers' Health?" *Business and Society Review* (1994).

65. "Office Ergonomics and Repetitive Strain Injuries: What You Need to Know," Ottawa Valley Physiotherapy, www.ovphysio.com (accessed May 25, 2006); Occupational Health and Safety Agency for Healthcare in British Columbia, www.ohsah.bc.ca/templates/index.php?section_copy_id=5396 (accessed May 25, 2006); S. Tenby, "Introduction to Ergonomics: How to Avoid RSI—Repetitive Strain Injury," Disabled Women's Network Ontario, http://dawn.thot.net/cd/20.html (accessed May 25, 2006).

66. U. Vu, "Steel Union Gathers Workplace Cancer Data," *Canadian HR Reporter* (June 2, 2008).

67. "Unions Stress Cancer Prevention," *Canadian HR Reporter* (February 28, 2005), p. 2.

68. D. Brown, "Killer Toxins in the Workplace," *Canadian HR Reporter* (April 23, 2001), pp. 1, 12.

69. A. Scappatura, "Enhanced Coverage for Firefighters," *Canadian HR Reporter* (May 18, 2009).

70. "EI Granted in Second-Hand Smoke Case," *Canadian HR Reporter* (May 19, 2003), p. 3; see also M.M. Finklestein, "Risky Business," *OH&S Canada* (September/October 1996), pp. 32–34.

71. T. Humber, "Snuffing Out Smoking," *Canadian HR Reporter* (April 11, 2005), p. 19, 23; *Towards Healthier Workplaces and Public Places* (Health Canada, 2004).

72. C. Hallamore, *A State of Unpreparedness: Canadian Organizations' Readiness for a Pandemic* (Ottawa, ON: The Conference Board of Canada, June 2006).

73. C.C. Cavicchio, "Action Plan for Dealing with a Global Pandemic," *The Conference Board Executive Action Series* (May 2009).

74. C. Hallamore, *A State of Unpreparedness: Canadian Organizations' Readiness for a Pandemic* (Ottawa, ON: The Conference Board of Canada, June 2006).

75. R.A. Macpherson, E. Ringsels, and H. Singh, "Swine Influenza: Advice for Employers Preparing for a Pandemic," *McCarthy Tetrault e-Alert* (April 29, 2009), http://news.mccarthy.ca/en/news_template_full.asp?pub_code=4502&news_code=1066 (accessed April 29, 2009).

76. C.C. Cavicchio, "Action Plan for Dealing with a Global Pandemic," *The Conference Board Executive Action Series* (May 2009).

77. D.J. McKeown and K. Ford, "The Importance of People-Focused Pandemic Planning," *Workplace News* (September/October 2006).

78. Ibid.

79. C. Harden, "Preparing for a Pandemic: The Total Rewards Angle," *Workspan* (July 2006).

80. *Violence in the Workplace*, Canadian Association of University Teachers (October 4, 2004); W.H. Glenn, "Workplace Violence: An Employees' Survival Guide," *OH&S Canada* (April/May 2002), pp. 26–31.

81. S. De Leseleuc, *Criminal Victimization in the Workplace* (Canadian Centre for Justice Statistics, Catalogue No. 85F0033MIE – No. 013, 2004).

82. "Male Nurses More Likely to Be Assaulted by Patients: StatsCan," *Canadian HR Reporter* (April 16, 2009).

83. S. Dobson, "Sexual Assault Prompts OHS Charge," *Canadian HR Reporter* (December 15, 2008); L. De Piante, "Watch Out for Dangerous Employees," *Canadian HR Reporter* (October 22, 2007); A. Feliu, "Workplace Violence and the Duty of Care: The Scope of an Employer's Obligation to Protect against the Violent Employee," *Employee Relations Law Journal*, 20, no. 3 (Winter 1994/95), pp. 381–406; G. French and P. Morgan, "The Risks of Workplace Violence," *Canadian HR Reporter* (December 18, 2000), pp. 27–28.

84. M.M. LeBlanc and E.K. Kelloway, "Predictors and Outcomes of Workplace Violence and Aggression, *Journal of Applied Psychology*, 87, no. 3 (June 2002), 444–453.

85. L. De Piante, "Watch Out for Dangerous Employees," *Canadian HR Reporter* (October 22, 2007).

86. S. Klie, "Screening New Hires Won't End Workplace Violence, Study Says," *Canadian HR Reporter* (November 21, 2005), pp. 1, 3; K. Acquino et al., "How Employees Respond to Personal Offense: The Effect of the Blame Attribution, Victim Status, and Offender Status on Revenge and Reconciliation in the Workplace," *Journal of Applied Psychology*, 86, no. 1 (2001), pp. 52–59.

87. A. Tomlinson, "Re-evaluating Your Workplace: Is It Safe and Secure?" *Canadian HR Reporter* (February 25, 2002), pp. 3, 12; L. Martin and D. Tona, "Before It's Too Late," *OH&S Canada* (April/May 2000), pp. 52–53.

88. P. Viollis and C. Mathers, "Companies Need to Re-engineer Their Cultural Thinking About Workplace Violence," *Canadian HR Reporter* (March 14, 2005), p. 19; D. Anfuso, "Workplace Violence," *Personnel Journal* (October 1994), p. 71; see also L. Martin and D. Tona, "Before It's Too Late," *OH&S Canada* (April/May 2000), pp. 52–53; H. Bloom, "Workplace Violence: The Myth That We're Helpless," *Workplace Today* (January 2002), pp. 36–37; W.H. Glenn, "Workplace Violence: An Employees' Survival Guide," *OH&S Canada* (April/May 2002), pp. 26–31.

89. D. Anfuso, "Workplace Violence," *Personnel Journal* (October 1994), pp. 66–77.

90. L. Young, "Managers at B.C. Telus Held Accountable for Wellness," *Canadian HR Reporter* (February 28, 2000), p. 9.

91. J. Taggart and J. Farrell, "Where Wellness Shows Up on the Bottom Line," *Canadian HR Reporter* (October 20, 2003), pp. 12, 15.

92. S. Klie, "Seven Oaks Hospital Relies on Healthy Staff," *Canadian HR Reporter* (October 23, 2006).

93. E. Buffett, "Healthy Employees Translate into Profits," *Canadian HR Reporter* (April 9, 2007).

94. A. Tomlinson, "Healthy Living a Remedy for Burgeoning Employee Absentee Rates," *Canadian HR Reporter* (March 25, 2002), pp. 3, 12.

95. S. Pellegrini, "The Next 25 Years: Wellness," *Benefits Canada* (June 2002), pp. 83–85.

96. C. Warren, "Healthy Competition Boosts Workplace Wellness," *Workplace News* (November/December 2007).

Chapter 15

1. Compdata Surveys, www.compdatasurveys.com/Products/Compensation.

2. N. Chhinzer and K. Ababneh, "Characteristics of the Unemployed in Canada: Leavers, Losers, and Layoffs," *International Business & Economics Research Journal*, 9, no. 12 (2010), pp. 1–15.

3. Statistics Canada, "Permanent Layoffs, Quits and Hirings in the Canadian Economy 1978 to 1995," Business and Labour Market Analysis Division, www.statcan.gc.ca/pub/71-539-x/71-539-x1995001-eng.pdf (accessed September 26, 2011).

4. A. Cowan and N. Stewart, "Compensation Planning Outlook 2011: Playing It Safe in the Face of an Unsteady Economic Recovery," The Conference Board of Canada (October 2010).

5. A. Heller, "The People Factor: Supermarkets' Investment in Return on People Provides Results in a Changing Labour Environment," *Supermarket News* (May 2004), http://subscribers.supermarketnews.com/mag/people_factor, (accessed September 26, 2011).

6. W.F. Cascio, *Responsible Restructuring: Creative and Profitable Alternatives to Layoffs* (San Fransico, CA: Barrett-Koehler, 2002).

7. W.F. Cascio, *Costing human resources: The financial impact of behavior in Organizations* (Boston, MA: PWS-Kent, 1991).

8. R.W. Griffeth, P.W. Hom, and S. Gaertner, "A Meta-Analysis of Antecedents and Correlates of Employee Turnover: Update, Moderator Tests, and Research Implications for the Next Millennium," *Journal of Management*, 26, no. 3 (June 2006), pp. 463–488.

9. J. Johnson, R.W. Griffeth, and M. Griffin, "Factors Discrimination Functional and Dysfunctional Sales Force Turnover," *Journal of Business & Industrial Marketing*, 15, no. 6 (January 2000), pp. 399–415.

10. S. Abbasi and K. Hollman, "Turnover: The Real Bottom-Line," *Public Personnel Management*, 29, no. 3 (2000), pp. 333–342.

11. S. Hartman and A. Yrle, "Can the Hobo Phenomenon Help Explain Voluntary Turnover?" *International Journal of Contemporary Hospitality Management*, 8, no. 4 (August 1996), pp. 11–16.

12. M. Stovel and N. Bontis, "Voluntary Turnover: Knowledge Management Friend or Foe?" *Journal of Intellectual Capital*, 3, no. 3 (2002), pp. 303–322.

13. W.H. Mobley, R.W. Griffeth, H.H. Hand, and B.M. Meglino, "Review and Conceptual Analysis of the Employee Turnover Process," *Psychological Bulletin*, 86, no. 3 (May 1979), pp. 493–522.

14. P.W. Hom and A.J. Kinicki, "Toward a Greater Understanding of How Dissatisfaction Drives Employee Turnover," *Academy of Management Journal*, 44, no. 5 (October, 2001), pp. 975–987.

15. P. Cappelli, *The New Deal at Work: Managing the Market-Driven Workforce* (Boston, MA: Harvard Business School Press, 1999).

16. S. Norris, and T. Williams, "Healthy Aging: Adding Years to Life and Life to Years," Government of Canada (October 27, 2000), http://dsp-psd.pwgsc.gc.ca/Collection-R/LoPBdP/BP/prb0023-e.htm (accessed September 26, 2011).

17. "Mandatory Retirement Fades in Canada," CBC News (October 18, 2010), www.cbc.ca/news/canada/story/2009/08/20/mandatory-retirement-explainer523.html (accessed September 26, 2011).

18. Ibid.

19. G. Golightly, "Preparing Employees for Retirement Transitions," *HR Professional* (December 1999/January 2000), pp. 27–33.

20. *1995 Canadian Dismissal Practices Survey* (Toronto, ON: Murray Axmith & Associates).

21. G. Golightly, "Preparing Employees for Retirement Transitions," *HR Professional* (December 1999/January 2000), pp. 27–33.

22. J. Famularo, *Handbook of Modern Personnel Administration* (New York, NY: McGraw-Hill, 1972), pp. 65.3–65.5.

23. N. Chhinzer and K. Ababneh, "Characteristics of the Unemployed in Canada: Leavers, Losers, and Layoffs," *International Business & Economics Research Journal*, 9, no. 12 (December 2010), pp. 1–15

24. N.C. MacDonald, "Progressing towards Just Cause," *Canadian HR Reporter* (September 22, 2008).

25. S. Rudner, "Just Cause Termination Still Not Clearcut," *Canadian HR Reporter* (March 23, 2009).

26. D. Bambrough and M. Certosimo, "Worker Fraud Usually Justifies Dismissal," *Canadian HR Reporter* (October 23, 2006).

27. L. Cassiani, "Dishonesty Not Always Enough to Terminate," *Canadian HR Reporter* (August 13, 2001), pp. 3, 6; P. Israel, "Firing an Employee for Dishonesty? Put Things in Context First," *Canadian HR Reporter* (August 12, 2002), p. 5.

28. "Proving Cause for Termination Getting Harder," *Workplace Today* (January 2001), p. 17; L. Harris, "High Standards Allow Employer to Fire Threatening Employee," *Canadian HR Reporter* (October 22, 2001), pp. 8, 10.

29. D. Bambrough and M. Certosimo, "Worker Fraud Usually Justifies Dismissal," *Canadian HR Reporter* (October 23, 2006).

30. A. Britnell, "Stop Employee Theft," *Canadian Business Online* (July 16, 2003), www.canadianbusiness.com (accessed May 29, 2006); J. Towler, "Dealing with Employees Who Steal," *Canadian HR Reporter* (September 23, 2002), p. 4.

31. "Air Canada Searches Employee Rooms," *Canadian HR Reporter* (February 10, 2003), p. 2.

32. J. Famularo, *Handbook of Modern Personnel Administration* (New York, NY: McGraw-Hill, 1972), pp. 65.4–65.5.

33. "Good Broker, Bad Decision," *Canadian HR Reporter* (July 17, 2006).

34. K.S. Cameron. "Investigating Organizational Downsizing: Fundamental Issues," *Human Resource Management*, 33 (1994), pp. 183–188.

35. Ibid.

36. Commerce Clearing House, *Personnel Practices/Communications* (Chicago, IL: CCH, 1992), p. 1410.

37. E.A. Lind, J. Greenberg, K.S. Scott, and T.D. Welchans, "The Winding Road from Employee to Complainant: Situational and Psychological Determinants of Wrongful Dismissal Claims," *Administrative Science Quarterly*, 45 (2000), pp. 557–590.

38. Y. Cohen-Charash and P. E. Spector, "The Role of Justice in Organizations: A Meta-Analysis," *Organizational Behavior and Human Decision Processes*, 86 (November 2001), pp. 278–321.

39. E.E. Mole, *Wrongful Dismissal Practice Manual*, Chapter 7 (Toronto, ON: Butterworths Canada, 1993).

40. J.R. Smith, "Worker Ordered to Pay $41.5 Million," *Canadian HR Reporter* (December 1, 2008).

41. K. Blair, "Sports Editor Scores 28-Month Severance," *Canadian HR Reporter* (April 7, 1997), p. 5.

42. M. Fitzgibbon, "Desperate for Workers? Watch Your Step," *Canadian HR Reporter* (January 28, 2008).

43. J. McAlpine, "Don't Add Bad Faith to Wrongful Dismissal," *Canadian HR Reporter* (May 6, 2002), p. 7; P. Israel, "Cut Down on Lawsuits Just by Being Nice," *Canadian HR Reporter* (November 18, 2002), p. 5.

44. N.C. MacDonald, "Record-Setting Wallace Award Overturned," *Canadian HR Reporter* (September 11, 2006).

45. J.R. Smith, "Top Court Strips Out Damages in *Keays*," *Canadian HR Reporter* (July 14, 2008); T. Giesbrecht, K. McDermott, and K. McNeill, "*Keays v. Honda Canada Inc.*" www.mccarthy.ca/article_detail. aspx?id=4053 (accessed June 27, 2008).

46. M.J. MacKillop, "The Perils of Dismissal: The Impact of the Wallace Decision on Reasonable Notice." Paper presented at the Human Resources Professionals Association of Ontario Employment Law Conference (Toronto, ON, October 1999), p. 18.

47. K. Blair, "Pay in Lieu Just the Beginning," *Canadian HR Reporter* (July 14, 1997), p. 5; see also K. Blair, "Dismissal Damages, Thy Name Is Mitigation," *Canadian HR Reporter* (February 9, 1998), p. 5.

48. M. MacKillop and L. Jessome, "Manage Disability Claims with Care," *HR Professional* (August/September 2005), p. 30; J.M. Carvalho, "$500,000 Punitive Damages Award Shocks Honda," *McCarthy Tetrault Report on Canadian Labour and Employment Law* (September 2005).

49. N.C. MacDonald, "The *Keays* to Punitive Damages," *Canadian HR Reporter* (November 20, 2006); T. Giesbrecht, K. McDermott, and K. McNeill, "*Keays v. Honda Canada Inc.*" www.mccarthy.ca/article_detail.aspx?id=4053 (accessed June 27, 2008).

50. E.E. Mole, *Wrongful Dismissal Practice Manual*, Chapter 3 (Toronto, ON: Butterworths Canada, 1993).

51. H.A.Levitt and V. Michaelidis, "Ex-Employee Granted $800,000 in Constructive Dismissal Case," *Workplace* (March/April 2008), p. 11.

52. H. Nieuwland, "Changing Employment Contracts," *HR Professional* (October/November 2008), p. 21.

53. J. McApline, "10 Steps for Reducing Exposure to Wrongful Dismissal," *Canadian HR Reporter* (May 6, 2002), p. 8.

54. E. Caruk, "What to Do If a Wrongful Dismissal Action Hits," *Canadian HR Reporter* (May 6, 2002), p. 10.

55. Sonny Weide, "When You Terminate an Employee," *Employment Relations Today* (August 1994), pp. 287–293.

56. D. Bell, "No Easy Way to Say 'You're Fired'," *Canadian HR Reporter* (June 15, 2009); J. Coil, III and C. Rice, "Three Steps to Creating Effective Employee Releases," *Employment Relations Today* (Spring 1994), p. 92.

57. S. Milne, "The Termination Interview," *Canadian Manager* (Spring 1994), pp. 15–16.

58. A. Saks, "Engagement: The Academic Perspective," *Canadian HR Reporter* (January 26, 2009).

59. J. Gibbons, *Employee Engagement: A Review of Current Research and Its Implications* (New York, NY: The Conference Board, 2006).

60. *Engaging Employees to Drive Global Business Success: Insights from Mercer's What's Working™ Research* (New York, NY: Mercer, 2007).

61. S. O'Neal and J. Gebauer, "Talent Management in the 21st Century: Attracting, Retaining and Engaging Employees of Choice," *WorldatWork Journal*, 15, no. 1 (2006), pp. 6–17.

62. J. Shaffer, "Measurable Payoff: How Employee Engagement Can Boost Performance and Profits," *Communication World* (July–August 2004).

63. Based on D. McElroy, "High Tech with High Touch: A New Communication Contract," *Canadian HR Reporter* (April 7, 1997), p. G6.

64. "Chrysler Workers Furious over CEO`s Letter," *Canadian HR Reporter* (May 4, 2009).

65. D. Jones, "What If You Held a Survey and No-One Came?" *Canadian HR Reporter* (July 16, 2001), pp. 19, 22.

66. D. Brown, "Getting the Hard Facts in Employee Attitude and Satisfaction," *Canadian HR Reporter* (November 1, 1999), p. 2.

67. A. Massey, "Blogging Phobia Hits Employers," *Canadian HR Reporter* (September 26, 2005), pp. 15, 17.

68. L. Harris, "Staffer Fired after Bad-Mouthing Colleagues, Management in Blog," *Canadian HR Reporter* (September 8, 2008); S.E. Sorenson, "Employee Blogging," *HR Professional* (April/May 2008), p. 16.

69. L. De Piante, "Blogging Guidelines for Employees: A Necessity in the Workplace," *Canadian HR Reporter* (April 23, 2007); S. Crossley and M. Torrance, "Indiscriminate Blogging and the Workplace," *Workplace News* (November/December 2007), pp. 12–13.

70. Based on D. McElroy, "High Tech with High Touch: A New Communication Contract," *Canadian HR Reporter* (April 7, 1997), p. G6.

71. S. Klie, "Blogs Connect CEOs with Employees, Clients," *Canadian HR Reporter* (November 17, 2008).

Chapter 16

1. T.T. Delaney, "Unions and Human Resource Policies," in K. Rowland and G. Ferris (eds.), *Research in Personnel and Human Resources Management* (Greenwich, CT: JAI Press, 1991).

2. S. Klie, "Wal-Mart Closes Union Shop in Quebec," *Canadian HR Reporter* (November 3, 2008).

3. L. Harris, "Union-Proof: How Some Employers Avoid Organized Labour," *Canadian HR Reporter* (October 22, 2007).

4. R. Morissette, G. Shellenberg, and A. Johnson, "Diverging Trends in Unionization," *Perspectives on Labour and Income,* 17, no. 2, Statistics Canada (Summer 2005); U. Vu, "Low Membership Keeps Unions on the Defensive," *Canadian HR Reporter* (February 13, 2006), pp. 4, 9.

5. C. Hallamore, "Globalization Shifts the Ground in Labour Relations," *Inside Edge* (Spring 2006), p. 14; see also C. Hallamore, *Industrial Relations Outlook 2006: Shifting Ground, Shifting Attitudes* (Ottawa, ON: Conference Board of Canada, 2006).

6. C. Hallamore, *Industrial Relations Outlook 2007: Finding Common Ground through the War for Workers* (Ottawa, ON: The Conference Board of Canada, 2007); S. Klie, "Labour Market Should Unite Business, Unions," *Canadian HR Reporter* (February 27, 2007).

7. L. Harris, "Unions Taking Up the Mantle of Women's Issues," *Canadian HR Reporter* (August 11, 2008); L. Harris, "Youthful Proposition from Unions," *Canadian HR Reporter* (October 20, 2008).

8. H.N. Wheeler and J.A. McClendon, "The Individual Decision to Unionise," in G. Strauss et. al., (eds.), *The State of the Unions* (Madison, WI: Industrial Relations Research Association, 1991).

9. H.S. Farber and D.H. Saks, "Why Workers Want Unions: The Role of Relative Wages and Job Characteristics," *Journal of Political Economy,* 88, no. 21 (April, 1980), pp. 349–369.

10. J. Kelly, *Rethinking Industrial Relations: Mobilization, Collectivism, and Long Waves* (London, UK: Routledge, 1998).

11. H.N. Wheeler and J.A. McClendon, "The Individual Decision to Unionise," in G. Strauss et. al., (eds.), *The State of the Unions* (Madison, WI: Industrial Relations Research Association, 1991).

12. Statistics Canada, "Unionization Rates in First Half of 2007 and 2008," (March, 3, 2010), www.statcan.gc.ca/pub/75-001-x/topics-sujets/unionization-syndicalisation/unionization-syndicalisation-2008-eng.htm (accessed September 26, 2011).

13. C. Fullager and J. Barling, "A Longitudinal Test of a Model of the Antecedents and Consequences of Union Loyalty," *Journal of Applied Psychology,* 74, no. 2 (April 1989), pp. 213–227; A. Eaton, M. Gordon, and J. Keefe, "The Impact of Quality of Work-Life Programs and Grievance Systems Effectiveness on Union Commitment," *Industrial and Labor Relations Review,* 45, no. 3 (April 1992), pp. 592–604.

14. L. Young, "Union Drives: Initiated Within, Prevented Within," *Canadian HR Reporter* (November 29, 1999), pp. 2, 14.

15. Based in part on L. Field, "Early Signs," *Canadian HR Reporter* (November 29, 1999), p. 14.

16. *Canadian Master Labour Guide,* 16th ed. (Toronto, ON: CCH Canadian, 2002).

17. A.W.J. Craig and N.A. Solomon, *The System of Industrial Relations in Canada,* 5th ed. (Toronto, ON: Prentice Hall Canada, 1996), p. 217.

18. Ibid., p. 218.

19. Ibid., p. 216.

20. J. Peirce, *Canadian Industrial Relations* (Toronto, ON: Prentice Hall Canada, 2000), p. 431.

21. The section on distributive bargaining is based on R.E. Walton and R.B. McKersie, *A Behavioral Theory of Labor Negotiations* (New York, NY: McGraw-Hill, 1965), pp. 4–6.

22. The section on integrative bargaining is based on R.E. Walton and R.B. McKersie, *A Behavioral Theory of Labor Negotiations* (New York, NY: McGraw-Hill, 1965), pp. 4–6.

23. Based on C. Kapel, "The Feeling's Mutual," *Human Resources Professional* (April 1995), pp. 9–13; see also S.D. Smith, "Taking the Confrontation out of Collective Bargaining," *Canadian HR Reporter* (September 10, 2001), pp. 11, 13.

24. U. Vu, "Interest Wanes on Interest-Based?" *Canadian HR Reporter* (February 28, 2006), pp. 6, 9.

25. J. Peirce, *Canadian Industrial Relations* (Toronto, ON: Prentice Hall Canada, 2000), p. 431.

26. C. Spurr, "A 'Perfect Storm': Stora Enso Lockout in Nova Scotia," *Shunpiking Online,* 3, no. 4 (May 3, 2006), www.shunpiking.com/o10304/0304-AC-CS-perfectstrom.htm (accessed June 1, 2006); "Keep Stora off Campaign Agenda: Mayor," *CBC News* (May 26, 2006), www.cbc.ca/ns/story/nsv-stora20060526.html (accessed June 1, 2006).

27. L. Diebel, "45-Minute Job Action Staged for International Hotel Workers' Day," *Toronto Star* (November 11, 2007), www.thestar.com/printArticle/275447 (accessed July 21, 2009).

28. See J.E. Grenig, "Stare Decisis, Re Judicata and Collecteral Estoppel and Labour Arbitration," *Labour Law Journal,* 38 (April 1987), pp. 195–205.

29. Based on M. Gunderson and D.G. Taras, *Union–Management Relations in Canada* (Toronto, ON: Pearson Education Canada, 2001), p. 429; J. Peirce, *Canadian Industrial Relations* (Toronto, ON: Prentice Hall Canada, 2000), p. 431.

30. M. Hebert, "Length of Collective Agreements," *Workplace Gazette,* 7, no. 4 (Winter 2004), p. 27.

31. *Canadian Master Labour Guide,* 16th ed. (Toronto, ON: CCH Canadian Ltd., 2002).

32. M. Hebert, "Length of Collective Agreements," *Workplace Gazette,* 7, no. 4 (Winter 2004), p. 27.

33. G. Sova, "How Long a Contract Should You Sign?" *Canadian HR Reporter* (February 28, 2005), p. 9.

Chapter 17

1. R. Runzheimer and G. Harper, "Workforce Mobility Management Saves Money and Increases Efficiency," *Workspan* (December 2007), pp. 76–81.

2. "Definition of 'Immigrant,'" Statistics Canada (November 2010), www.statcan.gc.ca/pub/81-004-x/2010004/def/immigrant-eng.htm (accessed September 26, 2011).

3. L. Grobovsky, "Protecting Your Workers Abroad with a Global Diversity Strategy," *Canadian HR Reporter* (November 1, 1999), pp. 15–16.

4. "Oil and Water," *Canadian Business* (November 8–21, 2004), pp. 14, 16; "Expect Corruption Overseas," *Canadian HR Reporter* (September 23, 2002), p. 9.

5. R.J. House, P.J. Hanges, M. Javidan, P.W. Dorfman, and V. Gupta, *Culture, Leadership, and Organizations: The GLOBE Study of 62 Societies* (Thousand Oaks, CA: Sage Publications, 2004); G. Hofstede, "Cultural Dimensions in People Management," in V. Pucik, N. Tichy and C. Barnett (eds.), *Globalizing Management,* (New York, NY: John Wiley & Sons, 1992), p. 143.

6. S. Klie, "HR Around the World," *Canadian HR Reporter* (November 6, 2006); K. King-Metters and R. Metters, "Misunderstanding the Chinese Worker," *The Wall Street Journal* (July 7, 2008), p. R11.

7. R. Little, "Foreigners Explore Pros and Cons Behind Vietnamese Work Ethic," http://vietnamnews.vnagency.com.vn/showarticle.php?num=)!SAY080808 (accessed September 4, 2008).

8. A. Yeo, "A Brief Look at the PRC Employment Promotion Law," *Human Resources* (December 2007), pp. 29–31; J. Yan, "A Snapshot of Chinese Employment Law," *Canadian HR Reporter* (November 6, 2006); "China's New Labor Contract Law," *Workspan* (March 2008), p. 12.

9. D. Matthews, *Severance Practices Around the World*. (Philadelphia, PA: Right Management, 2008); G. Avraam, A. Ishak, and T. Appleyard, "Terminating Employees Around the World," *Canadian HR Reporter* (April 6, 2009).

10. "Britain Introduces Corporate Manslaughter Act," *Canadian HR Reporter* (April 16, 2008).

11. A. Macaulay, "Culture, Safety and Privacy Norms Abroad Present Challenges for HR," *Canadian HR Reporter* (November 6, 2006).

12. E. Kelly, "The New Frontier," *HR Professional* (August/September 2008), pp. 24–28.

13. Discussed in E. Gaugler, "HR Management: An International Comparison," *Personnel* (August 1988), p. 28.

14. Wharton School, "Made in China," *Human Resource Executive Online* (February 26, 2008).

15. *2008/2009 Benefits Survey for Expatriates and Globally Mobile Employees* (New York, NY: Mercer, 2009).

16. M. Sim and L. Dixon, "Number of Women Expats Increasing," *Canadian HR Reporter* (May 21, 2007).

17. T. Shelton, "A Best-of-Breed Approach: Addressing the ROI and Retention Challenges of Global Workforce Management," *Workspan* (April 2009), pp. 50–54.

18. D. Bergles and R. Peterman, "Selling Relocation Used to Be Easier Than This," *Canadian HR Reporter* (September 27, 2004), p. 8; S. Cryne, "Are Short-Term Gigs Better Than Permanent Moves?" *Canadian HR Reporter* (December 6, 2004), pp. 1–2.

19. S. Dobson, "Enticing Employees to Go on Relocation," *Canadian HR Reporter* (May 18, 2009).

20. J. Head, "How Paper Can Protect International Relocations," *Canadian HR Reporter* (March 13, 2006).

21. *2005 Employee Relocation Survey: Domestic, Cross-Border & International Relocations* (Toronto, ON: Canadian Employee Relocation Council, 2005).

22. Ibid.

23. *Global Relocation Trends: Survey Report 2008*. GMAC Global Relocation Services.

24. G.N. Abbott, B.W. Stening, P.W.B. Atkins, and A.M. Grant, "Coaching Expatriate Managers for Success: Adding Value Beyond Training and Mentoring," *Asia-Pacific Journal of Human Resources,* 44, pp. 295–317.

25. G. Insch and J. Daniels, "Causes and Consequences of Declining Early Departures from Foreign Assignments," *Business Horizons,* 46, no. 6 (November–December 2002), pp. 39–48.

26. E. Krell, "Budding Relationships," *HR Magazine,* 50, no. 6 (June 2005), pp. 114–118.

27. P. Caliguri, "The Big Five Personality Characteristics as Predictors of Expatriates' Desire to Terminate the Assignment and Supervisor-Rated Performance," *Personnel Psychology,* 53, no. 1 (Spring 2000), pp. 67–88.

28. J. Selmer, "Expatriation: Corporate Policy, Personal Intentions and International Adjustment," *International Journal of Human Resource Management,* 9, no. 6 (December 1998), pp. 997–1007.

29. Discussed in C. Hill, *International Business: Competing in the Global Marketplace* (Burr Ridge, IL: Irwin, 1994), pp. 511–515.

30. C. Solomon, "One Assignment, Two Lives," *Personnel Journal* (May 1996), pp. 36–47; M. Harvey, "Dual-Career Couples During International Relocation: The Trailing Spouse," *International Journal of Human Resource Management,* 9, no. 2 (April 1998), pp. 309–330.

31. Based on B.J. Punnett, "International Human Resources Management," in A.M. Rugman (ed.), *International Business in Canada: Strategies for Management,* pp. 330–346 (Toronto, ON: Prentice Hall Canada, 1989);

L.G. Klaff, "Thinning the Ranks of the 'Career Expats,'" *Workforce Management* (October 2004), pp. 84–87.

32. V. Galt, "World Loves to Milk Canada's Executive Pool," *Globe and Mail* (September 5, 2005), p. B10.

33. S. Cryne, "The Changing World of the Relocation Specialist," *Canadian HR Reporter* (March 8, 2004), pp. 13, 15; G. Reinhart, "Preparing for Global Expansion: A Primer," *Canadian HR Reporter* (March 14, 2005), pp. 14, 17.

34. *Survey 2011 Global Assignment Policies and Practices*, KPMG, p. 9, www.kpmginstitutes.com/taxwatch/insights/2011/pdf/gapp-survey-2011.pdf.

35. Z. Fedder, "Short-Sighted Thinking Shortchanges Short-Term International Assignments," *Canadian HR Reporter* (September 25, 2000), p. 20.

36. S. Cryne, "The Changing World of the Relocation Specialist," *Canadian HR Reporter* (March 8, 2004), pp. 13, 15.

37. J.D. Daniels and L.H. Radebaugh, *International Business* (Reading, MA: Addison-Wesley, 1994), p. 767; Arvind Phatak, *International Dimensions of Management* (Boston, MA: PWS-Kent, 1989), pp. 106–107.

38. A. Bross, A. Churchill, and J. Zifkin, "Cross-Cultural Training: Issues to Consider During Implementation," *Canadian HR Reporter* (June 5, 2000), pp. 10, 12.

39. Ibid.; "New Labor Contract Law," *Workspan* (March 2008), p. 12.

40. E.M. Norman, "How Multinationals Doing Business in Asia Can Develop Leadership Talent During a Recession," *Workspan* (May 2009), pp. 35–43.

41. "More Multinationals Embracing Centralized Compensation Structures," *Workspan* (November 2006), p. 10; C. Reynolds, "Global Compensation and Benefits in Transition," *Compensation and Benefits Review* (January/February 2000), pp. 28–28; J.E. Richard, "Global Executive Compensation: A Look at the Future," *Compensation and Benefits Review* (May/June 2000), pp. 35–38.

42. L. Laroche, "Negotiating Expatriate Packages," *Canadian HR Reporter* (November 20, 2000), pp. 15, 19.

43. J. Cartland, "Reward Policies in a Global Corporation," *Business Quarterly* (Autumn 1993), pp. 93–96; L. Mazur, "Europay," *Across-the-Board* (January 1995), pp. 40–43.

44. K. Bensky, "Developing a Workable Global Rewards System," *Workspan* (October 2002), pp. 44–48.

45. A. Phatak, *International Dimensions of Management* (Boston, MA: PWS-Kent, 1989), p. 134; see also L. Laroche, "Negotiating Expatriate Packages," *Canadian HR Reporter* (November 20, 2000), pp. 15, 19.

46. K. Abosch, J. Schermerhorn, and L. Wisper, "Broad-Based Variable Pay Goes Global," *Workspan* (May 2008), pp. 56–62.

47. "Expatriates, Families Face Different Stressors than Stateside Counterparts," *Workspan* (October 2008), p. 18.

48. V. Frazee, "Keeping Your Expats Healthy," *Global Workforce* (November 1998), pp. 18–23; see also B. Barker and D. Schulde, "Special EAP Helps Expatriates Face International 'Culture Shock,'" *Canadian HR Reporter* (November 29, 1999), p. 20; L. O'Grady, "Using Technology to De-stress on International Assignment," *Canadian HR Reporter* (September 24, 2001), pp. 8, 12; R. Melles, "Lost in Translation," *Canadian HR Reporter* (March 8, 2004), p. 14; E.C. Heher, "Anticipating the Psychological Effects of Expatriate Life," *Workspan* (May 2006), pp. 54–56.

49. A. Bross and G. Wise, "Sustaining the Relocated Employee with an International EAP," *Canadian HR Reporter* (November 29, 1999), pp. 18, 19, 21.

50. M. Mendenhall and G. Addou, *International Human Resource Management* (Boston, MA: PWS-Kent Publishing, 1991), p. 366; see also M. Janssens, "Evaluating International Managers' Performance: Parent Company Standards as Control Mechanism," *International Journal of Human Resource Management,* 5, no. 4 (December 1994), pp. 853–873.

51. A. Lauffs, "Labor Relations in China," presentation to South China Morning Post Conference: Human Capital in Greater China (Hong Kong: December 2007).

52. M. Higginson, "Hungary's Low Labor Costs Still Lure Big Investors," *Budapest Business Journal* (April 10, 2006).

53. R. Sauer and K. Voelker, *Labor Relations: Structure and Process* (New York, NY: Macmillan, 1993), pp. 510–525.

54. Quoted from R. Sauer and K. Voelker, *Labor Relations: Structure and Process* (New York, NY: Macmillan, 1993), p. 519.

55. C. Storti, *The Art of Coming Home* (Boston, MA: Nicholas Brealey Publishing, 2001); S. Cryne, "Homeward Bound," *Canadian HR Reporter* (March 9, 2009).

56. "Views of Employees and Companies Differ on International Assignments," *Workspan Focus Canada 2006*, pp. 22–24; L. Stroh, "Predicting Turnover among Repatriates: Can Organizations Affect Retention Rates?" *International Journal of Human Resource Management,* 6, no. 2 (May 1995), pp. 443–456.

57. J. Keogh, "A Win–Win, from Start to Finish," *Workspan* (February 2003), pp. 36–39; D. Brown, "Companies Undervaluing Skills Learned During Relocation," *Canadian HR Reporter* (February 28, 2000), pp. 15, 21; J. Hobel, "The Expatriate Employee Homecoming," *Canadian HR Reporter* (June 1, 1998), pp. G5, G11.

58. D. McCutcheon, "Repatriation: Bringing Home the Troops," *HR Professional* (April/May 2009), pp. 33–34; P. Stanoch and G. Reynolds, "Relocating Career Development," *Canadian HR Reporter* (May 5, 2003), pp. 13, 15; L.M, "Global Talk," *HR Professional* (June/July 2006), p. 12.

59. Research and Evaluation Branch, Citizenship and Immigration Canada, "Canada Facts and Figures, Immigration Overview, Permanent and Temporary Residents 2010," www.cic.gc.ca/english/pdf/research-stats/facts2010.pdf (accessed September 26, 2011).

60. S. Lopes and Y. Poisson, "Bringing Employers into the Immigration Debate: Survey and Roundtable," *Public Policy Forum* (2004), www.toronto.ca/metropolis/metropolistoronto2005/pdf/lopesetal_audc.pdf (accessed September 26, 2011).

61. C.C. Miller, L.M. Burke, and W.H. Glick, "Cognitive Diversity among Upper Echelon Executives: Implications for Strategic Decision Processes," *Strategic Management Journal,* 19, no.1 (January 1998), pp. 39–58; S.K. Horwitz and I.B. Horwitz, "The Effects of Team Diversity on Team Outcomes: A Meta-Analytic Review of Team Demography," *Journal of Management,* 33, no.6 (December 2007), pp. 987–1015.

62. Society for Human Resources Management Survey Programme, 2001, p. 16.

63. Statistics Canada, "Earnings Differences between Immigrants and the Canadian-Born—The Role of Literacy Skills," (May 1, 2009), www.statcan.gc.ca/pub/81-004-x/2008005/article/10798-eng.htm (accessed September 26, 2011).

64. Ibid.

65. G. Picot, and A. Sweetman, "The Deteriorating Economic Welfare of Immigrants and Possible Causes: Update 2005," Statistics Canada, Catalogue No. 11F0019MIE, No. 262.

66. Statistics Canada, "Earnings Differences between Immigrants and the Canadian-Born—The Role of Literacy Skills," (May 1, 2009), www.statcan.gc.ca/pub/81-004-x/2008005/article/10798-eng.htm (accessed September 26, 2011).

67. Statistics Canada, "Longitudinal Survey of Immigrants to Canada: Process, Progress and Prospects," Housing, Family and Social Statistics Division (October 2003), http://dsp-psd.pwgsc.gc.ca/Collection/Statcan/89-611-X/89-611-XIE2003001.pdf (accessed September 26, 2001).

68. G. Larose and G. Tillman, "Valorizing Immigrants' Non-Canadian Work Experience," (Ottawa, ON: Work and Learning Knowledge Centre, 2009).

69. M. Fernando, "The Non-Accreditation of Immigrant Professionals in Canada: Societal Dimensions of the Problem," *Metropolis* (September 15, 1999), http://canada.metropolis.net/research-policy/conversation/MATAPAPER.html (accessed September 26, 2011).

70. J. Gilmour, "The 2008 Canadian Immigrant Labour Market: Analysis of Quality of Employment," Statistics Canada, Labour Statistics Division (November 23, 2009), www.statcan.gc.ca/pub/71-606-x/71-606-x2009001-eng.pdf (accessed August 11, 2010).

71. Ibid.

72. Ibid.

73. "Progress Report 2010," Foreign Credentials Referral Office, Government of Canada (August 5, 2011), www.credentials.gc.ca/fcro/progress-report2010.asp#bfn07.

74. C. Grondin, "Knowledge of Official Languages among New Immigrants: How Important Is It in the Labour Market?" Statistics Canada (April 2007), www.statcan.gc.ca/pub/89-624-x/89-624-x2007000-eng.pdf (accessed September 26, 2011).

75. Ibid.

76. M. Adamuti-Trache and R. Sweet, "Exploring the Relationship between Educational Credentials and the Earnings of Immigrants," *Canadian Studies in Population,* 32, no. 2 (2005), pp. 177–201.

Glossary

360-degree appraisal A performance appraisal technique that uses multiple raters including peers, employees reporting to the appraisee, supervisors, and customers.

A

achievement tests Tests used to measure knowledge or proficiency acquired through education, training, or experience.

action learning A training technique by which management trainees are allowed to work full time, analyzing and solving problems in other departments.

alternation ranking method Ranking employees from best to worst on a particular trait.

appraisal bias The tendency to allow individual differences, such as age, race, and sex, to affect the appraisal ratings that these employees receive.

aptitude tests Tests that measure an individual's aptitude or potential to perform a job, provided he or she is given proper training.

arbitration The use of an outside third party to investigate a dispute between an employer and union and impose a settlement.

attrition The normal separation of employees from an organization because of resignation, retirement, or death.

authorization card A card signed by an employee that indicates his or her willingness to have the union act as his or her representative for purposes of collective bargaining.

B

Baby Boomers Individuals born between 1946 and 1964.

balanced scorecard A measurement system that translates an organization's strategy into a comprehensive set of performance measures.

balance sheet approach A method of formulating expatriate pay based on equalizing purchasing power across countries.

bargaining unit The group of employees in a firm, a plant, or an industry that has been recognized by an employer or certified by a labour relations board (LRB) as appropriate for collective bargaining purposes.

bargaining zone The area defined by the bargaining limits (resistance points) of each side, in which compromise is possible, as is the attainment of a settlement satisfactory to both parties.

behaviour modelling A training technique in which trainees are first shown good management techniques, then asked to play roles in a simulated situation, and finally given feedback regarding their performance.

behavioural interview or behaviour description interview (BDI) A series of job-related questions that focus on relevant past job-related behaviours.

behaviourally anchored rating scale (BARS) An appraisal method that aims to combine the benefits of narratives, critical incidents, and quantified ratings by anchoring a quantified scale with specific narrative examples of good and poor performance.

benchmark job A job that is critical to the firm's operations or that is commonly found in other organizations.

biographical information blank (BIB) A detailed job application form requesting biographical data found to be predictive of success on the job, pertaining to background, experiences, and preferences. Responses are scored.

blind ad A recruitment ad in which the identity and address of the employer are omitted.

bona fide occupational requirement (BFOR) A justifiable reason for discrimination based on business necessity (that is, required for the safe and efficient operation of the organization) or a requirement that can be clearly defended as intrinsically required by the tasks an employee is expected to perform.

boycott An organized refusal of bargaining unit members and supporters to buy the products or use the services of the organization whose employees are on strike in an effort to exert economic pressure on the employer.

broadbanding Reducing the number of salary grades and ranges into just a few wide levels or "bands," each of which then contains a relatively wide range of jobs and salary levels.

burnout The total depletion of physical and mental resources caused by excessive striving to reach an unrealistic work-related goal.

business unionism The activities of labour unions focusing on economic and welfare issues, including pay and benefits, job security, and working conditions.

C

Canada/Quebec Pension Plans (C/QPP) Programs that provide three types of benefits: retirement income; survivor or death benefits payable to the employee's dependants regardless of age at time of death; and disability benefits payable to employees with disabilities and their dependants. Benefits are payable only to those individuals who make contributions to the plans or to their family members.

capital accumulation programs Long-term incentives most often reserved for senior executives.

career A series of work-related positions, paid or unpaid, that help a person to grow in job skills, success, and fulfillment.

career anchor A concern or value that a person will not give up if a choice has to be made.

career planning and development The deliberate process through which a person becomes aware of personal career-related attributes and the lifelong series of activities that contribute to his or her career fulfillment.

case study method A development method in which a trainee is presented with a written description of an organizational problem to diagnose and solve.

caucus session A session in which only the members of one's own bargaining team are present.

central tendency A tendency to rate all employees in the middle of the scale.

certification Recognition for having met certain professional standards. In labour relations, the procedure whereby a labour union obtains a certificate from the relevant LRB declaring that the union is the exclusive bargaining agent for a defined group of employees in a bargaining unit that the LRB considers appropriate for collective bargaining purposes.

change agents Specialists who lead the organization and its employees through organizational change.

Charter of Rights and Freedoms Federal law enacted in 1982 that guarantees fundamental freedoms to all Canadians.

classes Groups of jobs based on a set of rules for each class, such as amount of independent judgment, skill, physical effort, and so forth. Classes usually contain similar jobs—such as all secretaries.

classification/grading method A method for categorizing jobs into groups.

coinsurance The percentage of expenses (in excess of the deductible) that are paid for by the insurance plan.

collective bargaining Negotiations between a union and an employer to arrive at a mutually acceptable collective agreement.

collective bargaining agreement (union contract) A formal agreement between an employer and the union representing a group of its employees regarding terms and conditions of employment.

compensable factor A fundamental, compensable element of a job, such as skill, effort, responsibility, and working conditions.

competencies Demonstrable characteristics of a person that enable performance of the job.

competency-based job analysis Describing a job in terms of the measurable, observable behavioural competencies an employee must exhibit to do a job well.

conciliation The often mandatory use of a neutral third party who has no direct input on the negotiation process to help an organization and the union representing a group of its employees communicate more effectively with the aim of coming to a mutually satisfactory collective agreement.

construct validity The extent to which a selection tool measures a theoretical construct or trait deemed necessary to perform the job successfully.

constructive dismissal When the employer makes unilateral changes in the employment contract that are unacceptable to the employee, even though the employee has not been formally terminated.

content validity The extent to which a selection instrument, such as a test, adequately samples the knowledge and skills needed to perform the job.

contextual performance An individual's indirect contribution to the organization by improving the organizational, social, and psychological behaviours that contribute to organizational effectiveness beyond those specified for the job.

contingent/non-standard workers Workers who do not have regular full-time employment status.

contract workers Employees who develop work relationships directly with the employer for a specific type of work or period of time.

contrast or candidate-order error An error of judgment on the part of the interviewer because of interviewing one or more very good or very bad candidates just before the interview in question.

controlled experimentation Formal methods for testing the effectiveness of a training program, preferably with a control group and with tests before and after training.

craft union Traditionally, a labour organization representing workers practising the same craft or trade, such as carpentry or plumbing.

criterion-related validity The extent to which a selection tool predicts or significantly correlates with important elements of work behaviour.

critical incident method Keeping a record of uncommonly good or undesirable examples of an employee's work-related behaviour and reviewing the list with the employee at predetermined times.

D

data warehouse A specialized type of database that is optimized for reporting and analysis and is the raw material for managers' decision support.

decertification The process whereby a union is legally deprived of its official recognition as the exclusive bargaining agent for a group of employees.

deductible The annual amount of health/dental expenses that an employee must pay before insurance benefits will be paid.

deferred profit-sharing plan (DPSP) A plan in which a certain amount of company profits is credited to each employee's account, payable at retirement, termination, or death.

defined benefit pension plan A plan that contains a formula for determining retirement benefits.

defined contribution pension plan A plan in which the employer's contribution to the employees' retirement fund is specified.

Delphi technique A judgmental forecasting method used to arrive at a group decision, typically involving outside experts as well as organizational employees. Ideas are exchanged without face-to-face interaction and feedback is provided and used to fine-tune independent judgments until a consensus is reached.

developmental job rotation A management training technique that involves moving a trainee from department to department to broaden his or her experience and identify strong and weak points.

diary/log Daily listings made by employees of every activity in which they engage, along with the time each activity takes.

differential piece-rate plan A plan by which a worker is paid a basic hourly rate plus an extra percentage of his or her base rate for production exceeding the standard per hour or per day. It is similar to piecework payment but is based on a percentage premium.

differential or unequal treatment Treating an individual differently in any aspect of terms and conditions of employment based on any of the prohibited grounds.

differential validity Confirmation that the selection tool accurately predicts the performance of all possible employee subgroups, including white males, women, visible minorities, persons with disabilities, and Aboriginal people.

disability management A proactive, employer-centred process that coordinates the activities of the employer, the insurance company, and healthcare providers in an effort to minimize the impact of injury, disability, or disease on a worker's capacity to successfully perform his or her job.

discrimination As used in the context of human rights in employment, a distinction, exclusion, or preference based on one of the prohibited grounds that has the effect of nullifying or impairing the right of a person to full and equal recognition and exercise of his or her human rights and freedoms.

discrimination because of association Denial of rights because of friendship or other relationship with a protected group member.

dismissal Involuntary termination of an employee's employment.

dismissal for just cause An employer-initiated termination based on an employee's poor behaviours; in these situations, no severance, reasonable notice periods, or additional payments beyond what the employee has already earned are owed.

distributive bargaining A win–lose negotiating strategy, where one party gains at the expense of the other.

distributive justice Fairness of a decision outcome.

E

early retirement buyout programs Strategies used to accelerate attrition that involve offering attractive buyout packages or the opportunity to retire on full pension with an attractive benefits package.

e-learning Delivery and administration of learning opportunities and support via computer, networked, and web-based technology to enhance employee performance and development.

electronic HR (e-HR) A form of technology that enables HR professionals to integrate an organization's HR strategies, processes, and human capital to improve overall HR service delivery.

electronic performance monitoring (EPM) Having supervisors electronically monitor the amount of computerized data an employee is processing per day and thereby his or her performance.

electronic performance support systems (EPSS) Computer-based job aids, or sets of computerized tools and displays, that automate training, documentation, and phone support.

emotional intelligence (EI) tests Tests that measure a person's ability to monitor his or her own emotions and the emotions of others and to use that knowledge to guide thoughts and actions.

employee assistance plan (EAP) A company-sponsored program to help employees cope with personal problems that are interfering with or have the potential to interfere with their job performance, as well as issues affecting their well-being or the well-being of their families.

employee benefits Indirect financial payments given to employees. They may include supplementary health and life insurance, vacation, pension plans, education plans, and discounts on company products.

employee engagement The emotional and intellectual involvement of employees in their work, such as intensity, focus, and involvement in his or her job and organization.

employment insurance (EI) A federal program intended to provide temporary financial assistance to eligible persons who experience interruption to their work through no fault of their own.

employee opinion surveys Communication devices that use questionnaires to ask for employees' opinions about the company, management, and work life.

employee orientation (onboarding) A procedure for providing new employees with basic background information about the firm and the job.

employee self-service (ESS) Enables employees to access and manage their personal information directly.

employee share purchase/stock ownership plan (ESOP) A plan whereby a trust is established to hold shares of company stock purchased for or issued to employees. The trust distributes the stock to employees on retirement, separation from service, or as otherwise prescribed by the plan.

employee wellness program A program that takes a proactive approach to employee health and well-being.

employer branding The image or impression of an organization as an employer based on the benefits of being employed by the organization.

employment equity program A detailed plan designed to identify and correct existing discrimination, redress past discrimination, and achieve a balanced representation of designated group members in the organization.

employment insurance (EI) A federal program intended to provide temporary financial assistance to eligible persons who experience interruption to their work through no fault of their own.

employment (labour) standards legislation Laws present in every Canadian jurisdiction that establish minimum employee entitlements and set a limit on the maximum number of hours of work permitted per day or week.

empowerment Providing workers with the skills and authority to make decisions that would traditionally be made by managers.

enterprise-wide/enterprise resource planning (ERP) system A system that supports enterprise-wide or cross-functional requirements rather than a single department within the organization.

environment scanning An assessment of external factors influencing the organizations ability to find and secure talent from the external labour market including economic, competitive, legislative, social, technological and demographic trends.

environmental scanning Identifying and analyzing external opportunities and threats that may be crucial to the organization's success.

Equal pay for equal work Specifies that an employer cannot pay male and female employees differently if they are performing the same or substantially similar work.

equality rights Section 15 of the Charter of Rights and Freedoms, which guarantees the right to equal protection and benefit of the law without discrimination.

ergonomics An interdisciplinary approach that seeks to integrate and accommodate the physical needs of workers into the design of jobs. It aims to adapt the entire job system—the work, environment, machines, equipment, and processes—to match human characteristics.

ethnocentric staffing policy Policies that align wit the attitude that home-country managers are superior to those in the host country.

expatriate Employees who are citizens of the country where the parent company is based who are sent to work in another country.

expatriate assignment failure Early return of an expatriate from a global assignment.

external equity Employees perceives his or her pay as fair given the pay rates in other organizations.

F

fixed pay Compensation that is independent of the performance level of the individual, group, or organization.

flexible benefits programs Individualized benefit plans to accommodate employee needs and preferences.

forced distribution method Predetermined percentages of ratees are placed in various performance categories.

formal appraisal discussion An interview in which the supervisor and employee review the appraisal and make plans to remedy deficiencies and reinforce strengths.

Functional Job Analysis (FJA) A quantitative method for classifying jobs based on types and amounts of responsibility for data, people, and things. Performance standards and training requirements are also identified.

G

gainsharing plan An incentive plan that engages employees in a common effort to achieve productivity objectives and share the gains.

geocentric staffing policy Policies that aligned with the belief that the best manager for any specific position anywhere on the globe may be found in any of the countries in which the firm operates.

Generation X Individuals born between 1965 and 1980.

Generation Y Individuals born after 1980.

glass ceiling An invisible barrier, caused by attitudinal or organizational bias, that limits the advancement opportunities of qualified designated group members.

globalization The emergence of a single global market for most products and services.

grade/group description A written description of the level of compensable factors required by jobs in each grade; used to combine similar jobs into grades or classes.

grades Groups of jobs based on a set of rules for each grade, where jobs are similar in difficulty but otherwise different. Grades often contain dissimilar jobs, such as secretaries, mechanics, and firefighters.

graphic rating scale A scale that lists a number of traits and a range of performance for each. The employee is then rated by identifying the score that best describes his or her level of performance for each trait.

grievance A written allegation of a contract violation, filed by an individual bargaining unit member, the union, or management.

group life insurance Life insurance provided at lower rates for all employees, including new employees, regardless of health or physical condition.

group termination laws Laws that require an employer to notify employees in the event that they decide to terminate a group of employees.

guaranteed piecework plan The minimum hourly wage plus an incentive for each piece produced above a set number of pieces per hour.

H

halo effect A positive initial impression that distorts an interviewer's rating of a candidate because subsequent information is judged with a positive bias. In performance appraisal, the problem that occurs when a supervisor's rating of an employee on one trait biases the rating of that person on other traits.

harassment Unwelcome behaviour that demeans, humiliates, or embarrasses a person and that a reasonable person should have known would be unwelcome.

hiring freeze A common initial response to an employee surplus. Openings are filled by reassigning current employees and no outsiders are hired.

HR portal A single Internet access point for customized and personalized HR services.

HR technology Any technology that is used to attract, hire, retain and maintain talent, support workforce administration, and optimize workforce management.

HR technology strategy A plan that is aimed at increasing the effectiveness of HR programs, processes, and service delivery by shortening cycle times, increasing customer service levels, reducing costs, and adding new service capabilities.

human capital The knowledge, education, training, skills, and expertise of an organization's workforce.

human resources information system (HRIS) Integrated systems used to gather, store, and analyze information regarding an organization's human resources.

human resources management (HRM) The management of people in organizations to drive successful organizational performance and achievement of the organization's strategic goals.

human resources movement A management philosophy focusing on concern for people and productivity.

human resources planning (HRP) The process of forecasting future human resources requirements to ensure that the organization will have the required number of employees with the necessary skills to meet its strategic objectives.

human rights legislation Jurisdictions specific legislation that prohibits intentional and unintentional discrimination in employment situations and in the delivery of goods and services.

I

immigrant a person residing in Canada who was born outside of Canada (excluding temporary foreign workers, Canadian citizens born outside of Canada and those with student or work visas.

industrial engineering A field of study concerned with analyzing work methods; making work cycles more efficient by modifying, combining, rearranging, or eliminating tasks; and establishing time standards.

industrial union A labour organization representing all workers eligible for union membership in a particular company or industry, including skilled trades people.

in-house development centre A company-based method for exposing prospective managers to realistic exercises to develop improved management skills.

insubordination Willful disregard or disobedience of the boss' authority or legitimate orders; criticizing the boss in public.

integrative bargaining A negotiating strategy in which the possibility of win–win, lose–win, win–lose, and lose–lose outcomes is recognized, and there is acknowledgement that achieving a win–win outcome will depend on mutual trust and problem solving.

intelligence (IQ) tests Tests that measure general intellectual abilities, such as verbal comprehension, inductive reasoning, memory, numerical ability, speed of perception, spatial visualization, and word fluency.

interactional justice Fairness in interpersonal interactions by treating others with dignity and respect.

interest arbitration The imposition of the final terms of a collective agreement.

interest dispute A dispute between an organization and the union representing its employees over the terms of a collective agreement.

interest inventories Tests that compare a candidate's interests with those of people in various occupations.

internal equity Employees perceives his or her pay as fair given the pay rates of others in the organization.

intranet A network that is interconnected within one organization using web technologies for the sharing of information internally.

involuntary turnover Employer-initiated termination of employment, such as dismissal or layoff.

J

job A group of related activities and duties, held by a single employee or a number of incumbents.

job analysis The procedure for determining the tasks, duties, and responsibilities of each job, and the human attributes (in terms of knowledge, skills, and abilities) required to perform it.

job description A list of the duties, responsibilities, reporting relationships, and working conditions of a job—one product of a job analysis.

job design The process of systematically organizing work into tasks that are required to perform a specific job.

job enlargement (horizontal loading) A technique to relieve monotony and boredom that involves assigning workers additional tasks at the same level of responsibility to increase the number of tasks they have to perform.

job enrichment (vertical loading) Any effort that makes an employee's job more rewarding or satisfying by adding more meaningful tasks and duties.

job evaluation A systematic comparison to determine the relative worth of jobs within a firm.

job evaluation committee A diverse group (including employees, HR staff, managers, and union representatives) established to ensure the fair and comprehensive representation of the nature and requirements of the jobs in question.

job instruction training (JIT) The listing of each job's basic tasks along with key points to provide step-by-step training for employees.

job posting The process of notifying current employees about vacant positions.

job rotation A technique to relieve monotony and employee boredom that involves systematically moving employees from one job to another.

job sharing A strategy that involves dividing the duties of a single position between two or more employees.

job specification A list of the "human requirements," that is, the requisite knowledge, skills, and abilities, needed to perform the job—one product of a job analysis.

just cause An employer-initiated termination based on an employee's poor behaviours; in these situations, no severance, reasonable notice periods, or additional payments beyond what the employee has already earned are owed.

K

KSAs Knowledge, skills, and abilities.

L

labour–management relations The ongoing interactions between labour unions and management in organizations.

labour union (union) An officially recognized association of employees practising a similar trade or employed in the same company or industry who have joined together to present a united front and collective voice in dealing with management.

layoff The temporary withdrawal of employment to workers for economic or business reasons.

learning organization An organization skilled at creating, acquiring, and transferring knowledge and at modifying its behaviour to reflect new knowledge and insights.

leave of absence Allows those who may be interested in taking time away from work for a variety of reasons (e.g. personal, educational, etc.) to have a set period of time away from their position without pay, but with a guarantee that their job will be available upon their return.

local A group of unionized employees in a particular location.

lockout The temporary refusal of a company to continue providing work for bargaining unit employees involved in a labour dispute, which may result in closure of the establishment for a time.

Lost-time injury rate Measures any occupational injury or illness resulting in an employee being unable to fulfill the work full work assignments, not including any fatalities.

M

management assessment centre A strategy used to assess candidates' management potential that uses a combination of realistic exercises, management games, objective testing, presentations, and interviews.

management by objectives (MBO) Involves setting specific measurable goals with each employee and then periodically reviewing the progress made.

management development Any attempt to improve current or future management performance by imparting knowledge, changing attitudes, or increasing skills.

management game A computerized development technique in which teams of managers compete with one another by making decisions regarding realistic but simulated companies.

management inventories Records summarizing the qualifications, interests, and skills of management employees, along with the number and types of employees supervised, duties of such employees, total budget managed, previous managerial duties and responsibilities, and managerial training received.

management self-service (MSS) Enables managers to access a range of information about themselves and the employees who report to them and to process HR-related paperwork that pertains to their staff.

Markov analysis A method of forecasting internal labour supply that involves tracking the pattern of employee movements through various jobs and developing a transitional probability matrix.

mediation The often voluntary use of a neutral third party who has direct input on the negotiation process to help an organization and the union representing its employees reach a mutually satisfactory collective agreement.

memorandum of settlement A summary of the terms and conditions agreed to by the parties that is submitted to the constituent groups for final approval.

mentoring The use of an experienced individual (the mentor) to teach and train someone (the protégé) with less knowledge in a given area.

merit pay (merit raise) Any salary increase awarded to an employee based on his or her individual performance.

metrics Statistics used to measure activities and results.

metrics (workforce analytics) Statistical measures of the impact of HRM practices on the performance of an organization's human capital.

micro-assessment A series of verbal, paper-based, or computer-based questions and exercises that a candidate is required to complete, covering the range of activities required on the job for which he or she is applying.

mixed (semi-structured) interview An interview format that combines the structured and unstructured techniques.

multiple-hurdle strategy An approach to selection involving a series of successive steps or hurdles. Only candidates clearing the hurdle are permitted to move on to the next step.

must criteria Requirements that are absolutely essential for the job, include a measurable standard of acceptability, or are absolute and can be screened initially on paper.

mutual gains (interest-based) bargaining A win–win negotiating approach based on training in the fundamentals of effective problem solving and conflict resolution, in which the interests of all stakeholders are taken into account.

N

National Occupational Classification (NOC) A reference tool for writing job descriptions and job specifications. Compiled by the federal government, it contains comprehensive, standardized descriptions of about 40 000 occupations and the requirements for each.

negligent training Occurs when an employer fails to adequately train an employee who subsequently harms a third party.

nepotism A preference for hiring relatives of current employees.

networking An organized process whereby the individual arranges and conducts a series of face-to-face meetings with his or her colleagues and contacts, plus individuals that they recommend.

nominal group technique A decision-making technique that involves a group of experts meeting face to face. Steps include independent idea generation, clarification and open discussion, and private assessment.

O

occupation A collection of jobs that share some or all of a set of main duties.

occupational health and safety legislation Laws intended to protect the health and safety of workers by minimizing work-related accidents and illnesses.

occupational orientation The theory, developed by John Holland, that there are six basic personal orientations that determine the sorts of careers to which people are drawn.

occupational segregation The existence of certain occupations that have traditionally been male dominated and others that have been female dominated.

organizational climate The prevailing atmosphere that exists in an organization and its impact on employees.

organizational culture The core values, beliefs, and assumptions that are widely shared by members of an organization.

organizational structure The formal relationships among jobs in an organization.

organization chart A "snapshot" of the firm, depicting the organization's structure in chart form at a particular point in time.

outplacement counselling A systematic process by which a terminated person is trained and counselled in the techniques of self-appraisal and securing a new position.

outsourcing The practice of contracting with outside vendors to handle specified business functions on a permanent basis.

P

paired comparison method Ranking employees by making a chart of all possible pairs of employees for each trait and indicating the better employee of the pair.

panel interview An interview in which a group of interviewers questions the applicant.

pay equity Providing equal pay to male-dominated job classes and female-dominated job classes of equal value to the employer.

pay grade Comprises jobs of approximately equal value.

pay in lieu of reasonable notice A lump-sum equal to an employee's pay for the notice period provided to employees who cease working immediately.

pay ranges A series of steps or levels within a pay grade, usually based on years of service.

pension plans Plans that provide income when employees reach a predetermined retirement age.

performance analysis Verifying that there is a performance deficiency and determining whether that deficiency should be rectified through training or through some other means (such as transferring the employee).

performance management The process encompassing all activities related to improving employee performance, productivity, and effectiveness.

personality tests Instruments used to measure basic aspects of personality, such as introversion, stability, motivation, neurotic tendency, self-confidence, self-sufficiency, and sociability.

phased retirement An arrangement whereby employees gradually ease into retirement by using reduced workdays or shortened workweeks.

physical demands analysis Identification of the senses used and the type, frequency, and amount of physical effort involved in a job.

picket Stationing groups of striking employees, usually carrying signs, at the entrances and exits of the struck operation to publicize the issues in dispute and discourage people from entering or leaving the premises.

piecework A system of pay based on the number of items processed by each individual worker in a unit of time, such as items per hour or items per day.

point method A job evaluation method in which a number of compensable factors are identified, the degree to which each of these factors is present in the job is determined, and an overall point value is calculated.

polycentric staffing policy Policies that align with the belief that only host-country managers can understand the culture and behaviour of the host-country market.

portability A provision that employees who change jobs can transfer the lump-sum value of the pension they have earned to a locked-in RRSP or their new employer's pension plan.

position The collection of tasks and responsibilities performed by one person.

Position Analysis Questionnaire (PAQ) A questionnaire used to collect quantifiable data concerning the duties and responsibilities of various jobs.

pre-hearing vote An alternative mechanism for certification, used in situations in which there is evidence of violations of fair labour practices early in the organizing campaign.

pre-retirement counselling Counselling provided to employees some months (or even years) before retirement, which covers such matters as benefits advice, second careers, and so on.

primary sector Jobs in agriculture, fishing and trapping, forestry, and mining.

procedural justice Fairness of the process used to make a decision.

process chart A diagram showing the flow of inputs to and outputs from the job under study.

productivity The ratio of an organization's outputs (goods and services) to its inputs (people, capital, energy, and materials).

profit-sharing plan A plan whereby most or all employees share in the company's profits.

programmed learning A systematic method for teaching job skills that involves presenting questions or facts, allowing the person to respond, and giving the learner immediate feedback on the accuracy of his or her answers.

promotion Movement of an employee from one job to another that is higher in pay, responsibility, or organizational level, usually based on merit, seniority, or a combination of both.

Q

quitting Voluntary, employee-initiated resignation.

R

ratification Formal approval by secret-ballot vote of the bargaining unit members of the agreement negotiated between union and management.

ratio analysis A forecasting technique for determining future staff needs by using ratios between some causal factor (such as sales volume) and the number of employees needed.

realistic job preview (RJP) A strategy used to provide applicants with realistic information—both positive and negative—about the job demands, the organization's expectations, and the work environment.

reality shock (cognitive dissonance) The state that results from the discrepancy between what the new employee expected from his or her new job and the realities of it.

reasonable accommodation The adjustment of employment policies and practices that an employer may be expected to make so that no individual is denied benefits, disadvantaged in employment, or prevented from carrying out the essential components of a job because of grounds prohibited in human rights legislation.

recency effect The rating error that occurs when ratings are based on the employee's most recent performance rather than on performance throughout the appraisal period.

recruiter A specialist in recruitment whose job is to find and attract capable candidates.

recruitment The process of searching out and attracting qualified job applicants, which begins with the identification of a position that requires staffing and is completed when résumés or completed application forms are received from an adequate number of applicants.

red circle pay rate A rate of pay that is above the pay range maximum.

reduced workweek Employees work fewer hours and receive less pay.

regression analysis A statistical technique involving the use of a mathematical formula to project future demands based on an established relationship between an organization's employment level (dependent variable) and some measurable factor of output (independent variable).

regulations Legally binding rules established by special regulatory bodies created to enforce compliance with the law and aid in its interpretation.

relational database One piece of data is stored in several different data files so that information from the separate files can be linked and used together.

reliability The degree to which interviews, tests, and other selection procedures yield comparable data over time; in other words, the degree of dependability, consistency, or stability of the measures used.

repatriation The process of moving the expatriate and his or her family back home from the foreign assignment.

repetitive strain injuries (RSIs) Activity-related soft-tissue injuries of the neck, shoulders, arms, wrists, hands, back, and legs.

replacement charts Visual representations of who will replace whom in the event of a job opening. Likely internal candidates are listed, along with their age, present performance rating, and promotability status.

replacement summaries Lists of likely replacements for each position and their relative strengths and weaknesses, as well as information about current position, performance, promotability, age, and experience.

representation vote A vote conducted by the LRB in which employees in the bargaining unit indicate, by secret ballot, whether or not they want to be represented, or continue to be represented, by a labour union.

request for proposal (RFP) A document requesting that vendors provide a proposal detailing how the implementation of their particular HRIS will meet the organization's needs.

restitutional remedies Monetary compensation for the complainant to put him or her back to the position he or she would be in if the discrimination had not occurred (this includes compensation for injury to dignity and self-respect), and may include an apology letter.

retirees on call A program where retirees can continue to work on a part-time or as needed basis post-retirement.

rights arbitration The process involved in the settlement of a rights dispute.

rights dispute A disagreement between an organization and the union representing its employees regarding the interpretation or application of one or more clauses in the current collective agreement.

role-playing A training technique in which trainees act the parts of people in a realistic management situation.

S

scatter plot A graphical method used to help identify the relationship between two variables.

scientific management The process of "scientifically" analyzing manufacturing processes, reducing production costs, and compensating employees based on their performance levels.

secondary sector Jobs in manufacturing and construction.

selection The process of choosing among individuals who have been recruited to fill existing or projected job openings.

selection interview A procedure designed to predict future job performance on the basis of applicants' oral responses to oral inquiries.

selection ratio The ratio of the number of applicants hired to the total number of applicants.

seniority Length of service in the bargaining unit.

severance package A lump-sum payment, continuation of benefits for a specified period of time, and other benefits that are provided to employees who are being terminated.

sexual annoyance Sexually related conduct that is hostile, intimidating, or offensive to the employee but has no direct link to tangible job benefits or loss thereof.

sexual coercion Harassment of a sexual nature that results in some direct consequence to the worker's employment status or some gain in or loss of tangible job benefits.

sexual harassment Offensive or humiliating behaviour that is related to a person's sex, as well as behaviour of a sexual nature that creates an intimidating, unwelcome, hostile, or offensive work environment or that could reasonably be thought to put sexual conditions on a person's job or employment opportunities.

short-term disability and sick leave Plans that provide pay to an employee when he or she is unable to work because of a non-work-related illness or injury.

similar-to-me bias The tendency to give higher performance ratings to employees who are perceived to be similar to the rater in some way.

situational interview A series of job-related questions that focus on how the candidate would behave in a given situation.

situational tests Tests in which candidates are presented with hypothetical situations representative of the job for which they are applying and are evaluated on their responses.

skills inventories Manual or computerized records summarizing employees' education, experience, interests, skills, and so on, which are used to identify internal candidates eligible for transfer and/or promotion.

socialization The ongoing process of instilling in all employees the prevailing attitudes, standards, values, and patterns of behaviour that are expected by the organization.

social (reform) unionism Activities of unions directed at furthering the interests of their members by influencing the social and economic policies of governments at all levels, such as speaking out on proposed legislative reforms.

staffing table A pictorial representation of all jobs within the organization, along with the number of current incumbents and future employment requirements (monthly or yearly) for each.

stand-alone system A self-contained system that does not rely on other systems to operate.

statistical strategy A more objective technique used to determine whom the job should be offered to; involves identifying the most valid predictors and weighting them through statistical methods, such as multiple regression.

stock option The right to purchase a stated number of shares of a company stock at today's price at some time in the future.

straight piecework plan A set payment for each piece produced or processed in a factory or shop.

strategy The company's plan for how it will balance its internal strengths and weaknesses with external opportunities and threats to maintain a competitive advantage.

strictness/leniency The problem that occurs when a supervisor has a tendency to rate all employees either low or high.

strike The temporary refusal by bargaining unit members to continue working for the employer.

strike vote Legally required in some jurisdictions, it is a vote seeking authorization from bargaining unit members to strike if necessary. A favourable vote does not mean that a strike is inevitable.

structured interview An interview following a set sequence of questions.

succession planning The process of ensuring a suitable supply of successors for current and future senior or key jobs so that the careers of individuals can be effectively planned and managed.

supplemental employee retirement plans (SERPs) Plans that provide the additional pension benefit required for employees to receive their full pension benefit in cases where their full pension benefit exceeds the maximum allowable benefit under the Income Tax Act.

supplemental unemployment benefits (SUBs) A top-up of EI benefits to bring income levels closer to what an employee would receive if on the job.

survivor syndrome A range of negative emotions experienced by employees remaining after a major restructuring initiative, which can include feelings of betrayal or violation, guilt, or detachment, and can result in stress symptoms, including depression, increased errors, and reduced performance.

systemic remedies Forward looking solutions to discrimination that require respondents to take positive steps to ensure compliance with legislation, both in respect to the current complaint and any future practices.

T

task analysis A detailed study of a job to identify the skills and competencies it requires so that an appropriate training program can be instituted.

task performance An individual's direct contribution to their job related processes.

team A small group of people with complementary skills who work toward common goals for which they hold joint responsibility and accountability.

team-based job designs Job designs that focus on giving a team, rather than an individual, a whole and meaningful piece of work to do and empowering team members to decide among themselves how to accomplish the work.

team or group incentive plan A plan in which a production standard is set for a specific work group and its members are paid incentives if the group exceeds the production standard.

termination Permanent separation from the organization for any reason.

termination interview The interview in which an employee is informed of the fact that he or she has been dismissed.

tertiary or service sector Jobs in public administration, personal and business services, finance, trade, public utilities, and transportation/communications.

total employment rewards An integrated package of all rewards (monetary and non-monetary, extrinsic and intrinsic) gained by employees arising from their employment.

Traditionalists Individuals born before 1946.

training The process of teaching employees the basic skills/competencies that they need to perform their jobs.

transfer Movement of an employee from one job to another that is relatively equal in pay, responsibility, or organizational level.

transfer of training Application of the skills acquired during the training program into the work environment and the maintenance of these skills over time.

trend analysis The study of a firm's past employment levels over a period of years to predict future needs.

turnover The termination of an individual's employment with an organization.

U

unclear performance standards An appraisal scale that is too open to interpretation of traits and standards.

underemployment Being employed in a job that does not fully utilize one's knowledge, skills, and abilities (KSAs).

undue hardship The point to which employers are expected to accommodate under human rights legislative requirements.

unintentional/constructive/systemic discrimination Discrimination that is embedded in policies and practices that appear neutral on the surface and are implemented impartially, but have an adverse impact on specific groups of people for reasons that are not job related or required for the safe and efficient operation of the business.

union security clause The contract provisions protecting the interests of the labour union, dealing with the issue of membership requirements and, often, the payment of union dues.

union steward A union member elected by workers in a particular department or area of a firm to act as their union representative.

unstructured interview An unstructured, conversational-style interview. The interviewer pursues points of interest as they come up in response to questions.

V

validity The accuracy with which a predictor measures what it is intended to measure.

variable pay Any plan that ties pay to productivity or profitability.

vestibule or simulated training Training employees on special off-the-job equipment, as in airplane pilot training, whereby training costs and hazards can be reduced.

vesting A provision that employer money placed in a pension fund cannot be forfeited for any reason.

videoconferencing Connecting two or more distant groups by using audiovisual equipment.

voluntary turnover Employee-initiated termination of employment, such as quits, retirement, or resignation.

W

wage curve A graphic description of the relationship between the value of the job and the average wage paid for this job.

wage/salary survey A survey aimed at determining prevailing wage rates. A good salary survey provides specific wage rates for comparable jobs. Formal written questionnaire surveys are the most comprehensive.

want ad A recruitment ad describing the job and its specifications, the compensation package, and the hiring employer. The address to which applications or résumés should be submitted is also provided.

want criteria Those criteria that represent qualifications that cannot be screened on paper or are not readily measurable, as well as those that are highly desirable but not critical.

web-based application An application that can be accessed from any computer connected to the Internet.

wildcat strike A spontaneous walkout, not officially sanctioned by the union leadership, which may be legal or illegal, depending on its timing.

workers' compensation Workers' compensation provides income and medical benefits to victims of work-related accidents or illnesses or their dependants, regardless of fault.

workforce mobility The focus on managing the recruitment, relocation, and retention of employees who complete work-related tasks and activities outside of the core or primary head office or region of the company.

Workplace Hazardous Materials Information System (WHMIS) A Canada-wide, legally mandated system designed to protect workers by providing information about hazardous materials in the workplace.

work sharing Employees work three or four days a week and receive EI benefits on their non-workday(s).

work simplification An approach to job design that involves assigning most of the administrative aspects of work (such as planning and organizing) to supervisors and managers, while giving lower-level employees narrowly defined tasks to perform according to methods established and specified by management.

wrongful dismissal An employee dismissal that does not comply with the law or does not comply with a written or implied contractual arrangement.

Y

yield ratio The percentage of applicants that proceed to the next stage of the selection process.

Name and Organization Index

A

Abbasi, S., 419
Aboriginal Human Resource
    Council, 167
Aboriginal Inclusion Network, 167
Accountemps, 164
Adams, Billy, 468
Air Canada, 4, 314, 423
Alberta Alcohol and Drug Abuse
    Commission, 400
Alberta Human Rights
    Commission, 33
Alberta Milk, 345
Alberta Pacific Forest Industries, 226
Alcan, 226, 364, 467
Alcatel, 428
Alcoholics Anonymous, 399
All-China Federation of Industry and
    Commerce, 15
AltaGas Ltd., 352
American Federation of Labor
    and Congress of Industrial
    Organizations (AFL–CIO), 442
Anastasiadis, Philip, 37
Angus Reid, 360
Apple, 22
Ashland Canada Ltd., 287
Assessment Systems Corporation, 176
Assiniboine Credit Union, 485
Association of Canadian Pension
    Management, 365
Association of Canadian Search,
    Employment, and Staffing
    Services (ACSESS), 161
Association of Workers'
    Compensation Boards of
    Canada, 298, 358, 382, 398
AT&T, 60
Atlas-Graham Industries, 339

B

BackCheck, 197
Balsillie, Jim, 328
Banff Centre, 254–255
Bank of Montreal, 4, 216, 251,
    334, 372
Barling, Julian, 408
Becker, Brian, 8
Bell Canada, 364, 428
Bell Mobility, 39
Bellwood Health Services Inc., 399
Benefits Canada, 353
Benefits Design, Inc, 374
Benefits Interface, 353
BenefitsLink.com, 353
Best Software Inc., 69
Bhinder, Mr., 41
BHP Billiton, 230, 442
BlueSteps.com, 147
Bouchard, Gabriel, 144
Bow Valley College, 230
Brass Ring, 77
British Columbia Human Rights
    Tribunal, 33
British Columbia Teachers'
    Federation, 441
Brockbank, Wayne, 58
Brock University, 433

C

Calgary Health, 4
Canada Employment Insurance
    Commission, 354
Canada Industrial Relations Board,
    298
Canadajobs.com, 159
Canada Life Assurance Company,
    361
Canada Pension Plan, 357
Canada Pension Plan Investment
    Board, 332
Canada Post, 251, 313
Canada Safety Council, 390
Canadian Abilities Foundation, 167,
    168
Canadian Association for Retired
    Persons, 365
Canadian Association of
    Administrators of Labour
    Legislation, 46
Canadian Centre for Justice
    Statistics, 382
Canadian Centre for Occupational
    Health and Safety, 393, 395
Canadian Coalition for Good
    Governance, 312
Canadian Council of Human
    Resources Associations
    (CCHRA), 18
Canadian Council on Learning,
    215, 230
Canadian Council on Rehabilitation
    and Work, 167, 363
Canadian Employee Relocation
    Council, 474
Canadian Federation of Independent
    Business, 395
Canadian Forces Liaison Council
    (CFLC), 159
Canadian Human Rights
    Commission, 41, 276
Canadian Human Rights Tribunal,
    30, 314
Canadian Immigrant Integration
    Program, 486
Canadian Imperial Bank of
    Commerce (CIBC), 4, 70, 361
Canadian Industrial Relations
    Association, 18
Canadian Initiative on Workplace
    Violence, 408
Canadian Injured Workers Alliance,
    397
Canadian Labour and Business
    Center, 440
Canadian Labour Congress (CLC),
    405, 442
Canadian LabourWatch Association,
    440
Canadian LifeQuilt, 392
Canadian Management Centre, 232
Canadian Management Professionals
    Association, 251
Canadian National Railway (CN),
    41, 312
Canadian Pension and Benefits
    Institute, 375

Canadian Securities Administrators,
    312
Canadian Society for Training and
    Development (CSTD), 18, 214,
    225
Canadian Tire, 343
Canadian Trucking Human
    Resources Council, 230
Canadian Union of Public
    Employees, local 3903, 454
Canjobs.com, 159
CareerBuilder, 159
Career Edge, 157
CA Source, 158
Certified General Accountants and
    Professional Engineers Ontario,
    306
Certified Human Resources
    Professional (CHRP), 18
Chrysler, 432, 441
Cisco Systems, 225, 433
Citizenship and Immigration Canada,
    486
City of Richmond, 251
City of Waterloo, 174
CKR Global, 197
Coastal Pacific Xpress (CPX), 324
Company DNA, 343
Concordia University, 281
Confédération des syndicats
    nationaux (CSN), 442
Conference Board of Canada, 165,
    167, 215, 247, 330, 391, 406
Congyin, Lin, 15
Construction Labour Relations, 441
Construction Safety Association, 18
Construction Sector Council, 230
Creo, 339
Cronus Technologies Inc., 77

D

Dartmouth Work Activity Society,
    168
De Beers Canada, 442
Delfini, David, 147
Dell Computer, 227
Deloitte, 22
Deploy, 77
DHL, 472
DiSabatino, Jessica, 392
Dofasco Inc., 230, 433, 440, 462
Downe, William, 334
Drake Beam Morin, 430
Duffield, David, 70
DuPont, 389

E

EBA Engineering Consultants, 147
Eddie Bauer, 343
Ellis, David, 392
EmployAbilities, 168
Employee Benefit Research Institute,
    353
Encana, 157
Énergie New Brunswick Power, 159
Equal Pay Coalition, 314
Ernst & Young, 22, 157, 162, 210,
    373, 423

Estill, Jim, 434
ExecuTRACK Software Group, 77

F

Facebook, 162
Fairmont Hotels and Resorts, 16,
    145, 345
Family Services Employee Assistance
    Programs, 370
Farrell, Pauline, 382
Federal Contractors Program, 45
Federation of Trade Unions, 15
Fenuta, Mike, 396
Financial Post, 144
Fisheries Products International, 339
Follett, Mary Parker, 3
Foreign Credential Referral Office
    (FCRO), 486
Forensic Technology, 434
Forrester Research, 60
Fortune magazine, 296
Future Shop, 343

G

Gammas, Tommy, 37
Gao, Jennifer, 264
Gartner Inc., 60
General Electric, 254
Genesys Software Systems, 69
Goldman Sachs, 22
Google, 22, 58, 148
Gould, Stephen, 214
Govereau, Tracy, 37
Government of Canada, 28
Great Place to Work Institute
    Canada, 144
Grech, Tony, 396
Green Shield Canada, 362

H

Hackett Group, 80
Halifax Career Fair, 157
Halifax police, 455
Halogen Software Inc., 70, 83
Hanley, Wayne, 443
Harkness, Helen, 240
Harrison Hunter, 312
Hay Group, 300, 306
Healthy Companies International,
    231
Hedley, Bob, 254
Henteleff, Yude, 37
Herzberg, Frederick, 340
Hewitt Associates, 6, 144, 146, 306,
    373
Hewlett Packard, 4, 160, 375
Hire Authority, 158
HireImmigrants.ca, 167
Holiday Inn, 455
Holland, John, 240–241
Hollman, K., 419
Home Depot Canada, 159, 165
Honda Canada, 428
HR Dept, 8
HR Focus, 74
Huband, Charles, 37
Human Factors and Ergonomics
    Society, 403

Human Resources and Skills Development Canada (HRSDC), 103, 160
Human Resources Institute of Alberta (HRIA), 26
Human Resources Professionals Association (HRPA), 158
Human Systems Inc., 403
Husky Injection Molding Systems, 371

I

IBM, 4, 212, 371, 433, 476
Icarian, 77
IKEA, 83, 90, 371
Imagistics International, 76
Income Security Programs, 354
Industrial Accident Prevention Association (IAPA), 18, 395, 396, 397
Information and Privacy Commissioner of Ontario, 48
Innu Nation, 442
INSEAD, 476
Institute for Work and Health, 403
International Association for Human Resource Information Management, 60
International Data Corporation, 60
International Foundation of Employee Benefit Plans, 374
International Labour News, 441
International Labour Organization (ILO), 406, 450, 470
International Personnel Assessment Council, 217
International Personnel Management Association (IPMA), 18, 26
Investigative Research Group, 197
Issah, Sibaway, 167

J

J.P. Morgan, 22
Jaguar Land Rover, 284
Janzen, Dianna, 37
Jiumuwang Western-Style Fashional Clothes Co. Ltd., 15
Job Bank, 160
Job Match, 160
Job Postings, 157
Jobster, 159

K

Kanata Research Park, 371
Kelloway, Kevin, 408
Kelly, Bill, 382
Kelly Services, 164
KPMG, 22, 373, 473

L

L'Oréal Canada, 226
Labatt Breweries, 249, 250
Labrador Inuit Association, 442
La Senza, 343
Lau, Jennifer. See Subject Index, running case
Lawler, Ed, 60
Law Society of Upper Canada, 209
Learning and Development, 215
LearnInMotion.com. See Subject Index, running case
LeBlanc, Pierre. See Subject Index, running case

Lecavalier, Elisabeth, 434
Lewenza, Ken, 443
Loblaw, 145, 197, 443
Locke, Edwin, 343
London Business School, 476
Lorenzoni, Luca, 250

M

MacDonald Dettwiler and Associates Ltd., 342
Manitoba Human Rights Commission, 33, 37
Manulife, 485
Maple Leaf Foods, 254
Maverick Events Worldwide, 472
McDonald's, 145, 165
Mediacorp, 144, 352
Meralli, Yasmin, 372
Mercer, 58, 59, 306
Meyers Norris Penny, 166
Microsoft, 22, 157
Midvale Steel Company, 323
Minerals Council of Australia, 468
Minto Developments Inc., 345
Mission Possible, 472
Molson, 467
Monster.com, 6
Monster Canada, 144, 159, 306
Montana's Cookhouse, 345
Morris, Ken, 70

N

NASA, 225
National Adult Literacy Database, 230
National Center for Employee Ownership, 339
National Institute of Disability Management and Research (NIDMAR), 363, 398
National Quality Institute, 433
Nelson Motivation Inc, 341
New Brunswick Human Rights Commission, 34
Newfoundland and Labrador Human Rights Commission, 34
Newman, Jerry, 210
Niagara Institute, 251
Nicejob.ca, 159
Nissan, 97
Nixon, Gordon, 334
Noranda, 467
Northwest Territories Human Rights Commission, 34
Nova Scotia Human Rights Commission, 34
Nunavut Human Rights Tribunal, 34

O

O.C. Tanner Recognition Co., 343
Occupational Information Network, 105
Office Overload, 164
Ontario Human Rights Commission, 34
Ontario Human Rights Tribunal, 42
Ontario Ministry of Community and Social Services, 167
Ontario Ministry of Education, 212
Ontario Ministry of Labour, 440, 453
Ontario Nurses' Association, 441
Ontario Power Generation, 429

Oracle ERP, 70
Organisation for Economic Co-operation and Development, 314
Organization Plus, 69
OrgPlus, 77
Outward Bound, 232

P

PAQ Services Inc., 101
Parc Aviation, 164
Parker, Doug, 340
Paths to Equal Opportunity, 167
PCL Construction, 145
PeopleSoft, 64, 70, 74
People-Trak, 69
PepsiCo, 332
Pfizer Inc., 371
Pharos Restaurant, 37
Pitney Bowes Office Systems, 76
Precision Drilling Corporation, 312
PricewaterhouseCoopers, 22
Prime50, 165
Prince Edward Island Human Rights Commission, 34
Privacy Commissioner of Canada, 48
Procor Limited, 345
Procter & Gamble, 22, 157, 254
Psychometric Assessments, 186
Public Health Agency of Canada, 360
Public Service Grievance Board, 455
Purolator, 144, 214, 358

Q

Québec Commission des droits de la personne et des droits de la jeunesse, 34
Queen's University, 26, 408

R

Racism and Racial Harassment: Your Rights and Responsibilities, 40
RBC Financial Group, 162, 334, 345, 485
Recognition Plus, Inc., 343
Recognition Professionals International, 343
Recruiters Café, 144
RecruitSoft, 77
Research In Motion, 328, 345
Research Psychologists Press, 187
Reserve Employment Assistance Program (REAP), 159
Resources Consulting, 8
Retail Council of Canada, 231, 423
Right Management, 430
Rohm and Haas, 300
Roman Catholic Church, 33
Royal Canadian Mounted Police, 33
Royal Dutch Shell, 474
Rozeluk, Wendy, 58
RSI Clinic, 403
Runzheimer International, 467

S

Safe Communities Canada, 18
Sage HRMS Inc., 70
Saint Mary's University, 408

SAP, 70
Saratoga Institute, 68
Saskatchewan Human Rights Commission, 34
SaskEnergy, 254
Schein, Edgar, 242
Schuler, Cary, 77
Schuler, Rodney, 77
Schuler, Shaun, 77
Scotiabank, 144, 334
Secord, Amy, 250
Service Canada, 425
Seven Oaks General Hospital, 409
Sexual Orientation: Your Rights and Responsibilities, 41
Shepell.fgi, 370, 399
Sierra Systems, 214
simplyhired.ca, 159
Small Business Health and Safety (SBHS), 395
Snow Valley Edmonton, 345
Society for Canadian Women in Science and Technology (SCWIST), 167
Society for Human Resource Management, 59, 60
Software & Information Industry Association, 60
Sorin Group Canada, 129
Southern Alberta Institute of Technology (SAIT), 157
Southland Transportation, 145, 345
Spectrum Human Resource Systems Corporation, 69
Starbucks, 332
Statistics Canada, 230, 305, 467, 483
Steelcase Canada, 396
Stora Enso, 455
Stout, Kent, 352
Strength Tek, 409
Sunday Morning Post, 468
Sun Microsystems, 433
Superior Propane, 364
Supreme Court of Canada, 29, 314, 428
Swartout, Hank, 312

T

T.E. Financial Consultants, 421
Takada, Alemi, 164
Taleo, 77, 83
Taormina, Robert, 264
Tata, 284
Taylor, Frederick, 3, 323
Taylor, Steve, 396
TD Bank Group, 249
Technology Publications, 60
TELUS, 4, 249, 332, 373, 409
The Canadian Council on Rehabilitation and Work, 42
The Canadian Pandemic Influenza Plan, 406
The Expatriate Group, 474
The Financial Education Institute of Canada, 421
The Retirement Education Centre, 421
Thompson, Judith, 129
Thorndike, Robert, 262
Time Warner Inc., 74, 75
Tim Hortons, 144

Toronto Board of Trade, 305
Toronto Police Services, 74–75
Towers Perrin, 57, 369
Towers Watson, 296, 306
Toyota, 16
Transition Dynamics, 474
Transpavé, 385
Troilo, Palmerino, 34
Twaddle, Kerr, 37

U
Ulrich, David, 59
Ultimate Software, 69
Unilever Corporation, 81
United Food and Commercial
    Workers (UFCW), 443
United Steelworkers, 462

University of Alberta, 341
University of Macau, 264
University of Michigan Business
    School, 59
University of Ottawa, 230
University of Waterloo, 250
University of Western Ontario, 366
UPS Canada, 397
Urban Alliance on Race Relations,
    40
US Airways, 340
US Society for Human Resource
    Management, 18

V
Voisey's Bay Nickel Company, 442
Volareweb/Alitalia, 147

W
Walmart, 12, 440, 480
Watson Wyatt, 80, 144, 482
Waugh, Rick, 334
Web Hire, 77
Western Compensation and Benefits
    Consultants, 297
Wharton Business School, 254
Wild, David, 472
Women's Legal Education and
    Action Fund, 37
WORKink, 167
Workopolis, 159
Workplace Health Research Unit, 433
Workplace Safety and Insurance
    Board, 396, 397
Workplace Standards, 46

WorkSafeBC, 397
WorldatWork, 18, 294
World Economic Forum, 314
World Federation for Mental
    Health, 364
World Federation of People
    Management Associations
    (WFPMA), 18
World Health Organization, 413

X
Xstrata Nickel, 442

Y
York University, 454
Yukon Human Rights Commission, 34

boldface = key term
f = figure
t = table

A

Abilities @ Work, 167
Aboriginal people
  collective agreement, 442
  and employment equity, 46
  First Nations' rights, 29
  recruitment of, 166–167
  as untapped resource, 12
accidental death and dismemberment insurance, 359
accidents at work
  accident proneness, 390–391
  and age, 393
  chance occurrences, 390
  functional abilities evaluations
    (FAEs), 398
  and literacy, 391–392
  and perceptual vs. motor
    skills, 393
  and personal characteristics,
    390–391, 391*f*
  positive reinforcement,
    396–397
  prevention of, 394–398
  return to work, 398
  and selection testing, 394–395
  statistics, 382
  and top-management
    commitment, 395
  training and education, 395
  unsafe acts, 390, 394–397
  unsafe conditions, 390–391,
    394
  violence in the workplace,
    390*f*
  and vision, 391
  workers' compensation costs,
    397–398
accommodation, 35–36, 189
accountants, 5
achievement tests, 187
action learning, 249–250
action plan, 284
addiction, 189, 399
administration, 62–63
administrative support
  workers, 5
advertising, 162–163
affirmative action, 44
age
  and accidents, 393
  and discrimination, 42
  and recruitment, 165
  and workplace diversity, 12
agreeableness, 186
AIDA, 163
alcohol addiction, 189, 399

alternation ranking method,
  266, 269*f*, 278*f*
analytics, 80
annual bonus, 328–330
appeals, 422
application forms, 147–151,
  149*f*, 150*f*
appraisal bias, 276
apprenticeship training, 222
aptitudes, 241–242
aptitude tests, 184–185, 184*f*
arbitration
  of negotiations, 455, 456–457
  of rights, 458
artistic orientation, 241
asbestos, 405
Asia-Pacific region, 247
assignment letter, 471
associations, professional, 18
attendance, 63–64
attrition, 135
audiovisual techniques, 224
auditors, 5
auditory learning, 216
Australia, 468
authority, 108–109
authorization card, 447
autonomy and independence,
  242

B

Baby Boomers, 12, 13*f*, 325
Baby Busters, 13
background checks, 197–198
background information, 90–93
bad-faith conduct, 428
bad-faith damages, 428
balanced scorecard, 10
balance sheet approach, 477,
  478*f*
bargaining units, 440
bargaining zone, 451–452,
  451*f*
behaviour, as training measurement, 228
behavioural competencies, 310
behavioural interview, 191
behaviourally anchored rating
  scale (BARS), 271–272,
  271*f*, 278*f*
behaviour description interview
  (BDI), 191
behaviour modelling, 252–254
benchmark job, 300, 305
benefit formula, 367
benefits. *See* employee benefits
benzene, 405
bereavement leave, 355
Big Five, 186
Bill 168, 387
Bill C-45, 385

biographical information blank
  (BIB), 148
blended learning, 223, 226
blind ad, 163
bona fide occupational require-
  ment (BFOR), 32
boycott, 454
branding, 144–145
Bridging the Generation Gap,
  166
broadbanding, 308–309, 310*f*
buddy, 211
bullying, 36, 38, 39, 406
burnout, 402
business ally, 8
business intelligence, 58
business literacy, 231
business unionism, 441

C

Canada
  accidents at work, 382
  apprenticeship programs, 222
  education, 13–14
  employment law, 26–29
  employment trends, 11
  expatriate assignment failure,
    473
  global workers, management
    of, 482–487
  government jurisdictions,
    14–15
  immigrants, 467, 482–487,
    484*f*
  labour movement, 441
  labour shortages, 120–121,
    120*f*
  literacy, 230
  mental health costs, 400
  pension plans, 367
  productivity, 11, 215
  turnover, 416
  unemployment rates, 483*f*
  unionization rate, 444*f*
  workforce diversity, 11–14
  workplace violence, 407
Canada Labour Code, 297
Canada/Quebec Pension Plans
  (C/QPP), 298, 357
Canadian Management Professional (CMP), 251
cancer, 405
candidate-order error, 193
capital accumulation program,
  330
carcinogens, 405
career, 239
career anchor, 242
career counselling, 240
Career Handbook, 105
career management, 89

career planning and
  development
  career anchor, 242
  as component of total
    rewards, 296
  defined, 239
  evolution of, 240–245
  in learning organization, 243
  and life trajectory, 242–243
  management development. *See*
    management development
  new approaches to, 241–243
  promotions, 245–246
  roles in, 244–245
  skills and aptitudes, 241–242
  strategic importance of, 239
  transfers, 245
  and workplace diversity, 240
carpal tunnel syndrome, 405
case incidents. *See also* running
  case
  "Boss, I Think We Have a
    Problem", 490–491
  A Case of Too Little Training
    Too Late!, 236–237
  The Case of What Should
    Have Been Known, 204
  How to Downsize Successfully
    While Using HRP
    Fundamentals, 142
  An Inappropriate Email, 438
  Integration and Transfer of
    HR Functions Using HRIS,
    84
  Jack Nelson's Problem, 24
  A New Compensation Pro-
    gram to Motivate Perfor-
    mance, 349–350
  A New HR Professional's First
    Workplace Dilemma, 55
  A Performance Dilemma, 292
  Ramona's Health and Safety
    Nightmare, 413–414
  Salary Inequities at Acme
    Manufacturing, 320–321
  Solving a Potential Recruit-
    ment Dilemma, 172
  Strategy, 464–465
  Technology Plus's Benefit
    Dilemma, 380
  What Is a Human Resources
    Consultant to Do?, 118
  What Should Wilma and
    Frank Do?, 259–260
case study method, 252
cash plans, 339
caucus session, 450
centralization, 481
central tendency, 275
certification, 18–20, 18*f*,
  448–449

certification, of union, 448–449
Certified Personnel Consultant (CPC), 161
challenge, 242
chance occurrences, 390
change agents, 8
charitable causes, 343
Charter of Rights and Freedoms, 27, 28, 29
chief HR officer (CHRO), 9
chief talent officer (CTO), 9
childcare, 371
China, 15, 264, 468, 469, 470
classes, 301
classification/grading method, 301
classroom training, 223
client focus, 60
closed shop, 456
coaching/understudy approach, 249
cognitive abilities, 183–185
cognitive dissonance, 209
coinsurance, 360
cold calls, 162
collective bargaining
bargaining impasse, 453–455
bargaining zone, 451–452, 451*f*
collective agreement, 442, 455–457
conciliation, 453
contract approval process, 452–453
defined, 440, 449
distributive bargaining, 451, 451*f*
face-to-face negotiations, 450–452
and globalization, 481
integrative bargaining, 452
interest-based bargaining, 452
mutual gains bargaining, 452
preparation for negotiation, 450
steps in, 450
third-party assistance, 453–455
collective bargaining agreement, 28, 440, 442, 455–457
college/university-related programs, 251
colour discrimination, 40
combination plan, 336
commission, 335–336
commitment, 239
committee, appraisal by, 279
common-law partners, 41
communication
and employee engagement, 472
and employee separations, 432–434
compassionate care leave, 298, 355

compensable factor, 300, 302–304
compensation. *See also* pay plans
administration of, 65
as component of total rewards, 295
incentives. *See* incentive plans
international compensation, 476–480, 476*f*
and job analysis, 89
and motivation, 323–324
and strategy, 333–334
compensation policies, 299
competence, and promotion, 246
competencies
competency matrix model, 255
competency model, 7*f*
core competencies, 6–8, 58–59, 59*f*, 96
core competencies and, 310
defined, 96
and job analysis, 95–97
managerial competence, 242
and pay rates, 310–311
competency-based job analysis
defined, 95
examples of competencies, 96–97
overview, 95–96
reasons to use, 96
vs. traditional job analysis, 97
competency-based pay, 310–311
competency matrix model, 255
computer-based training (CBT), 225–226
conscientiousness, 186
consequences, 286
Constitution Act, 29
constructive discrimination, 32
constructive dismissal, 429
construct validity, 183
content validity, 182
contextual performance, 263
contingency planning, 80
contingent workers, 14
contract, 440
contract approval process, 452–453
contract law, 28
contract workers, 164–165
contrast error, 193
controlled experimentation, 228
conventional orientation, 241
cooperative education, 157, 158
core competencies
described, 6–8
examples of, 96
identified, 58–59, 59*f*
and pay rates, 310
corporate days, 352
corporate killing, 385
Corporate Manslaughter and Corporate Homicide Act, 469

corporate universities, 251
corporate websites, 159–160
cost/benefit analysis, 213
counselling services, 370
cradle-to-grave jobs, 420
craft union, 441
Crawford Small Parts Dexterity Test, 185, 185*f*
creativity, 242
credible activist, 6
credit unions, 370
Criminal Code, 385
criminal record checks, 174, 197
criteria, for selection, 177–178
criterion-related validity, 182
critical illness insurance, 360
critical incident method, 270, 270*f*, 278*f*
criticism, 284
cross-cultural training, 231, 475
cultural bias, 276
cultural factors, 468–469
cultural literacy, 231
cultural sensitivity training, 231
culture and change steward, 6–7
customer focus, 60
customer service training, 231–232

D

damage costs, 397
damages, 428
data warehouse, 61
decertification, 449
decision support, 67–68
deductible, 360
deductible formula, 329
defensiveness, 285
deferred profit-sharing plan (DPSP), 365
deferred share unit plan, 333
defined benefit pension plan, 365
defined contribution pension plan, 365
degree, of factor, 303
degree programs, 251
dehumanizing, 94
Delphi technique, 133
demographics, 444
derived score, 183
designated group members, 166–167, 174
designation, 18–20, 20*f*, 161, 251
development
as component of total rewards, 295
defined, 214
management of, 64. *See also* training
developmental job rotation, 249
diary, 103
differential piece-rate plan, 326
differential treatment, 30
differential validity, 182

corporate universities, 251
disabilities. *See* people with disabilities
disability benefits, 357
disability management, 363–364
disciplinary process, 421–423, 457
discrimination
in admission procedures, 217
on age, 42
bona fide occupational requirement (BFOR), 32–33
constructive, 32
defined, 30
on family status, 42
intentional, 30
investigation, 43*f*
legislation, 29–30
permissible, 32–33
prohibited grounds, 31*f*
on race and colour, 40
reasonable accommodation, 33
on religion, 40–41
remedies, 43–44
on sexual orientation, 41
systemic, 32, 32*f*
and training, 217
unintentional, 32
discrimination because of association, 31
dismissal, 422. *See also* termination
dismissal for just cause, 422, 429
distributive bargaining, 451, 451*f*
distributive justice, 426
diversity, of workforce. *See* workforce diversity
Don't Stop the Career Clock, 240
double cohort, 122
downsizing, 423
drivers of attraction, retention, and engagement, 432*f*
drug addiction, 189, 399
drug coverage, 360
duties and responsibilities, 108

E

early retirement buyout programs, 135–136
e-commerce, and sales compensation, 336–337
economic conditions, 11–16, 128
economic slowdown, 136
education, transferability of, 486
educational institutions, 157, 158
educational subsidies, 372
effectiveness and efficiency, 58
eldercare, 371–372
e-learning
computer-based training, 225–226

defined, 225
electronic performance support systems, 227
online training, 226
electronic database systems, 79. *See also* technology
electronic HR
electronic database systems, 79
IT/HR relationship, 60
electronic HR (e-HR)
cautions, 77–78
defined, 73
employee self-service (ESS), 74
talent management systems, 76
vendors, 76–77
web-based self-service applications, 74–76, 76*f*
electronic performance monitoring (EPM), 274
electronic performance support systems (EPSS), 227
email and internet usage policy, 50
Emotional Competence Inventory (ECI), 184
emotional intelligence (EI) tests, 183–184
Emotional Intelligence Questionnaire (EIQ), 184
Emotional Quotient Inventory (EQ-i), 184
emotional stability, 186
employee assistance plan (EAP), 370, 401, 477–480
employee benefits
administration of, 65, 375
benefit formula, 367
bereavement leave, 355
Canada/Quebec Pension Plans (C/QPP), 357
communication on, 375
compassionate care leave, 298, 355
as component of total rewards, 295
defined, 352
employee services. *See* employee services
employment insurance (EI), 353–354, 2989
flexible benefits programs, 373–375, 374*f*
for Generation Y, 362
government-mandated, 353–359
holidays, 358–359
importance of, 352–353
leave of absence, 355–357, 356*f*
long-term disability insurance, 363–364
maternity leave, 298, 355
mental health benefits, 364, 364*f*

paid breaks, 359
parental leave, 298, 355
pension plans. *See* pension plans
retiree health benefits, 362
sabbaticals, 365
severance pay, 354–355
short-term disability plans, 363
sick leave, 363
supplementary healthcare insurance, 360–362, 361*f*
termination pay, 354–355
vacations, 358–359
voluntary employer-sponsored, 359–369
workers' compensation, 357–358
employee commitment, 239
employee engagement, 6, 296, 432, 432*f*
Employee Feedback System (EFS), 433
employee handbook, 211
employee misconduct, 423
employee opinion surveys, 433
employee orientation
and cognitive dissonance, 209
content of, 211
defined, 209
and diverse workforce, 211–212
evaluation of, 213
executive integration, 213–214
mergers and acquisitions, 212
multi-location organizations, 212
online onboarding, 210
problems with, 212–213
purpose of, 209–210
responsibility for, 211
socialization, 209
special situations, 211–212
training process. *See* training
union vs. non-union employees, 212
employee privacy, 48–50
employee reaction, 213
employee recognition programs, 342–345, 344*f*
employee records, 66
employee referrals, 156
Employee Reliability Inventory (ERI), 394
employee retention, 239
employee self-identification form, 149*f*
employee self-service (ESS), 74, 75–76, 75*f*
employee separations
bad-faith damages, 428
and communication, 432–434
constructive dismissal, 429
cost of turnover, 417–418

discipline, 422
dismissal for just cause, 422–423, 429
fairness in, 426–431, 426*f*
group termination, 427
importance of, 416
involuntary turnover, 416, 420, 421–425
layoffs, 424–425
outplacement counselling, 430
punitive damages, 428–429
quits, 420–421
reactions to, 431
reasonable notice, 427–429
retirement. *See* retirement
severance pay, 431
termination interview, 430–431
voluntary turnover, 416, 418–421
wrongful dismissal, 426, 426*f*, 427, 429–430
employee services
childcare, 371
counselling services, 370
credit unions, 370
educational subsidies, 372
eldercare, 371–372
employee assistance plan (EAP), 370
executive perquisites, 373
family-friendly benefits, 372–373
food services, 372
job-related services, 371–373
other personal services, 371
personal services, 369–371
transportation, 372
employee share purchase/stock ownership plan (ESOP), 339
employee theft, 423
employee wellness programs, 409–410, 409*f*
employer branding, 144–145
employment (labour) standards legislation, 47–48
employment agencies, 161–162
employment at will, 26
employment contract, 211
employment equity, 44, 64
employment equity legislation
Aboriginal people, 46
designated groups, 46–47
overview, 44–46
people with disabilities, 46
and training, 217
visible minorities, 47
women, 46
employment equity program, 45
employment insurance (EI), 298, 353–354
Employment Insurance Act, 298

employment law. *See also* legislation
jurisdictions, 14, 27
legal framework for, 26–29
employment standards acts, 28, 189, 297
empowerment, 18
engagement, 296, 432, 432*f*, 472
enhanced language training (ELT), 231
enterprise resource planning (ERP) system, 70
enterprise-wide system, 70
enterprising orientation, 241
entrepreneurs and HR
family business, 127
HRIS software, 77
interviewing, 176–177
job analysis, 110
job descriptions, 110
occupational health and safety, 397
recognition and incentives, 343
selection testing, 176
succession planning, 127
environmental concerns, as environmental influence, 16
environmental influences on HRM
contingent workers, 14
economic conditions, 11–16
environmental concerns, 16
environment scanning, 122–123
external, 11–16, 122–123
globalization, 15–16
government, 14–15
internal, 17–18
labour market issues, 11–14
management practices, 17–18
non-standard workers, 14
organizational climate, 17
organizational culture, 17
technology, 14
environmental scanning, 8
environment scanning, 122–123
EQ map, 184
equality rights, 29
equal pay for equal work, 46
equity, 299
ergonomics, 95, 403–404, 404*f*
essential skills training, 230–231
ethnocentric staffing policy, 474
European Union, 367
evaluation
of job, 304
of training, 217, 218*f*, 227–230, 229*f*
evaluation form, 178, 179*f*, 196*f*
executive compensation, 312
executive development programs, 251
executive integration, 213–214
Executive MBA, 251

executive perquisites, 373
executive search firms, 161
expatriate, 467, 470
expatriate assignment failure,
    472–474
experience, 176
external equity, 299
external recruitment
    advantages of, 154
    cold calls, 162
    educational institutions, 157
    employee referrals, 156
    employment agencies,
        161–162
    executive search firms, 161
    former employees, 157
    Human Resources and Skills
        Development Canada
        (HRSDC), 160–161
    job fair, 158
    labour organizations,
        158–159
    methods, 156–163, 156f
    military personnel, 159
    online, 159–160, 162
    open house, 158
    planning, 154–156
    print advertising, 162–163
    professional associations, 158
    trade associations, 158
    walk-ins and write-ins, 162
    yield ratio, 155, 155f
extroversion, 186

F

factor weights and degrees, 303
fairness, in employee separations,
    426–431, 426f, 432
faking, 187
family business, 127
family-friendly benefits,
    372–373
family status, 42
family support, 471
feedback. *See also* performance
    appraisal
    formal appraisal discussion,
        282–285
    multisource feedback, 280
    ongoing, 264
    360-degree assessment, 77
    upward feedback, 279–280,
        280f
field placement, 157, 158
financial auditors, 5
financial crisis, 9, 136, 330, 366
fixed pay, 323
flexible benefits programs,
    373–375, 374f
food services, 372
forced distribution method, 266,
    269–270, 278f
forecasting
    Delphi technique, 133
    economic conditions, 128

gap analysis, 133
and HRIS, 67
labour demand, 130–134
labour market conditions,
    128–129
labour supply, 123–130
management inventories, 124
Markov analysis, 126–128,
    127f
nominal group technique,
    132–133
occupational market
    conditions, 129–130
qualitative approaches,
    132–133
quantitative approaches,
    130–132
ratio analysis, 130–131
regression analysis, 132
replacement charts, 124–125
replacement summaries, 125
scatter plot, 131, 132f
skills inventories, 124
staffing table, 133, 134f
succession planning, 126
trend analysis, 130
formal appraisal discussion,
    282–285
functional abilities evaluation
    (FAE), 185, 398
functional competencies, 96–97,
    310
functional illiteracy, 14, 230
Functional Job Analysis (FJA),
    103
fund size, 328–329

G

gainsharing plan, 339–340
general aptitude test battery
    (GATB), 241–242
general office workers, 5
generational differences, 12–13,
    13f
Generation X, 13, 13f, 165, 325
Generation Y, 13, 13f, 166, 223,
    325, 362
geocentric staffing policy, 474
geographical scope, 441
Germany, 470
glass ceiling, 44
global buddy, 472
*Global Gender Gap Report,
    2007,* 314
global HRM. *See also*
    globalization
    Asia-Pacific region, 247
    bullying, 39
    competitive advantage of
        HRM, 15
    considerations in, 474–481
    immigrant integration, 485
    leadership development, 247
    outsourcing, 81
    pension benefits, 367

performance appraisal, 264
recruiting from Europe, 147
globalization. *See also* global
    HRM
    balance sheet approach, 477
    within Canada, 482–487
    compensation, international,
        476–480, 476f
    considerations in, 474–481
    cultural factors, 468–469
    defined, 15
    economic systems, 469
    as environmental influence,
        15–16
    expatriate assignment failure,
        472–474
    industrial relations, 470
    intercountry differences,
        467–470
    international assignment
        types, 473f
    international EAPs, 477–480
    labour cost factors, 469
    and labour relations, 480–481
    and labour unions, 443
    legal systems, 469
    orientation, 475–476
    performance appraisal, 480
    relocation, 470–474
    repatriation, 481–482
    selection, 475
    staffing policy, 474
    and strategic HR, 467
    training, 475–476
    variable pay, 477
global nomads, 470
*Global Workforce Study,
    2007–2008,* 296
goal-setting, 272
going live, 73
golden parachute, 137, 373
government
    as environmental influence,
        14–15
    role of employment law, 26
grade/group description, 301,
    302f
grades, 301, 328
graphic rating scale, 266, 267f,
    275f, 278f
green causes, 343
grievance, 458, 459f
group description, 301, 302f
group incentive plan, 327–328
group interview, 98
group life insurance, 359–360
group registered retirement
    savings plan (group RRSP),
    365, 366t, 368
group termination, 427
guaranteed piecework plan,
    325
*A Guide to Screening and
    Selection in Employment,*
    180

H

halo effect, 193, 275
handbook, 211
happily employed, 160
harassment
    bullying, 36, 39
    defined, 36
    employer responsibility,
        38–39
    examples of, 38f
    harassment policies, 40
    psychological, 38
    sexual harassment, 37, 39–40
    as workplace violence, 406
hazardous materials, 386, 387f,
    388f
headhunters, 161
health and safety. *See* occupa-
    tional health and safety
health and safety committees, 384
health and safety programs, 358
healthcare costs, 360–362, 361f
healthcare insurance, 360–362
healthcare spending accounts
    (HCSA) are, 361
health promotion, 361
healthy work environment, 408
high-performance work system,
    96
hiring decision, 199–200
hiring freeze, 135
history of HRM
    human resources movement,
        3–10
    scientific management, 3
hobo phenomena, 419
holidays, 358–359, 467
horizontal loading, 94
HR portal, 74
HR technology, 57. *See also*
    technology
HR technology strategy, 80
human capital
    defined, 2
    importance of, 2
    life cycle of, 4
human capital theory, 151
human relations movement, 4
Human Resources and Skills
    Development Canada
    (HRSDC), 160–161
**human resources information
    system (HRIS)**
    administration, 62–63
    adoption, 71–72
    company background, 71
    compensation and benefits
        administration, 65
    components of, 62–65
    cost considerations, 72
    decision support, 67–68
    defined, 61
    employee records, 66
    employment equity
        information, 64

forecasting and planning, 67
functions of, 65–68, 66f
health and safety, 65
HR considerations, 72
implementation, 71f, 72–73
integration, 73
knowledge management, 64, 67
labour relations, 65
legal compliance, 66
management considerations, 71
organization management, 65
overview, 61
payroll, 65, 66
pension administration, 64
performance evaluation, 64, 64f
privacy and security, 73
recruitment and applicant screening, 180
recruitment and applicant tracking, 63, 148, 160
relationship with HRM, 61–62
report types, 68
selecting and implementing, 69–73
stand-alone system, 70
strategic alignment, 67
subsystems, 62f
talent management, 67
technical considerations, 72
time and attendance, 63–64, 63f
training and development, 64
types of, 69–70
users, 68f
human resources management (HRM)
core competencies, 6–8, 58–59, 59f
critical knowledge areas, 4, 6
cultural factors, 468–469
defined, 2
environmental influences on. See environmental influences
evolving role of, 9
and globalization, 467, 474–481
and global relocation, 470–474
history of. See history of HRM
and HRIS, 61–62
intercountry differences, 467–470
labour-management relations, 460–461
labour relations. See labour relations
measurement of value, 9–10
and non-HR roles, 5–6f
professionalism in, 18–20
responsibilities of, 4–8

role, evolving, 9
strategic role of, 2–3
and technology. See technology
unionization, impact of, 460–461
human resources management systems (HRMS). See human resources information system (HRIS)
human resources movement, 3–10
human resources planning (HRP)
balancing supply and demand, 134–139, 135f
defined, 120
environment scanning, 122–123
external candidates, 128–130
forecasting. See forecasting
importance of, 120–123
internal candidates, 124–128
job analysis, 88
labour demands, 120–121, 120f
labour shortages, 137–138
labour surplus, 135–136
model, 121f
steps in, 123
and strategic planning, 122
succession planning, 126
human resources records, 152
skills inventories, 152
human rights legislation
accommodation, 35–36, 36f
age, 42
case examples, 33–42
described, 29
on disability, 34–36
discrimination. See discrimination
enforcement, 42–44
explained, 30
family status, 42
harassment, 36–40
and job description, 109–110
job specification, 111
and pay equity, 315
and pay rates, 298
provincial codes, 27
race and colour, 40
and recruitment/selection, 180
religion, 40–41
and selection, 174
and selection testing, 395
sexual orientation, 41
and training, 217

I

identification of top talent, 9
illiteracy, 14, 230
immigrants
barriers to employment, 484–487
in Canada, 467, 482–487

and cultural bias, 276
and globalization, 467
increase in, 12, 129
job search difficulties, 484f
lack of Canadian experience, 484–485
literacy skills, 486–487
recruiting from Europe, 147
and safety training, 395
transferability of education, 486
as visible minorities, 47
impacts and benefits agreements (IBAs), 442
implementation
of HRIS, 72–73
of training, 227
implemented, 217, 218f
improshare plan, 340
in-basket exercise, 188
incentive plans, 344f
annual bonus, 328–330
development of, 340–342
eligibility, 328
employee recognition, 342–345
employee share purchase/stock ownership plan (ESOP), 339
for executives, 328–334
fund size, 328–329
gainsharing plans, 339–340
group incentive plans, 327–328
implementation of, 341–342
individual awards, 329–330
long-term incentives, 330–334, 331f
for managers, 337–338
merit pay (merit raise), 337
multiplier method, 329
for operations employees, 324–328
organization-wide incentives, 338–340
piecework, 324–327
for professional employees, 338
and profit-sharing, 329
profit-sharing plans, 338–339
for salespeople, 334–337
for senior managers, 328–334
short-term incentives, 328–330
split-award method, 329
stock options, 330–333, 332f, 339
team incentive plans, 327–328
types of, 324
when to use, 340–341
incident costs, 397
Income Tax Act, 361, 366, 368
independence, 242
individual awards, 329–330
individual interview, 98

individualized courses, 251
individual presentations, 188
industrial engineering, 94
industrial engineers, 5
industrial relations, 470. See also labour relations
Industrial Revolution, 94
industrial union, 441
informal learning, 222
information technology. See human resources information system (HRIS)
in-house development centre, 251
Innu, 442
instructional design, 217, 218f
apprenticeship training, 222
audiovisual techniques, 224
classroom training, 223
e-learning, 225–227
informal learning, 222
job instruction training (JIT), 223
on-the-job training, 222
programmed learning, 224
traditional techniques, 222–225
vestibule or simulated training, 224–225
insubordination, 423, 424f
insurance
accidental death and dismemberment insurance, 359
coinsurance, 360
critical illness insurance, 360
employment insurance (EI), 298, 353–354
group life insurance, 359–360
long-term disability insurance, 363–364
medical insurance, 360–362
integration
of executives, 213–214
of HRIS, 73, 84
of learning, 216
integrative bargaining, 452
intellectual capacity, 176
intelligence (IQ) tests, 183
intentional tort, 28
interactional justice, 427
interest arbitration, 455
interest-based bargaining, 452
interest dispute, 455
interest inventories, 187
internal equity, 299
internal labour, 124–128
international unions, 442
internet job boards, 159
internship, 157
interview
conducting, 283–284
guidelines, 98
for performance appraisal, 282–285

interview (*Continued*)
  selection interview. *See* selection interview
  supervisory interview, 199
  types of, 98, 282–283
intranet, 73, 80
Inuit people, 442
inventory shrinkage, 423
investigation costs, 397
investigative orientation, 241
involuntary turnover, 416, 420, 421–425
IT. *See* human resources information system (HRIS)
IT/HR relationship, 60

J
Japan, 327, 342
job, 88
  evolution of, 94–95
  redefinition of, 93
job analysis
  background information, 90–93
  communication and revision, 114
  competency-based, 95–97
  defined, 88
  diary, 103
  evolution of, 94–95
  functional job analysis (FJA), 103
  information collection, 98–105
  information sources, 105
  information verification, 105–106
  interview, 98–101
  job descriptions, 106–110
  job specification, 110–113, 113*f*
  log, 103
  National Occupational Classification (NOC), 103–105, 104*f*
  observation, 103
  participant diary/log, 103
  position analysis questionnaire (PAQ), 101, 102*f*
  practical approach, 110
  questionnaire, 98, 99–100, 99*f*, 101–103, 110
  selection of jobs, 93–97
  steps in, 90
  traditional vs. competency-based, 97
  uses of, 88–89, 88*f*
job classification, 301, 313
job description
  authority, 108–109
  duties and responsibilities, 108
  and human rights legislation, 109–110
  identification, 106
  National Occupational Classification (NOC), 110

performance standards, 109
physical environment, 109
relationships, 106
sample, 107*f*
summary, 106
working conditions, 109
job design
  competency-based, 95–97
  defined, 93
  team-based, 97
job enlargement (horizontal loading), 94
job enrichment (vertical loading), 95
job evaluation, 304
job evaluation
  classification/grading method, 301
  compensable factors, 300
  defined, 299
  job evaluation committee, 300–301
  point method, 301–305, 304*f*
  for professional employees, 313
  and wage/salary survey, 307–310
job evaluation committee, 300–301
job fair, 158
job identification, 106
job instruction training (JIT), 223
job offer, 200
job posting, 152, 153*f*, 154*f*
job-related services, 371–373
job-related stress
  burnout, 402
  employee assistance plan, 401
  environmental factors, 401
  personal factors, 401
  reducing, 401–402
  signs of, 400*f*
  too little, 401
  and workers' compensation, 402–403
job rotation, 95
job security, 441
job sharing, 136
job specification
  defined, 110–113
  sample, 113*f*
job summary, 106
job title, 110
just cause, 422–423
justice, organizational, 426

K
key position, 328
kinesthetic learning, 216
knowledge, 176, 178, 193
knowledge management, 64, 67
KSAs, 47

L
labour–management relations. *See* labour relations
labour congress affiliation, 442
labour costs, 7
labour demand
  balancing with supply, 134–139, 135*f*
  forecasting, 130–134
  and HRP, 120–121, 120*f*
labour equilibrium, 135
labour–management relations, 440, 460–461. *See also* labour relations
labour market conditions, 128–129
labour market issues, 11–14
labour movement, 441
labour organizations, 158–159
labour relations, 445*f*
  certification, 448–449
  collective bargaining. *See* collective bargaining
  and compensation, 298–299
  contract administration, 457–459
  desire for collective representation, 445–446
  disciplinary process, 457
  grievance resolution, 458, 459*f*
  and human resources information system, 65
  international labour relations, 480–481
  introduction to, 440
  and job analysis, 89
  labour relations (LR) strategy, 440
  legislation, 440–441
  process, 445–459
  response to union organizing campaign, 447–448
  rights arbitration, 458
  rights of employees, 448
  signs of union organizing activity, 447
  union organizing campaign, 446–446
  union recognition, 448–449
labour relations board (LRB), 441, 448–449
labour standards acts, 297
labour supply
  balancing with demand, 134–139, 135*f*
  economic conditions, 128
  external, 128–130
  forecasting, 123–130
  immigrants, 129
  internal, 124–128
  occupational market conditions, 129–130
  and selection, 175
  shortage, 120–121, 120*f*, 137–138, 368
  surplus, 135–137

labour union
  closed shop, 456
  collective bargaining. *See* collective bargaining
  and compensation, 298–299
  decertification, 449
  defined, 440
  and demographics, 444, 448
  eligibility of workers, 441
  employer response to, 447–448
  geographical scope, 441
  and global competition, 443
  and globalization, 481
  goal of, 441
  impact on HRM, 460–461
  international unions, 442
  labour congress affiliation, 442
  labour laws, 440–441
  and layoffs, 423
  local, 443
  maintenance-of-membership arrangement, 456
  membership trends, 443–444
  modified union shop, 456
  open shop, 456
  organizing, steps in, 446–446
  pre-hearing vote, 449
  Rand formula, 456
  reasons for joining, 445–446
  rights of employees, 448
  signs of organizing activity, 447
  steward, 443
  types of, 441–443
  union acceptance strategy, 440
  union avoidance strategy, 440
  union contract, 440
  unionization rate, 444*f*
  union recognition, 448–449
  union security clause, 455
  union shop, 456
  union substitution approach, 440
  union suppression approach, 440
  union vs. non-union employees, 212
  and white-collar employees, 444
language ability, 486–487
layoff, 136, 355, 423–425
leaderless group discussion, 188
leadership competencies, 96
leadership development, 254–256
leading questions, 193
learner content management systems, 226
learning
  measurement of, 228
  styles of, 216–217
learning management systems, 226
learning organization, 243

leave of absence, 136–137, 355–357
lecturers, 5
legal compliance, 66
legal framework, 26–29
legislation
  Bill 168, 387
  Bill C-45, 385
  Canada Labour Code, 297
  Charter of Rights and Freedoms, 27, 28, 29
  Constitution Act, 29
  contract law, 28
  Corporate Manslaughter and Corporate Homicide Act, 469
  Criminal Code, 385
  employee privacy, 48–50
  employee training, 215
  employment (labour) standards legislation, 47–48
  employment equity legislation. See employment equity legislation
  Employment Standards Act, 28
  enforcement, 42–44, 48
  and general public, 29–44
  human rights legislation. See human rights legislation
  Income Tax Act, 361, 366, 368
  labour laws, 440–441
  layers of, 27f
  objective of, 26
  occupational health and safety legislation. See occupational health and safety legislation
  Ontario Occupational Health and Safety Act, 387
  pay equity, 297, 314, 315
  and pay rates, 297–298
  pension plans, 366
  Personal Information Protection and Electronic Documents Act (PIPEDA), 49
  and recruitment/selection, 180
  tort law, 28
  workers' compensation law, 298
  and workplace violence, 407
level, of factor, 303
lies, 197f
life expectancy, 420
life insurance, 359–360
lifestyle, 242
life trajectory, 242–243
line of sight, 323, 338, 341
literacy, 14, 230–231, 391–392, 486–487
local, 443
lockout, 441, 454–455, 456
log, 103
logrolling, 279

long-term disability insurance, 363–364
long-term incentives, 330–334, 331f
Lost-time injury rate, 382

M
maintenance-of-membership arrangement, 456
management assessment centre, 187–188
management by objectives (MBO), 272–273, 278f
management development
  action learning, 249–250
  behaviour modelling, 252–254
  case study method, 252
  coaching/understudy approach, 249
  college/university-related programs, 251
  defined, 246
  developmental job rotation, 249
  in-house development centre, 251
  leadership development, 254–256
  management game, 253
  mentoring, 253–254
  outside seminars, 251
  role playing, 252
  succession planning, 247–249
  techniques, 249–251
management game, 188, 253
management inventories, 124
management practices, as environmental influence, 17–18
management replacement chart, 125f
management rights clause, 456
management self-service (MSS), 75–76
manager
  and career development, 244–245
  training, 232
managerial competence, 242
mandatory retirement, 420
manufacturing engineers, 5
market-pricing approach, 313
Markov analysis, 126–128, 127f
mass interview, 192
mass terminations, 423
Master of Business Administration, 251
material safety data sheet (MSDS), 388f
maternity leave, 298, 355
Mayer-Salovey-Caruso Emotional Intelligence Test (MSCEIT), 184
mechanical comprehension test, 184f
mediation, 453

medical examination, 189
medical insurance, 360–362
Meiorin test, 33, 35
memorandum of settlement, 452
mental health benefits, 364, 364f
mental health problems, 400
mentor, 211
mentoring, 253–254
mergers and acquisitions, 212
merit pay (merit raise), 337
metrics, 9–10, 68, 229–230
micro-assessment, 189
military personnel, 159
Millennials, 13
Minnesota Clerical Assessment Battery, 176
Minnesota Multiphasic Personality Inventory (MMPI), 186
Minnesota Rate of Manipulation Test, 185
minorities, 47
mixed (semi-structured) interview, 190–191
modelling, 252
modified union shop, 456
Monster.com, 6
motivation
  and employee selection, 176
  and learning, 216
  and money, 323–324, 341
motor abilities, 185
motor skill, 393
multicultural heritage rights, 29
multi-location organizations, 212
multiple-hurdle strategy, 175
multiplier method, 329
multisource feedback, 280
must criteria, 178
mutual gains (interest-based) bargaining, 452
Myers-Briggs Type Indicator, 186

N
narrative forms, 270–271, 278f
National CHRP certification requirements, 18f
National Occupational Classification (NOC), 103–105, 104f, 110
national unions, 442
needs analysis, 71–72, 217, 218–222, 218f
Neglected or Hidden study, 168
negligent hiring, 174
negligent misrepresentation, 199
negligent training, 217
negotiation. See collective bargaining
NEO Five-Factor Inventory (NEO-FFI), 186
nepotism, 156
Net Generation, 13

networking, 244, 244f
new-hire development process, 210
nominal group technique, 132–133
non-deductible formula, 328
non-permanent staff, 163–165
non-standard workers, 14
nonverbal behaviour, 193
notice, 354, 427–429
notification of candidate, 200
nurses, 342
nursing coordinators and supervisors, 5

O
objective tests, 188
observation, 103
occupation, 105
occupational health and safety
  accidents, causes of, 389–394
  accidents, prevention of, 394–398
  accidents, statistics, 382
  carpal tunnel syndrome, 405
  challenges in, 398–409
  committees, 384
  employee wellness programs, 409–410, 409f
  ergonomics, 403–404, 404f
  and human resources information system, 65
  importance of, 382
  job-related stress, 400–403, 400f
  legislation. See occupational health and safety legislation
  material safety data sheet, 388f
  metrics, 68
  positive reinforcement, 396–397
  repetitive strain injuries, 403–405
  selection testing, 394–395
  smoking, 405–406
  substance abuse, 399–400
  top-management commitment, 395
  toxins, 405
  training and education, 395
  video display terminals, 405
  violence in the workplace, 406–409, 407f
  viral pandemic, 406
  workers' compensation costs, 397–398
occupational health and safety legislation
  Bill C-45, 385
  committees, 384
  construction regulations, 383f
  Criminal Code, 385
  enforcement, 385
  purpose of, 383
  responsibilities, 383–384

occupational health and safety
legislation (*Continued*)
rights, 383–384
supervisor's role, 384–385
toxic substances, 386
Workplace Hazardous Mate-
rials Information System
(WHMIS), 386, 387*f*, 388*f*
occupational market conditions,
129–130
occupational orientation, 240
occupational segregation, 44
older workers, 165
onboarding, 209, 210. *See also*
employee orientation
online networking, 162
online onboarding, 210
online postings by job candidates, 198*f*
online recruitment, 159–160
online training, 226
Ontario Academic Credit
(OAC), 122
Ontario Occupational Health
and Safety Act, 387
on-the-job training (OJT), 222,
310
open-door policy, 460
open house, 158
openness to experience, 186
open shop, 456
operational executor, 8
operational HR, 10*f*
operationalizing, 62
organizational climate, 17
organizational culture, 17, 239
organizational designer, 7
organizational justice, 426
organizational structure, 91, 92*f*
organization chart, 91, 91*f*, 110
organization management, 65
organization-wide goal-setting
and appraisal program,
272
orientation. *See* employee orientation
outplacement assistance, 137
outplacement counselling, 430
outside seminars, 251
outsourcing, 4, 80

P

paired comparison method, 266,
269*f*, 278*f*
pandemic, 406
panel interview, 192
paper-based systems, 78
parental leave, 298, 355
passive job seekers, 160
pay equity, 313–315, 314*t*,
320–321
pay equity acts, 297, 314, 315
pay-for-knowledge system,
310–311
pay-for-performance plans,
323–324

pay grade, 305
pay in lieu of reasonable notice,
354
pay plans. *See also* pay rates;
rewards
fixed pay, 323
line of sight, 323
pay-for-performance plans,
323–324
pay rates. *See* pay rates
variable pay, 323, 323*f*
pay ranges, 308, 308*t*, 309*t*
pay rates
broadbanding, 308–309, 310*f*
compensation policies, 299
competency-based pay,
310–311
considerations in determining,
297–299
and equity, 299
establishing, 299–310
for executives, 312
job evaluation. *See* job
evaluation
for knowledge, 310–311
legal considerations, 297–298
for managers, 312
market-pricing approach, 313
our-of-line rates, 309–310
pay equity, 313–315, 314*t*,
320–321
pay grade, 305
for professional employees,
312–313
ranges, 308, 308*t*, 309*t*
red circle pay rate, 310
skill-based pay, 310–311
union influences, 298–299
wage curve, 307, 307*f*
wage/salary survey, 305–307
payroll technology, 65, 66
peer appraisal, 279
pension administration, 64
pension plans
benefit formula, 367
categories of, 365–368
deferred profit-sharing plan,
365
defined, 365
defined benefit pension plan,
365
defined contribution pension
plan, 365
designing, 367–368
funding, 368
government pensions, 298,
357
group registered retirement
savings plan, 365, 366*t*,
368
phased retirement, 368
portability, 368
supplemental employee
retirement plans (SERPs),
368–369, 369*f*
vesting, 368

people with disabilities
accommodation, 35–36
addiction, 189
and employment equity, 46
equality barriers, 12
and human rights legislation,
34–36
principles for assessment
accommodations, 181
recruitment of, 166–168
perceptual skill, 393
performance analysis,
219, 221
performance and recognition,
295
performance appraisal
action plan, 284
alternation ranking method,
266, 269*f*, 278*f*
appraisal bias, 276
appraisal tools, 278*f*
behaviourally anchored rating
scale (BARS), 271–272,
271*f*, 278*f*
central tendency, 275
by committee, 279
critical incident method, 270,
270*f*, 278*f*
criticism, 284
cultural bias, 276
defensive employees, 285
electronic performance
monitoring, 274
forced distribution method,
266, 269–270, 278*f*
formal discussions, 282–285
formal methods, 266–273
of global managers, 480
graphic rating scale, 266,
267*f*, 275*f*, 278*f*
guidelines for, 287
halo effect, 275
and improved performance,
285
interviews, 282–285
management by objectives,
272–273, 278*f*
mixing methods, 273
narrative forms, 270–271,
278*f*
paired comparison method,
266, 269*f*, 278*f*
by peers, 279
preparing for, 283–285
problems, avoiding, 277
problems and solutions,
274–277
rating scale problems,
275–277
recency effect, 277
and rewards, 329
sample form, 267*f*
by self, 278–279
similar-to-me bias, 277
strictness/leniency, 276
by subordinates, 279–280

by supervisor, 278
and technology, 273–274
360-degree appraisal,
280–282
unclear performance
standards, 275
validity and reliability,
274–275
who should do it, 277–282
written warning, 286
performance evaluation,
64, 77
performance expectations,
262–264
performance improvement plan
(PIP), 265*f*, 270
performance management
and competency-based
analysis, 96
defined, 262
ethics, 286–287
future of, 288
and job analysis, 89
legal issues, 286–287
process. *See* performance
management process
purposes of, 262
strategic importance of, 262
and technology, 273–274
performance management
process
appraisal and evaluation. *See*
performance appraisal
career development discussions, 286
coaching, 264
defining expectations,
262–264
feedback, 264
performance appraisal, 264
and performance measurement,
263
rewards/consequences, 286
sample performance improvement plan, 265*f*
steps in, 262
performance measurement,
263
performance pay, 340, 341. *See
also* incentive plans
performance share unit plan,
333
performance standards, 109
personal characteristics, and
accidents, 390–391, 391*f*
personal computers, 78. *See also*
technology
Personal Information Protection
and Electronic Documents
Act (PIPEDA), 49, 80
personality, 176, 186–187,
240–241
Personality-Related Position
Requirements Form (PPRF),
111
personal literacy, 231

personal networking, 244f
personal services, 369–371
phased retirement, 368, 420
physical abilities, 185
physical demands analysis, 111, 112f
physical environment, 109
picket, 454
piecework, 324–327
Plane Shift, 212
planning. *See* human resources planning. *See also* forecasting
point method, 301–305, 304f
poisoned work environment, 39
policies
   email and internet usage policy, 50f
   workplace violence policy, 407f
policy grievance, 458
polycentric staffing policy, 474
polygraph test, 189
portability, 368
portal, 74, 75, 80
position, 88
Position Analysis Questionnaire (PAQ), 101, 102f
position title, 106
positive reinforcement, 343, 396–397
praise, 342
predictive attrition, 58
Predictive Index, 176
pre-hearing vote, 449
pre-retirement counselling, 421
presentations, individual, 188
primary sector, 11
principles for assessment accommodations, 181
print advertising, 162–163
prior learning assessment and recognition (PLAR), 486
privacy
   and HRIS, 73, 80
   legislation, 48–50
Privacy Information Act, 80
private employment agencies, 161–162
procedural justice, 426
process chart, 93f
productivity
   defined, 11
   and health issues, 400
   and training and development, 215
productivity costs, 397
professional associations, 18, 158
professional employees, 312–313
professionalism in HRM, 18–20
professors, 5
profit-sharing plan, 329, 338–339
programmed learning, 224
progressive discipline, 422

projected turnover, 130
projective tests, 186
promotion, 138, 245–246
provident funds, 367
psychotoxic, 403
punitive damages, 428–429
Purdue Pegboard, 185
Purdue Test for Machinists and Machine Operators, 187

Q

qualified privilege, 198
qualifying period, 354
qualitative approaches, 130, 132–133
quantitative approaches, 130–132
questionnaires, 98, 99–100, 101–103, 110
quitting, 419–420

R

race, 40
Rand formula, 456
ranking method, 300
rapport, 194
rater training, 277
ratification, 452
rating scale problems, 275–277
ratio analysis A, 130–131
reaction, 228
reactions to dismissal, 431
realistic job preview (RJP), 199
realistic orientation, 241
reality shock, 209
reasonable accommodation, 33
reasonable cause, 384
reasonable notice, 354, 427–429
recency effect, 277
recognition, 342–345, 344f
recruiter, 144
recruiting yield pyramid, 155f
recruitment
   and applicant tracking, 63, 148, 160
   application forms, 147–151, 149f, 150f
   of contract workers, 164–165
   defined, 144
   of designated group members, 166–167
   and diversity, 165–168
   employer branding, 144–145
   from Europe, 147
   external. *See* external recruitment
   human resources records, 152
   importance of, 144–145
   internal, 151–154
   and job analysis, 89
   job posting, 152, 153f, 154f
   methods, external, 156–163, 156f
   methods, internal, 152
   non-permanent staff, 163–165

older workers, 165
process, 146, 146f
selection of employees. *See* selection
steps in, 146f
temporary help agencies, 164
of younger workers, 165–166
red circle pay rate, 310
reduced workweek, 136
reduction in workforce, 423
references, 197–198
referrals, 156
regression analysis, 132
regulations, 28
regulatory bodies, 28
rehabilitation programs, 358
relational database, 79
relationships, 106, 341
reliability, 182, 274–275
religion, 40–41
relocation, 245, 470–474
repatriation, 481–482
repetitive strain injuries (RSIs), 403–405
replacement chart, 124–125, 125f, 247, 247f
replacement costs, 397, 418
replacement summaries, 125
representation vote, 449
request for proposal (RFP), 72
restitutional remedies, 43, 44
restricted share unit plan, 333
restructuring, 89
results, of training, 229–230
résumé lies, 197f
retention, 239
retirees on call, 420
retirement. *See also* pension plans
   early, 135–136
   employers' responsibilities, 421
   mandatory, 420
   phased retirement, 368, 420
   as reason for turnover, 420–421
retirement age, 420
retirement benefits
   pension plans. *See* pension plans
   retiree health benefits, 362
retirement pension, 357
reverse mentoring, 254
rewards. *See also* compensation; incentive plans; pay plans
   benefits. *See* employee benefits
   categories of, 294
   components of, 295
   impact of, 296–297
   importance of, 294
   integrated package, 294f
   and performance appraisal, 286, 329
   positive reinforcement, 343
   and relationships, 341
   total employment rewards, 295f

rights arbitration, 458
rights dispute, 458
rightsizing, 423
risk-assessment programs, 361
role-playing, 225–226, 252
RRSP, 365, 366t, 368
Rucker formula, 340
rules and regulations, 9, 421–422
running case. *See also* case incidents
   The Better Interview, 203
   Does LearnInMotion Need an HRIS? 84
   Fair Treatment in Disciplinary Action, 437
   Getting Better Applicants, 171
   Going Abroad, 489–490
   The Grievance, 464
   The Incentive Plan, 348–349
   Introduction, 23–24
   Legal Issues, 54
   The New Benefits Plan, 379
   The New Health and Safety Program, 413–414
   The New Pay Plan, 319
   The New Training Program, 235–236
   The Performance Appraisal, 291
   To Plan or Not to Plan? 141
   What to Do about Succession? 258–259
   Who Do We Have to Hire? 117

S

sabbaticals, 251, 365
safety and health programs, 358
salary. *See* pay rates
salary grade, 328
salary-level cut-off point, 328
salary plan, for salespeople, 334–335
salary plus commission, 336
sales compensation
   combination plan, 336
   commission plan, 335–336
   in e-commerce era, 336–337
   salary plan, 334–335
sandwich generation, 372
scandals, 9
scatter plot, 131, 132f
scientific management, 3
screening. *See* selection
secondary sector, 11
second middle age, 240
security
   career anchor, 242
   and HRIS, 73
   of workplace, 408
selection
   background checks, 197–198
   criteria, development of, 177–178

selection (*Continued*)
defined, 174
evaluation form, 178, 179*f*
for global assignments, 475
guidelines for, 175
hiring decision, 199–200
and human rights, 174, 180
interview. *See* selection
interview
and the law, 180
multiple-hurdle strategy, 175
notification of candidate,
200
and people with disabilities,
181
preliminary screening, 180
process, 175–179
realistic job preview (RJP),
199
references, 197–198
résumé lies, 197*f*
screening, 180, 205–207, 408
selection ratio, 175
statistical strategy, 200
steps in, 177–178, 178*f*
strategic significance of, 174
supervisory interview, 199
supply challenges, 175
testing. *See* selection testing
selection interview
administering, 191–192
asking questions, 194–195
behavioural interview, 191
behaviour description interview (BDI), 191
closing the interview, 195
common mistakes, 192–194
conducting, 194–195
content of, 191
contrast or candidate-order
error, 193
designing, 194
evaluating the candidate,
195
evaluation form, 196*f*
halo effect, 193
importance of, 190
leading questions, 193
in management assessment
centre, 188
mass interview, 192
mixed (semi-structured)
interview, 190–191
negative emphasis, 192
nonverbal behaviour, 193
note taking, 194–195
objectives of, 190
panel interview, 192
planning, 192, 194
process for, 176–177
questions, development of,
178
questions, sample, 195*f*
rapport, 194
sequential interview, 191

similar-to-me bias, 194
situational interview, 191
snap judgment, 192
structured interview,
190, 191
structured sequential
interview, 191
structure of, 190–191
supervisory interview, 199
too much/too little talking,
193–194
types of, 190–192
unstructured interview, 190
unstructured sequential
interview, 191
selection ratio, 175
selection testing
and accident prevention,
394–395
achievement tests, 187
aptitude tests, 184–185,
184*f*
cognitive abilities, 183–185
emotional intelligence (EI)
tests, 183–184
examples of, 176
faking, 187
functional abilities evaluations
(FAE), 185
intelligence (IQ) tests, 183
interest inventories, 187
management assessment
centre, 187–188
mechanical comprehension
test, 184*f*
medical examination, 189
micro-assessment, 189
motor abilities, 185
personality tests, 186–187
physical abilities, 185
polygraph test, 189
reliability, 182
situational tests, 188–189
substance abuse tests, 189
validity, 182–183
work samples, 187
self appraisal, 278–279
seminars, 251
Senior Human Resources
Professional (SHRP), 18
seniority, 246, 457
senior managers, 5
separation costs, 418
separations. *See* employee
separations
sequential interview, 191
service/dedication, 242
service sector, 11
severance package, 137
severance pay, 354–355, 431
sexual annoyance, 39
sexual coercion, 39
sexual harassment, 37,
39–40
sexual orientation, 41

short-term disability and sick
leave, 363
sick leave, 363
Silent Generation, 12
similar-to-me bias, 194, 277
simulated training, 224–225,
225–226
situational interview, 191
situational tests, 188–189
skill-based pay, 310–311
skills and aptitudes, 241–242
skills crisis, 215
skills inventories, 124, 152
SMART goals, 343
smoking, 405–406
snap judgment, 192
social (reform) unionism, 441
social handicapping, 35
socialization, 209
socialization effects, 213
social literacy, 231
social networking, 162
social orientation, 241
social reinforcement, 252
split-award method, 329
staffing policy, global, 474
staffing table, 133, 134*f*
stand-alone system, 70
standards
data exchange and process
standards, 80
employment standards legislation, 28, 47–48
performance standards, 109
Stanford-Binet test, 183
statistical strategy, 200
stock options, 330, 332*f*, 339
straight piecework plan, 325
strategic activities, 60–61
strategic alignment, 58, 67
strategic HR, 10*f*
communication, 472
employee benefits, 352
employee engagement, 472
employee relations, 90
and executive compensation,
333–334
formal appraisal discussion,
284
and globalization, 467
labour supply, 129
management training, 250
occupational health and safety,
396
onboarding, 210
predictive attrition, 58
rewards program effectiveness, 296
role of HR, 9
training and orientation, 215
turnover, 434
union "super local", 443
younger workers, 166
strategic planning, 122–123
strategy, 2*f*, 8

strategy architect, 7
stress, 400*f*. *See* job-related
stress
stretch goals, 272
strictness/leniency, 276
strike, 441, 453–454, 455, 456
strike vote, 453
Stromberg Dexterity Test, 185
Strong-Campbell Interest
Inventory, 187
structured interview, 190, 191
structured sequential interview,
191
sub-factor, 302–304, 303*f*
subordinates, appraisal by,
279–280
substance abuse, 399–400
substance abuse tests, 189, 399
succession planning, 9, 126,
127, 247–249
suggestion programs, 433
supervisors, 5, 232, 278
supervisory interview, 98
supplemental employee retirement plans (SERPs),
368–369, 369*f*
supplemental unemployment
benefits (SUBs), 137, 354
supplementary healthcare insurance, 360–362
surplus labour, 135–137
surveys, 305–307
survivor benefits, 357
survivors, 427
survivor syndrome, 137
systemic discrimination, 32
systemic remedies, 43, 44*f*

T

talent, 9
talent management, 67, 76
talent manager, 7
*Tapping the Talents of
People with Disabilities:
A Guidebook for
Employers*, 167
task analysis, 219–221
task analysis record form,
219–221, 220*f*
task competencies, 96–97
task performance, 263
team, 97
team-based job designs, 97
team or group incentive plan,
327–328
teamwork, 232
technical competencies, 96–97
technical/functional career
anchor, 242
technology
client focus, 60
electronic HR. *See* electronic
HR
as environmental influence,
14

evolution of, 78–79
history of, 78–79
and HR role, 9
human resources information
system (HRIS). *See* human
resources information
system (HRIS)
impact on HR role, 59–61
importance of, 57–58
IT/HR relationship, 60
paper-based systems, 78
and performance appraisal,
273–274
personal computers, 78
standards, 80
strategic activities, 60–61
strategy, 80
transactional activities, 59
trends in, 79–81
web-based technology, 79
temporary help agencies, 164
termination. *See also* employee
separations
defined, 136
disciplinary process,
421–423
and employment law, 26–27
in labour surplus, 136
mass layoffs, 355
notice, 354
termination pay, 354–355
termination interview, 430–431
termination on abandonment,
449
terrorism, 467
tertiary sector, 11
testing. *See* selection testing
Test of Workplace Essential
Skills (TOWES), 230
theft, 423
Thematic Apperception Test,
186, 186*f*
360-degree appraisal, 77, 184,
280–282, 280*f*
time and attendance, 63–64
time-lapse data, 155
tort law, 28
total employment rewards,
294–297, 294*f*, 295*f*
toxic substances, 386, 387*f*,
388*f*, 405
tracking recruitment and
applications, 63
trade associations, 158
Traditionalists, 12, 13*f*, 325
training
apprenticeship training, 222
classroom training, 223
controlled experimentation,
228
costs of, 418
cross-cultural communication
training, 231
cultural sensitivity training,
231

customer service training,
231–232
decrease in, 215
defined, 209, 214
design of. *See* instructional
design
for diverse workforce, 231
effects to measure, 228–230
employee preparation,
216–217
essential skills training,
230–231
evaluation of, 227–230, 229*f*
first-time supervisors/
managers, 232
for global assignments,
475–476
for global business, 231
and HRIS, 64
implementation of, 227
instructional design. *See*
instructional design
and job analysis, 89
and learning styles, 216–217
legal aspects of, 217
literacy training, 230–231
motivation, 216
need for, 214–216
needs analysis, 217, 218–222,
218*f*
objectives of, 221
for older workers, 240
on-the-job training, 222, 310
performance analysis, 219,
221
process, 214
safety training, 395
for special purposes, 230–232
steps in, 217, 218*f*
task analysis, 219–221
for teamwork, 232
transferability of, 486
validation of, 227
workplace violence training,
408
transactional activities, 59
transfer, 138, 245
transferability of education, 486
transfer of training, 227, 252
transportation, subsidized, 372
trend analysis, 130
tuition refunds, 251
turnover
cost of, 417–418, 418*f*
defined, 416
dismissal, 422–423. *See also*
termination
involuntary turnover, 416,
421–425
layoff, 423–425
and managerial control, 419
projected turnover, 130
quits, 419–420
reasons for, 416–416, 417*f*
reduction of, 210

retirement. *See* retirement
strategic HR, 434
voluntary turnover, 416,
418–421

U

unclear performance standards,
275
underemployment, 47
understudy approach, 249
undue hardship, 33
unemployment rates, 483*f*
unequal treatment, 30
unfair practices, 441
unintentional discrimination, 32
unintentional tort, 28
union. *See* labour union
union acceptance strategy, 440
union avoidance strategy, 440
union contract, 440
union recognition clause, 455
union security clause, 455
union shop, 456
union steward, 443
union substitution approach,
440
union suppression approach,
440
United States employment law,
26–27
university professors and
lecturers, 5
university-related programs, 251
unlawful strike, 455
unsafe acts, 390, 394–397
unsafe conditions, 390–391, 394
unstructured interview, 190
unstructured sequential interview, 191
upward feedback, 279–280

V

vacancy costs, 418
vacations, 358–359
validation, 217, 218*f*, 227
validity, 182–183, 274–275
variable pay, 323, 323*f*
variable pay programs, 477,
479*f*
vendetta effect, 426, 426*f*
vertical loading, 95
vestibule training, 224–225
vesting, 368
videoconferencing, 224
video display terminals, 405
video surveillance, 49, 50*f*
violence in the workplace, 390*f*,
406–409, 407*f*
viral pandemic, 406
virtual teams, 97
visible minorities, 47
vision, 391
visual learning, 216
Vocational Preference Test
(VPT), 240–241

voluntary turnover, 416,
418–421
volunteering, 343

W

wage curve, 307, 307*f*
wages. *See* pay rates
wage/salary survey
commercial, professional, and
government, 305–306
defined, 305
formal/informal, 305
interpretation and use,
306–307
and job evaluation, 307–310
sample, 306*f*
walk-in, 162
want ad, 163
want criteria, 178
web-based application, 74
web-based self-service application, 74–76
web-based technology, 79
web-based training, 226
Wechsler test, 183
weight, of factor, 303
white-collar employees, 444
wildcat strike, 455
win-lose bargaining, 451
win-win approach, 452
women
Catalyst pyramid, 44*f*
drivers, 468
and employment equity, 46
Muslim, 41
and occupational segrega-
tion, 44
pay equity, 297, 313–315,
314*t*, 320–321
recruitment of, 166–167
in workforce, 12, 14
Wonderlic Personnel Test, 176,
183
workaholics, 401
work environment, 408
workers' compensation,
357–358, 397–398,
402–403
workers' compensation laws,
298
workflow process chart, 93*f*
workforce analytics, 80
workforce diversity
Aboriginal people, 442
and career development, 240
cultural bias, 276
and employee benefits, 362
and employee orientation,
211–212
health and safety, 393
incentive plans, 325
increase in, 11–14
and pay equity, 314
people with disabilities, 168,
181

workforce diversity (*Continued*)
   principles for assessment
      accommodations, 181
   and recruitment, 165–168
   and sexual harassment, 37
   and training, 231
   women. *See* women
   young workers, 393
workforce mobility, 467
working conditions, 109

work-life balance, 240,
   242–243
work-life programs, 295
Workplace Equity Information
   Management System
   (WEIMS), 66
**Workplace Hazardous Materials
   Information System
   (WHMIS)**, 236, 386, 387*f*,
   388*f*

workplace stress, 400–403, 400*f*
workplace toxins, 386, 387*f*,
   388*f*, 405
workplace violence, 390*f*,
   406–409, 407*f*
work samples, 187
work sharing, 136
work simplification, 94
write-ins, 162
written warning, 286

wrongful dismissal, 426, 426*f*,
   427, 429–430
wrongful hiring, 174

X
XML, 80

Y
yield ratio, 155

Photo Credits